The
POLITICS
of STATE
and LOCAL
GOVERNMENT

The Macmillan Company, New York

The POLITICS of STATE and LOCAL GOVERNMENT

SECOND EDITION

Duane Lockard Princeton University

Collier-Macmillan Limited, London

For Linda, Janet, and Leslie

PREFACE to the SECOND EDITION

ONE REALIZES THE DIZZY PACE of change in state and local government when one undertakes to revise a textbook in the field, even one only five years old. When the original edition of this book appeared the Supreme Court had just decided the first of the state legislative reapportionment cases, and I could only speculate about the implications of the decision. Federal grants-in-aid to state and local governments have grown three-fold in the intervening years; New York City's budget has soared from $2.5 to $6.7 billion, and although I have long been interested in the problems of the Negro American, the first edition has a curious (and a characteristically *white* American) obliviousness to the gravity of the problems of nonwhite citizens. The new volume, although it retains the basic approach and organization of the original, is a much changed book.

I wish to thank those who called my attention to errors in the first edition, and particularly to express my gratitude to Ray Baxter, my friend and research assistant, who gave me a student's critique of the book and searched out data for the revision. Finally, I want to thank Robert J. Patterson of The Macmillan Company for his unfailing co-operation and support.

D. L.

Princeton, N.J.

[vii]

PREFACE to the FIRST EDITION

THERE IS NO DEARTH of textbooks on state and local government. This one I add to the list with the hope that its emphasis on the political dynamics of these governments will serve a useful purpose. Writing it has, however, proved a difficult self-imposed assignment, for it is not easy to locate materials on the operational details of the tens of thousands of governments in this country. Still, as the footnotes and the bibliography on state and city politics attest, there are many such analyses, and I have leaned heavily on the researchers who produced them.

I owe a heavy debt too to many colleagues who read all or part of the manuscript, made innumerable constructive suggestions, thus saving me from errors both foolish and serious. I list these friends here in gratitude without seeking to implicate them in the sins of omission or commission that remain despite their best efforts. My colleagues William Beaney, Jameson Doig, and Walter Murphy of Princeton University; my former colleagues at Connecticut College, Marjorie Dilley and Louise Holborn; Morris Cohen of Clark University, and Malcolm Jewell of the University of Kentucky all read and criticized chapters in their respective fields of expertise. All the following read and commented on several chapters: James McGregor Burns of Williams, E. E. Schattschneider of Wesleyan, Eric Stevenson and Robert Wood of M.I.T. Herbert Kaufman of Yale and Nelson Polsby of Berkeley read major portions of the manuscript and both went well beyond the call of duty by sending many letters and notes of extensive and incisive criticism. Joseph Schlesinger of Michigan

State University read the whole manuscript and offered many helpful corrections and criticisms.

Others helped in many ways. John Strange, formerly my research assistant at Princeton University, did painstaking work on the bibliography and uncovered many errors in his careful reading of the final manuscript. The following colleagues were kind enough to supply me with election data and other information on their respective cities: Morris Cohen of Clark University, William Keefe of Chatham College, Maurice Klain of Western Reserve University, and Robert Salisbury of Washington University. Charles Adrian of Michigan State University kindly supplied me with materials on some aspects of Michigan politics. Brevard Crihfield, Executive Director of the Council of State Governments, helpfully complied with several requests for data. And I cannot fail to acknowledge my debt to two imaginative and untiring librarians for whom no request seemed too much: Hazel Johnson, Head Librarian of Connecticut College, and Helen Fairbanks, Librarian of the Woodrow Wilson School of Princeton University. I am grateful too to Rosemary Park, formerly President of Connecticut College, who arranged a leave from teaching during 1960–61 so that I could write. Mrs. Helen Wright, typist extraordinary, not only deciphered my scrawl and divined my intent but knew when I did not mean what I seemed to say. I wish also to thank the editors and publishers of *Political Science Quarterly* for permitting me to republish in revised form an article on the city manager which appeared in that journal, and the editor of *Fortune* for granting the privilege of quoting passages on the mayoral office by Seymour Freedgood in *The Exploding Metropolis*. The ones to whom the book is dedicated contributed in their special ways as did my wife, Beverly Lockard, during the many years it was an obtrusive house guest.

D. L.

Princeton, N.J.

CONTENTS

[xi]

LIST of FIGURES

[xiii]

LIST of TABLES

1. Politics and Nonnational Government

THIS IS A TEXTBOOK with a point of view: it has a thesis to expound and defend. It is a thesis rooted in a common fact of American history; namely, that most Americans take a dim view of politics. At best, most Americans tolerate politics as a necessary evil; at worst they regard it as a plague of corruption, compromise, and deceit. Disdain for politics has deep and honorable roots in our past. In his farewell address, George Washington vigorously condemned parties, lamenting the "baneful effects of the spirit of party generally." Down through the years since, our ablest politicians have—sometimes with tongue in cheek—denounced their opponents for stooping to politics. President Eisenhower was both adhering to tradition and expressing his own apparent feelings when he once said that "being President is a very great experience . . . but the word 'politics' . . . I have no great liking for that." Common hostility to politics has been so great that we have ever sought to restrict its sphere of influence to the smallest possible domain, and where we have failed to eradicate it, we have often pretended that we have. From pretense to myth is a short, easy step, and on myth a system of behavior can be based. Nowhere has the myth of no-politics-allowed been more pervasive than in state and local government.

Hence the sense of mission that motivated this book. My simple thesis is that there is an integral, necessary, and invariable relationship between the political process and the governmental process. Neither can be comprehended in isolation from the other. We have too long ignored this fundamental fact in discussing state and local government (and no doubt more importantly in constructing and operating those governments). In view of what appears on the agenda for these governments there is need for clear thinking about this essential interrelationship. Thus this book devotes as much space to analysis of the dynamics of political practice as it does to the fundamentals of the structure of government, and it seeks constantly to integrate these two elements of the total governmental process.

Since *politics* and *government* are central concepts of this book, they should—like the protagonists of a novel—be identified early and clearly. Accordingly the word *politics* as used here is not meant narrowly but broadly. It is *not* limited to elections, campaigning, or the maneuvering of political parties and interest groups. Rather, as Professor Harold Lasswell has aptly said: "The study of politics is the study of influence and the influential."[1] Thus defined, politics is involved in most of what goes on in the governing of human society, for people are constantly trying to influence those who can lay down and apply the rules. These attempts take countless forms, ranging from noble disquisition to tawdry backroom finagling. There are, of course, governmental actions that could hardly be called political—for example, the task of cleaning the snow from the city or state roads after a storm. But if the actual scraping away of snow is nonpolitical, it is about the only phase of the job that does not involve politics in some form or other. Whether snow-plowing is a job to be contracted to private firms or assigned to public personnel and government-owned equipment has often been a hotly disputed political question. Patronage (whether as personnel or contracts), ultimate responsibility for effectively clearing the highways, budgeting, supervision over personnel, overtime *versus* released time for sanitation or highway employees who battle the elements at all hours —these and dozens of other questions can become the focus of contests between men—can become, in short, the reasons why influence is brought to bear.

If politics is thus broadly interpreted, what can government be? Government will be used here to mean the broad tasks of ordering a society. Essentially, that is, *government* refers to the *people and institutions that make and enforce rules for a given society.* Obviously the political process, interpreted as influence and the use of influence, is

---

[1] Harold Lasswell, *Politics* (New York: McGraw-Hill Book Co., 1936), p. 1.

integrally connected with the governmental process—each concerns essentially the same end product: public policy. Although when we talk about government we normally think of formal public power to command, the deeper truth is that there is private government too. Corporations, labor unions, churches, and other organizations also wield governmental power—not only through their influence on those in public office, but also by their power to set rules of behavior that people often cannot avoid. Like pieces on a chess board, these various institutions may bring their power to bear in different ways—but regardless of the method used, the power is there. The bishop and the knight move differently on the chess board but each has power, as has the lowly pawn. In short, the test of power is the capacity to oblige others to take a particular action, not the manner in which the power is applied. In most cases the word *government* will refer to public government in the customary sense, however; when on occasion "private" government is meant, this will be made clear by the context.

Both politics and government are familiar words that evoke familiar stereotypes. *Politics* often connotes improper or venal behavior; the cartoonist's caricature of a politician, a cigar-chewing conniver whose selfishness is exceeded only by his deviousness, is a familiar figure in our folklore. *Government* has more ambiguous connotations: it is an object both of patriotic respect on the one hand and hatred and fear on the other. Awe and loyalty vie with apprehension over the threat of taxation, regulation, and perhaps even punishment. Because we have these preconceptions about politics and government, we find our prejudices getting in the way of serious analysis. We are not in the happy position of the geologist studying rock formations about which he has no emotional attitudes relevant to his study. He may come to his rock with preconceived and perhaps quite wrong ideas that may impair his analytical skill, but at least the blinders he wears are not emotional ones. For the student of political institutions, however, achieving a sense of neutrality toward the main concepts of his study is not easy, although it is a necessary precondition of penetrating comprehension. Research on political institutions is difficult enough under the best of circumstances in view of the variables of human behavior and the broad range of unknown or even unknowable elements (human motives, for example) that enter into the equations of politics. If the student cannot look at politics more or less neutrally—see it as a fact of life, a method of doing things whether good, evil, both, or neither—he will not get far. Hence the plea for as much objectivity as may reasonably be mustered.

But total objectivity is unattainable; every person, as E. B. White once said, slants his writing the way he leans. I hasten to say that I have definite preconceptions about the issues discussed in this book. I have tried to be fair in my presentation, but the student should be on his guard for the intrusion of my own values. Readers are invited to question any inference made, to challenge the reasoning, to examine the evidence presented, and to test any hypothesis offered against the facts of the community or state he knows or can come to know firsthand.

In a sense two different kinds of objectivity are involved in this discussion. On the one hand, the student is implored to refrain from leaping to unwarranted and unexamined conclusions about "politics" or "patronage" or the "public interest" just because these labels have some emotional connotation for him. On the other hand, it is admitted that "objectivity" in the fullest sense is an impossibility and that each of us is tainted in some degree by the subjective views we hold. To admit this is not to dive into a chartless sea of relativism nor to part company with rationality, logic, or efforts at "proof"; it is rather to emphasize these instead of merely "assuming" them.

Social Determinants and Ultimate Constitutions

In still another sense, however, values and ethical considerations are relevant to the study of state and local government. The student can analyze the workings of a governmental system only if he has some grasp of the values that people hold. Only when one begins to unravel the "ought's" and "ought not's," the vague but powerful sense of what "is" and what "isn't" done, can one get to an analysis of the real constitutional system operative within a given society. Aristotle, the father of political science, held ethics to be the basis of political systems. For Aristotle the constitution of a country really referred to its ethical pattern in the broadest sense. As Norton Long has said of Aristotle's theory of "constitution":

The state is characterized by its constitution exemplifying a particular conception of the good life, be it the wealth of oligarchy, the freedom of democracy or the martial spirit of a timocracy. The ethical principle embodied in the constitution sets the standard for distributive justice in the state, determines the nature and the composition of the politeuma, the ruling class, who in one sense are or personify the constitution, and informs the subordinate institutions with their appropriate roles in each particular type of constitution.[2]

After all, do not the ethical values of a community determine in large measure who has the right to run affairs? Reading the charter of a Southern town would poorly equip a researcher who wanted to know the power system of the community; it would not even tell him who was specifically excluded from prominent roles in government by reason of race.

This is not to say that the "constitution" in the formal sense of the term—that is, the documentary statement of powers and structure for a government—is not relevant. On the contrary, it is often of considerable significance, as we shall see in some detail in later analysis. But its significance lies in the fact that it grants special opportunities for the use of political powers. It sets the hurdle to be surmounted— or circumvented—granting special opportunities to some and putting special handicaps on others. What Robert Dahl has said of the national constitution is equally applicable here:

. . . Constitutional rules are mainly significant because they help to determine what particular groups are to be given advantages or handicaps in the political struggle. In no society do people ever enter a political contest equally; the effect of the constitutional rules is to preserve, add to, or subtract from the advantages or handicaps with which they start the race.[3]

Logically then, analysis of state and local government would seem to require as much attention to the social structure of a community as to the formal governmental structure. Of course, the study of fifty state governments and tens of thousands of local governments poses a formidable task. Collecting the constitutions of the states is easy enough, reading them all might be boring but not impossible. The collected charters and principal ordinances of all our local governments would be more than any one person could sensibly read and digest, although sampling the various types is feasible. But how can one get at the social-ethical patterns that we claim to be part of the ultimate "constitution"? This clearly is a task of a different order, for no two governments are ever alike. For all their formal comparability the fifty states

---

[2] Norton Long, "Aristotle and the Study of Local Government," reprinted in Edward C. Banfield, *Urban Government* (New York: The Free Press of Glencoe, Inc., 1961), pp. 21–2.

[3] Robert A. Dahl, A *Preface to Democratic Theory* (Chicago: University of Chicago Press, 1956), p. 137.

are essentially very different. While they are all part of one national government and subject to the same national Constitution, they are dissimilar in age, traditions, size, economy, wealth, political-governmental beliefs, and methods. Each state is the product of its own constitutional-political history and has accordingly developed unique answers to the universal questions of government. Governmental institutions characteristic of one region are insignificant or unused in another. Take the county as an example: in the South and West the county is a very important governmental unit; but in New England its role is minimal, and indeed in two states (Connecticut and Rhode Island) it has disappeared altogether. Alaska from the beginning has had no counties. Or consider the extent to which the political party is entrusted with power: in many states, particularly in the East, the party has considerable authority in both state and local affairs, but in some Western states, particularly those which emerged as states in the era of nonpartisan fervor, the party plays an entirely different role. (In Nebraska and Minnesota, for example, state legislators are elected without party labels, quite in contrast to New York or Connecticut where party considerations are uppermost not only in the election but also in the operations of the state legislature.) And in the two-party states of the country the manner of resolving public issues is remarkably unlike the ways of, for example, the one-party South. Often the accepted practice in one state is the taboo of the next.

Differences between the states, however, are as nothing when compared with the range of variation among local governments, which are so varied that comparison is ridiculously inappropriate at the extremes —e.g., New York City (budget requested for 1968–69: $6.7 billion) and a prairie town of a few dozen souls. One need not turn to such extremes to find remarkable differences, however; often local governments operating under identical charters (set forth sometimes by the state as the mandatory or optional charter forms for towns) will be quite unlike in actual practice. The decisive factors in shaping the ultimate pattern of government are not the authorizing charters but the political methods accepted by the citizenry. The same formal "constitution" (i.e., city charter) can be the basis of a relatively democratic and free polity or a near dictatorship. Both kinds of government exist in this country and the significant variables that distinguish them are not found in any constitutional document but in the social and ethical systems of the communities.

It follows then that intensive and systematic comparative analysis of state and local government is an exceedingly difficult task—or at least it is if we assume that the formal facts of structure and method are not the real essence of a government. Until recently scholars, reformers, and practitioners in a reflective mood have tended to emphasize the formal structure at the expense of the more vital if more elusive kinds of information about state and local government. The constitutional document could be analyzed, as could the administrative structure or the electoral laws, but the collecting and assessing of data on the more dynamic political phases of these governments was another matter. Some of it was done, of course, and it is an important asset for contemporary scholarship. Nevertheless, the volume of material on the formal aspects of state and local government is about ten times greater than the volume of material on the informal political aspects.[4] Consequently much that is said in the following discussion is perforce tentative and may seem annoyingly uncertain. But until extensive and systematic comparative analyses of the political realities of these myriad governments are made, there must be tentativeness and uncertainty— as of course there will be to some extent even after extensive comparative study, given the amount and the elusive character of the data.

In part to accommodate for this lack of amassed information on the "ultimate constitutions" of our nonnational governments, case studies are presented or referred to throughout the book. These detailed examinations of actual events of decision-making in specific situations emphasize the peculiarities of the specific situation and generally do not provide broad generalization. Case studies serve, however, two significant purposes: they provide sustaining evidence to illustrate generalizations made elsewhere, and they emphasize the importance of the operational as opposed to the formal side of government.[5]

---

[4] Many textbooks discuss state legislatures, for example, almost solely in terms of legislative procedure; one text written over a decade ago devotes a whole chapter to the *workings* of state legislatures without once using the word *party*.

[5] There is much to be said for student preparation of case studies in the analysis of state and local government. The materials for such study are after all readily available. Local and state officials are often flattered to be sought out by the student who seeks "practical" knowledge from the fountainhead and will usually cooperate in providing information and advice. The student who actually reads a city charter, a few ordinances, a budget, some news clippings on a disputed issue and then does some interviewing to get an understanding of what happened and how it happened will probably have learned more about state and local government than the student who spends an equivalent amount of time reading a textbook on state and local government, the one in hand included. An excellent and inexpensive paperback volume by William H. Riker—*The Study of Local Politics* (New York: Random House, 1959)—provides ideas for research and explains how to carry out research projects. It also contains useful advice on conducting interviews and instruction on elementary statistical methods. E. E. Schattschneider and Victor Jones offer instruction about and demonstrate the use of many resource materials in their book, *Local Political Surveys* (New York: Holt, Rinehart and Winston, Inc., 1962).

These brief introductory comments on the methods of political analysis of state and local government will, it is hoped, be of some value in interpreting the observations on operational reality as they are presented in the ensuing chapters.

2. State and Local Government in an Age of Change

THE TWENTIETH CENTURY is an age of change. Not that social change is a new phenomenon; in truth no society remains static, if for no other reason than that social existence is to a considerable extent dependent upon physical circumstances which inevitably change over time. Extreme drought over a sustained period of time can change the social life of an area; new implements of agriculture, new means of travel or communication, have equally profound effects on social organization. Change therefore is characteristic; what is unique about our time is the unprecedented speed of change, which is primarily the consequence of the unparalleled speed of technological change.

Modern developments in communication provide interesting illustrations of the point. As the creation of a practical printing press introduced new communications possibilities and unexpected political problems to the fifteenth century, so the development of electronic media of instantaneous communication is having a profound social effect on the twentieth century. As a matter of fact, it is probably impossible at present to appreciate fully the sweeping effects of the last half-century's advancements in communications. As we can evaluate better than could his contemporaries the results of Gutenberg's invention, so future generations will better be able to evaluate the importance of television, radio, facsimile reproduction, automatic translators, and other modern means of conveying information.

Each new major technological discovery opens the way to other discoveries, and the application of scientific knowledge to production and resource development makes new advances possible. New power sources invite new means of transportation; new materials open the way to new machinery; conceptual discoveries point the way to other tangential or analogous ideas. Application of scientific knowledge provides wealth with which to experiment and develop in other directions, both intellectual and economic. Modern technological progress moves by geometric progression, and therefore social change tends to do likewise.

Perhaps one of the most significant of the "new" factors of our life is the sheer fact of numbers. We can feed, clothe, protect, and keep alive hitherto unimaginable numbers of people, and we have communications resources sufficient to keep them all in some kind of contact with each other. A primary difference between our kind of huge society and the sprawling Roman Empire is that through our instantaneous communication it is possible for the citizen in New Mexico, for example, to hear about a hurricane hitting New England, and to read in his paper of production problems in Detroit, racial conflict in Mississippi, irrigation developments in Idaho, the same day they occur.

For this huge and closely interrelated economic and social system we pay a price. Part of that price is the complexity we encounter when we attempt to make necessary rules to facilitate the interrelationships and minimize the inevitable conflicts that arise. The more complex the system the greater the number of places where things can go wrong, and the greater, significantly, the number of places where individuals can make the most of their potential power by threatening to interfere with the whole by stalling some crucial element of it. The greater the community the more numerous the interests that potentially conflict. The greater the numbers of people involved and the more remote the areas to be served from the place where "decisions" are to be made, the greater are the difficulties in devising policies that accord with the needs of the individuals of a given area.

The "Necessity" for Nonnational Government

Our communications may be sophisticated and virtually instantaneous, our transportation system a marvel, and our sense of community one of the wonders of the world; nevertheless there are serious problems encountered in making policies to serve the interests of so many people. The fact is that it is impossible to make all the decisions at the center of the government, even if we desired to do so—which, given our traditions, we do not. (More will be said on this subject in Chapter 3.) As a consequence of war, depression, international tension, and the gradual expansion of federal governmental power to meet these and other crises, the focus of interest has turned toward the city on the Potomac to such an extent that it would almost seem that the *only* government is the national government. This is not the case, and in hard practical terms it cannot be the case, for however clever and effective the people sitting at the center of the government may be, they do not know about the problems at the street corner, the needs of a local school system, or the requirements for Dry Gulch County's irrigation system. There must be local and regional governments to meet local and regional needs. We can, and certainly we shall, debate the extent to which power over the irrigation system and the schools ought to be centralized. But there can be no debating the proposition that there has to be an on-the-spot agency of some sort with relative freedom to use discretion in making decisions as dictated by local conditions. Even if the "need" for such governments is not conceded, it is clear that our traditions and existing institutional patterns will dictate the continuance of nonnational governmental units with considerable independent authority.

An Agenda of Challenge

Those myriad governments face a complex maze of challenging problems. The centers of older cities are rotting away faster than they are being rebuilt. Slums, spreading like an epidemic, are but one example of the issues that will have to be faced locally. There are many more, and it will serve to demonstrate the place of nonnational government to discuss briefly some of the problems that are on the standing or anticipated agendas of these governments.

Nonnational governments are going to have to cope with four basic challenges in the next few decades. Perhaps the most pervasive of these is the *challenge of numbers*—the crowding into metropolitan centers of enormous numbers of people. Concurrent with, and in part aggravated by, the concentration of population in metropolitan areas is the *challenge of social instability and unrest.* Mobile population, segregated social classes, segregated racial groups, breakdown of community ties that tend to restrain irresponsible and antisocial behavior—these and similar social problems pose serious and difficult tasks for local government. Third, there are *economic challenges* which are going to have to be met by these governments, and finally there are some difficult *political challenges* that must be overcome in order adequately to meet some of the other challenges.

1. *The Challenge of Population Pressure.* Everyone knows that the United States has within the last fifty years become a predominantly urban society. Just before the Civil War only 15 per cent of the people lived in cities; at the beginning of the twentieth century only 40 per cent were urban dwellers. Not until 1920 did half the people live in cities. Today two-thirds of the population is urban, and the process of urbanization is not slowing down but accelerating. The present process of urbanization is different from that of the past when it was the city center that expanded with great speed. Now the area lying outside the core of the metropolis receives most of the population increase, while the centers of most cities are static or are losing population. As superhighways and mass transportation systems spread into the countryside, it is technologically feasible to live farther and farther from the city center. As of 1966 a majority of all metropolitan residents lived in the suburbs (59.4 million in the center cities and 65.8 million in the suburbs), according to a Census Bureau estimate. Figure 2–1 shows the distribution of Standard Metropolitan Statistical Areas in the nation.

There is every reason to expect that the process of concentrating population in the metropolitan area will continue in the years ahead, as metropolitan areas continue to account for about three-quarters of the growth of the national population. If this same rate of growth continues, our metropolitan areas between 1960 and 1975 will have added a total population increase equal to the 1960 *total metropolitan population* of New York (10.5 million), Chicago (6.1), Los Angeles-Long Beach (6.7), Philadelphia (4.0), Detroit (3.7), Boston (2.5), and Baltimore (1.7). In fifteen years, that is to say, we shall probably add some 30 million people to the number now living in metropolitan areas. The task of creating facilities for 30 million people within fifteen years is a sobering prospect.

Some evidence of the problems of the central cities themselves is found in the migration to the suburbs of thousands of families every week. In the twenty-three largest metropolitan areas (all with total population in excess of a million people) fifteen of the central cities lost population during the decade 1950–60, while simultaneously the surrounding regions of all 23 grew. A few central cities gained (Atlanta,

46.5 per cent; Houston, 56 per cent; and San Diego, 63 per cent), but the common pattern was not just a relative but an absolute loss of population. The fifteen other largest cities had an average loss of population of 7.5 per cent, with the losses ranging 15 per cent in Boston to nearly 3 per cent in New York City. Yet without exception every one of these metropolitan areas *as a whole* gained population, resulting, of course, from the huge growth in the suburban areas. The average increase in the areas beyond the core cities was 56 per cent, ranging from the Minneapolis–St. Paul boost of 114 per cent to Boston's 17 per cent.[1]

What real difference does this make for local government? Consider first the problems involved in supplying services for the masses of people locating in these suburbs—the streets, fire departments, police and welfare services, schools, recreational facilities, housing, water supply, and transportation. The costs are staggering, the administrative and policy problems involved are complex and challenging. Consider the problem of the slowly declining water table that may make the very existence of these huge metropolitan complexes impossible in some areas unless ways are found to supply potable water at an economic cost. (In 1900 the nation used 40 billion gallons of water a day; in 1930 it needed 92 billions, but in 1960 it used 312 billion gallons of water every day. The demand projected for 1975 is 453 billion, or 32 per cent more than natural resources will provide.[2])

Although these might seem to be primarily problems for the governments of local communities to deal with, they are not so local as they first appear. Will local resources suffice for building the schools that swiftly expanding communities need? Is there a sufficient tax base to pay for new schools when there is little within the town borders but residential housing? And will it be possible to "go it alone" on water supply when the need for water is area-wide and the supply is limited, and perhaps available only by transporting it ten or a hundred miles? Here the larger units of government will come into the act, either as authorizers—as in the case of the state government—or as doers—as in the case of counties or states that by one means or another take over functions that once were local responsibilities.

2. *The Social Challenge.* A large city is a reservoir of humanity; there is a steady human current, a constant inflow and sometimes a

---

[1] See *The New York Times*, June 21, 1960. The data are from the 1960 Census.

[2] See *The New York Times*, October 23, 1960. This article reports that a 1957 United States geological survey found 1000 communities already forced to restrict water consumption.

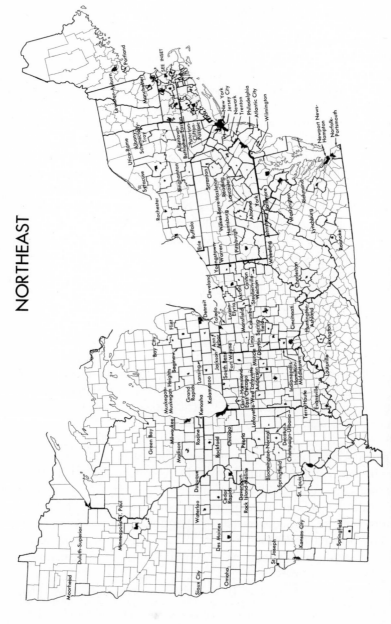

NORTHEAST

Figure 2-1. Standard Metropolitan Statistical Areas of the United States and Puerto Rico, 1967
Source: *U.S. Bureau of the Census.*

SOUTHEAST

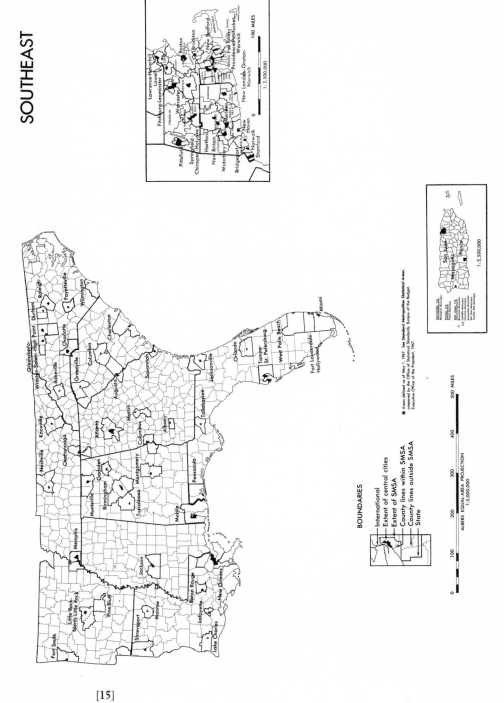

BOUNDARIES

International
Extent of central cities
Extent of SMSA
County lines within SMSA
County lines outside SMSA
State

ALBERS EQUAL-AREA PROJECTION
1:5,000,000

0   100   200   300   400   500 MILES

* Areas defined as of May 1, 1967. See Standard Metropolitan Statistical Areas, prepared by the Office of Statistical Standards, Bureau of the Budget, Executive Office of the President, 1967.

Greensboro-Winston-Salem-High Point
Durham
Raleigh
Fayetteville
Wilmington
Charlotte
Charleston
Columbia
Greenville
Asheville
Knoxville
Nashville
Chattanooga
Augusta
Macon
Atlanta
Savannah
Columbus
Albany
Jacksonville
Tallahassee
Orlando
Tampa-St. Petersburg
West Palm Beach
Fort Lauderdale-Hollywood
Miami
Pensacola
Montgomery
Gadsden
Birmingham
Huntsville
Tuscaloosa
Mobile
Memphis
Jackson
Baton Rouge
New Orleans
Lafayette
Lake Charles
Shreveport
Monroe
Pine Bluff
Little Rock-North Little Rock
Fort Smith

100 MILES
1:2,500,000
0

Lawrence-Haverhill
Lowell
Fitchburg-Leominster
Worcester
Boston
Brockton
New Bedford
Fall River
Providence-Pawtucket
Warwick
New London-Groton-Norwich
New Haven
Hartford
New Britain
Waterbury
Bridgeport
Norwalk
Stamford
Pittsfield
Springfield
Chicopee-Holyoke

San Juan
Mayagüez
Ponce

1:2,500,000

[15]

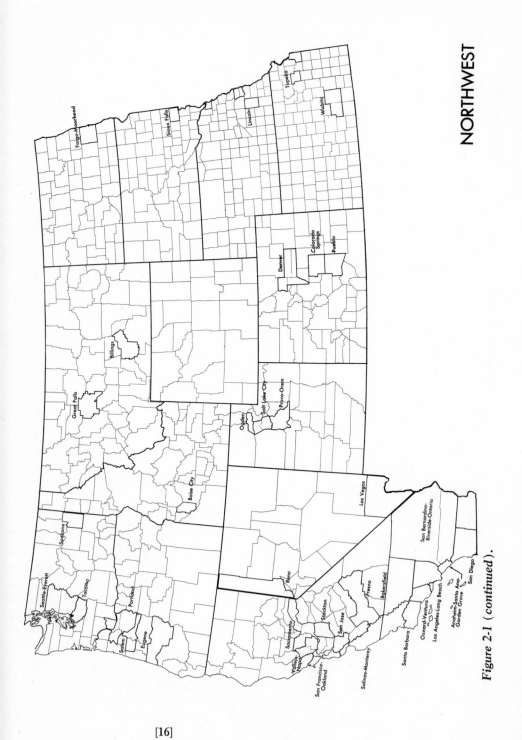

Figure 2-1 (continued).

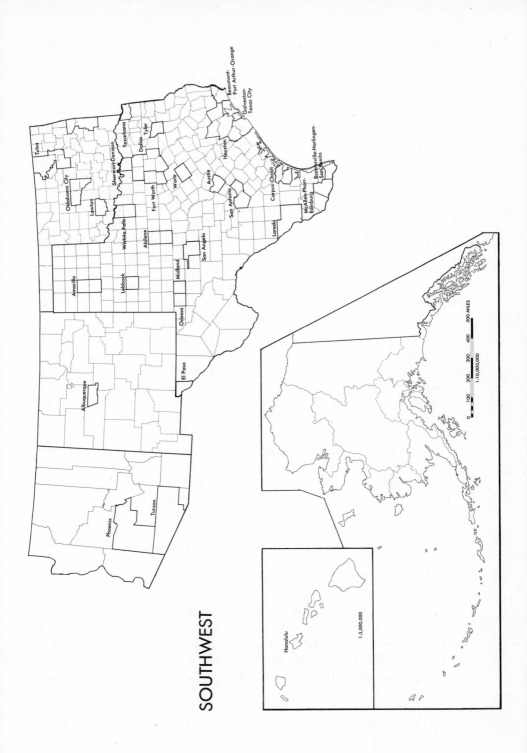

SOUTHWEST

greater outflow of migrants. Over half of the nation's counties had a net loss of population in the 1950's. From Puerto Rico and Mexico, from the farms of the South and Midwest and the deserted mining towns of the Appalachians, and more slowly from the waiting lists limited by our immigration laws, people flow into the urban centers in search of jobs—better jobs, or perhaps any job at all. Detroit and Los Angeles, for example, are magnets drawing seekers of advancement whether they are trained engineers or unskilled near-paupers. The persistent need for the talented and the unskilled alike brings a constant flow to the various parts of the metropolis. The affluent tend to locate in the suburbs; the remainder, having no other choice, take what they can get in the center of the city. And all that many of them can get is an overcrowded tenement in a slum area. Every large city in the United States struggles to cope with the social consequences of degraded and degrading physical surroundings, although the extent of the problem varies, largely with the age of the city.

Gradually these population shifts are producing a racially segregated metropolitan way of life. As nonwhites are compressed into the center city, the whites escape. For the first time in history the white population of metropolitan center cities actually declined between 1960 and 1966, the Census Bureau estimates. (It was only a decline of 0.3 per cent, but it accompanies an increase in suburban white population of 21.3 per cent, and a nonwhite center city increase of 23.9 per cent![3])

The constant turnover in population in the large cities is well-illustrated by the flux of people in the largest of our cities, New York. A 1957 population survey showed that since the 1950 census the city had lost 416,000 whites, while adding 320,000 nonwhites.[4] In the past quarter-century, according to Professor Oscar Handlin, the number of Negroes and Puerto Ricans in the metropolitan region of New York has increased by some 250 per cent, and he predicts a further increase of 60–75 per cent in the next two decades. Together the two million Negroes and Puerto Ricans now constitute just under one-fifth of the total metropolitan population.[5]

The living conditions of the great majority of Negroes and Puerto Ricans in the center of New York is surely not a matter of national pride. Uprooted and feeling unwanted, many of them live a marginal existence. The moral codes that restrained behavior in the simpler societies from which they came are often broken down in the alien and

---

[3] See *City*, July, 1967, p. 2.

[4] Oscar Handlin, *The Newcomers: Negroes and Puerto Ricans in a Changing Metropolis* (Cambridge, Mass.: Harvard University Press, 1959), p. 42.

[5] *The New York Times*, October 26, 1959.

hostile new surroundings of the metropolis. Both the restraints and the support of more traditional community life wither in the confusion of the crowded city. Families are broken up in the process of migration, and parents lose control over adolescents, who are sometimes more knowing about the "new" environment than their parents. Juvenile delinquency and crime rates are high among the newcomers—and the more crowded and undesirable the neighborhood, the higher the crime rate. The connection between living conditions and crime is suggested by the different delinquency rates for the five boroughs of New York (see Table 2–1).

TABLE 2-1
Delinquency Rates and Living Conditions in New York City, 1960*

	Delinquency Rate (per 1000 Population Aged 6–20)	Population Density (per Square Mile)	Percentage of Housing Dilapidated and Substandard
Manhattan	59.3	77,190	26.0%
Bronx	45.1	33,135	12.1%
Brooklyn	41.2	34,570	14.6
Staten Island	36.0	3,699	12.6
Queens	30.9	16,014	4.2

* See Calvin F. Schmid, "Urban Crime Areas," 25 *American Sociological Review* 527 (1960).

No one needs be reminded of the social costs and the bitter hatred these conditions have wrought—the quasi-rebellion and rampant destruction in city after city are monuments for our time. Nor is the problem restricted to nonwhites alone. The squalor and unrest are true too of recently arrived hill country Americans, who strangely constitute a "foreign" element in their native land. One unkind description of the "invasion" of some 70,000 "hillbillies" into Chicago says: "Of all the migrant waves that have swept Chicago in the 125 years since the city mushroomed from the swamps, none have [sic] seemed so alien or posed such social problems as a recent influx of native-born white Americans." They arrive in Chicago, according to one source, at the rate of a thousand a week.[6] Another exaggerated picture was presented by the Chicago Tribune which said:

The Southern hillbilly migrants . . . who have descended like a plague of

[6] "Anglo-Saxon Migration," 69 *Time Magazine* (March 18, 1957), 73.

locusts in the last few years, have the lowest standard of living and moral code (if any), the biggest capacity for liquor, and the most savage tactics when drunk, which is most of the time.[7]

Equally unflattering remarks are made about migrating Negroes, Puerto Ricans, and others.

Relevant to the mixture of ethnic and racial groups is the question of racial integration of school systems and other facilities, one of the foremost moral-social-political problems of our day. Although the formal authority behind the integration of local school systems is an order of the United States Supreme Court, the actual handling of the problem is not a national but preëminently a state and local task. Whether to integrate, how rapidly, or how much, are political questions precisely because they stem from social conflict. Normal community relations dissolve and give way to unconventional actions ranging from noisy protest and threats to bombing and shooting. It is not, however, the role of the courts to guide the community through its difficulties in overcoming the deeply seated prejudices nor to parry the thrusts of politically powerful forces that would upset any local efforts to preserve the school system by compromising on the integration point. These tasks are left to harassed local school boards, sheriffs, mayors, governors, superintendents of schools, and the like. The imagination, courage, and political-governmental skills involved in achieving the reality that the formal court order demands are formidable indeed. When the Supreme Court ordered integration with "all deliberate speed," it in effect decentralized the administration of the change by allowing discretion to federal district judges who in turn have to deal with local authorities. (Not insignificantly the Court thus also fragmented the opposition to integration in the South.) In any event the order initiated an enormous task for state and local government, and not only in the South but wherever there are significant numbers of Negroes.

One could go on listing the challenges that contemporary social developments place on nonnational governments—the achievement of integration in Northern communities as well as Southern ones, the artificiality of the suburban community and the middle-classless urban centers (where the rich can live in penthouses above the squalor, the poor cannot help staying, and from which the middle-class elements flee to the suburban hinterland), and others—but discussion of these

---

[7] Quoted by Albert W. Votaw, in "The Hillbillies Invade Chicago," 216 *Harper's Magazine* (February, 1958), 64ff.

points may be deferred. The essential point is clear: the conditions of modern mass society pose problems for *all* levels of government.

3. *The Economic Challenge.* Although some people may not realize it, the federal government is not the only source of public policy affecting the economy. The corridors of the state legislature are filled with lobbyists who would never make the mistake of assuming state government has no effect on the economic interests they represent. Bankers, contractors, retailers, and labor leaders who regularly confer with city councilors are under no delusions about the potential effect of local power on their economic interests. The regulation of banking is a major duty of the state government; the statutory regulation and supervision of the insurance industry—including even that part of the business involving interstate transactions—is explicitly relegated to the states by the federal government. Services, regulations, prohibitions, and direct subsidies all affect business conditions.

One of the difficulties in carrying out these various duties is the fact that states are in a sense in competition with each other, as are cities. The demands for taxes to undertake the functions necessitated by a growing and ever more complex society are enormous, and the political feasibility of any tax increase is, of course, always limited. When a local government begins to canvass the possible tax sources on which it can draw, it is faced with one problem that Congress does not face. If a state proposes a new tax levy, it is threatened with the possible loss of industry to states in which the tax burden is not so heavy. The threat is often more bluff than substance, but the stakes for the state that may lose thousands of jobs are so high that politicians must hesitate before possibly committing political suicide. What is true of taxation is equally true of business regulation, control over industrial pollution of air or streams, regulation of labor conditions, or the provision of welfare needs for the indigent or the unemployed. The fear of acquiring a reputation for being "unfriendly" to business is a constant political force.

Even if this were not true, the fact that the states are so different in economic resources poses a problem for their very existence as viable units of government. If the states cannot find the resources to undertake functions that the majority of the people apparently demand, then some alternative means of financing the projects must be found, and that alternative is usually a Congressional appropriation. And if the money comes from the national treasury, inevitably there will be accompanying standards of performance required as a precondition of financial assistance. Thus a degree of control over a particular service or governmental program passes from the regional to the national government. There are, as we shall see in later discussion of this problem, sharply divided views as to the merits of granting such powers to the national government, but if greater equality of, say, educational opportunity *and* maximum local control are both desired, unevenness of economic resources poses a problem. The wide range of variation in the wealth of the states is apparent from Table 2–2, which presents various cultural-economic indices.

4. *The Political Challenge.* If responsible management of economic development and the finding of the resources necessary to conduct desired programs for economic and social improvements are to be successfully achieved, we shall need great political ingenuity, courage, and leadership—more than most of our states and municipalities have shown in recent decades. Since much of the remainder of this volume is devoted to examination of the implications of the foregoing proposition, a brief introductory examination of it is appropriate.

Because apathy is relatively great, because it is always easier—at least in the short run—to evade action than to buck the resisters, the tendency is to muddle along, ignoring problems rather than devising means of coping with them. Because it is always difficult to tackle the entrenched interest group protecting its advantages, whatever they are, the tendency is to leave such problems for the *next* governor, mayor, or city council rather than risk political difficulties that a vocal minority can undoubtedly arouse. If greater efficiency requires tackling the civil service-protected job holders, or the equally formidable patronage holders or seekers, then perhaps the program should wait a while. If the open land that can be sold for housing and industrial development is needed for recreational parks to accommodate the advancing population, the short-run, lower-tax, easy way out may seem more inviting than the alternative of planning ahead and insisting on short-run denial for long-run advantage. In short, the courage to plan ahead, the wit and leadership required to make enough people see the need of facing the realities of mass society may turn out to be the crucial challenge facing state and local government.

But suppose a disbeliever flings the challenge back and asks how these "needs" are to be determined? What standards determine that this is a "reality" that "must" be met? It is obvious that these "realities" are not objective facts that every rational person would have to accept. Some may say, for example, that the problem of diminishing water supply is a relative one. It is relative, of course. In many a North African village the water supply consists of a peddler wandering through the dusty streets with a leather water bag on his shoulder, shouting his

TABLE 2-2
Comparative Cultural-Economic Indices

	Connecticut	New York	Oregon	Minnesota	Colorado	Mississippi	West Virginia	United States
Per Capita Personal Income (1964)*	$3155	3037	2484	2512	2512	1369	1860	2460
Per Capita Total Revenue (1965)*	$ 389	481	461	437	454	283	310	384
Amount of Total Revenue per $1000 of Personal Income (1965)*	$ 122	154	180	186	177	197	159	151
Per Pupil Expenditures (1965)	$ 637	876	612	577	513	317	367	532
Median School Years Completed (1960)**	11.0	10.7	11.8	10.8	12.1	8.9	8.8	10.6
Physicians per 100,000 population (1965)*	178	211	148	148	176	74	101	151
Selective Service Rejection Rate (per cent disqualified) (1965)*	35.3	46.8	39.9	33.8	37.8	53.3	50.8	43.6

* Data drawn from *Statistical Abstract*, 1966.
** Bureau of the Census, *County and City Data Book* (Washington, D.C.: Government Printing Office, 1962), p. 3.

price for a cup of water. Moslem religious laws demand the washing of hands and face five times a day, but water is so scarce that rubbing oneself with sand is a permissible substitute. The contrast between such conditions and the typically wasteful use of water in this country illustrates poignantly the "relativity" of needs. Slums, unsanitary conditions, substandard schools, lack of recreational facilities—these and a thousand other "deficiencies" one could name all must be considered in terms of their relative importance and in terms of the ability of the community to correct them. Even the preservation of human life itself has to be weighed in the scales of relativity. If we wished to spend the necessary resources we could end the deaths that occur every year at railroad crossings simply by building an overpass at every crossing in the land. But we don't want to spend the money and therefore such accidents continue to take lives. The same is true with regard to the social, economic, and psychological costs of slums, inadequate education, and so on.

Why talk about "needs" of cities and states in the future then? If these are relative matters, then the question of whether or not the political leadership can be produced to cope with them may not be of much importance. But to admit that these are relative matters is not to write them off as unimportant to the values and desires of the people concerned. The point is that the problems do not have to be presented as "absolutes" in order to emphasize their significance. The slum riots of recent years present an enormous challenge to "do something" before the social fabric of the whole society is ripped to shreds—and that seems to be an "absolute." Yet even here the establishment of priorities and the facing off of one program against another is inevitable. Priorities and need in short are part of the continuing political process, not "givens" with which you begin.

No one should underestimate the difficulties of achieving adequate political initiative and leadership to meet these challenges. The difficulties are formidable and the temptation to evade them is inviting and ubiquitous. Some of the main difficulties can be categorized thus: political party problems, obscurity of some governmental agents and units of government, the problems of achieving coordination of policy among governments, the favorable fighting ground on which certain vested interests are entrenched, and, finally, the technical difficulties to which imagination and foresight must be applied.

In general, American political parties are weak and ineffective or worse, although there are places where parties are well-organized and reasonably responsible. In some states, it is clear—although the information on the point is not, oddly enough, very full or instructive for many parts of the country—that the parties are little more than names behind which factional rivalries are conducted. In some areas the parties are still notoriously corrupt and a few old-style bosses still survive. And in more areas than not, especially in the lower levels of government where fewer and fewer peope are involved, there is no effective second party, and the advantages of two-party competition are consequently lacking. Particularly at the state government level, political parties are important potential contributors to the development of public leadership, but all too often this potential is unfulfilled.

It follows that the more apathetic people are about a given government or function of government, the wider is the discretion of those who hold formal power in the agency or government involved. The more obscure and unobserved an agent the greater the temptation to misuse his power. Many units of government (the thousands of coun-. ties, the tens of thousands of small municipalities and independent school districts) are often *terra incognita* to the very residents to whom supposedly they are "close" and by whom supposedly they are controlled. Political control over government is difficult to achieve when the public cannot name its officials and knows nothing of their actions.

The more numerous and obscure governments become, the greater the difficulty in achieving coordination between them for the conduct of programs that transcend the powers of any one government. Preachments for the parochial point of view and against the common development of a region—for water resources development, for example, or area-wide economic development and zoning coordination—are very hard to overcome politically. The demagogue, willing to attack in defense of home-town or immediate interests and to defy a scheme to collaborate with someone downriver or across the valley, always has a certain advantage. Cooperation to eliminate pollution may be hard to obtain from the upriver towns that are doing the polluting. Devising means to overcome such attacks, and inventing means to provide some kind of political unity for undertaking area- or region-wide cooperative programs is a considerable challenge.

There are so many kinds of securely emplaced special interests to act as political barriers that one knows not where to start in illustrating the point. Incumbent civil servants help scuttle a proposal for change because it appears to threaten their job security. Scattered and sometimes wasteful agencies beyond the control of responsible leaders in state or local government, arouse their "clientele" to fend off attempts to cut administrative costs and inefficiency. Economic interests collaborate with constitutionally or traditionally entrenched political forces to warp policies to their special desires. There are officials whose handsome salaries are based on fees for services that could be provided more cheaply and just as efficiently in other ways. Often these fee-paid jobs are major sources of political party revenue which means that the beneficiaries of the fees have defenders they can depend on to stop reform drives. This is especially true where the annual "take" is enormous as it is with New York City marshals, some of whom earn as much as $100,000 per year.[8]

This courage, imagination, and leadership must be produced in the middle of political battling, pulling, and hauling, where there is ever-

---

[8] See *The New York Times*, January 22, 1968. The *Times* also reported on December 17, 1951, that many other states had fee-paid employees with incomes larger than their state's governors. See also Lawrence Leder, "The Fee System Gravy," 47 *National Municipal Review*, 374 (1958).

present fear of defeat at the next election, fear of too much centralization, fear of high taxes and poor service. Amidst the swirl of contests for power, prestige, and preferment, decisions must be made with foresight and imagination. Involved technical questions may be political questions as well, and therefore the knowledge of the engineer or the public health specialist or the urban architect must be combined with the skills of a political leader. To lead a fight for aesthetic values in a community where the loudest voices demand minimum taxes rather than civic beauty may seem too much to ask of political leaders, but aesthetic values need a loud voice too. The aesthetic qualities of the today's cities are important, particularly because of the social aridity that often characterizes the huge city—yet transmitting artistic values in the hurly-burly of political debate is no mean task.

Thus the political leader of a city or a state that would produce not only a safe and convenient life for its citizens but a life of beauty and meaning has to be able to understand the technician and the artist. He must be able to translate the technical and obscure into the comprehensible; he must protect his specialists from predatory raids by fellow politicians and the short-run-Johnny whose specialty is today and to whom tomorrow is someone else's worry. The political leader must understand, utilize, and protect the technicians if he is to succeed in twentieth-century society.

Decentralization and the Distribution of Powers Among Governments

3.

As EVEN A CASUAL STUDENT of American history would recognize, the proper distribution of powers among governmental units has been one of the most vigorously debated issues of our national politics. As early as the seventeenth century, colony-mother country disputes presaged this theme, and the Revolutionary War was, after all, largely a quarrel with England about which powers should be allowed to the colonies and which retained in London. The Articles of Confederation, the Constitution, Federalist and anti-Federalist controversies, the doctrines of nullification and those of inseparable union, long constitutional contests over the commerce clause and the state police power—all these and many other notable events of our political development concern the optimum allocation of authority between governments. Not only is this issue one of the most pervasive in American political history, but its importance is enormous, and especially so in comparison with other countries where centralized power has been accepted for so long that such debates as do arise about the distribution of powers do not have the depth of historical attachments and the passion of conviction that they do in the United States.

For all our attention to the question, however, it does not follow that we achieve great sophistication in most discussions of power distribution. Thus federalism becomes a "given" in our argument and is not seriously questioned. (Federalism means, not the federal government, but the system of delegating certain powers to the national gov-

[27]

ernment and reserving certain others to the states.) We all are in favor of "home rule" and control at the "grass roots," but we are not always certain what these terms imply. Professor Roscoe Martin, tongue in cheek, has propounded the rule ". . . that the grass-roots character of a given phenomenon (place, event, program) increases directly with the square of its distance from Washington."[1] But how often do we examine this principle and its implications?

Occasionally someone like the late Harold Laski, British critic of American institutions, directly challenges the wisdom of federalism, but such effrontery is rare. Laski concluded that effective and vigorous government was made difficult by federalism, and "that the institutional apparatus of American federalism maximizes the difficulty" of achieving "creative leadership in the positive state." [2] Others asked questions of a rather searching character during the Depression when the Supreme Court used the concept of federalism to negative many anti-Depression measures of the New Deal, but when the Court relented, we settled back to normal attitudes once again. Such dissatisfaction as now exists about federalism is usually expressed in more moderate terms. The questioning is not directed at the fundamental doctrine but at its proper interpretation or adaptation to current controversies and conditions.

Government "Close to the People"

Let me illustrate a fairly common difficulty that follows from dependence upon unexamined assumptions about the decentralization of power. It is often assumed that the closer power is to the people the greater will be their interest in and control over it. This assumption runs into difficulty when we begin to test it empirically. Is the public in fact more interested in state and local government than about the more remote national government? Is proximity the "cause" of citizen interest? By ordinary tests of public attitudes it would appear that even among citizens who show any interest at all in public affairs—and many do not, of course—a greater proportion concern themselves with national than with state or local matters. Inquiries among citizens of a middle-sized Michigan city some years ago indicated that among those interviewed, only two of the fifty-six who were active in public affairs

---

[1] Roscoe Martin, *Grass Roots* (University, Ala.: University of Alabama Press, 1957), p. 3.

[2] Harold J. Laski, *The American Democracy* (New York: The Viking Press, Inc., 1948), p. 121.

listed state issues as the ones that interested them most. Fifty-nine per cent of the respondents considered national affairs the most "serious." [3]

Apathy toward government is no novelty, of course; the significant point is that there is greater apathy about state government than about the more remote national government. News media emphasize national politics more than state politics, it is true, but this is doubtless a response to existing public interest. The urgent questions of war and peace, the drama of the presidency, the histrionics of a Senate filibuster, attract more attention than the debate in last night's city council meeting or a close vote in the state legislature. Evidence of the acceptance of this state of affairs is that in common parlance the word *government* alone is increasingly used to identify national government; to refer to nonnational government a modifier is needed.

Perhaps the most convincing evidence of the differences in public interest are the variations in the number of voters who can be persuaded to participate in city, state, and national elections. National elections, most particularly presidential elections, draw the greatest number of voters to the polling places; state elections arouse fewer participants and local elections fewer still. V. O. Key, Jr., compared voting for president with voting for local officials in the 324 towns of Massachusetts and found that "in a few localities the local vote amounted to less than 10 per cent of, and in a few it exceeded, the presidential vote. About half the local elections attracted a vote of less than 70 per cent of the presidential vote." [4] New York City voters react about the same way. In the period 1948–58 their average turnout for gubernatorial elections was 78 per cent of the city's average turnout for presidential elections; in mayoralty elections the turnout was 72 per cent of the presidential average.[5]

Federalism: Decentralization and Centralization

For the federal government to be uppermost in the minds of its countrymen is an inversion of historical precedent. Not only did the states

[3] Ralph H. Smuckler and George M. Belknap, *Leadership and Participation in Urban Political Affairs* (East Lansing, Mich.: Government Research Bureau, Michigan State University, 1956), p. 30.

[4] V. O. Key, Jr., *Politics, Parties, and Pressure Groups*, 4th ed. (New York: Thomas Y. Crowell Company, 1958), p. 627.

[5] Calculated from election data in Wallace S. Sayre and Herbert Kaufman's *Governing New York City: Politics in the Metropolis* (New York: Russell Sage Foundation, 1960), p. 126.

precede the national government, but the states also did most of the "governing" in the United States for a long time after the Constitution was adopted (how long after it would be difficult to say—a century at least, probably more). De Tocqueville, the French commentator on America of the Jacksonian era, observed that the real government of the United States was not found in the national capital: "The federal government scarcely interferes in any but foreign affairs; . . . the governments of the states in reality direct society in America." [6] This was the time in the evolution of American concepts of government when a federal statute providing money for internal improvements such as highways and canals was widely thought to be unconstitutional. Late in his life Jefferson contemplated urging nullification resolutions by the states should such a law be passed. This was a time when the national government had more revenue than it could readily spend—a result of high tariffs and low federal expenditures. In peacetime annual surpluses were the rule, occasionally as much as a 50 per cent surplus of income over outlays.[7] In 1836, when the surplus mounted unusually high, part of it was turned over to the states. Jeffersonian ideas emphasized the importance of localism, and although Jefferson's actions in office were not always consistent with the ideas he expressed when out of office, his doctrine nevertheless took firm root in the new nation. To be sure, Jeffersonian decentralization doctrines were flexible—a good many people (including Jefferson) professed or ignored them depending on whether the particular use of national power was to their liking. This is still true. A good test of it can be found in regional newspapers. The typical editorial expresses antipathy to federal spending, turning glib and angry phrases about galloping, creeping, or other gaited motion toward enveloping centralism. But another issue of the same paper, without mentioning the dangers of encroachment, will plug for greater federal outlays for TVA expansion, farm subsidies, aircraft manufacture, drought relief, or some other locally based "need" which is self-evident to the people whose jobs depend upon its being met.

Jefferson's theories were less important than the facts of physical space and the inadequacy of means of intercommunication between parts of the country in determining that the states would retain the

---

[6] Alexis de Tocqueville, *Democracy in America*, Phillips Bradley, ed., Vol. 1 (New York: Alfred A. Knopf, 1945), p. 254.

[7] See Lewis H. Kimmel, *The Federal Budget and Fiscal Policy, 1789–1958* (Washington, D.C.: Brookings Institution, 1959), p. 315. See also A. H. Birch, *Federalism, Finances and Social Legislation* (London: Oxford University Press, 1955), pp. 8–13.

greater share of governing responsibilities. Thus Jefferson wrote to Madison in 1794 on the occasion of his return to Monticello:

I could not have supposed, when at Philadelphia, that so little of what was passing there could be known even at Kentucky, as is the case here. Judging from this of the rest of the union, it is evident to me that the people are not in a condition either to approve or disapprove of their government, nor consequently to influence it.[8]

In that year sending a message from Philadelphia to Georgia took 13 days, to Kentucky as much as a month.[9]

Although it would have been technologically feasible to expand the province of the national government after the Civil War, there was not much impetus to do so. It is true that Congress passed the Morrill Act in 1862, providing aid to the states for establishing state colleges, and that agricultural services by the national government began at that time. In the main, however, expansion was very slow. Indeed, in view of the unprecedented sweep of federal powers during the Civil War, it is surprising that there was so little expansion after the war. Of course, constitutional traditions were against expansion, and during this era, *laissez-faire* ideas were increasingly popular. Proponents of federal action—and there were such, of course—had not only to overcome the ideological obstacles of the time but also to face the powerful and well-entrenched political forces of an expanding industrial and financial empire. Only after long, patient struggling was the Sherman Antitrust Act of 1890 navigated through the shoals of Congress. Notwithstanding this "invasion" of hitherto unregulated business practice, there was no rush of regulatory legislation following it. As a matter of fact, there was no speed demonstrated in applying the antimonopoly act itself— two decades passed before much effective action was taken against the monopolies.

It hardly needs be said that the national government has had a spectacular boom in the twentieth century. Three wars have enlisted the interest of the mass of the people in an inescapable way, arousing nationalistic sentiment and focusing unprecedented attention on Washington. War necessitated expansion of powers to accommodate the sweeping inclusiveness of modern warfare. Likewise the full impact of

---

[8] Quoted by Leonard D. White, *The Federalists* (New York: The Macmillan Company, 1948), p. 481.
[9] *Ibid.*

industrial capitalism and an inordinately complicated economic life brought other expansions of power from the Pure Food and Drug Act of 1906 to the Securities and Exchange Act of 1934 to the Taft-Hartley Act of 1947.[10]

Indeed, there were so many changes in federal power, and these changes were in such contrast with the character of the governmental system prior to 1900 that many people worried lest this growing behemoth destroy the very fundamentals of our social and economic fabric. Thus the National Association of Manufacturers in a pamphlet called *Bring The Government Back Home* expresses its fear:

The increasing concentration of political and economic control in the federal government is destroying the economic and governmental environment which is essential to the survival of the American system of free enterprise and to the preservation of the American constitutional system of a union of states. Unless the trend toward ever bigger government is halted, and until it is reversed, the states and private business alike face the prospect of ultimate, complete domination by the federal government. And complete federal domination IS totalitarianism.[11]

While this is hardly an unprejudiced viewpoint, it is an argument that has raised grave fears in the minds of many people. The impression appears to be fairly common that the federal and the state-local governments have been on opposite ends of a seesaw—if the federal powers increased, only one thing could happen to nonnational powers: they must decline as dramatically as the central government's powers increase.

This reasoning sounds logical, but the evidence does not sustain it. Both state and national governments have vastly expanded their activities in the past half-century.[12] As the Eisenhower-appointed Commission on Intergovernmental Relations pointed out:

---

[10] For an excellent review of the evolution of federal-state powers, see L. D. White, *The States and The Nation* (Baton Rouge, La.: Louisiana State University Press, 1953), pp. 1–33.

[11] Quoted in William Anderson, *The Nation and the States: Rivals or Partners?* (Minneapolis, Minn.: University of Minnesota Press, 1955), pp. 5–6.

[12] A comparison of federal and state-local government employment is instructive here. In 1900, state and local governments employed 73 per cent of all public employees, and in 1949—notwithstanding the enormous expansion of the federal bureaucracy—state and local governments still accounted for half of all such employment. State and local employment had increased by 407 per cent in comparison with a federal rise of 1005 per cent. See Solomon Fabricant, *The Trend of Government Activity Since 1900* (New York: National Bureau of Economic Research, 1952), p. 29.

The States and their subdivisions bear directly more than two thirds of the growing fiscal burden of domestic government. In recent years their activities have been increasing faster than the nondefense activities of the National Government.[13]

Between them state and local governments now spend around $100 billion a year, far more than is spent by the national government on nondefense items. As V. O. Key has observed:

. . . the conclusion emerges that, as the prophets of doom proclaimed the passing of the states during the ferment of the New Deal, state governments were expanding their staffs, enlarging the scope of their activities, spending more and more money, and in general enjoying a boom as such things go in governmental circles.[14]

Substantially the same thing can be said of the municipality; modern social and economic conditions have enormously expanded the number and scope of activities undertaken by municipal governments to cope with ever-mounting problems.

At the beginning of the century nonnational expenditures usually ran at two to three times the national costs of government, and the role of grants was small indeed—only $7 millions in 1902. By 1942 grants had become more important (amounting to $887 millions) and due to New Deal governmental programs the federal outlay nearly equaled that of the states and localities. But note in Figure 3–1 how the rate of state and local expenditures has soared to a level twice the federal rate. (Note that federal grants are shown separately and are not included in either state-local or federal figures.)

Can one infer from the records of expenditures that a governmental unit has a significant role to play—that this is a reasonable measure of its activity and thus of its importance? Admittedly a government that was no more than a conduit through which money was channeled would appear to be significant when it was not if one looked only at its financial reports. But if one broadens the scope of inquiry slightly and examines other characteristics of these governments the obvious sources of confusion can be eliminated. Thus the data on public debt and public personnel confirm the impression that the state and local

---

[13] The Commission on Intergovernmental Relations, *Report* (Washington, D.C.: Government Printing Office, 1955), p. 36.

[14] V. O. Key, Jr., *American State Politics: An Introduction* (New York: Alfred A. Knopf, 1956), p. 7.

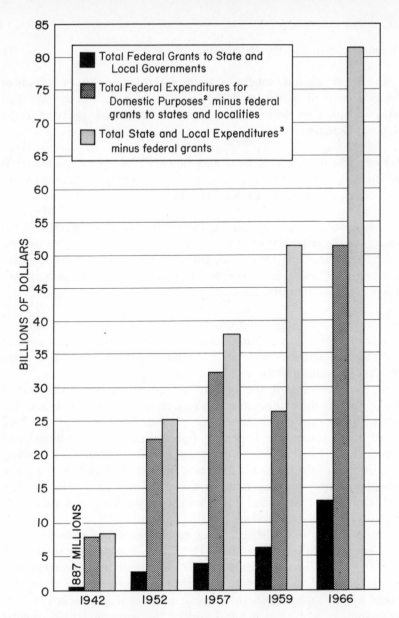

Figure 3-1. Comparative Growth of Federal and State-Local Expenditures for Domestic Purposes (1942–66)[1]

[1] Sources: *Historical Statistics of the United States, Colonial Times to 1957*, pp. 721 ff.; *Statistical Abstract*, 1961, pp. 403 ff.; *Statistical Abstract*, 1967, pp. 422 ff.

[2] Federal Expenditures exclude (1) major military, (2) international relations, (3) grants to state and local governments.

[3] Excludes from state and local expenditures two self-sustaining operations: (1) insurance trust funds, (2) liquor store funds; and amounts equal to federal grants to states and localities for the year in question.

governments continue to be active and important, for it is the sole responsibility of states (and ultimately state taxpayers) to handle their own indebtedness, and state and local government personnel act in the name of the states and localities as they govern (see Table 3–1.) Notice that federal debt has risen relatively slowly since the end of World War II, whereas the debt levels of nonnational governments have increased by almost six times the 1944 debt. The public employment record makes the same point even more dramatically since many of the civilian employees of the federal government—such as those in the Defense and State Departments—are performing tasks not directly related to domestic affairs. Moreover federal civilian employment has declined since the war while state-local employment has more than doubled.

Similarly, an inventory of state and local functions is an impressive record since these governments conduct the world's hugest educational and highway systems, maintain judicial, welfare, police, health, and rec-

TABLE 3-1
Comparative Debt Levels and Public Employment
For Federal and State-Local Governments*

| | Debt | | Public Employees | |
| | Federal | State-Local | Federal** | State-Local |
Year	(in millions)		(in thousands)	
1942	72,422	19,706	2664	3251
1944	201,003	17,479	3365	3172
1952	259,105	30,100	2583	4522
1957	270,527	53,039	2439	5608
1959	284,706	64,110	2234	6387
1965	317,274	99,512	2588	8001

* Source: *Historical Statistics of the United States, Colonial Times to 1957; Statistical Abstract*, 1960, 1961, 1966.

** This includes only civilian employees of the federal government, although civilians in defense or international jobs are not excluded.

reational facilities for our mobile and sometimes turbulent society. Most regulation of industry, banking, commerce, utilities, labor, and protection of public safety fall to these governments. Their programs of research, conservation, preventive health, social work, housing, and urban planning are vast in scope and significant for the day-to-day lives of all Americans. Patronizingly setting state and local government aside as insignificant agencies concerned only with sewers, sidewalks, and vague state statutes is a monstrous mistake.

The skeptic may say, however, that statistics on expenditures, debts, and employment and the catalogue of functions are unconvincing because the federal government is increasingly the financial supporter of these programs. It is argued that this aid is tantamount to federal control and consequently weakens state and local government. This is a widely held point of view and deserves attention. In many ways this question is at the heart of the contemporary federal system. In the first place it is certainly true that many of the undertakings alluded to above are financed in good part from federal funds, and indeed many of them would not have been initiated without the federal government's economic stimulus. Encouraged by financial assistance, cities have gone into urban renewal programs, tearing down slums and replacing them with decent housing or commercial developments, with two-thirds (and, for smaller cities since 1961, three-fourths) of the cost of these programs provided from federal funds. State highway, welfare, education and other programs have been boosted by aid from Washington. Grants from the central government amounted to 10 per cent of the expenditures of the states in 1953, and in some earlier years, particularly during the Depression, the percentage of federal contributions to the total expenditures of the states (not local governments in this case) ran as high as 30 per cent. Still as the data plotted in Figure 3–1 demonstrate, the proportion of grant-in-aid money in state and local expenditures remained under 10 per cent, except for 1959 which goes slightly over that figure as a result of the initiation of the new program of federal aid to states for building interstate highways. Even with the expansion of grants in the mid-1960's the proportion of state-local expenditures from Washington was only 13.8 as of 1966.

The volume of grants is, however, only the roughest index of their significance. Opponents of federal grants are surely correct in their contention that the availability of this "easy" money (in the sense that state and local officials can spend money that they do not have to raise themselves) encourages nonnational governments to venture into programs that otherwise they would not undertake. Consider, for example, the fat carrot that Congress was persuaded to place before the donkey when it passed the 1956 Federal Aid Highway Act. A state legislature, by appropriating 10 per cent of the cost of a highway, can get from the federal government the remaining 90 per cent of the cost. In the urban renewal program, a city can tear down its slums and rebuild and have up to three-quarters of the net cost of the project financed by Washington. Opponents of such programs object to them on several grounds. In the first place the projects can more readily be undertaken since the barrier of financing is lowered. Secondly, grants tend to transfer the financing of government from the resources available to states and municipalities (which are in general more limited) to the federal graduated personal and corporate income tax which, if limited, still does not have to be set in the light of interstate and intermunicipal competition for industry. That is, states set their tax rates in fear of other states with perhaps lower taxes who may entice industry away, whereas the federal government has no such direct competitors. Third, grant programs work toward a kind of redistribution of wealth in the country by taking more from the rich states than is returned to them and giving the poorer states more than they contribute. When residents of wealthier states complain that their particular state has to pay more than a dollar for a dollar's worth of federal aid they are factually quite correct. Fourth, the administration of the distribution of grants naturally costs money, and antagonists of the system point to this as "waste" in the sense at least that the money is not directly devoted to the programs themselves. Finally, and certainly not the least important, the grants involve certain federal controls.[15]

It is the latter complaint—the effect of federal controls—that is the chief ground for objection to grants and it therefore is appropriate to assess briefly the implications of those controls. In the first place no grants are made without conditions being stated as prerequisites to be met by the state or locality before the cash is handed over. There is almost invariably a demand that the money granted be used only for specified purposes, that matching money be contributed by the participating governments (ranging from 50-50 shares to the 90-10 arrangement mentioned above for the highway program), that certain standards of administrative practices be met (thus in many states civil service status and protection are granted solely for employees involved in federally aided programs and for no others), and finally that minimum conditions of various kinds be met regarding the actual conduct of the functions aided by the grants. These minimum conditions naturally vary enormously depending upon the programs; they may involve the quality of materials and methods used in constructing highways, the minimum standards for rehousing slum dwellers forcefully

---

[15] The literature on grant-in-aid operations is extensive. A short summary of the programs in operation as of 1955 can be found in the Report of The Commission on Intergovernmental Relations, sometimes called the Kestnbaum Report (for its chairman, Meyer Kestnbaum) (Washington, D.C.: Government Printing Office, 1955), Chap. 5, and pp. 302–09. See Chap. 5 for adverse opinions on the grant program. For a rousing attack on grants by a former Governor of New Jersey and member of the commission, see Alfred E. Driscoll, "The Biggest Con Game in Politics," *Reader's Digest* (December, 1956), 33–38; (January, 1957), 63–67.

ejected from their homes, or a complete and accurate reporting of the operations that must be made available to the federal agency.

To what extent do these various controls actually turn over to the federal government the authority and ultimate responsibility for conduct of the functions involved? Is the fear well-grounded that in the end the grantor takes over the actual program and thus diminishes the significance of the grantee? Although it is not inconceivable that this could happen, there is little ground for believing that it has. On the contrary, a case could be made for the proposition that the use of grants has sustained and strengthened the states and localities for the simple reason that their range of activities could not possibly have been so extensive if dependent solely on their own financing. The grants have in some degree made them more significant governments. It is also contended that the minimal conditions demanded have frequently improved rather than hurt the state and local governments, since they have had to keep records through which the corrupt could be rooted out and since they have had to reduce waste by trimming their administrative personnel to meet the limits on this cost factor demanded by the federal law.

Even if these arguments are not acceptable—and they certainly have mixed applicability to the various states—however, the fact is inescapable that the federal agencies have not done all that legally they might have done to demand compliance. Indeed there are many complaints that the powers of the agencies to demand compliance have been too little used. In the urban renewal program, for example, the federal Urban Renewal Administration is often quite vexing to local officials about the dotting of *i*'s and the crossing of *t*'s in filling out the myriad forms required and have also closely second-checked the sensitive financial negotiations for property acquisition which are usually standing invitations to corruption. Nevertheless, Renewal officials have been lenient in enforcing aspects of the "workable program" that each community must submit for approval. Although the rules call for definite plans to relocate the dispossessed, the federal agency has not demanded compliance of most cities. In welfare program administration as well, the federal government has a mixed record of insistence and neglect where minimum conditions are concerned. In the celebrated controversy in Newburgh, New York, where in 1961 the city manager instituted what were widely deemed harsh measures to cut the relief roles, the Secretary of Health, Education, and Welfare, Abraham Ribicoff, disavowed any intent to cut off aid to either that city or to the state of New York, through which the federal funds were directed. A good illustration of the hesitancy of the federal agents to make demands is found in Paul Ylvisaker's case study of the origination of federal aid to welfare programs in Blue Earth County, Minnesota.[16] There the federal government's administrators could have made much more rigorous demands on the state and local officials, but they forebore to do so—and the reason is fairly clear: the cooperation of local and state officials was needed by the federal official. Blunt demands and threatened sanctions against nonconforming officials could perhaps wreck a program that the federal agency wanted to see succeed by evoking headlines heralding the conflict and bringing angry Congressmen (who also vote on appropriations for federal agencies) banging at the administrator's door, complaining of the arbitrariness of federal demands.

The same is true of other programs. The staff of the Urban Renewal Administration are hesitant to make too rigorous demands, since they are understandably desirous of keeping urban renewal operating at a fast pace—thus inviting future demands for expansion of the program—rather than fighting out relocation procedures or other substantive questions that may delay rather than accelerate operations, and may produce controversies that will alienate Congressional support. This is particularly the case where federal funds are in effect being used to entrench racial segregation in housing—should the agency fight it out and lose appropriations or should it avert its official eyes and keep the program going by staying out of trouble? Without attempting here to go further into the politics of intergovernmental negotiations that arise from these federal "controls," the point is that the legal authorization for the application of controls and the actual application of them are two different, if closely related, things. The conceivable effect (based on the letter of the law) is infinitely greater than the potential effect (based on the political realities). This, it should be emphasized, is not to say that there is *no* impact from these controls; in many respects the controls have been effective both for the "improvement" of nonnational operations and for enforcing national policy upon resisting local officials. Whether one likes this kind of control or not is a matter of personal values, but it can hardly be argued that the controls have wholly cut the ground from under the states and the localities.

Other arguments, however, have been leveled at the so-called categorical grant program (meaning conditional grants rather than open-ended grants to be spent as desired). It is argued, for example, that the red tape and endless paperwork to justify state or local expenditures

---

[16] Originally issued as one of the Inter-University Case Programs series, it is reprinted in Harold Stein, ed., *Public Administration and Policy Development* (New York: Harcourt, Brace and World, Inc., 1952), pp. 89–106.

represents a vast waste of talent that might be used profitably rather than frittered away filling out forms with seven carbon copies. There is some truth in this accusation, as any local official who has been involved in a grant program will testify. They complain about the demands of the "Feds" for useless mountains of paper. A personal experience may illustrate the point. As a member of a state task force I once had occasion to petition the U.S. Office of Economic Opportunity for funds to do needed research on some problems of migratory farm labor, and I produced a simple, and I thought straightforward, statement of my needs. This got a hasty rejection in Washington, and only after the request had been transformed into a document the size of a small book was it looked upon favorably.

There are, however, two sides to this story. All bureaucrats have to protect themselves—not only from Congressmen, who become dangerous when disturbed, but also from other petitioners who may have political pressure but insufficient standing or reason to substantiate their requests. Therefore, the bureaucrat has to build a record to defend his every move. It is also noteworthy that the habits of self-protection can lead to a kind of fussy overattention to minute detail that takes the place of attention to the more important fundamentals.

Moreover, there is grave concern that the multiplication of conduits through which grants-in-aid are allocated will result in overlapping and utter confusion. Grant programs numbered about 60 in 1955 when the Commission on Intergovernmental Relations reported, but now there are more than 400 of them, and many suspect that more than a little confusion has crept into their operations. This concern, supplemented by a curious blending of conservative and liberal opinion, has resulted in pressure for "revenue sharing," a scheme whereby the states would receive a proportion of federal tax revenue to use as they see fit—more or less. At least the money would not be tied up in the kinds of legal restrictions and detailed specifications that grant programs now normally involve. Support for this idea has come from conservatives who dislike the categorical grant programs and would like to see the states have funds to strengthen themselves rather than allow the federal government to set goals and methods because it provides funds. And it also has support from liberals like Walter Heller, former chairman of the President's Council of Economic Advisers, who contends that the enormous needs for resources at the state and local levels would make it wiser to direct excess federal income tax revenues (developed as a result of economic growth) to these pressing needs of the public sector of the economy than to resort to tax reductions, which he, no doubt rightly, assumes there would be enormous Congressional pressure to do.

The war in Vietnam made the proposal a moot issue, for the war more than absorbed any excess revenue, but should the war end or abate the debate will no doubt mount again. There are many angles to revenue sharing and there is no space to go into them all here. This brief summary statement of pros and cons will have to suffice.

Charge: That revenue sharing would turn over funds to the least competent and least innovative element of government—the states.

Response: Case not proved merely by asserting it; the evidence is mixed. While states have deficiencies, there are also real assets and it is noteworthy that they have had the courage in the course of the past two decades to increase taxes repeatedly to provide the money for an enormous expansion of governmental activity. In state after state the number of students in public higher education institutions has doubled in a few years time; many innovations in civil rights legislation took place in states before Congress could be persuaded to pass its first twentieth-century civil rights act; in highway accident prevention, in pollution control and in other areas the states have as often led the federal government as the contrary.

Charge: That revenue sharing would only lead the states to slack off their tax efforts and let the federal money fill in.

Response: The ceaseless demand for services at the state level and the willingness of the states to enact taxes to meet them does not suggest states would rest on their oars if thus assisted.

Charge: The states might use the money for low-priority or (in the view of some) utterly objectionable programs.

Response: They might, but money is being spent for some of these low-priority programs in all states already and it is no solution to deny funds for expansion of other needed ventures.

Charge: Revenue sharing would be destructive to the morale of state government—to spend money not raised would sap their vitality as governments.

Response: The evidence doesn't support the charge. The use of categoric grants does not appear to have ruined state governments, so why should revenue sharing? In Canada, where revenue sharing has been used, the provincial governments have become more, not less, independent over the years. And, to take another example, the states have poured enormous amounts of money into local school districts via grants, but the school district has not lost its independence or its relative autonomy as a result.

Charge: To share revenues in this way would terminate the ability of the federal government to use Title VI of the Civil Rights Act to enforce desegregation in programs using federal money.

Response: This would be a problem (to those who want to have such power exercised, of course) if all categorical grants were being terminated. Since they are not, at least under most proposals for revenue sharing, the ability to use Title VI would not be affected.

Charge: The states would use the money and the cities that desperately need help would be left out. (Note: governors generally support revenue sharing and mayors oppose it for just this reason.)

Response: This is a problem, but it can be avoided by providing in the law that a specified percentage of the shared revenue be allocated to the cities of a state. A little ingenuity can rectify that shortcoming.[17]

Quite apart from the grant question, however, one must realize that the three levels of government are not worlds apart but are integrally interconnected in their activities—not just as a consequence of grants-in-aid but as a result of nearly two centuries of *shared powers*. I cannot find a way of saying this better than the late Morton Grodzins said it:

> The American form of government is often, but erroneously, symbolized by a three-layer cake. A far more accurate image is the rainbow or marble cake, characterized by an inseparable mingling of differently colored ingredients, the colors appearing in vertical and diagonal strands and unexpected whirls. As colors are mixed in the marble cake, so functions are mixed in the American federal system.[18]

He goes on to point out the innumerable ways in which collaboration among the three branches of government proceeds. A single official may at various times be an agent of each of the three levels of government (his example is a city sanitary officer):

> From abattoirs and accounting through zoning and zoo administration, any governmental activity is almost certain to involve the influence, if not the formal administration, of all three planes of the federal system.[19]

This is a point that will be elaborated when a more extensive analysis of federalism is undertaken (see Chapter 4). For the moment, suffice

---

17 On revenue sharing, see Walter Heller, *New Dimensions of Political Economy* (New York: W. W. Norton, 1967), Chap. 3: Joseph A. Pechman, "Financing State and Local Government" (Washington, D.C.: The Brookings Institution, 1965). See, for arguments on both sides "Revenue Sharing and Its Alternatives: What Future for Fiscal Federalism?" Report of the Congressional Joint Economic Committee, 90th Congress, 1st Session, July, 1967.

18 Morton Grodzins, "The Federal System," in *Goals for Americans* (Englewood Cliffs, N.J.: Prentice-Hall, Inc., 1960), p. 265.

19 *Ibid.*, p. 266.

it to say that the interrelationships of national and nonnational government are complex both in conception and operation and that the contention that nonnational government is withering away is ridiculous and unsupported by fact.

If by some magic the states and the municipal governments were spirited away, we would have to reinstate them for the sake of efficiency alone, to say nothing of any other values they serve. In practical terms it is not impossible to govern so huge a number of people without decentralizing much of the decision-making. The Russians centralized control over virtually every aspect of the Soviet political and economic system, only to discover that such centralization was not only inordinately expensive but that it also led to unrealistic decisions based on inadequate understanding of what was needed in remote areas. Keeping both the top and the bottom of the hierarchy reasonably informed of what was or ought to have been going on produced bureaucracy, red tape, and confusion. In 1956, therefore, the Russians—in spite of their desire to exert discipline and policy control according to Communist Party dictates—resorted to decentralization of powers to the Soviet "Republics" in several aspects of their governmentally controlled economy. One keen observer of trends in the Soviet economy, David Granick, believes the decentralization was motivated by a desire to *increase* the effectiveness of central control. The red tape and mountainous detail that rigid centralization involved produced not only uncertainty through too remote control but also some ignoring of the rules out of necessity. The ludicrous length to which overcentralization could lead is illustrated in a tale Granick relates:

A former lawyer for a Soviet bakery, who is now a Russian refugee, tells the story of the bakery needing more flour than its normal allotment during the period shortly before the Second World War. A request was put through channels, and in time it was approved. The approval bore the signature of V. M. Molotov, Chairman of the Council of People's Commissars. It was as though the President of the United States were to approve the purchase of oil to heat a New York Post Office Substation.[20]

To say that governments of some kind must exist at lower than the national level is not to resolve the question, however. For there are infinitely varying degrees of autonomy or subjection to central control that can be applied to such governments. At the margin a seemingly

---

[20] David Granick, *The Red Executive* (Garden City, N.Y.: Doubleday & Co., 1960), p. 162.

independent government may be denied any independence of action. Let us set up a hypothetical situation: assume a subunit of government with presumably separate power to undertake certain functions and with its own agencies and personnel for carrying them out. Theoretically the how, when, and where of conducting the functions are left to the discretion of local officials. Within this broad framework there may be the most extreme variations. On the one hand the choice of local officials and local experts may be subject to central government control; the local government may not be allowed to pick among alternative possibilities. Furthermore, the supposed discretion to undertake functions may be hedged about with numerous directives from the central government that vitiate the theory of independent choice. Superior governments may exert control over local budgets and taxation, from reviewing details to exercising summary veto. It is obvious that the kinds of controls here described are not applied to American state and local governments except in marginal degree. Nonnational governments enjoy a considerable degree of autonomy, although the actual extent of this discretionary power varies from state to state just as it varies according to the issue involved. That is, some states apply relatively more stringent controls over what local governments may do, and the states themselves are much freer to decide what the law should be than they are to apply it. There is relatively little restraint on the state in the definition of crime, for instance, but as to the application of that law to individuals the Supreme Court uses the Fourteenth Amendment concept of "due process of law" to review the fairness of trials.

The relative independence of local and state governments—their opportunities to develop their state and local economies in their own ways, to handle race questions in widely varying ways, to undertake thousands of functions that often put them at crosspurposes with each other and with the federal government—is both an asset and a problem. Why it is an asset hardly needs further illustration. Nor is it difficult to appreciate the problems that are involved. Too much working at crosspurposes strains the system and fotsers efforts to expand central control. In a sense this raises a paradox of a huge society. The paradox is this: will the confusion and working at crosspurposes of local autonomy be worse than the confusion and bureaucratic duplication of centralized control? Naturally no categoric answer is possible; the question is unanswerable. Society's response will vary from crisis to crisis, from contest to contest. It is unlikely that a pragmatic society like ours will formulate any categoric answer and then attempt to conform to it. Rather it will centralize this function, refuse to centralize that one, decentralize another, and waver back and forth on others, depending on the forces of the moment and on the gravity of the question and thousands of other minute but significant variables that influence decision-making in a democratic society.

Does that mean that attempts to weigh the implications of these gradual steps are futile in the long run? If society is going to go on deciding pragmatically rather than in terms of a more rational set of principles, why then make the effort to conceptualize the matter at all? There is, I would argue, reason to analyze these problems of centralization and decentralization, notwithstanding the pragmatic behavior of democratic government. In the first place analysis in general terms has its impact on decisions about particulars. Each of us is the victim of idea-mongers who have implanted ideas in our heads. The famous economist John Maynard Keynes, whose economic theories now shape the fiscal policy decisions of his opponents as well as those of his champions, once wrote:

The ideas of economists and political philosophers, both when they are right and when they are wrong, are more powerful than is commonly understood. Indeed the world is ruled by little else. Practical men who believe themselves to be quite exempt from any intellectual influences are usually slaves of some defunct economist. Madmen in authority, who hear voices in the air, are distilling their frenzy from some academic scribbler of a few years back. I am sure that the power of vested interests is vastly exaggerated compared with the gradual encroachment of ideas.[21]

Not only are we the victims of theorists and "madmen in authority," we also have a difficult time in comprehending what is going on about us. Proposals are made not in the quiet of the study but in the thick of controversy. And when one attempts to assess the implications of a move or series of moves regarding centralization, it is by no means easy to interpret the significance of particular events. What are the implications of a decision to transfer to a metropolitan area body complete power over water supply in a metropolitan region? Is this a step toward breaking down local democracy by withdrawing a kind of power once held locally, or is it a means of assuring firmer control over a complicated question that cannot be dealt with through communities competing with each other for water supply? Does it contribute, that is to

---

[21] John Maynard Keynes, *General Theory of Employment, Interest, and Money* (New York: Harcourt, Brace and World, Inc., 1936), pp. 383–84.

say, to centralization or decentralization? From the perspective of a watershed basin official or a state agency it might seem to be a decentralizing move; from the local angle the opposite.

Moreover, often the tendency when dealing with such issues is to mount the soap-box and attack the problem with propaganda rather than analysis. Paul Ylvisaker comments:

. . . most of what has been said on the subject (of distributing powers among governments) has been provoked in the heat of battle over whether or not to adopt or keep some variety of the system. As a result, we have inherited a congeries of expedient claims, supported only by casual examples and fragmentary arguments chosen on the run . . . [22]

Consider this outburst on federal grants-in-aid from the Indiana General Assembly in 1947:

We are fed up with subsidies, doles and paternalism. We are no one's stepchild. We have grown up. We serve notice that we will resist Washington, D.C., adopting us.

"Be it resolved by the House of Representatives of the General Assembly of the State of Indiana (the Senate concurring), That we respectfully petition and urge Indiana Congressmen and Senators to vote to fetch our county courthouses and city halls back from Pennsylvania Avenue. We want government to come home.

"Resolved further, That we call upon the legislatures of our sister States and on good citizens everywhere who believe in the basic principles of Lincoln and Jefferson to join with us, and we with them, to restore the American Republic and our 48 States to the foundations built by our fathers."

William Anderson observes that:

It is perhaps worthy of mention that the Indiana legislature did not follow up this somewhat bombastic resolution by a refusal to accept further federal grants-in-aid, or by granting more home rule powers to the counties and cities of the state.[23]

---

[22] Paul Ylvisaker, "Criteria for a 'Proper' Areal Division of Power," in *Area and Power, A Theory of Local Government*, edited by Arthur Maass (New York: The Free Press of Glencoe, Inc., 1959), p. 30.

[23] William Anderson, *op. cit.*, pp. 6–7.

The "Proper" Focus of Powers: Some Tests

Any worthwhile approach to the problems of proper location of powers among governmental units will have to eschew categorical, sweeping generalizations and look to more rigorous forms of reasoning. What does it mean to say we "want government to come home"? "Come home" in what sense? Physically? If so, that doesn't mean much in itself. "Closer" in the sense that people will be more aware of activities of governments near at hand? But do proximity and "awareness" always coincide? Data cited earlier suggested that people are less aware of state than of national government operations. Do people feel closer to a county government, which, though physically right at hand, is often vague in every other sense—its personnel, policies, even its very existence may be unrealized. Such unexamined "propositions" serve little purpose.

To evaluate existing or proposed institutional arrangements, the facts of a situation are only part of the process of evaluation; values are also involved. What is a "reasonable" economic base for a service? What is a reasonable cost to pay for a particular function? Obviously the desire of the individual for that particular activity influences the amount he is willing to expend for it. If he does not value education highly, he may be unwilling to accept expenditures for programs that others feel are minimal necessities. But the beginning of rational analysis on such a question must be the collection of the relevant data concerning it. Whatever the values of the individual—excepting one who is so closed-minded that he will not give any consideration to evidence (and such individuals are probably more scarce than, in the midst of political controversy, we are likely to assume), the accumulation of factual information is the beginning point. One must know the terrain before maps can be drawn. What is the nature and scope of the problem? When, how, and why was the problem raised? How much will proposed plans cost? What operational methods have been employed in the past and with what results? What is proposed in the new arrangement? How have similar plans worked elsewhere? Are the comparisons apt, or were the conditions in another jurisdiction so different as to make the comparison less valid and instructive? The collection of such questions and of some kinds of answers in factual terms is a prerequisite to rational analysis.

Apart from values concerning specific public policies (*e.g.*, being favorably disposed to improvements in educational systems), there are broad values that appear to be sought through decentralization in general. It is therefore necessary to consider centralization or decentralization proposals in terms of these sometimes competing values. Although these values are more implicit than explicit, they nevertheless do appear to shape our thinking about the proper locus of powers. These values appear to me to be the following:

1. Minimizing arbitrariness in governmental rulemaking
2. Maximizing democratic control over government
3. Maximizing efficiency in governmental operation

Quite clearly these values can conflict with each other—to make the most of one may mean limiting the achievement of another. In practical terms, of course, no one value is ever sought exclusively. We take a "yes, but" attitude, and more or less consciously sacrifice one goal or value to achieve another. Contradictory or not, however, each is sought and from time to time is given varying degrees of consideration by citizen and official alike.[24] It should not be assumed, however, that these are put forward as guides to practical action. They are general propositions and mutually contradictory in some degree. Laying down "guides" of that sort is a dubious proposition as the Commission on Intergovernmental Relations proved in their Report. Attempting to state conditions that would "justify National action within the National Government's delegated powers, when the lower levels of government cannot or will not act," they listed five guides. One of them says there is warrant for federal action "when a State through action or inaction does injury to the people of other States."[25] But that is not much help to anyone trying to decide what policy ought to be, for what constitutes enough "injury" to warrant action? The last of their rules is broad enough, if liberally interpreted, to bring about a policy not unlike that of the Reconstruction policy toward the South, for it advocates federal action: "When States fail to respect or to protect basic political and civil rights that apply throughout the United States." Precisely to avoid such confusion, therefore, the values I listed above are intended not as guidelines to action but as ways of analyzing arguments concerning the proper allocation of political power in our system.

---

24 These values vary slightly from those presented by Paul Ylvisaker in his essay referred to above, but the main source of my idea was in that essay. I have varied the terms and the application of them in order to serve a somewhat different purpose. His is a fuller analysis than is possible here. See "Criteria for a 'Proper' Areal Division of Powers," *op. cit.*, pp. 27–49.

25 *Op. cit.*, p. 64.

1. Minimizing Arbitrariness. *Ex hypothesi* it would seem that the man most remote from the scene is least likely to be cognizant of local conditions and desires, and therefore most likely to make an arbitrary decision that does not accord with local realities. Bureaucracy reaches its most ludicrous depths when the remote administrator directs the man on the spot to proceed with the impossible, local conditions notwithstanding, Literature, like history, is filled with examples of such blundering, both tragic and comic.[26]

Decentralization also serves to soften the rigidity of the law by permitting minorities to moderate, postpone, or even to refrain from undertaking a kind of program to which there are local objections. It is an unspoken assumption of federal grants to states that any government offered aid may refuse to accept it. To be sure, such decentralization leads to an untidy situation, and many people disagree violently with a system that allows programs to be subject to such hit-or-miss application. There are difficulties implicit in it, particularly where the law raises deeply moral questions, as does the desegregation question. In practice, permission to evade the terms of the Fourteenth Amendment was granted the state governments, particularly—but not exclusively— in the case of the Southern states. The Amendment explicitly forbids states to make invidious distinctions between people (denial of "equal protection of the law"), but flagrant race discrimination was permitted nevertheless. Even though the Fourteenth Amendment is now being more rigorously interpreted, States and localities, both North and South, are in effect permitted to postpone, moderate, and openly to evade the application of the desegregation ruling. Effective measures to end centuries of segregation are difficult to conceive, enact, and apply, but *immediate* desegregation will come from no source. There may therefore be some merit in permitting various approaches to the problem, depending on local circumstances. Nonenforcement may be an extreme form of decentralization of powers, but it remains as an important aspect of the general prevention of "arbitrariness." For "arbitrariness" is partially at least subjective; one man's arbitrariness is another man's reasonableness.

Significantly also a minority may have an opportunity, where power

---

[26] The grim extermination of tens of thousands of German soldiers in the battle of Stalingrad presents a terrifying example of how stupid overcentralization can be. Hitler insisted on maintaining detailed control over army movements, denying field commanders normal discretion to conduct campaigns. Of course, the worst stupidities of that campaign were the product of madness rather than centralization but it was the overcentralization that produced the hopeless situation out of which it was brutally decided not to extricate the men. Theodor Plevier, in his powerful novel *Stalingrad*, depicts the unbelievable consequences of this gross failure of dictatorship.

is dispersed, to capture control over significant, if lesser, units of government, thereby preventing the complete elimination of a perhaps important political element from participation in government. As a consequence of having some share in power, the minority—whether it be a party group or a regional faction or some other distinctive but relatively numerous grouping—may acquire both a sense of responsibility and an opportunity to condition the making or the application of policy. A group completely without power is more likely to make irresponsible claims and charges than if it too shares in power and acquires thereby an awareness of the difficulties, limitations, as well as rewards that power-holding implies.

2. *Achieving Democratic Control over Government.*   Again as a hypothesis, it would seem correct to assume that the more points at which pressure can be applied to those who make policy, the greater the chance of exerting effective control. One government possessing full power, if such can really be imagined, would be difficult of access by the citizen and failure to impress agents of the single government would be the end of the matter. The reverse of this, where each group had full opportunity to throw sand in the gears, would, of course, be equally disastrous. Still, an official who lives across town may be accessible in a way that an official in the state capital or Washington often is not.

The effectiveness of control depends admittedly on more than the number of "check points" that can be established. Whether or not the agents who have power are willing to defer to those who object or plead for remedy is dependent on a number of factors. One of the most important of these is the traditional attitudes that exist regarding such complaints. If the tradition condones under-the-table payments as a *sine qua non* of action, then the degree of decentralization may be of no great importance. (Or it may possibly make matters worse.) Surely one of the factors that is crucially important in this respect is the character of the political system of a particular country or region. The more autocratic and closed a political system is, the greater the likelihood that *who* complains will matter more than how serious is the complaint. Although these are difficult factors to assess, they must nevertheless be considered in analyzing a decentralization problem.

As an example of the problems that can arise in connection with decentralizing the operation of a particular program, take the case of certain of the laws that were proposed as remedies for the economic difficulties of the 1930's. To turn over the funds for relief work projects to some local or state governments was to risk seeing the money misused. Some of it was used with political favoritism rather than poverty as a principle of eligibility. There were constant battles between the

Secretary of the Interior, Harold Ickes, and Harry Hopkins, Roosevelt's confidant, on this point. Ickes, erstwhile Republican muckraker, wanted guarantees that all funds would be carefully accounted for and that political favoritism would be at an absolute minimum. Hopkins was determined that the maximum be done for economic improvement even if some misuse of funds by local or state authorities was encountered. (Actually both policies were followed, but Ickes won often enough to convince some observers of American state and local politics that one of the greatest goods of the anti-Depression programs was that they tightened up accounting practices in local and state governments and prevented some of the more blatant kinds of misuse of funds that had been easier to achieve previously.) To discuss such programs without considering the character of the traditions and the political practices of localities and states would be to overlook a crucial element of the scene, however vague and subjective such factors may be.

An important consideration is the reduction of the probability of massive error by reducing massive power. If a government has very wide and singular power to do the "wrong" as well as the "right" thing, and if it does err, the very inclusiveness of its power compounds the difficulty. If some of the power is effectively decentralized, then the error may be committed in several places but not so easily throughout the whole country. In short, by limiting power, the opportunity for an all-encompassing error is reduced. Again, there is another side to this proposition: incapacity to take an inclusive and incisive action which is "right" may be an invitation to serious errors where subordinate units either intentionally or innocently ruin the program by "wrong" actions.

Finally, on the point of democratic control, consider the possibility that in some matters more humane and enlightened policies may be effected by decentralization rather than through one central government. The obvious example is legislation to protect the civil rights of minority groups. Such legislation is not passed in the South, but the South's position in the national politics is such that it can use its minority position to block legislation for the whole country by bargaining with conservative elements who wish to defeat liberal economic policies. (This was true even when the South went down to defeat on the Civil Rights Act of 1964. Because the old coalition stood firm, it forced modification of the laws so as to make the federal law considerably less effective than most state laws on fair employment practices.) But in states where tradition, population concentrations of particular racial groups, and other political factors make it feasible to pass such legislation, it can be achieved. In fact, the only effective legislation to enforce fair hiring practices and prevent racial discrimination in employment has been state legislation. A few states with a social climate that made possible such advances for human dignity set an example which other states have followed widely in recent years. If decentralization can involve denial of rights by recalcitrant states that will not accept a long-delayed demand for compliance with the Fourteenth Amendment, it is also true that decentralization permits experimentation and localized advances in the assurance of rights that would have been nearly inconceivable if the decision had to be worked out through the democratic compromising of the national government.

An illustration of this point is found in Great Britain where the problems of racial conflict are growing, although far less severe than in this country. There, a highly centralized political system has been incapable of taking resolute action, because the national parties feel threatened by any proposal for significant legislation. The absence of federalism appears to help not at all.

3. *Maximizing Efficiency.* Basically, efficiency refers to the maximum output for minimum input, although it often is used in discussions of administration and governmental organization in such vague and stereotyped ways that its original meaning is entirely lost. It comes in some instances to mean "good" administration or governmental organization without further specification. As used here, the term refers to administrative methods that get the desired tasks done with a minimum of duplication and delay and a maximum of technical proficiency. It is obvious that this is not a goal to be sought at the exclusion of all others, for in many respects the pursuit of efficiency would render impossible democratic control or might increase official arbitrariness. An administrator released from supervision by elected officials or freed of the need to respond to citizen complaints might operate with greater dispatch and with less red tape, but thus isolating administrators from citizen "pressure" is surely not an unmitigated blessing.

It hardly needs proving that there are aspects of the existing governmental system that are inefficient in the sense that they involve duplication and delay, and are often technically inefficient. It is true that the public is little inclined to rise up in anger over the problem of inefficiency—of wasted resources, excess tax loads, social costs (as in matters of public health, for example). Only when situations become dramatically critical is there likely to be much attention focused on the problem by the typical citizen. This is quite understandable in view of the complexity of the governmental system itself and the difficulty that even the most "expert" of analysts find in assessing the problems involved. Furthermore citizens are accustomed to existing standards and systems, and if there are indeed some inefficiencies in the way estates of the deceased are handled by the local magistrate, for example, many would still prefer to see the function kept as a local operation rather than transferred elsewhere for the sake of efficiency and economy.

Some programs, of course, are difficult if not impossible to establish on any kind of effective basis without some degree of centralization. James Fesler, in his perceptive discussion of this problem in his book, *Area and Administration*, says:

> Administrative efficiency is a . . . factor relevant to solving the function-area equation. For many governmental functions efficiency requires the development of a staff of officials of diverse skills; otherwise the people are denied the fruits of expertness developed in the specialized channels of education and experience. . . . A staff of specialists will have an adequate work-load only if it has a large clientele. And a large clientele exists only in the larger governmental areas, the exact size depending on population density and, more especially, on the density of the phenomena with which particular governmental functions are concerned.[27]

In other cases efficiency may be impossible to achieve on local levels for technical reasons—scattered action may be self-defeating. Programs for water supply and conservation, to take a random example, may be very difficult to set up on a decentralized basis for the simple reason that each small part of the region may have what superficially at least appears to be conflicting interests with each other part of the area. The need for a rational and efficient means of handling the problem may make it necessary to move well beyond the local government level for a satisfactory repository of the power to develop and control water supply.

Another perfect example of this kind of difficulty is found in the economic practices of state and local governments in a time of economic difficulties. In the depression of the 1930's, states and local governments offset the "pump-priming" activities of the national government (the theory being that by putting money into circulation through federally financed building projects and the like, the whole economy would be reinvigorated) by cutting state and local expenditures and reducing the number of employees to the barest minimum.

---

[27] James Fesler, *Area and Administration* (University, Ala.: University of Alabama Press, 1949), pp. 24–25. Fesler has also argued cogently against the typical pro-decentralization bias, contending that the decentralizers often ignore the defects of decentralization or merely assume its virtues. For a different view of the problem from that presented here, see his "Approaches to the Understanding of Decentralization," 27 *Journal of Politics* 536–66 (1965).

In the depressed thirties, the fiscal policies of these governments exerted a deflationary rather than an expansionary effect on the economic expenditures, and especially construction outlays, were severely reduced, borrowing was restricted, and taxes weighing on consumption were substantially increased.[28]

Efficient governmental action in many spheres demands a highly coordinated and integrated approach, and on the surface at least the greater the number of governments involved the greater the problem of achieving an integrated program. It is one of the elementary facts of life that the American governmental landscape is crowded with countless local governments. They exist legally and usually cannot be denied their quota of authority without a vigorous struggle. Governmental units seem to have a élan that is hard to extinguish; once in existence they tend to perpetuate themselves. They acquire, as a consequence of existence, an almost organic quality with a will to continue to exist.

Nor does their sole source of support come from those on the public payroll. Others in the community who have no monetary involvement often support continuance partly because it is traditional and familiar. The familiar way of doing things gives a sense of security. One hears the argument that the existing methods with known faults are preferable to a new system with who knows what unanticipated shortcomings to offset the promised rewards of change.

Given the durability of governmental units, it is no surprise to find that the number of governments existing in the United States decreases very slowly in response to the declining population of rural areas (half of all counties lost population in the 1950's), nor has the technical feasibility of larger governmental units as a result of improved means of transportation and communication produced a sharp reduction in the number of governments. We have more than 90,000 governments in this country, most of them serving surprisingly small numbers of people. As a matter of fact, 52 per cent of the municipalities in the United States in 1962 had less than 1000 people in them, and 84 per cent had less than 5000. Since rural areas terminate few municipalities and suburbanization produces new ones, there were over a thousand more municipalities in 1962 than in 1952, according to a Census Bureau count. So too with "special districts"—governmental bodies concerned with such problems as water supply, sanitation, irrigation, and fire protection. In the five years after 1962 the number of special districts increased by almost 3000, an increase of 16.2 per cent.

---

[28] Alvin H. Hansen and Harvey S. Perloff, *State and Local Finance in the National Economy* (New York: W. W. Norton and Company, 1944), p. 49.

The exception to this proliferation of governments is found among school districts, the number of which has decreased by 80 per cent (from 108,500 to 21,800) since 1942. Nevertheless, there are still 15,000 districts with fewer than three schools in them. Many districts, as a matter of fact, do not operate any schools at all, providing only tuition and transportation for their children to attend other school systems.[29]

The question may well be asked whether governmental units make sense when they serve so few people. Can efficiency be maintained when there are such obvious limits to the personnel and financial resources with which to undertake the functions? Roscoe Martin points to the curious fact that:

. . . one state maintains a vast superstructure of local government while another equally populous makes out with one-tenth as much, one state harbors 6000 school districts while another has none, one state preserves a thousand townships while another abolishes all such units—and all in the name of the twin gods of efficiency and democracy.[30]

Martin also poses criteria for judging the necessity for the existence of a local government. He argues that there must be functions of sufficient "number, variety, and significance to challenge the interest of both public servant and the citizen." Logically he also contends that there must be a sufficient population to provide the public some choice in filling the offices of government. Third, he pleads for "geographical adequacy"—area commensurate with the communication means existent and adapted to the functions to be performed, conditions that obviously change with the passing of time. He also lists "fiscal adequacy," meaning, of course, a sufficient tax base to produce needed revenue for operation. He holds that there should be "technical competence," arguing that "if a unit of government is not large enough, in terms of variety of functions to be performed, size of population, and fiscal resources, to permit a measure of administrative specialization, then its right to continued existence deserves to be challenged."[31] Finally he argues that the governments should be "general rather than special"—that governments should have general jurisdiction, handling local government problems of all sorts for a given area rather than

---

[29] See *1967 Census of Governments*, "Preliminary Report, CG-P-2" (Washington, D.C.: Government Printing Office, 1957).

[30] Roscoe Martin, *Grass Roots* (University, Ala.: University of Alabama Press, 1957), p. 50.

[31] *Ibid.*, p. 52.

creating a series of special governments assigned specific and limited tasks.

To pose such criteria is to invite attack. What would the answer be to someone who asked: "Suppose we don't want to be 'efficient'? Suppose we would prefer to have control over the administration of our schools, or local management of relief cases, even if we are not so efficient, rather than let some outsider run our affairs? To illustrate the point, consider Leonard White's description of a battle that turned largely on the question of efficient methods of handling welfare aid programs.

In 1946 the Social Security Administration began a drive to require the states to adopt uniform state-wide standards of assistance for programs jointly financed by the state and the federal government, and to make these standards mandatory upon all local social security agencies. . . . The Social Security Administration, in the interests of the best attainable program, asked New York to impose a single uniform standard, irrespective of locality, for aid to dependent children, for old age assistance, and for aid to the blind and to the permanently and totally disabled. The state also was required to terminate local election of country and city welfare commissioners in favor of appointment after open competitive examination; to relax local residence requirements for these positions; and to allow a dismissed or demoted employee to appeal to an administrative board. . . . The state was notified that unless these uniform state-wide standards were accepted, no federal funds would be forthcoming [for any of these programs].[32]

Conforming to local practices, New York State preferred to handle its programs for the small rural upstate towns differently from those for the larger urban centers. At some sacrifice in efficiency, that is to say, the state wished to go its own way. In the end the national agency got most of what it demanded in a compromise agreement, so that the concept of efficiency took precedence over localism.

The problem with criteria like those set forth above is that they are looked upon as technical matters—if not by their creators, then by others who rely on them as they seek to reform local government. Consider the criterion concerning adequate population. How much does it tell us? What difference does it make in the final analysis how many candidates are offered for offices to be filled? In a small community talent and inclination for public office is obviously limited and necessarily the choice will be limited, but this may begin to apply in communities of many thousands. In a community of a few hundred it might

---

[32] Leonard White, *op. cit.*, p. 82.

be argued that intimate knowledge of candidates for office is an asset not available to larger communities and that this not only compensates for but is more important than a wide range of choice among candidates. How could this be refuted, at least on the level at which it is cast in the orginal criterion? Not at all, in my view.

Consider next the criterion concerned with technical competence which challenges the right to existence of a government that is not large enough to provide "administrative specialization." It could be argued that this places the cart before the horse—local governments should not serve but be served by administrators or administration. Of course, Professor Martin is emphasizing specialization and expertise in performing complex tasks, not seeking to restructure government to fit administrative whims. But he would be hard put to explain to a skeptic why a small community that chose to forego the "benefits" of expertise ought not to keep a less complex but satisfactory (to them) kind of governmental system. In short there is no way to "prove" that efficiency is a value that ought to be more prized than localism.

The problem in setting up criteria for the evaluation of governments is that the process presupposes a value system on which, implicitly, the criteria must rest. Had Professor Martin's criteria for the *raison d'etre* been drawn by an ardent advocate of localism and extreme decentralization, the list would have been different indeed. Does this mean, since it is easy to establish a counter-list of criteria, that efforts to establish criteria for judging local government performance are futile in the long run, rendering the whole thing confusing at best and self-defeating at worst?

Such a conclusion does not follow, if one turns to the basic point from which this argument took off—that is, the point of values which people seek to maximize. It is true that if you and I set forth to argue whether a given governmental program should be operated from Washington, the state capital, or the county seat, basing our respective arguments on criteria that are mutually exclusive, we will get nowhere. Each of us may erect logically impeccable arguments, but because the first assumptions from which we moved were contradictory, the two ultimate positions will be entirely unlike. Therefore if two people are to discuss intelligently a question like decentralization, it will be necessary to come to some kind of agreement, or at least to make our value assumptions reasonably clear.

Weighing the value implications of a particular proposal is no simple undertaking. The desire for local autonomy, the desire to avoid arbitrary decisions, the desire for reasonable efficiency in decision-making, all can conflict in a given situation, and where one ultimately comes out—in an abstract evaluation, at least—would depend upon the importance the individual gives to particular values. In consideration of a case that is not abstract (the hypothetical case raised for illustration of a point) but concrete (the question of whether in *your* state highway construction responsibility ought to be removed from the county and given to the state highway department), other factors may be involved. For now particular interests come into the picture (your income depends on a highway contracting business, or you live on dirt roads that the county had done nothing about, and so on), and the force of tradition comes into play ("Well, we've always done it that way, I don't see any reason to go off on some blue-sky project to change what we are familiar with.")

In matters of decentralization, as in comparable questions that we debate in state and local government (should the governor's power to control his subordinates be increased? should the city consolidate with the county? should we adopt the city manager system? and so on), the approach is not a mere matter of expertise. The expert in state and local government can advise and assist by explaining the meaning of terms or the practices that exist elsewhere or by illustrating pitfalls or advantages implicit in specific proposals. But he cannot put the questions of what to do in a jeweller's scales and give a precise reading of their relative weights. The student who learns this point early and therefore ceases to look for neat formulae that will resolve the knotty problems of contemporary state and local government will that much sooner get to the point where he can assess the problems effectively. Either implicitly or explicitly, the value factor will always be present; to recognize its existence and its significance is the first step toward understanding.

4. The Politics of Constitutionalism: I

A DISTINCTION must be made between what earlier was called the "ulti-mate constitution" of a community and the constitution in the more conventional sense of the term. *Constitution* usually means the docu-ment itself, although strict accuracy demands that more than the literal document be included in the meaning since the interpretations of a constitution can sometimes be more important than the words of the instrument *per se*. To use a common example to illustrate the point: the United States Constitution outlines the procedure by which the president is to be elected, but this in itself does not provide much in-sight into the constitutional-political realities of how we fill that office. Indeed, from the document itself there is no reason to deduce that the people themselves need have any part in the process of selection, that point having been left vague by the framers of the Constitution. But for anyone today to propose that the people be excluded from choosing the president, that the choice be left to the state legislatures as was the practice in the early days of the Republic, would surely produce out-rage and inevitable claims of unconstitutionality. Hence not only the document but the belief systems and interpretations of the document constitute the "constitution" of a government.

By "ultimate constitution" something more inclusive is intended. The term refers to the broad ethical norms that dictate behavior in the political realm. Interpretation of the Commerce Clause is a matter of formal constitutionalism; discrimination against particular elements of the society—their tacit exclusion from participation in government—is a matter of the ultimate constitution. Legal authority for an agency to provide a public service or to regulate certain business practices is, or can be, a matter of formal constitutionalism; the sense of what is right for a government to do and not to do—in civil liberties or in ownership of economic resources, for example—become matters of ethical values, the "ought" or "ought not" factors, not questions of whether the legal authority exists to undertake a particular function. It is such ethical propositions that I call the "ultimate constitution."

The Context of Politics

To some it may seem indiscreet to discuss the "politics" of constitutions, but, particularly where states and local governments are concerned, nothing could be more appropriate. To be sure, we do have political disputes about the United States Constitution, yet such contests are conducted with an apologetic air, with constant protestations of faith in the "true" constitution which the opposition is undermining. The fundamental constitution is beyond dispute, even though dispute rages on specific points; the Constitution *per se* is an uncontested given in the governmental equation. State constitutions and local charters normally occupy less hallowed ground; they are accepted as subject to controversy partly because they are so detailed in their provisions that the day-to-day conduct of government more frequently raises constitutional questions. The more detailed the provisions, the more likely that the constitution will have to be revised to meet new situations; conversely, the simpler and briefer the constitution, the greater the possibility of adapting to changes without direct amendment. As the history of the relatively brief and simple United States Constitution illustrates, the possibilities of amendment by interpretation—which has been the life of the document—are enormous when all the details are not spelled out but only the broad outlines are proposed.

State and local constitutions, on the other hand, are elaborately detailed in most cases, rarely trusting to generality of expression common to the product of the 1787 Convention. They provide in detail for specific functions, how they are to be conducted, and by whom. Change in the administrative system of a state department of education may require a constitutional amendment; broadening the authority of the city health department often requires revision of the city charter.

Our tendency to revere constitutional documents sometimes leads us to overlook one significant fact about them: they not only provide certain basic rules about how politics is to be conducted; they also materially affect the locus of power in the community. The constitution sets handicaps and allots advantages to various players, and particularly in the case of the nonnational constitutions there is no settled agreement about the distribution of these favors and shackles. Like a team of six-footers in basketball, searching for ways to "equalize" the game through rules that minimize the advantages of being seven or eight feet tall, some element in the political lineup is always seeking to revise the rules to curtail some other element that either is, or seems to be, in a favored position. A serious proposal, for example, to equalize the population of districts from which state legislators are chosen, in order to terminate the overrepresentation of rural areas, is an invitation to a political donnybrook because representation is a high stake. Similarly, proposals to introduce a city manager system or to remove the party labels from city election ballots will produce a fight at city hall.

Constitutionalism: Characteristics and Purposes

Constitutions, whether for nations, states, or localities, all share certain common characteristics and common objectives. First, they prescribe the essential structure and distribute powers among agencies of the government in question. Second, they provide both explicit and implicit limits on government. Third, they are aimed at assuring stability in government. Fourth, they attempt to establish an optimum quantity of power to meet such contingencies as may arise. Fifth, they usually exemplify permanence and superiority to ordinary law. Sixth, they are intended in varying degrees as inspirational or consensus-building statements.

Prescribing the Structure of Government. Perhaps the most obvious purpose of a constitution is the establishment of the basic structure of government, the setting forth of significant provisions for major agencies and their respective duties and interrelationships. The extent to which those institutions and functions are described varies widely, but in general, it is true that the federal Constitution is the least detailed of our constitutions, the local charters the most detailed, and the state constitutions somewhere in between. How power is distributed by the constitution depends on many conditions, not the least of which is the influence of the current doctrine as to the "best" method of running a government. It is too frivolous, perhaps, to say that this goes by fad or fashion, but at times attachments remarkably similar to "fashion" seem to set the thinking of a constitution-making assembly. Which groups gain dominance in a constitutional convention or on the committee drafting a new city charter also provide significant indices to the character of the document. A group of conservative businessmen might reflect their *laissez-faire* ideas by consciously limiting the areas in which the government could act, or might exhibit their ideas on taxation through provisions that make it difficult to levy higher taxes or to borrow (by requiring an unusual majority on these motions, for example). Labor groups generally oppose the city manager form of government, presumably because they fear the city manager will be less subject to the kind of pressures they can utilize—the threat of the ballot box—and more susceptible to the persuasions of businessmen. In short, the structural details of a constitution are not only intrinsically important but also significant as indicators of the character of the political elements that combined to produce the document.

Limiting Governmental Power. By direct prohibition and by other means constitutions limit the powers of government. The most obvious example of direct prohibition is the Bill of Rights, a classic statement of prohibitions, copied in one way or another in state constitutions. Local charters do not have specific bills of rights; rather they characteristically contain innumerable explicit and implicit prohibitions scattered throughout the document. Explicit prohibitions are not limited to bills of rights; they are often in other sections as well (see Sections 9 and 10 of Article I of the United States Constitution), and in the case of the state constitutions prohibitions are numerous, scattered throughout the document, and frequently picayune in nature. Prohibitions, it should be noted, are not only categoric denials of power to do certain acts, but also are procedural in the sense that certain means of governmental action are forbidden. For instance, denial of a jury trial may be directly forbidden, while the taking of property by government may be permitted only with just compensation.

Implicit limitations of power may involve placing one kind of authority in opposition to another. Granting power to two elements of the government, both of which must agree before an action can be taken, or making a grant of power to an agency conditional upon the acceptance by another power center in government—these too limit government. The greater the distribution of fragments of authority to small elements of the government by constitutional fiat, the more limited in effect will be the ensuing policy-making powers of the political community in question.

Stability in Government. Stability, continuity, and orderliness are uniform desires of government makers. The extent to which one of these goals is uppermost in the minds of the framers of constitutions varies of course; some people readily sacrifice other values to assure stability and order, others do quite the reverse. But to all, stability has utility, for man's constant tendency is to stave off the unsettling change of the world around him by imposing stability and order in social relations. Thus even in the bylaws of the Tuesday Afternoon Needle and Knitting Society there are provisions for a term of office, for orderly replacement of leaders, for records to show how things were done last year as an example to the membership and leaders of today and tomorrow.

Not only in formal provisions but by the very existence of an agreed-upon set of rules the constitution tends to emphasize stability. People's expectations of orderly management of public affairs is a valuable asset of a government, and in the early stages of the existence of a government (for example, the newly independent nations of Africa) it is difficult to get acceptance of a new constitution and the regime operating under it since no pattern of stable expectations has been established. So too with a government which has lost the respect of its citizenry, because the normal expectations were not realized in practice. When the social order breaks down—as it did in the spring of 1861 in the United States or in the spring of 1958 in France—the stability factor of the constitutional system has failed to survive the strains placed upon it.

Constitution-makers can only to a limited extent assure stability in drawing up constitutions. The social, political, and economic considerations within which a constitution operates will be at least as decisive if not more so for producing stability as anything in a constitutional document. The hold that a constitution can get on the people with the passage of time, the extent to which they cannot imagine making fundamental changes even in time of stress (*e.g.,* the violent reaction to Franklin Roosevelt's Court-packing plan in 1937) transcend in significance any particular provision of the literal constitution.

Because state and local constitutions are not often threatened with violent overthrow, it should not be assumed that the factors of stability are not relevant to those units of government. In the first place they can be wracked by violence in extreme cases—the Dorr Rebellion in Rhode Island, for example, or race riots, or extreme uses of force as by the late Mayor Hague in Jersey City, his quasifeudal domain.[1] These can lead to problems of instability, and indeed such conditions are anticipated by constitutional provisions which permit unusual powers to control violence, and at the same time try to prevent uncontrolled authority which might lead to desperate acts of violence against incumbents.

Power, But Less Than Absolute Power. This aspect of constitutionalism is meaningfully applicable only in societies that reject the propriety of absolute or dictatorial power being lodged in any group or individual. A Fascist or Communist constitution may pay obeisance to many of the ideas of traditional parliamentary democracy, but on this fundamental point they depart and leave no doubt as to the proper locus of ultimate authority—it is to be in the overlords who run the party and who embody mystically or otherwise the will of the society. In societies not characterized by dictatorial ideology, the search for the optimum way of granting power is a constant quest.

The goal is to grant enough power to meet such contingencies as may arise but to give less than absolute power since that in itself is regarded as a danger. To prevent arbitrary use of emergency power, yet not to render formal authority powerless to deal with emergencies, is a formidable challenge for the writers of constitutions. The object is to find the proper location and quantity of power to assure stability and order and simultaneously prevent the arbitrary and capricious use of that power to the detriment of liberty. Which is to say, of course, that the goal is impossible to achieve. No writer of any document, nor any practicing politician can do more than guess well, provide as best he can for the times and circumstances he knows or can imagine, and then hope his ideas will not be misused to produce either anarchy or tyranny. Statements on parchment must, moveover, be interpreted and applied by men in the heat of controversy, subject to pressures of an unforseeable political context, operating in uncertainty from necessarily limited knowledge of what to expect next. Even though the goal is impossible to reach, we will go on trying to state the optimum power distribution.

Permanence and Superiority Over Ordinary Law. Constitutions are almost invariably thought of as relatively permanent and beyond revision by the routine methods of amending ordinary law. In some instances constitutional change requires no more difficult steps than are needed to amend an item of ordinary statutory law, yet even then the common understanding is that the constitution is special and that un-

---

[1] See Dayton David McKean, *The Boss* (Boston: Houghton Mifflin Co., 1940).

hurried deliberation should be a prerequisite to constitutional change. For example, in England, with its unwritten constitution, there is no formal difference between changing ordinary law and changing constitutional provisions, but any attempt to alter what is thought to be the constitution, even though it be such merely by long-accepted agreement, inevitably produces demands for delay in view of the fact that it is the fundamental law.

In a sense this merely means that some kinds of political controversy get settled on a relatively permanent basis. Disputes about the taxing power, civil rights, executive authority, and other matters that would tend to make a shambles of the political system if they were constantly open to dispute are accepted as relatively unchangeable and not open to controversy. In effect this is exactly what the newer society has not achieved, why it may be said to be in the process of achieving a constitution. This does not mean that these shelved matters are beyond dispute even in a settled constitutional system, and in most systems many points that are fundamentally accepted will be subject to minor modifications in the ongoing process of application of the rules of the constitution to the day-to-day politics of the society. Yet it is important to appreciate that these "permanent" elements are shelved controversies.

In American practice, keeping the controversies shelved is assisted by raising hurdles to amending the constitutions. This is true even in the case of the local charter, which with its wealth of detail is both a constitution and a statutory code, although the hurdles to alteration of a charter are usually not so high as for other constitutions.

Constitutions are also commonly considered as superior to ordinary law, and are used as a standard to measure the law's validity. Ordinances of the city council are subordinate to the city charter; the work of the state legislature may be challenged in the courts as inconsistent with the provisions of either the state or federal constitutions. In some countries the function of determining whether the statutory law is consistent with the constitution is not a judicial function as it has become in the United States, but almost universally the understanding is that the routine law should conform to the "higher" law of the constitution. The implementation of the superiority of the higher law is difficult or impossible where a determined group, with a powerful and united following, decides to achieve its ends without the inconvenience and delay of formally amending the constitution. Such methods are more common in unstable societies, particularly those in the early stages of political independence. In such countries, leaders of the moment, unwilling to take the chance of ultimate defeat by exercising patience, may in effect negate the concept of a "superior" law. It should not, however, be assumed that overriding the strict terms of the constitutional rules is limited to governments of newly independent states. American states and localities have often done substantially the same thing. Several examples of high-handed disregard of the letter of the constitutional law will be cited in case studies presented below.

Constitutions as Inspirational Statements. Constitutions are intended to serve as the core of a myth system, eliciting the support of the present generation and of future generations as well. They therefore often contain pious proclamations, unenforceable provisions, and other high ideals of the society that may not be attainable but that are to be hopefully sought. And in order to have the society committed to the idea, the makers of constitutions embody the ideals in the fundamental law to be studied, believed, and ultimately revered as right and proper. Preambles of constitutions are perhaps the classic example of this function—they are unenforceable, they provide no basic law, but they announce in lofty terms the principles of the community. Similarly, provisions of bills of rights are stated unconditionally, although in practice they are not observed in the absolute terms in which they are stated. That is, the constitution of a state may forbid interference with freedom of press or freedom of speech, but the law may provide several curbs on both kinds of activity. The courts say that the terms of the constitution are not meant as absolutes, however they may be stated; society inevitably will seek to protect itself against what it considers immoral or disrupting activity and therefore a law which seemingly contravenes the constitution may be validated.

Even in local charters, there is usually some window-dressing, often in the early part of the charter, which appears to provide the city with all manner of sweeping powers to undertake a wide range of functions. These sweeping terms are then nullified or at least modified by the document itself, by provisions of the state law or the state constitution, or by court interpretation which rule that the powers of subordinate units of government must be read narrowly rather than in the broad manner in which they may read parts of the constitution of the state. The reasons behind this narrowness of interpretation will be considered in some detail later; for the present it offers an interesting example of the general tendency to use basic laws as noble statements.

There is, by the way, no intent to impute dishonesty or immorality to the writers of constitutions who proclaim what they cannot enforce. For the most part, the framers of democratic constitutions are not callous about what they say; they are not, like the writers of dictatorial constitutions, merely out to catch human flies with honeyed constitutional terms. The statement of lofty ideals, the announcement of intent beyond the possible achievements of the moment, is not done wholly to deceive, although the guarantees of the Fourteenth Amendment of the United States Constitution were paper promises for the better part of a century—and in some respects continue to be only that. It is also done with intent to inspire support for a regime that the framers hope will achieve stability and justice, as they see and understand these goals. To observe that there is a propaganda element in constitutions is not therefore to condemn them but to face a reality and one of some importance for providing a sustaining support for the constitutional regime itself.

American Constitutional Traditions

Probably no other nation in the world is more devoted to the idea of the written constitution than is the United States. That attachment is in large part the consequence of the deep roots which the Constitution itself has struck in our national traditions. For our attitude toward this document is little short of idolatry: no crown jewels ever got more loving attention. It was not always so, however. As the historian Ralph Henry Gabriel points out, in the early years of the nineteenth century the Declaration of Independence was a more highly emphasized symbol than the Constitution, for the former was, after all, not subject to dispute, which in the pre-Fort Sumter decades could hardly be said of the Constitution. The Fourth of July was a moment for lauding the Declaration of Independence; but there was no "Constitution Day." "A few liberals were, in fact, beginning to complain," writes Gabriel, "that the younger generation was growing up without adequate knowledge of that great document because its text was to be found in few school books."[2] After the Civil War, which was fought at least in part on a Constitutional point, the document became the more symbolic of nationhood to the victorious majority of the nation; its founders were rendered into demigods by reverential historians, and conservatives in particular began to find in the document firm support for doctrines they favored. Said the not particularly radical Calvin Coolidge:

---

[2] Ralph Henry Gabriel, *The Course of American Democratic Thought,* 2nd ed. (New York: The Ronald Press Company, 1956), p. 99.

The Constitution of the United States is the final refuge of every right that is enjoyed by an American citizen. So long as it is observed those rights will be secure. Whenever it falls into disrespect or disrepute, the end of orderly organized government as we have known it for more than a hundred and twenty-five years will be at hand. . . . To live under the American Constitution is the greatest privilege that was ever accorded to the human race.[3]

High regard for the Constitution reinforced support for the idea of constitutionalism. The basing of what was almost a secular religion on that document after the Civil War did not alone produce the emphasis we place on constitutionalism, for a background of constitutionalism existed prior to the Convention of 1787. Indeed, it is clear that the product of that convention owed much to ideals of constitutionalism common in the country at the time and very much in the minds of the members as they arrived in Philadelphia. Because we place such uniquely heavy emphasis on the idea of written constitutions, not only at the national but at the state and local levels as well, it is important to consider at least briefly the historical basis of constitutionalism in this country.

The origins of our notions of constitutionalism are not American at all, but derive largely from the political contests of medieval England.[4] When the feudal barons forced King John to sign a document which came to be revered as the Magna Carta, they had no ideas even remotely similar to our concept of government limited by a constitution, and the baronial rights reaffirmed in that document were ultimately to be the least important aspect of the occasion. The barons, as one of the two groups sufficiently powerful to extort such concessions from the King (the other being the clergy), made him promise that in the future the "customary privileges, franchises, and liberties of the barons shall not be infringed as they have been in the past." [5] Out of political conflict came a constitutional principle as succeeding centuries reinterpreted the baronial guarantees in terms of later ideas rather than

---

[3] Quoted by Gabriel, *ibid.*, p. 444.

[4] This is not to pretend that the ideas of medieval England are the sole ideological basis of our constitutionalism, for concepts drawn from both Greek and Roman political writings—particularly as regards the "natural law" component of constitutionalism—are also significant. In operational terms, however, these ideas exerted less direct influence upon American developments than did the growth of Anglo-Saxon jurisprudence; for this reason the heritage stemming from the Magna Carta is emphasized more than that from Athens or Rome.

[5] Charles H. McIlwain, *The High Court of Parliament and its Supremacy* (New Haven: Yale University Press, 1910), p. 54. See Chap. 2, "The Fundamental Law," for an excellent essay on the development of the British constitution.

those appropriate to feudal institutions. In due time the Magna Carta became the very essence of constitutionalism, symbol of the duty—at first of the King and later of the Parliament—not to transcend the fundamental law which assured every Englishman certain basic rights.

Thus by the time English colonies were founded in America, constitutionalism was a commonly accepted idea. Not that there was universal agreement on what constitutionalism amounted to; as the English Civil Wars were to demonstrate, there was not even agreement on what the English constitution itself meant. The Common Law—a body of rules common to the whole realm, hallowed by custom, and independent of any legislative or royal enactment—was generally accepted, although exactly what it was was not quite so clear. Ultimately, it did not turn out to be what Sir Edward Coke tried to make it in his battle with the Stuart King James I; it was Coke's contention that the Common Law stood as a higher law, above the King and Parliament. Should the King and Parliament act contrary to the Common Law, their acts would be void. This position, so familiar to Americans accustomed to American constitutional law, did not prevail in England; and ultimately not even Coke himself was willing to accept its full implications. Out of the political turmoil of the seventeenth century, British political institutions took shape, becoming a system of legislative supremacy and rejecting both the only written constitution in the history of that nation (the Instrument of Government of 1663, proposed by Cromwell), and the practice of depending on written constitutions as well.

At the time that British politicians were rejecting formal constitutional rules in a written document, they were simultaneously acting so as to reinforce the idea of written constitutions in their American colonies. By the granting of colonial charters to the companies establishing settlements here, and later by granting more elaborate charters to the growing colonies, the habits of dependence on a written code for the regulation of governmental organization and operation became more entrenched among the colonial people. While it is true that the earliest charters were vague and very limited in their provisions, they were nonetheless the basic directives for the conduct of government among people who were, at a minimum, many weeks travel removed from the fountainhead of formal authority in London. It is the judgment of Benjamin F. Wright that these charters were very probably:

. . . the decisive step in the development of the American variety of constitutions. . . . For these charters were to serve, in one way or another, sometimes for a few years, sometimes for over a century, as instruments of government beyond the power of the colonists to alter.[6]

These constitutions were, however, granted by royal action with varying degrees of participation by the colonial people. One interesting exception to this was the Connecticut Colony's early constitution, which dates from the winter of 1638–39 and has been called the first popularly drawn constitution. Called the Fundamental Orders of Connecticut, the document included a surprising amount of detailed direction for the establishment and operation of the government of the new colony. The detailed provisions of this document distinguish it from the much more famous Mayflower Compact, which was less a constitution than a general agreement to have a government—an agreement, so to speak, to draw up a constitution in due time. The important point, however, is that whether drawn by the colonists or conferred by royal prerogative, charters were present in all the colonies and inevitable habits and expectations grew up around them. Such development was not an inevitable accompaniment to federalism: in Canada, for instance, the provincial governments do not have constitutions in the sense that the states in this country have. There is in a sense only one written constitution in Canada—that of the Dominion, called the British North America Act of 1867, with its subsequent amendments. The powers of the provinces are generally set forth in that document. Such constitutions as the provinces have are subject to revision by the provincial legislatures by ordinary legislative enactment (except where those enactments might interfere with the powers of the Dominion itself).[7]

Thus when the bonds with England were cut by the Declaration of Independence, the new states, at the invitation of the Constitutional Congress, began drafting replacements for their earlier charters. Before the end of 1776 eight states had adopted new constitutions, and Rhode Island and Connecticut had revised their charters at least sufficiently to take account of their newly announced independence. In 1777 two more states followed with new constitutions and three years later Massachusetts did likewise.[8] There seemed to be no doubt of the need for

---

[6] Benjamin F. Wright, "The Early History of Written Constitutions in America," in Essays in History and Political Theory (Cambridge, Mass.: Harvard University Press, 1936), p. 346.

[7] See Patrick Kerwin, "Constitutionalism in Canada," in Government Under Law, edited by Arthur E. Sutherland (Cambridge, Mass.: Harvard University Press, 1956), p. 453. See also R. M. Dawson, The Government of Canada, 2nd ed. (Toronto: University of Toronto Press, 1954), pp. 80, 90–91.

[8] In 1776 Massachusetts had revised its 1691 colonial charter.

new constitutions. "Rarely, if ever, did they debate the desirability of having a constitution. Rather they assumed that such documents were necessities." [9]

Measured by today's standards the first state constitutions were crude and incomplete; neither the content nor the means chosen to draft and adopt these constitutions would seem acceptable to present-day citizens. In the first place, a cardinal point of today's constitutionalism was missing: popular participation in at least the approval of the constitution. These early documents were drawn up in the state legislatures and were not submitted to the voters. It did not seem incongruous for the legislature to decide this, partly because there was no precedent to the contrary (the Crown had theretofore decided such matters), and partly because the only clear repository of authority of the time was in fact the legislature. Illustrative of their conception of what these constitutions were to be is the vagueness that characterized the provisions for amending the constitution. Some provided no means of amending at all, others provided impossibly complicated means, others merely left amendment to the legislature. In other cases unusual majorities were demanded for an amendment (*e.g.*, five-sevenths of the legislature in Delaware) or passage by successive legislative sessions was required.

Popular sovereignty—in the sense of the appropriateness of public authorization of a constitution—was often referred to, but little used in practice.[10] Massachusetts made a significant contribution to the development of popular constituent power when in 1778 the legislature submitted to the voters in town meeting (*i.e.*, a state referendum) a constitution which the legislature itself had drafted and approved. The voters turned it down, suggesting a convention specially selected for the purpose of drafting a new constitution. Accordingly a constitutional convention, representative of the towns of the state, was held and its handiwork was approved by the voters in 1780. Later, as the right to vote was expanded and the potential power of masses of voters grew, belief in popular sovereignty became almost universal, but the Massachusetts actions stand as innovations with considerable significance for

---

[9] Benjamin F. Wright, *Consensus and Continuity, 1776–1887* (Boston: Boston University Press, 1958), p. 9. See also Allan Nevins' history of the states in this period, *The American States During and After the Revolution, 1775–1789* (New York: The Macmillan Company, 1924), especially Chap. 4, "The Writing of the State Constitutions."

[10] The Maryland constitution, for example, declared "that all government originates from the people, is founded on compact only and instituted solely for the good of the whole." All the early state constitutions and the earlier colonial charters are available in F. N. Thorpe, *Federal and State Constitutions, Colonial Charters, and Other Organic Laws* (Washington, D.C.: Government Printing Office, 1909).

the nature of the constitutions.[11] For if the people were the ultimate creators of the constitution, even though indirectly so, then the constitution became the sovereign instrument occupying a higher place than routine legislation.

These early constitutions are interesting as evidence of the thinking then current on questions of governmental practice and institutions. The writers of these documents consistently emphasized legislative power and not only because the legislators themselves were doing the writing. Their enemy had been the King—at least in the demonology of wartime excitement—and it was easy to transfer his alleged misuse of power to the threat of executive power in general. Moreover, the colonists had had their fill of executive authority in the form of royally chosen governors whose wide powers from the Crown brought them into conflict with local politicians.[12] As tensions grew between London and the colonies mutual antagonism between the King's agents—the governors—and colonial legislative bodies grew more intense, and accordingly the prestige of executive authority declined and fear of its misuse spread.

There is thus an anomaly in these early constitutions: they establish in many instances virtual legislative supremacy while simultaneously proclaiming the doctrine of separation of powers. Were they maliciously being misleading? The answer lies in the political realities they faced, the traditions they knew, and the fact that they—not unlike other generations of politicians—were able to live with certain contradictions partly because they did not recognize them as such. There were those who recognized the discrepancy, however, and—fearing undue legislative authority—complained of the error. Thomas Jefferson was alarmed at the great power of the legislature granted by the Virginia constitution, contending that:

. . . the concentration of these [powers] in the same hands is precisely the definition of despotic government. It will be no alleviation that these powers will be exercised by a plurality of hands, and not a single one. One hundred and seventy three despots would surely be as oppressive as one.

Separation of powers was then very popular—a popularity due in large part to Baron Montesquieu's *Spirit of the Laws* which was widely

---

11 Evidence of the early acceptance of popular constituent power are the terms of the Tenth Amendment, which delegates certain powers to the United States government, and reserves others to the states "or to the people."

12 In Connecticut and Rhode Island governors were elected; elsewhere they were appointed by the Crown.

read in America. Even the Virginia constitution to which Jefferson objected provided that "the legislative, executive, and judiciary departments shall be separate and distinct so that neither exercise the power properly belonging to the other." Other constitutions also recognized the doctrine, emphasizing the need to keep the departments "forever separate and distinct" as those of North Carolina and Maryland both put it. Massachusetts made the point plainer still by decreeing separation in order that "it may be a government of law and not of men."

Separation of powers was given no substance, however, as most of the early state governments were practical examples of legislative supremacy. Chief executives had very little independent power (only one governor was granted a veto) and they often were bypassed in making significant appointments. Moreover, in most cases governors were appointed by the legislatures, which were thus able to maintain a measure of control over them. Also the powers exercised by the legislatures were very broad, for—acting consistently with the traditions of pre-*laissez-faire* governments—they controlled prices, regulated trade practices, and otherwise involved themselves in economic affairs, even in some cases to the extent of attempting to overrule the courts in property dispute cases. In general the legislatures were to remain the dominant power in the states for most of the ensuing century. Observers in the latter part of the nineteenth century noted that the bulk of state power still rested with the legislature.

Another aspect of the state constitutions—in this case a more familiar trait—was the inclusion of bills of rights. Most of them asserted such rights of citizens as freedom of speech, press, and religion, and provided various procedural guarantees as well, particularly for those accused of violation of laws (jury trials and freedom from bills of attainder and compulsory self-incrimination, among others). Here, as in other aspects of these early efforts at constitution-writing, the state constitutions were to become models for the Constitutional Convention of 1787 and for the First Congress which wrote the federal Bill of Rights.

Both directly through explicit copying of provisions of the state constitutions and indirectly through what were deemed horrible examples to be avoided (*e.g.*, the weak executive) the state constitutions set patterns for the Constitutional Congress as it drafted a replacement for the Articles of Confederation. Under the Articles the primary power to govern rested with the states, of course, and the difficulties they found in cooperating with each other, the lack of concentrated authority in the national government to deal especially with commercial development led to fears of disunion and demands for altering the character of the union between the states. Thus the Constitution sharply increased the potential authority of the national government and limited the power of the states to undertake activities that were deemed injurious or unjust. Acquiring clear power to control actions of citizens directly rather than acting through the agency of the states, the United States government now became a true government with direct relationships with the people. The exact range of national power was by no means determined by the Constitution, however explicit the language of Article I may seem when it allocates powers, for the location of power among the national and state governments was a matter to be decided through endless political combat and a civil war. Nor are the boundaries of federal power settled now; indeed, they can never be settled since the language of the Constitution is open to constant controversy as the society adapts itself to new circumstances and new problems. Thus the Constitution marked a major change in the constitutional relationships between the central and the state governments, but was no final determination of these powers. Time, events, and politics redraw the pattern from generation to generation.

Federalism and Constitutionalism

What the men who wrote the Constitution intended the relationships between the central and the state governments to be and what we as a nation have from time to time believed they intended are by no means always the same things. Occupied with problems of their times and not being clairvoyant, the framers of the constitution could not have envisioned the social and economic conditions that would inevitably alter their proposed government. They could hardly have guessed the extent to which the interpretation of one generation would be practically abandoned by a succeeding generation. It is a common and understandable although mistaken practice to read back into the events and even into the minds of the men of the Constitutional Convention circumstances and ideas which are current later. Strange as it sounds, in all probability the founding fathers were not believers in federalism in the twentieth-century use of that term. While they no doubt were in agreement that both the central and state governments had to exist and that some means had to be provided for sorting out the functions to be allotted to them, there is less and less certainty that there was wide agreement on the details of what those allocations were to be. The more intense the dispute on an issue in the Convention, the more likely that compromise settled the point and correspondingly the less likely that the clear and unmistakable "intent" of the whole body can be discerned. Although "federalism" has come to mean that the national government is in some respects supreme, such was not the universal understanding when the document was written nor in the decades immediately following. Powerful political forces of that era contended that the national government was the agent of the states. They argued that the states, having preceded the national government, having sent state delegations to the Convention, and having ratified the Constitution, must therefore have "created" the new government, from which it "followed" that the central government was in a degree subordinate to the states. No better evidence of this can be found than the Kentucky and Virginia Resolutions in which Jefferson (from the background as an instigator) urged the idea that the states themselves should decide what was constitutional and what was not by in effect suspending the enforcement of federal law within a state when it determined a law to be unconstitutional.

Federalism, then, like other aspects of the Constitution, is constantly subject to revision because new circumstances make new demands on government; and in time men come to believe that what seems necessary to meet the conditions of their own time must have been what the wise founding fathers intended. So we go back to what they said, search diligently among their letters, diaries, and other papers to convince ourselves that they surely must have meant what we want them to mean. All schools of politicians and their respective scholarly collaborators have had their turns at such historical "revisionism," but the long history of efforts to reread the events of the summer of 1787 need not be repeated here. I should cite, however, one very recent and quite novel attempt partly because it represents a reading of those events so diametrically opposite to the tack taken by the Virginia and Kentucky Resolutions. This interpretation says all the preceding attempts had misread the intent of the framers—that they really were trying to set up a system of highly centralized power and not a federal system at all. Professor William Crosskey, whose doctrine this is, contends, for example, that the constitutional grant of power to Congress to regulate commerce was meant as a general power to regulate all commercial activity, not just interstate commerce. With elaborate evidence to back up his reading of the document, he says the history of its interpretation has been one long mistake motivated by "political" considerations.[13]

---

[13] William W. Crosskey, *Politics and the Constitution in the History of the United States*, 2 vols. (Chicago: University of Chicago Press, 1953). Perhaps it is more than a coincidence that Professor Crosskey begins his book with a discussion of the evils that follow from the wrongful reading of the Constitution. One must,

Even if he is right, which is doubtful, it is not likely that he can change the Constitution, for textual analysis of either the document iteslf or of the surviving paper evidence surrounding it is a weak tool to employ against nearly two centuries of practical (not speculative) interpretation.

In order to facilitate discussion of the meaning of federalism, perhaps the most advantageous course is to establish the elements of a "model" of federalism. A model in social scientific analysis is not necessarily an exercise in definition, although it is partly that, nor is it the postulation of an ideal toward which it is recommended that a society strive, although it can implicitly be that too. The broader use, and the one intended here, is to formulate from the far-ranging literature of federalism several principles which characterize it as one system of government distinct from others.[14] Here then are characteristics of a model of federalism:

1. A union of states in which there is a legal right and practical means for the state units to continue existence and operation in some degree independently of the others or of the whole.

2. A central government with authority for foreign affairs and certain domestic authority exercised directly on the people, and with supremacy at least sufficient to assure its dominance when broader interests come into conflict with state ones.

3. A distribution of powers between the two levels of government consistent with principles 1 and 2 above, neither level of government having exclusive control over the distribution of powers or the means of altering that distribution.

4. Some documentary description of the central government-state relationships and the power distribution, and an agency at least somewhat distinct from either the state or the central government to handle inevitable disputes as to the border lines of power.

Such a model, it is self-evident, is not wholly a legal proposition nor is it solely a political description; it is, on the contrary, an attempt to

however, be impressed with the erudition he brought to his task and the enormous volume of evidence he details to support his case.

14 For a more thorough discussion of the uses of models in social science, see Austin Ranney and Willmore Kendall, *Democracy and the American Party System* (New York: Harcourt, Brace and World, Inc., 1956), pp. 18ff. See also M. A. Gersheck and Daniel Lerner, "Model Construction in the Social Sciences," 14 *Public Opinion Quarterly* 710–23 (1950).

signify the practical necessities, both legal and political, since each in-volves the other, requisite for such a system of government.[15] The Soviets describe theirs as a federal system of government, but the facts of its operation are not consistent with the criteria of the model, since the Communist Party is clearly stated to be the one basic source of power in the nation. Also, practical subordination of regional govern-ments (the "Republics") to the dominance of Moscow is inconsistent with all of the elements of the model except the second. Nor would government under the Articles of Confederation, at the opposite ex-treme, be consistent with the model. Any purely unitary system, such as that of Great Britain, would be excluded for lack of both a document and a tradition to sustain the idea of partially independent lesser gov-ernments. In formal terms no lesser government in Britain has inde-pendent powers, nor indeed any powers but those allowed by Parliament. In practical terms, it may be true that certain powers are decentralized in England and have been for so long that their removal would almost amount to a constitutional amendment. To centralize certain functions would invite an enormous political battle, tradition being to the contrary. We may therefore speak of the degree to which formally nonfederal governments approach federal practices, but the absence of both the legal and the political restraints that derive from constitutional-traditional practice and belief makes the distinction be-tween the federal and the unitary system clear. Thus when Great Britain was making a decision to terminate the National Fire Service, which had been organized during World War II, the debate was not conducted in terms of constitutional propriety so much as in terms of proper location for best service. A comparable debate in the United States, given our federalist beliefs and traditions, would inevitably have been a constitutional debate as well as a political one.[16]

Federalism, by distributing power as it does, results in minimizing governmental power at times because the decision to pursue a given

---

[15] For an excellent introductory statement of the principles of federalism, see William Livingston, *Federalism and Constitutional Change* (London: Oxford University Press, 1956), Chap. 1. See also the articles in Aaron Wildavsky, ed., *American Federalism in Perspective* (Boston: Little, Brown & Co., 1967).

[16] In lengthy House of Commons debates on the bill to "return" the fire services to local authorities, the argument against the bill did not directly revolve on a constitutional point, but emphasized rather that the Government was breaking a promise made in wartime to return the function to the same local areas from which it was taken. Instead, went the complaint, the service was being given to other and larger units of local government. In one hundred pages of Parliamentary debate on the bill there does not appear to be one reference to any constitutional point; rather the past promise, centralization, and efficiency are the key points. See *House of Commons Debates (Hansard)*, Vol. 435, (1947), pp. 1422–1519.

policy has to be made not once, but over and over as many times as there are states in which to debate and decide. Denying the central government certain kinds of power, or making it act through the state governments is to delay, or occasionally even to nullify, a potential exercise of governmental power. Any central government, federal or unitary, must depend upon the cooperation of lesser governments in order to achieve many of its objectives. But in the case of federal governments the lesser units have much stronger means of resisting the central government than their counterparts in unitary systems. The distribution of powers in federalism supplies legal as well as political weapons to minimize central government power. The business community resorted to court action to nullify two versions of federal child labor laws, contending that such legislation went beyond the appropriate sphere of national power for the reason that the control of child labor was a matter properly within the province of the states. The Supreme Court accepted this argument and as a result federal action against child labor was postponed for nearly three decades after Congressional majorities were ready to act.[17] More recently labor unions have attacked state laws providing the so-called right to work on the grounds that these state laws violated several provisions of the United States Constitution, a point the Supreme Court did not find acceptable.[18]

The various aspects of decentralization which were discussed in Chapter 3 are in many ways relevant to the subject of federalism. We need not repeat in detail here the arguments about moving decision-making closer to the region where the decisions have to be lived with, or the opportunity to adopt and administer those laws which an area wants most and to reject policies not in keeping with local desires, or the problems of coordinating policies where variations can cause difficulties. These conditions are not peculiarities of federalism alone, they are aspects of decentralization and may be present in the absence of federalism. The point with regard to federalism as concerns decentralization is that federalism becomes a method of minimizing the exercise of powers by providing legal and political barriers and giving them constitutional status.

It should be noted that the traditional relationship between the state

---

[17] *Hammer* v. *Dagenhart*, 247 U.S. 251 (1918), and *Bailey* v. *Drexel Furniture Co.*, 259 U.S. 577 (1922). This doctrine of limitation was abandoned unequivocally by the Court in *United States* v. *F. W. Darby Lumber Co.*, 312 U.S. 100 (1941). But 24 years was, some people thought, a long time to wait.

[18] See *Lincoln Federal Labor Union* v. *Northwestern Iron and Metal Co.*, 335 U.S. 525 (1949).

government and municipalities constitutes a near classic case of non-federal government—of a unitary system, that is. The constitutional position of a municipality is that of a frank subordinate; it has its existence and its powers by consent of the legislature. In theory if the state legislature wished to terminate the legal existence of Boston or of a Kansas hamlet, it has the legal right to do so. But it has no political right and, practically speaking, no political opportunity to do so. It is true that dissolution of municipalities has occurred—occasionally to defeat creditors by recreating a new municipality without assuming the debts of the dissolved one, although the Courts were usually unwilling to accept such maneuvering.[19] And in some cases the courts have held that a legislature cannot either create a municipality nor terminate the existence of one without the agreement of the citizens involved.[20] The question of the "legal existence" of a municipality is peripheral, however; the more important point is that the community has relatively little independent power to perform any governmental act unless it has authorization from the state. There are advocates of local federalism whereby the powers of local government would be more sharply defined and protected from interference by the state legislature and from all the common practices of narrow reading by the judiciary.[21]

While state-local federalism has not by any means been achieved, the ancient doctrine of complete subservience of the locality to the state has been greatly modified. The Supreme Court in 1923 said that "A municipality is merely a department of the state and the state may withhold, grant, or withdraw powers and privileges, as it sees fit. However great or small its sphere of action, it remains the creature of the state."[22] But this unequivocal statement overstates the case probably for 1923, and certainly for the present. Not only has the Home Rule

---

[19] See, for example, *Shapleigh* v. *San Angelo,* 167 U.S. 646 (1897).

[20] See *State ex rel Favis* v. *Town of Lake Placid,* 109 Florida 419 (1933).

[21] See, for example, the position taken by Rodney L. Mott in *Home Rule for America's Cities* (New York: American Municipal League, 1949), pp. 11–13.

[22] *Trenton* v. *New Jersey,* 162 U.S. 182 (1923). Interestingly the city of Trenton attempted to retain its control over a water supply system by claiming rights under the Fourteenth Amendment. Since business corporations had been allowed by the courts to claim rights to protection of property as "persons" within the meaning of the Civil War Amendment, the City claimed it had a proprietary or quasibusiness standing as a consequence of having acquired ownership of a once-private water company. For the state to take over the water supply was not, in the view of the United States Supreme Court, to take Trenton's property without due process of law, since the city, as a subordinate of the state, had no standing to make such a claim. As Mr. Justice Cardozo made even more explicit in 1933, a municipal corporation "has no privileges or immunities under the federal Constitution which it may invoke in opposition to the will of its creator." *Williams* v. *Mayor and City Council of Baltimore,* 289 U.S. 36.

movement enlarged the legal means of the municipality to initiate certain reforms or programs, the expression of the home rule idea has undoubtedly had its political effect on officials who either become persuaded of the values of local independence or who judge such notions to be sufficiently widely believed to make them worthy of recognition in fact as well as in pronouncement.

More will be said in Chapter 5 about the signifiance of the home rule doctrine and its impact on local government, for in that chapter there is an attempt to show something more concrete about the politics of state constitutionalism. Having presented some of the background and some of the underlying ideas of constitutionalism and federalism, I now turn to some of the salient characteristics as well as the significant problems of the actual constitutional arrangements of the states.

The Politics of Constitutionalism II:
5. The State

AMERICAN REVERENCE for constitutionalism is combined with an abiding faith that structural arrangements of government can produce good government. The formal structure of government seems to fascinate us more than the political methods by which a government operates. When citizens brood over failures of their local government, they consider changing the form of government rather than examining the political temper of the community. Although our notions of what constitutes the "best" system of organization have changed from time to time, we retain faith in structural reform. Our passion to find the right formula has induced an enormous amount of research, thinking, writing, and pleading about the structure of government, particularly about government below the federal level. In two hundred state conventions and countless city charter commissions, the "right formula" has been sought after like a Holy Grail.[1] One can trace the changing

---

[1] The estimate of two hundred constitutional conventions is that of Albert L. Sturm in *Methods of State Constitutional Reform* (Ann Arbor, Mich.: University of Michigan Press, 1954), p. 116. On state constitutional reform generally, see W. Brooke Graves, *Major Problems in State Constitutional Revision* (Chicago: Public Administration Service, 1960), which contains a useful bibliography. A fascinating study of the politics of a constitutional convention is Carl B. Swisher's *Motivation and Political Technique in the California Constitutional Convention, 1878–79* (Claremont, Calif.: Pomona College, 1930).

notions about the right structure of government by briefly recounting the evolution of state constitutional change over the nearly two centuries of state constitutional development.[2]

At first (see Chap. 4), fear of an overpowerful executive led to constitutions which granted dominant power to the legislature. But in time disaffection with the legislature, combined with a growing faith in separation of powers, led to restrictions on legislative power and to expansion of executive and judicial authority. When state legislatures took particularly distasteful actions, the reaction was a constitutional provision to forbid such legislation. Other amendments limited the authority to charter banks and denied authority to alter the salaries of high officials (salaries were specified in the constitution instead). When legislatures endangered the credit of states by borrowing and spending beyond annual revenue, specific debt limits were put into the constitution.

Other constitutional means were applied to restrain the legislatures. The governor's powers were expanded: he was given the veto power and greater (although by today's standards, very limited) control over the executive branch. The authority of the judiciary expanded too. Gradually the courts assumed wider authority to pass on the validity of state laws, and to supplement this some state constitutions said specifically that the court's powers included judicial review—that is, specific authority to override legislation inconsistent with the state constitution.

The principles of the long ballot led to constitutional provisions for the popular choice of a wide range of officials—judges, governors, many major administrative officials and a host of lesser agents. Not only was direct election provided for, but the terms of office were made brief so that return to the people for reapproval would be frequent. Later party primary election provisions went into many constitutions in further pursuit of the principle of popular control.

The post-Civil War era brought further constitutional limitations in an effort to curb the widespread dishonesty in government. The ethical standards of politics then were lower than at any time before or since. Bribery of legislators by railroads and other financial interests was common, and buying a legislator was apparently not as difficult as keeping him bought.[3] So the public reacted by further limiting the legislature. Legislative sessions were made biennial rather than annual, and the

---

[2] The same can be done for the evolution of our ideas about municipal government (see Chap. 6).

[3] See the outraged novels of Winston Churchill (the American one) for fascinating vignettes of late nineteenth-century political skullduggery in New Hampshire, particularly *Coniston* and *Mr. Crew's Career*.

number of days they would be permitted to meet was stated specifically; the frank assumption was that the less time they spent at the state house, the less damage they could do. The more outraged the people became, the easier it was to apply "corrective" limitations in the constitution. The pattern is clear: general restraints in bills of rights, implicit restraint through enlargement of executive and judicial powers, explicit prohibition of particular kinds of laws, and limitation through detailed statement of legislative procedure and curtailment of legislative sessions.

That the restrictions were put into the constitution to prevent skullduggery does not necessarily mean that they were effective in preventing it.[4] Often, as York Willbern has said, they locked the barn door after the horse had been stolen, and "there is little indication that the restrictions helped." He continues:

> The muckrakers indicated that state government was at a low ebb by the end of the century. Reform has come as a political and not a constitutional development. It has been based upon better reporting and better leadership. Generally, civil service and merit systems and budgeting and better accounting came not ordinarily as constitutional restrictions on legislatures, but as acts of the legislature itself, spurred by the political environment. Strong leadership by governors with popular support has done most of it.[5]

Failure to achieve the goals of the framers of the limitations, however, does not mean that the restrictions had no effect. The gradual swelling of details, of minutely specific authorizations to undertake particular kinds of action, and the proliferation of restraints continue to shape the conduct of state government.

The post-Civil War decades are unusually important years in the history of state constitutionalism. There was more constitution-writing then than during any other period of our history. Twenty-four states acquired the constitutions they still have; many other states also wrote constitutions in that period which have since been replaced by subsequent documents.[6] Since in this era there was so much well-

---

[4] On the effects of these limitations, see James W. Hurst, *The Growth of American Law* (Boston: Little, Brown and Co., 1950), p. 234. See Chaps. 10 and 11 of this volume for an overall assessment of state constitution-making and many realistic insights into the process.

[5] York Willbern, "Suggestions Concerning a Study of Historical Development of State Constitutions." A paper presented at a seminar of the National Municipal League, September, 1957, p. 6 (mimeographed).

[6] In the period from 1866 to 1897 there were fifty-one state conventions. It was a period of constant constitution-making and remaking in the South where the end

founded distrust of politicians, the constitutions that were drawn reflected the public distrust in the profusion of detail used to diminish the discretion left to legislators. The resulting constitutions came more and more to look like statutory codes rather than the fundamental law documents that they presumably were. The extreme detail of present-day constitutions can be traced to developments during this period.

Some Problems of State Constitutions

Although it is inevitably necessary to generalize about the fifty state constitutions, the differences between them are so great that nearly any generalization has to have within it an implied set of exceptions to cover the variations. Thus it is generally true that state constitutions are quite long, although many of the older ones are not. Some are confusing and even contradictory and so detailed they almost defy comprehension, but others are relatively simple, codified, and comprehensible. Given the variations among these constitutions, any student of them should look at some of the actual documents and some of the comparative data on them in order to form his own judgments.[7]

State Constitutions: Long and Profusely Detailed

A written constitution is normally conceived to be a relatively brief document setting forth the fundamental structure of a government and the important limitations which are placed upon it. The model of

---

of the Civil War, Reconstruction, and then the end of Reconstruction toppled one regime after another; there was a spurt of new state formation (nine new states were formed); and in other states there was political unrest that invited constitution-writing activity. See Sturm, *op. cit.*, pp. 114–15, for the dates of state constitutional conventions.

[7] In most states there is a state publication, variously called a manual, bluebook, or register, which contains the state constitution. The biennial publication of the Council of State Governments, *The Book of the States*, contains current information about constitutional development and also shows in tabular form comparative data about constitutions. Another invaluable source is the *Index Digest of State Constitutions*, produced by the Legislative Drafting Research Fund of Columbia University. The latter volume is a ready source of comparative information on all the constitutions as of 1960. An excellent short description and analysis of state constitutions is to be found in a pamphlet published by the National Municipal League, and written by Robert B. Dishman, *State Constitutions: The Shape of the Document*. After looking at some of the actual documents, it would be instructive to examine the model state constitution issued by the National Municipal League.

brevity and effectiveness is the United States Constitution. Simplicity and lack of detail are its hallmarks. Very few state constitutions are that brief, and some fill a small volume instead of fifteen pages or so for the federal Constitution. The Louisiana constitution is 350,000 words long —enough to equal a very fat novel in length and to exceed by far any novel ever published in dullness.

The subjects that find their way into state constitutions are varied and sometimes curious indeed. The California constitution limits the powers of the legislature concerning the length of wrestling matches. The Georgia fundamental law announces a $250,000 reward for the first person to strike oil in the state. Louisiana's constitution proclaims Huey Long's birthday as a perpetual state holiday.[8] Many state constitutions provide in minute detail for the governing bodies of specific counties and municipalities, and if any change in local government is to be made, it can only come through a constitutional amendment. Amendments proliferate as the details become more explicit, for the more minute the prescriptions the less leeway there is for adaptation through interpretation, and—like the statutory law which the detailed constitution comes to resemble—it is necessary to alter the constitution in order to adapt to changing circumstances. Hence the constitutions in force now have been amended more than 3000 times, and in some instances it is necessary to read the constitution backwards, like a Chinese newspaper, in order to see what the last word is on a specific point, moving back the daisy chain of amendments to the original provision. Voters are often asked at a general election to pass judgment on half a dozen or more amendments, often so involved in phrasing that they are impossible to comprehend. Making fun of the practice of adding countless amendments, a research organization once entitled a publication analyzing thirty-one proposed constitutional amendments to be voted on in one election: "Biennial Bingo, or 31 more in '54."[9]

Does it matter that constitutions are long and detailed? Do the restraints on the manner of exercising state powers have any long-run significance? How in fact does the elaboration of detail affect the way a government operates? This is, after all, the important question to be asked about the length and complexity of state constitutions. That they are long *per se* is not necessarily a negative quality. And if increasing the complexity of their terminology has some sound and necessary

---

[8] These and other oddities are cited by Robert Dishman, *op. cit.*, pp. 15–18.

[9] Cited by Karl Bosworth in "Law Making in State Governments" in *The Forty-Eight States* (New York: The American Assembly, 1955), p. 90.

reason, no one ought to cavil about that. After all, constitutions are not written to be read for pleasure, and even the simplest of them—the United States Constitution—can baffle the untrained reader who is not familiar with the legal jargon and sometimes archaic words (how many men on the street could tell you what "letters of marque and reprisal" [Article I, Sec. 8] are?). Some may regret that state constitutions are not easy reading for a high school civics class, but the loss is not overwhelming. The importance of the length, complexity, and tangle of detail of state constitutions is deeper than that.

Substantially the reason the complexity is important is that it allots an advantage to some contestants in the political process and a handicap for others. By inviting litigation the wealth of detail plays into the hands of those who want to prevent a particular law from going into effect. And, although a legislative majority may have approved it, and the governor's signature may be authentic, there are always possibilities that the courts can be persuaded to invalidate a law on grounds that some minute aspect of constitutional procedure was not properly complied with. If so, dissenters to a law may carry the day and the legislation be cancelled, for it may be impossible to mount once again the necessary peak of interest that pushed through the legislation in the first place. At the least, a delay of from one to two years is likely since re-enactment must await the next legislative session.

Here is a situation that illustrates the possible consequences of overelaboration of detail in a constitution. In Louisiana, a few years after that state had by various means got out from under the direct rulership of the Huey Long political machine, a governor instituted a move to reorganize the executive branch to improve its efficiency.[10] Since the state constitution provided in great detail for the creation of and the interrelationships between the various major agencies of the executive, it was necessary to resort to a constitutional amendment in order to make the change. The governor had to battle powerful opposition to get approval of the amendment, but finally it was approved both by the legislature and in a popular referendum, and accordingly he recast the state's administrative structure. Immediately the validity of an action of an administrator was challenged in a taxpayer's suit, claiming that the constitutional amendment was itself invalid, even

---

[10] The reforms, initiated by Governor Sam Houston Jones, were aimed at increasing the governor's control over a far-flung administrative complex. While not without political implications, the reforms appear to have had at least the honest intention of raising the effectiveness of the government. See Allan P. Sindler's discussion of the fight over reorganization in his *Huey Long's Louisiana* (Baltimore: Johns Hopkins Press, 1956), pp. 158–60.

though duly passed by the people, because it had dealt with more than one subject and because the legislature had not specified precisely at which election the amendment would be submitted to the voters. In a federal court such a suit would be thrown out for want of proper standing to bring suit,[11] but state courts do entertain such suits and the Louisiana courts found no fault with this one. Indeed, they blithely invalidated the amendment on the grounds that it had covered more than one subject (and how could it do otherwise if its objective was to reorganize scattered administrative agencies?), and because of the unclarity about which election the legislature intended for the referendum. This sounds like a very close and proper reading of the constitution, something the court might say that it felt itself obligated to do in view of the explicitness of its language. The trouble is that the Supreme Court went on to say that the margin in favor of the amendment had only been 6667 votes.[12] If the court's argument is in fact constitutional, then the size of the majority is utter irrelevant. If the court is making a frankly political decision, then the meager margin is of some significance.

State courts, it must be emphasized, are less inclined than are federal courts to take a liberal attitude in interpreting the limits of legislative authority. Even though the United States Supreme Court has often been willing to go rather far in reading the Constitution in such a way as to defeat the intent of Congress, it is nevertheless true that the Court in theory—and most of the time in practice as well—seeks to read legislation so as to make it constitutional if it reasonably can do so. That is, the Justices say in effect that they are ready to assume that the Congress *meant* to act constitutionally, and that if there is a way to read the legislation as constitutional, they will do so.[13] Some state courts share this attitude, but many of them come close to taking an opposite tack. In part, however, the negative approach may be accounted for by the very specificity of the constitution, which is an invitation to close reading. No doubt it has often been the intent of the writers of constitutions to restrict the legislature's discretion, and

---

[11] *Frothingham* v. *Mellon*, 262 U.S. 447 (1923).

[12] *Graham* v. *Jones*, 3 So. (2nd.) 761 (La. 1941). See the brief discussion of the case in Charles Aiken, "State Constitutional Law in 1941–42," 36 *American Political Science Review*, 667, 668 (1942). The student of state constitutions will find a wealth of useful information in the series of annual articles of the same title as the one just cited. The series ran in the *Review* from 1927–49.

[13] The classic statement of this doctrine was made by Justice Brandeis in *Ashwander* v. *Tennessee Valley Authority*, 297 U.S. 288 (1936); his comment is sometimes called the "Ashwander Rule."

state courts may merely be acting in the spirit of the constitution in their restrictive rulings.

Surely the abundance of detail is an open invitation to litigation, and to nullification of legislation. But the mood of the courts toward the enactment of legislation is often so negative that they reach beyond the specifics to general provisions in order to invalidate laws. They have, for example, much more frequently than federal courts employed the doctrine of separation of powers to negate state laws.[14] The allied doctrine of improper delegation of powers has similarly been frequently used by state courts. For example, the South Carolina legislature was once told it could not allow the state highway commission to determine which of two alternative methods of financing a highway project was preferable on the grounds that this was an illicit delegation of legislative authority.[15] As Professor J. A. C. Grant once observed:

Since many practitioners of the law tend to confuse the terms "unprecedented" and "unconstitutional," statutes calling for action of a new and novel sort are as certain to be contested as those which challenge well established rules of constitutional law.[16]

Not only will the law be challenged, but the opinion of the judges of the advisability of the legislation may affect its chances for survival. Hypothetically the value and the wisdom of legislation is of no consequence to the courts, but is obviously often taken into account. Although the more free-wheeling practices of the laissez-faire-oriented courts of earlier days (and lasting up until the late 1930's) have been moderated, there are still instances of state invalidation of legislation because of the we-don't-think-it-is-a-good-idea rule.[17] As recently as

---

[14] See Charles G. Haines, "State Constitutional Law in 1931–32," 26 *American Political Science Review* 660–64 (1932), for a good discussion of the use of this rule in state courts.

[15] *State* v. *Moorer* 150 S. E. 269 (1929).

[16] "State Constitutional Law in 1935–36," 30 *American Political Science Review* 692 (1936).

[17] Oliver P. Field shows the decline of reversals since 1930 in *Judicial Review of Legislation in Ten Selected States* (Bloomington, Ind.: Bureau of Government Research, Indiana University, 1943). He cites the following numbers of reversals by decades (p. 14):

Decade	Reversals
1891–1900	193
1901–10	241
1911–20	170
1921–30	174
1931–40	87

Significantly no less than 55 per cent of all reversals since 1771 (total of 1406) took place in the period 1891–1930.

1946 the Kentucky courts used the vague concept of "natural freedom of contract" as the basis for overthrowing legislation regulating burial insurance contracts. Courts have overruled the two state attempts to force employers to give paid time off for their employees to vote on election day.[18] An observer of state courts remarked some years ago that regulatory measures "still provide a fruitful source of litigation." [19]

The elaboration of constitutional authorizations of specific powers has another significant effect—it can lead to the necessity for further detail and further confusion and legal uncertainty. That is, the more detailed the provisions on a specific question the greater the likelihood that it will be necessary later to modify the constitution because circumstances have changed. Constitution writers cannot foresee all the possible exceptions or additions that may become mandatory in a few years or decades.

In general, state constitutions do not need to authorize particular kinds of laws. But if the wealth of detail grows sufficiently complex, it may become necessary to authorize specifically a particular kind of legislation for the simple reason that so many kinds of legislation are authorized that doubt may be cast on the constitutionality of a law unless it is possible to point to some authorizing constitutional provision. This is a strange turn of events, since the one "advantage" of the state constitutions over the federal is that they are constitutions of general powers and do not therefore have to depend upon any list of specifically delegated powers as Congress must look to Article I, Sec. 8, in which most of its powers are listed. The states originated as governments of general sovereign powers and therefore it was unnecessary to enumerate their powers; and the traditional interpretation of state constitutions remains that even now, although the practice of inserting constitutional authorization for specific programs has tended to controvert this standard doctrine. Thus thirteen states have found it useful or necessary to state in their constitutions more or less detailed authority for state and local government collaboration with the United States

---

18 The United States Supreme Court refused to alter a Missouri Court ruling that such a statute was valid in *Day-Brite Lighting Co.* v. *Missouri*, 342 U.S. 421 (1952). The Court said: "Our recent decisions make plain that we do not sit as a super legislature to weigh the wisdom of legislation nor to decide whether the policy which it expressed offends the public welfare." Justice Jackson, however, disagreed in this case and cited cases in Kentucky and Illinois in which such laws had been invalidated.

19 See Foster Sherwood, "State Constitutional Law in 1948–49," 43 *American Political Science Review* 735 (1949). He cites a Maryland case in which a legislative authorization of denial of the right to build a filling station in a neighborhood where a majority of the residents object was denied validity on grounds that this was an unjustified use of the police power. He cites other illustrative cases.

in urban redevelopment programs. Elsewhere, the states have either not authorized the program at all or have done so under the general powers of the legislature. Where resort to an amendment is necessary, all the difficulties of the constitutional amendment process are encountered—delay, unusual majorities and possibly therefore a shackling of state government.

Restraints on the Legislature

An interesting chapter in the story of constitutional restraint on legislatures is the effort to minimize or even to forbid borrowing by the state. Nearly all the state constitutions now provide some kind of restraint on borrowing,[20] although the effectiveness of the limitations is not very impressive on the whole. When one examines the total debt loads of the various states there is no distinguishable difference between the more and the less restrained states. Apparently the various hurdles that are put before the officials or the voters (since they must often approve borrowing in referenda) are not insurmountable. The restrictions vary from the requirement of unusual majorities in the legislature for approval (a three-fourths vote is necessary in Delaware) and specifically stated dollar limits to flat prohibitions of borrowing with stipulated exceptions.[21] In effect some states can resort to borrowing only when a constitutional amendment is passed. This is, with minor exceptions, the case in Louisiana, and yet the bonded debt of that state is relatively high. In many states the barriers to borrowing are evaded by issuing bonds without the full faith and credit of the state behind them; the result is that an abnormally high interest rate is necessary and wastes funds.[22]

There is, of course, no special virtue in borrowing instead of staying within the annual revenue estimates; but on the other hand, there is no

---

[20] Four states provide no direct limitation: Connecticut, Mississippi, New Hampshire, and Tennessee.

[21] See B. U. Ratchford, "Constitutional Provisions Concerning State Borrowing," 32 *American Political Science Review* 694–707 (1938) in which the provisions of each state with regard to borrowing are summarized. Similar limitations on taxing authority are in many constitutions. See Glenn D. Marrow, "State Constitutional Limitations on Taxing Authority of State Legislatures," 9 *National Tax Journal* 126 (1956); and Frank M. Landers, "Constitutional Provisions on Taxation and Finance," 33 *State Government* 39 (1960).

[22] James A. Heins, *Constitutional Restrictions Against State Debt* (Madison: University of Wisconsin Press, 1963).

convincing reason why a state should not borrow under certain circumstances and for certain kinds of programs. Borrowing may indeed be the only way to finance some very necessary capital expenditures for large projects such as mental hospitals or buildings for higher education. Furthermore, borrowing for such capital programs is a way of making future users pay a share of the costs of their own facilities. While even high hurdles can be surmounted when there is a sufficient drive to resort to borrowing, the hurdles unquestionably favor the interests of those who would say no to public projects. The argument that the hurdles prevent fiscal disaster is not particularly impressive, since they are in fact surmountable. The importance of the limitations lies in the political fact that they give an advantage to one element and a handicap to another.

The political significance of the constitution is well-illustrated in the sometimes feverish efforts of special-interest groups to find sanctuary in the constitution for their particular concern. As a result of such efforts many constitutions contain a wide range of guarantees and prohibitions for the protection of interests powerful enough to push their way into the fundamental law. As Robert Dishman has pointed out, a survey of a constitution may identify the state's powerful interests—those strong enough to wangle their way to "privileged or protected status . . . in the constitution."[23] Veterans, labor unions, farmers, church groups, the gasoline industry, and hundreds of other economic, social, and professional groups have managed to get special exemptions from taxation. For instance, veterans use their political power to assure many different kinds of benefits; the gasoline industry has succeeded often in limiting to highway uses alone the income from gasoline taxes. Other special interests protect their place in government by the "earmarking" of certain revenues for special funds to be spent for the particular purposes of the interest. Hunters want the returns from hunting licenses reserved for restocking the game they kill; special funds are set aside for education, welfare, and other purposes. The result in some states is that less than half of all state revenues are available to the legislature to appropriate as they think necessary.[24] Labor unions seek guarantees of the right to belong to unions and to bargain collectively, and, conversely, management seeks "right to work" guarantees intended to assure the right *not* to belong to a union. The importance of achieving constitu-

---

[23] Dishman, *op. cit.*, p. 7.

[24] Indeed, as of 1965 in more than a dozen states two-thirds or more of state revenues are earmarked, running as high as 86, 88, and 90 per cent in Louisiana, Wyoming, and Alabama respectively. See Supplement to *State Expenditure Controls: An Evaluation* (New York: Tax Foundation, Inc., 1965), p. 53.

tional status for such privileges is obvious; no ordinary legislative majority can eliminate the ground gained by the interest. The advantage always lies with those who oppose constitutional change, since unusual steps are demanded to get an amendment passed, thereby placing the advantage with the minority who would stop action.

The reapportionment revolution and renewed agitation for constitutional reform has produced a number of constitutional conventions in recent years. Significant changes came in Connecticut, New Hampshire, New Jersey, Rhode Island, and Tennessee. A number of other states have appointed commissions to recommend changes or have begun the convention procedures as of late 1967 (Georgia, Idaho, Kentucky, and North Dakota have had recent commissions; Maryland, Pennsylvania, and New York had conventions in session in 1967).

The Politics of Amendment

The extent to which constitutions are amendable is an important factor to consider in weighing their political effect. The difficulty of altering constitutions varies widely; in some cases it is relatively easy, in others it is nearly impossible. Complex and slow amendment procedures raise difficulties for the operation of state government, since the more detailed character of state constitutions renders the inflexibility a more serious problem than it might be with a constitution that was vaguer in its provisions. To take an extreme example, the State of Tennessee has an amending process that is most difficult—indeed almost impossible—to operate. Not only must a majority of all members elected to the legislature approve the amendment twice (and the second time by a two-thirds vote), but in an ensuing referendum it must be approved by a majority equal to or larger than a majority of those voting for governor. The more customary procedure is to require approval by a majority of those voting on the amendment, but under the Tennessee system (used by five other states as well) the person who votes in the general election but not on the referendum may thereby cause defeat of the amendment since *a majority of all those voting in the general election* is required for passage of the amendment. Thus in Tennessee not one single amendment was added to the constitution between its adoption in 1870 and 1953. In 1953 the situation became serious enough to allow the creation of a constitutional convention which submitted eight amendments to the voters.

The most common means of amending is to provide for approval of the amendment by two-thirds vote in the legislature and then for approval by a majority of the people voting on it in the next election. A handful of states allow amendment after approval of a majority of those voting in the legislature and a majority of the people voting in a referendum. Delaware is the only state not requiring submission of amendments to the people, allowing amendment by vote of two-thirds of those elected to the legislature in two successive sessions.[25] At the opposite extreme fourteen states (nine of them are western states) permit the initiation of an amendment by petition, bypassing the legislature entirely.

Except in Tennessee and perhaps half a dozen other states where the hurdles for amendment are fairly high, the relative difficulty of the amendment process does not seem to determine the frequency with which constitutions have been amended. Some of the more easily amended ones have not had excessive amendments added to them; others somewhat more difficult to amend have numerous amendments. As of 1965, California, Louisiana, South Carolina, and Texas—all of which require a two-thirds legislative vote plus public approval in a referendum in order to amend—had had the following number of amendments proposed and adopted:

State	Year of Adoption of Constitution	Proposed Amendments	Adopted
California	1879	600	350
Louisiana	1921	607	460
South Carolina	1885	364	251
Texas	1876	254	158

No doubt the complexity of the constitution is a more significant producer of amendments than the ease or difficulty of the amending process.

Constitutional restraints—both directly through prohibitions and indirectly through difficult amending procedures and other procedural specifications—were applied because men were fearful of what legis-

---

[25] For comparative data on the means of amending constitutions, and for other relevant data on them generally, see the current issue of *The Book of the States*. This contains regular articles on the developments of the past two years in state constitutions, summarizing the major changes in the various states. For earlier generally similar articles see the series in the *American Political Science Review*, "State Constitutional Development," which ran from 1929–37.

lators might do if allowed unlimited powers. There was ground for the fear, as we have noted, but the record does not indicate that the restraints had the effect their proponents hoped for. If the ethical standards of a state's politics are low, the constitution cannot raise them. No better evidence of this can be found than the history of Louisiana skullduggery. Louisiana's constitution bristles with restrictions and explicit instructions on all manner of subjects, but they have not tamed the politics of the state noticeably. As V. O. Key once said:

Few would contest the proposition that among its professional politicians of the past two decades Louisiana has had more men who have been in jail, or who should have been, than any other American state. Extortion, bribery, peculation, thievery are not rare in the annals of politics, but in the scale, variety, and thoroughness of its operation the Long gang established, after the death of the Kingfish, a record unparalleled in our times.[26]

No other state can quite match Louisiana's flamboyant chicanery, yet there are competitors for this sorry prize. There is little reason to conclude that the states with elaborate constitutional restraints have come any closer to achieving honesty and responsibility than those without restraints. Again the political climate of the community is a more persuasive force than its constitutional document.[27]

Constitutions: Politics and Purposes

It is possible to overstress the hobbling of government by constitution. Often in emphasizing the negative qualities of constitutions, critics fail to see the political realities that may in some cases dictate the continuance of some of the constitutional provisions. In the past, before the U.S. Supreme Court ordered reapportionment, the retention of an apportionment system which favored rural areas may be accounted for in many states by tacit public approval of this constitutional means of stopping change. As one who has campaigned for alteration of legisla-

---

[26] V. O. Key, *Southern Politics in State and Nation* (New York: Alfred A. Knopf, 1949), p. 156.

[27] When the political situation reaches the extreme that it did under Huey Long, constitutions have little meaning. During his governorship one opponent shoved a volume before Huey, saying, "Maybe you've heard of this book. It's the Constitution of the State of Louisiana." "I'm the Constitution around here now," Long replied. Quoted by Arthur Schlesinger, Jr., in *The Politics of Upheaval* (Boston: Houghton Mifflin and Co., 1960), p. 17.

tive apportionment in one of the then unfairly apportioned states in the nation (Connecticut), I no longer can entertain the naive notion I once had—that the rigged apportionment is retained solely because any amendment must come through the legislative chamber which the small towns or other favored districts control. The combination of apathy, vague approval, and vigorous approval of the existing apportionment outweigh the opinions of supporters of change in the scales of political controversy. In other states the initiation through popular petitions of amendments to alter unfair apportionment was not strikingly successful. In several glaring cases the public has been persuaded to vote down such amendments even though they appeared to be voting against their own self-interest. This, I hasten to emphasize, does not mean that the special privileges are unimportant. The point is that the constitutional factors must be weighed realistically and considered in terms of a state's political realities.

The advocates of more effective state government cheered to the rafters when the Kestnbaum Commission announced its opinion on the obsolescent and negative character of state constitutions. Had not the Commission been appointed by a conservative president who wished to stem the flow of power from state government to Washington? Here certainly spoke an unbiased voice, pleading for the very improvements that the "do-something" elements in various states had been advocating for decades. And what did the Kestnbaum Commission say about state constitutions? Commenting on the need for more effective state government, if the states were to maintain their rightful place in the scheme of American government, the Commission said:

In addition to reapportionment, there are a number of other measures that would enable State legislatures to become more effective instruments of policy formation. In this age of rapid change, legislative bodies are called upon to deal with an increasing number of complex and technical issues. Most State legislatures are not, however, in a position to give the time and study that many of these issues should have. Most of the States impose constitutional limitations on the frequency and length of sessions. . . .

Perhaps the chief obstacles to legislative flexibility are those created by over-detailed provisions of State constitutions, designed to correct specific actions of past legislative sessions. Some of these provisions rigidly prohibit certain forms of legislative action; others contain elaborate restrictions and prescriptions of an essentially statutory nature. Some of them attempt to regulate in detail such rapidly changing or technical matters as the powers of corporations, the routes of the State highway system, and the conduct of State and county administration. Some interfere with the full use of modern tools of budgeting, accounting, auditing, and personnel administration . . .

It is abundantly clear that restrictions and limitations of the type described have engendered at least as many errors and excesses as they have prevented. Removing these limitations would be an important step toward strengthening State government.[28]

The only "difficulty" with the statement is that it can be taken too uncritically. The important political point underlying the statement may not be appreciated if the standard American error of overemphasizing the formal constitutional aspects of the question obscures its political aspects. "Removing these limitations," said the commission, "would be an important step toward strengthening State government." It would be a "first step" in the sense that a vigorous political follow-through would be necessary if the states are to fulfill their role more effectively. Yet in another sense, it cannot possibly be a first step, for a prior battle is going to have to be fought. It is a battle with some political conservatives who take the inconsistent position that the powers of government should not be centralized but should be kept at the state level, while simultaneously exerting their power to prevent the improvement of state government. Their position is understandable, even if not entirely logical. What they are saying is that they really do not wish to see certain kinds of power exercised at all, and that they rate more highly their chances of preventing undesired action if the power to decide is dispersed to the various states. (A not unreasonable position, after all; the history of state politics and government is testimony to the effectiveness of the nay sayers.) There is no reason why a convinced conservative who does not want to see regulatory power exercised over his activities should become an overnight convert to vigorous state government. (The more important question for the man who will lose money as a consequence of a water pollution program is not which government will force him to cease polluting streams but whether any government will do so.) This is, of course, a continuing "battle" that is never to be finally won, but there is every advantage in recognizing the political forces that are at stake in the larger battle. Clarification of these fundamental positions may lead to clearer thinking by both conservative and "do-something" elements, permitting them to come closer to cooperating in working out the basic strategy for state government improvement.

One final point should be made concerning state constitutionalism —a point dealing with strategy in a broad sense. There is a basic ques-

---

28 The Commission on Intergovernmental Relations, *Report* (Washington, D.C.: Government Printing Office, 1955), pp. 41–42.

tion of the rightful purpose of a constitution—should it be a repository of certain fundamental principles of a people or a detailed statutory code? Should it contain only fundamental points, such as the basic form of the government, certain profoundly held beliefs about what a government should not do, and then stop? But how can we keep to the fundamentals, assuming there is a desire or convincing reason to do so? A suggestion made by York Willbern some years ago in the course of a National Municipal League seminar on state government has interesting possibilities. He tentatively proposed that a distinction be made between the fundamental and the nonfundamental parts of a constitution. Those parts that are fundamental—the basic distribution of power, the bill of rights—might be distinguished from the quasistatutory provisions. The fundamental parts of the constitution might be made amendable only by the unusual majorities and special procedures that a state chooses to demand, but after fifteen years the more "legislative" elements of the constitution could revert to the status of ordinary legislation and would be changeable by ordinary legislative majorities.[29]

Thus if a special provision for the protection of a forest preserve is put into a constitution, a subsequent generation might be able to change its views without having to convince an unusual majority to concur. If the conservation measure has become a straitjacket to subsequent development—and although I happen to be very partial to the protection of woodlands in a time of encroaching urbanization, I can conceive of times and circumstances when reconsideration of land policy might be wise—then the demands of a future majority ought to be able to alter the law. So too with education and other special concerns that the public feels tenderly about; if the interested public wants to retain constitutional status for a provision, it requires no more than a majority vote. Special privileges that at any given moment seem to need protection but which in the long run may be deemed not actually to need or merit the privilege granted may then not have the right to protect their place by minority vote. (That is, they cannot stop alteration of the constitution by voting "no" in the legislature and winning the vote because they compose just over one-third of the members voting—which is what a two-thirds rule means, of course.)

Naturally there would be much debate about what constitutes a

---

[29] Seminar on Constitutional Studies in New York, September 7, 1957. "What this would mean," Willbern has said in a subsequent letter, "would be that the amending clause would provide for two methods of amendment—a difficult method for some items, with the easy method perhaps being applicable only after the passage of a term of years." Letter to the author, November 3, 1960.

"fundamental" or a "statutory" provision, and marginally this proposal partakes of the "gimmick" characteristics so common to our governmental thinking. It has, however, the significant quality of attempting to sort out the permanent from the passing, and it seeks to minimize the rigidity of constitutional practice where rigidity offers no evident value. As York Willbern has rightly said: "I think we could exercise a great deal more ingenuity about the *levels* of sanctity which we mean to ascribe to particular kinds of constitutional provisions." [30]

---

[30] *Ibid.*; italics in original.

6. The Politics of Constitutionalism III: The Municipality

IN THE DISCUSSION of state constitutional politics it was safe to assume a general knowledge of the nature and the overall functional role of the states, but familiarity with the municipality's constitutional position cannot be assumed. This unfamiliarity does not result from apathy toward local government; the evidence suggests that citizens interested in public affairs are more likely to be concerned with local than state politics. Rather it results from the bewildering complexity of local constitutionalism and the wide range of variety of local governments. Each state has its own local government traditions. Even the terminology gets confusing since the same word takes on different meanings in different states. Procedures of one state are unknown in the next. It is necessary therefore to say something about the wide array of local government institutions in the United States before attempting to assess the municipality's constitutional position.

Local Government Types: Variations on Themes

Municipal government is commonly used in reference to all governmental units beneath the state government—county, city, township, and so on. While there are historic differences between the municipal corporation—which means a community with continuity and a corporate being recognized as having certain rights in the law—and agencies (such as the county) created to perform the duties assigned to it by the state and as an agent of the state, the distinction means less and less as the years go by. It meant something when the lines of jurisdiction of government were less clearly set than they now are, or when new governments were being rapidly created in unsettled territory, or when judicial reliance on the historic doctrines of the municipal corporation was much more common than it is today. Today both the county and the city frequently serve as agents of the state. Thus we may meaningfully call *municipal* all the various local government units that are common today.[1]

TOWNS AND TOWNSHIPS

Somewhat less than half the states have local units of government called "towns" (mostly in New England) or "townships" (mostly in the Mid-Atlantic and Midwestern states). The New England town, one of the earliest governmental institutions developed in colonial America, was a closely knit society located in a fairly small area and governed ultimately as a simple direct democracy. The characteristic town meeting was a gathering of the townsfolk to act as their own legislative body; little authority was delegated to the three "selectmen"—the board of interim agents who considered affairs between town meetings. Consid-

---

[1] There are distinctions in the law of certain states between what is and what is not a municipal corporation, and this *legal* distinction has importance in the law of those states. It does not follow, however, that there is, even in the states that make such a legal distinction, a political disinction of any significance. See Jefferson B. Fordham, *Local Government Law* (New York: The Foundation Press, 1949), pp. 15–17. He argues that the traditional distinction is no longer important. He states the standard classification of municipal corporations and public quasicorporations this way:

Incorporated cities, towns, villages and boroughs constituted the first class; everything else fell within the second. At the root of this distinction were four factors: (1) the notion that counties and other quasicorporations were almost exclusively state agencies administering matters of state concern as distinguished from the large sphere of local business with which municipalities dealt, (2) the assumption that the agencies to be labelled quasicorporations were less complete forms of corporate organisms; (3) the notion that municipalities, unlike a county, for example, possessed, at least in a limited sense, a private as well as a public character; and (4) the theory that while municipalities were established only at the request or with the consent of the inhabitants counties and other quasicorporations were created by the state without the consent of the inhabitants.

Fordham concludes that "Whatever factual basis the old classification may have had previously it stands seriously undermined today."

erable authority still is granted to the New England town, and proportionately little power is allowed the New England county. In Rhode
Island and Connecticut the county is no more than a territorial designation; all governmental powers are located either in the state or the cities,
towns, and special districts. The whole territory of the New England
states (with minor exceptions in the far northern parts of the region)
is divided into towns—there is no "unincorporated," county-governed
terrain between municipalities. The practice of incorporation varies;
some have specific charters, others depend upon special state legislation passed with regard to the specific town and upon general legislation
empowering all towns and cities to undertake various functions. In the
larger towns, particularly in the suburban regions, the classic forms of
town-meeting government have been modified greatly, but not quite
lost as the inhabitants attempt to adapt the governmental form intended for hundreds to the tens of thousands.[2]

The township, although generally patterned after the New England
town, has less power and usually is not so vigorous a unit of government
as the town. In a few states there is a "township meeting" roughly
comparable to the New England town meeting, but even where it exists
its powers do not equal those of the prototype.[3] The township has a
board of supervisors or trustees as a governing body whose powers vary
depending upon whether the law provides for a township meeting. This
distinction may be more formal than real, however, for in some cases
the township meeting is so sparsely attended that the local officials outnumber citizens in attendance with inevitable results as to control over
policy. The township, because it shares powers with county and other
units of government, has not acquired the vitality and traditional acceptance common to the New England town.

There are other local government forms scattered over the country;
for example, the "hundred" (roughly equivalent to the township)
which survives from ancient English usage in Delaware or the "village"

---

[2] On the New England town in general, see John F. Sly, *Town Government in
Massachusetts* (Cambridge, Mass.: Harvard University Press, 1930); Lane W.
Lancaster, *Government in Rural America* (New York: Van Nostrand Press, 1937),
pp. 42–54; Robert S. Babcock, *State and Local Government and Politics* (New
York: Random House, 1957), pp. 95–104.

[3] For a listing of the states which have towns and townships, see the latest annual
volume of the *Municipal Year-book* (Chicago: International City Managers Association). With minor exceptions the township is common from New York to the
Dakotas and Kansas. There are 66 of them in Washington. For a general discussion
of the township see Lancaster, *op. cit.*, pp. 70–79, and Clyde F. Snider, *American
State and Local Government* (New York: Appleton-Century-Crofts, 1950), pp.
356–61.

which has different meanings from place to place. In a few states the term *borough* is applied to small municipalities which lack the status of cities but which are something more than villages. Any attempt to categorize all the peculiarities of small town and rural government would be pointless here; any serious study of local government will necessitate looking at the detailed structure of one or more actual states and not a perusal of superficial description of practices in all the states.[4]

THE COUNTY

The structure, authority, operational methods, and representativeness of county governments are too varied to permit a simple description. True, all but three states[5] use the county in some form for general administrative purposes; but after this generalization, difficulty sets in. For present purposes it is fortunately unnecessary to go into great detail about county government. In general there is some kind of county board, usually although not invariably popularly elected, and that board has (again usually) general taxing powers and authority to undertake various kinds of activity. In the Southern and Western states where county government is a key element of local government, county officials have powers over highways, education, law enforcement, and welfare services. In addition, the county often has regulatory powers over zoning, for example, or liquor licenses.

The county governing body—variously called the "board of supervisors," "commissioners," or "judges"—usually shares its powers with other boards or elective officials who have authority over various functions such as roads, libraries, hospitals, and law enforcement. The powers of all county government are dependent upon acts of the state legislature, and although there has been occasional success in achieving county home rule, this reform has not gone far. Although not chartered as are the cities and some lesser municipalities, in most parts of the country counties are not merely administrative agencies. According to Paul W. Wager:

---

[4] The constitution of most states offers a starting point for the examination of the structure and terminology of loacl government. See, for example, the New York State Constitution, Article IX, and the *Index Digest of State Constitutions*, pp. 736–65.

[5] Connecticut, Rhode Island, and Alaska have no counties as organized units of government; in certain other states some counties are so sparsely populated as not to be organized for governing purposes (North and South Dakota). It should be noted too that the "parish" in Louisiana is the equivalent to a county elsewhere.

They have always been recognized, as units of local government with a considerable degree of autonomy. In addition to the services which they are required to perform, there are others whose performance is optional. Even in respect to the mandatory functions they are allowed so much discretion as to manner of performance that it may amount in fact to a determination of what is done. . . . Within the limits established by the constitution or statutes, . . . the county determines its own tax rate. Thus, despite the limitations and controls imposed by the state, a county enjoys a large measure of self government.[6]

The county has no host of admirers who consider it a good example of American local government; the confusion and, frequently, the obscurity of county operations are not conducive to efficiency. With rural population declining and in New England with the county being squeezed out of power by the towns and cities and states, the county has been losing in power and popular prestige. In recent years there has been a revival of interest in the county as a possible metropolitan area government in which to centralize functions once dispersed to the smaller units of an area. Here and there counties are taking over local government services, at times through contractual agreements between county and city; in other instances the county becomes the chief unit of government for a metropolitan area. (There will be further discussion of this development in Chapter 16 where metropolitan problems are examined.) It is noteworthy that the rise of suburbs has not necessarily sounded the death-knell but rather has invited a re-examination of the potentialities of county government.[7]

THE SPECIAL DISTRICT

Spread across the country in ever-increasing numbers are special district governments which are not municipalities in the conventional

---

[6] Paul W. Wager, *County Government Across the Nation* (Chapel Hill, N.C.: University of North Carolina Press, 1950), p. 9. This volume, which Professor Wager edited and to which he contributed several essays, is the best place to start for a survey of county government. There are separate chapters on each state, except for Alaska and Hawaii. See also the treatment of the county by Clyde F. Snider, *op. cit.*, pp. 304–24; Lane Lancaster, *op. cit.*, pp. 54–70, gives a sense of the political process of the county and its commonly called "court house gang"—*i.e.*, the clique that dominates county government, especially in the South. More up-to-date is Herbert S. Duncombe, *County Government in America* (Washington: National Association of Counties Research Foundation, 1966); it is, however, largely a descriptive and factual account, not an analysis.

[7] For a survey of this development, see M. B. Feldman and E. L. Jassy, "The

sense but which assume an increasingly large share of the burdens of local government. The essence of the special district is the specialization of function it connotes: there is no attempt to give it integrated powers; rather it is established for limited and specific functions and granted the taxing and fiscal powers necessary to perform the task. Thus there are fire districts, mosquito control districts, and other districts concerned with such myriad projects as sewerage, water supply, transportation, weed control, irrigation, education, bridge construction and maintenance, and housing. One species of special district has declined in number through consolidation in the past few decades—the school district, of which there are fewer than half the number that existed twenty years ago. (The decline of the school district is in response to several factors: the high costs of education induce consolidation for economy; state educational grants often allow a premium for consolidation; and the interest groups concerned with education have in general pushed for consolidation in their desire to offer a richer educational program.) Apart from school districts, however, the rise of suburbs, and the demands for various functions that newly-developed areas now need (transportation, sanitation, water supply, and so on), have led to the establishment of quasigovernments to deal with each problem in a specialized way.[8]

Operating usually with an appointive board in control of policy, and with independent taxing and bonding power, the special district is often criticized for its lack of responsibility to the public. And since the special district operates necessarily on only a part of a given community's problems, there is at times a lack of integration of policy, and, it is often claimed, an unwise distribution of available tax resources. The absence of any overall control over the allocation of resources and the increased difficulty of achieving coordination of policy have produced much criticism of the special district.[9]

Urban County: A Study of New Approaches to Local Government in Metropolitan Areas," 73 *Harvard Law Review* 526–82 (1960).

[8] There are numerous reasons for the development of these special district governments—the distrust of existing units of government, the desire for services in areas which are not coterminous with existing governmental boundary lines (either less than or more than one municipality being involved), and the desire to render a particular function of government independent of the existing government and its politics. The best treatment of the whole problem of special districts is that of John C. Bollens, *Special District Government in the United States* (Los Angeles: University of California Press, 1957). He discusses the causes of the growth of special districts, pp. 5–15.

[9] See Bollens, *supra*, pp. 247–63. (See also Chap. 16.)

Both because the student is more familiar with city government than with other kinds of local government, and because the ensuing pages will deal in considerable detail with the historical evolution of urban government, not much need be said about the city at this point. State laws (or the state constitution) describe the minimum conditions for cities, although in some states there is no formal listing of conditions under which municipal charters are granted by special act of the legislature. The governmental characteristics of the approximately 5000 places classified as urban by the Census Bureau vary greatly, and for that matter even the legal definition of what constitutes a city varies from state to state.[10] The complexities as well as the general character of city-governing patterns will emerge in the following discussion of the constitutional framework of local government.

Municipal "Constitutionalism"

For several reasons it is difficult to discuss the constitutional system of local government. In the first place what must be considered as the constitution of a typical local government is not a single document and its interpretation through laws and traditions that have grown up around it. There are many sources of constitutional law for the local government, not just one main source. Not even where a charter is granted to a municipality can that be considered as *the* constitution, for the state laws and the constitution also delegate powers, limit and regulate their exercise, and otherwise specify the character of local government.[11] In addition, federal law and the federal constitution restrain, condition, and regulate (although they do not empower) local government. In the absence of a charter from the state, a municipal government looks either to special legislation passed with regard to that particular town (in the states that permit such legislation) or to general statutes for the prime sources of its "constitution." In addition, of course, judicial rulings interpreting all these various elements of

---

[10] For a table showing the various requirements of state law regarding municipal corporations, see Harold F. Alderfer, *American Local Government and Administration* (New York: The Macmillan Company, 1956), pp. 41–48.

[11] For an illustration of the way state law sets standards for local operations, see the report of the Advisory Commission on Intergovernmental Relations, *State Constitutional and Statutory Restrictions on Local Government Debt* (Washington, D.C.: Government Printing Office, 1961).

municipal constitutions become an important part of the constitutional system—perhaps, as will be illustrated later, even more important an element than is the case with the federal court rulings on national powers, dramatic as those rulings often are.

Yet there are sufficient similarities between the constitutional systems of the states and those of the municipalities to warrant the use of the term *constitutionalism* with reference to the latter. This is particularly true where there is a local charter, which—although it does not often become an object of awe and reverence as is the case of the state and national constitution—does elicit much attention from citizens interested in local affairs. In the minds of people active locally, the charter is analogous to other constitutions and truly becomes the "fundamental law" of the city.

THE EVOLUTION OF THE MUNICIPAL CHARTER

The law of municipal corporations has its origin in Roman colonial practice. To manage its empire Rome made the cities that it took under its control municipal corporations and allowed them certain powers of local self-management. The fall of Rome almost extinguished urban life, and with it the legalistic niceties that had characterized Roman municipal law. Towns and boroughs in England became incorporated municipalities in a "muddle-through" fashion. At first certain privileges were granted to towns that managed either to buy, bargain for, or otherwise gain some concessions from the Crown. These rudimentary agreements said nothing more than that the king recognized certain customary practices of the locality and would not interfere with them. (Compare the Magna Carta in this respect.) Gradually, however, the charters became more and more precise as to powers and procedures and the resulting governments could rightly be called "corporations" more or less in the modern sense. Regularizing charters appears to have emerged in the fifteenth century, although there is some debate among historians about the actual date.[12]

By the time of the settlement of the colonies, however, the munic-

---

[12] C. W. Tooke calls the granting of a charter to Hull in 1439 the beginning of the modern corporate charter, in "Municipal Corporations," *Encyclopedia of the Social Sciences* (New York: The Macmillan Company, 1935), Vol. XI, p. 87. But this conclusion is possibly in error; the actual existence of municipal corporations seems to have preceded that date. See Frederic W. Maitland, *Township and Borough* (Cambridge: Cambridge University Press, 1898), p. 18. London was recognized as a legal entity in the twelfth century, but "even this precedent was not followed widely in granting charters until the fifteenth century," says Harvey Walker in *Federal Limitations on Municipal Ordinance Making Power* (Columbus, Ohio: Ohio State University Press, 1929), p. 4.

ipal corporation with its charter was a commonly accepted institution. In conformity with English practice, some of the early charters followed the practice of the "close" corporation—that is, a self-perpetuating ruling body which exercised all the power of the municipality with no public participation in its choice or its operations.[13] New York and a few other cities started off with such charters, although more democratic replacements soon were granted. In Philadelphia the closed corporation system lasted 85 years.[14] In nearly all colonies local government charters were granted by the executive and not the legislature. In some cases the cities pleaded vainly for charters, which they were denied by colonial governors, and in virtually all cases the cities felt their powers were far too restricted by the charters, thus preventing them from coping with the problems of early urbanism.[15]

The governments of colonial cities were dominated by the wealthy merchant group and the quasiaristocratic groups. Unlike the more typical city, Boston elected a wide range of officials in the town meeting; in the judgment of one historian, "nowhere in the entire world did so

---

[13] This had become the standard procedure in England: the charter appointed members of the ruling body by name, and the surviving members appointed successors in a permanent system of control by the inner clique. This practice continued until the Reform Act of 1835.

[14] See the Philadelphia charter of 1701 in which William Penn followed English precedents in naming the original officials in the charter itself. The councilmen and aldermen were given life appointments, and they were to select from among the aldermen one to act as mayor with a one-year term. This charter remained in effect until 1776. See Thomas H. Reed and Paul Webbink, *Documents Illustrative of American Municipal Government* (New York: The Century Co., 1926), p. 49–58. On the origins and development of American ideas on local government, see Anwar Syed, *The Political Theory of American Local Government* (New York: Random House, 1966).

[15] These problems had in some cases become formidable, for several American cities had reached a population of 10–20,000 or more before the Revolution, and their public health, law enforcement, and other municipal problems frequently could not be met under the limitations of the charters—both with regard to financial provisions and the substantive powers granted. See the excellent history of colonial cities by Carl Bridenbaugh, *Cities in the Wilderness: The First Century of Urban Life in America, 1625–1742* (New York: The Ronald Press Company, 1938); and *Cities in Revolt, Urban Life in America, 1743–1776* (New York: Alfred A. Knopf, Inc., 1955). See the latter for a discussion of Charles Town's unsuccessful efforts in the 1760's to achieve city status. Evidence that the problem of too-limited powers was a continuing restraint on post-Revolutionary cities is seen in Richard C. Wade, *The Urban Frontier: The Rise of Western Cities, 1790–1830* (Cambridge, Mass.: Harvard University Press, 1959). Wade found, for example, that the Cincinnati charter had to be revised in major degree five times between 1815 and 1827, each time enlarging the scope of powers to deal with expansion of the city. Similar problems are cited for St. Louis, Pittsburgh, and Louisville. See also Ernest S. Griffith, *History of American City Government: The Colonial Period* (New York: Oxford University Press, 1938), for detailed discussion of governmental institutions.

large a number of the populace participate in the government of their city as elected officers."[16] In time the town meeting in Boston, to which all freemen were eligible to come, was taken over by the "caucus," an early-day political machine. Gentlemen of the town complained in 1768 that the "lowest mechanics discuss upon the most important parts of governments with the utmost freedom which being guided by a few hot and designing men, became the constant source of sedition." [17] But this was an exception; in other cities control over policy was not so widely dispersed. In Charles Town, South Carolina, an observer from Boston in 1773 assessed the colonial assembly which was unwilling to grant the demands of the city:

Who do they represent? The laborer, the mechanic, the tradesman, the farmer, the husbandman or yeoman? No. The representatives are almost if not wholly rich planters. The Planting interest is therefore represented, but I conceive nothing else (as it ought to be).[18]

In the years following the Revolution, American city government continued to reflect its colonial origins in many respects, but the constitutional theories and the political ferment of the time also began shaping local government. Thus, the power to grant charters passed from the governor, then in disrepute, to the increasingly powerful state legislature. This development was not necessarily a bonanza for the cities since the legislatures, composed of primarily rural representatives, did not take a sympathetic view of urban needs. Powers to tax and to undertake services and regulatory activities which the cities deemed necessary to meet their needs were often refused by the legislature. And, reflecting the growing interest in separation of powers, local charters made more explicit distinctions among kinds of powers, and the powers were distributed more precisely among the various institutions of local government. Whereas the council had once had in its hands almost all the powers of local government—legislative, executive, and occasionally judicial powers as well—now powers were specified for particular bodies. The mayor, who once had been chosen by the council, was now more commonly elected by the people. And the proportion of the people who were permitted to participate in the choice was widened constantly. Suffrage in the colonial and early post-Revolu-

---

[16] Carl Bridenbaugh, *Cities in Revolt, op. cit.,* p. 6. He was referring to the practices of the middle of the eighteenth century.

[17] *Ibid.,* p. 222.

[18] *Ibid.,* p. 219. Italics in original.

tionary War cities had usually been quite restricted, but in the nineteenth century the barriers to voting were broken down until in most places status as a taxpayer was no longer a prerequisite to voting.

Concurrently with the expansion of the suffrage, and particularly in the Jacksonian era, the number of public officials subject to popular election grew. The Jacksonians, or at least the most zealous among them, devoutly believed that rotation in office was a virtue in itself. They thought widespread office-holding was intrinsically good, certainly more important than emphasizing qualification for a particular task. So the list of local officials popularly elected grew longer and longer.

Although the mayor's power was enhanced by his popular election and by the placement of some administrative duties in his office, this trend was curtailed by the development of special boards—both elective and appointive—which were given independent control over education policies and the operation of water supply systems, police and fire departments, and other services. The legislature itself controlled some of the special boards rather than empowering the local government to make appointments to them. As the executive power was dispersed, the mayor's significance declined, and in time there developed what subsequently was called the "weak mayor" system, a local government in which there was no well-organized executive and a general dispersal of powers. Many governments of the period resembled the federal government, with bicameral city councils and a mayor's veto which could be overridden by a two-thirds vote of the legislature. Separation of powers plus dispersal of powers to boards and lack of executive political or administrative power combined to limit the effectiveness of city government.

The post-Civil War period is as important in the history of municipal government as it is in the history of state government. Cities were probably more corrupt and more disgracefully mismanaged during this period than were the states. Political machines like the Tweed Ring in New York and the Philadelphia Gas Ring plundered on an heroic scale. Votes from the bedraggled immigrant slum-dwellers kept the machines in power. When the machine got access to the public coffers and control over city contracts and franchises, it then had ample money with which to be the helping hand to the poverty-stricken immigrants—a basket of food, a bucket of coal, a menial job. So a bargain was struck: favors for votes. But as the odor of corruption intensified, the cry for reform rose louder. About 1890 the age of municipal reform began, and in the fight for "good government," charter revision became a foremost weapon.

At first the reformers moved against the corrupt politicians, and often were able to dislodge them from city hall, but the corruption went so deep and the cooperation of the business community with the crooked politicians was so profitable to both that stable political backing for the reform attempts was hard to achieve. In city after city the reform element won, only to have the boodle agents regain power in a short time. Commenting on turn-of-the-century attempts at reform, William B. Munro, one of this country's leading scholarly observers of city government, hit the keynote of the reform movement. He observed that:

. . . competent and honest officials found themeslves unable to accomplish much during their brief interludes in power, since they were hampered by the complicated system of checks and balances which city charters had set up in an endeavor to prevent official crookedness.

Municipal reform therefore did not advance appreciably in the United States until the opening years of the twentieth century. At that time it entered a new era by directing its assaults not merely against corrupt office-holders but against those complications of city government which made good administration virtually impossible under any political regime. The new reform movement demanded home rule, simplification of city government, elimination of party designations from the ballot and the introduction of business methods into municipal administration.[19]

This statement expresses well the mood of the reformers—it emphasizes the need for structural change and administrative improvement and the desire to get party politics out of city government.[20] Note that Munro says nothing about the political backing necessary to overthrow the plunderers or to maintain power once they had won city hall. Whether Munro and the reformers themselves were right about what caused improvement in city government, the important point is that they thought the key factor was structural and not political. When they sought to remedy a bad situation in a city, it was the state laws

---

19 William B. Munro, "Municipal Government," *Encyclopedia of the Social Sciences,* Vol. XI, p. 114.

20 It is at least a questionable assertion that the "complicated system of checks and balances . . . had been set up in an endeavor to prevent official crookedness." The introduction of checks and balances into city government had in good part come to local government in frank imitation of the national government; not with the intent of preventing crookedness but out of respect for separation of powers as a means to liberty. Undoubtedly restraints put on the city in the era of the free-booters were intended to hamper the crooks, but the basic elements of check-and-balance government antedated the worst of the corruption.

regulating the city that they concentrated on, not the city's social and political character. They looked to the city charter and set about tinkering with it in order to make it work right. Nothing is more characteristic of twentieth-century thinking about municipal government than the constant—sometimes almost evangelic—effort to find the right, the ideal *form* of government. Organizations like the National Municipal League, founded in 1894, contributed energy, intelligence, and devotion to the search for the way to good government.[21] The story of the League and its various local counterparts is an integral part of the evolution of American municipal charter.

THE "COMMISSION" PLAN

Early in this century the "commission" plan captured the imagination of municipal reformers. It seemed to offer relief from the dilution of administrative responsibility characteristic of the weak mayor-council government. The simplification of government under the new plan was dramatic, and it had the further virtue of conforming to the pattern of the business corporation which was a persuasive asset in that era of adulation of business. The system had originated in Galveston, Texas, following the wrecking of the city by a devastating hurricane in 1900, which posed seemingly impossible tasks for the existing debt-ridden and near-bankrupt government. To meet the emergency, the state legislature authorized the governor to suspend the existing government and replace it with a "commission" of five outstanding citizens to act as a temporary government. When the emergency had passed, a means was sought to continue more or less the same kind of government that had brought the city through the crisis. The governor appointed three commissioners and the city elected two, but the courts invalidated this procedure as inconsistent with the Texas constitution. So in 1903 all five commissioners were elected, and the commission plan got its formal initiation. First Des Moines,. then many other cities adopted the elements of the system devised in Galveston, and with varying degrees of

---

21 Frank Mann Stewart has written a history of the League in *A Half-Century of Municipal Reform: The History of the National Municipal League* (Berkeley and Los Angeles: University of California Press, 1950). The leading figure of the League was Richard S. Childs, who for well over a half-century has been an organizer, promoter, and an inventive thinker in the movement. See his *Civic Victories, The Story of An Unfinished Revolution* (New York: Harper & Row, 1952). The monthly *National Municipal Review* (since 1959, the *National Civic Review*) is a regular publication of the League and a source of valuable articles on municipal affairs.

effectiveness it continues now to operate in cities across the country.[22] Many cities adopted the plan during the second decade of the century, incongruously the same decade during which a movement away from the plan began and several cities abandoned it.

Difficulties in operating the commission plan led to disillusionment. The high spirit of experiment and adventure that accompanied the introduction of the system waned in time and with it quite frequently went the community's political support and cooperative mood. The system's potential flaws became more apparent when it had to operate in "normal" circumstances. For one thing the system lacked the administrative leadership the reformers sought. Rather than tightening control over the administrative machinery, the system in many cities led to greater dispersal of administrative power. Especially where the public elected commissioners for specific departments, but also where the departmental responsibilities were decided after election, the frequent tendency was for each commissioner to become very protective of "his" department. The commission operated less as a committee of administrative overseers than as a board of individuals bargaining with each other. A commissioner became the captive of the fire, police, or parks departments, and he sat in the board of commissioners as a bargaining agent for his sector of the government. Logrolling ("You vote for my budget requests and I'll vote for yours"), uncoordinated policy, and slipshod administration were not uncommon. Although there are still more than 200 cities with population in excess of 5000 that employ the commission system, it seems to be losing ground to other kinds of local government.[23]

THE RISE OF THE CITY MANAGER SYSTEM

Even before the commission system had attained its peak in popularity, the scheme that was to supplant it in the enthusiasm of the reformers was taking shape: the city manager system. Actually the manager

---

[22] A brief recapitulation of the rise and decline of the popularity of the commission plan is in Childs' *Civic Victories, op. cit.*, pp. 134–40.

[23] For annual surveys of the kinds of local government in the various cities of the country, see the *Municipal Year Book*, published by the International City Managers' Association in Chicago. The *Year Book* in 1940 showed that 17 per cent of the cities had commission governments; in 1966 the proportion was down to 8 per cent, although the number of local governments using the system had not declined as sharply as this makes it appear. The difference in proportion is the result of an increase in the total number of municipalities. Most of the commission plan cities are in Illinois, New Jersey, and Pennsylvania.

system was grafted onto the commission system and originally it was called the "commission-manager" system. Richard S. Childs usually is credited with being the "inventor" of the system, although he says he did no more than to adapt to the commission plan a system commonly used in business and even in government where, for example, a school board hires a professional manager (*i.e.*, the superintendent of schools) to run the school system under the board's general direction.[24] In any event, as Childs points out, there was one city manager in operation before he devised the so-called Lockport plan in 1911; in Staunton, Virginia, the town fathers in 1908 had employed a manager of local government who was responsible for general administration and was to report to the mayor and to the bicameral city council. Childs proposed the hiring of a manager by a commission, thinking of this as a direct analogy with the business corporation's general manager operating under the corporate board of directors. His proposal was made for the upstate New York town of Lockport, which didn't adopt the system because the New York State legislature turned it down. But Lockport's plan was publicized widely by the National Short Ballot Organization (of which Childs was the secretary) and other towns began to adopt it—the first being Sumter, South Carolina. Within three years the idea had spread to about fifty cities, and it has continued to grow gradually ever since. Four-fifths of the cities of over 5000 population now have managers.[25] There have been abandonments, of course, but new adoptions have been far more numerous. Probably no other twentieth-century innovation in municipal government has been more popular. This popularity is attributable to the system's emphasis on the manager and his professional and independent status, on its nonpartisanship, and its much publicized effort to keep administrative affairs and policy-making in separate spheres. More will be said subsequently about the manager and the council and their relationships with each other (see Chaps. 11 and 14). For the present it is enough to note that the manager is hired by the council, is subject to its direction, and that he is the chief executive in the administrative work of the city. As the model city charter of the National Municipal League states in one of its provisions (commonly copied verbatim by local charter drafting commissions): "Except for the purpose of inquiry, the council and its members shall deal with the administrative service solely through the

---

[24] See Childs, *op. cit.*, pp. 143–47.
[25] The 1966 *Municipal Year Book* says there are 1245 cities with the manager system—or 40.3 per cent of all cities of more than 5000 people.

city manager and neither the council nor any member thereof shall give orders to any subordinates of the city manager, either publicly or privately." [26]

Most cities operate with a mayor-council system, although the variations among these governments are very great. From one end of the spectrum, the weak mayor system—where administrative power is dispersed—to the other end—the strong mayor plan—where there is a considerable concentration of power in the hands of the chief executive there are a great many shadings of difference. The formal differences between the weaker and the stronger executives may in some cases, however, be less determinative of the effectiveness of the government than the mayor's political position. If the mayor is granted great formal powers—through for example, a veto power, wide appointment authority, and control over the major elements of the administrative heirarchy—he may or may not be able to produce a vigorous and effective government. Whether or not he succeeds will be influenced in good part by his own qualities of leadership and by his political position in the city. If he is the minion of a strongly entrenched and irresponsible party organization, he may not be politically free to exercise the appointive and executive powers that the charter allots him. On the other hand, if he has a strong personality and a substantial political following, a mayor may be able to transform the city's government in spite of the impediments of a weak-mayor charter. As subsequent illustrations will indicate, a government's potentiality has to be measured as much by its political foundation as by its formal structural elements. This is not to say that administrative cumbersomeness is irrelevant, or that a mayor's veto or lack of appointive powers are not significant. Clearly a mayor's potential power is curtailed when there are a number of elected officials who have independent control over particular phases of local government. Such fragmented organization inevitably invites uncoordinated policy making. But, given the right political push, a "badly" structured government can be passably effective; given the

---

[26] Article II, Sec. II, *Model Charter*, 1948 ed. The League was reluctant at first to accept the city manager plan, maintaining for several years its attachment to the strong mayor plan. In 1915, however, the League rewrote its model charter and proposed the manager plan, calling it (as was then common) the "commission-manager" plan. Not the least significant of the proponents of the plan are the managers themselves through their organization, the International City Managers Association. The group was formed in 1914 when eight of the seventeen then operating managers met to organize it. See Child's, *op. cit.*, p. 147.

wrong political push, even a well-structured one will go sour. This is a basic truth that many of the fervent reformers forgot.

The Politics of Charter Reform

Who are the reformers and who their enemies? What are the align-ments among advocates of the various remedies for local government ailments? Obviously, since we are talking about thousands of different communities over a long period of time, there is no uniformity in the alignments, but significant similarities recur regularly. Particularly in the early part of the century, when the commission plan was popular, busi-ness groups frequently supported it. There were, however, powerful businessmen who fully supported, even if usually *sub rosa*, the en-trenched agents of corruption. As the old style predatory practices be-came less and less defensible in the twentieth century, business backing of the bosses weakened. (It didn't disappear entirely; indeed, it still exists in many places.) Thus the vanguard of the reform movement often was occupied by Chamber of Commerce leaders, or by other organized groups in the business community. Often the reform efforts were coordinated by an overall "good government" organization which led the political forces for change. It was and still is common for such movements to enlist the enthusiastic help of the young professionals and other members of the middle class who derive a sense of achieve-ment from their reforming efforts.

The other side—those who would preserve the existing system, what-ever it may be—is usually led by those who would lose their jobs if the system were changed. Since they have access to the formal power of government, they are often quite effective in forestalling reformist efforts. This does not mean that they use foul play—although they may do that too; it means rather that they can dispense contracts and other patronage, thereby influencing the ambitious or the "practical" —the ones who accommodate themselves to the realities of the existing power situation for purposes of self-advancement. Not unnaturally the existing party organizations are usually found on the side of the stand patters—or in the case of the existing city manager systems, often in the camp of those who would replace it. A party organization adapts itself to power as best it can, and a manager is more likely to be aloof toward a party than a mayor—who probably has some ambitions the party can help satisfy—would be.

Labor often—although not invariably—opposes the city manager system. No doubt a primary source of their coolness toward the system is that it is often sponsored by the business community. Labor groups frequently battle with local political organizations, and they therefore frequently take a neutral position on manager plan adoption proposals. That is, neither the business-sponsored character of the proposal nor the defense of the status quo by the political parties appeals to labor. The result is that it often does nothing.[27]

The Politics of Charter-making

No municipality is autonomous. The structure, procedures, and powers of all municipalities are in varying degrees set by forces beyond municipal control. The city must not only conform to laws passed by the state legislature and the provisions of the federal and state constitutions, it also is subject to varying degrees of supervision by state administrative agencies. Also, the courts invariably have broad powers to weigh the validity of local actions. The city's freedom to determine its own powers and procedures has clearly grown during the course of American municipal history, and in some states the discretion for the city is relatively broad. In others, however, municipal authority comes strictly from the legislature and any alteration of a city charter or expansion of local powers is beyond the legal competence of city officials.

Although the methods of making and revising municipal charters vary greatly from state to state, it is possible to distinguish several types of state action on charters.[28] The main methods, listed here according to the increasing degree to which they grant local discretionary control over local powers, are these: (1) special legislation for individual cities; (2) classification of municipalities with different charters pro-

---

27 See the case study of J. D. Williams, *The Defeat of Home Rule in Salt Lake City* (New York: McGraw-Hill Book Co., 1960), for an illustration of the ambiguous position in which labor sometimes finds itself.

28 It is difficult to be certain of the actual methods in some states—at least if one must depend upon the reports of methods supposedly applied. For in truth what the constitution or law of a state may prescribe as the sanctioned method may not in fact be the one commonly used. Neatly tabulated lists of state methods of charter adoption or amendment must be taken with an occasional grain of salt. What purports to be a grant of power to the locality may turn out to be nothing of the kind since the method of using local authority may be so unworkable as to make adoption of a charter by it impossible. Broad generalizations, if carefully made, can correctly describe the general practices across the country, but anyone desirous of knowing the practice of a given state had better turn to specific constitutions, statutes, charters, and articles on the procedures of a given state.

vided for the different classes of cities; (3) optional charters provided by the legislature with local choice allowed among the alternative forms; and (4) home rule by legislative act and by constitutional provision.

1. *Special Legislation.* During the late eighteenth century when authority over the cities passed from the colonial governors to the new state legislatures, the custom of granting charters on an individual basis was not changed—the legislature merely took the place of the governor and specified powers and procedures for the cities. These legislative acts developed into the practice that we now call "local special legislation"; laws were passed with reference to specific cities, and each city had to persuade the rurally dominated legislature to alter its charter to meet the needs of growing urban centers.

Abuses of the power of the legislature became increasingly common, however, and demands for curtailment of this power became insistent. The use of "ripper" legislation (*i.e.*, abolishing locally accepted laws, ignoring local desires, and substituting the will of the state legislature) made the demand the more insistent. Some of the interference was motivated by honest concern for the proper government of the cities, but much of it came from the tawdriest kind of dishonesty. Thus legislators granted bribing speculators the right to operate transportation facilities on specified city streets, disregarding the desires of local authorities for the development of the city. "In California the legislature habitually made it mandatory for cities to erect municipal structures of a specified cost at a designated place." [29] In many states local special legislation dominated the time and attention of legislators; local bills often constituted half or even two-thirds of all the bills passed in a session.

Actually, some limitation of this power already existed in some states, the first dating from 1812. In time various restraints were put into state constitutions. These included the outright prohibition of special acts, the limiting of subjects on which special legislation could be passed, and several safeguards in the procedures by which such legislation could be adopted (*e.g.*, demanding a notice to the community involved and a public hearing on the substance of the bill, and—in some cases—a further provision that the act would take effect only upon acceptance by local authorities). Limitations of varying effectiveness were gradually applied in most of the states. In some cases the

---

[29] *State-Local Relations* (Chicago: The Council of State Governments, 1946), p. 144. The ensuing pages of this volume, a report of a special committee to investigate state-local relations, provide a brief but instructive introduction to the various methods by which states empower municipalities.

legislature found its way around the limitations and continued—with the sanction of the courts—passing local bills. In some states no restrictions were applied, and at present the New England states and several Southern states place few limitations on special legislation.[30] Although old style "ripper" legislation is not very common any more, it does turn up occasionally. For example, the Long machine in Louisiana took political revenge on the New Orleans political organization by restricting the city's taxing power and fixing the salaries of specified (Long machine-approved) local officials.[31] A more common problem of special legislation is the practice of delegating to the legislative delegation from the specific city the power to veto any proposed change in the city's charter. In cases where the legislative delegation and the city administration belong to different parties, this can lead to unedifying contests. One means of veto is the practice of "losing" bills that were supposed to be passed, but which somehow got tucked away in a local legislator's pocket during the last hours of a legislative session. Finally, special legislation leads to logrolling among legislators. Thus the merit that the system would seem to have—individual consideration of the needs of cities—is often negated for the simple reason that the legislature does not frankly assess the proposed legislation at all. The assessment is of the proposers and opponents, not of the content of the bill.

2. *Classification of Municipalities.* The first alternative to dependence upon special legislation was expansion of the area of general law for municipalities. But this posed difficulties in that the needs of various communities were not uniform. Demonstrable differences between municipalities (in size, economy, age, and so on) required some

---

[30] See *ibid.*, p. 150, for a table citing the formal limitations on state passage of special legislation.

[31] See Lennox L. and Helen R. Moak, "The Rape of New Orleans," 37 *National Municipal Review* 412 (1948). Say these critics of the Long regime's efforts: "Without doubt the legislature has combined in this act all the worst features of the aldermanic and commission forms of government. It will be a form untried in any major American city." It is noteworthy too that the power of the legislature over local government has been applied occasionally in the desegregation controversies—removing local powers, or attempting to do so, in order to prevent the enforcement of federal court integration orders. A dramatic case in point concerned the power of the Alabama legislature to set the boundaries of a locality. The state had altered the boundaries of Tuskeegee, the home of the famous Negro college, Tuskeegee Institute, from a conventional rectangle to a weirdly shaped, twenty-seven sided figure for the apparent purpose of excluding all Negroes and no white persons from the city, thereby preventing the Negroes from voting in the town. The Supreme Court of the United States sent the case back to trial in Alabama and gave the strong impression that they considered this a violation of the Fifteenth Amendment, notwithstanding the customary state authority to set city boundaries. See Bernard Taper, *Gomillion* v. *Lightfoot* (New York: McGraw-Hill Book Co., 1962).

alternative to provision of a single set of state regulations for all cities. One of the answers was the classification system. By this means the legislature would establish several categories of cities (normally based on population) and provide different charters for each class. This system had the merit of permitting some flexibility—although, it was soon argued, not enough. Classification by size of community did not allow for variations in local economies or in geographic location (*e.g.*, a seaside city demonstrably has different problems from an interior market town). The apparent intent of the classification system can, however, be ingeniously—not to say ingenuously—circumvented by the simple expedient of setting up a class in which there is but one city. Philadelphia, Pittsburgh, and Indianapolis are examples of single-city classifications.[32] Most states continue to use classification in one way or another, although they may provide means other than classification for acquiring a local charter.

3. *The Optional Charter System.* An alternative and somewhat more flexible method of conferring local charters is to provide a number of charters from which the municipality is permitted to choose. This system permits, of course, considerable state control over the exact form and powers of local governments. By specifying most of the powers of local government through general legislation applicable to all (or to certain classifications of) cities, this system achieves control over local activities. But the municipality is also granted the opportunity to choose the essential form for its government from among the alternatives offered. In some states the alternatives are fairly limited, in others the choices are extensive. In Massachusetts there are five "plans" from which to choose by local referendum; New Jersey provides fourteen alternatives.[33] Most states allow some cities to choose alternative charters, but few allow all cities to make choices from among any extensive

---

[32] All kinds of ruses are devised to create these one-city categories. Although the courts often speak of population size as the appropriate method for making classifications, they frequently accept other standards. At times legislatures have classified cities according to the amount of local debt, the form of existing local governments, and even street names to achieve what are in effect special laws for certain localities. See the discussion of this practice in William Anderson and Edward W. Weidner, *American City Government* (New York: Holt, Rinehart, and Winston, Inc., 1950), pp. 138–43. One of the clearest and most succinct of the treatments of this subject is that in Ernst B. Schultz, *American City Government, Its Machinery and Processes* (New York: Stackpole and Hack, 1949), pp. 122–24.

[33] Cambridge, Massachusetts, went through a period of political turmoil during its adoption of the so-called Plan E government (city manager system) in the late 1930's. For an account, see Frank G. Abbott, "The Cambridge City Manager," in *Public Administration and Policy Development*, edited by Harold Stein (New York: Harcourt, Brace, and World 1952), pp. 580–91.

range of possibilities.[34] It would appear that the optional system is gaining in popularity at present, particularly in states which have not yet been persuaded to accept formal home rule.

4. *Home Rule.* *Home rule* is a term used in both a general and a technical way. In its general usage it implies wide scope for local government without supervision from the state, an opportunity for maximum local discretion and minimum direction from above. In a more technical sense the term refers to the practice by which local governments may draft and adopt their own charters. Home rule is thus a modification of the traditional relationship between the subordinate municipality and the sovereign state. Whereas the traditional doctrine decrees full authority to the state to grant or to deny powers to a municipality, home rule grants at least to some extent an *imperium in imperio*—a "sovereign within a sovereign." The traditional position was stated by a scholarly jurist from the Iowa bench, Judge John F. Dillon, who said:

Municipal corporations owe their origin to, and derive their powers and rights wholly from, the legislature. It breathes into them the breath of life, without which they cannot exist. As it creates, so it may destroy. If it may destroy, it may abridge and control. Unless there is some constitutional limitation on the right, the legislature might, by a single act, if we can suppose it capable of so great a folly and so great a wrong, sweep from existence all of the municipal corporations of the state, and the corporations could not prevent it. We know of no limitation on this right so far as the corporation themselves are concerned. They are, so to phrase it, the mere tenants at will of the legislature.[35]

Home rule in effect abridges this sweeping authority of the legislature, granting to the municipality certain powers and certain rights to draft its own charter and decide its own procedures. Home rule provisions in a constitution do not, however, grant antonomy or anything like it to municipalities. On the contrary, home rule grants but limited powers and rights, and local exercise of those powers and rights is in some degree subject to control and regulation by the legislature, the judiciary, and even the executive.[36]

---

[34] In some states, the municipality is given a choice between several general law charters or local initiative to draft a "home rule" charter. This is true in both Colorado and Nebraska, for example.

[35] *City of Clinton* v. *Cedar Rapids and Missouri River R.R. Co.,* 24 *Iowa* 455, 475.

[36] The literature of home rule is extensive—its tone sometimes ponderous and legalistic, sometimes evangelistic and pleading. The classic statement of the doctrine

In one form or another 36 states provide for home rule, although it must be said that home rule in some states is meaningless. The constitution may permit or even command the legislature to enact home rule legislation, but it does not follow that the legislature will comply. The legisatures of Georgia, Nevada, and (and for many years) Pennsyvania ignored constitutional authorization of home rule. In Georgia, for example, after much confusing legislation and litigation over a mandatory constitutional home rule provision (*i.e.*, one that directed rather than permitted the legislature to pass such a law), the State Supreme Court held the provision unconstitutional. Then a new "permissive" home rule constitutional amendment was passed in 1954, but not until 1966 was an implementing statute enacted. Although the Pennsylvania home rule provision went into the constitution in 1922, not until recently was anything done to effectuate it.

Several states began with statutory home rule and later adopted it constitutionally; only Florida still has statutory home rule in effective operation.[37] Many advocates of home rule are inclined to dismiss legislative home rule as unsatisfactory on the ground that it leaves too much to the discretion of the legislature and too little to that of the municipality. Since legislative home rule can be wiped out by legislative action just as easily as it was created, it is therefore said to provide too little protection for local interests. One could argue, however, that home rule by statute has more significance than a constitutional provision which the legislature refuses to implement or under which it passes enabling laws that the municipalities cannot successfully apply.

About one-half of our state constitutions allow home rule, but the

---

is H. L. McBain's *The Law and Practice of Municipal Home Rule* (New York: Columbia University Press, 1916). An evangelical message on the subject is Rodney L. Mott's *Home Rule for America's Cities* (Chicago: American Municipal Association, 1949). A recent survey of home rule law with summaries of constitutional and legislative provisions in twenty-nine states is the article by John R. Kerstetter, "Municipal Home Rule," *Municipal Year Book*, 1956, pp. 256–66. A useful summary of the leading problems of the subject will be found in Ernst B. Schultz, *op. cit.* pp. 121–40. For a treatment of the legal aspects of home rule, see Fordham, *Local Government Law, op. cit.*, pp. 74–113.

[37] In Florida about one-third of the cities eligible to act under the statute have used it successfully. See Kerstetter, *op. cit.*, p. 258. In Connecticut there was a long and confusing battle over the home rule statute—about which more will be said subsequently—but in recent years there have been a number of successful adoptions of charters under the revised home rule act. Thus by 1967, 154 municipalities had appointed charter-drafting commissions under the 1957 version of the law; in 72 of these recommended major revisions or entirely new charters be adopted, and in 36 cases, major changes were approved by the voters. In other instances the voters had rejected the changes. See Connecticut Public Expenditure Council's *Connecticut's Home Rule Law*, August 1967, p. 4.

variations among these provisions are enormous; they range in fact from quite extensive local discretion to provisions that are quite useless. In some cases the provisions are too cumbersome to apply; in other states cities are little inclined to use the opportunity for the simple reason that they have sufficient flexibility to act under general law and feel no need for a locally drawn charter. This is said to be the case in Wisconsin, Oregon, and California, for example.[38]

One of the fundamental differences among constitutional home rule systems is how much the state legislature is allowed to participate in the implementation of the system. The more complex system is "self-enforcing." The dozen states which have "self-enforcing" home rule attempt to bypass the legislature by writing into the constitution the essential methods by which localities may adopt charters and do not depend on future legislative action to spell out details of application. (Indeed the first constitutional home rule amendment—that of Missouri in 1875—was of this type.) The "nonself-enforcing" system leaves the details of implementation to the legislature, either allowing or commanding the legislature to pass implementing statutes to provide methods for local use of home rule.[39]

The language of the grant of home rule is, of course, very important, and much litigation has arisen about the meaning of such terms as "all laws and ordinances relating to municipal concerns" (Michigan), "powers of local self-government" (Ohio), "in respect to municipal affairs" (California). Home rule involves a distinction between the general powers of the state and local affairs—the former is the domain of the state and the latter that of the municipality. But what does a court do when it faces a dispute about local control of traffic on a state highway which runs through the middle of a city? Is that a local matter because the street is in the city, or a state matter because it concerns a state highway? Are the working hours and conditions of local employees entirely a matter of "municipal affairs" or does the state's power over labor and public employment supercede the powers of the city?[40] The most ardent home rule promoters insist that specification of local powers should be included in the state constitution, notwithstanding the invitation to dispute and litigation that such specification involves. They are unwilling to leave the detailing of local powers to the judgment of the legislature, primarily because they do not trust

---

[38] Kerstetter, *op. cit.*

[39] About half the nonself-enforcing systems are mandatory, the other half permissive.

[40] See Rodney L. Mott, *op. cit.*, pp. 9–12, concerning the range of home rule powers.

legislators to be lenient toward the municipality. Unless there is a constitutional grant to the cities, argues Professor Arthur Bromage:

. . . what is to prevent the legislature from setting, for example, a minimum salary scale and maximum hours of employment for all home rule cities? . . . What is to prevent the legislature from prohibiting the development of municipal ownership of utilities?

The answer, he says:

. . . must be found in legislative grace or tolerance, or in the power of a state municipal league to influence legislators from [sic] passing laws applicable to all home rule cities and crippling in effect.[41]

Legally, of course, there is nothing to prevent the legislature from acting arbitrarily; the crucial point becomes a political consideration. At least one political consideration in the minds of those who oppose the Municipal League's specification of local powers is the conviction that

. . . there should be a policy-making power in a state, short of the general electorate, competent to make the decisions as to adaptation and devolution of governmental powers and functions to serve the changing needs of society.[42]

Such developments as the rise of metropolitan areas with their intergovernmental problems have led to the conviction that flexibility in state powers is more crucial than an absolute grant of irremovable powers to the municipality. Therefore the home rule proposal of the American Municipal Association would allow to any home rule city the same powers which the legislature can grant to non-home rule cities, but all powers would be subject to limitations by the legislature.[43] In

---

[41] Arthur W. Bromage, "Home Rule—NML Model," 44 *National Municipal Review*, 132, 133–34 (1955). Bromage is defending the National League's model state constitution's system of granting home rule against that of the American Municipal Association which rejects the distinction between general powers and local powers.

[42] Jefferson B. Fordham, "Home Rule—AMA Model," 44 *National Municipal Review* 137, 140 (1955).

[43] More precisely the language of the model constitutional provision is this:
A municipal corporation which adopts a home rule charter may exercise any power or perform any function which the legislature has power to devolve upon a non-home rule charter municipal corporation and which is not denied to all home

short, the American Municipal Association, in spite of the not entirely encouraging record of the state legislature, still is ready to sacrifice specificity of powers for greater legislative flexibility to cope with the problems of the future.[44]

Control Over Local Powers: Stakes and Contestants

So far the discussion of city charters and powers has considered primarily the form and procedures of local constitutionalism and has dealt with political forces only vaguely. This does not mean that political forces are unimportant, or that those who have high stakes in major contests over local authority are not stirred to activity when their positions are threatened. Nor should we ignore the political significance of those whose stake may be small but whose interest in local affairs and zeal for improvement compensate for their lack of "selfish" interest. They lobby, write articles, appear before hearings, and otherwise promote the cause of reform. In some cases the zeal and interest become so strong that they relinquish their amateur standing and become professional pleaders attached to some reform organization. Contestants with heavy stakes in the operation of city government may be less conspicuous than the reformers, but they respond because their interests are, for them, vitally important. It is true that the battlers may have a wrong conception of the proposals being made, and that they may be quite wrong in their assessment of the probable consequences of proposals on, for example, home rule, but the wrongness of their evaluation of a situation does nothing to diminish the fervor with which they fight. Their fears—of higher taxes, burdensome debt, irresponsible political machines, elimination of party activity, loss of patronage—are real and must therefore be put into the scale of evaluation of any contest over local powers.

The effort to get home rule in Connecticut will illustrate some of the fears and forces involved in such contests. The Connecticut General

---

rule charter municipal corporations by statute and is within such limitations as may be established by statute.

The hand of the lawyer is evident in this *Model Constitutional Provision for Municiapl Home Rule* (Chicago: The American Municipal Association, 1953).

[44] It does not follow that specification of "self-government" power for the municipality (*e.g.*, in the Ohio Constitution) will prevent legislative enactments which appear to infringe upon this power. Thus in 1960 the Ohio legislature passed a bill (which, but for a veto by the Governor, would have become law) providing a mandatory 56-hour workweek for Ohio's firemen.

Assembly passed a statute in 1915 granting unusually broad power to municipalities; it permitted a city to decide the "organization of its government" and to "exercise such powers and [perform] such services as may be necessary and convenient for its welfare." But a commission set up to investigate the act in 1923 reported "no record of any municipality having adopted a charter or an amendment under this law," except for one town that initiated action and then—feeling insecure about the validity of the new charter—went to the General Assembly and asked for a special act restating exactly what they had done for themselves.[45] The law was repealed, unlamented, in 1923.

In Connecticut—and in many other parts of the country—interest was revived in home rule after World War II. A heavy volume of special legislation was presented at every session of the legislature, much of it dealing with such picayune matters as the appointment of dog catchers or the construction of sidewalks in a village. Although "ripper" legislation was uncommon, there were battles in the late stages of every biennial legislative session when warring factions from cities maneuvered by every conceivable means to pass or kill special bills. The chairman of the Committee on Cities and Boroughs had a powerful position and his bulging pocketful of local bills caused great concern to lobbyists and legislators anxious to keep a bill in his pocket or get it to the floor. At times bills were "lost" in transit between the two houses on the last day of the session with the result that the bill died but no one knew whom to blame. Partly as a consequence of the proposals for home rule by the 1949–50 Commission on State Government Organization, and through the efforts of pro-home rule groups (League of Women Voters and Connecticut Public Expenditures Council, particularly), home rule once again became a topic of conversation in legislative halls in Hartford.

In 1951 a bill was passed granting home rule by statutory authority, but the grant was made with one legislative hand and withdrawn by the other. The law was next to impossible for a municipality to use since it required a favorable vote in a referendum in which 51 per cent of the persons on the voting lists voted on the issue. The catch was that virtually no referendum issue can get the attention of that many voters. In most city elections the total turnout of electors does not reach

---

[45] See the *Report* of the Commission on Uniformity of Municipal Charters, Hartford, Connecticut, 1923, p. 28. The Commission laid the failure of the law to the persistent habit of using special legislation, the unclarity of the law itself, and the general lack of familiarity with home rule procedures. See also the unpublished report to the Commission on Government Organization on "State-Local Relations in Connecticut," by Fred V. Cahill and Duane Lockard, State Library, Hartford, Connecticut, for the background of home rule in Connecticut.

51 per cent and thus if literally everyone voting on the measure said "yes," the proposal would still fail to pass. Opponents of one charter change ran newspaper advertisements recommending that opponents not vote; elsewhere the word was more discreetly passed. Nowhere did the act work successfully.[46] In addition, the law was so inadequately drafted that the courts scarcely knew how to apply it when it was contested in litigation.[47]

The 1953 session of the General Assembly bowed to pressures and amended the act, now making its use difficult but not quite impossible. The new version provided that the approving majority had to be "at least 26 per cent of all the electors qualified to vote." This still left the proponents of change with a formidable obstacle to surmount, even though it prevented defeat of a change by nonvoters. One survey before the passage of the home rule act showed an average of 29 per cent of the voters voted on local referenda; if such proportions held true in the future, the proponents would be able to win only if they could muster support of about 90 per cent of those voting! Accordingly there were very few successful applications of the law, and in several cases majorities were beaten by the mimimum 26 per cent requirement— once where there was a three-to-one approval by the voters.

Efforts to liberalize the act in the 1955 session failed. The sponsor of the bill proposed a minimum of 15 per cent voting in favor, compromised for 20 per cent to try to save the bill, but could not even get that. The fate of the bill was sealed by leaders of the House of Representatives who refused to allow the bill to come to the floor for a vote. In the Senate even a gesture toward revision—and it would have been no more than a gesture since the House action had already been decisive—was stifled by two Democratic senators from New Haven who threatened to tie up the Senate by parliamentary tactics for the remainder of the session unless the bill were returned to committee. They balked for fear the bill would permit revision of the New Haven charter in a way desired by the Democratic mayor, Richard Lee, whom the senators distrusted. The House did, however, pass a constitutional home rule amendment through its first stage in 1955 by giving it majority approval. In 1957 the amendment needed two-thirds approval of both houses before submission to a statewide referendum in 1958, but that

---

[46] See Duane Lockard, "Home Rule for Connecticut's Municipalities," 29 *Connecticut Bar Journal*, 51, 53 (1955).

[47] See the critical comments of both the majority and a dissenter of the Connecticut Supreme Court bench in *Ex rel. Rourke v. Barbieri*, 139 Connecticut 203 (1952).

approval did not come. Instead, the original amendment was replaced with a new version, delaying approval at least until 1960, assuming that two-thirds of both houses would approve in 1959. They did not approve in 1959, however; instead a third version of the amendment was initiated. Indeed, not until a 1965 constitutional convention was a home rule provision inserted in the Constitution and even that was not to go into effect until July 1969![48]

Why the gestures of compliance but acts of evasion? The answer is to be found in the fears of influential political elements in the state. They are uncertain what this new gimmick will involve; they would rather not take chances with gains they now have achieved or advantages they now enjoy. Many politicians in both parties are skeptical of home rule because they are apprehensive of opening up a new source of power. Under the old conditions, regular politicians were important agents for negotiation with the legislature for local bills. With home rule in effect, knowledge of and ability to manipulate in the legislature are devalued. Moreover, facilitating the alteration of local government might lead to interference with patronage, the introduction of city manager government, or other unwanted disturbance of the status quo. These opponents are joined by financial conservatives, who fear higher taxes and burdensome debt may result. They may not be exactly sure if or how home rule would change the fiscal arrangements of a city, but they are familiar with the existing arrangements and would rather not invite trouble by changing the rules.

Certain interest groups are threatened, or feel threatened, by home rule. For example, local employees often oppose it because they are uncertain whether hardwon benefits may be jeopardized. As a leader of the firemen's association once wrote to a state senator in Connecticut: ". . . we are fearful that [the proposed law] might lower the requirements on a referendum so much that many of our rights such as pension rights, which are the product of special acts of the legislature, could be done away with by an unthinking, impulsive minority." Legislators are loath to forego power over local affairs not only because they

---

[48] The story of evasion in Connecticut has not been repeated everywhere by any means, yet in most states one way or another has been found to minimize the extent of devolution of power to municipalities. In Rhode Island, for example, a home rule amendment dating from 1951 is still relatively ineffective; there the courts have played a major role in curbing the use of the amendment. Even in some of the states where home rule has been generally accepted, there are long records of obstruction and a certain amount of day-to-day harassment. In New York the courts have narrowed the scope of home rule drastically—according to one observer, it has been "interpreted out of existence by judicial decision." W. B. Richland, "Courts Nullify Home Rule," 44 *National Municipal Review*, 565–70 (1955).

often feel a genuine need for supervision of local communities that may exceed the legislator's idea of the bounds of proper policy, but also because they like being in a position of power and get satisfaction from having local interests appeal to them for legislation. Although legislators may be harried by badgering local groups with irreconcilable demands, they are nevertheless put into the spotlight by the demands. To many a representative from a small community, his hour on the stage and his place on the front page of the weekly newspaper are the major rewards for his legislative service and few things are more likely to put him there than a lively dispute about local powers. This prerogative is not lightly abandoned.

Making Local Law by Judicial Interpretation

The subordinate position of the municipal corporation in the hierarchy of government places the heavy hand of potential judicial restraint on its every action. If it is proposed that the city pass an ordinance to eliminate discrimination in housing or to control smog and air pollution, the question of whether the ordinance *ought* to pass is sometimes easier to settle than whether legally it *can*. Limitations and uncertainties abound and doubts about the validity of local enactments can always be raised. The costs and delays of litigation challenging the authority of the city to undertake new services or regulatory action therefore constitute a major political force in municipal government.[49] The city attorney (or the corporation counsel, as he is often called) becomes a key official, and often a very negative force, for his reputation is at stake every time the city undertakes an action that may be successfully challenged in the courts. He recommends cautiously as indeed both his professional training and the facts of the law incline him to do.

The sources of restraint are more numerous for the municipality than for either state or national governments. The former must heed both the state and national constitutions, of course, and any of its actions are deemed the equivalent of state action for purposes of national constitutional law. Moreover, the taxpayer's suit is readily available to the challenger of city acts but less so for the state.

---

[49] Says a foremost legal scholar: "Judicial review of legislative, executive and administrative action is extensive and crucial at all levels of government, but we find it to be most detailed and most pervasive at the local level." Fordham, *Local Government Law*, p. 36. See also "Taxpayers' Suits: A Survey and a Summary," 69 *Yale Law Review*, 895 (1960).

When the city seeks to regulate noisy sound trucks on its streets, freedom of speech is suddenly involved.[50] Regulation of itinerant peddlers, banning incitement to riot by inflammatory speeches, racial discrimination on municipally owned facilities, and hundreds of other city activities can raise questions of federal constitutional law. The state constitution and state statutes also impose specific restrictions, but more significantly, as we have noted, they delegate specific powers to the municipality. As a government of strictly delegated powers, the municipality possess only those powers clearly apportioned to it by the constitution or the laws of the state. The standard of interpretation of local powers is enunciated in the famous Dillon's Rule.

It is a general and undisputed proposition of law that a *municipal corporation possesses and can exercise the following powers, and no others:* First, those granted in *express words;* second, those *necessarily* or *fairly implied* in or *incident* to the powers expressly granted; third, those essential to the accomplishment of the declared objects and purposes of the corporation—not simply convenient, but indispensable. Any fair, reasonable, substantial doubt concerning the existence of power is resolved by the courts against the corporation, and the power is denied.[51]

In short, the city is subjected to the strictest construction of its powers. If the city charter, the general law of the state, or a decision by a state court does not clearly justify a particular power, the exercise of it by any municipality is in grave doubt. The potential power that this grants to conservatively minded judges is apparent. In the past they frequently made hash of local efforts to govern, often going to ridiculous lengths to invalidate local ordinances.[52] Application of the "rule of reasonableness"—not so common now as in the past, but by no means now absent from decisions—leaves to the judge the decision as to the propriety of local enactments, and it is often claimed that the courts pose themselves as super-city councils to weigh not the strict legality but the appropriateness of ordinances.

There has undoubtedly been greater lenience toward municipal

---

[50] *Saia v. New York*, 334 U.S. 558 (1948) and *Kovacs v. Cooper*, 336 U.S. 77 (1949) both concern attempts by municipalities to save the ears of its citizens from the blaring of sound trucks.

[51] John G. Dillon, *Commentaries on the Law of Municipal Corporations*, 5th ed. (Boston: Little, Brown and Co., 1911), Vol. 1, Sec. 237. Italics in original.

[52] See the excellent brief discussion of this point in Charles M. Kneier's *City Government in the United States*, 3rd ed. (New York: Harper & Row, 1957), Chap. 9; and also that by Ernst B. Schultz, *op. cit.*, pp. 58–80. For instructive detail and analysis, see *Corpus Juris Secundum*, Vols. 62–64 on "Municipal Corporations."

powers shown by the courts in recent years than was the case in the past. The depression and the growth of urban problems in recent decades have unquestionably loosened the bonds of judicial restraint beyond anything anticipated by Judge Dillon who enunciated the standard rule of interpretation. Nevertheless, long complicated charters and greatly detailed authorizing laws are still necessary to satisfy the city attorney and the bonding houses who will take city bonds only when they have legal advice that the laws are valid, and, of course, to meet the demands of the courts.[53] Litigation remains an important threat and therefore a crucial political force in the government of municipalities.

---

[53] An interesting, if ambiguous, provision of the 1947 New Jersey constitution says: "The provisions of this Constitution and of any law concerning municipal corporations formed for local government, or concerning counties, shall be liberally construed in their favor." The ambiguity derives from following provisions which nearly restate Dillon's rule. See Art. IV, Sec. VII, par. 11.

7. The Political Process: I

LIKE ARIADNE'S THREAD, politics has been the guide line through the preceding chapters, yet it is necessary to emphasize politics even more directly now in an explicit examination of the nature of the political process. Politics is concerned with the use of influence, with the myriad ways in which human beings attempt to induce others to do their bidding. I shall speak of political power as in effect the probability that one person will be able to get another to do what he wishes—that is, A has power over B in a certain situation when he can make B do something that without A's interference B would not have done.[1] This seems simple enough, but it is not as clear as it seems, for students of political interrelationships are by no means agreed on the meaning and character of political power. (A possible source of confusion over the word *power* lies in the fact that it is used two ways: first, as described

---

[1] This adheres closely to the method of analysis of comparative political power proposed by Robert Dahl in "The Concept of Power," 2 *Behavioral Science* 201 (1957). The student of politics who wants to examine actual power situations is urged to read this article which presents a closely reasoned method for the analysis of power, emphasizing the *base, means, amount,* and *scope* of power. See his comment on power in *Modern Political Analysis* (Englewood Cliffs, N.J.: Prentice-Hall, 1963), pp. 50–54; 69–71. See also the imaginative and pioneering works of Harold Lasswell on political power. His *Power and Society* (New Haven: Yale University Press, 1950), written with Abraham Kaplan, is particularly useful in the present context.

in the preceding sentences; second, as legal authority to do some governmental act [e.g., the powers of municipality]. The tyranny of language is such that the same word must be used to mean very different things, and occasionally it will be necessary to use both meanings within the same context, but hopefully confusion can be avoided.)

There is no space here, nor is there necessity, for an elaborate account of current thought about political power, but the subject is too central to this book to be put aside lightly. Since a primary objective here is to give the student a clearer view of the meaning of political power and to facilitate his efforts to locate and evaluate power in a given situation, a review of recent scholarly dispute about political power follows. It may at least give prior warning to the student who will read many a sweeping and misleading commentary about the nature of local political power.

The "Power Elite" Theory

One approach to the study of local power may be called an elitist explanation of power. Those who hold this view find that there are relatively few crucially important top leaders in any city or larger community (even extending to the whole nation in some efforts at description) who are the real wielders of power in the community. They are inclined to accept, and they have made serious efforts to validate, the commonly uttered remark, "You know, there are really about a dozen men who run this town." These theories represent a further development of and indeed are attempts to prove with empirical evidence the ideas of Gaetano Mosca and Vilfredo Pareto, two late nineteenth-early twentieth-century social and political theorists, who were convinced, as Mosca put it, that "In all societies . . . two classes of people appear—a class that rules and a class that is ruled."[2] On the face of it there is an element of self-evident truth in this position. It is

---

[2] Gaetano Mosca, The Ruling Class (New York: McGraw-Hill Book Co., 1939), p. 50 (first published in 1896 as Elementi di Scienza Politica). Pareto argues that "every people is governed by an elite, by a chosen element in the society. . . ." See his The Mind and Society (New York: Harcourt, Brace, and World, Inc., 1935), p. 169 (first publishd in 1916 as Tratto di Sociologia generale). Something of the same sort is involved in Robert Michels doctrine of the "iron law of oligarchy," which, he contends, cannot be escaped in the management of political parties. See Political Parties: A Sociological Study of the Oligarchical Tendencies of Modern Parties (New York: The Free Press of Glencoe, Inc., 1949) (first published in 1915).

surely true, even in democratic societies, that there are some men who have more power than others. A system of representation implies greater power for the representative than for the represented, and, even if this were not true, there are differences between men which make some of them into leaders and others followers. The ambitious, articulate, and energetic few tend to move into the positions of leadership and to dominate others. This is true of a nation as it is of a bowling league. All this can be accepted as reasonably provable by empirical tests.

But the catch comes when this tendency for the few to rise, like cream, to the top is translated into a rigidified system which suggests that the rulers are a relatively permanent group who regularly control the destinies of the mass of nonleaders. In some societies—the dictatorial ones, whether nations or smaller groups like gangster mobs—the circulation into and out of the ruling clique may be very slow indeed, but in more democratic societies it has yet to be proved that there is a static and unchanging element that asserts continuous control over policies. There is a second catchpoint here too: the contention that power tends to flow only in one direction: from the top downward. Robert Michels, who was a contemporary of Pareto, conceived of the dominant leadership cliques of the European leftist parties he studied as relatively immune from influence by the mass of the party following. But subordinates do have power over superiors, however paradoxical that may sound. In many ways the leadership is dependent upon the followers to cooperate in the common endeavor, whatever it may be, or else the whole effort and therefore the leader himself will have failed. Many a martinet military officer has been taught this lesson by aggrieved subordinates. As a consequence of this need for cooperation —and it affects a dictator as well as a Boy Scout troop leader—the follower has some degree of influence over the superior. Coercion through terror can diminish the reciprocal lower-to-upper power nearly to the vanishing point, but in nondespotic regimes it is clear that there is nothing like a one-way flow of power.

Still the relative difference in the degree of power wielded by the county sheriff and by a rural Negro in Alabama, the difference in the power of a chairman of a huge corporation and that of a janitor in a tenement house are demonstrable and impressive. The important question for present purposes is not whether there are differentials in power —that point is perfectly clear—but how power is used and by whom. Is the average community dominated by relatively few leaders who decide all the important questions among themselves?

Those who take the elitist approach to community power argue that there is a relatively permanent "top leadership" which decides the important questions. A pioneering work of this type was *Middletown*,[3] by Robert and Helen Lynd, which examined the social, economic, and political behavior of Muncie, Indiana. They found a great concentration of power in a few families and in the business elite. Many subsequent analyses of power in local communities have been based upon assumptions drawn from the work of the Lynds. More recent investigations owe much to a reopening of the search by Floyd Hunter who contributed a somewhat more objective or at least more systematized method of investigation. His book, *Community Power Structure*,[4] was a study of the power of the elite of Atlanta (he called it "Regional City"), where he found not only that there was an elite but that the business community dominated this "top leadership." Following Hunter's lead, several other sociologists and a few political scientists made investigations of other cities where, with detailed interviews and other research methods, they sought to identify controlling cliques.[5] One of them said he was testing the hypothesis that "key influential leaders in a community influence policy by acting in concert through cliques."[6] He found evidence of such a clique, as did the other researchers, although there were variations in the number of top leaders, differences in their composition (especially in the extent of businessman domination of the group), and differences in the extent of control. One of them found a bifurcation of the community's power structure, stemming from withdrawal of the economic dominants from active direction of the political and civic life of the community." [7] One survey showed

[3] Robert and Helen Lynd, *Middletown* (New York: Harcourt, Brace, and World, Inc., 1929). They followed this with *Middletown in Transition* (New York: Harcourt, Brace, and World, Inc., 1937).

[4] Floyd Hunter, *Community Power Structure* (Chapel Hill, N.C.: University of North Carolina Press, 1953.)

[5] The elitist literature is voluminous and no attempt is made to provide a complete bibliography of it. Some examples are Robert O. Schulze and Leonard U. Blumberg, "The Determination of Local Power Elites," 58 *American Journal of Sociology* 292 (1957); Roland J. Pelegrin and Charles H. Coates, "Absentee-Owned Corporations and Community Power Structure," 61 *American Journal of Sociology* 413 (1956); Robert O. Schulze, "Economic Determinants and Community Power Structure," 23 *American Sociological Review* 3 (1958); Delbert C. Miller, "Decision Making Cliques in Community Power Structures: A Comparative Study of an American and an English City," 64 *American Journal of Sociology* 299 (1958); Robert E. Agger and Vincent Ostrom, "The Political Structure of a Small Community," 20 *Public Opinion Quarterly* 81 (1956); Morris Janowitz, ed., *Community Political Systems* (New York: The Free Press of Glencoe, Inc., 1960); Kent Jennings, *Community Influentials: The Elites of Atlanta* (New York: The Free Press, 1964).

[6] Miller, *op. cit.*, p. 299.

[7] Schulze, "Economic Dominants and Community Power Structure," *op. cit.*, p. 8.

substantially negative findings, but he was not following Hunter's methods, having done his research at about the same time that Hunter was doing his.[8]

The "Pluralist" Alternative

The publication of these findings has triggered a vigorous and voluminous response, so voluminous in fact that it threatens to take up more space in scholarly journals than the original research reports did. Rejecting both the methods and the results of the elitist analysis, most of the critics have argued for a more pluralistic alternative explanation —that is to say, they argue that what prevails is a more dynamic system of power interrelationships involving the interactions of many groups in contest with each other with policies resulting from their conflict-and-compromise rather than from any single stable group dictating policies to the remainder of the community.[9] They object to the term *structure* as Hunter uses it, claiming that this implies a stability and consistency of power control by a single group that they have not found to exist.

---

[8] James B. McKee, "Status and Power in the Industrial Community: A Comment on Drucker's Thesis," 58 *American Journal of Sociology* 364 (1953). McKee, reporting on the steel manufacturing city of Lorain, Ohio, found no particular group dominating the city; he identified several groups with varying degrees of power. "The pyramidal model, with power and authority located at the apex," he said, "is inaccurate and misleading," at least as a description of Lorain.

[9] The literature criticizing the elitist school is too extensive to be listed here in full. Most of the more recent items cited contain general bibliographies in their footnotes, and the interested student will have no difficulty in tracking down the articles of the controversy. Among the critical pieces are the following: Herbert Kaufman and Victor Jones, "The Mystery of Power," 14 *Public Administration Review* 205 (1954), a critical review of Hunter's study; Talcott Parsons, "The Distribution of Power in American Society," 10 *World Politics* 123 (1957), a long review of C. Wright Mills' *The Power Elite*, in which Parsons rejects Mills' elitist explanation of American national politics; Daniel Bell, *The End of Ideology* (New York: The Free Press of Glencoe, Inc., 1960), Chap. 3 ("Is there a Ruling Class in America? *The Power Elite* Reconsidered"); Robert A. Dahl, "Critique of the Ruling Elite Model," 52 *American Political Science Review* 463 (1958), and *Who Governs? Democracy and Power in an American City* (New Haven: Yale University Press, 1961); Norton E. Long, "The Local Community as An Ecology of Games," 64 *American Journal of Sociology* 251 (1958); Nelson W. Polsby, "Three Problems in the Analysis of Community Power," 24 *American Sociological Review* 796 (1959), "The Sociology of Community Power: A Reassessment," 37 *Social Forces* 232 (1959), *Community Power and Political Theory* (New Haven: Yale University Press, 1963); Peter H. Rossi, "Community Decision-Making," 1 *Administrative Science Quarterly* 415 (1957); and Raymond E. Wolfinger, "Reputation and Reality in the Study of 'Community Power,'" 25 *American Sociological Review* 636 (1960).

One of the basic premises with which the elitist study begins is that "decision-makers are likely to remain the same from issue to issue," but this proposition, says one critic, has "never met adequate empirical test."[10] The complaint is that the researchers go into a community assuming there is such a structure and then ask questions of local citizens which invite them to identify the leaders who constitute the supposed leadership clique. The respondent is asked to name "persons of influence" whom nearly everyone would admit are important decision-makers on major matters; then the list is narrowed down by placing in the highest category of leadership those who are nominated most frequently as a "person of influence." (Hunter uses the list of nominated influentials as judges of the "top leadership.") This makes the test of the original hypothesis dependent upon beliefs about other individuals rather than upon the demonstrated activities of an individual, yet the reputation that X has for wielding great power may very well be quite different from the facts of how much power X can exercise in a specific situation. Moreover when interviewees are asked to nominate the ones who have great power, the natural tendency is to try to supply the information asked for, not to respond by the question-begging inquiry as to whether in fact the community actually has an elite that possesses broad powers. It would be useful to examine in detail exactly what kind of influence the top leaders do bring to bear on the making of decisions. This the protagonists of the elitist persuasion have sometimes done, but their tendency is to imply that in the absence of specific findings of a positive role for the topmost leaders that it must have existed in the very nature of things. The following comment on power structure theory is instructive:

In another situation we find the community aroused about a different kind of problem. It may be smoke control or rat control or narcotics control, or it may be enforcement of a housing code. Many of the organized groups in town go on record as opposing the undesirable situation and urging community action. The newspapers, radio and television support the movement, and there is a great hullabaloo. Yet nothing happens. Agencies or local government which could take effective action do not do so. One wonders why. If we look beneath the surface we may find that certain people of power in the community whose vested interests are threatened have, under cover, informally, and in certain patterned relationships with each other, worked out a way to keep anything from happening.[11]

---

10 Polsby, "The Sociology of . . ." p. 232.

11 Gordon W. Blackwell, "Community Analysis," in *Approaches to the Study of*

It is of course always possible that a block may have been thrown by "certain people of power," but the fact that their blocking is done behind the scenes makes this easier to assume. There are so many slips between conceiving of a project and its consummation that behind-the-scenes sabotage is all too easy an explanation and too ready a "proof" of the existence of a static power elite. As Robert Dahl has said,

> If the overt leaders of a community do not appear to constitute a ruling elite, then the theory can be saved by arguing that behind the overt leaders there is a set of covert leaders who do. If subsequent evidence shows that this covert group does not make a ruling elite, then the theory can be saved by arguing that behind the first covert group there is another, and so on.[12]

Research done in New Haven, Connecticut, by Dahl and several associates attempted to discover whether a ruling elite actually managed the affairs of that city. Instead of approaching the question through the reputations for power of certain individuals, Dahl tested the hypothesis that if the "leaders on issue A turned out to be the same as leaders on issue B and on issue C, then the 'power structure' of New Haven would be identified."[13] But the results of the investigation showed there was very little overlap in the groups of people who were leaders in promoting three important kinds of programs in the city. The leaders in matters of public education were not the same leaders involved in urban redevelopment, and those concerned with political nominations were still another group.[14] In summary one of the investigators reported that:

> . . . in none of the three issue-areas could we detect the faintest hint of what Hunter described for Regional City, the Lynds for Middletown . . . namely, the more or less covert determination of community politics by a politically homogeneous economic and social elite.[15]

Politics, edited by Roland Young (Evanston, Ill.: Northwestern University Press, 1958), p. 308.

[12] Robert A. Dahl, "A Critique of the Ruling Elite Model," *op. cit.*, p. 463.

[13] Polsby, "Three Problems . . ." *op. cit.*, p. 799.

[14] See Dahl's *Who Governs? Democracy and Power in an American City, op. cit.*, Chaps. 8–12 especially.

[15] Polsby, "Three Problems . . .," *op. cit.*, p. 803. Interesting evidence on this point can be drawn from another analysis of a community power structure done by Floyd Hunter and two colleagues. They studied the city of Salem, Massachusets, while that city was making a self-study of its health problems. The search team attempted to identify the top leadership of Salem in essentially the same manner

Lively debate continues as to the relative merits of these two competing ways of looking at community power.[16] In my opinion the
protagonists of the proposition that small cohesive cliques control
American cities have yet to prove their case. Their dubious research
methods and the indefiniteness of some of their concepts and terminology undercut their "proof." A shifting series of leadership groups,
such as Dahl found in New Haven, appears to be nearer an accurate description of the realities of American urban politics. It is obvious, however, that the degree of concentration of power varies from community
to community. Dahl's work was done, it is worth remembering, in a
stable New England community, whereas some of the other community
power studies were carried out in rapidly expanding cities. In an older
more stable city it is conceivable that a greater dispersion of power
might prevail since inertia or even near *immobilisme* would be likelier
to develop in an old city than in an expanding one where the role of
business promoters might well be more significant. Nevertheless Dahl
and his supporters have been unable fully to meet and controvert the

---

as Hunter had previously done in Atlanta. They came up with forty nominees as
major leaders, and these people were then asked to name the ten most powerful
among themselves. This done, presumably the chief power-wielders of the city were
at hand. Yet on the committee to survey health needs were only two of the top
ten and two of the next thirty. And the research team subsequently reports that only
eleven of the forty "can be identified as having had some part in the study and
action process in relation to the health needs under scrutiny." Floyd Hunter, Ruth
Schaffer, and Cecil Sheps, *Community Organization: Action and Inaction* (Chapel
Hill, N.C.: University North Carolina Press, 1956), p. 237. It could be claimed,
of course, that health services were not an important item of community concern
and that therefore the real bigwigs would not care one way or another, but it does
not appear from the context of the book that the problem was deemed unimportant:
considerable sums of money were likely to be spent as a result of the survey, and
the substantive questions of public policy were of considerable interest to the community as a whole at least once the survey was under way.

16 See articles by Dahl, Peter Rossi, and Charles Adrian in *Social Science and
Community Action*, edited by Adrian (Lansing, Mich.: Michigan State University,
1960); and the interesting attempt to rescue Hunter's basic method presented by
Lawrence J. R. Herson, "In the Footsteps of Community Power," 55 *American
Political Science Review* 317 (1961). Further bibliography on community power
is to be found in Herson's detailed footnotes. See also the balanced assessment of the
theory and of power in Syracuse, New York, by Frank J. Munger in *Decisions in
Syracuse* (Bloomington, Ind.: Indiana University Press, 1961), Chaps. I, XIV; and
William V. D'Antonio and Eugene C. Erickson, "The Reputational Technique
as a Measure of Community Power," 27 *American Sociological Review* 362 (1962).
See also the late Arnold M. Rose's *The Power Structure* (New York: Oxford University Press, 1967) for a broad sweep of the literature and an attempt at drawing
up a kind of balance sheet on the controversy. Other noteworthy works on this
subject are Robert Presthus, *Men at the Top* (New York: Oxford University Press,
1964); Robert Agger, Daniel Goldrich, and Bert Swanson, *The Rulers and the
Ruled* (New York: John Wiley, 1964).

argument that a test of power based upon examination of issues on the agenda is inadequate because it cannot take account of various means employed to keep unwanted issues from surfacing.[17] Thus neither side of the argument can be taken as "proved." Perhaps the best approach for students seeking to decide which of the two alternative positions comes nearest to being an accurate description of reality in the state or locality in which they are studying would be to attempt a cooperative research project to test the degree of concentration of power in a community close at hand. In the meantime a skeptical attitude toward sweeping generalizations about the elite "who really run this city" would seem advisable.

Action and Inaction: Community Equilibrium

Whatever the merits of the power elite theory there is no doubt about the existence of innumerable groups that influence policy-making in all parts of government. We permit and our traditions encourage free association for political purposes, and the ever more complex economic and social system of our time seems to offer, and ultimately almost to demand, organization of specialized groups for promotion of their interests. The village blacksmith and the miller did not belong to trade associations or to labor unions although both were in business and both were laborers; in a simpler society there was less need for organization to protect specialized interests since a face-to-face community involved a different order of social and economic interrelationships than does the modern urban-industrialized system. As David Truman has pointed out, organization begets organization, for when an interest group achieves its goals it may thereby create a disadvantage for another group thus inspiring counter organizational efforts to redress the balance.[18] Thus at least in the sense that there are many interests in competition with each other both directly and indirectly, ours may be said to be a pluralistic system.

Indeed, there are so many competing groups, so many disparate voices and pressures, that one marvels at the stability and orderliness

---

[17] See Peter Bachrach and Morton Baratz, "Two Faces of Power," 56 *American Political Science Review* 947 (1962), and also Bachrach's *The Theory of Democratic Elitism* (Boston: Little, Brown, 1967).

[18] David B. Truman, *The Governmental Process, Political Interests and Public Opinion* (New York, Alfred A. Knopf, Inc., 1951), pp. 52–62. This is a definitive work on interest groups in American politics.

of the governmental system. But it is normally stable, and in fact sometimes discouragingly so to the advocate of some reform measure or general change of direction of public policy; it almost seems at times that
nobody is ready to support the noble cause that has fired the enthusiasm of some people to whom the importance of a special cause is self-
evident. The young lawyer bent on judicial reform, the League of
Woman Voters leader determined to get election laws changed, the
civic-minded businessman interested in promoting a city manager system—all such advocates are driven to occasional despair by the unhear-
ing public whose attention they cannot attract.

The cards are stacked against the innovator. Not only are there legal
and governmental devices for slowing down innovation (law suits to
challenge constitutionality of new policies, vetoes, two-thirds majority
requirements, and so on), there are also social factors that handicap the
proponent of change. There must, for example, be a considerable
amount of public interest aroused to support important changes, but
the general public, even when aware, is little inclined to go forth to
battle for the righteous cause.[19] The known situation, even if undesirable, is at least known and not fraught with the uncertainties of
perhaps unsuspected disadvantages that new notions may harbor.

There is a kind of equilibrium that settles over a community—a state
of calm acceptance of the status quo which is hard to break.[20] And
that acceptance can extend to most odious circumstances—crooked
police departments, corrupt administration, gross inefficiency. One of

---

[19] Robert Dahl reported that in New Haven "after several years of public discussion and debate over charter reform, when a sample of registered voters was asked
in 1959 whether they personally would do anything if a revision of the charter was
proposed that would make the mayor stronger, over 40 per cent of those who dis-
approved of such an idea said they would do nothing to oppose it, and nearly
three-quarters of those who approved said they would do nothing to support it." As
Dahl said, these appeared to be honest responses since less than half the voters who
went to the polls bothered to vote on the charter referendum—which failed. See his
"Reflections on Community Consensus," a paper presented at the American Political Science Association Convention in New York, September 1960 (mimeographed),
pp. 16–17. For an analysis of "latent" public opinion and political innovation, see
V. O. Key, Public Opinion and Democracy (New York: Alfred A. Knopf, Inc.,
1961), Chap. 11.

[20] Wallace Sayre and Herbert Kaufman, Governing New York City (New York:
Russell Sage Foundation, 1960), pp. 716–19, observe that the politics of New York
City discourages change; they see "tendencies toward stasis" because any change
brings some risk of cost (in money, power, and prestige) to some participants in the
city's total governmental sphere. Also they attribute this condition to unwillingness
of officials to put themselves in the line of fire by pressing for changes that have
aroused the ire of some people, and finally they comment on the "tortuous path"
that any change must navigate before it can be effectuated. In essence their observations parallel the general point being made here.

the major sources of this equilibrium in a community is the tendency of people to adjust their lives to circumstances as they find them. The annals of war and tales of natural catastrophes suggest that people are capable of managing in the face of incredible adversity. People seem capable of making their at least temporary peace with almost any kind of condition; even inmates of Nazi extermination camps "cooperated" with their executioners rather than take risks and die in rebellion.[21] The ambitious ones will find ways of adapting their operations to the fact of a crooked police department; a contracting firm—in the interest of business success—will bribe building inspectors in order to expedite their operations. So too with slum conditions, sloppy and inefficient administration, or rank injustice; such conditions are adapted to by compliance with the malpractices involved or they are accepted apathetically as the conditions that exist. A shell of protection gets built around the status quo, good or bad.

If this is the case—if there is a tendency to equilibrium in a community—then how does anything ever get done? After all, cities do change, states do adopt new constitutions and embark on new projects, and reform governors and mayors do induce changes. The answer is, of course, that there is a tendency to equilibrium but no inevitability of its being unbreakable. Galveston, faced with an incredible job of reconstruction, pulled itself together and remade a city; New York City, appalled at the outrages of the Jimmy Walker regime, did the unconventional and rejected the Democratic party at the height of its national popularity by electing the inimitable Fiorello LaGuardia in 1933. Disgust, fear, and anger over the conditions of a government can lead to a new spirit in a community—a spirit which, as long as it lasts, makes possible public acts that otherwise would have been inconceivable. Without any formal change in the structure or character of the government, the impossible suddenly gets done. Intransigence gives way to cooperation; a sense of community possibilities overrides the bickering of conflicting groups.

There is, as Dahl has pointed out, a considerable amount of "slack"

---

[21] Bruno Bettleheim, once an inmate of both Dachau and Buchenwald, comments on this passivity in the face of death in a disturbing but significant article. "The Ignored Lesson of Anne Frank," 221 *Harper's Magazine* 44 (November, 1960). To be sure the bestial treatment and starvation rations they received would not be likely to leave them with much opportunity for rebellious action, but when certain death was ahead and indeed continually before their eyes, it is significant that they did not try more frequently to annoy their tormentors. See also John Hersey's novel, *The Wall*, and Alfred Kazin, "Eichmann and the New Israelis," 24 *The Reporter* 24 (April 27, 1961).

in the typical community's political system. Potential resources for affecting policy are not drawn upon to the fullest extent.

Very few people seem to exploit their resources to the limit in order to influence political officials; even political officials often have resources available to them which they do not fully use. But precisely because of the existence of these slack resources, a great many significant, abrupt, short run changes in the distribution of influence can be brought about; for whenever some one in the community begins to exploit his available and hitherto unused resources much more fully and efficiently than before, he gains markedly in influence.[22]

Given a stimulus to action, the pattern of *stasis* can be broken. There is a tendency to overlook the importance of this intangible source of motivation—this sense of mission that can change torpor to temper. Motivation by way of excitement and a sense of community is often ignored by those who attribute improvements, if such they be, to change in the form or structure of government. This is perhaps a natural result of the persistent practice of overemphasizing the importance of form, and the concomitant habit of overselling formal changes with consequent need to "prove" that the promised improvements have in fact materialized. It is difficult to disentangle the consequences of a change to a strong mayor charter, for example, from the consequences of the political momentum and community spirit involved in promoting the change. It is perhaps sufficient to warn that sweeping claims for new forms might well be examined with an eye to the political context which brought the change about.

But political honeymoons, however joyous, do not last forever. In time the wave of community feeling dissipates, a new equilibrium settles in, and stable patterns are re-established. After the new broom has swept clean, the dust settles, and once again the shell of protective adaptation and apathy gathers to insulate the status quo. The alternation between the placid and the vigorous and active is, of course, not always clear and sharp, and in some communities the word "alternation" may be inapt since the intervals between mood changes may seem interminably long.[23] Yet the tendency for this kind of community spirit to come and go seems to me a significant feature of local government

---

[22] Robert Dahl, "The Analysis of Influence in Local Communities" in *Social Science* . . . , *op. cit.*, p. 36.

[23] See James Reichley, *The Art of Government, Reform and Organization Politics in Philadelphia* (New York: The Fund for the Republic, 1959).

particularly.. Analysis of broad political sentiments of this kind may make explicable events that otherwise would defy explanation.

The "Game of Politics"

Newspapermen like to talk about the "game" of politics—partly, I suppose, because it suggests a slightly cynical attitude toward politics and politicians, a little cynicism being an important working tool of a political reporter. There is, however, neither facetious intent nor cynical implication in the use of the term here. It is used because it is helpful to think of the political process as a kind of elaborate game in which there are contestants vying with each other under more or less specific formal and informal rules, pursuing varying strategies in order to win certain objectives or rewards. There are particular skills that are widely recognized as requisite to a good performance and certain others that are frowned on as illegitimate. Certainly the game has its aura of challenge and there is not a little fun as well as some grief in the playing of it. The game is played with all seriousness, of course, and the deploying of forces and mapping of strategy are done with an air of gravity often beyond the call of duty. (Politicians—good ones anyway—usually have a sense of humor, but they play their big roles with great solemnity.) In the succeeding pages the players and some strategies will be introduced; in succeeding chapters much of the analysis will turn on this "game" metaphor.[24]

The Players

The range of player-contestants in the politics of a pluralistic society is enormous, and the best one can do is to categorize the types of players

[24] I hasten to distinguish the phrase I use here from the "theory of games" and strategic analysis theory that has grown up in recent years and has become a very recondite form of analysis of public policy. It is not that form of analysis that I am referring to, of course. For an introduction to the methods and purposes of this analytical approach, see Richard C. Snyder, "Game Theory and the Analysis of Political Behavior," in *Research Frontiers in Politics and Government* (Washington, D.C.: The Brookings Institution, 1955), pp. 70–103. More pertinent to the immediate understanding is the work of Sayre and Kaufman, *Governing New York City, op. cit.* Sayre and Kaufman present a working example of game analysis of politics, emphasizing the players, strategies, rules, and results of the playing of politics in New York City.

and attempt to describe the general characteristics of the various categories. The major contestants can be summed up this way: political party organizations, public officials (executive, legislative, and judicial), the organized bureaucracy, interest groups (a sweepingly inclusive set!) and "publics" that from time to time show cognizance of issues.

1. *Political Party Organizations.* A political party is an organization which seeks power primarily through attempts to supply the personnel of government. A party certainly cannot be meaningfully understood as the mass of people who vote for party candidates, for most voters have precious little sense of commitment to party and they have little to do with its day-to-day operations. In fact, the party may not even consist of the people who formally belong to it, since often the people who register with a party do so only in order to vote in primary elections. Many of these "registered" party members feel quite free to abandon the party when they feel like voting for the opposition, while still retaining their full party membership. Although party members have varying degrees of potential influence on intraparty matters, they usually do very little about them. They do not vote in the party primary elections in anything like the proportions in which they vote in general elections (with the exception of some Southern one-party states where the primary *is* the election). Many, perhaps most, party members could hardly care less about the operations of the party.

In short, to analyze the party one must look to the organization that makes it tick.[25] If the casual voters for the party and the membership broadly speaking cannot be said to constitute the party, the organizational group that provides its leadership can. For they are the workers, the major deciders of party policy, the most influential backers of nominees for public office, the nucleus that makes the party into a viable agency of public power. This organizational nucleus is comparable to the owners and managers of a baseball club; it is the owners and managers—not the fans—who really constitute the baseball club and likewise it is the leadership of the parties and not the voters who manage the political party. Popular usage of course gives a blessing to the image of popularly controlled parties, and politicians never weary of pointing out how their party is truly "democratic" and controlled by the people themselves while all evidence indicates the opposition party is manipulated by dubious characters who leave no role for the membership. This notion is constantly reiterated—both by idealists and by hardened campaigners.

---

[25] This is the thesis of E. E. Schattschneider, who puts the point very well in his *Party Government* (New York: Holt, Rinehart, and Winston, Inc., 1942), pp. 35–64.

There are, however, so many different kinds of political party organizations in this country that it is difficult to say exactly what one means by the statement that the "organization" rather than the "people" controls the party. The next two chapters assess a wide variety of local and state parties. Some organizations are virtually dictatorial in their power—tightly organized and rigidly controlled, primarily for the benefit of the chief owner-operators of the organization.[26] Such machines are less common now than in the past, but they still do exist. At the other extreme are parties too disorganized and ineffective to merit the name *party*. Yet even the name of the party means something (it is, for example, a way onto the ballot that otherwise may be unattainable where minor parties and independent candidacies are not encouraged by electoral laws), and control over it is usually the stimulus for some degree of organized effort. Practically speaking, party organizations range between the two extremes of autocracy and virtual nonexistence.

The prime purpose of organization is to enable the party to gain control over the machinery of government. To control government it is necessary to get the "right" men into office (*i.e.*, your candidates, not the opposition's), and to do that there must be effective means of nominating candidates, getting them elected, and dealing with them effectively once they have been elected, for the elected ones are appointers and this, too, is a means of control. If, for example, a party cannot organize itself effectively for nominating its candidates, then it ceases to be a party in practical terms. When a party breaks into factional splinters, and cannot agree on one candidate even after formal designation has been made, then that party is defeating its essential purpose, since it thereby invites defeat through splitting up its vote (in the sense of leadership, specialization, and resources) for the convenience of the opposition. Organization is necessary for effective campaigning, for negotiating appointments, and indeed for keeping the very party alive.

Thus the party acts in its own behalf. One of its essential features is its tendency to operate as an interest group making demands on government to satisfy its organizational needs—mainly, although not solely, the need for patronage to feed its aspiring workers.[27] Stephen K. Bailey, who served as mayor of the college community of Middletown, Con-

---

[26] This appears to be the case in Albany, New York, where a classic, if anachronistic, machine still reigns. But Albany is not alone; see the discussion of local machines in Chapter 9.

[27] V. O. Key has described this phase of party operations well in his *Politics, Parties, and Pressure Groups*, 4th ed. (New York: Thomas Y. Crowell Co., 1958), pp. 381–405.

necticut (pop. 30,000), has said of his patronage problems that he was ready to meet the party requests on marginal but not on really important problems of the city's destiny. Thus he refused to compromise on a zoning change request, was challenged by his party treasurer and the party boss "who . . . got very mad . . . and hauled me up for questioning." He told them:

Look, gents, there are things we render unto Caesar and there are things we render unto God. If the john breaks down in the City Hall I will get a Democratic plumber, because Democratic plumbers are ten times better than Republican plumbers. But if you are going to begin fooling around with what this city is going to look like ten years from now, I'm going to make the decision, not you.[28]

Those who labor—or many of them anyway—want rewards and the party leadership is alert to all possible means through which government can supply jobs or other rewards to help sustain a good working force for the party. The practice of using just any living and breathing but deserving party worker for even technical jobs in government, while not gone, is less frequent than in the past. The use of franchises, contracts, and governmental purchasing for the faithful is still with us, even if diminished from the excesses of the past. Though contemporary politicians may be more restrained and their opportunities more limited, it remains true that providing the personnel of government and getting favors still is characteristic of party operations. (For one thing, it is a source of great pride to have landed jobs for others—as with fishermen, the size and number of the catch is an endless subject of conversation.) Does this mean then that the party has no other reason for existence? This has often been claimed, but it simply is not the case. The self-serving ways of the party are significant, but that does not say all there is to be said by any means.[29] Parties, for example, reflect attitudes of the people of a community. They may not do so with ideal fidelity; they may in fact repress the views of some elements of the community and exaggerate those of others. But invariably attitudes widely held in the community or those of groups that are in politically strategic situations condition the behavior of the party. Thus Southern parties reflect

---

[28] In the colloquy of *Tragedy and the New Politics*, edited by Hallock Hoffman (New York: The Fund for the Republic, 1960), p. 24.

[29] E. E. Schattschneider has argued effectively against this limited view of parties in "The Functional Approach to Party Government," in *Modern Political Parties*, edited by Sigmund Neumann (Chicago: University of Chicago Press, 1956), pp. 198ff.

Southern *white* attitudes on racial questions. A politician who goes far beyond the consensus on such matters is in trouble and the party organization will shy away from him. Disputes over nomination are common in the South and it would be idle to attribute such disputes to patronage concerns. It is worth recalling that there are over 500,000 elective offices in state and local government, almost half of them subject to nomination by parties. Contests for nomination involve more than patronage. Increasing or trimming the school budget, integration or segregation, tax policy or welfare practices, and other issues all may be involved in nomination or party control controversies.

It is true that nothing like ideological uniformity exists in American parties. National parties especially are beset by deep divisions and wide gulfs separate the more liberal from the more conservative factions in each party. Such extreme division is not so common in state and local parties although it does happen; in Texas there are ultraconservative and left-wing liberal groups, both of which call themselves Democrats; some Western states have been represented in Washington by one very liberal and one very conservative Senator, both Republican. How then can the party be said to be really striving for any kind of policy position when there are such divergences within its own ranks? The answer is that the party itself becomes an object of contest between groups of politicians who seek control in order to pursue their policies. Segregationist elements seek control over the Democratic parties of Southern states; liberal farm-labor elements have sought control of the Democratic party in Midwestern states; conservative business and rural groups have collaborated to control the Republican party in many states. Again, to interpret these exertions as aimed solely at patronage is to misinterpret the whole process. Policies and power to affect policies are constant stakes in party contests.

Thus in the total competition of the political process—in the "game of politics"—the party organization operates in its own behalf and as a reflector of attitudes toward policy matters. Sometimes the two roles become intermixed—the party seeks enlargement of a particular activity of government in anticipation of more jobs for the faithful, while it simultaneously reflects what it deems to be a popular attitude that will win it favorable public response with which it hopes to acquire or retain power through elections. The manner in which the party plays its roles and the effectiveness with which it does so varies widely, of course, but the roles are constant and significant factors in the overall process. Indeed, even when the party chooses to remain out of a fight, hoping to incur no wrath when tempers are riled, this too has significance. A potentially significant force sidelined is an important consideration in the assessing of factors involved in a contest.

2. *Public Officials.* The major public official—the executive, judicial, or legislative officeholder—plays the game in his own behalf and not necessarily as a party organizational leader. Although they are likely to be party members and usually leaders in the organization, public officials do not think of themselves as primarily party leaders. Their public positions, their ambitions and desires for personal gain or particular policies, force officials to seek a standing independent of the party. Thus the governor of a state may be the titular figure in his party, but he must present to the world a different face from that of a party mogul. Nonoffice-holding party politicians have a more or less singular concern with the welfare of the party, and are expected—routinely by the public, absolutely by party associates—to work in the party's behalf. A governor's notion that he would like to go to the United States Senate, be re-elected, or appointed to the bench will tend to make him move in ways that he would not if he were a party leader without the responsibilities and the *conspicuousness* of being an office holder.

Although officials seek to project an image of themselves as somewhat independent of the party, there are nevertheless many officials whose personal following constitutes whatever organization a party has in a given area. Since in many places the party organization has atrophied to practically nothing, officials fill the vacuum by developing a personal organization. This is particularly the case where multifactional politics prevails. In Florida, for example, the Democratic party is strong in votes but weak in organization, and campaigns tend to be a matter of every-man-for-himself as half a dozen or more candidates seek the Democratic party nomination for important offices. Under these circumstances, practically the only "party organization" that exists is the following of the individual or aspirant officeholder.

There are, however, many public officials who are not party-oriented and who may indeed be antiparty. Officials elected on genuine nonpartisan credentials against party opposition and appointed officials, such as city managers and judges, may feel no sense of attachment to any political party and therefore may not be responsive to party appeals —or may indeed react negatively to such an appeal.

The primary strength of the official is his formal authority to act. He thereby acquires what is often called legitimacy, which is to say that the official is accepted by the public as vested with the proper powers of the society and that habit, tradition, and the symbolism of the society back up his use of power. Even those inclined to disagree with a given policy will tend to sustain the public official in his right to take an action they detest. Courts are respected greatly by Americans, and often therefore a detested court decision will be accepted more readily just because the court ordered it. That is, the legitimacy of the Court system is very great. In short, the public official has the keys of the kingdom in his hand; because he in a sense is a manifestation of the state itself, his actions are accepted in part as actions of the state. Once he has acted, even though there be disagreement and perhaps even resistance to his orders, the fact that he has an official position makes it "natural" to comply and "wrong" to resist.

Significantly, higher public officials can attract attention to their statements and can thus make themselves heard during any political controversy. This capacity to command attention is a very important source of power when there is great emphasis upon public understanding and public support for policies. In a system of government that responds to the ballot's force, public response to pleas for support on a given policy can become a very significant element in a struggle. Therefore the official's capacity to get the press to publicize his utterances becomes a prime advantage of his power position. The press normally reports any significant comment by the mayor, and the governor's office can always assemble the press corps within minutes when the governor has decided to make a statement on an urgent issue. News is made according to who says it as well as by what is said. The more prominent the official, therefore, the more likely his pronouncements are to receive wide coverage, and accordingly the more powerful player he is in the game of politics.

3. *The Bureaucrats.* The word *bureaucrat* is not used here with any negative connotation; it merely refers to persons who operate the permanent civil service of a government. Although in American usage the word is often a form of denunciation, that practice has no place in a serious attempt to comprehend governmental processes. Bureaucrats —like politicians, deacons, and showgirls—are of many kinds; it is only decent therefore to reserve judgment until we know who and what we're talking about.

In most contests over public policy, the bureaucracy gets involved in one way or another—sometimes deeply and sometimes only tangentially. The potential power of the bureaucrats derives from several aspects of their position. They are in the first place permanent; other players tend to come and go—legislators are replaced, the parties may alternate with each other in majority control, and many appointive and elective officers step on and then off the field where politics is being played—but the bureaucracy goes on forever. Because the bureaucrats are permanent and usually are experts, they are normally more knowledgeable about the subject matter of their particular province than are their transistory supervisors; consequently their opportunity to "control" their superiors rests in some measure on their possession of expertise which the supervisor has to depend on.

The permanent civil servant has a major investment in his agency, and he will seek to protect it in his relations with others outside the agency. His personal concern for his own well-being—his promotion, recognition, income, job security—is obvious, of course. And the bureaucrat high enough in the hierarchy to make responsible decisions is probably also devoted quite sincerely to his agency's cause. A high policy official who has worked his way up the ladder of his department has a sense of *esprit de corps* not unlike that of a soldier in a crack military outfit. He will defend its interests as his own, and sometimes the two will be virtually inseparable. So too the dedicated engineer in the highway department, or the director of social workers in the welfare department. Their psychic investment in the agency becomes a motivation to fight in behalf of its program.

A bureaucracy tends to have a life of its own; it tends to become an organic whole with a sense of common commitment among its membership and a readiness to close ranks and protect the common interest. And because it is more or less organic and self-protecting as well as systematic and deliberate, it therefore has means to defy orders through noncooperation of various kinds. A command to trim manpower can be handled by delaying execution, hoping that the one who commanded will forget his unwise decision. A decision to transfer a function from one agency to another can be resisted in all sorts of ways—prominent and popular figures may threaten to resign if the order goes through, interest groups close to the agency may build up pressure against the order. Thus a command to a state university by a state board of education might be evaded by delaying execution, by pleading that the board consider the implications of the order, by arousing the alumni organization of the university to stand off the threat.[30]

Although it is common to speak of the bureaucracy as not involved in the political process, it is impossible to come to such a conclusion if politics means what we have said it does in these pages. Contests for preferment, for power over various programs, battles over appropriations for one program versus another—in our terms all these are political fights, and such fights more or less routinely concern the bureaucracy. The bureaucrats then are powerful, permanent, knowledge-

---

[30] See, as a case in point, Samuel Halperin's A *University in the Web of Politics* (New York: McGraw-Hill Book Co., 1960). This case study sharply illustrates the interplay of bureaucratic and other political forces.

able, and paradoxically both respected and distrusted players of the game.

4. Interest Groups. As we have said, interest groups beget interest groups, and the more complicated our society the greater the invitation to form interest groups for self-protection and self-promotion. Interest groups are thus numerous beyond belief. Some of them are unscrupulous in their insistence on their own ends with the result that the very notion of organized interest groups has a negative connotation for many people. Historically there has been enough unscrupulous activity on the part of groups seeking to serve their own interests at the expense of wider publics to explain the general attitude toward interest groups. The negative stereotype is furthered by the use of the words *pressure group* to characterize all such groups, for pressure—as David Truman has pointed out—suggests a mildly sinister kind of activity.[31] Since in fact interest groups are anything but alike in their composition, methods, and objectives and since we seek here to evaluate as dispassionately as possible, it is wiser to use the less prejudicial term *interest group* rather than *pressure group*.

What is an interest group? It is a group of people who share common attitudes and who make "certain claims upon other groups in the society for the establishment, maintenance, or enhancement of forms of behavior that are implied by the shared attitudes."[32] Some kinds of shared attitudes produce no interest groups, of course—the lovers of apple pie have not organized into a group—and some groups share attitudes and band together but make no claims on society and may therefore not be a meaningful interest group (*e.g.*, a philatelic society, a lodge of Elks, a hiking club). But if some threat arouses the concern of the group it may then begin to make demands. Thus a birdwatchers' club may go along for years without the slightest effort to make demands on government or other groups, but the mass use of insecticides may stir the concern of the members and they set off to arouse the public and the government to the dangers and the vital need for action. Thus a gathering of kindred spirits becomes an interest group.

There is, as David Truman has pointed out, an inevitable tendency for the interest group to turn to government for resolution of its problems.[33] For government today is the most inclusive of all forms of

---

[31] Truman, *op. cit.*, pp. 38–39. Harry Eckstein, however, defends the term *pressure group* as an appropriate usage, and one not particularly likely to produce a negative attitude; see his *Pressure Group Politics* (London: Allen and Unwin, 1960), p. 10.

[32] Truman, *op. cit.*, p. 33.

[33] *Ibid.*, pp. 104–06.

human organization; it covers more subjects and has more sweeping powers than any other kind of human organization. Therefore groups turn to government, and as one group satisfies its goals through governmental action others are invited to do so—not only through imitation but also in self-defense. The more effective specific groups are in achieving their goals through government the more inevitably are competing groups forced to resort to government. Thus both labor and management in the past resisted—and still talk about resisting—the use of governmental power to resolve the difficulties that arise between them. But as one side or the other achieves a governmental decision in its favor, the other side seeks to reverse that decision or modify it so as to make it easier to live with.

It scarcely need be observed that interest groups can at times be enormously effective in promoting their ends. Their successes have been so dramatic that there is a tendency to describe them as almost omnipotent. It may serve to warn against this kind of glib generalization (particularly with regard to groups that achieved what the generalizer wanted to prevent happening) to comment on some of the assets and liabilities of such groups in action. In the first place, the prestige of the group is an important consideration: some groups start off with a good reputation and others work uphill because the public is suspicious of them. Thus doctors and ministers come into a battle with favorable reputations that opens doors (and ears) for them. On the other hand, labor organizations, liquor dealers, and people opposing jail as a treatment for narcotic addiction are in an exactly opposite position—they are distrusted from the first. Instead of being associated with morality, security, and good health, they evoke negative stereotypes.

Second, the size and unity of a group are important considerations. Is the group inclusive of most elements of the particular interest, or is it a splinter element in competition with many other small groups? Is the group cohesive and tightly organized and able to present a strong and convincing show of concern and unanimity? Whether or not it can show cohesiveness is in part at least a factor that varies with the subject of the moment. If there are deep divisions within a group, it may even have to sit out the game on the sidelines since it would be impossible to get the organization to resolve its inner disputes sufficiently for it to make any kind of successful showing. Thus a Parent-Teachers Association might avoid a controversy about education that divided its members along religious lines. In a Connecticut controversy about children being provided bus transportation to parochial schools, the PTA steered clear of the fray—and indeed when a state officer of the group made a statement on the controversy, there was violent objection from members and ultimately the official had to claim that she spoke not for the group but for herself.[34] If, on the other hand, a group is intensely concerned and in agreement on a given issue, the effectiveness of the group is likely to be at its maximum. An interest group leader like a military commander, is usually no more effective than the support he can get from his followers.

Naturally the leadership and financing of a group also condition its success. If it has the leadership to make the most of its assets and to argue effectively for the positions taken, and the cash to pay for the propagation of its viewpoint, it may achieve things that a large but badly led and poorly financed group could never manage. (There are other factors influencing interest group operations, of course, but discussion of these can be deferred until succeeding chapters where the operations of groups will be considered in more detail.)

It is significant that interest groups play the game at all stages. They may initiate a proposal by publicizing it in various ways or they may begin to build opposition to a proposal almost immediately upon its announcement, using the tools of publicity in the prepolicy-making stage to lay the groundwork for activities to come. The interest group may involve itself with political parties, giving assistance to the party organization and its candidates in the campaign—hoping of course, for a cooperative attitude once the candidates win election. The party is also approached on general policy matters in order to influence its leaders to speak up for the "right" points. The interest group participates in the familiar process of lobbying, a process which is sometimes considered—quite wrongly—to be its sole activity. When the legislative battle is over, the scene shifts to the executive branch. It is almost as important for the interest group to get the "right" administrators appointed as it is to get the law passed, for execution of the law requires many interpretations and subordinate rule-making decisions. Through these administrative decisions, the ultimate meaning of the law is determined. Finally, it is possible to negate the law by challenging the authority upon which it is based. Occasionally court interpretation may whittle down a law to make it relatively meaningless.[35]

The interest group, like the other players we have talked about, has

---

[34] See the excellent case study of this controversy in Theodore Powell's *The School Bus Law, A Case Study in Education, Religion and Politics* (Middletown, Conn.: Wesleyan University Press, 1960), pp. 192–93.

[35] A very interesting example of the use of the courts by interest groups is found in Clement Vose's study of Negro and white interest groups using the courts to decide racial disputes, thereby making positive law on the subject in the absence of legislative action. See his *Caucasians Only* (Berkeley, Calif.: University of California Press, 1959).

a tendency to play from self-interest, strictly speaking. From the nature of most interest groups, it is obvious that the policy goals they seek are self-interest in character, but there is a sense in which the group's leadership gets involved for its own sake. That is, the leaders of the group will worry about the continuity of the group itself before committing it to positions that might splinter it even though the leaders may be very concerned about the policy involved. The question they ask is whether this issue is so important that it justifies risking the very existence of the group; might it not be better to lose today and live to fight another day? The concern over the continuity of the organization affects the leadership of the group, since they have a good deal invested in the organization. Not unlike the bureaucrats and their agencies, the leaders of special groups have their own welfare, income, and sense of mission tied up in the group. This may lead in fact to some make-work to show how busily headquarters is serving the welfare of the dues-paying membership. Thus the staff spends part of its time thinking up things to worry about, and having produced a list of troubles they serve their own and the group's interest by defending it against real and imaginary onslaughts.

5. *The "Publics."*   The awkward sounding word *publics* is used here in preference to the word *public* since the latter suggests a misleading conception of the role of society at large in political activities. Although we are prone to talk about the influence of the public on policy, the fact is that if we mean by *public* anything near the whole adult population we are talking nonsense. For the whole adult population is almost never aroused to concern over public affairs. Somewhat less than seven in ten of all eligible adults participate in the most widely publicized opportunity for the public to exert its direct influence on policy—namely, the election of a President of the United States. And, as we have observed, proportionately fewer potential voters take the trouble to turn out for state and local elections.

Not only is there no unanimity of concern among the people, even the people who do show some interest in public policy cannot concern themselves with all the questions of the hour. There are too many questions and the attention-span of any individual is too limited. Some people are aroused about schools and there is a "public" that can be depended on to react to news about school developments. The public involved ranges from those with a mild and rather vague concern to those whose concern seems to be all-consuming. There is a public that shows up to discuss judicial reform, a public that responds to a milk price increase, another that rises to the defense of the civil service system—and it may very well be that there is no overlapping at all in the three groups. It is true that if the civil service system is being seriously threatened the interest will suddenly widen and the resultant public will be many times larger than the number involved on routine matters. But even that enlarged group will still constitute a minority of the population, and perhaps a surprisingly small minority if we actually tried to find out the number of people who have any real interest in the question.

Even though the separate "publics" may not be large numerically, they cannot be ignored as political actors. These publics are played to constantly by the other contestants for the simple reason that they are believed to possess power. Does the deference shown these publics make sense? Have they real power? Naturally the amount of power and the effectiveness of its use varies with the public and the situation, but in general there is potential power here. In the first place our traditions demand a certain deference to the people. There is some confusion and even contradiction in the common conception of popular sovereignty, but, confusion or not, no one is likely to get far arguing that the best way to make decisions in this country is to ignore public attitudes. There is, however, more to it than mere belief. Through elections, through direct presentation of the views of nonofficial persons (*e.g.*, by protest appearance of citizens at hearings or an avalanche of mail to legislators or executives), through grumbling that in various ways makes an impression on formal decision-makers—through all these and other methods the publics do make themselves heard. Thus, although ill-organized and perhaps quite unorganized, individual citizens sharing certain viewpoints become players in the game.

Strategies of the Game

Strategy for a particular contest depends upon the players, the subject matter, and the prevailing sentiments of the time. The elements of strategy are therefore varied and dynamic, however much attempts to discuss and categorize them may suggest that they are static. Politics is played by ear and intuition, not from a well-marked sonata score. Social change constantly alters the circumstances of the game, and therefore the canny player must anticipate gradual changes in the rules of the game, new players, and new strategies that hitherto may never have appeared. (Of course, strategy can take one just so far; Casey Stengel once said he was a better manager on the days when Mickey Mantle was in the outfield.) What is said here concerning the strategies of the game is descriptive, not prescriptive; hopefully the student observer of the game will add his own examples of strategic thinking. Merely to illustrate the variable character of strategies available, consider the following four general approaches: alliances, publicity, compromise and maneuver, and the use of threats and rewards.

1. *Alliances.* It is obvious that in a pluralistic system the formation of strategic alliances is vitally important. A player pressing for a given policy will seek to get the support of parties, interest groups, and public officials in any and all conceivable combinations. The necessity is at all times to give the impression that an overwhelming number of people representing many diverse interests are in agreement on the policy point and that they all demand (or protest) an action. The protagonists in battle may not always be scrupulous about leaving exactly the right impression about the extent of the supporting forces he alleges to be in his camp, and in fact shrewd players tend to discount the enthusiastic claims of a mass following by a personal arithmetic reserved for assessing such exaggeration. The alliances in a given battle may be remarkably different from those in the next contest, and the cliche "strange bedfellows" is nowhere more frequently used than in the description of alliance patterns of politics.[36]

It is sometimes difficult to tell who is using whom in the heat of controversy. A public official may ask an interest group to put pressure on him publicly to do something that he wants an excuse to do. Seemingly objective and detached bureaucrats, pretending to be uninvolved in political activity, may resort to vigorous means to get the clientele of their agency aroused and active. The teachers and the Parent-Teachers Association, the state agriculture department and the Farm Bureau Federation, the state employment service and the AFL-CIO, attempt to set common policies and to provide mutual support as needed. The kinds of alliance that develop may also be of dubious character—such as, for example, covert alliance between the leaders of major parties to put on sham battles and then divide the spoils without the inconvenience of a real fight. This, of course, is most likely to happen when one party is so weak that it does not feel capable of winning anything in open elections and is therefore tempted to "cooperate" with the stronger party in order not to be left out altogether. Alliances with the underworld, with race track or liquor interests, are often made but rarely advertised; many a governor has been pushed into a vague yet effective alliance with race track elements in order to get his budget through

---

[36] This commonly observed shifting of sides incidentally lends no support to the power elite theory cited earlier.

—perhaps promising not to request an increase in the state's percentage of the race track's "take" as a *quid pro quo* for assistance on the budget in the legislature.[37]

2. *Publicity.*   Since there are publics to be attracted, interest group memberships to be stirred up and activated for the fray, and—in the case of elections—many people who have to be persuaded, the use of publicity becomes very important. The skillful manipulation of words so as to give the desired impression and induce the proper response— which, if you like, may be called propaganda—is a common implement for playing the game. It does seem that the techniques of presentation of political messages have become more and more sophisticated—per- haps frighteningly so—within the last few generations. Presumably it has always been true that the cleverest debater and the most cunning demagogue have been able to influence policy as a consequence of their eloquence or rhetorical skills, but with the ubiquitous and instantaneous communications media of today's world, the place of the symbol manipulator seems to be more crucial than ever. No doubt the new im- portance of word-smiths is attributable to the concurrent rise in im- portance of popular power (*e.g.*, the transfer of the power to elect United States Senators from the state legislature to the voters, in 1913, and the spread of the initiative and referendum, and the wide use of the party primary law—all came in this century) and the development of unprecedented means of communication. Opportunity and instru- mentality crossed paths.[38]

The intricacies of word *manipulation* cannot be discussed in detail here. Suffice it to say that the means of presenting and of endlessly repeating slogans, sly suggestions, noble sentiments and oversimplified pie-in-the-sky promises are almost endless in variety. We shall have more to say of this when we discuss politicial campaigns (see Chap. 8). Note, however, that the same devices are regularly used in nonparty and noncampaign efforts to shape policy. Bureaucrats, corporations, labor unions—even some more or less notorious figures—hire experts to present a favorable picture of their activities to the public. Not infre- quently there is a bogus element in the presentation, using the truth rudely if not actually prevaricating. Often shadow organizations are created, with appropriately high-sounding names, to be the source of information that would not be well-received from its true source. Such activity was involved in a notorious contest between the railroads and

---

[37] See Lockard, *New England State Politics*, p. 161.

[38] On this development, although with primary emphasis on national politics, see Stanley Kelley, Jr., *Professional Public Relations and Political Power* (Baltimore: Johns Hopkins Press, 1956).

the trucking industry as they fought over laws limiting the weight and size of trucks permitted on Pennsylvania highways. So outrageous were the front organizations created for the purpose of misleading the public and the legislators and governor who were to decide the question, and so outlandish and unfair were the tactics of presentation of the railroad side of the story, that the railways were convicted under the Sherman Antitrust Act, although the verdict was subsequently reversed.[39] Not all uses of publicity are equally obnoxious, of course; the presentation of argument can be rational, ethical, tasteful and yet effective, and frequently it is. The uses of publicity are infinitely variable, as are its effects. Under today's conditions no player can afford to ignore the potential power of public relations.[40]

3. *Compromise and Maneuver.* The game demands ability to compromise, to maneuver in order to make the most of a situation and to anticipate the turn of events. The adamant and unyielding persons or groups in politics may or may not achieve their goals in a given contest. But the nature of a pluralistic system, right or wrong, demands a degree of flexibility and give-and-take; the player unwilling to yield to the opposing elements from time to time is likely to be frozen out of the game in one way or another. The minor party that continues to demand—without appreciable results—some relatively unrealistic course of action is heading for futility. Being unwilling to operate in the real situation which demands more a give-and-take attitude, the absolutist group in effect shuts itself out.

There is a common tendency to condemn political compromising, to dismiss politics as morally dubious since "principles" take second place to compromise for sake of expediency. But there is compromise and compromise, and before condemning or giving blanket approval to compromising it is appropriate to think about the nature of the process involved. Any society of wide scope and complexity is necessarily going to have to compromise in making decisions; the diversity of interests

---

[39] This unhappy chapter in American politics is recounted by Robert Bendiner in "The 'Engineering of Consent'—A Case Study," 13 *The Reporter* 14 (August 11, 1955). Bendiner quotes *Tide*, an advertising magazine, as saying, "Understandably, the pre-trial deposition-taking [the early presentation of evidence in the case] in the trucker suit . . . has quite a few PR [public relations] men wondering about ethics and behavior of the business." The conviction was reversed by the Supreme Court in 1961 (see *The New York Times*, February 21, 1961). A fuller account is available in an excellent case study by Andrew Hacker, "Pressure Politics in Pennsylvania," in *The Uses of Power*, edited by Alan F. Westin (New York: Harcourt, Brace, and World, Inc., 1962).

[40] For a general analysis of the effect of publicity on public opinion, see V. O. Key, *Public Opinion and American Democracy* (New York: Alfred A. Knopf, Inc., 1962), especially Chaps. 9–11, 14–15, and 20.

and values makes compromise a condition for the continuance of the system. Some kinds of political compromise are, nevertheless, ethically insupportable; they can be placed in the same moral category with the compromising of the truth by the patent medicine advertising. On the other hand, some political compromising is, by comparison with commercial huckstering, virtually noble. A compromise to break a deadlock may get the compromiser into difficulty with his following, yet the compromise may be an act of statesmanship and a means to a commendable gain for the group. The dynamics of a typical political controversy are such that the chances for killing action are enormous; the result is that the player committed to getting positive action is especially likely to face the uncomfortable alternatives of "half a loaf or nothing." And in that situation the excellent becomes the enemy of the good, for the proponents of the best proposal may do the bidding of opponents of any action by refusing to compromise. This is such a common and simple situation that no lengthy examination of the point would seem necessary, except for the persistent tendency of people to consider such matters in strictly black and white terms—and of course to condemn compromises that do not conform to the white side of the either-or proposition. Nor is clarification of the problem aided by the tendency of politicians—especially defeated ones—to heap abuse on others who did compromise. Very often this is defensive counterattack so as to minimize the credit due the compromiser for having brought home the bacon even if it was a bit moldy. But assuredly it does not aid understanding of the realistic alternatives.

If there is a way out of this impasse, it is not immediately clear to me. If on the one hand there is too much exaggeration of the tendency to compromise, a too-lenient attitude might do equally grave harm to the political system. Certainly the commonly posed query of whether or not a given case involves a compromise of principle is no adequate test. The supposed test is that only a compromise not affecting basic principles is excusable. It is easy to show why this does not resolve the dilemma. The opposing camps in racial integration controversies claim respectively the principle of segregation and the principle of equality. But any significant action which sought to find a *modus vivendi* to work out a local impasse on the integration question would certainly be a compromise that did affect principle. Any condoning of Negro children in white schools affects the segregation principle; any acceptance of less than full integration affects the equality principle. Thus the test of principle is no test at all, except for absolutists who will not budge and would not consider compromise in the first place. Therefore the actual situation, the history of events, the players, and even a good guess at the probable future effects of the compromise may be far better measures of what ought and what ought not be objects of compromise. Still, whether condemned or condoned, compromise will go on as a practical aspect of democratic politics.

Finally, it is significant that we operate with a system of very complicated rules which put a premium on ability to anticipate the hazards of the labyrinthine channels of decision-making. As we said previously in discussion of the constitutional complex, and as we shall say later in discussion of legislative rules, the very complexity of the system of rules penalizes miscalculation about its details. A single misstep can spell the defeat of a project since it may be impossible to get the stage set again, with all the necessary stars, audience, and supporting cast reassembled to repeat the performance. Thus the strategic plans call for consideration of all the possible traps that the rules impose. This includes everything from seeing to it that the formalities of statutory form are observed to anticipating and forestalling an infinite number of parliamentary traps that can waylay a bill. Appropriate maneuvering to adapt to the existence of complex rules becomes an integral part of the strategic planning of the effective player.

4. Threats and Rewards. There are many prizes which can be bestowed or dangled as possible rewards, just as there are many kinds of retribution to be used on the uncooperative. Political objectives are sought in part through rewards and sanctions deployed to influence behavior. The rewards range from a pat on the back, recognition from the high and mighty, and interest group support for candidates to financial deals both acceptable (logrolling on budgets, for example) and unacceptable (a bribe). And the threats run the gamut from the implied promise that a politician will "sit on his hands" in the next campaign through outright threats or use of violence if demands are not met.

The currency of rewards and punishments in the political game is used with varying subtlety and finesse. An interest group may tell legislators that it will oppose them in the next election "unless." A mayor may threaten a subordinate with dismissal unless he agrees with some policy the mayor is backing. A popular subordinate may threaten the governor with resignation—with resultant politicial difficulties unless the governor gives in on a point. Such inverse order influence is, as we have observed elsewhere, an important, if not always conspicuous force in political relationships. Thus Robert Moses, long the majordomo of the New York City and New York State park, recreation, transportation, city development and planning, and several other programs, managed to retain his position in both city and state government regardless of which party controlled the elective positions. He was powerful, widely admired, scrupulously honest, and admittedly efficient; he built a power base that the governors and mayors had to acknowledge and almost invariably had to give in to in a showdown. The late Newbold Morris, a colleague of Mr. Moses in the regime of Mayor Fiorello LaGuardia, said LaGuardia often addressed Mr. Moses as "Your Worship," although others of his closest associates "who have worked with him for a quarter of a century still refer to him and address him as Mister Moses." [41] Frequently when the Mayor and Moses disagreed, the Mayor received but never accepted Mr. Moses' resignation. Some compromise always kept him on the job. Finally LaGuardia in a playful mood had his secretary mimeograph some forms which said in effect: "I, Robert Moses, hereby resign as . . . (fill in job being resigned at the moment) as of this date . . . (fill in date)." Subsequent mayors may not have had LaGuardia's sense of humor about this most unusual "subordinate," but all have shared the Little Flower's dependence upon him.

The strategic use of such threats and rewards—to use them effectively yet not overplay the hand—is the mark of the master player. The empty threat to visit dire punishment that all know cannot be delivered may do more harm than good. The promise of undeliverable rewards may bring more headaches than the prize was worth. Some threats and rewards are covert and not obvious to the observer—and some of them, being frankly illegal, could not be otherwise—but much of this strategic bargaining is apparent or can be inferred from the behavior of the people involved. Since the range of prizes and punishments and the pattern of their employment are so varied, no further elaboration of this strategic factor need be attempted here; ensuing chapters will further illustrate their importance.

---

[41] Letter to the author from Mr. Morris, January 13, 1961.

The Political
Process II:
8. The State

THIS CHAPTER deals primarily with state parties, their organization, strength, operations, weaknesses, and potential. It is not true that when the party situation has been described, the whole of a state's political system has been encompassed. Yet it is possible to trace from the party's features the major outlines of a state political system. If parties are weak, splintered, and ineffectual organizations, the state's politics is thereby importantly affected. Since in every state major offices are chosen under party designations, the question to be answered—even where the party is admittedly disorganized and lacks commanding power— is how the chief Democrats and Republicans use the machinery of their respective parties in *attempting* to influence competition for the major prizes that are attainable only under the auspices of the party. However meager the role of the formal party leaders, the play of forces within the party is perhaps the most significant index of a state's politics. The organization and leadership, the electoral strength and general reputation, the factional patterns and degree of cohesion, the traditions, and even the personalities of the leaders of political parties, are important determinants of a state's political pattern.

To appreciate the significance of party is not to deny the relevance of other elements of the political process, for in many respects parties are but reflectors of other political forces that shape the contours of the political map.[1] The particular traditions of a given area—for example, the sectional voting habits and the belief system on which these depend—obviously determine political conditions. This is dramatically true, of course, in the one-party states of the South and in some of the strongly Republican-oriented Northern states, where a self-perpetuating traditional set of beliefs strongly incline the mass of the population toward one party and toward certain principles of social behavior associated with that party (not as dramatically true for Vermont, for instance, as for the South, but true nevertheless). In several Midwestern states, nonpartisanship has deep historical roots and the politics of these states has been shaped thereby. Likewise, beyond the party pattern as such, the kinds of interest groups that emerge in various states lead to striking differences in political conditions. For example, a state with a large urban population and with much of its labor force employed in manufacturing is likely to have strong unions which become very important political forces, but in a predominantly agrarian state labor unions make demands that may never be heard—at least not loudly enough to matter. Not only the demands but the methods of farm groups differ from those of labor, and so the politics of predominantly agrarian states differ accordingly. Interest groups affect and are affected by the party system, however, and the ensuing discussion will consider this pattern of interaction.

State Politics: Autonomous or Dependent?

Does it make sense to speak of the politics of the states as independent of the tides of national politics? In one sense, the answer must be no. The states are not, as V. O. Key has correctly argued, independent governments but units of the federal system:

Within the states public attention cannot be focused sharply on state affairs undistracted by extraneous factors; political divisions cannot occur freely on state questions alone: national issues, national campaigns, and national parties project themselves into the affairs of states.[2]

---

[1] The Bibliography contains items on the parties and politics of the individual states.

[2] V. O. Key, *American State Politics: An Introduction* (New York: Alfred A. Knopf, Inc., 1956), p. 19. This book is the most significant work yet written on state politics; it cuts through the underbrush of misinterpretation and woolly as-

The political machinery of the national parties is essentially the machinery of the state and local parties. Important debates on domestic politics almost invariably result in mixing national and state politics. Clearly also voting in national elections affects state politics, sometimes decisively. The tides of national party popularity which elect and defeat presidential aspirants simultaneously determine the fates of local candidates—scoundrels and innocents alike. No period better illustrates this than the early New Deal era when state Democratic parties, basking in the reflected popularity of President Roosevelt, fashioned local victories that surprised the victors no less than the vanquished. Nor was it merely a case of the pull of presidential coattails—candidates dragged to victory by straight ticket voting for the attractive name at the head of the ticket. Especially in the early 1930's the Democratic party's national popularity was such that the aura prevailed even when state law provided for election of state officials at dates other than November in even-numbered years. (In normally Republican Maine, Democratic governors were chosen in September of 1932 and 1934.)

Does it follow then that there is no genuine independence of state politics? In spite of the evident impact of national politics, there is still an element of independence and of individuality in the politics of each state. *Autonomy* is too strong a word to describe the degree of separateness of state politics, but it is wrong to conceive of the states as completely tied to the national political system. State parties are, after all, parties in a federal and not a unitary system; there is a considerable range of discretion, both legally and in practice, left to the state parties. Accordingly one finds a wide range of differences in state parties; indeed, as we shall see, there is a bewildering array of variations in state party practices and strengths. Distinct constitutional patterns and traditional political peculiarities of individual states impart a certain insularity to each state's politics. Thus the politicians of a state count on a favorable response from many people merely by emphasizing the rightful independence of the state from outside interference. Apparently the demagogic potential of this appeal is often quite strong. Take the case of the late John Rankin, a fire-eating demagogue of the old school, who was displaced as a Mississippi Congressman in 1952 by a reapportionment which put him in competition with a popular candidate. Rankin

---

sumptions that have been features of this topic. This chapter and other parts of this volume lean heavily on the thoughtful analyses and the empirical evidence found there. On the place of state parties in the federal system of government, see David B. Truman, "Federalism and the Party System" in *Federalism Mature and Emergent*, edited by A. W. Macmahon (Garden City, N.Y.: Doubelday & Company, 1955).

is said to have lamented unto the day of his death that Northern newspapers ignored him in that race, denying him the opportunity to advertise himself by the interfering non-Mississippi enemies he attracted.

In practical terms the insularity of state politics is enhanced by the character of the national parties—that is, they are not truly national parties but collections of loosely federated state parties with the dominant power decentralized in the states rather than centralized in the national parties. As E. E. Schattschneider has pointed out:

> Decentralization of power is by all odds the most important single characteristic of the American major party; more than anything else this trait distinguishes it from all others. Indeed once this truth is understood, nearly everything else about American parties is greatly illuminated.[3]

Control over nominations both for Congress and for the presidency is not within the power of the national party organization but is retained by state and local party organizations. The national party committees are important—so far as they have any real significance—because of the local power of the members who sit on the committee, not because of any authority of the committee as a whole. National conventions are enclaves of state political potentates, not a gathering of national figures who tell the state organizations what to do. This localizing or decentralizing of political power is not accidental by any means; it is rather the reflection of our political history and the tendency toward separatism that has always been a part of our governmental tradition but which has survived more effectively in the parties than in the government. This jealously guarded power has the inevitable tendency of insulating state politics from national control. While it is certainly true that the voters are swayed by national political tides, the state and local political organizations retain their hegemony and go their separate ways.

The extent to which national tides affect state politics varies from state to state, depending largely on whether or not it has competitive parties. In one-party areas national sweeps have little impact. A Republican national trend must be very strong indeed to win majorities in the traditionally Democratic South. On occasion, the Republican party does win southern states in presidential contests, and Republicans are beginning to threaten in statewide elections in many states. Although Republicans won the governorship in Arkansas and Florida (and nearly

---

[3] E. E. Schattschneider, *Party Government* (New York: Holt, Rinehart and Winston, Inc., 1942), p. 129.

so in Georgia) in 1966, national tides still have only minimal impact in such areas.[4] More often local situations produce the deviation or, as in upper New England, a gradual change of party loyalties may bring unexpected results when combined with an unusual candidate or dramatic situation.[5] Conversely, the more competitive a state's parties are and the closer the margin of victory is likely to be, the more influential are the shifts of sentiment in national politics. Then the impact of national elections is exaggerated rather than minimized. National tides can also have a considerable impact on majorities in state legislatures particularly because this tends not to be a conspicuous office and there is a tendency for the head of the ticket to swing majorities with him.[6]

An example is the situation in Connecticut during the 1950's. As Figure 8–1 shows, the tides of presidential voting had a decisive effect on partisan control over the General Assembly. The Eisenhower sweeps in 1952 and 1956 and the Kennedy victory in 1960 inflated majorities of their respective parties in the legislature, although there was nothing about the national election directly relevant to the disputes of the legislature. Thus in 1954 the Senate had 20 Democrats and 16 Republicans, but after the 1956 election (when President Eisenhower won 64 per cent of the vote in Connecticut) the tables were turned and the Republicans controlled that chamber by 31 to 5. Although the previous membership of the Senate (which served from 1955 to 1957) was not a perfect assemblage of legislators, they were not so remiss as to deserve such sweeping repudiation. But, of course, it was not in fact a repudiation but the fortunes of national affairs and President Eisenhower's popularity.

Gubernatorial elections no less than presidential ones have an effect

---

[4] Key observes that in the eleven Confederate states only two Republican names (both from Tennessee) can be found in the lists of governors during the first half of the twentieth century. *Op. cit.*, p. 22.

[5] A Democratic Congressional candidate won the single seat in the United States House of Representatives from Vermont in 1958. He was defeated in 1960. It was the common opinion among observers of Vermont affairs that the Democrat won in 1958 less on his own merits than on the demerits of his Republican opponent. In any event his victory doubtless signals the beginning of the end for Vermont's one-party status, for the Democratic party has been increasing its percentage of the vote regularly, occasionally winning more than 45 per cent of the vote for state offices. In 1958 Democratic candidates across the country did well and the Vermont breakthrough can therefore be attributed in part to national tides, laid on top of the increased Democratic vote. Confirmation of this trend came in 1962 when a Democrat won the governorship; and he was re-elected in 1964 and 1966, each time with a substantial margin. Maine and New Hampshire are now more competitive also.

[6] More will be said on this in discussion of split party control between governors and legislatures. See Chap. 10.

on legislative elections, and in recent years gubernatorial majorities have offered a counterfoil to presidential voting. It can at least be claimed that there is a relevant connection between gubernatorial and legislative campaigns, although a popular governor at the top of the ticket can

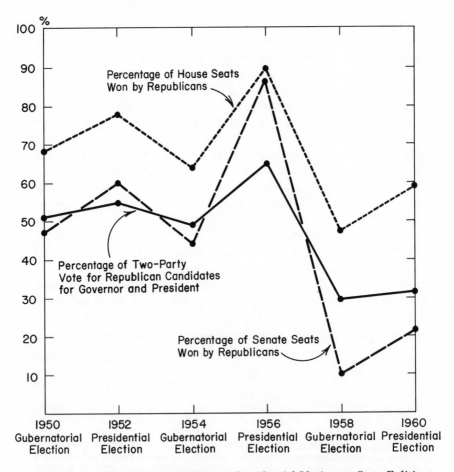

Figure 8-1. The Variable Impact of Presidential Voting on State Politics: The Case of Connecticut, 1950–60

have a sweeping impact that transcends any reasonable claim for inter-connection between the two campaigns. Note, for example, the marked decline of the Republican membership of the Senate in 1958, when

Governor Ribicoff won re-election by an unprecedentedly high margin. The Connecticut House of Representatives, which then varied its party proportions in a moderated fashion owing to the number of safe Republican seats in that house, was controlled by the Democrats for the first time since 1876 as a result of Ribicoff's victory. Democratic control proved to be politically significant in policy terms, since it allowed the passage of acts which, it is safe to say, could not have been passed had the Republicans controlled it. On the face of it this is neither good nor bad, although arguments can be offered that it represented a catastrophe (according to the Republicans in the campaign of 1960) or an unalloyed blessing (according to Democrats on the hustings). The point, of course, is not whether the results were good or bad, but that changed party control did make a difference.[7]

Voting for state legislators is often relatively blind voting—at least as compared with voting for more conspicuous officials such as governor or United States Senator. The latter are public figures whom even the vaguely interested citizenry will have heard about. As spotlighted officials they managed to resist the sweeps of national politics by attracting split-ticket voting.[8] Historically there has in fact been an increasing tendency for voters to resist the temptation to stick closely to the party ticket for all offices and instead to elect popular figures in state elections even when they are drawn from the minority party. Key points out that over the past seventy-five years there has been a decline in the "capacity of parties to carry states simultaneously for their candidates for President and for governor." He found that in states which hold presidential and gubernatorial elections simultaneously, "the proportions of elections that produced pluralities for presidential and gubernatorial candidates of the same party by groups of presidential elections have been as follows: 1880–92, 93.1 per cent; 1896, 89.5 per cent; 1912–24, 81.2 per cent; 1928–40, 77.8 per cent; 1944–52, 75.5 per cent."[9]

---

[7] See Key's further illustrations on these points as regards Missouri and Oklahoma, *op. cit.*, pp. 31–33, 41–44.

[8] Joseph A. Schlesinger has found that there are a good number of other state officials besides the topmost figures who manage to run counter to tides and stay in office over long periods of time, winning constant re-election whatever may be the fate of other candidates. See his article "The Structure of Competition for Office in the American States," 5 *Behavioral Science* 197 (1960) and his book, *Ambition and Politics* (Chicago: Rand McNally, 1966).

[9] Key, *op. cit.*, p. 48–49. This undoubtedly does reflect a greater tendency to selective ticket-splitting and indicates voter discrimination between state and national politics, but it may also reflect the fact that there are now more competitive states than there were in the past. That is, in a one-party state much ticket-splitting could be obscured by continual failure to produce a majority for the deviant candidate, whereas in competitive states relatively small percentages of ticket-splitters can shift majorities.

Detailed examination of the 1960 presidential election illustrates the willingness of voters to pick and choose between the presidential and gubernatorial candidates of the same party. In that election there was considerable variation between presidential and gubernatorial voting, with President Kennedy exceeding the vote of Democratic candidates for governor in eight states but trailing the gubernatorial candidates in the other nineteen states that were holding simultaneous elections for governor. The variation was not very great in six states (two percentage points or less), but in about twelve states the deviation was quite wide and in nine states it was sufficient to provide split results—*i.e.*, a governor of one party and a presidential majority for the other. Compare this with the figures Key calculated above for the historical trend: in 1960 the same party won both offices in 66 per cent of the states, and Key's lowest average—for the period 1944–52—was 75.5 per cent. The 1960 presidential election, as one of the closest in the history of the office, might be expected to show a very high proportion of split results, yet that election showed less deviation than that of 1956, at the height of President Eisenhower's popularity, when only 44 per cent of the states voted a governor and president of the same party. This is the result of the tendency in recent years for Democratic gubernatorial candidates to run ahead of Democratic presidential candidates, which has generally been true in most states since 1944.[10]

The inclination of voters to make distinctions between national and state politics—or at least between national and state candidates—can be examined more carefully by distinguishing between the states that schedule their gubernatorial elections concurrently with presidential elections, thereby maximizing the impact of the presidential election campaigns on state elections, and those that do not. (Local decisions to alter election dates, while almost invariably presented as attempts to avoid undue influence of national upon state politics, are not always dictated by such noble motives: usually involved are simple calculations as to the relative advantage of the party with the votes to decide the question.) It would appear that the states which elect governors during presidential elections would have a higher correlation between state percentages for president and governor than would states that do not. This is not the case in the period since 1944, although the difference in correlation of percentages for the two groups is small. Among the

---

[10] As information to be presented subsequently will show in detail, there are only nine states in which the Democratic candidates for governor have not done better on the average than Democratic candidates for president—in all the remainder —omitting Alaska and Hawaii, which were not states during most of that time— the intrastate Democratic strength was apparently greater than the national strength.

states with simultaneous elections there is an average difference between the two offices of 9 per cent, and in the states with nonsimultaneous elections the average difference is 7.2 per cent.[11] These averages suggest a higher proportion of ticket-splitting than is common across most of the country because the averages include the great deviations in the one-party southern states that are responding increasingly to the enticements of Republican presidential candidates while continuing to elect Democratic state officials. (The four southern states electing their governors during presidential elections averaged a deviation of 22 percentage points [presidential less than gubernatorial vote, of course]; the three southern states choosing their governors in the off years had a 20-point variation.) Excluding the southern states, the percentages decline sharply, although the differences between the two types of elec-

TABLE 8-1
Variations in Voting for Governor and President in States
Electing Governors for Two-Year Terms, 1944–60*

State	Average Democratic Percentage of Two-Party Vote for President	Average Democratic Percentage of Two-Party Vote for Governor	
		In Presidential Years	In Nonpresidential Years
Arizona	48	56	52
Iowa	44	47	46
Kansas	37	43	48
Massachusetts	52	52	52
Michigan	47	51	50
Minnesota	50	46	47
Nebraska	38	39	42
New Hampshire	44	45	43
New Mexico	49	50	52
North Dakota	40	38	37
Rhode Island	53	57	55
South Dakota	41	39	42
Vermont	35	38	36
Wisconsin	45	47	47

* The voting data were largely gleaned from the three volumes of *America Votes*, edited by Richard Scammon (New York: The Macmillan Company, 1955, 1958), Vols. 1 and 2 and (Pittsburgh: University of Pittsburgh Press, 1960), Vol. 3.

---

[11] This is the result of calculating the average percentage of the two-party vote for the Democratic candidates for governor and for president in the elections from 1944–60, finding the percentage point deviation state by state and then calculating an average of the state deviations. There are fourteen states which throughout the period elected governors in nonpresidential year elections and eleven that chose them only in simultaneous elections, and the remaining states had mixed presidential year and nonpresidential year elections for governor.

tions are not significant: simultaneous elections, 1.6 points; nonsimultaneous, 3.8 points.

It is interesting to compare the voting tendencies in the states that have two-year terms for governor, meaning that they elect governors during both the presidential and nonpresidential years. Again it would seem likely that there would be a greater similarity between gubernatorial and presidential voting when the elections are held simultaneously than there would be between the vote for president and the vote for governors who ran in the off-years. Yet as Table 8–1 shows, in the fourteen states which consistently had two-year terms for governor during the period 1944–60, only four states—Kansas, Nebraska, New Hampshire, and New Mexico—showed a greater similarity between presidential and gubernatorial averages in the nonpresidential years than in the presidential years. Since these data report averages, the degree to which voters do pick and choose in elections is minimized through cancelling out. The material in Table 8-2 illustrates sharply the extent of discriminatory voting.

In summary then it is certainly valid to say that the states do not function as autonomous political units; as integral parts of a federal system they are subject to restraints and myriad influences external to the state. And since national politics plays an increasingly large role in

TABLE 8-2
Percentage Point Differences in the Vote for Democratic Candidates for Governor and for President in Selected States, 1944–60

	1944	1948	1952	1956	1960	Average for the Five Elections:
Arizona	20	6	2	11	4	8
Iowa	4	7	7	10	5	7
Kansas	6	3	11	23	5	10
Massachusetts	1	5	3	15	15	8
Michigan	5	7	6	11	1	6
Minnesota	15	11	0	6	2	7
Nebraska	17	7	8	7	2	8
New Hampshire	5	0	2	11	2	4
New Mexico	2	1	2	6	1	2
North Dakota	10	5	8	3	9	7
Rhode Island	3	4	4	8	5	4
South Dakota	8	8	1	3	7	5
Vermont	9	9	15	15	3	10
Wisconsin	4	6	2	10	4	5
Average by Elections:	10	7	6	12	6	

our lives, it is inevitable that the dramatic crosscurrents of national politics should influence state affairs, especially since state and national
elections are often held simultaneously. Yet it is evident that state politics do have a certain independence of national politics. The differences
in presidential and gubernatorial voting are illustrative as a counter-
balance for the impression that national party tides determine all. It is
true that the increasing number of states with competitive parties
maximizes the impact of this split voting, but that such sharp deviations
occur is significant. In the operation of state parties, as basic blocks in
a decentralized party system, there is also broad latitude for discretion
and independence among state parties.

The Classification of State Party Systems

Thus far little attempt has been made to distinguish between the
various types of state parties. Although we commonly talk of the American party system, in truth there are vital distinctions among these
systems, and indeed no meaningful study of state politics is possible without some effort at comparative analysis of state parties—which, of
course, requires some effort at classification of the various types. Classification is no simple process. This is so for several reasons: we know too
little about the manner of operation of many of the states; we have
not agreed upon the criteria for distinguishing among the various kinds of
state political systems; we are faced with an array of different classification systems which make sense individually but are mutually incompatible. The difficulty is further compounded, of course, by the bewildering
variety in the politics of the various states. The economic, social, and
historical differences among the states produce a variety of political
systems, and accordingly there are variations not only in party strength
from state to state but great differences in attitude toward parties and
in party methods, effectiveness, and organization. And all these factors
are significant variables in the assessment of any state's politics.

The commonest form of classification of state party systems is to
distinguish between the one-party states and the competitive states, but
this turns out to be an overly simple distinction since it is not clear
where the line should be drawn between the "almost" competitive and
the "almost" one-party states. As one examines the voting behavior of
the various states, it also becomes apparent that there are sometimes
consistent variations in the way a state reacts in national as compared

with state politics which may require more than one measure of the degree of competition. Moreover it is difficult to say what the time span for a comparison should be. If the time period is long, the classification may neatly describe what has been rather than what is since obviously states do change in their political outlook. If the time period is too short, the classification may reflect an interim wave and not the long-run tendencies of a state. Thus some arbitrary decisions have to be made and therefore for obvious reasons no system of classification has yet been universally accepted.[12]

The classification system most useful for present purposes does three

---

[12] In the past decade there have been several attempts to classify state party systems by more systematic methods. Austin Ranney and Willmore Kendall in 1954 suggested a three-class system in which distinctions were made between the one-party states, the modified one-party states, and the two-party states—using as their criterion the proportion of elections for president, United States senator, and governor won in each state. This offered a rough measure of the extent to which competition existed, particularly where they presented data on the proportion of elections which the second parties won at least 30 and 40 per cent of the votes. See "The American Party Systems," 48 American Political Science Review 477 (1954); the essence of this is repeated in their Democracy and the American Party System (New York: Harcourt, Brace, and World, Inc., 1956), Chap. 7. Joseph A. Schlesinger proposed an alternative method in 1955, classifying the states according to the presidential and the gubernatorial voting tendencies by an ingenious method which plotted the percentage of times a party won the governorship in the period 1870–1950 against the percentage of elections in which there was a change of party control of the office, and repeating the process for the presidency for comparison. See "A Two-Dimensional Scheme for Classifying the States According to Degree of Interparty Competition," 49 American Political Science Review 1120 (1955). V. O. Key uses a technique somewhat similar to that of Ranney and Kendall to classify certain states in American State Politics, op. cit., pp. 98–99.

Robert T. Golembiewski took a new approach in 1958 employing three criteria: the proportion of seats held by minority parties in state legislatures, the consistency with which one party comprises the legislative minority in legislative houses over a period of time, and the tendency for governors to be of the same party as that which controls the legislature. Thus he divides the states into one-party, weak minority-party, and two-party states. This is naturally a measure of intrastate politics rather than state-in nation politics. There are several instances in which his categories do not jibe with those of Ranney and Kendall. See Golembiewski's "A Taxonomic Approach to State Political Party Strength," 11 Western Political Quarterly 494 (1958). Key presents a variant method employing the percentage of seats in state legislatures in Politics, Parties, and Pressure Groups op. cit., 4th ed., pp. 314–15. Schlesinger has refined his earlier techniques by analyzing the vote for nine different officials; he presents rather surprising findings of sharp variations in the voting for such disparate offices as secretary of state, auditors, and comptrollers, suggesting that perhaps the easy generalizations about differences in party systems deserve to be reconsidered in terms of these offices which do not rise and fall with overall party voting tendencies. See "The Structure of Competition for Office in the American States," 5 Behavioral Science 197 (1960). See also the useful distinctions made by Edward F. Cox in "The Measurement of Party Strength," 13 Western Political Quarterly 1011 (1960).

things: emphasizes current political trends, shows relative party voting strength, and gives weight to the factional or organizational character- istics of state parties. If one is concerned with party systems as indica- tors of something more than what will happen on election day and is also concerned with the likely influence of party on the way the govern- ment runs, then such a classification system seems appropriate. Al- though other students of state politics have been willing to rank the states on a continuum from the most to the least competitive, this seems to me dubious. There are too many changes that in a relatively short time can make such precise rankings nearly meaningless. And if one took the average Democratic vote of a given state over a ten-year period and it was shifting from a Republican to a marginal state, the resulting average might conceal rather than clarify the current status of the state's party system. Therefore in Table 8-3 the states are listed in groups of five in alphabetical order in each group. The time period in- volved is 1946 to 1966 and presidential, gubernatorial, and state legisla- tive elections are considered in ranking the states. In addition, the organizational pattern of a state's politics is considered. That is, if a state's parties tend to be strongly led and well organized, and legislators are given to voting as a party bloc in the state legislature, then a higher group ranking is given a state. Conversely, a competitive state in which leadership is weak and the party counts for little in the legislature, is ranked lower than a state with an equal degree of competitiveness but with stronger party organizations. Similarly at the lower part of the scale, where the noncompetitive states appear, the degree of factional- ism assists in sorting out states. Where factionalism is most rampant and the confusion of the party system at its highest the state is given a lower ranking; where clearer bifactional division occurs, the state is given a higher ranking.[13]

What difference does it make whether a state has competitive parties? Does it matter beyond the obvious difference in the way campaigns are conducted? Does the existence of competition really matter where the

---

[13] Admittedly this process is arbitrary to a degree; and being subjective, my classifications are certainly debatable. Thus Arkansas for a number of years was not widely multifactional while Governor Orval Faubus reigned, but it appears to have returned to its multifactionalism with his departure from the governor's office, a point demonstrated by the inability of the ordinarily dominant Democrats to hold onto the governor's chair in the 1966 election. Although Florida elected a Repub- lican in 1966, it remains a multifactional state in Democratic affairs, again dem- onstrated by the contribution that multifactionalism made to that Republican victory. It is conceivable that other states will continue trends established in the last few elections and will no longer fit their present classifications, but this must be left to future determination.

TABLE 8-3
Patterns of State Party Competition*
(Arranged Alphabetically in Groups)

GROUP I

Competitive Parties, Much Party Voting in Legislature
Connecticut
Massachusetts
Michigan
New Jersey
New York

GROUP II

Competitive Parties, Considerable Party Voting in Legislature, but not as Much as in Group I
Delaware
Indiana
Ohio
Pennsylvania
Rhode Island

GROUP III

Competitive Parties, Moderate Party Voting in Legislature
Colorado
Hawaii
Illinois
Montana
Wisconsin

GROUP IV

Competitive Parties, Little Party Voting in Legislature
Alaska
California
Maryland
Minnesota
Washington

GROUP V

Some Competition, Little Party Voting in Legislature
Arizona
Nevada
New Mexico
Oregon
Wyoming

GROUP VI

Little Competition, Little Party Voting in Legislature
Idaho
Kentucky
Missouri
Utah
West Virginia

GROUP VII

One Party Domination, Party Voting Rare
Iowa
Kansas

TABLE 8-3 (*Continued*)

Maine**
Oklahoma
New Hampshire**

GROUP VIII

One-Party Domination, More than in Group VII, and Party Voting Equally Rare
Nebraska
North Dakota
South Dakota
Tennessee**
Vermont**

GROUP IX

No Practical Competition in Intrastate Politics, Bifactional Division Frequent
Georgia**
Louisiana**
North Carolina**
South Carolina**
Virginia**

GROUP X

No Practical Competition, Multifactional Division Frequent
Alabama***
Arkansas***
Florida***
Mississippi***
Texas***

* Based upon the closeness of electoral competition for the Presidency, the Governorship, and state legislature 1946–66; the degree of party voting on legislative roll calls; and the extent of bi- or multi-factional alignment. There is no precise statistical measure of these combined factors due to the vagueness of roll call data and the shifting patterns of factionalism. Therefore no effort is made to rank the states from 1–50, since the rankings would be too arbitrary to be statistically reliable.

** States where bifactional division in the dominant party is common, although in most cases this is less true today than in the past.

*** States where multifactional division in the dominant party has been common.

operation of government is concerned? Does it affect the kind of policy that is produced? The late V. O. Key, Jr. believed competition did make a difference, and he said in his *Southern Politics* that the absence of competition in the South facilitated the control over governmental policy by the "haves" in the society as opposed to the "have nots." He said that "A loose factionalism gives great negative power to those with a few dollars to invest in legislative candidates. A party system provides at least a semblance of joint responsibility between governor and legislature. The independence of candidacies in an atomized politics makes it possible to elect a fire-eating governor who promises great accomplishments and simultaneously to elect a legislature a majority of whose members are committed to inaction."[14] Unfortunately Key never followed up this statement with any empirical effort to test its validity, to see whether, that is, there really is any difference between political systems as to their policies where the have nots are concerned. In a small way I tried to test the proposition in a book on New England state politics, but with a sample of but six states the results were at best only tentative.[15] That analysis indicated that the two-party states in the southern half of New England tended to have programs more liberal toward the poor than did the less competitive three northern states. The thought was that the very conspicuousness of competitive party leaderships would have that effect. That is, if leaders feared that they might be retaliated against because they refused to act favorably toward the "have nots," they might therefore be more likely to act favorably than if the confusing uncertainties of a one-party factional system easily covered up responsibility for who did what. As Key said, "The factional system simply provides no institutional mechanism for the expression of lower bracket viewpoints." And he added that "The great value of the two-party system is not that there are two groups with conflicting policy tendencies from which the voters may choose, but that there are two groups of politicians."[16]

Other scholars were not convinced, however, and did further empirical research to test the idea. Professors Dawson and Robinson collected data for a wide number of welfare and related programs and compared the states in the degree of liberality they showed for those benefits. Then they ran correlations between the program "payoffs," so to speak, and the degree of party competition. They found a positive correlation, but when they compared the payoff rankings with data on the socio-economic characteristics of the states they found an even higher correlation, suggesting that the key factor might not be the character of the party system but the all-important factor of whether the resources were available to allow for the high payoff.[17]

This does not, however, entirely undercut the notion that there may

---

14 V. O. Key, Jr., *Southern Politics in State and Nation* (New York: Alfred A. Knopf, 1949), p. 308.

15 Duane Lockard, *New England State Politics* (Princeton: Princeton University Press, 1959), pp. 226–37.

16 Key, *Southern Politics, op. cit.*, pp. 309–10.

17 Richard E. Dawson and James A. Robinson, "The Politics of Welfare," in Herbert Jacob and Kenneth Vines, eds., *Politics in the American States* (Boston: Little, Brown, 1965), pp. 371ff. Others followed this lead. Thomas Dye using statistically sophisticated methods on an enormous amount of data came to similar

be a relevant connection between the party competition and payoffs, even though on the surface it seems to do so. For the states that are the richest are also the most competitive, and the poorest the most one-party. Therefore, when we measure competition against the policy payoff, we are inadvertently also comparing economic capacity and vice versa.[18] I am led personally to believe that the competition factor has some significance here because of the evidence we have of party leaders actually behaving as if they were afraid of the next election and pressing their followers to take specific actions because of that fear. I have myself witnessed party leaders often angering their own followers when they insist on certain policies as necessary for winning the next election. Indeed, I have seen leaders do this even when the policy in question was very distasteful to them. Because they were in the spotlight of publicity they acted, as they believed, to save the greater cause: winning the next election. How often this happens and how much it may contribute to policies responsive to the have-nots there is no way of demonstrating by any statistical means, but it can hardly be irrelevant.[19]

In any event the dissenting views of these scholars serve one very useful purpose: they force reconsideration of a concept of the party that was too simplified. The party, like other single facets of politics, is but part of a complicated and highly interested series of institutions, beliefs, and practices that form a political *system*. The influence of party, therefore, must be evaluated in terms of the operations of the system not in isolation. Thus one should observe the great differences between two-party systems as there are among one-party setups. It is necessary to establish subcategories of party systems within the basic classifications established above—necessary in order to examine in any detail the comparative effects of different party systems on policy. There are at least five different kinds of party systems, each with distinctly different connotations for state politics. Some of the variations are suggested in the outline below:

---

conclusions; see his *Politics, Economics, and the Public: Policy Outcomes in the American States* (Chicago: Rand McNally, 1966). Richard I. Hofferbert presents similar findings in "The Relation Between Public Policy and Some Structural and Environmental Variables in the American States," 60 *American Political Science Review* 73 (1966).

[18] Statisticians call this problem "multicollinearity." That is, when two factors are closely interrelated, it is nearly impossible to say whether the relationship of either one with a third variable is stronger than the relationship of the other.

[19] See my longer comment on this problem in a volume to be published by Harvard University Press in honor of the late Professor Key and to be edited by Oliver Garceau. And see also John Fenton, *People and Parties in Politics* (Glenview, Ill.: Scott, Foresman, 1966), Chap. 2.

I. Competitive States

    A. Cohesive and strongly led organizations, characterized by one or more of the following:
        1. Clearly identified and continuous leadership.
        2. Leadership control over ascent up the ladder of promotion.
        3. Centralized party finances and centralized operation of party campaigns.
        4. Great party influence in the making of legislative policy.

    B. Splintered and weak organizations, characterized by:
        1. Wide factional cleavage.
        2. Frequent conflicts over nominations; little centralized control over promotion for the ambitious.
        3. Little party leadership influence in the making of legislative policy.

II. The One-Party States

    A. One faction predominant, characterized by:
        1. One faction that is continuous and well-organized, other factions being vague and transitory.
        2. Dominant faction leaders having great influence on nominations.
        3. Dominant faction leaders exert some influence over legislative policy.

    B. Bifactional structure, characterized by:
        1. Two factions more or less continuously in competition with each other.
        2. Some questions of policy get debated in primary contests between factional candidates.
        3. Moderate to minor legislative policy identification of factions.

    C. Multifactional structure, characterized by:
        1. Many factions, discontinuous and vague in composition.
        2. Emphasis on personality conflicts in primary contests.
        3. Confused policy-making in which it is very difficult to fix responsibility.

This is admittedly not a set of categories to which states can be easily assigned; this classification process requires no mere tabulation of statistical information but assessment of detailed, subjective, and qualitative information. Difficulties of application arise—such as the fact that in some states the two parties are so different that they would have to be fitted into different notches rather than into one. For example, in Massachusetts the Democratic party fits category I,B and the Republican I,A. The major advantage of such a classification system is that it highlights distinctions between the different systems and suggests criteria for evaluating the politics of a given state.[20]

Party Operations: The Nomination

The nominating process is the "crucial process of the party," E. E. Schattschneider rightly observes:

> The nature of the nominating procedure determines the nature of the party; he who can make the nominations is the owner of the party. This is therefore one of the best points at which to observe the distribution of power within the party.[21]

Without effective means of designating the party's choice for office, a party is destined to self-defeat. Since parties designate in some form or other the few who are eligible for consideration at general elections, they play a crucial role in determining who is to hold office. By making nominations, the parties reduce the public's choice to two for each office, or even one "choice" where no opposition candidate is offered. Since the party role in narrowing alternatives is important, so also are the methods by which the parties make their choices. These methods are infinitely varied, and it will serve to illustrate some of the key aspects of state politics to assess briefly some of these variations.

In the first place, the formal aspects of the nomination process are not for the parties alone to determine; party nominations, in American practice at least, are subject to legal controls. This has not always been the case; in the beginning of popular politics in this country

---

[20] A somewhat more detailed presentation of this classification system and a tentative application of it is found in Lockard, *New England State Politics, op. cit.,* pp. 324–26. A good indication of the organizational patterns of a state can be found by examining the primary contests that occur in parties over a period of time. When contests for nomination for governor and other major officers are frequently two-way battles, this suggests bifactionalism; races consistently showing crowds of candidates contending indicates multifactionalism, of course. The absence of contests may show the existence of organizational leadership. None of these is conclusive proof that any of these patterns exist; supplementary information can be gleaned once the indicators are located. Caution is advised about making inferences where incumbents are running, since incumbency tends to depress challenge.

[21] E. E. Schattschneider, *Party Government,* p. 64.

nominations were privately conducted. From the pre-town meeting caucuses in Tom Dawes garret about which John Adams made his famous complaint, to the southern Democratic attempts to exclude the Negro from participation in the "White Primary" of those states—the nomination process was deemed a private affair.[22] But the state gradually widened the legal controls over the nomination process and even the federal government took cognizance of the primary when the Supreme Court in a series of decisions from 1927–53 reversed a precedent and made primaries a public affair, thereby restraining Southern politicians from employing the tactics that kept the primary "white." The key decision was Smith v. Allwright which made the primary irrevocably a public and not a private matter.[23]

The laws of the fifty states provide fifty different ways of nominating candidates; no two systems are exactly alike, although one can discern similarities among general types. Basically nominations are made by convention, by direct primary elections or combinations of the two.[24] The state convention has declined in importance as the primary has gained in popularity; in some states the convention is an empty gesture serving no particular purpose beyond the drafting of a platform that will not be much noticed and the designation of unknown party members to serve as members of the electoral college if the party wins the presidential election. In a few states—such as Connecticut, New York, and Indiana—the convention is an important agency since it nominates the most powerful figures of state politics, but there are only about a dozen states which use conventions, and in some of these the powers of the conventions are quite limited.[25] In most cases there is what is called an indirect primary for choosing delegates to the conventions,

---

[22] Adams complained of the meetings of the so-called Caucus Club where "selectmen, assessors, collectors, fire wards, and representatives are regularly chosen before they are chosen in the town." There, he added, "they smoke tobacco till you cannot see from one end of the garret to the other." Quoted by Schattschneider, *ibid.*, p. 41.

[23] 321 U.S. 649 (1944). See Key, *Southern Politics*, pp. 619ff., on this development.

[24] This excludes one method still used in some areas for local nominations—that is, the caucus in which all eligible party members gather in a meeting to designate one of their number as a candidate. This is not very widely used now, but does persist in some New England areas and in a few other states.

[25] In almost all cases the convention is circumscribed in some way—that is, the offices for which the convention may nominate do not include all statewide offices (*e.g.*, Michigan), the convention decision may be challenged in a primary (*e.g.*, in Connecticut), or the convention may be able to do no more than recommend its choice to the voters in an ensuing primary. The biennial *Book of the States* (Chicago, Council of State Governments) gives a state-by-state tabulation of the various methods of nomination in effect. A good review of nomination methods is in V. O. Key's *Politics, Parties and Pressure Groups*, Chap. 14.

but most people pay little attention to it with the result that normally only a handful of the party faithful decide who will be delegates.

Direct primaries, which date from the late nineteenth century, spread gradually across the country, starting in the South in the 1870's, extending to Wisconsin (1903) and Oregon (1904), and then to the Eastern seaboard states. All states had primaries in some form or degree by 1955, when Connecticut joined the fold.[26] At first, the chief motivation of the direct primary movement was the return of some element of public participation in the choice of officials where one party had become so dominant that its convention made the only political decision. In time the objectives of those advocating primaries were broadened. As the parties fell more and more into public disrepute in the late nineteenth century and the early part of the twentieth century, the advocates of primaries began to emphasize the need to curtail the powers of the party bosses and to espouse the idea of turning over to the people the power to nominate. The Muckrakers and the Progressives took over the advocacy of the primary, seeking thereby to undermine the existing party organizations. They were often successful, at least temporarily, in dislodging their enemies with it. The importance of the primary then as now was that it offered an alternative means to power other than winning support of the organizational leaders. Since the degree to which the primary has limited party leadership varies with the type of primary adopted, it is advisable to consider briefly the various kinds of primaries.

One of the most significant distinctions between primaries is that between the open and the closed primary, which essentially means whether or not the primary is open to all eligible voters or is closed except to party members.[27] Open primaries operate in several different ways: the voter is allowed to choose the party he prefers and votes entirely within that party, or he is offered a single ballot on which the lists of candidates contending within both parties appear and the voter is then allowed to vote for one person for each office, crossing back and forth between the party lists if he desires. The latter system, called a "blanket" primary and used only in Washington State, is the ultimate in diminishing the significance of the party organization in choice of candidates; it not only eliminates the question of party membership

---

[26] Key, in his *American State Politics* (pp. 87–97), gives the best brief history of the rise of primaries that I know of. For the story of how the last of the states capitulated, see Duane Lockard, *Connecticut's Challenge Primary: A Study in Legislative Politics* (New York: McGraw-Hill Book Co., 1959).

[27] See the detailed analysis of open and closed primary systems in C. A. Berdahl, "Party Membership in the United States," 36 *American Political Science Review* 16–50, 241–62 (1942).

but offers a cafeteria-style list of hopefuls from which to pick.[28] Somewhat similar to the open primary is the so-called cross-filing system used in California until 1959. By this device a Republican candidate could file to run in the Democratic primary as well as in the Republican one, and the more popular candidates—particularly incumbents—often eliminated the necessity to compete in the general election by winning the primaries of both parties. This became more difficult to do in 1952 when the law was amended to require that candidates state their party affiliation on the ballot beside their names. This has had the result of sharply diminishing the chances of winning the nominations of both parties.[29] This was the first step toward the abolition of the system which had its origins in the era of progressivism in 1913.

The closed primary system, which is the method of all but about half a dozen states, presumably allows only registered party members to participate, but there are some states in which "crossing-over" (also called "raiding" and "colonizing") is possible. Exactly how common or how effective the "raiding" process is, it is difficult to tell, but there are apparently instances of organized efforts to get members of a party to vote in the primary of the opposite party in order to help nominate the "least" desired—that is, the least formidable—candidate. It is said that this process went on in 1946 when the late Joseph E. McCarthy first was elected to the United States Senate—the Democrats voted in Wisconsin's open primary for McCarthy as the easier Republican to beat in the general election. If they actually did influence his ultimate election in this way, many of them must have rued their activities in due time. In 1962 Texas Republicans by public advertisement openly encouraged their members to raid the Democratic gubernatorial primary and vote for the liberal candidate, hoping thereby to improve Republican chances in November. It does appear, however, that most closed primaries are in fact closed.

---

[28] That is, it is the ultimate unless one reserves for that designation the "nonpartisan primary" which is close to being a contradiction in terms. This refers to the first round of elections in a nonpartisan balloting system in which the number of candidates is reduced for the final election.

[29] In the period 1940–52, according to Joseph Harris, 84 per cent of the state senate candidates won the nominations of both parties in this fashion. See Joseph P. Harris, *California Politics* (Stanford, Calif.: Stanford University Press, 1955), pp. 39–42. Robert J. Pitchell reports in detail on the rise and decline of the cross-filing system in "The Electoral System and Voting Behavior: The Case of California's Cross-Filing," 12 *Western Political Quarterly* 459 (1959). He shows that the total number of candidates who won both nominations declined sharply—from about two-thirds to less than a quarter of all candidates. Thus the percentage of double nomination winners runs as follows: 1950: 68.7 per cent; 1952: 71.8 per cent; 1954: 26.2 per cent; 1956: 24.4 per cent.

Two further terms commonly used to describe types of primaries should be explained: the *runoff primary* and the *challenge primary*. The former is an elimination contest, used in Southern states, where the primary is tantamount to election, to decide between the two leading contestants when neither has managed to win a majority in the first primary. The term *challenge primary* is applied to a system which allows the party organization tentatively to designate candidates who will stand as the final nominees unless there is a challenge to these endorsees in a primary election. Several states use variations on this method, the most recently developed one being that of Connecticut.[30] The basic objective of this style of primary is to preserve the party organization's function as nominator while simultaneously providing a stick with which to discipline the party when it steps over what rebels think are the bounds of propriety. This, in short, moves from exactly the opposite thesis of the cross-filing or blanket primary system which denies the value of the party organization rather than sustaining it.

Thus, in a sense, the challenge primary represents a deviation from what Schattschneider calls a hypertrophy of the nominating process.[31] This hypertrophy of nominating procedures is probably a basic cause of the atrophy of party organization. Is it possible to show that the primary as an alternative means to power has diminished the place of party in our politics? Although it is difficult to assign the causes of such a decline to any single factor, V. O. Key developed an impressive array of evidence to suggest a connection between this decline and the spread of the primary. His major evidence is the disappearance of local party organizations in districts where there is one-party dominance. (This is, of course, not limited to the South—in every state there are counties, cities, and towns dominated by one party.) At least one reason why nominations may not be made in such places is a sense of hopelessness, but this is not enough of an explanation, for in some areas nominations do go on being made by the underdog party. But such nominations are made only where there is an organization effective enough to take the trouble. If nominations continue to be made where the primary is little used and nominations fall off where it is used, one has some ground for inferring that perhaps the primary is a contributing cause. To cite Key's data, here are the "proportions of legislative seats uncon-

---

[30] For a brief description of this law, see Duane Lockard, "Connecticut Gets a Primary," 44 *National Municipal Review* 469 (1955); for a brief review of the initial operation of the law see the same journal, Vol. 45, p. 494. The National Municipal League has sponsored a somewhat similar type of primary. See *A Model Direct Primary Election System* (New York: National Municipal League, 1951).

[31] Schattschneider, *op. cit.*, p. 99.

tested at the general elections" for four states, the first two of which adopted primaries late or in a limited way and the second two of which adopted primaries fully and early.[32]

	1908	1948
Connecticut	2.4%	4.8%
Indiana	1.0	5.0
Ohio	1.8	18.5
Missouri	1.4	21.4

Key warns against assuming that this correlation proves that over-emphasis on nomination by primary has been *the* cause of the decline of party, yet he does say that the "data make it difficult to reject the hypothesis that the creation by direct primary legislation of new channels to power, more readily accessible and less readily monopolized than antecedent procedures, operates over the long run to modify the nature of the informal structure of party leadership in biparty systems."[33] The modification of party to which Key refers has been a change conducive to atrophy of party organizations.

Does this show then that the primary has in fact done what its sponsors hoped it would—remove from the party leadership the control over nominations and turn it over to the people? It would be safe to say that the primary has frequently removed the monopoly over the channels to power once held by party leaders, but it does not therefore follow that that leadership is everywhere shorn of significant power over nominations or that the "people" have gained control over nominations. Party leaders often maintain considerable influence over the primaries by giving their influential backing to prospective candidates through formal or informal means. Whether or not party organizations can assert this power depends upon the nature of the party as well as upon the nature of the primary. Evidence of this is the case of the Massachusetts Democratic party. Deeply divided by factional strife, Massa-

[32] Key, *American State Politics*, p. 190. In New Hampshire an even more exaggerated decline took place between 1908 and 1950: in 1908 2.1 per cent of the seats were unchallenged and in 1950 the proportion had jumped to 59 per cent. See Lockard, *New England State Politics*, pp. 55–57, and also Malcolm E. Jewell, "Party and Primary Competition in Kentucky State Legislative Races," 248 *Kentucky Law Journal* 517 (1960). See also his paper presented at the 1962 convention of the American Political Science Association, "Competition and Factionalism in Southern Legislative Primaries and Elections."

[33] *Ibid.*, p. 194.

chusetts Democrats consistently opposed the institution of a state convention to recommend candidates for a primary to follow the convention, while the more tightly organized Republicans have consistently supported a convention. The reason is obvious, of course: the Republicans had the organizational muscle to make good use of the convention, whereas the Democrats feared the convention as an invitation to bitter battling. With the institution of conventions in 1954, Republicans managed to assert more effective control over their nominations (as evidenced by the sudden diminution of the number of candidates contesting for offices in the state primaries), while the Democrats held conventions that erupted into fistfights and produced few effective endorsements.[34] Given these variations within a single state, it is therefore difficult to pass judgment on how far the primary has actually gone in denying the organization its powers; in many cases it has apparently contributed to the total elimination of the organization, but in others the organization has learned to live with and to dominate the primary.

As to whether the primary has turned nominations over to the "people," the answer is readily apparent: it has not—at least if we are talking about operational control over the nominating process. That the mass of the people have relatively little interest in the typical primary is evidenced by the low turnout for most primaries. Of course, one must qualify the degree to which the people exert effective influence through the primary by distinguishing between the one-party and the competitive states. There is no doubt that in the one-party states, although the proportion of potential voters participating may not be very impressive in some cases, the primary is nevertheless a great gain in popular influence since the alternative is virtually no popular role at all. It is true that competitive states can have primaries that are decisively important and that the voter's influence can be significant in the most dramatic of these contests. The turnout may not match that of the general election but it may often amount to a million or more voters in the larger states. Campaigns are intensive and expensive and roughly comparable to general elections. In this case the "people" obviously have a significant opportunity to affect the decision. Still, the typical case in the competitive states is very different; usually the drab and unexciting "contests" draw so few participants that it would be taking an unjustified liberty with the language to call that "control" by the people. Thus V. O. Key calculated the voting participation in primaries as compared with general elections in fifteen nonsouthern states and the

---

[34] See Lockard, *New England State Politics*, pp. 132ff., on this development in Massachusetts. See John Fenton on the variable roles of the primary in his *Midwest Politics* (New York: Holt, Rinehart and Winston, 1966).

tremendous difference between the turnout for the two kinds of elections is impressive. Less than 35 per cent of the potential electorate voted the combined Democratic and Republican primaries between 1926 and 1952 in no less than 73.9 per cent of the elections, but of the general elections in that period only 3.9 per cent had such a scant turnout. At the other extreme—those elections which got 60 per cent or more of the people to vote—only 1.7 per cent of the primaries qualified in comparison to 55.1 per cent of the general elections.[35] Often the primary seems to draw only the most faithful of the workers of the party who ratify the decisions of the organization.[36] In other cases, especially in the less competitive or the one-party states, exciting primary races may produce a very heavy turnout and a significant role for the voters in making nominations. In short, the primary does most to enhance the "people's" participation in one-party states and little affects popular power in most competitive-state races.

Perhaps the most significant aspect of the primary has been the opening the channels to public office to those who do not have the blessing of party leaders. With money, a following, and a "personality" a candidate can appeal directly to the people and win. These "left-handed banjo players," as V. O. Key used to call them, may have further contributed to the atrophy of parties.

Party Operations: The Campaign

I once heard a campaign speech open with the story of a truly tired campaigner who, sitting on the side of his bed with a sock in hand and a quizzical look on his face, heard his wife ask, "What's wrong, dear?" To which he replied, "Tell me, am I going to bed or getting up?" This is a bit farfetched, but in the midst of a campaign it is certainly not uncommon for a campaigner to arise before the sun does. Politicians in the thick of a campaign are usually uncertain how they stand; they are never sure if their ammunition is hitting the target and, if so, with what effect. To the campaigner, the race seems to involve everybody and everything he comes into contact with; to the world, neither the candidate nor the race exists until recognition is inescapable. Forcing people to take notice

---

[35] Key, op. cit., p. 135. See also K. H. Porter, "The Deserted Primary in Iowa," 39 American Political Science Review 732 (1945).

[36] This is particularly true of primary elections for party officials—local and county chairman, for example. Most voters appear to care very little about who runs a party.

is the most important part of the campaign, but it is hard to achieve. The following is, if not typical, at least as a realistic day of campaigning for a candidate for a state senate seat in a district of some fifty thousand people.

5:00: Rise to go to a machine tool factory to greet workers at the gate in the company of the candidate for Congress.

6:30: Have coffee with the candidate for Congress, speculating about how things are going; nobody knows.

7:00: Back home to write up press releases on yesterday's talks to be left with the reporters on the way back to town.

8:00: Drive to the printers office for conference on the composition of a flyer to be used the Sunday before election; pained discussion of how and when this will be paid for.

9:30: Drive to the radio station to cut tapes to be played as one minute spot announcements; pained financial discussion.

10:30: Drive to a home in a housing project where loyal workers have invited a dozen housewives to meet the candidate over a cup of coffee. (By the end of the campaign, coffee and cookies taste like lye water and mud pies, but you smile and thank warmly.)

12:00: Back to town, jump on a bus, pay the fare and ride ten blocks, shaking hands down both sides of the aisle; then jump another bus and ride back ten blocks, shaking more hands.

1:00: Luncheon talk at the Kiwanis Club meeting (strictly nonpartisan remarks); much handshaking and friendly introductions to living persons over twenty-one years old.

2:30: Dash into party headquarters and warmly praise the workers who are stuffing envelopes and licking stamps.

3:00: Join the candidate for sheriff and make a tour of the shopping center, passing out red, white and blue pencils with "Send Sam to the Senate" printed on them. (Not fully paid for yet either.)

5:00: Home for a clean shirt and to remind (*i.e.*, insist) the family to be available Saturday afternoon for the Federated Woman's Political Club campaign picnic at the lake.

7:00: Dinner and a short speech at the Polish Club; nobody seems to marvel at, nor even to notice, how you managed to connect that noble spirit, Ignace Paderewski, with the current campaign for the state senate.

9:00: Only an hour late for the rally in the next town; set speech to the faithful who have heard it before but applaud warmly.

11:00: Conference at the hotel bar with the major leaders of the party and some other candidates. Major question is, how are things going? Nobody seems to know.

12:30: Home to look over the newspaper, review some campaign material from state headquarters, fall asleep while reading. . . .[37]

Candidates for higher office do not have to do so much of their own dirty work—like arguing with the printer or running off their own news

---

[37] If this seems extreme, note this news item: "While campaigning for governor, Joseph Ward was able to get home only occasionally. One night his two-year-old daughter Charlotte suddenly spotted her father's image on the television screen and exclaimed: 'Mummy, that man comes here.' "—*The New York Times*, February 21, 1961.

stories, typed two-finger style, but they have infinitely greater headaches
—one of which is trying to run a campaign while coordinating a staff
which is supposed to be doing all the menial chores but may not be. In
short, campaigning requires organization, although whether the organization is personal or coordinated with that of other candidates through
the party depends upon local circumstances. In some states, the lone-
wolf operation is standard and all effort tends to be individualistic; the
party's campaign and all other candidates are ignored, and the rule of
every-man-for-himself applies. In other states, the financing, planning,
and conduct of campaigns are coordinated and every effort is made to present a united front against the opposition. Of course, the degree of coordination of a campaign is inevitably limited by the fact that each
candidate has his own style of campaigning, and, since candidates tend to
be prima donnas, there is always somebody who, in Navy parlance, "didn't
get the word"—or didn't want to. Yet in the cacophony which is a campaign the wrong thing said is usually drowned out by the surrounding din
of voices.

The problems—both ethical and practical—of conducting election
campaigns are so numerous and complicated that to be brief one must be
superficial, yet the power potential of election is so vast that the risk of
superficiality must be taken.[38] The essential problem is to project a favorable image to as many potential voters as possible, alienating few and
persuading many that the candidate in question is the best choice. To get
this favorable impression across to people who are defensive and skeptical
toward the blandishments of politicians and who are often not terribly
concerned with who wins elections is no mean undertaking. The means
of communicating with this amorphous public may be marvelous, but
the very fact that the voter is pummelled from all sides makes him
resistant to campaigning. There are so many people and so many means
of getting messages to them that the complexity (and cost) of the
campaigning process seems to grow with the passing years. But there are
now, as there were in the campaign of 1840 when the battle cry was
"Tippecanoe and Tyler Too," certain essential and relatively unchanging
features of the campaigning process.

Essentially campaigning involves the adroit use of the media available
for communicating the most positive side of the candidacy with what
money can be rounded up to do the job and with such manpower as can
be mustered. The media of communication are infinitely more abundant
than ever before: television, radio, magazines, billboards, leaflets, news-

---

[38] The rationality, probity, and some ultimate implications of campaigning are
analyzed with insight by Stanley Kelley, Jr., in *Political Campaigning: Problems of
Creating an Informed Electorate* (Washington, D.C.: Brookings Institution, 1960).

papers, rapid transportation which enables the candidate personally to come into contact with vast numbers of people. While the newer means of communication, such as television, may be conducive to irrelevancy— the candidate's fine family rather than his possible policies—it does force the candidate to address himself to the whole community and not to segregated units of it to which he can make different and perhaps contradictory appeals. There are many in the electorate who strongly contend that seeing the moving picture of a candidate's face on the screen gives them insight into his character. The kinds of media that can be employed depend, of course, on the size of the constituency. A candidate running for representative of a small town has no need for television, and a candidate for governor who depended on door-to-door canvassing would be wasting his time.

The methods employed through the media are infinitely varied, but the major tactic is the presentation of a favorable image of the candidate through appropriate manipulation of words and symbols. In short, campaigning involves propaganda. The candidate seeks to make people believe what he wants them to believe and to act on that belief. Campaigning is an adversary proceeding, a form of relatively polite warfare —the source of the word *campaign* is military, of course—and therefore the nicely reasoned, coolly objective presentation of all sides of issues can hardly be expected of candidates. Indeed, reasoned discourse is so unexpected that an approach to such is a pleasant and perhaps rewarding innovation. To "accentuate the positive and eliminate the negative" is standard form as a candidate seeks to associate himself with favorable symbols (liberty, free enterprise, patriotism, national destiny, economic progress) and to evoke positive response thereby.

The stakes in a campaign are so high that there is strong temptation to find something positive to accent whether there is much there or not. There is a well-nigh inevitable urge to find out what people would like to hear and to tell them that rather than to assess a situation boldly and try to win by facing realities and offering leadership to cope with the future. It is quite possible to manipulate symbols so as to leave an essentially false impression which may help win campaigns but at the same time diminish public faith in the democratic process itself. A candidate not overburdened with scruples about the limits of decency in campaigning has at his command today an awesome array of means to his ends—the falsified photograph which suggests his opponent is something he is not, the subtly but constantly reiterated innuendo, the irresponsible charge without foundation but with great amplification through the myriad media of communication. Such tactics have apparently won elections on occasion.[39]

It is common to attribute to public relations experts the "decline" of political morality in campaigning. But the responsibility cannot be theirs alone, nor even chiefly, since the campaigner must ultimately bear responsibility for what gets said and done in the campaign. Campaigning is similiar in some respects to commercial advertising in which there is some question about the guiding ethical principles, to say the least. But campaigning is also very different from advertising; the objectives are of a different order and so are the responsibilities. Most politicians probably recognize this, but there are always those who do not and will therefore resort to whatever tactics seem most likely to get results. One public relations man is reported to have said: "The generality of candidates . . . only know that they're ambitious and not much else. We take it from there."[40] This is an exaggeration, of course, one that glorifies the role of the word-smith beyond its common contribution to campaigns. But, suggesting as it does a willingness to turn over to the adviser a responsibility for content, it raises serious ethical and practical questions whenever it occurs.

The multiplication of not only the means of communication but also of the electorate itself has sent campaign costs higher and higher. It probably is true that the proportionate cost of campaigning has decreased rather than increased as a result of the newer means of communication—one half-hour on television may be expensive but it reaches an incredible number of people—but the gross costs soar and therefore candidates must worry about money: where to get it, how to get it, how to use it most advantageously, and how to minimize the fact that somebody had to finance the campaign and may therefore want recognition because he did contribute. These are among the toughest problems of campaigning.[41] Although state laws limit campaign expenditures and require reporting of all such expenditures, it is safe to say that the laws

---

[39] See Stanley Kelley, *Professional Public Relations and Political Power, op. cit.,* pp. 109–43, on the Butler-Tydings campaign for the United States Senate in Maryland in 1950. This suggests the lengths to which conscious falsification can go.

[40] *Ibid.,* p. 234. See also Robert J. Pitchell, "The Influence of Professional Campaign Management Firms in Partisan Elections in California," 11 *Western Political Quarterly* 278 (1958).

[41] Oregon and North Dakota print at public expense campaign pamphlets in which candidates are given space to have their say; California prints such a document for all items on the ballot for referenda. Stanley Kelley expresses the opinion that the laws of the first two states have helped the "poor man" candidate even in a contest with the well-financed one. He also is of the opinion that all these have materially improved the level of a campaign discussion. *Political Campaigning,* p. 41.

are observed in the breach more than in compliance. This is partly because the laws are often not reasonable—placing impossible restrictions on the amount of money a candidate may spend—and partly because a live-and-let-live attitude has been adopted on the matter.[42] In almost half the states corporations may contribute to campaigns for state and local offices, as labor unions may in all but four states—in contrast to federal law which forbids such contributions in federal elections.

Waging a statewide campaign, especially since it may mean two elections, a primary and the general, may in larger states cost more than a million dollars or more which means that the candidate and his party must solicit help and thereby incur obligations. There can be no escaping the fact that campaign contributions can lead to obligations which may be "paid off" through policy actions of the elected official. At its worse this may lead to gross distortion of the interests of the community in behalf of perhaps the worst elements of the society—the gamblers, for example—and at the more innocent level it may involve the harmless recognition of the financial angel with some honorary plum. The high cost of campaigning therefore opens the way to misdeeds, but this is not to say that invariably the payer of the piper gets to call the tune. It simply does not follow that a candidate to whom money has been given is thereby bought. The giver may not have intended a purchase in the first place, but even if he did the *quid pro quo* may not be forthcoming for any number of reasons. The main reason, however, is easily understood: Money is important and it is a means to influence, but votes are necessary too and activities that jeopardize votes are dangerous in the extreme to the politician who expects to make a career of officeholding. In a sense, campaigns are not limited to the weeks just before elections; they are waged the year round. The governor finds it expedient to accept speaking engagements before Chambers of Commerce, at county fairs, party functions, and commemorative events, for the impression he makes with his appearances and with the policies are the reserves to be called upon in the

---

[42] The definitive work on money in politics is Alexander Heard's *The Costs of Democracy* (Chapel Hill, N.C.: University of North Carolina Press, 1960). An attempt to provide a more workable political finance control law in Florida is described in E. E. Roady's article, "Florida's New Campaign Expense Law and the 1952 Democratic Gubernatorial Primaries," 48 *American Political Science Review* 465 (1954). Also instructive are Herbert Alexander's dissertation, "The Role of the Volunteer Fund Raiser: A Case Study in New York in 1952," Yale University Library, 1958; and John White and John Owens, *Parties, Group Interests and Campaign Finance: Michigan '56* (Princeton, N.J.: Citizens Research Foundation, 1960). The Citizens Research Foundation has published many excellent short monographs on campaign spending; readers interested in this issue will find them most helpful. See also the *Book of the States* for a table presenting state by state provisions on campaign expenditures (for 1966–67, pp. 28–31).

weeks of formal campaigning. If the governor concedes so much to his financial backers that negative impressions are created, he jeopardizes his position. Admittedly the chances of concealing concessions are good and leave latitude for maneuver, but this should not obscure an important fact about money in politics generally: it is one among many means of influencing players in the game but is not the absolute force it is sometimes supposed.

Finally a campaign needs manpower—people to do all manner of chores necessary for a campaign. A campaign requires the enlistment of a great number of volunteer workers to do innumerable tasks—arrange meetings, organize activities generally (somebody has to keep the schedule straight, type letters, maintain liaison with the press, distribute literature, make arrangements with television stations, and so on). Although the proportion of the population actually willing to do this kind of work is limited—less than a tenth of the people do any active political work—the contribution of those who do labor is indispensable.

What good does it all do? Does campaigning really make any difference in the long run? Politicians certainly think so, and are deadly serious in their approach to the process, but that doesn't necessarily make it what they think it is. The blunt fact is that most people appear to have made up their minds about how they will vote by the time nominations are made—and in some cases even before. For most people vote the same party ticket election after election and in the short run are surprisingly consistent—perhaps three-quarters or more of those who vote in two successive elections vote the same way. And there is no evidence that campaigning persuades many voters to change their minds. Campaigns serve another function, however, and one of considerable importance: they stir up the regulars, arouse their interest, and get them to talking about the campaign—thereby assuring that they will take the trouble to vote on election day. For those without strong convictions about parties, issues, or candidates, the campaign may serve to make them aware that something is going on, and hopefully their latent interests may be aroused and they may be persuaded to participate. Thus nobody quite dares not to campaign at all, for if the other side does campaign, silence may be disastrous, unless of course the opposition is so inept or unfavored as to be insignificant.

Elections are won chiefly by persuading the vaguely interested and the frankly uninterested to participate. The most strongly committed can be depended upon to vote and to follow their partisan convictions almost regardless of what the campaign produces. They are rarely open to persuasion. And indeed the so-called independents, who value their sense of detachment and lack of partisanship, are often about as regular in their voting habits as are the partisans. They may shift slightly more often and may split their tickets more frequently, but they are not as numerous as is sometimes supposed, and therefore they are not as likely to be as influential a factor in elections as the folklore of politics would have us believe. The independents are far fewer in number than those who float in and out of the electorate from year to year, and it is the latter therefore who are more often decisive.

Nonvoting thus assumes major importance in the analysis of American politics. There are certain elemental facts about voting participation that we ought to consider here, and Figure 8-2 shows some of those facts. Nonvoting is most common among those of low income, poor education, and low status. Voting regularity is most frequent among those of high status, high income, and good education. A recent analysis of voting registration in New York City showed a definite correlation between the wealth of the neighborhood and the high percentages of voter registration. In Manhattan, for example, the districts with the lowest income and the greatest proportions of Negroes and Puerto Ricans had less than half their eligible population registered, but the wealthier districts had 60–70 per cent of their eligible registered.[43]

The Republican party draws its most reliable support from the higher socioeconomic groups and the Democrats from the lower ones. This is not to say that there are no rich Democrats and no poor Republicans, for each of us knows of many illustrations to prove that there are, but the tendency is remarkably consistent for the bulk of these groups to go their separate ways. Thus even when the Republicans are most popular, as for example when President Eisenhower was winning by a landslide in 1956, the lower economic groups gave him much less support than the high income groups did. There are many more people in the low income brackets than in the high ones (although the top and bottom extremes shown in Figure 8-2 are roughly equal proportions of the population), with the consequence that there are more people inclined toward the Democratic than toward the Republican party across the country generally. Why then do Democrats not have all national elections won before they begin? The reason is the variation in turnout; lower economic groups do well to turn out as many as 50 per cent of their potential votes whereas the upper income groups, as the diagram indicates, vote to the extent of 80 or 90 per cent. This should not be taken to mean that all those of lower income who stay at home are lost votes for the Democratic party, for that is

---

[43] See *The New York Times*, June 30, 1962.

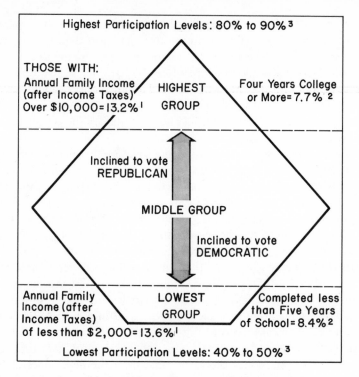

Figure 8-2. Voter Participation and Party Inclination Relative to Income and Education Levels

[1] Source: *Statistical Abstract*, 1962, p. 330; the data in both cases are for 1960.
[2] Source: *Statistical Abstract*, 1962, p. 117; data are for persons over 25 years of age as of 1960.
[3] Source: Robert E. Lane, *Political Life* (New York: The Free Press, 1959), pp. 48–49. The original source of most of Lane's data was the work of the Survey Research Center at Michigan University.

not the case. Many a hard-working Democrat labored on election day to turn out a big vote in 1952 and 1956 only to find that his faithful Democratic friends were voting for President Eisenhower.[44] Fear born of economic crisis, the attraction of a dramatic personality, or other strong motivations can pull voters from their normal learnings—certainly in presidential elections, and sometimes in elections for lesser offices as well. In most situations, however, the lower-class penchant for voting Demo-

---

[44] See the analysis of this process by scholars at the Survey Research Center at the University of Michigan, Angus Campbell, Philip Converse, Warren Miller and Donald Stokes, *The American Voter* (New York: John Wiley & Sons, Inc., 1960), Chap. 5. This is the most sophisticated yet of the analyses of voting behavior.

cratic and the upper-class allegiance to the Republican party are basic facts of our politics.[45]

The State of State Politics

The public attitude toward state politics is not particularly favorable. There are several reasons for this, the most prominent of which is that it is often a quite justified opinion. There is a great deal of timidity, confusion, and evasion of responsibility in state politics, and although there are dedicated and able people at work in these vineyards, there are an impressive lot of opportunists playing the field. Worse still, there are in the politics of many states those who take advantage of their position in the legislature or a government bureau to supplement their income dishonestly. No doubt the negative attitudes are also in part the result of the low visibility of state affairs; the public little hears nor long remembers the good that state government does but its evil actions make the front page. A crooked treasurer is news; an honest and efficient one is not. Thus, where low visibility in general prevails and only the more conspicuous events are seen at all, the impression may be even more negative than the reality warrants.

Yet the reality is bad enough. In too many states the public impression of a drab, evasive, or corrupt politics is more or less accurate. Frequently the quiet and obscure political situation in a state conceals from public scrutiny great influence in the government on the part of a few interest whose narrow concern prevails over more inclusive but less strategically placed groups. In the past, even more than now, certain kinds of interests —particularly those dealing in natural resources such as natural gas and oil, water power, timber, and minerals—dominated state governments. In the heyday of expansion of the American economy, the purchase of public officials was a common practice and many state governments fell under the almost complete control of coal interests, copper companies, or railroad combines. It was understandable—particularly in the case of the extractive industries—that they should come to involve themselves so deeply in state affairs: public ownership of mineral or water rights made it necessary to deal with government, and in an era of expansionist enthusiasm and not very high political ethics the quickest and surest

---

[45] This has, of course, not always been the case; before 1932 the Republican party's hold on the middle class was firmer than it now is, and the lower economic groups were much more Republican before the Depression broke the spell that had existed from the post-Civil War era down to the 1920's.

way of controlling the desired rights was merely to purchase the officials who had the power to grant them.

Happily this is not a widespread problem today; few states, if any, sink to that level. A wider variety of competitive forces clash in a more pluralistic order, rendering the strangleholds of the past difficult—if not impossible—to achieve. Yet there are powerful groups which take advantage of the calm and inconspicuous operations of state politics to further their desires. In hard fact, state governments are often quite unresponsive to the needs and desires of the people without wealth and organized power. Such people find it difficult to influence governmental policy. This is not the only level of government where this is true, but it is a particularly chronic problem in many states.

In general the one-party states present the least responsive and most corrupt political systems. The factional confusion of noncompetitive politics is made to order for well-placed and powerful interests who strike bargains with irresponsible politicians and in inconspicuous ways manage to achieve their objectives, often with total disregard for the interests or desires of wider elements of the society. Seemingly low-pressure, inactive government may conceal backstage politics of the most objectionable sort. Thus the oil interests in Louisiana have long found it advantageous to reward deserving politicians with oil stocks. And in recognition of the potential importance of public utilities, Huey Long began his rise to fame by serving on the Public Service Commission. (Note: the power to regulate is also the power *not* to regulate.) The late Eugene Talmadge, when he was Governor of Georgia, put on a great performance in pretense of concern for the little man, but as Key said of him: ". . . like many professed champions of the forgotten man, in the showdown [he] turned up on the side of the fellows who did the forgetting."[46]. The business community and Talmadge liked each other very much, and for reasons that were not hard to find once the policies were being made. In Alabama there are always politicians who take to the stump to berate the "Big Mules" who are said to dominate the state, but the Big Mules go on and effective counterorganization does not appear. It should not be assumed that one-party government is merely another term for dishonesty and corruption in government. The Virginia state government is said to respect a code of honesty, and the same is true of one-party Vermont. In neither state is the government as responsive to the needs of the citizenry as many would have them be—especially in the case of Virginia —but the qualities of the two communities and the character of their political leaders have prevented a decline into skullduggery.

---

[46] Key, *Southern Politics*, p. 116.

It does not follow that two-party states are free of such practices. In many states with competitive politics the level of chicanery is indistinguishable from that in many one-party states. The state of California has parties that are relatively evenly matched in voting strength, yet until very recently it had a reputation for legislative morality that would have won the state no laurel wreaths. Artie Samish, who began as a liquor lobbyist, reportedly parlayed his position into one of the near-command over the legislature, controlling decisive votes indirectly in contest after contest over important legislation. Samish came to grief in 1953 when he was convicted of income tax evasion, but before the federal government took him out of politics, he had managed for a decade to assert extraordinary power in California's politics.[47] No doubt part of his power derived from the confusion and undisciplined individualism of California's nonpartisan atmosphere. His main source of power was his control over the large sums of cash he could offer legislators who needed campaign contributions in order to stay in office. Other examples could be cited. For example, in Rhode Island the press has reported several times on members of the House of Representatives who, although recorded as "present" in the House chamber, were in truth working behind the two-dollar window at certain horse tracks, the owners of which were eager to have a friendly legislature. The records for probity of Illinois and Massachusetts, both competitive states, would not pass stringent tests, to say the least.[48]

The point, however, is not that the existence of party competition is an unfailing remedy for the evils that can settle over state politics. All too frequently parties in competitive states are ill-led, faction-ridden, corrupt, and inefficient. The potential contribution of these parties is not even approached, let alone realized. Yet where there is competition there is a possibility for improvement, for the simple reason that the ins are opposed by the outs and each tries to turn to its advantage any indiscretion of the other. The visibility of the major parties and the pressures of election uncertainty are disciplinary rods and may induce a certain caution. One must grant that this leaves a broad avenue open for irresponsibility and that state parties can and do often join in unholy alliances of agree-

---

[47] See Lester Velie, "The Secret Boss of California," *Collier's* (August 13 and August 20, 1949). Velie's article led to legislation in 1949 and 1950—once the publicity had been spread, legislators dared not ignore the situation. See also William Buchanan's substantial analysis of the California situation in his *Legislative Partisanship: The Deviant Case of California* (Berkeley: University of California Press, 1963).

[48] On Massachusetts political morality, see Murray Levin, *The Compleat Politician* (New York: Bobbs-Merrill Company, Inc., 1962). See also Edgar Litt, *The Political Cultures of Massachusetts* (Cambridge, Mass.: M.I.T. Press, 1965).

ment not to exploit the possibilities of the competitive situation. They make agreements, for example, that the outs of the moment will not complain about the ins using insurance premiums on state property insurance policies as a patronage reward to faithful insurance men-party workers, with, of course, reciprocity expected when outs become ins.[49] Yet on the whole it does appear that the threat of election day enhances the opportunity of the mass of the electors, or potential electors, to bring pressure to bear on the official holders of governmental authority. It is perfectly true, as we have observed earlier, that a great proportion of the voters do not participate in politics even to the extent of voting biennially. In a one-party situation, the apathetic and the active alike are hard pressed to find any effective means to get at those they consider responsible for whatever they dislike. Once aroused, even the apathetic elements become potentially powerful in a competitive situation for the simple reason that there does exist an organized opposition, hungry for office and ready to exploit the misdeeds of the incumbents.

If this is the case, then how do we move toward achieving two-party competition in state politics? Apparently there is nothing we can do to change the climate of politics by conscious actions; the social, economic, historical, and political conditions of a community determine whether or not there will be competition. Traditional attachments deep in the history of a community align voting habits that change only very gradually. Uniformity of interests may solidify the position—as, for example, the historic one-crop economy of the South and devotion to the low tariff of the Democratic party, by the same token, the development of strong labor unions and the movement of the Democratic party in recent generations to a position sympathetic with labor's demands has led other areas to one-partyism (although in no state is there a labor-dominated one-party situation). Northern agricultural regions combine agrarian conservatism with Republican attachments that go back to the days when leaders of the Grand Army of the Republic shouted, "Vote as you shot, boys, vote as you shot!" There are, in short, a number of fortuitous factors that appear to determine the political predilections of a state at any given time.[50]

Changing deeply set party voting habits is difficult and only the most extreme situations can impel the deeply habituated voters to break with

---

[49] Standard practice in Connecticut until 1963 when, following an investigation of abuse of the insurance gratuity game, it was abolished.

[50] V. O. Key has examined these phenomena in some detail in his *American State Politics*, Chap. 8; see also his study of the persistence of traditional voting attachments in "Partisanship and County Office: The Case of Ohio," 47 *American Political Science Review* 525 (1953).

the past. One-party dominance tends to be self-perpetuating since the ambitious who are inclined toward a political career usually follow either the politics of their families—and in one-party regions the odds are naturally in favor of the dominant party—or, if they have no deep convictions, the ambitious are likely to choose the dominant party so as to get somewhere rather than to fight nobly but inevitably lose. A party's lost reputation may be hard to regain, especially since the opposition is not likely to let the voters forget the record of past infractions. (Thus Democrats prefer to run against Hoover's Depression record, and Republicans against Truman's "five-percenter—mink coat" scandals.) In addition, the development of national party positions, reflecting trends of national political attitudes, may place the national party so decidedly at odds with local sentiments that building up the second party becomes extremely difficult. Thus the liberalism of the national Democratic party is often muted by the local Democratic parties in such states as Maine and North Dakota, while the Lincoln tradition has not been the most notable asset of Republican organizers in the South.

Yet there is a definite trend toward the development of two-party politics nearly everywhere in the nation. This is the understandable result of the nationalizing of our politics, the increasing mobility of Americans from one part of the country to another, the instantaneous communica-

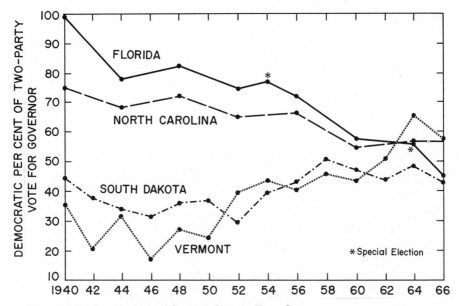

Figure 8-3. The Decline of Sectionalism in Four States

tion of information to the whole nation, the gradual wearing away of traditional attachments to party, and the distribution of industry and commerce across the nation. Sectionalism, which is a basic cause of state one-partyism, is in decline and has been for many years. Although sectionalism has been strong in this century, the second half of the century seems destined to see its rapid erosion. Political trends certainly suggest this. Note the trends in gubernatorial elections set forth in Figure 8-3. The Southern states are those with some semblance of a Republican minority party, a condition that is not uniform over the South by any means.[51]

How far the gradual increase in party competition will go remains to be seen. Whether or not that development improves the quality and responsiveness of government will depend in good measure upon the improvement of existing party organizations in the various states. And in part that improvement is likely to come about only if there is a general reversal of the broadly embraced conviction that parties are worthless or worse than worthless. Whether or not these events take place is an important consideration for the success of the federal system of government, for the state governments will be effective and acceptable agencies of government only so long as they possess political systems that give responsive government.[52]

---

[51] Douglas Gatlin presents interesting evidence on party competition in North Carolina showing a correlation between socioeconomic diversity and party competition. See his paper "Socioeconomic Bases of Party Competition in North Carolina," presented at the 1962 Convention of the American Political Science Association.

[52] A hopeful sign that conditions of party organization may be improving is the fact that within recent decades party organizations in such states as Michigan, Minnesota, Pennsylvania, Connecticut, Maine, and California have improved vastly. Francis Carney, for example, tells an interesting story of the drift of California away from the staunchly antiparty attitudes that had been common there at least since the time of Hiram Johnson and the Progressive movement and toward the gradual development of the Democratic party into something that operates as an organization. See his *The Rise of the Democratic Clubs in California* (New York: McGraw-Hill Book Co., 1958), one of the Eagleton Case Studies in Practical Politics.

9. Municipal Politics

POLITICAL SCIENTISTS have not devoted much of their time to local politics. Why this is so is not easy to say, since the material for study is close at hand and the complexity of the subject offers a challenge. Perhaps the fascination of other aspects of political life and the diversity of governmental systems have kept urban politics from being studied with fervor and intensity equal to that devoted to state and national politics, parties and pressure groups. Here is a fact which illustrates the prevailing situation: unlike presidential and state elections, mayoralty elections have never been the object of sufficient interest to justify extensive compilation of comparative statistics for investigation; on nearly every other phase of local government there is an abundance of data (down to the salaries of fire chiefs and the number of paid days vacation allowed to city employees), but ward-by-ward voting data are exceedingly hard to find.[1]

---

[1] Only recently have data on urban voting in general elections been collected and published. Admittedly the collection of voting data in general has not been done very systematically until recent years, but even now the most conspicuous deficiency in the amassing of these elementary details is the lack of urban voting data. A beginning on the kind of job that needs doing is Richard A. Scammon's series called *America Votes*, four volumes of which have been issued. The first two were published by The Macmillan Company, the others by the University of Pittsburgh Press. For the major cities of the country Scammon has collected voting data for presidential, senatorial, and gubernatorial elections on a ward-by-ward basis. Still, there are no available compilations on municipal elections. Very useful, if as yet only a beginning, are the mimeographed studies being issued by the Joint Center for Urban Studies

Accordingly there are few comparative analyses of municipal politics. Most of the writing on the subject deals with a single city's politics, often in journalistic style.[2] The subject of urban bossism has been the one phase of urban politics studied in depth, yet even that has not been searchingly assessed in comparative terms. What follows is thus more an invitation to take municipal politics seriously than a satisfactory discussion of the subject.

Some Distinguishing Characteristics of Municipal Politics

In one sense, municipal politics is merely politics—the process of exerting influence on public decision-making. Whether the men around the table are cabinet members or city council members, the interrelationships between them which we call "political" are essentially similar. Yet some features of the political process are more characteristic of local affairs than of politics on a broader scale or on a wider territorial and population base, and it may be useful to mention some of these features to set the framework for the analysis that follows.

In the first place personalities play an unusually important role in municipal politics.[3] In a local community it is not only possible to have face-to-face contact between the leading figures of public affairs, it is almost inevitable. In the politics of wider areas, face-to-face meetings are necessarily less frequent.[4] Moreover, the issues about which contests arise

---

at M.I.T. and Harvard under the editorship of Edward C. Banfield. Twenty-two cities were surveyed, and data on political organization, recent policy developments, election statistics, and other similar subjects have been collected. Professor Banfield has summarized information on a number of these cities in his book, *Big City Politics* (New York: Random House, 1965). See also the data and analysis of urban voting in large cities by Charles E. Gilbert and Christopher Clague, "Electoral Competition and Electoral Systems in Large Cities," 24 *Journal of Politics* 323 (1962).

[2] See Robert Daland, "Political Science and the Study of Urbanism," 51 *American Political Science Review* 491 (1957), p. 507.

[3] See Sidney Verba's *The Small Group and Political Behavior* (Princeton, N.J.: Princeton University Press, 1961), for an insightful analysis of interpersonal political relationships.

[4] The smaller the town, the greater the importance of face-to-face relationships. For an incisive analysis of the politics of a small upstate New York town in which the effects of personality clash and of extensive face-to-face contact between the citizenry are outlined, see Arthur J. Vidich and Joseph Bensman, *Small Town in Mass Society* (Princeton, N.J: Princeton University Press, 1958). For a less systematic but illustrative assessment, see Granville Hicks, *There Was a Man in Our Town* (New York: The Viking Press, Inc., 1952), and the same author's

in a city or small town are often more personal in nature than those of higher levels of government. School and playground conditions and the control of noise, smog, crime, dirt, or disease are all matters that may arouse deeply personal concerns or even passionate antagonisms. Note that the street scenes outside schools undergoing integration are dominated by mothers whose faces express more of their emotions than words can convey. The question of whether a block is to be zoned for industry, for commercial development, or for residences may spark bitter personal controversy. The threat of war or the adequacy of the state's conservation policy are important matters to be sure, but their seeming remoteness and complexity put them at arm's length in comparison with the question of traffic light for Johnny and Mary's safety on the way to school.[5] The immediacy of many of the problems of local government and the close personal contacts between the participants in local decisions give a special flavor to local politics.

The politics of the locality is even less autonomous and distinct from that of other political spheres than that of the state. The municipality is the base of several political and governmental systems and therefore cannot escape involvement in the politics of the state and nation. The party organizational units are the same for municipal as for national politics, and in most—although not in all—communities, there is a common core of party activists who man the organizational duty posts in municipal as in state or national political campaigns. Moreover, the city depends upon the state for authority to undertake its programs, which inevitably involves each in the politics of the other. The extent of state supervision of municipal affairs varies, but in some states it is quite broad—involving, for example, state control over the municipal police (as in Boston and St. Louis). Yet it is true that there is still some autonomy, still considerable discretion for local decision-making. Certainly this is true by comparison with most other countries where local discretion is usually much more circumscribed. The fact that American municipal discretion is curtailed should not, in short, lead to the erroneous conclusion that independent local power is nonexistent.

Another politically significant feature of most local governments is their tendency to splinter governmental functions into separate bits

---

earlier study of small town life: *Small Town* (New York: The Macmillan Company, 1946).

[5] The heat that such personal problems can arouse is well-illustrated by the case of the lady who was prominent in the affairs of the Italian-American society of her town and who sought unsuccessfully to have the city amend its zoning ordinances so that she could develop a piece of land she owned. Of an undertaker who as a council member had voted against her she said: "He's seen the last body he'll ever embalm from the Italian Sisterhood."

which are passed to independent boards or commissions with power to conduct that phase of government relatively independently of the other aspects of public policy. Thus school boards are often given independent taxing and budgetary powers as well as general authority to operate schools, and they can use these powers without regard to the conduct of the rest of the city's government. In Los Angeles such miscellaneous functions as management of airports, harbors, libraries, recreation and parks, water supply, and public power are all independently financed and independently conducted. The objective of such independence is, of course, to insulate the function from politics, an objective that independence may or may not achieve. The separation of such functions as education, utilities, fire protection, health, and recreation from the overall responsibilities of the executive and legislative agents of the community is politically important for several reasons. It means that there are many centers of power which may only with difficulty be brought together for effective cooperation in facing problems. It may also mean that the particular clientele of the agency in question will find it easier to achieve their desires by concentrating on the half-dozen people who run an agency rather than having to convince the city council and chief executive who have other, competing interests to consider. There are boards and commissions with relatively independent power on other levels of government in the United States—for example, the independent state and federal regulatory commissions—but even these semi-judicial agencies lack the range of discretionary power often allotted to the special district on the municipal level. For one thing the members of the independent regulatory commission are not normally elective officials who enjoy their own sources of popular support; for another, these state and federal agencies do not have independent revenue authority— the power to levy taxes and draw up their own budgets—which many local boards and commissions have.

Two other significant characteristics of local government should be mentioned: the widespread use of nonpartisanship in electing public officials and the frequent use of referenda in deciding questions. Discussions of both of these factors follow, and no further comment on them is necessary at this stage except to emphasize that nonpartisanship inevitably affects the important process of leadership recruitment and that the use of referenda turn the decision-making process away from the formally constituted officials and tends therefore to affect fundamentally the use of power in the community.

In order to survey and assess some of the leading features of municipal politics, bossism, nonpartisanship, political behavior, local interest groups, and the use of referenda will be discussed in turn.

Bossism

Occasionally a polite debate stirs when someone announces that bossism is now at long last a thing of the past. Thus a reporter for *The New York Times* some years ago wrote a requiem to bossism called "Exit the Boss, Enter the 'Leader,' " making the point that modern conditions militate against the old-style boss and favor instead the more respectable leaders —who manage a political organization, to be sure, but do so more responsibly and usually as prominent officeholders (like Thomas E. Dewey as the Governor and forceful leader of the New York state Republican party).[6] Other students of the phenomenon of bossism dissent and claim, as does Dayton McKean, that "The system of boss and machine, so often pronounced to be moribund, nevertheless persistently refuses to die."[7] So too Robert S. Allen, referring back to the condemnation of urban politics by Lincoln Steffens in the *Shame of the Cities* (1904), said in 1947 that our cities are still "corrupt and content." Behind pretentious façades, he said, is the "same old story of boodling bosses and businessmen, of horrendous slums, of dirt and filth, disease and vice, of gross and shameless waste, of mismanagement and misrule, of crass disregard of public health and human dignity."[8]

What then is the reality? Is bossism fading from the scene or is it still prevalent? Both sides to the argument have some of the truth, for bossism in the old style is no longer so widespread or significant a feature of urban politics as it once was, and yet to pronounce the last rites for bossism is still premature. One must search hard now to find the kinds of colorful bosses that enlivened the local political scene a generation or so ago. "Hinky Dink" Kenna, "Bathhouse John" Coughlin, and "Big Bill" Thompson are all gone from the Chicago scene, replaced by the powerful but very different incumbent Mayor Richard Daley. "Little Ed" and "Brother Bill" Vare, long the bosses of Philadelphia, were replaced by one man not unlike them in some respects—Congressman William Green—and another who is their antithesis—Mayor Richardson Dilworth. And so it goes in city after city; the Hague machine has had no successor in Jersey City; Tammany Hall is weak, rent with dissension, a pale shadow of its former self; Kansas City has had no replacement for

---

[6] Warren Moscow, *The New York Times Magazine* (June 22, 1947).

[7] Dayton McKean, *Party and Pressure Politics* (Boston: Houghton Mifflin Co., 1949), p. 268. McKean, author of the best study of a boss ever written—*The Boss* (Boston: Houghton Mifflin Co., 1940), dealing with the incredible Frank Hague of Jersey City—presents an excellent brief review of the subject in Chap. 12 of his text, *Party and Pressure Politics.*

[8] Robert S. Allen, ed., *Our Fair City* (New York: Vanguard Press, 1947), p. 4.

the Tom Pendergast machine, nor Memphis for the Ed Crump organization.

There are, however, some bosses still in operation. Albany, New York, has a tight machine in the O'Connell organization. There are bosses in the Negro communities of some cities; a good example of that is "Good Jelly" Jones. (That local bosses often have chummy nicknames is no accident: their power rests on their close relationships with their neighbors—they are accessible, helpful, friendly, and gregarious people, or at least they start out that way.) Jones is a Negro politician in Nashville to whom the usually publicized Negro causes are of no concern; his source of power is assistance to the needy, not devotion to civil rights. When they need help, he says, "I don't turn them down."[9] In return his friends do not forget him on election day, and in classic style Good Jelly can deliver his neighborhood to whichever candidate seems the better investment. He trades votes for cash. Civil rights conscious Negroes resent Jones' unconcern with ideology, but he says, "My folks, they're not the integration type. They're not interested in all that. All they want is a little food."

Yet for Jones, like others of his genre, the future looks threatening. The lawyer who defends Jones in his periodic bouts with the law says: "You take this city, growing all the time, and the city limits going out, and the Negro making a little more money all the time—a thing like Jelly got, it's getting to be less and less important all the time. Five, ten years from now there probably won't be any Good Jelly. Pretty soon both sides will be too busy worrying about this middle-class vote to pay for Jelly. That's where the next battle will be."[10] This states the essential reason for the decline of classic bossism: the clients and the means to play the game are fading away.

If we mean by bossism the form of local politics so prevalent a generation or two ago in most of our cities and (contrary to the usual notion that bossism is a singularly urban phenomenon) in much of the rural countryside, it has clearly declined.[11] What was that form of bossism?

---

[9] David Halberstam has written a fascinating profile on Jones, called "Good Jelly's Last Stand," 24 *The Reporter* 40–41 (January 19, 1961). Jones has lost his political power, it is now reported; according to a Nashville observer (Robert H. Birkby), he can no longer "deliver the votes."

[10] *Ibid.*, p. 41.

[11] The old-style boss system has declined but the number of strong machines that linger on testifies to the strength of the causes of bossism originally. The O'Connell machine lives on in Albany, Boss Kenny rules Jersey City, and a strong machine still rules Atlantic City. There are many others—and rural machines as well, in the opinion of Roscoe Martin. See *Grass Roots*, p. 65. See also Anthony Lukas, "Boss Pollock: He Can't Be There But He Is," *The Reporter* (July 19, 1962), pp. 35ff. (on James Pollock of Baltimore).

The essence of bossism was service for a price, and political spoils were the means by which the system was kept operating. Just as Good Jelly helps his people, so the standard operating procedure of the old-style boss was to make himself available to those in need—whatever the need. Some needed work; some, a basket of food; some, rent money; some, advice and intercession when the police arrested a wayward son. As a social service agency, the boss was humane and indispensable to "his" people, who were often immigrants bewildered by the surroundings in which they found themselves and frequently faced with near starvation. Martin Lomasney, a Boston ward boss who died in 1933, defined his own role succinctly when he told Lincoln Steffens: "I think there's got to be in any ward somebody that any bloke can come to—no matter what he's done—and get help. Help, you understand; none of your law and your justice but help."[12] A reputation for being helpful even at the risk of being thought crooked—for being a Robin Hood—was indispensable, as the inimitable James Michael Curley proved. For decades Curley won elections in Boston, although most people—including many who voted for him—thought he was dishonest. But he was also thought to be generous and ready to help anyone in need. A pair of scholarly researchers found that:

Taxi drivers . . . , bell hops . . . , minor workers in his machine all agree that Curley is probably the easiest "touch" in the city, always ready with a dollar bill or better in the face of a hardluck story. And it is of more than passing interest that three of the respondents interviewed in the course of our opinion survey reported that Curley has given them amounts up to ten dollars in the darkest days of the Depression when they were completely "broke." A reputation for such generosity must be understood in the context of a great city where anonymity and competition are the order of the day. It is of such stuff that the charisma of a city boss is made.[13]

---

[12] *The Autobiography of Lincoln Steffens* (New York: Grosset and Dunlap, [originally published by Harcourt, Brace in 1931]), p. 618. See also the essay by A. D. Van Nostrand, "The Lomasney Legend," 21 *The New England Quarterly* 435 (1948).

[13] Jerome S. Bruner and Sheldon J. Korchin, "The Boss and the Vote: Case Study in City Politics," 10 *Public Opinion Quarterly* 1, 19 (1946). This side of Curley is related with a layer of sentimentality in the thinly disguised picture of him in the Edwin O'Connor novel, *The Last Hurrah* (Boston: Little, Brown & Co., 1956). Curley himself becomes maudlin in his own *I'd Do It Again* (Englewood Cliffs, N.J.: Prentice-Hall, Inc., 1957), in which he manages to erase some of the kindlier tones that O'Connor has painted into his portrait. The literary side of Boston politics came full circle in a biting satire by former Massachusetts Governor Foster Furcolo, *Let George Do It* (New York: Harcourt, Brace, and World, Inc., 1957), published under the pseudonym of John Foster.

In short, the reason bossism survived—and indeed in some places still thrives—is that it serves a useful function to some people in the community. As the sociologist Robert K. Merton has recognized, the official governmental machinery may be so remote or bound down by legalistic restraints that the machine, "through its local agent fulfills the important social *function of humanizing and personalizing all manner of assistance to those in need*."[14] By providing means of advancement for those denied other ways to get ahead in the world, the machine serves a vitally important function for the economically and socially deprived members of the community. It will not bother the conscience of the one who is assisted that the machine uses illegal or "corrupt" methods to aid him. So far as the beneficiary is concerned, he has been helped and he will remember it.

For services rendered, a *quid pro quo* was expected. A good ward or city boss could deliver "his" people with regularity and dependability. Issues were not important; the voters were quite ready to do their benefactor a favor in return for his interest in and help for them. Voting the boss's way seemed a small enough return. Lomasney, for example, was able to carry his ward in 1905 for a Republican named Frothingham in spite of the disinclination of his Irish constituents to have anything whatever to do with the Back Bay Yankee aristocracy. Boss Lomasney swung his voters away from the Democratic candidate for mayor (President Kennedy's grandfather, John Fitzgerald) in the course of factional conflict in the Democratic party. Lomasney failed to defeat "Honeyfitz," as Fitzgerald was called, but he carried 95 per cent of his ward for the Republican.[15]

To keep the machinery operating, money and patronage were necessary. The money came in through "contributions" of various kinds, sometimes through the involuntary contributions of those for whom jobs had been found (the system called for "contributing" 2 per cent of the salary). Money came in from the distribution of favors—such as franchises to operate transportation systems—that those with power could bestow. The boss got patronage from any and all sources, such as from businessmen who had to hire pick and shovel men and who found it good business to cooperate with the bosses. Patronage came from all levels of government. This was an important factor in the boss's operation: he was locally based but he was involved in city, county, state, and

---

14 Robert K. Merton, "The Latent Function of the Machine," from *Social Theory and Social Structure* (New York: The Free Press of Glencoe, Inc., 1957), pp. 71–81. Italics in original. Reprinted in Edward C. Banfield, *Urban Government* (New York: The Free Press of Glencoe, Inc., 1961), pp. 180–90.

15 Van Nostrand, *op. cit.*, pp. 444–45.

national politics for the simple reason that each provided patronage. If his party or faction was on the losing end at one level of government, his attachments to the others could provide the means to weather the misfortune.[16]

The decentralization of American national parties therefore plays into the hands of the boss: he is at the bottom of the pyramid, he has contact with all the elements of the party system, but he usually is beyond the authority of any higher echelon of the party. He has and uses the weapons of discipline to keep control over his organization, but he is usually free of effective control or discipline from above. To the boss, therefore, the important thing is to maintain control over his local party organization— to win primary elections which to him are more crucial than general elections. This is not to say that he has no concern with general election victories—indeed, he would prefer to win and thereby reap any rewards such a victory might offer. But if he has a choice between his party's winning with a candidate antagonistic to his interests or losing the election, he will not have much trouble making up his mind what to do. He "goes fishing" or "sits on his hands"—that is to say, he does nothing in the campaign.[17]

Patronage still exists and the party leaders are eager to get it to dispense to the faithful; American parties continue to be decentralized and local leaders continue to be largely immune from disciplinary control from above; the poor and insecure support local politicians with their votes in return for small favors and even for advice in a confusing and threatening world. Often a political leader will achieve his leadership role because he takes the time and trouble to hear people's complaints and will attempt to get assistance for them in some fashion. Thus a recent study of community leadership indicated that the lower-class sections of Philadelphia tended to look to local politicians as their leaders far more than did the

---

[16] E. E. Schattschneider emphasizes this point in his analysis of bossism in *Party Government, op. cit.*, pp. 170–86.

[17] See the excellent analysis of the power position of bosses and methods employed in sustaining it by Harold F. Gosnell in *Machine Politics: Chicago Model* (Chicago: University of Chicago Press, 1937). A boss, as Gosnell points out, is a hard man to down. An interesting account of an attempt to outwit a Chicago ward boss named Johnny Powers is given by Anne F. Scott in "Saint Jane and the Ward Boss," 12 *American Heritage* 12 (1960). Saint Jane is Jane Addams, who with all her determination and resourcefulness and her courageous allies at Hull House never managed to unseat Powers. See also the colorful descriptions of bosses presented by J. T. Salter in *Boss Rule* (New York: McGraw-Hill Book Co., 1935). An article by William E. Mosher, "Party and Government Control at the Grass Roots," 24 *National Municipal Review* 15 (1935), presents some useful material on the backgrounds of local political leaders. See the more recent and detailed study by William J. Keefe and William C. Seyler, "Precinct Politicians in Pittsburgh," 35 *Social Science* 26 (1960).

upperclass neighborhoods who were more likely to turn to professional people (physicians or lawyers). It is also significant that the lower classes were more inclined to look to politicians when they sought advice than were the upper classes.[18]

Present-day suburban party leaders illustrate the point that a middle- and upper-class neighborhood does not turn to the politician as a symbol of honorable leadership. As Robert Wood points out: "The suburban 'boss,' when he appears, . . . bears little resemblance to the traditional American image."[19] Handouts, marginal patronage employment, and a political clubhouse to hang out in offer no inducement to the typical suburban middle-class resident. The suburban political leader plays a more restrained role than did the old time boss, although some of them have considerable power.[20]

The point made by McKean is valid: there are still bosses, still functions for them to perform, and this is likely to continue for a long time to come. The structure of our political system, the traditions of our politics, the facts of our social structure, the existence of patronage and political favors—all sustain the role of the boss.

But the system is not what it once was, and the basis of the boss's power is under attack. The social welfare role of the boss is now largely performed by the government itself. The unemployed worker who receives a compensation check does not need a boss to give him a basket of food or rent money to tide him over. The destitute get assistance from the welfare departments and need curry no political favor to get a

---

[18] See Ira DeA. Reid and Emily L. Ehle, "Leadership Selection in Urban Locality Areas," 14 *Public Opinion Quarterly* 262 (1960). The more bureaucratized the process of aiding those in need becomes, the more important becomes the role of intermediator between citizen and bureaucrat. Reform groups battling party machines often emphasize this "service" role. In urban areas where the middle classes "reclaim" a formerly lower-class area (*e.g.*, Greenwich Village in New York City), there is less demand for such services. On this and other aspects of reform, see James Q. Wilson, *The Amateur Democrat* (Chicago: University of Chicago Press, 1962).

[19] Robert Wood, *Suburbia* (Boston: Houghton Mifflin Co., 1959), pp. 169–70. Wood's general discussion of suburbian bossism (pp. 166–75) is particularly recommended.

[20] Charles Adrian's assessment of Orville Hubbard, a boss from a suburb of Detroit, gives one a chilling sensation. See his excellent case study in *Governing Urban America* (New York: McGraw-Hill Book Co., 1955), pp. 126–31. J. Russel Sprague, erstwhile boss of the Republican party in Nassau County, is an interesting example of suburban bossism: the machine is honest, efficient, and ruthless. As Warren Moscow says of it: ". . . a particularly neat combination of city machine and county organization, smart enough to keep people happy and bury its own dead." *Politics in the Empire State* (New York: Alfred A. Knopf, Inc., 1948), p. 138.

relief check.[21] Other innovations have caused bosses equal trouble. Patronage has been drying up at all levels of government. There are exceptions, where the patronage tree still bears heavy fruit (as in Pennsylvania), but particularly in municipal and federal government the jobs that were once the basis of the boss's aid to unskilled workers are now largely beyond the reach of party leaders.[22] The development of accounting systems and the use of federal funds in state and local projects (necessitating occasional federal audit of local projects) have quashed some money-making schemes of the past. Immigration has ceased to be an important source of new voters who need help and repay the favor with a supporting vote on election day. Although Puerto Ricans tend to play that role in some areas, literacy laws have put many Spanish-speaking migrants beyond the pale, politically. The Negro and the white hillbilly offer some of the same kind of opportunities for the urban boss that the old immigrants did, but they are not as alien to American customs as were the Eastern Europeans of half a century ago and are unlikely therefore to remain manageable for as long a period.

Thus, higher economic standards, the elimination of the masses of immigrants, and the assimilation of the older migrants and their children have sharply restricted the potential clientele of the boss. A changing electorate, new means of communication, and perhaps even new notions about politicians have helped the "leader" and hurt the boss.[23] Thus one finds many mayors today who, far from being yes-men for overlord bosses, are political powers in their own right.[24] Thus a politician like the flamboyant Fiorello LaGuardia of New York City could meet and conquer the bosses on their own ground for he could appeal to the voters in a colorful and engaging way that was invincible. The catalogue of modern mayors of this type is long indeed: the late David Lawrence, once mayor of Pittsburgh; Mayor Richard Lee of New Haven; Senator Joseph

---

[21] The point is well-made by a character in *The Last Hurrah* who says it was not the local politicians who beat Skeffington but Franklin Roosevelt with his social welfare laws (pp. 374–75).

[22] Local leaders sometimes express disdain for patronage posts at the higher levels (for which perhaps a college education may be useful if not indispensable) and a preference for the privilege of awarding pick and shovel jobs for which greater gratitude may be anticipated by the dispenser. See Wilson, *op. cit.*, Chap. 7 on this point; and also Charles Gilbert, *Governing the Suburbs* (Bloomington: Indiana University Press, 1967), pp. 252–59.

[23] See the local politician's view of the changing character of his job and a report on his tactics in Richard T. Frost, "Stability and Change in Local Party Politics," 25 *Public Opinion Quarterly* 221 (1961).

[24] For a picture of one of the turn-of-the-century tame mayors, see the article by Bruce Bliven, "The Boodling Boss and the Musical Mayor," 11 *American Heritage* 8 (December, 1959). This is the lurid tale of Boss Abe Rueff of San Francisco and his bandleader mayor, Eugene Schmitz.

Clark and Richardson Dilworth, former mayors of Philadelphia; Vice President Hubert Humphrey, former mayor of Minneapolis; and others.[25]

Finally, on the subject of bossism and leaders this point should be emphasized: although it is common to speak sweepingly of bosses and of the pervasive power of such leaders as Thomas Dewey in New York, it should always be kept in mind that both bosses and leaders are players in the game of politics who must make their accommodations with other performers and other forces. They are not omnipotent now, nor were they ever, even though some of the more flamboyant of the earlier bosses came uncomfortably close to monolithic power.

Nonpartisan Politics

Nonpartisanship was among the many reforms spawned by the widespread disgust with the corruption, extravagance (without much to show for it), and the oligarchical and irresponsible power wielded by bosses in both state and local government early in this century. The "good" people of a city—the upper social and economic levels—were appalled at the power of the bosses and distressed at the success with which the bosses could get support from the mass of humanity then jammed into the burgeoning cities. To the upper crust it seemed self-evident that the lower classes were being led astray by unscrupulous politicians, that the true "good" of these people was not served by such political leadership. The party organization seemed to be the root of the evil, the cause of corruption and bad government.

Very few of the reformers had the perspicacity to see, as Lincoln Steffens did, that the roots ran deeper—that bossism was a social phenomenon responsive to community conditions.[26] Rather it was somewhat

---

[25] On Lawrence, see Frank Hawkins, "Lawrence of Pittsburgh, Boss of the Mellon Patch," 213 *Harper's Magazine* 55–61 (August, 1956); on Lee, see Jeanne R. Lowe, *Cities in a Race with Time* (New York: Random House, 1967), pp. 417–52, and Allan Talbot, *The Mayor's Game: Richard Lee of New Haven and the Politics of Change* (New York: Harper and Row, 1967); on Clark and Dilworth, see James Reichley, *The Art of Government* (New York: Fund for the Republic, 1959). The last is a thorough study of the decline of the old Republican machine in Philadelphia and the rise of the reform Democratic group. The mixture of reform and Democratic machine elements in more recent years is also detailed, making the whole an exceptionally useful study of bossism, reform, and counter-reform, as it were. On Dilworth, Clark, and Lawrence, see also Joseph Kraft, "Pennsylvania's New Breed of Politicians," 217 *Harper's Magazine* 48 (October, 1958).

[26] This comes across eloquently in the third part of his *Autobiography, op. cit.*

naively assumed that if the boss were denied his chance to use the party ticket to elect his crew, then the boss system would disappear. Thus it was proposed that city elections be held without benefit of party labels so that honest citizens would have a chance to win office without having to win the favor of the minions of the party machine.

So the idea of nonpartisanship flourished—at least on the local level, although not so successfully in state government. Nebraska and Minnesota adopted the nonpartisan ballot for their state legislatures, but elsewhere nonpartisanship is little used by the states except for occasional nonpartisan judicial elections. In municipal government, however, the system has become very common; Charles Adrian has estimated that a majority of all elected officials of all levels of government combined are chosen in nonpartisan elections.[27] Sixty-four per cent of the cities with more than 5000 population have nonpartisan elections. In council-manager cities the percentage of nonpartisan cities is even higher—84 per cent—although in mayor-council cities a bare majority—51 per cent —still have partisan nominations and elections.[28] The nonpartisan system appears to be gradually spreading—at least since 1940. At that time 56 per cent of the cities were reported to have nonpartisan elections; in 1949 the figure had increased to 56.9 per cent; by 1966 it was 64 per cent.[29] Much of this increase appears to be the result of the increasing adoption of the council-manager system which so often carries with it the nonpartisan ballot system.

What were the professed aims of the advocates of nonpartisanship? They appear to have sought the following four general objectives.[30]

1. To take "politics" out of local government.
2. To raise the caliber of candidates for elective offices.
3. To restrict local campaigning to local issues, ruling out extraneous national or state issues.
4. To eliminate straight ticket voting for candidates, emphasizing the individual candidate rather than his party affiliation.

---

[27] See Adrian's excellent survey and research suggestions in "A Typology for Nonpartisan Elections," 12 *Western Political Quarterly* 449–58 (1959). See also the fuller survey of both the history and prevalence of nonpartisanship by Eugene C. Lee, *The Politics of Nonpartisanship: A Study of California City Elections* (Berkeley, Calif.: University of California Press, 1960), Chap. 3. See also Gilbert and Clague's comments on nonpartisanship in large cities, "Electoral Competition . . . ," *op. cit.*

[28] *Municipal Year Book*, 1966, p. 95.

[29] Figures are taken from the *Municipal Year Book* for corresponding years.

[30] See the "principles" of nonpartisanship as stated by Lee (*op. cit.*, Chap. 12) in his assessment of the system. He presents a fuller and more detailed analysis.

To what extent have these goals been achieved? It is difficult to be certain about some of them, partly because of a lack of detailed study of the functioning of nonpartisan as compared with partisan electoral systems. In recent years several scholars have begun to investigate nonpartisan elections systematically, although their work is of necessity tentative because of the vast diversity of operational patterns about which we know little as yet. Given this obvious limitation, let us attempt to determine the extent to which the high hopes of the proponents of nonpartisanship were justified.

1. *Taking the Politics out of Local Government.* In the sense in which the word *politics* is used in this book, this goal is meaningless. If politics means the use of influence to condition the making of public policy, then politics does not disappear with the elimination of party labels. Politics as the use of influence is not, however, the common usage of the word; it connotes, as observed elsewhere, many other things. The confusion surrounding the term stems at least in some measure from the writings of men like Richard S. Childs, a lifelong, zealous, and active advocate of municipal reform. Childs, reporting on experience with nonpartisan elections in 48 cities, concluded by saying: "This testimony covering over 500 elections demonstrates that politics without politicians is actually with us."[31] Using *politics* and *politicians* to mean *party affairs* and *party politician* is a common but unfortunate usage, appropriate perhaps for a campaign against party labels, but not for analysis.

The nonpartisan system *may* remove some kinds of party politics. It *may* remove the party as an active organization from the nominating, campaigning, and policy-making processes, although in some cities the party leadership merely moves into the background and operates from behind the scenes. This appears to be the case to a considerable degree in Minnesota, where the state legislature is elected without party labels. There parties recruit and give aid to candidates for the legislature. Most legislators join one of two caucuses—the Liberals (Democrats) or the Conservatives (Republicans)—and state legislative politics goes on in much the same way that it does in states using partisan elections. Significantly, the leaders of the factions are often prominent members of their respective parties, the leadership of one faction having recently been held by a national party committeeman and later by a state party chairman.[32]

---

31 See his *Civic Victories* (New York: Harper & Row, 1952), p. 303. The quotation is taken from an appendix of the book which reprints an article he had written in the *National Municipal Review* in 1949, entitled "500 Nonpartisan Elections."

32 See Ralph S. Fjelstad, "How About Party Labels?" 44 *National Municipal Review* 359–64 (1955). Charles R. Adrian discusses both the Minnesota and the Nebraska experiments in "Some General Characteristics of Nonpartisan Elections," 46 *American Political Science Review* 766–76 (1952). See also G. Theodore

In Nebraska, legislative elections and legislative behavior appear to be free of partisan improvement.

When nonpartisan balloting is adopted, one of several alternatives develops in local politics.[33] The first alternative is the simple transformation of major parties from legal participants in the electoral and political processes to informal (whether overt or covert) participants. Thus Chicago has "nonpartisan" elections for its City Council but the Democratic party is the decisive force in city elections.

The second alternative is that the dominant party operates as an important force but the minority party casts its lot with some civic association to form an opposition coalition. This until recently was the case in Cincinnati, where the dominant Republicans have opposed the City Charter Committee and the Democratic minority; similarly in Hartford, Connecticut, the dominant Democrats oppose both the Citizen's Charter Committee and the Republicans.

In some places a third alternative appears in which the major parties are inactive but one, two, or more local groups spring up to support candidates. Such groups vary in the extent to which they maintain continuity as organizations. Many of them are closely related to the national parties. One recent study of a Massachusetts city found two groups which the author called the "Progressives" and the "Nonpartisans" that opposed each other consistently, and he also found that there was a very high correlation between Progressives and Democrats and between Nonpartisans and Republicans.[34]

A fourth situation involves no continuous groups but is instead a tendency for candidates to band together and run as a slate, using a combined campaign.[35] Such slates often get backing from interest groups. The

Miteau, *Politics in Minnesota* (Minneapolis: University of Minnesota Press, 1960), Chap. 3.

[33] Charles R. Adrian in "A Typology for Nonpartisan Elections," *op. cit.*, sets up four types of political systems that result from nonpartisan elections. His categories are employed here, except that I introduce variations based upon majority party dominance in cities.

[34] J. Lieper Freeman, "Local Party Systems: Theoretical Considerations and a Case Analysis," 64 *American Journal of Sociology* 282 (1958). A roughly comparable situation prevailed in another anonymous town studied by Oliver P. Williams and Charles R. Adrian and reported on in their article, "The Insulation of Local Politics Under the Nonpartisan Ballot," 53 *American Political Science Review* 1052–63 (1959). Their town, called Alpha, has a Citizens' Committee most of whose leaders were Republicans; there was considerable correlation between voting for Citizens' Committee candidates in local elections and Republican voting in state elections. There was also a sporadically active opposition group.

[35] On slate system operation see, for example, a case study by Marvin A. Harder, *Nonpartisan Election: A Political Illusion?* (New York: McGraw-Hill Book Co., 1958), which presents a detailed study of a Wichita, Kansas, nonpartisan election

slate system appears to be fairly common practice. In his report on non-partisan election practice, Richard S. Childs found only three of 48 cities in which parties, covertly or openly, had any great effect, but in nearly half the cities the slate system was in use.[36]

Finally, it is not uncommon for local elections to be run without either the parties or other groups actively supporting candidates. The individual candidate runs on his own, collecting his own money and conducting an independent campaign through whatever local connections he can arrange. Ethnic group associations may be of some significance in these campaigns. The extensiveness of the every-man-for-himself system is not known precisely, but Childs reported that in 22 of the 48 cities, campaigning was an individual undertaking.[37]

Thus if by removal of "politics" from local government we mean the removal of the party from an effective role in local elections, it appears to be true that adoption of the system often eliminates the parties. In varying degrees they may covertly—or, in some cases, openly—participate, but the scattered and not very conclusive evidence available suggests that parties are usually reduced to minimal roles. The fading away of parties, however, is rarely a matter of shattering a powerful political instrument. Quite often local parties are so disorganized and divided that they are insignificant. It is probably true that the cities with weak and disorganized parties are those in which the party ceases to play a significant role when nonpartisan elections are initiated, and that parties with greater unity and strength and a tighter organization survive the transformation in some form.

2. *Raising the Caliber of Candidates.* Does the elimination of the parties result in a marked improvement in the quality of candidates who can be persuaded to run for office? Disregarding the manifest difficulty of measuring so subjective a factor as the "caliber of candidates" and assuming that at least in broad terms such measurement is feasible, there does not seem to be much clear evidence that a change in election system does dramatically change the quality of candidates offered. No doubt ample and convincing evidence can be found that the introduction of a new kind of local government structure *accompanied by the introduction of the nonpartisan election system* has often produced a remarkable improvement in the quality of candidates offered and elected. But it is no easy matter to prove that the change was the consequence of the election

---

in which a slate was a factor of some importance. The title by the way is misleading; this is a case study of an election and not an analysis of whether or not nonpartisan elections are an illusion or a reality.

[36] Childs, *op. cit.*, p. 302.

[37] *Ibid.*, p. 300.

system and not the consequence of other simultaneous developments. A new charter is the result of an aroused electorate, and this invites able and perhaps hitherto apolitical people to be candidates. Men who would not otherwise consider running do so because they are now interested in local affairs and their hopes are high. There is usually a letdown, however, when the excitement and newness wear off; someone has to grapple with long-standing, contentious, and obstinate questions. It is in this post-honeymoon season that the real test comes. To make a convincing case for the proposition that the election method enhances candidate quality, it would have to be shown that in the long run there is a distinguishable difference between the kinds of candidates the two systems produce. This has not been done. There is evidence that some able candidates are brought forth by the prospect of being able to run without having to bend a knee to the party, but there are also cases in which the parties recruit candidates who would not be willing to run unless they had the assurance of organized support rather than having literally to promote themselves—which, particularly among novice politicians, is often not a promising prospect.[38]

A scrap of evidence on this point is provided by the city of New London, Connecticut. The city has had the council-manager system since 1921; it is an old and stable city of 34,000 population with a slight Democratic margin in voting. The parties are moderately well organized, or at least the Republican party is; the Democratic party is intermittently faction-ridden and not very effective in recruiting candidates or in supporting them. At the inception of the manager system, a nonpartisan election system was provided, but in 1933 the charter was amended to permit party nominations for the Council—the only elective offices. There does not appear to have been much change in the character of the candidates offered after the new system was inaugurated, but there is some difficulty in assessing this from the distance of thirty years. A new opportunity to test this question was offered in 1953 when a campaign was started to go back to nomination by petition, eliminating the party label on the ballot at the same time.

Considerable support for the change was provided by the League of Women Voters, a local group calling itself the New London Civic Association, and the local newspaper, through numerous editorials. Only the two parties spoke in defense of the system. The usual flurry of propaganda efforts preceded a referendum on the question. The local newspaper, the New London *Day*, ran an ad in its own columns urging a "yes" vote,

---

[38] Lee's conclusions regarding nonpartisanship in California cities is that the integrity and ability of candidates appear to be "above average." *Op. cit.*, p. 170.

saying that candidates "elected on their own under a nonpartisan charter will (1) owe a direct responsibility to the taxpayers [Note: not to the voters but to the taxpayers], (2) call 'em as they see 'em—regardless of party affiliations. . . ." There were the customary attacks on "well-oiled political machines" and "king makers," and promises of improvements that would be hard to achieve even under the best of circumstances. The two parties cooperated in defense of the *status quo*. They raised questions about who would support candidates if parties were eliminated (hinting that it would be some secret interests or "splinter groups and aggrieved individuals"). The Republicans asked in an ad: "Who wants control of New London and why do they want it?" They added that "A Vote in Favor of this Referendum is a vote for the Destruction of the American Way of Life." But the voters were not convinced. They removed the parties formally from the election process by a vote of 887 to 779—only 11.4 per cent of the voters participating.

In September of 1953 the first nonpartisan election since 1933 took place. The New London Civic Association backed two candidates for the city council, one a Republican and one an independent. One of them had been a long-time council member and an active Republican leader; the other was an intelligent young businessman of considerable ability who had not previously been active in politics. Five other candidates ran, making a total of seven candidates for the three vacancies: one was a Democrat who had been in and out of office since 1925, three others were less well-known Republicans, and the last was a nominal Democrat. A majority of the vote cast was required for election; consequently only one person—the experienced and well-known Republican candidate—was elected in the first election, making a runoff necessary. The four highest of the remaining six ran in this election. The result was that the one experienced candidate (who was also very well-known as a Democratic politician) was elected and the most able of the four candidates (the one backed by the Civic Association) was eliminated. So the results could hardly be called an impressive showing for the new system.

Succeeding elections showed no notable change in the kind of candidates who won. In fact, the main result was that the same candidates who had won before as partisans now won as nonpartisans. More and more questions were raised about the system, particularly about the necessity for runoff elections and about some awkward and unclear provisions in the new law. In time interest began to flag; the New London Civic Association found it difficult to get members to attend meetings; in one case not until the very last minute had enough candidates filed petitions for the school board to fill all the vacancies due to occur. Accordingly the parties moved to reinstate the party nomination process and in 1957 another referendum returned the parties formally and legally to the electoral process. Whom did the parties nominate then? Practically the same men ran who had been running under the petition system, with one or two additions to fill out the tickets. New London's experience suggests that underlying political conditions and personalities were more determinative of the "caliber" of candidates than was either election system.

3. *Keeping to Local Issues.* One innovation more than any other has excluded state and national party issues from local elections: the providing of separate days for local elections. Where both elections occur on the same day, inevitably there is a tendency for national issues and national politics to influence local voting.[39] In partisan local elections held at a time other than the general election day, there is certainly some connection between national party affiliation and local voting habits, but this is not necessarily a matter of national issues replacing local ones. Few local campaigns are waged around such questions as the tariff, atomic energy, or national health insurance; none at least has come to my attention. The real question therefore is not the influence of issues but loyalty to national parties. Emotional attachments to national parties is a force of considerable importance; national issues present no problem.

4. *Eliminating Straight Ticket Voting.* Does the removal of the party label eliminate ticket voting? It does not eliminate it, but it does diminish the practice to a considerable although quite variable extent. The removal of the label makes ticket voting more difficult for the simple reason that voters respond to a party symbol readily but to a list of names only with difficulty. As both party machines and reformers were well aware, the organization of voters is aided through convenient identification of the party list and made far more difficult when voters must memorize a list of names scattered in alphabetical arrangement among other names.

The assumption that voters will become more discriminatory—that they will pick carefully from among individuals rather than blindly casting a straight ticket vote—if they are denied the party guideline, is not wholly sound. For some voters the denial may force them to make more discriminatory choices than they might otherwise make. But for many others the system results in equally, if not more, arbitrary voting since they had some ideas about the party but do not know the qualifications nor even the names of candidates. There is in fact some evidence, especially where the long bedsheet type ballot is offered the bewildered voter, that the position a candidate has on the ballot can become a

---

[39] Yet even presidential victories do not pull into office all local officials holding to the victor's coattails. See V. O. Key's analysis of this regarding county officials in his "Partisanship and County Office: The Case of Ohio," 47 *American Political Science Review* 525–32 (1953). See Lee, *op. cit.*, pp. 181–84.

decisive factor: whoever comes first on the list reaps extra votes. This is essentially voting by lot and does not indicate a high order of rationality is a necessary concomitant of the removal of the party labels.[40]

Nor does it follow that the removal of the party label removes all tendency to single out and support candidates from the voter's own party. Republican wards seem to favor Republican candidates, and Democratic wards are partial to Democrats. One study of voting in local elections in four Michigan towns indicated a considerable correlation between the voting in certain wards for Republicans in state elections and the voting for Republican local candidates running in nonpartisan elections. The same study also indicated, however, that minority party members have a better chance of winning against a predominant party candidate in non-partisan elections than in partisan elections.[41] Thus in certain heavily Republican suburban communities an occasional Democrat gets elected when the ballot is nonpartisan. In his recent study of nonpartisanship in California, Eugene C. Lee found that Republicans have a better chance than Democrats of winning in city elections, notwithstanding the fact that most registered voters in California are Democrats, not Republicans. In six California cities he discovered that although only 42 per cent of the registered voters were Republican, 69 per cent of the mayors and councilmen elected over a period of nearly twenty-five years were from the GOP.[42] In some cities Republicans constituted only one-third of the registered voters, yet half to three-quarters of the elected officials. In short, nonpartisanship has not eliminated ticket voting, but it has diminished it.

One criticism of nonpartisanship is that it is difficult under that election system to hold officials accountable. The argument is that the voter does not have the opportunity to hear organized criticism of incumbent officeholders from an opposition party, and that the positions

---

[40] There is convincing evidence that location on the ballot can be a boon or burden. In a very detailed and precise analysis of ballot position, D. S. Hecock and H. M. Bain, Jr. showed that, particularly for inconspicuous offices on long ballots, the accident of having first place on the ballot list could mean an increase in votes. See their analysis in *Ballot Position and Voter Choice; The Arrangement of Names On the Ballot and Its Effect on the Voter's Choice* (Detroit: Wayne University Press, 1956). Further commentary on this practice is offered in Howard White, "Voters Plump for First on List," 39 *National Municipal Review* 110–11 (1950). In recognition of the value of ballot position, many states require rotation of names on ballots.

[41] Williams and Adrian, "The Insulation of Local Politics Under the Nonpartisan Ballot." *op. cit.* They report: "Several known Democrats won nonpartisan elections during our study period in cities where no Democrat has carried a local partisan race within living memory." See also G. W. Pearson, "Prediction in a Non-Partisan Election," 12 *Public Opinion Quarterly* 112–17 (1948). Pearson reported that voters in Denver were frequently unable to identify the party affiliation of candidates whom they were supporting.

[42] Lee, *op. cit.*, p. 55.

of individual incumbents on a city council are well-nigh impossible to keep track of even for the interested citizen. To sustain this contention there is evidence that incumbent city councilmen in nonpartisan cities manage to stave off defeat longer than do councillors in partisan cities. Unless one assumes that nonpartisan officials are naturally so virtuous that defeat is less likely for them than for partisan officials—which is hardly tenable—then the higher rates of re-election in nonpartisan systems suggest that accountability is harder to achieve under such systems. Charles Gilbert and Christopher Clague found significantly higher ratios of survival for nonpartisan city council members than for partisan ones. Further, they found that there was a lesser tendency to suffer defeat in both election systems when the members ran *at large* rather than from districts.[43] Thus where the voter lacks personal contact with his councilman and where the cue of the party label is removed, there is apparently the least possibility of holding the official accountable. Achieving accountability is always difficult; the evidence from the large cities that Gilbert and Clague analyzed suggests it is more difficult than ever when parties are absent.

NONPARTISANSHIP AND THE PARTY SYSTEM

One significant factor sometimes overlooked in discussion of nonpartisan elections is their impact on the total party organization. The local organization of the major party is an important element of the party's structure. Local offices and activity in local politics provide experience for the ambitious novice who aims at higher positions. But if the local political system is truly severed from the party organization, the ambitious one may have to choose between local activities and party activity, and if he chooses the former he may be effectively eliminated as a potential candidate for partisan offices. Admittedly this is not an absolute by any means; many politicians manage to move from "nonpartisan" politics to party politics—as Herbert Humphrey did in moving from the mayoralty of Minneapolis to the United States Senate.[44] The opportunity to move from nonpartisan into party activities is often closed, whereas there is a tendency for partisan local elections to push local officials into other party affairs. One author, complaining about the shortcomings of partisan local elections, observed that: "Councilmen are

---

[43] Gilbert and Clague, *op. cit.*, pp. 341–44.

[44] Robert L. Morlan, "City Politics; Free Style," 38 *National Municipal Review* 485–90 (1949). Joseph Schlesinger's extensive research on the career pattern of governors and U.S. Senators shows that local elective office is not a common form of political experience for those who rise. See his *Ambition and Politics* (Chicago: Rand McNally, 1966), p. 73.

drawn into party work for state and national as well as local elections."[45] In view of the intergovernmental politics of our federal system, it seems to me that such intermingling of experience is not appropriately a matter for complaint but for applause.

Closing a channel of recruitment is not the only significant effect of nonpartisanship on the party system. The elimination of local activities also has contributed to the general weakening of party organizations that has been taking place in recent decades. If we take seriously the party's role in democratic politics, this may be of some importance, although it is difficult to say precisely what effect the removal of local party labels has had on party organization. It must, however, have contributed something to the atrophy of local organizations.

The rhetoric of the adversaries battling about whether partisanship ought to be initiated or retained in a city is not necessarily very enlightening to anyone seeking to understand the system. For the claims of both proponents and opponents are often speculative and exaggerated. Communities debating the merits of the system should, as Eugene Lee has rightly said, "examine [their] own problems, needs and resources. . . . The size of the city, the character of its population, the quality of its civic institutions, the integrity of its press—these and countless other matters will determine which type of ballot and which kind of politics will result in the most political life for the community. . . ."[46]

Some Patterns of Local Politics

Attempts to generalize about the politics of the infinitely varied localities of the United States should involve, although it has not always done so, a considerable humility. We know too little about the realities of the exercise of political power to warrant dogmatism. The social composition of a community, to choose just one illustrative example, conditions the manner of its politics. Consider two adjacent towns with roughly equal population and yet utterly different social composition. One is a "dormitory" suburb of New York, with an upper-middle class population, no industry and none desired, and a very high educational level and with all the pseudo and real sophistication that this may involve. The other is a mill town with decaying slums, most of whose workers are employed in factories, and the majority of whose population consists of immigrants

45 Arthur W. Bromage, "Partisan Elections in Cities," 40 *National Municipal Review* 250–53 (1951).
46 Lee, *op. cit.*, p. 184.

and second or third-generation Americans. No one in his right mind would expect the politics of the two towns to be similar. The economic interests, ideological commitments, habits of social interaction, and conceptions of what is rightly political and what must be kept nonpolitical all dictate different kinds of politics for such varied communities. This, to be sure, is a painfully obvious point, but it is often overlooked by commentators on local politics.

It does not follow from this that there are no similarities in the politics of local governments; hypotheses may be offered for comparative analysis of local politics, and validation of these may reasonably be sought through research. Diversity does not prevent comparative analysis, it only complicates it. Some tentative hypotheses about local politics will be offered.

1. *In local politics there is a tendency for one party to have a consistent majority in elections.* This politically significant fact is the simple consequence of the basic factors that induce people to be Democrats and Republicans—the many social, traditional, economic, and other motivations behind partisan choice. As the municipality is the smallest unit of government, there is greater likelihood that it will contain sufficient numbers of similarly inclined partisans to provide a consistent balance of power favoring one party. The larger the unit of government, the greater the mixture of social and economic strata and accordingly the greater the chance of population diversity sufficient to provide stable two-party competition. The small suburban community, the industrial center, and the small rural town are all likely to exhibit one-party tendencies.

This does not imply, however, that the dominant party in numbers of votes on election day must therefore dominate the politics of a community. In the first place, local political parties are often so disorganized and weak that they amount to little in local government contests. This is most frequently true in communities operating under nonpartisan ballot systems, of course. Thus the Democratic party of Los Angeles, although it has more registered voters on its lists than has the Republican party, still cannot take advantage of its numerical superiority because of— among other things—its organizational weakness. (Republican mayors predominate, although they do not necessarily run as Republicans.)

The tendency to one-party dominance does not necessarily foreclose the minority from all participation, however. Where councils are chosen by districts, the minority party may maintain representation in order to criticize the majority.[47] As noted in the discussion of nonpartisanship, the

---

[47] Connecticut law now requires minority representation on local governing boards by not permitting either party to run a full complement of candidates.

tendency to emphasize personal popularity in local elections permits the minority party candidate to win surprisingly often. This probably occurs less frequently where the party label is involved, but the personality factor works there too and constitutes a way to overcome the majority's natural advantage. Minorities can also reap rewards when the majority's local misdeeds become pungent and wrath is aroused. It took LaGuardia two tries to unseat the Democratic organization in New York City, and he did it—significantly—in 1933, when the Democratic party was basking in the reflected popularity of the New Deal's early glow. In Philadelphia reform elements gathered around some seemingly improbable Democratic novice politicians to unseat an apparently permanent Republican machine in 1949. In St. Louis, San Francisco, Buffalo, and Cincinnati, party turnover in power has occurred in recent years.[48]

2. *In the main, large cities are Democratic, suburbs and rural communities are Republican.* This is true in the main, but exceptions to the generalization are important to bear in mind. In 1958, Democratic candidates for governor carried the thirteen largest cities in the North by an average vote of nearly two to one.[49] Suburban regions are normally just as Republican even if not more so.[50] And the Republican proclivities of the small town and farming regions are legendary. Yet to each of these "rules" there are important exceptions. Most obvious of all perhaps is the sectional Democratic faithfulness of the rural South; such headway as has been made by the Republican party in the southern states has taken place not in rural but in urban and suburban areas. In the large cities of the North, Democratic majorities are not invariable by any means. It might be said that the 1952 and 1956 Republican majorities scored by President Eisenhower in cities were atypical, as indeed they were, but in the 1948 election—when President Truman won at least in part because of the strong urban support he garnered—there were many cities with majorities for Governor Dewey. Indeed, of 78 nonsouthern cities with populations in excess of 100,000, no less than 21 voted Republican.[51] Nor is it justified to assume that all suburban towns are Republican in inclination. Their partisan tendencies are determined by the same kinds of fac-

---

[48] See Gilbert and Clague, *op. cit.*, pp. 328–29. Douglas Gatlin, reporting on party competition in North Carolina, found that the extent of competition in local politics was much higher in cities than in small towns, presumably as a result of the greater socioeconomic diversity of the city. See his paper, "Socio-Economic Bases of Party Competition in North Carolina," presented at the 1962 convention of the American Political Science Association.

[49] Drawn from data in Scammon, *op. cit.*, Vol. 3.

[50] See, for example, the summary of data on this presented by Wood, *Suburbia*, pp. 139–140.

[51] See the tabulations in *The Political Almanac, 1952*, edited by George Gallup (New York: B. C. Forbes and Sons, 1952), pp. 29–32.

tors that decide the political odds of other communities, and it is wrong to assume that all suburbs are alike in composition.[52] The wealthiest and most exclusive of the suburbs are overwhelmingly Republican in state and in local elections; more socially diversified suburbs are less Republican —and some of them are in fact resoundingly Democratic. It is often contended that the Democratic migrant to the suburbs soon drops his Democratic allegiance in order to conform to the prevailing Republican social milieu of his new neighborhood. No doubt this does happen in some cases, but there is considerable evidence to indicate that partisan attachment whether Republican or Democratic, tends to survive a move to suburbia.[53]

3. Local campaigns for office tend to emphasize personal popularity rather than issues. Personal relationships are obviously important in local politics; the constitutency is relatively restricted and the possibility of a candidate's depending upon personal acquaintance is therefore greater than it would be in contests for higher offices. A candidate is often inclined to make the most of his various group associations—religious, residential, social and fraternal, and occupational as well as political—in order to attract votes. And where political attitudes are not structured by firmly held political beliefs, the potential significance of personal relationships becomes all the greater. Moreover, the nonpartisanship and multi-factional party strife common to so many municipalities is most conducive to emphasis on the personal qualities of the candidate rather than upon issues. It is instructive to recall that in state political campaigns the greatest dependence upon personal popularity combined with relative neglect of issues in campaigning occurs in the Southern states with multi-factional one-party system. Local politics fits the same pattern apparently.

An examination of the voting returns in a given city soon indicates that there are often remarkable correlations between ethnic neighborhoods and the votes received by ethnic candidates. Irish candidates seem to do

---

[52] This point is made effectively and briefly by G. Edward Janosik in his article "The New Suburbia," 31 *Current History* 91 (1956). Robert Wood in *1400 Governments* (Cambridge, Mass.: Harvard University Press, 1961), not only shows there are such differences but also illustrates their significance.

[53] Several studies have concentrated on this phenomenon. See Wood, *op. cit.*, on his theories of "conversion" as opposed to "transplantation" (*i.e.*, no change in party alignment), pp. 135–49. Jerome Manis and Leo Stine, in "Suburban Residence and Political Behavior," 22 *Public Opinion Quarterly* 483 (Winter, 1958–59), contend that suburban residence is not a significant determinant of voting alignment. This is also the position of Bernard Lazerwitz, who based his conclusions on material gathered by the Michigan Survey Research Center in the course of the 1952 and 1956 voting behavior studies. See his "Suburban Voting Trends: 1948 to 1956," 39 *Social Forces* 29 (1960). Fred Greenstein and Raymond Wolfinger argue for a greater potential role for conversion in their article, "The Suburbs and Shifting Party Loyalties," 22 *Public Opinion Quarterly* 473 (Winter 1958–59).

well where the auld sod is popular, Jews get bonus votes in wards where Yiddish is heard on the street, Negroes gain in the segregated neighborhoods where *Ebony* outsells *Life*. Close examination of the voting returns in any city large enough to have distinct ethnic and racial neighborhoods that correspond with ward or precinct voting lines will illustrate this point clearly, although extraordinary variations do show up at times.

It is common to dismiss as unworthy the practice of choosing a candidate because of his ethnic background. If this is considered as merely one among many reasons for choosing candidates—placing it alongside the desire to guard personal economic interests, keep tax rates low, favor "sound" businessmen candidates, and so on—it looks a little less evil. The Negro, for example, may want very much to have a Negro representing him on the city council because he feels no one else will truly represent his personal desires. Or a person from an ethnic group that has not been given "recognition" in local politics may feel, sometimes with a passion quite incomprehensible to one of Anglo-Saxon background, that electing "one of his own kind" in itself represents his most important political desire. It is true that outlandish and irrational appeals are made to attract such support, and also to say that at least marginally such emphasis may deepen community schisms. Yet the desire of the minority groups to choose one of their own to represent them should hardly be dismissed with scorn any more than should the comparable desire of middle-class neighborhoods to choose candidates reflecting their own ideals.

The more dramatic instances of ethnic candidates winning unusual margins in "their" respective regions has led to some unwarranted assumptions about ethnic voting. Ethnic group leaders have not been loath to stretch the truth in selling political leaders the idea that their followers will desert en masse to the opposition unless a representative of their group is given recognition on the ticket. The deliverability of ethnic groups is far less possible in reality than these leaders either realize or admit. Having a name beginning with or ending with *o* or ending with *–ski* is often a benefit, but that does not mean the votes of the Irish, Italian, or Polish ethnic groups are deliverable to the opposition should proper recognition be denied. The deliverability of a group is in any event a dubious proposition today, and in the past no doubt the more impressive "deliveries" were assisted by vote frauds of various kinds. The more significant point is that in local elections where party lines are not drawn, other factors—such as ethnic associations—assume greater importance.

If ethnic associations do result in bonus votes (an Italian-American in Boston changed his name to Foley and considerably increased his percentage of the vote), why then do not all ethnic candidates win equal

favor in "their" wards? The answer is that when ethnic associations become most important, the voter's motivation involves more than simple
similarity of names. The ethnic candidates scoring a first, or the one who
has come in some degree to represent a signal advance for the ethnic group
in an area (an ethnic variant on "local boy makes good") is the one who
reaps unusual rewards at the polls. Take the case of the Italian-American
community in Rhode Island which responded warmly to John O. Pastore
when he became the first Italian-American to run for Governor. Compare
his vote in 1946 in districts with heavy Italian population with the received by his Irish-American predecessor as Democratic candidate for
the same office two years earlier:

	McGrath	Pastore	Percentage Point Difference
In 34 Italian Districts	64.2%	69.9%	+ 5.9
In 31 Irish Districts	69.1	59.8	− 9.3
In 17 French Canadian Dist.	72.7	60.1	−12.6
In 6 Yankee Districts	43.4	34.8	− 8.6

Both McGrath and Pastore won their election contest, but in the case
of Pastore he could not have won without the extra votes he got in
Italian neighborhoods. Similarly, the first Italian-American to run for
governor of Rhode Island on the Republican ticket could not have won
the office without unusual Italian-American support. Of 17 of Provi-
dence's most heavily Italian districts, Mr. Christopher Del Sesto, the
Republican candidate for Governor in 1956, pulled the normally Demo-
cratic-voting Italians to majorities for himself in 14 districts. In all of
them Mr. Del Sesto ran well ahead of his Yankee running mate for
Lieutenant Governor; in one such district the Yankee trailed by 19 percentage points behind Del Sesto.[54]

---

[54] Data on the ethnic composition of the electorate in Rhode Island is probably
more complete than that of any other state since the State Board of Elections has
compiled a document called a "Survey of Rhode Island Electors." By examination
of the names on electoral rolls, the percentage for each group is set forth for every
precinct in the state. The heavy concentrations of ethnics in Rhode Island makes
for great emphasis on this by politicians, and presumably this accounts for the
official curiosity that serves the researcher's purposes as well as the politician's. For
details on the 1956 and 1958 elections in which Mr. Del Sesto won the governorship twice but managed to serve only the second term owing to some dubious
maneuvering by the Democratic incumbent, Dennis Roberts, see Lockard, *New
England State Politics, op. cit.*, pp. 193–203, and also Chap. 11, "Ethnic Elements
in New England Politics," for further evidence and discussion of ethnic voting
generally.

The voting returns from three precincts in Boston in the 1959 city council illustrate the remarkable sensitivity that minorities can show for one of their own kind. Mr. Elam, needless to say, is a Negro candidate.[55]

	Percentage of the Precinct Vote for:		
	Ianella	Foley	Elam
In an Italian District	73	14	7
In an Irish District	19	64	12
In a Negro District	23	29	72

4. *The roles played by political parties in municipal politics vary widely, but it is possible to classify party activities in four general categories.* Such classifications are of course not absolute, and it is apparent that communities shift from one category to another—sometimes within relatively short time periods. But for purposes of analysis such groupings are useful.

(a) *The strong political machine dominating politics.* As noted in the discussion of bossism, such organizations are rarer by far today than in the past, and although they vary in their effective control, are still very strong machines in many cities and towns which dominate the political scene. In Chicago a strong machine, with business community support and only ineffective opposition, controls the politics of that city.[56] Enough has been said of this style of politics in the discussion of bossism to obviate the necessity of further comment here.

(b) *Cities with competitive parties, reasonably well organized.* In view of the prevalent tendency for cities to have one-party predominance

---

[55] These data are drawn from a table presented by Edward C. Banfield and Martha Derthick, eds., *A Report on the Politics of Boston, Massachusetts* (Cambridge, Mass.: Joint Center for Urban Studies of M.I.T. and Harvard University, 1960), p. II-24 (mimeographed). The Italian precinct is Ward 3, Precinct 2; the Irish: Ward 6, Precinct 1; the Negro: Ward 9, Precinct 4. For a perceptive discussion of the persistence of ethnic voting, see Michael Parenti, "Ethnic Politics and the Persistence of Ethnic Identification," 61 *American Political Science Review* 717 (1967).

[56] Wilson, *Negro Politics* (New York: The Free Press of Glencoe, 1960), Chap. 3, gives a good description of organization in the process of discussing Negro politics in Chicago. See also Alfred De Grazia's description of a Republican challenge to the organization when Robert Merriam ran against Mayor Richard Daley: "The Limits of External Leadership Over a Minority Electorate," 20 *Public Opinion Quarterly* 113 (1956). For some reason the article does not identify Chicago or the names of candidates, perhaps in imitation of some sociologists, but if it is not the Daley-Merriam race he is talking about, there must be two Chicagoes in the Midwest.

in voting, it is obvious that regularly competitive parties are not the rule by any means. Competition does occur with regularity in some cities; however, many others have intermittent periods of vigorous competition. Thus in recent years there has been continuous competition in such cities as Philadelphia, Buffalo, Cincinnati, Indianapolis, and New Haven. In many cities, including some small ones, party competition is lively.

(c) *Cities with nominal nonpartisanship but with active parties.* Not in open violation of the law, but in disregard to the clear intent of the law, parties often successfully operate in local affairs where supposedly they are banned. In Kansas City, Denver, and Hartford, for example, parties operate with varying effectiveness—the nominally nonpartisan ballots notwithstanding. In Kansas City, in fact, the notorious Pendergast machine operated for fifteen years under "nonpartisanship," as did the reform government that succeeded it, and the postreform organization that won control of the council in 1959.[57] In Denver the political parties have increasingly participated in city politics in recent years. In the 1930's and 1940's the parties were little involved in the organizations that successive mayors built to support their power; it was said to be a kind of "bipartisan" government. More recently the parties have been openly involved in mayoralty elections and in the overall politics of the city. Said the *Rocky Mountain News* in 1957, "The city election, under the charter, is nonpartisan. Despite that, however, it usually boils down to a two-party affair with the Democratic and Republican organizations lining up on both sides of the fence."[58] In a great many cities similar backstage operations determine important features of city politics.

(d) *Municipalities in which parties as a consequence of disorganization or extreme factionalism have little to do with local politics.* This state of party affairs is by no means limited to communities legally requiring nonpartisan elections, for it is not unusual for parties to be so divided and disorganized that they can exert no effective power in local affairs. Thus, in Boston, city council candidates may use local factional Democratic machinery to a minor extent in their campaigning, but for all its Democratic leanings the city of Boston has no Democratic organization that dominates its politics.[59] In many smaller communities the major parties

---

[57] See Kenneth E. Gray, *A Report on Politics in Kansas City, Missouri*, edited by Edward C. Banfield (Cambridge, Mass.: Joint Center for Urban Studies of M.I.T. and Harvard University, 1959) (mimeographed).

[58] Quoted by Kenneth E. Gray in *A Report on Politics in Denver, Colorado*, edited by Edward C. Banfield (Cambridge, Mass.: Joint Center for Urban Studies of M.I.T. and Harvard University, 1959), p. II-22 (mimeographed), See Gray's general discussion of party activity in the "nonpartisan" government of Denver.

[59] See Banfield and Derthick, *op. cit.*, on the weakness of the Democratic party in Boston.

steer clear of local politics, leaving to local quasiparty organizations with other names and other memberships the functions of local politics. There are often correlations between the membership of these groups and the membership of national parties, but often not even this is significantly true since in some areas the numerical predominance of one party is so great that divisions do not follow national party lines. In certain larger cities, too— and particularly so on the West Coast—the conduct of local politics appears to have no attractions for the regular party organizations. Thus, in Los Angeles, a politics of every-man-for-himself prevails; it is true that the major officials of the city are usually known as Republican or Democrats, but the extent of party promotion of their candidacies is limited and party activity in local affairs generally is minimal. As one observer has said, Los Angeles "has always been governed by ad hoc groups which come together to elect a Mayor, disband after election, and leave him with no more power than that vested in him by the charter and that arising from the force and persuasiveness of his personality."[60] He competes with councilmen who have their personal organizations and who play individualistic politics to the hilt, neither asking nor receiving significant support or opposition from the parties.

5. *Efforts to initiate or to maintain "nonpolitical" operations in municipal government tend to divide communities along class-status lines with upper-class elements favoring and lower-class elements opposing these procedures.* Nonpartisanship in elections is not the only device devoted to minimizing the "political content of city and town government. Several other institutional arrangements are aimed in greater or lesser part at trimming the power of the politician and emphasizing the "professionalization" of local government. The civil service system in preference to patronage is an example. So is the city manager system which by transferring the executive functions to an expert manager seeks to remove "political influence." Reformers often promote the election of city councilmen on an at-large basis rather than choosing them from individual wards since the latter method is assumed to play into the hands of local political organizations and diminish the chances of getting an overall view of the city's problems. Finally proportional representation (a system of balloting whereby the voter expresses weighted choices for candidates, providing a better opportunity for minority representation and making it difficult for party organizations to depend upon a simple ticket or slate to put its candidates across) has

<hr>

[60] James Q. Wilson, *A Report on Politics in Los Angeles*, edited by Edward C. Banfield (Cambridge, Mass.: Joint Center for Urban Studies of M.I.T. and Harvard University, 1959), pp. II-15 (mimeographed).

been supported either as an adjunct to other nonpartisan devices (such as the city manager system) or on its own merits.

There is considerable evidence to support the inference that upper social groups support such changes in public referenda and lower ones oppose them. Take the case of Worcester, Massachusetts, where in 1960 the electorate abandoned the proportional representation method of electing city councillors. Proportional Representation came to Worcester in conjunction with the city manager system in 1947 and it was defended as an appropriate election system for that form of local government. At the same time Democratic politicians in particular campaigned against the Proportional Representation system openly and against the city manager system covertly. The vote to repeal the system in 1960 correlates with the socioeconomic status of the residents of various wards, as the following table shows.[61]

Worcester Wards	Monthly Rental Value of Homes (1950)	Percentage of Owner Occupancy of Homes (1950)	Per Cent Democratic for Atty. General (1958)	Per Cent for Retention of Proportional Representation (1960)
1	$41.30	63%	33%	54%
10	50.74	43	37	54
3	28.52	16	73	28
5	24.73	20	74	27

A similar pattern has been observed elsewhere—in Cambridge and St. Louis, for example. The St. Louis situation suggested to Robert H. Salisbury the hypothesis that "where the community is large and diverse in population, reform is likely to have quasi-class connotations and be an instrument of middleclass values, negatively received by the lower and lower middle income groups."[62]

---

[61] The data for this table are drawn from Robert H. Binstock, *A Report on Politics in Worcester, Massachusetts* (Cambridge, Mass.: Joint Center for Urban Studies of M.I.T. and Harvard University, 1960), pp. I, 20, 21 (mimeographed), and the *Worcester Evening Gazette*, November 9, 1960.

[62] Robert H. Salisbury, "The Dynamics of Reform: Charter Politics in St. Louis," 5 *Midwest Journal of Political Science* 260 (1961). See also Brett W. Hawkins, "Public Opinion and Metropolitan Reform in Nashville," 28 *Journal of Politics* 408 (1966), where he shows the following distribution of educational levels according to their percentage of support for metropolitan consolidation in 1962.

Educ. Level:	1–8 yrs.	9–11 yrs.	12 yrs.	Some College	Coll. Grad.
% for	33.3	57.7	71.4	80.8	85.7

No doubt these differences appear partly because the old-line politicians are put on the defensive by such proposals and can get their strongest support from their own home bailiwicks. Conversely it is easier to sell the reforms among middle- and upper-class groups because the reform leaders are also drawn from the upper ranks. Undoubtedly the opposition reflects lower-class apprehension that the reforms may diminish their relative power in city politics (e.g., an at-large election system might well make it less possible for a Negro to be elected to the city council, and labor unions might be apprehensive about the possibly enhanced power of the business elements of the community should a city manager system be instituted). By the same token, the reformers' emphasis on efficiency, maximum value for the tax-dollar, and "nonpolitical" government is more attractive to middle- and upper-class elements than to lower-class residents who have close contacts with ward politicians and less concern with the tax rate.

The differences between upper and lower layers of society today bear close resemblances to the divisions between the Progressive Reformers of the early part of this century and the immigrants who supplied the voters for bosses and were therefore the natural enemies of the reform group. Richard Hofstadter says that the Yankee assumed:

. . . a popular democracy with widespread participation and eager civic interest. To him politics was the business, the responsibility, the duty of all men. The immigrant, by contrast, coming as a rule from a peasant environment and from autocratic societies with strong feudal survivals, was totally unaccustomed to the active citizen's role.[63]

The abstractions, the issue-orientation so congenial to the reformer and the traditional Yankee were either incomprehensible or anathema to the immigrant—a point the bosses were quick to realize. The bosses attended the weddings and the religious festivals, and made every effort to emphasize rather than diminish the ethnic background of his constituency. The bosses could reach the ethnic pride and inspire loyalty in the newcomers, but the Progressives with their high ideals touched no responsive note among the immigrant groups.

While it would be absurd to contend that precisely the same situation exists today when immigration has been reduced to a trickle and

---

[63] Richard Hofstadter, *The Age of Reform: From Bryan to F. D. R.* (New York: Vintage Books, 1960), p. 182. Hofstadter's analysis of the tensions between the reform group and the immigrant deserve the attention of students of modern city politics.

where second- and third-generation descendants of the earlier immigrants often seek to be more American than Daughters of the American Revolution (*e.g.*, the ultra-Americanism of the late Senator Joseph McCarthy), there is still much in Hofstadter's thesis that is pertinent for contemporary urban politics. The tendency to see politics as a matter of personal loyalties constantly baffles the intelectual do-gooder who enters local politics. His concern for issues and substantive questions of policy is alien to the on-going politics in the lower-class ward. He may be tolerated or even employed to best advantage, but usually neither the indigenous leaders nor the intellectual will really understand the motivations of the other.

If this is true, then how have so many reforms been approved? The lower ranks of society outnumber the upper ranks, which ought to make it hard to adopt such schemes—at least when they are submitted to referendum, as usually they are. The answer to this question is hard to nail down, but it is important enough to merit some effort at explanation.

In the first place it is probable that the innovation of many of these devices was associated with campaigns against truly odious political machines which were not only corrupt but often tied in with criminal elements and otherwise guilty of repulsive actions. As Oliver Garceau has said of the Kansas City of the Pendergast era:

It was a violent, bloody and dangerous period in Kansas City. . . . The police were thoroughly corrupted and would not protect the citizen. Elections were remembered by the number of deaths, and lesser acts of violence. The worst plague for the common citizen was kidnapping. Much more than half were never reported even locally. People went to what seemed, to an outsider, like fantastic lengths to floodlight their grounds, bar and bolt their houses, double check on every member of the family who left the house for however short a trip, travelled about the town only in groups, never except in emergency alone. This was by no means the fantasy of a few, but the settled practice of those in the upper middle neighborhoods. . . .[64]

Memories of such political machines are easily stirred and, where the memories are not vivid, the folklore of bossism is pervasive enough to provide an excellent base for campaign activities in behalf of reform.[65]

---

[64] From a prefatory comment to Gray, *op. cit.*, p. 2.

[65] During a contest in Cincinnati over the repeal of proportional representation,

Still, that is hardly adequate to explain the prevalence of "non-political" governmental devices if there is genuine antagonism to them among the lower-class elements of the urban population. Does variation in voting turnout account for the success of reform? Perhaps the lower-class elements simply fail to get their way because they do not vote in proportion to their numbers. Earlier (see Chap. 8) we observed that in general elections the proportion of upper-level voters exceeds that of lower-class voters: the lower the status, the less the rate of turnout on election day. Perhaps in city elections the relative voting strength of the upper elements increased in comparison with the lower-class wards because lower-class groups will not have been urged to vote so constantly as in national elections. This does appear to be the case, and there is furthermore a revealing distinction between voting in city elections and voting on referenda.[66]

This hypothesis was tested in half a dozen cities by comparing the voting turnout in city elections with that in state elections. It was apparent that a higher proportion of upper-class voters made it to the polls in both kinds of elections; in some cases the proportions varied considerably. In Pittsburgh, Cleveland, St. Louis, Worcester, Cincinnati, and Kansas City, it was apparent that the upper-class wards outvoted the lower-class ones, often by as much as ten to fifteen percentage points (calculating the vote cast as a percentage of the population of the respective wards). For both groups the percentage of the vote cast declined in city elections as compared with state elections, but the rate of decline was not appreciably greater in the lower-class than in the upper-class wards, and in a few cases the decrease was greater in the upper-class wards.[67] The following data show turnout in city elections as percentages of the turnout in state elections either one year before

---

a reporter was sent to Kansas City to "give a firsthand account of the shenanigans of the Pendergast machine." He sent back reports which received headlines as:

PENDERGAST GANG PREYED ON AGED, SICK AND POOR
ESPIONAGE ON THE NAZI PLAN USED BY KANSAS CITY BOSS

Quoted from Ralph A. Straetz, P.R. *Politics in Cincinnati* (New York: New York University Press, 1958), p. 246. This book is a useful study of a city's struggle not only over proportional representation but of the interesting "reform" v. machine context within which proportional representation battles were fought.

[66] It will require more comparative research on this problem than has yet been done before any certainty on this point is justified. In particular it would be enlightening to have students research referenda involving nonpolitical devices to test whether there is a marked differential between kinds of wards in voting turnout.

[67] Eugene C. Lee (*op. cit.*, pp. 133–38) found a correlation between Republican registration and turnout in state and local elections. Republicans voted relatively more heavily than Democrats in city elections.

or one year after the 1958 state elections, depending upon the date of the city election.[68]

City	Type of Wards	City Election Turnout as Percentage of the 1958 State Election Turnout (Averages)
Worcester	4 Lower-Class	93
	3 Upper-Class	91
Cincinnati	4 Lower-Class	88
	4 Upper-Class	84
Kansas City	3 Lower-Class	86
	3 Upper-Class	87
Pittsburgh	3 Lower-Class	72
	3 Upper-Class	72

However, voting on referenda gave a further advantage to the upper-level groups for not only is the proportion of lower-class voters less, but the proportion of such voters who vote on the issue also is less. The voting variations in a referendum in New London, Connecticut, in 1953 on the question of whether or not to adopt a nonpartisan election is an illustration of the point. The referendum carried by 53 per cent of the vote cast, but the two-lower class wards of the city voted "no" (actually 33 and 37 per cent "yes" votes), whereas the upper-class ward gave 59 per cent support to the measure. The proportions of voters turning out in the lower and upper wards are revealing: 7.5 and 9.0 per cent of the registered voters in the lower-class wards went to the

---

[68] The voting patterns of the Northern Negro provide an interesting parallel to this point. In general Negroes—even those who are registered to vote—do not turn out on election day in proportions equal to those of the non-Negro community. Oscar Glantz has shown in his study of Negro voting in seven large industrial cities that an average of about 83 per cent of all registered voters voted in the presidential elections from 1948 to 1956, whereas the average turnout of Negroes was 73 per cent. See his "The Negro Voter in Northern Industrial Cities," 13 *Western Political Quarterly* 999 (1960). Interestingly, where whites vote in fewer numbers the Negroes do likewise, and Negroes have the highest percentage of turnout where the whites were also voting heavily—as in Kansas City where both the whole community and the Negro community had the highest percentages in the seven cities studied.

An interesting variation turns up when one examines the voting in Negro wards for city elections: frequently the Negro wards have a higher proportion of turnout for city elections as compared with state elections than do white upperclass wards. This occurs primarily when excitement is aroused in Negro wards by the presence of a Negro candidate on the ticket.

For a somewhat different analysis of "class" variation in referenda voting, see Kenneth M. Vines and Henry R. Glick, "The Impact of Universal Suffrage: A Comparison of Popular and Property Voting," 61 *American Political Science Review* 1078–87 (1967).

special election (it was held in June, which tended to reduce the turn-out) while the upper-class ward showed a turnout of 14.9 per cent—nearly twice that of the first ward cited. If this is a common pattern—and the research on the question is yet to be done—it may help explain the success of reform.

Interest Groups and Local Politics

Interest groups are manifestly important actors in local politics. As the initiators of demands upon other elements of the community, press-ing for recognition of their requests, interest groups obviously are at the heart of the political process.[69] In a pluralistic community where there is no single dominating power that forces conformity in totalitarian style to the dictates of the regime, interest groups assume great im-portance. Indeed it says something important about the primacy of interest groups that totalitarian regimes can tolerate no independent organizations, which, however innocent-sounding, may become sources of counterorganization against the regime. Thus Hitler proceeded through a program of *Gleichschaltung* coordination to force all or-ganizations in Germany to conform to Nazi doctrines and to accept approved Nazis as key members of organizations.[70] All organizations have potential political significance, and in a society where the forma-tion of interest group organizations is, if not specifically encouraged, at least not hampered, it is hardly surprising that they play a key role in local affairs where face-to-face relationships encourage organized, co-operative efforts to achieve the common objectives of groups of people.[71]

---

[69] Robert H. Salisbury discusses the manner in which the interest groups in St. Louis condition the pattern of party competition and indeed the whole politics of the city in "St. Louis Politics: Relationships Among Interests, Parties, and Govern-mental Structures," 13 *Western Political Quarterly* 498 (1960).

[70] This should not be taken to mean that interests do not exist or that they have no importance in the politics of totalitarianism. A dictator has to take account of important interests in his community—the military, for example, or the churches, workers, and peasants. The "account" taken is, to be sure, of a different order, but even for a dictator there are limits as to what can be ordered done since some degree of cooperation is necessary to achieve his goals. Even terror cannot be a complete substitute for cooperation.

[71] The degree of proliferation of social organizations in communities appears to vary, although the number in all communities of any size would probably surprise the uninitiated. Hundreds of organizations exist even in areas with less than 10,000 population, and in metropolitan centers organizational proliferation verges on the incredible.

The manner in which interest groups operate and a measure of their effectiveness are set by the kind of political system a community has. In a city with multicentered politics, interests groups will operate in one way; in a city with clearly visible and powerful political leadership they operate in others. In a city like Detroit which has nonpartisan elections and in which there are several competing major forces—manufacturing interests and downtown financial interests and the CIO unions, to name a few—has a multicentered politics; no powerful political machine dominates the political scene. It is not obvious to whom one must turn to get authoritative support for a proposed project or rather it is obvious that one must turn in all directions for support. Here multi-faceted bargaining is characteristic. The same appears to be true in Los Angeles, which also has nonpartisan elections and no clearly organized party machinery dominating the city's politics.[72] New Haven, prior to the election of Mayor Richard C. Lee, had a multicentered politics in which the decision-making centers were numerous and power was spread widely. When Mayor Lee took over he created what Robert Dahl has called an "executive-centered" politics.[73] With political power concentrated in the hands of the mayor, the behavior of interest groups changed; the great political and administrative power of the mayor made it mandatory that any interest group try to win the mayor's approval of any policy they want to propose. This does not mean the mayor's support is the only alliance a group seeks, of course, but the existence of a powerful centralized authority manifestly alters interest group strategy.

Whether a city has a loose and many-centered politics or a powerful organization or political leader dominating the scene, there is always bargaining among various interests, between interests and leaders in government, and between interests and the bureaucracy. Bargaining patterns also vary with different kinds of politics. In a city with focused leadership, bargaining goes on in an atmosphere of deference to the power potential of the leadership. Direct negotiations with the leader or his deputies become necessary for all interests. Other negotiations of course continue to be needed, but the fact that there is a more centralized leadership may reduce the importance of other bargaining. A mayor who chooses not to push his leadership thereby makes other kinds of bargaining more vital—perhaps nearly the whole decision-making process. James Q. Wilson, discussing the variations in Negro politics in the North, says at one point:

---

[72] See the interesting comparative analysis of the politics of Detroit, Chicago, Los Angeles, and New York presented by James Q. Wilson in *Negro Politics, op. cit.*, and *The Amateur Democrat, op. cit.*

[73] Dahl, *Who Governs, op. cit.*, pp. 200–14.

In many major cities, white political leaders have been reduced more and more to simply seeking office and ratifying decisions which are welded together by outsiders. Some strong-mayor cities (such as Chicago, for example) have political leaders (like Mayor Richard Daley) who are real powers in their own right and who can both propose and dispose. But typically the civic groups propose and the political leaders acquiesce when they can do so without provoking excessive controversy. . . .[74]

The effectiveness of an interest group is also dependent upon its own characteristics: its size, wealth, prestige, cohesion and unity, strategic position in society and politics, and the compatibility of its beliefs with those of the community in general. The nature of the demands a particular group makes may, however, assume equal importance in the bargaining process with the intrinsic qualities of groups. Take as an example a local controversy over fluoridation of water supply to minimize tooth decay. Doctors and dentists usually promote such projects, and when they appear at hearings to plead for fluoridation they come with many assets. They have the aura of science about them as well as the prestige of the healer. But if the doctors' demands run counter to beliefs *intensely* held by opposing forces, all the scientific prestige of the medical societies may not suffice.[75] A chapter of the National Association for the Advancement of Colored People may build up a large membership, get good leadership and wide backing in the Negro community for their proposals, but their proposals may be so alien to the deeply set beliefs of the community that politicians will not dare go far in meeting them. Affluent groups that we might expect to have great effectiveness may lose out when pitted against groups with a large following, especially when thoughts about election day pass through the minds of political leaders.

This is not to say that certain kinds of interest groups do not have decided advantages over others. The affluent and respected business and banking interests "downtown" do indeed have opportunities at the bargaining table not allotted to those who work at the lowly menial tasks in city hospitals. Indeed the latter will be lucky if they can be faintly heard shouting two blocks away from the bargaining table. Yet the very interests that often seem invincible—bankers or industrialists— do lose frequently. The affluent may lose when a perhaps more numerous or clamorous element convinces politicians that playgrounds, rent

---

[74] Wilson, *Negro Politics*, *op. cit.*, p. 311.

[75] On controversies over fluoridation, see James S. Coleman, *Community Conflict* (New York: The Free Press of Glencoe, Inc., 1957), p. 19; and Bernard and Judith Mausner, "A Study of the Anti-Scientific Attitude," 192 *Scientific American* 35–39 (February, 1955).

control, or an increase in the hospital worker's rate of pay are expedient. The prizes of the political game, it is worth reiterating, are not few and simple but many and complex, which ought to be a warning against sweeping generalizations about the potentialities of particular interest groups. The character of demands, the politics of a particular city, the groups involved and their characteristics, the particular context of a given controversy—all have somehow to be fitted into the equation of probability.

THE CLASSIFICATION OF INTEREST GROUPS

Through classifying various kinds of local interest groups, the character of the groups and their operational methods may be made clearer.

Business Groups. One sometimes hears sweeping remarks about the "business interests" in the city. Which business interests? Bankers? The entertainment industry? Parking lot owners? Filling station operators? Chain store managers? The proprietor of a dress shop on a side street? Are the interests of all these elements so uniform as to be thus easily lumped together? Even the director of a chamber of commerce, although he would not advertise the fact, would have to admit that only in a very vague and general way can his organization represent all these conflicting views. The retailer's interest in more downtown parking is not compatible with the demands of the parking lot owners whose income a city parking lot might endanger. Neither do all bankers or all real estate men share common views on questions of banking and real estate, let alone on questions that are tangential to their business concerns. "Downtown" business often is pitted against shopping centers on the fringes of a city. In short, in talking about business interests or any other collection of interest groups, it is well to keep in mind that there are great differences among different business interests and that it is rare, not customary, for most of the business community to share a common view on a local controversy.[76]

---

[76] See the instructive discussion of the peculiar position of the managers of the branch plants of the huge corporation by Norton E. Long, "The Corporation, Its Satellites, and the Local Community," in *The Corporation in Modern Society*, edited by Edward S. Mason (Cambridge, Mass.: Harvard University Press, 1959), pp. 202–17. As Long points out, the manager of an absentee-owned corporation has loyalties to his business organization that divert him from the role he might play if he were a permanent fixture in the community and not a bird of passage who will gladly move tomorrow across the country because that is the way to move up in the company. "In a short thirty years," says Long, "we have passed from a corporate order whose managerial style derived from the so-called 'robber barons,' the divine right Bayers, and the public-be-damned Vanderbilts, to the business-school-trained, public-relations-conscious professional of the highly specialized complex corporate bureaucracy of today." (At p. 205) Lumping the transient manager of a

Diverse and sometimes divided as business interest groups are, this is no indication that particular elements of the business community are powerless in local politics. On the contrary, in many cities combinations of businessmen through various methods exercise very wide authority in local affairs. The businessman in a city has the prestige of his position, the financial means to support local causes (*e.g.*, a public utility's contribution to a urban improvement committee), and a potentially significant power in the tax bill they pay annually. They can (and frequently do) threaten to leave town unless they get what they want. No politician wants to be blamed for indirectly raising the tax burden because he chased off the revenue-laying goose. How do you get re-elected by people whose jobs have been terminated, apparently by refusal to comply with the needs of the business that departed?

Evidence of the persuasiveness of this kind of threat is found in the dramatic results of a threat in 1957 by the Esso Standard Oil Company to leave Bayonne, New Jersey, if an anticipated tax increase were levied. (Esso employed 1800 people and paid a fourth of the city's taxes.) This threat followed by two years the departure from town of another oil company, and the anticipated increase in tax rate was intended to compensate for some $10 million in lost taxable valuation resulting from the flight of that company. (The dear departed had paid 17 per cent of the city's tax bill.) Shortly after the loss of that company other industries in town formed the Bayonne Citizens Association ("citizens," notice, not "businesses") to "seek reforms and economies."[77] This subsequently became an even more dignified-sounding organization when it was retitled the Bayonne Economic Research Council.

Taking a line similar to that of the industrial group, the local newspaper contended that, although city workers were underpaid, the city's civil service was overstaffed. The police department, the schools, and other agencies were claimed to have more personnel than the average for towns of the size of Bayonne (some 80,000 people). Instead of an average of 9.8 public employees per 1,000 population Bayonne had 13.3. Accordingly instead of the proposed tax increase, the business men asked for economies to reduce costs to about 90 per cent of the previous year's budget.

Faced with these demands, the five city commissioners and the school board complied by proposing the following austerity measures:

---

corporation satellite plant with a local banker or a local owner-entrepreneur of a manufacturing company can lead to gross misinterpretation. See also R. J. Pellegrin and C. S. Coates, "Absentee-owned Corporations and Community Power Structure," 61 *American Journal of Sociology* 413 (1956).

[77] *The New York Times*, January 15, 1957. This account is based on stories in *The Times*, January 12, 13, and 15, 1957.

1. Reduce the days of work allowed for city laborers by one day per week, thus cutting their pay by $10 to $15 a week
2. Cut $260,000 from the Public Safety budget by not filling vacancies
3. Retire 35 school employees; make economies on textbooks, all athletic programs; reduce the janitorial services of schools, thus reducing some $617,000 from the school budget
4. Reduce the allotment for the Memorial Day parade from $2,000 to $500

Said the Mayor in frank assessment of the situation: "We can't take a chance again. The Board of Education should be ready with its budget on Monday. Myself and my fellow Commissioners have come forward with reductions in our department requests."[78] At a special session in the offices of the Board of Education industrialists and a dozen members of the city's clergy discussed possible cuts in the city's budget. Pleading for public support for the slices that had to be made, a priest said for the assembled clergy:

We believe the gentlemen in office in town are honest and basically trying to do a good job. But because of the pressure put on them by individuals, they can't do the job they want to do. They will do the right thing if they get some moral help to protect them from the opinion of the people.[79]

Rough calculations indicated that some $1.3 million had been trimmed from the budget, which brought from the manager of the Esso plant the approving statement that the officials "had done a good job"; the economy campaign had been "on a high level without leveling criticism at anyone," he said. The omens were good for Bayonne: the manager announced that his plant would continue its modernization plan.

Labor Groups. The diversities among business groups are matched by those in labor unions which, although they share certain common features, have striking differences among them. As evidenced by bitter jurisdictional disputes, unions are often dramatically antagonistic toward each other, and, short of that, there are vast differences among them, depending upon their ideological orientation and traditions, their internal organization, and the industry involved. Some unions, mainly those with a CIO background, take stands on a broad range of public issues, attempt to encourage their membership to participate in politics, and the leadership often throws the weight of the union behind specific

---

[78] *The New York Times,* January 13, 1957.
[79] *The New York Times,* January 15, 1957.

local projects such as public housing or slum clearance. Other unions involve themselves very little in public affairs, and many of them—far from taking radical positions—are inclined to be conservative in outlook. This is particularly the case with some of the craft unions, the local units of which keep strictly to union business of wages, hours, and working conditions, and scorn involvement in any politics which does not directly concern the union. Thus differences among unions, large and small, militant and tame, tightly knit and loosely affiliated, are many and significant.

Unions are less concerned with local politics than they are with state or national politics since in the latter arenas legislative and administrative proposals that vitally and directly concern labor are constantly being considered. In some cities labor unions make a strenuous effort to move into local politics, and occasionally it works, but in most cities unions are marginal factors. In Milwaukee, for example, unions are said to play a significant role, but in Detroit—although the United Automobile Workers have tried hard to exercise strong power in the city— the nonpartisan politics of the city appear, according to several observers, to have severely limited the effectiveness of the UAW's efforts. Labor sometimes becomes involved in campaigns to oppose the city manager plan. Illustrative of this point is a contest in Salt Lake City over the drafting of a new charter for that city in 1957; proponents of the change sought labor support, but were informed it could be had only by prior agreement to write a new charter calling for a strong mayor rather than a city manager plan.[80]

Naturally local government employees unions constitute an exception to the generalization that unions steer clear of most local issues. Yet even these usually take a fairly narrow interest in matters beyond the scope of their particular field of employment, whether they are teachers, sanitation men, police men or zoo attendants. Occasionally local public employee groups get deeply involved in general politics, however; thus the Boston firemen support particular mayoralty candidates, although not through formal endorsement. Teachers unions are becoming much stronger and deeply involved in city politics. There does appear to be an increasing tendency for such unions to take a closer look at the budget and revenue processes in the city, which may well develop into wider involvement in local politics generally.

Other Economic and Social Groups. A vast array of other economic and social interests gives rise to significant organizations. Professional

---

[80] J. D. Williams, *The Defeat of Home Rule in Salt Lake City* (New York: McGraw-Hill Book Co., 1960), p. 6 (one of the Eagleton Case Studies in Practical Politics).

groups, such as lawyers, doctors, and dentists, come to government making demands from time to time when issues concerning their specialties arise. Bar associations make recommendations about judgeships or court procedures, doctors on hospital conditions, dentists on fluoridation. Veterans groups and other social groups may make demands—to fire a "disloyal" teacher or to change the school curriculum. Churches assume roles of varying importance depending upon the city and the issues that arise. A controversy about the transportation of parochial school children by city school buses can catapult religious groups into politics with great heat and fervor. Yet when that issue is settled one way or another, it may be a long time before church groups are directly involved in local politics again. The exception to this would be certain communities in which the place of the church is especially important, such as Salt Lake City where the Mormon Church has a great deal of influence, or Boston, where the Catholic Church enjoys a comparable position.[81] Likewise ethnic and racial groups exercise some power on certain kinds of questions. In the inner councils of political parties, ethnic groups can often bargain for the nomination of ethnic candidates as "recognition" (an important form of currency in the business of politics) for a particular nationality group. And in matters not only of places on a ticket but of other issues of concern to Negroes, such groups as the NAACP and the Urban League may play a role.[82]

The underworld element should not be overlooked in listing the major interests operating in a city. They may not do much publicly, but their influence, especially in larger cities, is often considerable. Gamblers and slot-machine czars have large investments to protect. Money is their main means of adapting to the forces seeking to ban their activities, but occasionally force is also applied, evidence of which can be seen in the systematic use of violence in the waterfront activities

---

[81] *Ibid.*, p. 4ff. Williams calls the Mormon Church one element of a triumverate of the city's political life, along with a newspaper and the Chamber of Commerce. See also the cogent comments on the Mormon Church in Jonas, *Western State Politics, op. cit.*, pp. 73–81. Important as the Roman Catholic hierarchy can be at times in the politics of a city such as Boston, more moonshine than reality goes into some of the sweeping statements about the "all-pervading" power of the Church. When its full power is turned on in matters of public morals, its authority is formidable indeed, but its full power is not often turned on for on most issues the Church takes no evident stand at all.

[82] James Q. Wilson shows that the nature of the party organization in a city has an effect on the manner in which Negro politicians pursue their goals; when they get into a stable and powerful organization such as that in Chicago, they tend, says Wilson, to compromise more than when they have to fight for their places continually in a weaker organization such as the New York City Democratic party. In the latter case a more aggressive form of politics is likely. *Op. cit.*, pp. 34–37.

of criminal elements. Law enforcement agents, city executives, labor leaders, and shipping officials must perforce take into account the potential for and use of violence by mobsters.

"Problem" Interest Groups. The members of each of the interest groups discussed above either share common economic interests that bring them together, or are members of social groups reflecting some personal attributes and essential characteristics of the individual which motivate organizational effort to defend the shared interest. There are other groups, many of them especially important in local politics, which are not formed around shared economic interests or by shared personal characteristics, but by a shared *concern* for a particular problem. Thus some organizations are centered around the welfare problems of the community—the Community Chest, United Fund, and other welfare service organizations. Parent-Teacher Associations form around a common interest in education, just as other groups are organized to combat juvenile delinquency, promote public parks, or aid mentally retarded children. These groups may not beat paths to the politician's door, but at intervals they become deeply involved in politics. A proposal to educate the mentally retarded child to the limits of his abilities can mean a lively political contest involving, for example, the embattled group interested in the welfare of the retarded child, PTA organizations, the board of education, the city council (since a new educational program or perhaps a new building must be approved and financed), and many others whose areas of concern may touch upon this problem. Thus it is with literally hundreds of groups in larger communities and with dozens in small places.

"Good Government" and Reform Groups. No doubt the seeming ubiquity of "good government" groups (which the irreverent party regulars used to call the "goo-goo" boys) is a lasting heritage of the Muckraker-Progressive movement of the early part of this century, but whatever their origin, such groups are often major political forces in today's municipal politics. The names by which they go and the roles they play vary greatly from city to city, and it may serve to illustrate the variations among them to describe summarily some of the major types of reform-good government organizations.

Perhaps the most significant of these groups are those that have for all practical purposes become political parties, although it might be argued that when they do so they cease to be interest groups in the usual sense. Still the spirit of reform and shiny idealism continues to march such a group as the City Charter Committee (commonly called the Charterites) in Cincinnati, even though it serves as a major party in opposition to the regular Republican organization in that city.[83] Not all efforts at transformation into a party succeed by any means. Thus the Hartford Citizen's Charter Committee finally dissolved in the face of its continued failure to compete successfully with the Democratic party in the city which has, though informal endorsement of candidates, come to dominate the city council. Finally in a 1967 referendum nonpartisan council elections were abandoned entirely.[84]

Similar groups operate with narrower objectives, such as the promotion of community development or redevelopment. Thus the Greater Philadelphia Movement operates as a nonpartisan group to foster improvement of the metropolitan area of Philadelphia. Municipal Leagues, Citizens Action Committees, Civic Associations, and variously titled groups operate with varying effectiveness in cities across the country. Some of them serve as research and information agencies of considerable value—for example, the Cleveland Bureau of Governmental Research and the Milwaukee Citizen's Research Bureau.

One "reform" group of occasional importance is the taxpayers' association or league which has a conservative orientation and seeks the greatest possible value from the taxpayer's dollar. This is an objective often shared by many good government groups listed above, but the taxpayers' associations often do not display general concern for broad civic reforms but concentrate instead on fiscal matters. In contrast to taxpayers' groups is the League of Women Voters, local units of which campaign ceaselessly for reforms in local government and in political procedures. Limiting its attention to relatively few subjects and providing both its membership and the public at large educational material on these topics, the League is a scrupulously nonpartisan and persistent —if something naïve—pleader on the reform front.

Direct Democracy: More Power to the People?

Direct participation of the public in initiating and approving legislation is far more common in the United States than in most democratic countries. Direct participation is, however, a characteristic of state and local government and has only marginally been employed by the national

---

[83] It is, however, being threatened now since the Democratic party organization decided in 1959 to run a Democratic slate after more than 30 years of cooperation with the Charter group.

[84] *The New York Times*, December 10, 1967.

government (in the case of agricultural price support referenda among participating farmers).[85] This practice, like the efforts to "democratize" American parties, is in good part a consequence of our strong belief in popular sovereignty. In the eighteenth century, state governments submitted constitutions for popular approval, and Connecticut in 1818 made constitutional amendments subject to popular approval. Other states followed in time. In the Jacksonian era, democratization of parties, the long ballot, and the spoils system were further developments of popular participation in government.

In the late nineteenth century, emphasis on direct legislation resulted from dissatisfaction with the state legislatures and boss-ridden city councils. The move to enlarge the public's role and to diminish that of the elected official was thus not only consonant with a respected tenet of American political thinking, it was a practical matter of "fighting the crooks." Since elected officials could not be trusted, the reasoning ran, alternative ways to achieve legislation and to countermand undesired legislative acts should be provided. In time nearly half the states and most cities provided for referendum procedures, and, although the initiative is less prevalent, there are many jurisdictions in which legislation or constitutional amendments may be initiated by popular petition and then submitted to referendum. Direct legislation is more common in the Western states than in the East but is used in some degree in all parts of the country.

Conservatives have generally feared and opposed direct democracy. In the Jacksonian era they quite rightly saw these devices as attacks on the semiaristocratic features of early American government (e.g., bureaucratic posts for sons of the landed gentry), and—fearful of placing too much power in the hands of propertyless voters—they resisted these innovations. At the turn of the century, owners of utilities and other businesses were apprehensive that the people through direct legislation might take advantage of property interests generally. It was their not unreasonable assumption that they could stifle such legislation when it had to pass through a legislature where—as a last resort—the persuasive powers of bribery could contain radicalism. When Oregon's initiative and referendum system was first used to set a special assessment on Portland municipal street improvements, the action was attacked in court as unconstitutional on the grounds that it was a denial of a "republican form of government" which the United States Constitution requires each state to maintain. (The argument was that a

---

85 See Ralph M. Goldman, "The Advisory Referendum in America," 14 *Public Opinion Quarterly* 303 (1950), for a discussion of national referenda as well as a brief survey of the historical development of the referendum in this country.

republican form of government necessarily implied representation; a system of direct legislation, it was contended, denied this guarantee.) But the courts rejected the suit and sustained the law.[86]

In the long run, however, the people have not used the referendum for "radical" purposes very often—or at least not unless the word *radical* is very loosely used. Liberal proposals have frequently been initiated, only to have conservatives beat the proposals and retain control of the situation through vigorous publicity campaigns. In despair over the effectiveness of such campaigns, the late Senator Richard Neuberger once said:

In recent years California, the state where initiative and referendum now are used most frequently has voted down bills to create a state housing authority, to redistrict the legislature on the basis of present-day population, to repeal a consumer's sales tax, and to adopt a state FEPC forbidding racial discrimination in employment. These setbacks, all by overwhelming margins, have given pause to liberals and welfare workers.[87]

The Politics of Direct Democracy. Resort to the referendum is merely an indication that somebody in a given contest calculates that he will have a better opportunity to achieve his goals that way than by some other method. The motivations to use an initiative or to demand a referendum are essentially these: (1) to circumvent obstruction in a legislative body or in some other agency of government (*e.g.*, the governor's veto),[88] (2) to reverse a decision reached by some public agency by challenging through an appeal to the populace;[89] (3) to "pass the buck" and avoid responsibility for making a decision on a contentious proposition (e.g., a city council may dodge an issue by letting it go to referendum). As an alternative agency of decision-making, the referendum can assume considerable importance.

---

[86] *Kadderly* v. *Portland*, 44 Oregon 145 (1903). A similar question was brought to the Supreme Court of the United States in 1912 and was again rejected: *Pacific States Telephone and Telegraph Co.* v. *Oregon*, 233 U.S. 118. The basis of the court's opinion was that this was a "political question" and therefore nonjusticiable.

[87] Richard Neuberger, "Government by the People," 85 *The Survey Graphic* 490 (1950).

[88] See two studies by Gordon E. Baker on efforts to get reapportionment through initiative after failing to get legislatures to apportion more fairly. In Oregon the effort succeeded; in Washington it led to results only indirectly. "Reapportionment by Initiative in Oregon," 13 *The Western Political Quarterly* 508 (1960), and *The Politics of Reapportionment in Washington State* (New York: McGraw-Hill Book Co., 1960) (one of the Eagleton Case Studies in Practical Politics).

[89] Referenda on water fluoridation often arise in this manner, as to challenges on expansion of educational facilities.

Many opponents of the referendum process expressed fears that it would lead to major changes in state and city politics. They were afraid that it might lead to minority rule through special interest group campaigns, that it would lead to sloppy legislation drawn by inexpert laymen, and that it would destroy legislative responsibility. The evidence does not appear to sustain the anticipated forebodings. First, projects backed by minorities apparently are no more likely to be won through referenda than otherwise. Second, sloppy legislation is regularly adopted by state legislatures, and, although this is no "excuse" for similar legislation being proposed from other sources, in the judgment of some students of the subject there is no greater problem of poor legislative draftsmanship from the one source than from the other. Third, there is no clear evidence to suggest that the use of the referendum has destroyed legislative responsibility, since the states using the referendum most have had only the vaguest kind of legislative responsibility—if one means by that some degree of collective responsibility for actions taken. The states involved have been those with the greatest degree of nonpartisanship and with little party discipline in the legislatures, and if there has been a decline in legislative responsibility in those states it would be presumptuous indeed to assign that to the practice of using referenda.[90] On the matter of responsibility, Senator Nueberger raises an interesting point: the legislature of Oregon passed a sales tax five times only to have it reversed each time by a referendum vote.[91] This would seem to suggest so little opportunity to affix reasonable responsibility on legislators that an alternative mode of action would appear justified.

One other criticism of the referendum is that it is a source of major confusion to voters who often cannot act sensibly on the more complex issues. There is validity to this. Highly complex proposals on banking and taxation, at times nearly impossible to express in simple language, do baffle voters. Even the most conscientious of citizens might have reason to be baffled if he had to decide on the appropriateness of complex legislation like that dealing with "Oil and Gas Conservation" and put on the California ballot in 1956. An official state publication distributed to voters made the bill available—all 29 small-print, double-column pages of it. But a citizen might be excused if he tuned out when he came early in the bill to sections such as:

---

[90] In a review of the chief criticisms leveled against the referendum, Joseph La Palombara and Charles Hagan conclude that the critics have failed to make their case. See their article, "Direct Legislation: An Appraisal and a Suggestion," 45 *American Political Science Review* 400 (1961).

[91] Neuberger, *op. cit.*, p. 493.

When used between the word "oil" and "gas," the word "and" includes the word "or" and the word "or" includes the word "and." The use of the plural includes the singular and the use of the singular includes the plural. . . . "Unit Agreement" shall mean and include any unit agreement, any unit operating agreement, consent agreement. . . ."[92]

It is true that legislators too can be confused by technical terms and involved language, but as compared with the layman the legislator has at least the opportunity to familiarize himself with legal language by constant exposure. But voters are quite understandably less inclined to acquire ability to cope with legalese. Voters may also act irrationally on questions put to them. They may say "yes" to a project but "no" to the request for funds to sustain it.[93] More serious, however, is the criticism that the complexity of issues makes it possible to mislead voters through publicity and scare campaigns into voting in seemingly self-defeating ways.[94] This raises an important point about the referendum: the politics of the referendum campaign.

The Politics of the Referendum-Issue Campaigns. Voter confusion about the meaning of proposed issues is an important consideration in the conduct of campaigns, whether in support or opposition. Widening the scope of the decision-making arena inevitably means the inclusion of a higher percentage of people to whom the proposal will mean little or nothing. Taking advantage of this referendum, campaigners raise doubts on the basis of the inherent complexity of an issue and then urge a negative vote in view of those doubts.[95] An advertisement run late in a Salt Lake City campaign on home rule said simply: "Confused? Many are. Play Safe—When in Doubt, vote NO!"[96] Public relations firms which specialize in running referendum campaigns are alert to the vote-winning potential of this confusion and set about to make the most of it, not by seeking to clarify the issue but by sowing every possible doubt. In a 1948 campaign for reapportionment of the

---

[92] "Proposed Amendments to Constitution, Propositions and Proposed Laws . . . 1956," State publication, Appendix p. 6. To peruse a copy of this biennial publication is to sympathize with the more conscientious of California voters.

[93] Legislators often show a similar kind of less-than-rational behavior, however, so this is not as "condemning" as it appears. That is, they vote for a project in one roll call and reject it in effect in the next when its funds are cut off.

[94] See John S. Radabaugh, "Tendencies of California Direct Legislation," 42 *Southwestern Social Science Quarterly* 66 (1961).

[95] See, for example, Maurice A. Lohman and Wm. C. Sayres, "Why People Vote 'No'": *Case Study Observations* (Albany, N.Y.: The University of State of New York, State Education Dept., Division of Research, 1960).

[96] J. D. Williams, *op. cit.*, p. 12.

California Legislature, so effective was the doubt-sowing operation that the very counties that stood to gain most in the reshuffling of legislative seats voted overwhelmingly against the measure.[97]

The way in which confusion and latent antagonisms in the minds of voters can affect referenda is well-illustrated by battles over the fluoridation of water supply. All told, some 1600 cities and towns have undertaken to add fluoride to drinking water (proportions of one to one million parts of water) to reduce children's dental cavities. After long testing the evidence is most imposing that such treatment does have a positive effect in saving children's teeth and that the fluorides thus administered are harmless, yet when the proposal to fluoridate has been submitted to the public, in about 60 per cent of the cases it has been turned down.[98] The evidence suggests that the less educated lower classes vote against fluoridation partly because they distrust the proposers of the plan and partly because they are more convinced by the more direct if less scientific attacks on the process than by the highly scientific defense. Much is made of the fact that the fluorides are literally poisonous when ingested in quantity, but of course so is the chlorine in the water supply of most cities. Thus one broadside against fluoridation in Northampton, Massachusetts, closed with the ominous warning that: "J. Edgar Hoover, head of the FBI, has warned the public to be on guard against any attempts at poisoning of public water supplies."[99] The gullible were not told that the warning was made during the Korean War and had no conceivable reference to the use of fluoride.

Part of the antagonism to fluoridation, like that aroused over proposals to improve educational facilities, presumably results from the frustrations produced by the social and economic difficulties of lower-class life. Aggressiveness and bitter, if latent, antagonism toward the elites that have great influence in the community have often been found

[97] On the effectiveness of one public relations firm in fighting issue campaigns, see the description of the team of Whitaker and Baxter of California by Stanley Kelley, *Professional Public Relations and Political Power*, Chap. 2.

[98] The figures are those of Thomas F. A. Plaut who said in 1959 that of 336 referenda the "no" vote prevailed in 201 cases and the "yes" vote in 135. See his article "Analysis of Voting Behavior on a Fluoridation Referendum," 23 *Public Opinion Quarterly* 213 (1959). A brief bibliography on the subject is contained in the footnotes of this article (see especially pp. 213–14).

[99] Mausner, *op. cit.*, p. 37. Note also the emotional heat and social divisiveness that accompanied the California referendum to repeal that state's fair housing law in 1964. A similar fight in Berkeley and other cities caused great tension. See Duane Lockard, *Toward Equality* (New York: The Macmillan Company, 1967), pp. 68–72, and Lynn W. Eley and Thomas W. Casstevens, *The Politics of Fair-Housing Legislation* (San Francisco: Chandler Publishing Co., 1968).

among these people.[100] One student of community conflict has concluded that some of the aversion to fluoridation plans stems from simple antipathy toward the incumbent administration which proposed the plan. The antagonism seems to prevail even when the proposal does not actually come from the administration; the distinctions about origination of the plan are not put across and the anti-those-in-power sentiment prevails even when the administration is not involved. He surmises that the disgruntled ones are likely to be nonvoters in most referenda, but if aroused they would vote "no." Therefore, he says, the greater the turnout, the greater the likelihood of defeat. From data on a number of fluoridation votes he found a marked correlation between large turnout and defeat. Where the turnout was large, nearly two-thirds of the proposals lost; where it was small a majority of the proposals won.[101]

What is the political significance of the fact that referenda usually draw fewer voters than do elections of officials? In the first place, any notion that the referendum turns over to the whole populace, or even to a majority of the adults, the power to legislate is grossly in error. Usually the number of voters participating is a minority of the registered voters, and of those who potentially are eligible voters. Even when voters are already at the polls to vote in presidential or gubernatorial elections, they often do not choose to vote on referendum questions; between 1948 and 1954 V. O. Key found that in about four out of ten elections in California less than three-quarters of the voters at the polls voted on issues on the ballot.[102] In city elections the proportions are generally even smaller since in those elections the total turnout is less. Particularly in city elections then this low turnout might seem to give a determined minority group a decided advantage since its power would be enhanced by full participation. Although more research would be necessary on the point before one could say with certainty whether this advantage does accrue to small blocks of voters, writers on this subject, emphasizing state government but referring to local referenda as well, contend that this does not give undue advantage to the minority.[103]

---

[100] See James S. Coleman (*op. cit.*, p. 19) for a discussion of this problem and for further references on evidence of these attitudes.

[101] *Ibid.* And many referenda do fail. The Investment Bankers Association reported that in 1961 only 68 per cent of the school bond issues were approved by voters.

[102] V. O. Key, *Politics, Parties and Pressure Groups, op. cit.*, p. 630.

[103] La Palombara and Hagan, *op. cit.*, pp. 414–19. See also V. O. Key and Winston W. Crouch, *The Initiative and Referendum in California* (Berkeley, Calif.: University of California Press, 1939). See, however, the evidence cited above regarding city government reform referenda and class variations in voting on them.

The Recall. Akin to the initiative and referendum is the recall, a means by which an elected official may be removed from office before the expiration of his term through a special election. It is in effect an impeachment process by the public rather than by other officials. Originated early in this century in California, the practice ultimately spread to several other states and more extensively to local governments, but it never acquired the popularity of the referendum, and outside California does not appear to be much used. Where it is possible to start recall proceedings, however, any group displeased with an official's action has a weapon of considerable potential political significance. For there is no requirement that charges brought against an incumbent be shown to be reasonable or that they express probable cause for removal before the recall election takes place: it is necessary merely to get a specified number of voters to sign a petition for recall, and the campaign is under way. The forms of balloting on the question vary—in some cases the recall is conducted simultaneously with an election to fill the vacancy should the voters remove the officer and in others the question of recall alone is on the ballot. But whether the recall campaign is on removal only or on replacement as well, campaigns are likely to be lively and at times quite bitter.[104]

The potential importance of the recall would seem to be great in that an official can be forced to defend himself at any time against a sustained attack that could result in his having to spend an enormous amount of money in a camapign not only to retain his office but perhaps to defend his reputation against what may be baseless charges. Yet it does not appear that there is extensive use of recall even as a threat. This point has not been the subject of recent research, however, and while it is probably true that the recall has little ultimate importance there have been too few systematic studies of the practice to warrant any great confidence in the conclusion.[105]

---

[104] The recall attempt aimed at a San Francisco mayor in 1946 illustrates the range of techniques that can get involved in such contests. See the brief case study on this affair by Charles Adrian in *Governing Urban America, op. cit.,* pp. 90–92. See also Stanley Kelley, *op. cit.,* pp. 48–49 on the role of the public relations firm of Whitaker and Baxter in this campaign.

[105] The most recent attempt at thorough analysis of the subject dates from 1930: F. L. Bird and F. M. Ryan, *The Recall of Public Officers: A Study of the Operation Of the Recall in California* (New York: The Macmillan Company, 1930).

The Politics of the State Legislative
10. Process

THE TEMPTATION to talk about state legislatures collectively is inescapable. All legislatures pass laws, respond to and resist interest groups, party leaders, governors, bureaucrats, and others who urge the approval or rejection of particular measures. Yet the differences among state legislatures are striking. Legislatures reflect different sets of political and social forces, traditions, and practices. The legislature is always the focus of the law-making process, but there is nothing inevitable about the character of the demands made, the way in which they are made, or about the kinds of bargaining and maneuvering in response to them. The questions posed, the ways of seeking solutions, the distribution of power within the legislature vary greatly from state to state.

The fifty legislatures are, in short, all things. Some are powerful, some are weak. Some are authoritative on questions on which others are powerless. Some legislatures shine with the putrescence of corruption from a less than honorable element of the membership that gives a distinctive appearance (and odor) to the whole; others have a higher proportion of honorable and honest members than most institutions, political or otherwise. Some are efficient and well-organized for their functions while others are nearly chaotic in their ineffectiveness. Some are dominated by disciplined and powerful parties, others are torn by dissidence and factional rivalry. Most legislatures have their moments of timidity and toughness, of evasiveness and responsiveness, irresponsibility and responsibility.

[255]

It is not these variations alone that pose difficulties for the student of the state legislative process. The further difficulty is that certain kinds of data about them—the formal, structural, procedural details —are readily available while their operational characteristics are obscure and for most states unavailable without some laborious searching for and interpretation of more or less subjective information. The politics of the legislature (*i.e.*, the way in which power is exercised in these institutions) is elusive, whereas the formal procedural facts are concrete, objective, and handily collected and tabulated. This offers a temptation to concentrate on the obvious and outward aspects of the legislature to the neglect of political processes. It is both feasible and profitable to undertake comparative analysis of legislative operations, but if the analysis is restricted to the outward phenomena the conclusions inevitably must have an air of unreality about them. The accumulation of factual information about the length of legislative sessions, the tenure of members, the volume of legislation enacted, or the size of legislative bodies has little importance unless these data are assessed in terms of their political consequences. What does the length of tenure of members have to do with the exercise of power in a legislature? Who gains and who loses by a constitutional requirement of a two-month limitation on the duration of a legislative session? The importance of these features of legislative structure or procedure have importance not as abstractions but as they affect the exercise of power over somebody.

But how can one analyze the operations of legislatures if the information on them is incomplete and not readily available? Assuming that it is important to go beyond the formal arrangements to the more dynamic features of who manages to get whom to do what and by what means, how can one acquire such data? The only answer now is that one must concentrate sufficiently on a few states to know something of their operations so that in time it will be possible to evaluate generalizations about legislatures in general—for such generalizations will be offered, whatever the state of our knowledge. This is not, however, an invitation to know the tree and forget the forest; on the contrary I maintain that the forest can never be appreciated unless some tree serves as a frame of reference, a source of perspective for evaluating hypotheses and propositions about legislatures generally. Existing case studies and other evaluations of state legislative politics permit the student to see some particular trees, and such literature may always be supplemented by examination of state legislative institutions near at hand.[1]

---

[1] The footnotes of this chapter and the bibliographical appendix of this book offer some leads to this literature. It should not be assumed, by the way, that legislative methods—the formal law-passing procedures and the constitutional and rules limita-

The State Legislature: Institution in Eclipse?

A television documentary on the state legislature a few years ago asked whether the legislature still served the purposes for which it was intended. The answer to that depends, naturally, on what it was intended to do. If it was "meant" to be a well-spring of public policy, a primary initiator of rules, a master of the public purse, then it is not unreasonable to say that it no longer serves its intended purposes fully. What the framers of the constitutional provisions establishing the legislatures "intended" is not so neatly ascertainable as this question suggests. The common habit of overemphasizing the rational element in the creation of an institution is at work here. Undoubtedly there were many different intentions in the minds of those who voted in early state conventions for the particular legislative institutions that may conveniently be said to be the basis of the "purposes intended." A radical-minded man and an aristocratically-inclined conservative may have had utterly contradictory objectives and yet both may have voted "yea." Significantly also it is well to remember that legislative like other political institutions are in no small measure the product of evolutionary processes: the rough outline is filled in by trial and error, contest, and compromise over time. Therefore the "intent" of the "originators" may have little meaning for a society a century or more removed. In any event it is obvious when one examines the duties of and the powerful role played by the state legislature of the early nineteenth century that the legislature of today presents a striking contrast. The earlier prototype was the dominant political agent in the society, far more decisive than the governor or the bureaucracy or the courts. By comparison, the legislature of our day has peripheral power; it shares authority with other agents and occupies a much less exalted place in the eyes of the public and in contests over policy.

The reasons for this shrinkage in relative power are complex. Legis-

---

tions on the legislatures—are unimportant. This is rather a suggestion that the importance of these devices is not a matter of abstract reasoning but a dynamic question of power which can be most effectively understood when seen in the context of an ongoing political system. The details of legislative procedure, which are presented more fully in most textbooks on state government, can also be found in the biennial *Book of the States* which presents current information on such matters as session-length, volume of bills, veto procedures, apportionment, party affiliation of members and other features of all state legislatures. For a general assessment of the institution, see Malcolm Jewell, *The State Legislature* (New York: Random House, 1962). See also Alexander Heard, ed., *State Legislatures In American Politics* (Englewood Cliffs, N.J.: Prentice-Hall, 1966).

latures, like other political institutions, are evolutionary by nature: they change with the political, social, and economic circumstances of which they are both a part and a reflection. The development of a complex and huge economic system and of a corresponding social system poses new questions for government to deal with. Attitudes about public policy, the methods deemed appropriate and perhaps even necessary to cope with the problems of an industrial society have changed the nature of government and therefore of the legislatures. A bureaucracy of unprecedented size and scope of power now exists; experts are not only more numerous, they are deferred to and granted wide discretion. In a simpler past more was left to the legislature than is now possible to leave there. Legislators possess neither the expertise nor the time, if they knew enough about so many highly technical matters, to consider the details of regulating insurance or banking, for example; of necessity such matters are delegated to administrators. To illustrate the point consider the quandary in which certain Connecticut legislators found themselves some years ago. They were told late in their session that new rules for teacher certification were soon to be promulgated by the state department of education, and they were given the provisions that were to be included. When the legislators—within whose power it lay to disapprove the rules—asked when the formal promulgation would be made so that the legislature might approve (or, some of them hoped, disapprove), they were told the rules would be made final some weeks after the session ended. Thus the earliest opportunity for legislative consideration of them would be about eighteen months later, when they would have been in effect long enough to be established policy that would have to be abrogated. Here as in innumerable other cases the administrator possesses discretionary power which can be exercised relatively independently of the legislature. Similarly, policy initiation has largely passed from the legislator to the governor, the expert, or the interest group.

But, it might be argued, does not the legislature still control the purse strings to which any department head must pay attention? It is indeed true that the legislature still formally must ratify the budget, but, as with Congress, most state legislatures are ratifiers and not initiators of appropriations. Budget-making is generally the duty of bureaucrats subordinate to the governor, and once the budget has been submitted to the legislature, little modification results. This is not to say that the legislature is powerless in budgetary matters or that pleaders for ap-appropriations can ignore the legislators but rather that the legislature becomes one of the places where such pleas can be made, one in which the plea is for *revision* of previously prescribed proportions. Thus even in its most traditional role, indeed the very role that gave rise to the legislative institution originally, the legislature has slipped in importance.[2]

Still, is the legislature not the "representative" body that draws power from the people precisely because of the close connection between the voters and their elected representatives? This to be sure is one source of strength, but it is by no means a sole legislative prerogative, for the governor claims to be representative and in fact such is his popularity that he can often persuade a good many voters that he, not the legislature, "really" represents their interests. In a simpler society, where in all probability the legislator was known to most of his constituents, a kind of direct "representation" was possible, or at least the opportunity for such was infinitely greater than it is in the mass society of today. It is common today for citizens not even to know the names of their state representatives, and only a small proportion must know their representatives personally, especially in the urban centers. But the governor they do "know," at least by name. Through the media of modern communication he is almost ubiquitous, making pronouncements on all kinds of policy and not uncommonly claiming to reflect the actual will of the people.

Governors are particularly inclined to make such claims—and they are more likely to be accepted widely where the legislature is not apportioned equally. Before the Supreme Court invalidated malapportionment of state legislatures in 1962 (in *Baker v. Carr*) and then oversaw the wholesale revision of apportionment systems, most states had badly malapportioned legislatures leading inevitably to a certain amount of public distrust of legislators. Where a small portion of the population had more than its proportionate share of legislative strength and a large

---

[2] It is interesting to note that parliamentary history began when English kings in need of cash summoned notables from the English countryside in hopes they would aid them in gathering the money necessary to conduct their affairs. It is true that the notables were assembled in the hope also that they would help facilitate the establishment of centralized government over the island, but it was the need for money that induced kings to call new parliaments when none had been held for long periods. And they were not held for long intervals by some kings because it was soon apparent to the knights, clergy, lords, and burgesses that the king needed their support. Once this became clear, demands could be made, at first subtly, later adamantly, as preconditions to the approval of the needed taxes. And of course this was ultimately parlayed into legislative supremacy, reducing the once omnipotent sovereign to a figurehead. But the process did not stop there. The present Parliament has only the most remote control over budgets, the power of the purse now having passed to the Cabinet. For an instructive resume of the origins and evolutions of parliamentary institutions, see Charles A. Beard and John D. Lewis, "Representative Government in Evolution," 26 *American Political Science Review* 223 (1932), reprinted in *Legislative Behavior*, edited by John C. Wahlke and Heinz Eulau (New York: The Free Press of Glencoe, 1959), pp. 22–30.

part of the people—particularly those in large cities—had less than their fair share of the seats of the legislature, the governor often cast himself in the role of the representative of the underrepresented urban majority of the population. And the legislature consequently suffers in its prestige in no small measure. As V. O. Key said,

Many factors have conspired to produce the low status of the American state legislature. Yet, among these factors, its unrepresentative character must be assigned a high rank. A body that often acts reluctantly under executive pressure and whose chief purpose often seems to be one only of negation cannot but in the long run lose prestige. A body that is condemned by its constitution to the defense of a partial interest in the state becomes, if not a council of censors, something other than a representative body in the conventional sense.[3]

Without attempting to elaborate the point further it is evident that the pressures on the contemporary legislature are formidable. There is no reason to assume that the legislature is strong enough to withstand them permanently; it may yet succumb. That the legislature is granted specific recognition in the state constitution is no guarantee of continued viability as a political institution for we have ways of adapting constitutional terminology to political realities so as to make the institutional system conform to those realities. If the legislature goes on losing prestige, there is nothing in the past history of the institution to suggest that it will prove resistant to the process of evolution that has brought it to where it is now. Form it may retain, but the power it has may be lost to other agencies, and like the British House of Lords or the American Electoral College, the state legislatures could come to mean little.

Yet it would be inaccurate to assume that what could take place has taken place. The legislature is nowhere powerless and insignificant. Challenged and with less relative power as a policy-maker than it once had, the legislature is still an agency of considerable consequence. The legislative process in all states still has political pertinence.

The Legislative Function

The function of the legislature that consumes most of its time and that in the opinion of most people is its sole duty is, of course, the enactment of statutory law—the formal pronouncement of rules of public

---

[3] Key, *American State Politics: An Introduction, op. cit.,* pp. 76–77.

policy which society is to obey or—in the case of nonregulatory law—
is to be served by. The volume and the scope of such law is enormous,
ranging from the trivial to the most vital matters, but it would be a mistake to assume either that the legislature has no other function than
the passage of such rules or that the legislature's output constitutes the
full body of the law. No doubt the legislature is the seminal source
of the basic rules which control social conduct and which prescribe
the services and privileges to which the citizen is entitled, but it is not
the only source of such rules. The constitution, over which the legislature has but limited control, is also a major source not only of broadly
prescriptive rules (on matters of structure of government, for example)
but of restrictive provisions (the bill of rights) and often quite detailed
quasistatutory regulations. The courts are a source of law, notwithstanding the polite fiction that courts do not make but only interpret it. The
traditional common law was, after all, a body of judge-made law, produced decision by decision. Likewise the executive is responsible for a
large portion of our law—through executive orders and administrative
regulations establishing "sublaws," so to speak (filling in the details of
statutory laws). Finally, the people themselves through the initiative
and referendum share in the law-making function in varying degrees.

Writing, revising, promoting, attacking, and ultimately enacting
statutes on general matters of public and sometimes private concern are
not the only functions of the legislature by any means. The legislature
initiates constitutional amendments and shares in maintaining supervision over the operations of the executive branch. Also, the approval
of administrative appointments (and in some states the direct filling of
some administrative positions) falls to the legislature, and there is constant demand on legislators to intercede on behalf of constituents. And
though the legislature usually plays a secondary role in matters of fiscal
policy—reacting to the proposals of the governor and his fiscal agents
—that role is not an insignificant one. For the initiation of any new
program not included in the governor's proposed budget can only be
achieved in most states by getting the appropriations and taxation committees to look favorably upon the project. In short, the legislature is
in one way or another involved in all aspects of state government.

The Perspective of the Legislator

Although there are some who make the legislature a career, the
typical legislator—if there is such a thing—is a bird of passage: he

hasn't been in the legislature long and he isn't going to stay long. Nearly half the approximately 7,660 legislators in office at any given time are first-termers, many of them bewildered by the obscure terminology and complex etiquette of legislative procedure. The first-termer lacks experience in reading laws and bills for quick understanding which, as anyone who has struggled with the opaque and sometimes archaic language of the law knows, is not an easily acquired art. He is likely to be amazed at the pressure that builds up as the session progresses—pressure on his time, on his nerves and energy, on particular measures that—were he not in the legislature—he probably would never have considered likely areas of dispute. In this whirling kaleidoscope of bits and pieces of issues and personal and group conflicts, he is expected to act rationally, responsibly, and wisely, Or at least he is expected to act thus by the hornbook rules promulgated by those who never got closer to the legislative process than the spectator's gallery. Whether the legislator will feel any special sense of responsibility as he votes on the state budget (the aggregate of which for all states runs to more than $50 billion annually) or on the passage of the more significant of the 25,000 pieces of legislation (from the more than 120,000 introduced) normally enacted by legislatures every biennium depends upon the individual and his particular outlook. It may therefore be worthwhile to look at the overall position of the legislature, not from the perspective of the observer, but from that of the participant.

It is obvious, of course, that there is no such thing as a single perspective on the legislature: the member's conception of his own proper role determines how he sees the legislative process, and the illusions that members bring with them to the state capitol are by no means identical. Some see their task in terms of an idealized, if fuzzy, conception of a rational man whose task it is to meditate on all questions, resist all special interest pressures, and decide all issues on their "merits" regardless of the pressure brought to bear by anybody—even including constituents. Others see themselves as the chosen delegates of some special element of the society—farmers, laborers, insurance and real estate businesses, or the party organization—and they fully expect to act accordingly. The lack of research assistance, the pressures applied by the party leadership, or the need to keep political fences mended while simultaneously doing the homework of the session, will look very different to different types of legislators. Thus with all the aspects of legislative life: in the perspective of some members certain "problems" would seem utterly irrelevant, yet to some members each of them is an important aspect of his role.

Take the problem of homework. The legislator who takes seriously the need to keep up with all that is going on will sooner or later find he has overreached his grasp: even in the small state he will simply be unable to keep up with all the questions at issue. And in the larger states it is inevitable that no single person can fully inform himself about the thousands of bills and resolutions posed during a session. (In Connecticut over 3000 bills were presented in 1955, and the number doubled in the next ten years to over 6000. Nor is there much help provided in the way of research assistance or staff aides. No state provides anything like the amount of assistance provided a member of Congress; in most states there is little assistance of any kind, secretarial, research, or other. Time is limited sharply since most states have biennial sessions often limited to a few months' duration. The volume of business is great for many reasons, not the least of which is the long delay between sessions, and thus an enormous array of issues have to be decided in a relatively short time. The job of being a legislator is perforce a part-time one for most members for the simple reason that the income paid legislators is inadequate to support a family during the months the legislature is in session. This hardly facilitates concentration on his legislative task.

Constituents want favors, intercession with bureaucrats (both innocent and occasionally not so innocent), or patronage. Others want legislators to speak at the next meeting of the PTA or the 4-H club or the Sons of Italy's annual dinner. Patronage squabbles often require an enormous amount of time, particularly for the member who has ambition and a desire to go on in political life. He cannot ignore the bickering over appointments for he often possesses power to influence these decisions, and, if he ignores the faithful who have helped him win election, he will be thought ungrateful; if he allows a bad appointment to be made with his implicit backing, he may have to bear responsibility for it if the appointee proves a bad choice. Moreover, the legislator's desk is piled high with minor requests that he feels dutybound to respond to in some fashion. It is well enough to say that the time of a busy legislator should not be diverted for answering the questions of a man wanting his license plates to bear his initials or to respond to a junior high school class who would like to visit the legislature next Tuesday, but the fact is that legislators do not allow such requests to go unanswered. Recalling my own experience, I once wrote:

One constituent, writing in to request a minor but time-consuming chore of me, said he knew I was busy and he did not want to waste my time, but could my office do it for him? My office! I had no office staff and indeed no office except for a corner in my hallway at home, where unsorted and unfiled letters, brochures, notes, and thousands of legislative bills constantly threatened to bury my children under a paper cascade.[4]

What a new legislator soon finds is that there is no choice but to depend on his colleagues to inform him about issues assigned to their committees; and, like it or not, he is reduced to following their advice unless he knows the subject well enough to have an opinion. It is a source of surprise to many new members how many issues they are too ignorant to have an opinion about—the nonlawyer, for example, faced with the details of a corporation code or a revision of inheritance-estate laws. He also discovers that there are a good many issues so trivial that he need have no firm opinions about them—trivial, that is, from his point of view although not from somebody's point of view, for all issues matter to somebody: fishing regulations in a state park, barber licensing, revising the charter of a city at the opposite end of the state, and so on. The problem of too little time and too many duties result in his emphasizing the major problems that indirectly encompass many lesser items (the budget or major reforms or a constitutional convention) and selected other questions that arouse his attention. Some members never appear to show any particular concern beyond perhaps a few farm bills, some local bills that they want desperately for their own communities, or horse-racing legislation, while others take on sponsorship of relatively more important and more complex matters such as judicial reform, mental health problems, and education.

It does not take long for the novice to learn that legislative politics is not a lawn party but serious and hard-fought contests over issues that are vital to the contestants. The stakes are high and the players go after their objectives not in the manner of a Sunday afternoon croquet player but with the fire and determination of a World Series shortstop. Every advantage is pressed; bargaining to get support for bills often puts wholly unrelated measures into jeopardy when X announces that his followers will sandbag Y's legislation unless X's bill is guaranteed passage in return. The legislator has to face the half-a-loaf-or-none kind of tough decision not just once or twice a session, but often several times a week. A legislator may feel that his political future depends

---

[4] Duane Lockard, "The Tribulations of a State Senator," 14 *The Reporter* 24 (May 17, 1956). As to self-perceptions of state legislators, see John C. Wahlke, Heinz Eulau, William Buchanan, and LeRoy Ferguson, *The Legislative System: Explorations in Legislative Behavior* (New York: John Wiley & Sons, Inc., 1962). Legislators in California, New Jersey, Ohio, and Tennessee were intensively interviewed and their roles analyzed. For a most perceptive and productive use of the "role perception" of legislators, see James D. Barber's *The Lawmakers* (New Haven: Yale University Press, 1965).

upon his bringing home the bacon to his district: a new bridge or highway, improvement or expansion of area recreational facilities. Another may feel that action to improve psychiatric care for inmates of jails and prisons or expanded programs for the treatment of the chronic alcoholic, the improvement of educational or mental health facilities should take precedence over highways and bridges. A good deal of bargaining between people with such disparate interests, both inside and outside the legislature, is inevitable; for neither can convince the other that his order of priorities is the "right" one. Thus the tough decision, the compromise solution which sacrifices expansion of the enforcement staff of the civil rights commission for an increase in the minimum wage, or which allows more for highways than A thinks is necessary but which he must concede to B in order to get his desired appropriation for aid to the mentally retarded.

There is, to be sure, a common tendency to take a superior attitude about such swapping, to editorialize on the iniquity of those who would dare to pose the sacred needs of education or conservation against judgeships or highways. Since there is no way to establish a single and uniformly recognized order of priorities—at least not in a democratic society—the process of playing off the precious (subjectively speaking) against the immaterial will go on. This is not to say that I have no order of priorities, nor that I would not battle for the superiority of my values over others; it is rather an admission that there are other orders of values and that the holders of these also represent significant elements of the society. The battler for aesthetic values who deplores and seeks to prevent the proliferation of gaudy highway signs defacing the beauty of the countryside has my complete agreement and sympathy but I cannot see that *ipso facto* these values are going to be persuasive to others who (a) may have an investment in outdoor advertising, (b) may want to get the income for the leasing landholders and the state that the signs may bring, (c) may not care one way or the other about the relative aesthetic merits of road signs and open fields. A legislator seeking a highway for his area, even at the expense of better mental health services, can defend his request on the basis of economic growth and development and there is no question but that such claims have great public support. If we leave the contests in the legislative arena open to the free play of the varied forces of our society, it seems clear that one man's noble venture is going to have to contest with another man's ignoble one. Bargaining, in short, will go on.

A major demand on the legislator's time comes from contests between interest groups to which the public pays little attention but which demand considerable time and attention from the legislator for the simple reason that the contestants are so embroiled and embattled that they will not leave the legislator alone. The law can be used to improve the competitive position of economic interests by placing restraints on competitors, a fact all too well appreciated by lobbyists for business and professional groups. Their pleas are not stated in terms of relative competitive position, yet that is exactly what is involved when large garages attempt to exclude small ones from making major automobile repairs; when liquor stores seek to prevent the sale of liquor in drug stores; when druggists seek to sell liquor at later hours than are permitted the liquor stores; when farmers, oystermen, dentists, engineers, and countless others get into squabbles over their "internal" affairs. The arguments are put in terms of public safety, health standards, free enterprise, or fair trade, and the legislator is subjected to a drumfire of telegrams, letters, telephone calls, personal pleading, and propaganda on such bills. Should automobile dealers be allowed to sell insurance on the cars they sell? For some reason—all connected with the highest of motives of public welfare naturally—insurance men doubt the ability of auto dealers to advise wisely on insurance and they therefore propose to prohibit the sale of automobile insurance by car dealers. Not only does this bring forth vigorous pleas from the auto dealers and insurance men in the legislator's district, but a legislator who has no particular connection with either business soon notices that his colleagues who do have connections frequently become unashamed lobbyists within the legislature. While the incidence of outright bribery and corruption in most American legislatures is nowadays slight, the practice of acting on behalf of one's own economic interest—in the most flagrant disregard of the moral obligation to avoid conflict of interest—is all too common; indeed, it is unusual to see a legislator refrain from taking advantage of his inside position.

Why should he avoid involvement in such questions, he asks? Does he not "know" more about insurance than those in the law or in education or in retail business? Does he complain when the lawyer pleads his own cause, or the banker his? True, he is knowledgeable about his special field and he expects others to do as he does. Moreover, the claim is not infrequently made that the particular interest emphasized is not a *special* interest but tantamount to the general welfare of the public (*e.g.*, education as supported by a teacher, or elaborate trial procedures by a lawyer). Whether there is a "solution" to this problem of inside lobbying I do not know; surely the temptation is great in view of the part-time character of the legislator's job in most states and in view of the nature of the questions that constantly arise for solution. There simply does not appear to be much in the way of a conception of conflict of interest among legislators.[5] Perhaps if such a notion were emphasized more, legislators might accept this as a limitation on the more extreme forms of abuse. If the public in general shows no special concern with the problem, however, there is unlikely to be any particular change in the attitude or behavior of legislators.

If such are the trials of being a legislator, why then does anyone stay more than one term? Is it because he finds ways to make the job "pay" by nefarious means? Such an assumption often is made by those who hear complaints about the difficulties of legislative life. "If it's so bad," I have heard it said, "why do they stay on? Must be getting something out of it for themselves on the side." This cynical assumption is rarely warranted, although it would not be valid to say that it is never applicable. For the overwhelming majority of members who serve and stay on notwithstanding the "hardships," there is no question of illicit income involved. There are many rewards, but not necessarily economic ones. For it is worth remembering that there are psychic rewards of being called "Senator," or being asked to help with some important public problem, getting one's name in the paper regularly as a decision-maker. And like men and women who spend their spare time working for the Red Cross or the Community Chest, the legislator gets his reward in part from a sense of doing something intrinsically worthwhile.

"Group Theory" and Legislative Politics

"The legislature referees the group struggle," writes Professor Earl Latham, "ratifies the victories of the successful coalition, and records the terms of the surrenders, compromises and conquests in the form of statutes."[6] In Latham's view the politics of the legislative process is primarily a matter of the colliding of groups of various kinds; once the

---

[5] It is interesting to compare British parliamentary practice where conflict of interest goes even further: members of Parliament are sponsored by interest groups. This is not deemed improper, even though other acts to which Americans would take no serious exception (leaking to the press, quite inadvertently, a minor detail of a forthcoming tax bill) are punished harshly. It is significant, however, that no single member of the House of Commons—except cabinet members—possesses the independent power of American legislators. Bound in by party discipline, even the sponsored member working for his group may be less effective than a nonsponsored insider here.

[6] Earl Latham, "The Group Basis of Politics: Notes for a Theory," 46 *American Political Science Review* 376 (1952). Reprinted in *Political Behavior*, edited by Heinz Eulau, Samuel Eldersfeld, and Morris Janowitz (New York: The Free Press of Glencoe, 1956), pp. 232–45.

collisions have occurred and the forces of each group have registered, the legislature then solemnizes the resultant positions in statutory form. He hastens to add that the legislature in the adjustment of group interests "does not play the part of inert cash register, ringing up additions and withdrawals of strength; it is not a mindless balance pointing and marking the weight and distribution of power among contending groups. Legislatures are groups also and show a sense of identity and consciousness of kind that unofficial groups must regard if they are to represent their members effectively. In fact," he adds, with regard to Congress (a point equally true of state legislatures), "each of the two houses of the Congress has a conscious identity of special 'house' interest, as well as a joint interest against the executive establishment."[7]

This conception of the role of groups in the legislative process contains some difficulties for the student attempting to comprehend the nature of the political currents of a state legislature, and therefore it is useful to begin analysis of legislative politics by assessing some of the implications of this doctrine of group primacy. There is no disposition here to suggest that groups are not significant forces in the making of policy, nor is there any quarrel with the proposition that the legislature also constitutes a group and that legislators sometimes decide issues partly in order to defend legislative prerogatives. The difficulty with this theory is that the processes of policy-making in a legislature involve more than group phenomena and that the legislature is neither an inert cash register nor just another "group."

Unhappily there is inadequate space here for a thorough analysis of the difficulties with the group theorists' attempts to reduce all to group phenomena. But it is necessary to take at least a brief look at this body of theory and some of the implications which flow from it, since it is increasingly common to look at the legislature as if in fact it did involve little more than a sounding board or computer on which the various forces are registered. Group theory derives largely from the work of Arthur Bentley, who undertook to provide a complete system for the explanation of the governmental process by focusing on group phenomena.[8] To Bentley the group was of the essence: "The great task in the study of any form of social life is the analysis of these groups. . . .

---

[7] *Ibid.*, p. 391.

[8] The classic of the field is his book. *The Process of Government* (Chicago: University of Chicago Press, 1908). At the time Bentley wrote this book, pluralist political theory was popular, and in one sense he took off from the pluralist position of such men as Harold Laski and G. D. H. Cole who were in revolt against both the individualist theories of the nineteenth century and the classic theories of idealism.

When the groups are adequately stated, everything is stated. When I say everything I mean everything."[9] In one sense this proposition can lead to a truism: that man, as Aristotle said a long time ago, is a social animal. It is certainly true that human behavior is essentially group-based: we grow up in a family group, attend schools and churches, live in a community, are members of a nation. Clearly our thinking and behavior are conditioned by these influences. A completely isolated person is not a human being; a child reared apart from all other human beings is not recognizably human for it cannot speak, think, or act humanly.

But it is no truism the group theorists are aiming at, although they do make use of the elementary facts of group association and of the influence of all kinds of groups on human beliefs and behavior. The theory is an attempt to explain why and how political decisions are made and to explain this on the basis of a kind of calculus of competing political pressures. As Bentley says at one point:

It is possible to take a Supreme Court decision, in which nothing appears on the surface but finespun points of law, and cut through all the dialectic till we get down to the actual groups of men underlying the decisions and producing the decisions through the differentiated activity of the justices.[10]

As the stork-brought-the-decision myth (the court merely "interprets") distorts the judicial process by discounting the force of preconceptions of judges and the play of political forces outside the courtroom, Bentley's decisional analysis by calculus of relative group forces is nearly as extreme an exaggeration. The judicial process is affected by the personal idiosyncrasies of judges, for example, and by the intellectual force of the law itself. Judges often decide questions in what seem surprising ways, given their supposed predilections, since they apparently seek consistency with some doctrine of the law or in some other way respond to intellectual forces that are unexplainable in terms of group pressures. While legislators are more prone to respond to group pressures than are judges (we plan it that way, after all, through the election process), it is an inadequate explanation of the behavior of legislators to say that it all boils down to someone bringing pressure to bear.

It is true that the more recent advocates of group theory have modified the extreme positions that Bentley took on his calculus of pressures, and that they have emphasized more heavily the non-interest

---

[9] *Ibid.*, pp. 208–09.
[10] *Ibid.*, p. 205.

group kinds of group phenomena. That is, they have emphasized, for example, the nation-state as a kind of group exerting ideological force on the individual. David Truman as the major protagonist of group theory among contemporary political scientists has stressed the "potential interest group"—a collection of people who share certain interests but who have not yet come together to make demands on the society, but when pushed far enough will mobilize and demand.[11] The potential interest group has seemed to some to play the role of *deus ex machina*, a way of saving the day for the group theory when otherwise no feasible way of explaining political decisions in terms of group pressures is available. For example, how can actions by government to serve the interests of the voteless migratory worker (admittedly a rare event but it does happen occasionally) be accounted for in terms of group pressure? The potential-interest-group explanation is that the potential power of elements not organized is recognized in anticipation of their possible and undesired mobilization.[12]

Even though modern group theorists assert that their theory is not an attempt to reduce all politics to the play of interest groups as such, there is enough about the language they use and the overtones of their presentation to lead the unsuspecting to interpret what they say purely in terms of interest group struggle. While the comment by Professor Latham (see p. 267) does not say the struggle is between specified interest groups, one needs to watch the context closely not to fall into the mistake of interpreting the matter just as Bentley firmly believed it could be: as a matter of relative power among groups to be weighed and evaluated more or less by quantitative methods.[18] As critical com-

---

[11] Truman's *The Governmental Process* (New York: Alfred A. Knopf, Inc., 1951), is the most thorough analysis of the empirical evidence on interest groups ever made, and it is also the most formidable presentation of the group theory extant, since he refines, expands, and revises Bentley's theses to more defensible positions. His concept of the potential interest group is summarily stated on pp. 34–35 and is spelled out throughout the remainder of his book. It will be recalled perhaps that the terms and interpretation of the nature of interest groups used in the present volume were adapted from Truman's book (see Chap. 7).

[12] As Truman states the proposition: "The unacknowledged power of such unorganized interests lies in the possibility that, if these wide, weak interests are too flagrantly ignored, they may be stimulated to organize for aggressive counteraction." *Ibid.*, p. 114.

[13] Reducing the problem to a kind of calculus, Charles Adrian has said:

In fact, *public policy* might be defined as the end result of the interaction of the various interested pressure groups upon one another. It is the sum of the vector forces, where each vector represents the total force and direction of each group as determined by its age, respectability, size of membership, wealth, ability of leadership, skill at lobbying, inside connections, intensity of interests, and other pertinent factors.

Governing Urban America, 2nd ed., *op. cit.*, p. 121. Italics in original.

mentators on the group theory have been saying in recent years, the emphasis on the group is a significant advance in our understanding of the political process, but the group does not therefore displace other phenomena of equal significance.[14]

An unyielding faith in the proposition that all decisions must be the result of pressure brought to bear by some kind of organized group can lead to misinterpretation by letting assumption take the place of empirical evidence. The following comment on the state legislature of New Jersey is an interesting case in point: "Ordinarily the judges do not bring much pressure on the legislature," said a participant-observer in that institution. "There is no organization of judges to look after their interests. They must have exerted some influence to have forced their salaries up to the levels they now enjoy, but no record exists of this activity."[15] If their salaries went up, they must have exerted pressure in some fashion to get them raised, whether there is any evidence that they did or not. There are alternative explanations, some of which would be consistent with the group theory (other groups—lawyers, civic reform groups may have made the demand instead of the judges), and some not so consistent (that the need for honest and devoted judges required salaries roughly comparable to those a competent lawyer might earn, a conviction that could gain currency without judges or any other interest group consciously beating the drums for it). The judges may indeed have had backstage ways of subtly pressing for salary increases, but need it be assumed that they did in the absence of any evidence on the point?

Another example will illustrate in a different way the folly of making all legislative decisions turn on interest group pressures. In the last days of the 1955 session of the Connecticut General Assembly a messenger from the Governor (Abraham Ribicoff) entered the Democratic Senate caucus room with word that the Governor had decided to support a bill concerning the treatment of sexual deviates in prisons and mental institutions, and he hoped that the Senate (controlled by a Democratic majority) would support the bill. His "hope" under most cir-

---

[14] Critical comment on the group theory has been increasing in recent years, and the student is referred to that literature if he wishes to pursue this problem. See, for example, Peter H. Odegard, "A Group Basis of Politics: A New Name for an Old Myth," 11 *Western Political Quarterly* 689 (1958) and Stanley Rothman, "Systematic Political Theory: Observations on the Group Approach," 54 *American Political Science Review* 15 (1960). See also the discerning comments of Harry Eckstein in *Pressure Group Politics* (London: Allen and Unwin, 1960), especially pp. 1–40, 151–63.

[15] Dayton David McKean, *Pressures on the New Jersey Legislature* (New York: Columbia University Press, 1938), p. 151.

cumstances would be fulfilled without much dissent, even oral dissent, for there is a tradition of party discipline and great party voting consistency in Connecticut legislative politics. But that day the senators blew the roof off and ranted and raved at the messenger (who was himself within a few years to be Governor—John Dempsey) and almost bodily threw him out of the caucus room. Why? Because of some group interest pressed so strongly that the senators had to respond? Because of some backstage swap that bargained the sex deviate treatment bill for some other, perhaps unrelated bill? None of these was in the least involved. What had happened was simple and readily explained.

The fate of the bill rested on two factors: its promoter and the fatigue and frustration of the senators. The bill had been promoted almost single-handedly by a Republican member of the House of Representatives—a relentless, indeed tireless woman advocate of more sensible treatment of these psychiatric cases. Every senator had been the victim of countless entreaties on the issue from her, and toward the end of the session some of them had begun to duck behind a pillar when she approached. *There was very little organized support for the bill.* When Governor Ribicoff finally consented to find a place for her program in his budget, he did for her what he refused to do for many Democratic senators who had been urging him to sponsor their pet projects. This took place, it should be noted, in the last days of a five-month session when nerves were edgy, and to add to the tension it was a sweltering humid June day. There was virtually no consideration of the merits of the issue. The frustrations of a group of tired, harried legislators, not interest group pressures, determined the fate of the bill. It never got to the floor for a vote.

Aspects of Power in the Legislature

Inside dopesters "know" who has "real" power in the legislature; their sweeping generalizations about the unrestrained "control" of the governor, the education lobby, or the bankers are familiar, impressionistic, and often quite wrong. Impressionistic observations are often valuable to the student of the legislative process, for their impressions may point to significant truths. Assessing the power relationships in a legislative body demands more than vague impressions, however; it requires not only a knowledge of the play of forces, but some reasonable criteria and methods of analysis.

To develop such an approach to the study of the legislative process, the first step is to stipulate what is meant by "power" in the legislature. Power in the legislature is no different from power elsewhere, so we may return to the usage employed earlier: power is the probability that one person will be able to induce another to do his bidding—the relative effectiveness of one person in getting others to do what they might not otherwise have done. Power then is a social phenomenon associated with some individual or group of individuals—we may call them *actors* as we used that term in discussing the strategies of the game of politics —and it has some source, is based upon something possessed by the actor that inclines the respondent person to comply. The possible bases of power are infinite: prestige or respect, wealth or other control over rewards, punishment or terror, legitimacy or formal authority. The employment of these bases of power require some means, some instrumentality of action to render the base of power an active force rather than a potential one. *Actors, base of power,* and *means of using power* are key terms for the assessment of the legislative process and it is therefore necessary to turn to a brief consideration of them.[16]

The Actors.   Naturally no categoric list of actors in the legislative process can be assembled: the actors change with the issues of the session as do the singers with the operas of the season. On a given matter some actors, the initiators and main protagonists and chief opponents of a policy, play primary roles and commit themselves and their resources to the success or defeat of a program. Others play a more peripheral role, or may start on the edges and ultimately be drawn more deeply into the affair. Thus a governor may not have much concern with a horse racing bill or a conservation issue at first, but may be dragged into it by circumstances that make his participation politically imperative. Conversely a governor may initiate a particular administrative reform about which others at first show little concern, but as the affair progresses the number of forces in combat on the issue may be very wide as individual members of the legislatures are cajoled into taking a position or as interest groups find the proposal affects them.

In short, the actors can be a most inclusive cast: legislators, interest groups and their representatives, governors, parties and party leaders, bureaucrats, and "publics." The "publics" in the sense of a group of

---

[16] This means of analysis is derived from the previously cited ideas of Robert A. Dahl contained in his article, "The Concept of Power," 2 *Behavioral Science* 201 (1957). Dahl proceeds in this article to develop an elaborate methodology for the evaluation of the relative power of legislators, but so many hypothetical elements (assumptions about roll call votes, and so on) have to be imported into the case before it becomes a method of quantitative analysis that his more elaborate methods of analysis are less fruitful than the elements upon which he based them.

people who get aroused on a particular subject and begin to make demands may perhaps be one of the most elusive and irregular of the actors, but, given the importance of election day and the consequent desire to anger as few people as possible, the impact of the "publics" can be quite significant. To some elements in the contests of the legislature it is important not to broaden the range of participation of actors —a controversey between two is simpler than one between three or more contestants. Broadening the scope of involvement may, on the other hand, be indispensable to others who anticipate the certainty of defeat unless they can recruit support outside the inner circle. Advocates of laws to forbid the pollution of streams will seek to convince the sportsmen's clubs that they have an interest in clean streams, doctors that public health depends upon it, conservationists that pollution is the destruction of resources, political parties that clean rivers are good politics. Conversely the polluters may very well desire—until the fat has hit the fire when their best bet may be counterrecruitment—to keep the controversy narrowed to few participants in anticipation of an unpublicized victory which, as a matter of record, they usually win. The range of actor participants is thus not a marginal but a crucial factor. E. E. Schattschneider, who calls this inclusiveness-exclusiveness factor *scope*, argues that this "factor overthrows the familiar simplistic calculus based on a model of a tug of war of measurable forces."[17]

Bases of Power. This is the heart of the matter: the effectiveness of any actor is a function of his base power. Maneuver, strategy, energetic exertion are meaningless unless there is some base of power that other players in the game recognize. There has to be some foundation—or belief in a foundation, for deceptions may be involved—of power in order to get compliance. Thus the existence of a party organization with considerable control over rewards (political advancement, patronage, and the like) that are important to legislators and other politicians constitutes a formidable source of power. A governor, who has prestige and a platform guaranteed him by reporters ever eager for copy for the next press deadline, has a base of power. The bases of power are infinite in number, and it may be useful to pose some categories of potential power of special relevance in the legislative arena.

1. *Legislative Rules and "Structure" as Bases of Power.* The rules of procedure and the constitutional structure of legislatures grant an

---

17 E. E. Schattschneider, *The Semi-Sovereign People, A Realist's View of Democracy in America* (New York: Holt, Rinehart, and Winston, Inc., 1960), p. 6. Schattschneider uses the concept of scope as a base for a critical descriptive analysis of the American political system. See especially Chap. 2, "The Scope and Bias of the Pressure System."

advantage to the fellow who does not want action to be taken. Take the power potential inherent in bicameralism—the practice of having a two-chamber legislature (which prevails in all states except Nebraska). The very fact that bills must pass both houses in identical form—that, in short, the bill must go over two hurdles and not one—is a source of power. Differences between the constituencies represented, differences in party control, jealousies between the two houses often impede action. Those who would kill a bill thus have two shots at the target. Of all the reasons offered for imitating Nebraska and adopting a unicameral legislature, the one that makes most sense in practical terms is that it would eliminate the buck-passing, the opportunity to kill legislation by hanging it up in a back-and-forth game between the two houses. This is an old and familiar game especially where the two houses happen often to be controlled by opposite political parties.[18]

The rules of a legislature are, as observed earlier, utterly incomprehensible to many a fledgling legislator, and indeed some of those who stay on and gain legislative experience never learn the rules in detail. This, needless to say, is an asset to the member who learns how to play the rules to best advantage. Parliamentary procedure is elaborated not for the purpose of confusing but for that of making the process of legislation orderly and fair, and yet the complexity of the procedural rules

---

[18] Unicameralism is also urged as a money-saving device, as a way of focusing public attention on the legislature more effectively since there would be but one house to watch, on the grounds that fewer legislators will mean fewer bills and therefore more careful consideration of those introduced, and as a way of eliminating the conference committee. None of these seems terribly convincing to politicians accustomed to a two-house system, or at least one may assume this since unicameralism has been requested repeatedly in most states especially since 1934 when, at the urging of U.S. Senator George Norris, Nebraska adopted a unicameral, nonpartisan legislature. The literature on the "Nebraska experiment," as it used to be called, is voluminous and hortatory. The *National Municipal Review* annual indexes will lead the curious to many such articles. A. C. Breckenridge assesses Nebraska's experience in *One House for Two* (Washington, D.C.: Public Affairs Press, 1958). See also the report of the Committee on American Legislatures of the American Political Science Association, Belle Zeller, ed., *American State Legislatures* (New York: Thomas Y. Crowell Company, Inc., 1954), pp. 47–60, 240–56. The Committee recommends the adoption of unicameralism. It is interesting to speculate why unicameralism, so logical and tidy in the abstract, has made so little progress. Doubtless political realists who employ bicameralism to good effect have had something to do with its failure to get anywhere, and the rather disembodied arguments in its behalf are not entirely persuasive. Yet it is likely that the long-standing bicameral tradition (and the consequent inability to foresee the results of the change) has been of equal or greater significance.

An argument in behalf of unicameralism has been put forward in some recent state constitutional conventions, and in my opinion it has some persuasiveness. It is that such a drastic change in operations of the legislature would force reconsideration of the functioning of the body, might necessitate development of staff sources, and thereby considerably improve the legislature.

is open to clever use by the one who knows how to speed up or slow down the proceedings through the proper motion, objection, or maneuver.

The rules also may offer means to an individual or to a small group to override the will of a majority in the legislature. Thus where committees are not required to report legislation back to the floor, and especially where sessions are short, the opportunity exists to kill legislation by pigeon-holing. Rules committees may have complete control over access to the floor for action.[19] Rules requiring unusual majorities to approve borrowing or appropriating funds naturally become the basis of power of those who would limit expenditures. As Table 10-1 on legislative procedure shows, there are many places to waylay bills and many bases to be touched before a bill gets home safe.

2. *Campaign Contributions, Patronage, and Political Support as Bases of Power.* In general the more important the party organization is in a state's politics the less important is the campaign contribution for the legislator and vice versa. If the real contest over legislative seats comes in a primary election for reason of a lack of any significant contest in general elections in one-party states, the legislator has got to find finances to run his campaign. Interest groups in many states are foremost sources of necessary campaign funds. Thus the lobbyist has a subtle means of persuasion. This was the primary source of the awesome power wielded by the erstwhile "boss" of the California legislature, Artie Samish. The crossfiling system and the nonparty character of California politics left the legislator singularly dependent upon Samish or others who could provide the funds to conduct costly campaigns. Samish, as agent for a number of economic interest groups, doled out the necessary cash in return for strategic support on legislation.[20] Where the party has great control over nominations legislators have less reason to expect challenges in primary contests and therefore less need of scraping up a campaign fund. Even where money is not much involved, however, interest groups often have a resource for persuasion in implied support (or conversely a threat of opposition) in elections, and this can be applied to the party leaders as well as to individual legislators. Of course it also follows that the party organization where it has funds, control over nominations, and patronage to dispense or in marginal cases where it can successfully appeal to the party loyalty of legislators has a considerable source of power. More will be said on this subsequently.

3. *Bureaucracy-Clientele Cooperation as a Base of Power.* As a final

---

[19] See Eugene C. Lee, *The Presiding Officers and Rules Committees in the Legislatures of the U.S.* (Berkeley, Calif.: University of California Press, 1952).

[20] See references to Samish in Chap. 8, p. 199.

example, consider the potential power of the bureaucracy through their clientele or following in the public. Although nominally the bureaucrat is "nonpolitical" and would only at the behest of a governor or other "political" superior take the initiative in promoting or opposing legislation, the realities of contemporary state politics belie the neutral appearance. The bureaucrat must be subtle in his politicking and he ordinarily will, if possible, avoid coming into direct and open conflict with the governor or other political leaders, but this does not put him out of the game by any means. A major source of bureaucratic power is the support that can be aroused by getting the clientele that is served by the agency active in demanding policies favored by the bureaucracy. Thus the state department of education can depend on public support from prominent individuals and powerful organizations intimately concerned with education; the agriculture department gets help from the farmers, the welfare department from professional groups and various organizations concerned with public welfare, the labor department from labor unions. The bureaucrat may appear to be making his case strictly on the basis of expert judgment and without obvious sources of support, but the legislator realizes the importance of the alliance of the agency and its supporters as a constant source of power. Evidence of the potency of this form of power was clearly demonstrated in state after state in the post-World War II era when so-called Little Hoover Commissions were established to find ways of streamlining and improving the administrative structure of state government. Almost invariably the proposals threatened the independence, power, budgets, prestige of administrative agencies, and, accordingly, the clientele came to the defense of the beleaguered agencies with great success. In very few states did the proposals get far and agency-clientele cooperation was a major reason why.

Means of Exercising Power. This refers, as we said, to the instruments for applying power—the media for utilization of the potential power of the base. Thus the cracking of the whip of discipline in the

TABLE 10-1
A Summary of Legislative Procedure for Bill Passage

1. *Introduction of bill in House*	This, and all the following, could equally well begin in the Upper Chamber and then go to the Lower House rather than vice versa.
2. *Assignment to committee*	Usually done by the presiding officer, but occasionally by a special committee for that purpose.

TABLE 10-1 (con't.)
A Summary of Legislative Procedure for Bill Passage

3. Public hearing	In three states this is a joint (House and Senate) Committee hearing. The proportion of bills given hearings varies, but important ones usually are. All interested persons are allowed to testify.
4. Executive Session of committee*	Here the bill is discussed, amended, pigeonholed (in some states all bills must be reported out), or reported to the House with a favorable report or an unfavorable report. Generally an unfavorable report is the decisive action; the chamber merely ratifies the committee's conclusion.
5. Bill placed on calendar*	A calendar is in effect a list of bills to be voted on.
6. Caucus	This is by no means an invariable procedure; in some states there is no party caucus and even where one does exist it may not consider all or even most bills. Regional or factional caucuses take the place of party caucuses in some one-party states. This is the stage at which bills die in reality in many states.
7. Floor debate, amendment, and vote*	Means usually exist for getting bills that are deemed very important out of order on the calendar and brought up for action more rapidly than the routine calling of the calendar would permit.
8. Sent to the upper chamber*	Here Steps 2 through 7 are repeated, except in the few states which use joint committees, where assignment to committee is of course eliminated.
9. If passed without amendment, the bill can go to the Governor for his approval or veto*	If vetoed, the bill returns to the house of origin for reconsideration; an unusual majority is usually required to override a veto. The governor may decide to let it become law without his consent.
OR If amended, the bill goes back to the house of origin*	When returned, the house can accept the changes or ask for a committee of conference, an ad hoc committee drawn from the membership of both houses.
10. Consideration by conference committee*	Here compromise may be worked out for acceptance or rejection by the two houses.
OR No conference committee is appointed, and the bill is amended and shuttled back and forth between the chambers.*	This can lead to the demise of the bill without its being clear who was "responsible," if it "dies" on the calendar or in transit between the chambers at the close of the session.

* A bill can be defeated at any of these steps along the way.

Handwritten annotations: Thrid READiNg And VOTE · Conference Committe · 11. Effective date · Bill pass But EVERY thing is No agree on it goes to this Comittee

legislature by the party leaders is a means of bringing the organization strength into effect. Logrolling (you support our bill and we will support yours) is a means of bringing not only party but interest group and even the individual legislator's power into play. Thus a legislator may utilitize his position on a committee to stall a specific bill until late in the session in order to bargain with some other group or powerful figure in behalf of his own local bills or other pet projects. In short, all the standard devices of strategy and maneuver are means for the exercise of power.

The Influentials in the Legislature

The distribution of power in the fifty state legislatures is by no means uniform; in some states there appears to be considerable concentration of influence over legislative decisions on major matters, in other states influence is much more dispersed and transitory. Yet in all of them there are some legislators and some nonlegislator-actors (lobbyists, party figures, governors) with great power on some kinds of questions. The number and kinds of issues on which leadership can effectively be asserted varies, but the fact that some men are more persuasive than others, have been around longer, have the respect of others, have formal positions that entitle them to take the lead and perhaps in some measure decide some questions for the whole body—these facts place much greater power in the hands of a few than in the hands of the many. These few I call the "influentials" for lack of a more suitable term. The influentials—whether individuals or groups—can be and with varying frequency are routed by the many. In some instances influentials avoid involvement, in some they will try but fail to lead, and in other cases the very nature of the legislative process will place what at times will prove to be decisive power in their hands. How frequently the few will be able to take advantage of their potential and be decisive is dependent on many variables: the political system and traditions of the state, the issues involved, the intensity of public attitudes on the matter, the traits of the influentials themselves. Thus in the Mississippi legislature a member with long experience, a leader in the White Citizens Council movement, and a close ally of the governor is likely to be looked to by both friends and opponents of a bill aiming, let us say, to liberalize welfare allowances from which Negroes might benefit considerably. Similarly a majority leader of the Republican party in the upper house of the New York legislature is invariably a man of

great power, and on a broad range of issues his position, if not determinative, is at least one of the most decisive forces at work in the legislature. The base of power and the manner of bringing the power to
bear may vary widely in the two states, but the existence of the power
is in both cases a fact of prime importance.

To what extent is the authority of the influentials a matter of party
power? It is obvious that the one-party states do not have cohesive
party organizations with power to control the legislature. Where one-
party politics prevails, divisions on public policy are patently not
along party lines, since there is virtually no opposition and the major
party organization is often little more than a holding company for factions
and individualists wanting to use the party name on election day.
Divisions tend to follow regional, factional, or interest lines. Thus in
some twenty states there is relatively little party organization influence.

What about the remaining thirty-odd states? The common impression has been that the parties amount to very little even there, but
recent scholarship has cast doubt on the assumed powerlessness and
insignificance of the party organization in the legislature. It is quite
conceivable that the party is much more important in most states than
the standard textbook version of legislative politics would suggest. For
the usual position, following a conclusion reached by A. Lawrence
Lowell in 1901, is that the legislature is virtually free of significant party
influence. Lowell studied the tendency of legislators to vote together
consistently as party groups in the British House of Commons and then
returned to this country and proceeded to make the same kind of survey in Congress and in several state legislatures. He found in effect
that the amount of party voting declined as he went along: it was highest in London, less in Washington, and almost nonexistent in some of
the states he studied.[21] He did find party voting in the New York legislature but in such states as Massachusetts he found virtually no party
cohesion among legislators. It is strange but true that generations of
political scientists in the decades following Lowell's survey took his
work as final and looked no further. Thus as much as fifty years later
Lowell was being cited as gospel without any attempt to check whether
the intervening years might have changed the situation. Reputable
scholars stated that the divisions in state legislatures showed far less
evidence of party influence than was the case in Congress (1950), that
the caucus is used more in Congress than in the state legislature (1939),
that legislation in the states was largely a nonpartisan matter with party

---

21 A. Lawrence Lowell, "The Influence of Party upon Legislation in England and
America," *Annual Report of the American Historical Association*, 1901.

lines meaning far less than in Congress (1950). Is this the case in fact? It doubtless is the case where there is no party competition at all, although that does not appear from the contexts to be what these writers were referring to. And it probably is the case in some states with party competition, but it is a far cry from being the case in all the latter states. *On the contrary, in many of these states the influence of party is far greater than it is in Congress.*

The fact of the matter is that in many states party influence is the most significant determinant of policy decisions in the legislature. While the parties do not always initiate policies nor do they often frame the bills and proposals made (although they do both in some instances), any wise promoter of a bill will turn first to the leaders of the party and seek their support on the well-founded assumption that their support is crucially necessary. It may be possible to defeat the party leadership and recruit the necessary support from the membership of the legislature without regard to party lines, but in states where there is significant party organizational strength no experienced actor would ever fail to seek the support of the party leadership, and if their support is not available, he will seek their neutrality as the next best alternative. Only as a last resort will the promoter seek to challenge the party leadership; legislators expect a party position to be established on all major legislation and they often will not commit themselves firmly on issues until the position of the leadership is clear.[22]

This is not to suggest that the position of the leadership is one of absolute power nor that any kind of monolithic authority exists in the states where the party has power. The leadership is no stronger than the support it can muster, and nowhere is the power of the leadership sufficient to induce uniform support on all questions. Still, the weapons of discipline are not forgotten by the ambitious: defiance of the leadership can sometimes be a ticket to political oblivion. Although the following observation on the power of the party in Connecticut was made when I was an *outside* observer of legislative operations, the truth of the statement was confirmed by the later experience of being in the Connecticut Senate:

As a final resort, party leaders in Connecticut will at times discipline legislators either because of factional shifts which cut the ground from under the individual or because of disloyalty to the party program. Discipline can extend to a denial of renomination for the General Assembly, and, of course,

---

[22] A labor lobbyist in Connecticut once reported that efforts to commit legislators on bills frequently met this response: "Well, let's wait and see what the leaders do on this."

denial of higher offices on the state level, but in more subtle ways it can make the individual very ill at ease while in the legislature, both through social pressures and through refusal to grant legislative time for pet projects which the legislator wants to enact for his home town. Disciplinary action is not brought against every legislator who happens to step out of line (for some, refusal of renomination would be impossible, since they control the local nominating machinery), but for a good many legislators, and especially the ambitious ones, it remains a fearsome weapon and its ominous existence in the party armory is not easily forgotten.[23]

I would modify this by emphasizing that in practical terms the actual use of the harsher sanctions against the nonconformist is not a matter of common practice but a rarity, partly because there are relatively few opportunities to exercise them. Discipline is a little like an electrified fence around a field for grazing cattle—the power need not always be turned on; once stung by the fence, the cattle refuse to go near it. (And legislators convey warnings to the newcomers to the corral.) Moreover and equally important, an ethos about any legislative body conditions the attitudes of members: if the commonly accepted practice is to work together as party groups then there is a strong temptation to go along with the prevailing pattern. The use of discipline to command party cohesion is probably less important than the habit of conforming because that is the way things are done. Conversely, a tradition of independence in a legislature has the effect of rendering difficult the initiation of party leadership control.

Briefly, then, what are the bases on which party cohesion and consistency in party voting rest? First, there has to be reasonably effective party organization and leadership and competition between parties. Second, there has to be ideological similarity within the party to get agreement on policies. How often do these conditions prevail in the various states? It is not yet clear how many states do have effective party leadership and how many highly dispersed power, but recent findings suggest that several states show high levels of party cohesion in roll call voting from which it may be assumed that party organizations are taking positions on issues. The following are suggestive brief comments quoted from observations on various states:

[New Jersey] If a group is wise, it goes to the party leaders and not to the members of the committee in charge of the bill. The committee will almost

---

[23] Duane Lockard, "Legislative Politics in Connecticut," 48 *American Political Science Review* 166 (1954), 173.

always follow the advice of the leaders. . . . Party control of legislation is therefore much more stringent than in Congress.[24]

[New York] The legislators are not robots, but the rule of the leadership, overriding the whims or personal desires of the members, has meant that on *important* issues . . . members can be coerced, if necessary, in voting the way the welfare of the party or the state as a whole dictates.[25]

[Rhode Island] In both Houses of the General Assembly caucuses are held regularly. . . . Breaking with the decision of the caucus is not a common practice; normally a decision made there sticks. The leaders of the parties negotiate and compromise with each other and then the results are taken to caucus where support is lined up—often after the most strenuous argument.[26]

[Ohio] [Data on party voting suggest that] "party conflict is frequent in the Ohio legislature and that the parties attain high levels of internal unity often enough when in opposition to each other to provide definite alternatives to the voters of the state. They are responsible in the sense that they are internally united and in conflict with each other.[27]

[On roll call voting in the states of Massachusetts, New York, Pennsylvania, Ohio, Illinois, Washington, Missouri, and Colorado] In many of the American states with a strong two party system, during sessions when party balance in the legislature is not one-sided, partisan considerations influence to a significant degree the legislature voting on issues about which there is some measure of disagreement.[28]

Does the last statement quoted contain a joker clause—the reference to party divisions on issues "about which there is some measure of disagreement"? By one means of measurement of the effect of party it would appear that the party has little relevance as a force in the legislature because in many states there are more occasions on which the party blocs in the legislature vote alike than those on which they vote in disagreement with each other. William Keefe considers this to be evidence of the insignificance of party in the legislative process. His studies in Illinois and Pennsylvania led him to conclude that in those

---

[24] Dayton D. McKean, "A State Legislature and Group Pressures," 179 *Annals of the American Academy of Political and Social Science* 124 (1935), 130.

[25] Warren Moscow, *Politics in the Empire State* (New York: Alfred A. Knopf, 1948), p. 170.

[26] Lockard, *New England State Politics, op. cit.*, p. 218.

[27] Thomas A. Flinn, "The Outline of Ohio Politics," 13 *The Western Political Quarterly* 702 (1960), 720.

[28] Malcolm Jewell, "Party Voting in American State Legislatures," 49 *American Political Science Review* 773 (1955), 791. See also the evidence for Michigan by Robert G. Scigliano, *Michigan Legislature* (East Lansing, Mich.: State College Governmental Research Bureau, 1955), pp. 31ff.

states the parties had an effect on the organization of the legislature and on certain kinds of questions but that in most phases of law-making the parties have little effect.[29] He found that:

. . . nonpartisanship is much more in evidence than partisanship in the formation of public policies of the state of Pennsylvania. Most of the decisions taken on the floor in the General Assembly are unanimous. In the Senate unanimous roll call votes amounted to 81.6 per cent of all those taken; in the House the percentage was 69.7[30]

How can one reconcile the statement by Jewell that party voting is reasonably high in Pennsylvania and Keefe's observation? The problem is not a difficult one, for two different things are being measured. Keefe calculates the number of times the parties show great unity (80 per cent of the party voting the same way) when in opposition to each other (called a "party vote"), and he calculates the number of times this degree of cohesiveness (in both parties) occurs as a percentage of the total number of roll calls. Jewell calculates the percentage of times the parties are sufficiently cohesive to have a "party vote" (using a 90 per cent agreement criterion as Keefe used 80 per cent above) but uses as his base not all roll call votes but the votes on which there was significant division. Jewell, in other words, excludes as irrelevant all the unanimous votes and all votes on which 90 per cent of both parties voted the same way, whereas Keefe includes these and makes his calculation on the basis of all roll call voting. Which is the more meaningful test? Particularly in view of the fact that the rules require a roll call vote on final passage of all bills in Illinois and Pennsylvania (and many other states), the exclusion of unanimous and nearly unanimous votes is reasonable. After all, there is no reason to expect the parties to be opposed on all kinds of questions: it is obvious that the parties do not disagree on all matters and certainly they could hardly be expected to disagree on many of the picayune measures a legislature has to decide. Local bills and minor bills concerning gasoline stations, beauticians, barbers, and watchmakers are not by their nature deeply divisive matters, and if the rules demand a roll call on final passage, the only

---

[29] See Keefe's articles, "Party Government and Lawmaking in Illinois General Assembly," 47 *Northwestern University Law Review* 55 (1952), and "Parties, Partisanship, and Public Policy in the Pennsylvania Legislature," 48 *American Political Science Review* 450 (1954). See also his review of legislative behavior studies, "Comparative Study of the Role of Political Parties in State Legislature," 9 *The Western Political Quarterly* 726 (1956).

[30] Keefe, "Parties, Partisanship . . . ," *op. cit.*, p. 463.

way legislators can vote is unanimously. In fact, it is common where the rules require roll calls to have a motion made to have the last recorded (usually unanimous) vote stand for the present issue and if there is no disagreement this *pro forma* resolution substitutes for a roll call. (In some states, by tacit agreement, the clerk merely reads the first and last names on the legislative roster with the same effect as the *pro forma* motion.) To contend that the parties are evidently powerless because they do not disagree on these minor and insignificant matters is like belittling the prowess of a heavyweight because he has never yet hit a ringside patron: neither has he aimed at one.[31]

Exactly how much party voting there is in states beyond the dozen or so that have competitive politics and have been systematically studied there is no way of being sure, at least until someone does more research. In Minnesota, for example, an inkling of the probable influence of party in unexplored states is found in the fact that the nonpartisan system of election does not bar party voting in the legislature. Republicans call themselves "conservatives" and Democrats are the "liberals," and the two sides caucus and often vote along party lines. Professor Theodore Mitau found in analyzing votes on three issues over a period of time that there was considerable cohesiveness shown among the liberals and somewhat less among the conservatives.[32] Moreover, judging from newspaper accounts of legislative struggles in such states as Wisconsin and Michigan, where party competition has been increasing in recent years, there does appear to be considerable party unity shown.[33] Clearly, as Malcolm Jewell's evidence illustrates, there is a greater amount of party voting in the legislatures of the more populous and urbanized states than in the more rural states, which is probably a reflection of the types of issues and parties that develop in the two kinds of states. The issues that arise in the large urban states are likely to resemble those that divide the national parties—the major economic and social controversies of the time. In rural states the uniformity of economic interests often produces few contests and a relatively bland

---

[31] Elaboration of the details of findings of roll call voting need not be detailed here: suffice it to say that there is a considerable variation between the degree of party consistency in Massachusetts and New York on the one hand and Missouri and Colorado on the other; yet in neither is the role of the party a negligible factor. Roll calls are not the only means of testing the extent of party effect in the making of public policy, of course; other kinds of observation are important as supplemental checks. Yet impressionistic observations in the absence of roll call vote analysis can sometimes be as misleading as the roll call data; see, for example, the generalizations made by the Committee on State Legislatures of the American Political Science Association. *American State Legislatures, op. cit.*, Chap. 12.

[32] Mitau, *op. cit.*, pp. 69–71.

[33] See Scigliano, *op. cit.*

kind of politics. This is what several students of Missouri politics find, for example. Neither urban-rural nor party divisions are common in the Missouri legislature, and reflection on this situation led Professor Robert H. Salisbury to a general hypothesis about state legislative politics:

The character of state politics—intensity of competition for office, articulation of representative and constituency, etc.—will be a function of the range and intensity of conflicts of interests in the state.[34]

To repeat, the power of even the effectively led party organizations in legislatures is far from monolithic. Even where the party is strongest —as in Connecticut and New York—interest groups patently have great power of persuasion and they initiate issues.[35] Obviously also the parties stand clear of some contests and do nothing simply because there seems to be no profit in getting involved. Or the resolution of the differences between competing interests may be so technical or so embittered that party leaders advise the representatives of interest groups to resolve their differences and then return for ratification of their agreement. That is, the legislature sometimes invites them to provide a means of doing exactly what Latham says the legislature does as a standard practice—ratify agreements reached by interest groups. Oliver Garceau and Corinne Silverman report on a typical example of this kind in a study of workmen's compensation legislation in Vermont. Most Vermont legislators knew remarkably little about what was going on in the bargaining, and indeed only a few of them knew anything about the competing groups in the battle. But once the informal leaders of the Vermont legislature had satisfied themselves that a "reasonable" compromise had been reached on the bill, it passed without difficulty.[36] Vermont, of course, has one-party politics and parties mean virtually nothing on most questions in the legislature; even so, not all issues are left to be resolved by such outside bargaining processes. In states with strong party organizations also there are cases where the interest groups

---

[34] Salisbury, "Missouri Politics and State Political Systems," *Research Papers, 1958* (Columbia, Mo.: University of Missouri Bureau of Government Research, 1959), p. 23.

[35] See Harmon Zeigler, "Interest Groups In The States" in Jacob and Vines, eds., *op. cit.*, pp. 101ff.

[36] Oliver Garceau and Corinne Silverman, "A Pressure Group and the Pressured: A Case Report," 48 *American Political Science Review* 672 (1954). V. O. Key cites an instance in Arkansas where the legislature in 1947 passed a formal resolution requesting that all veterans' groups submit a "just, fair, reasonable and adequate consolidated veterans legislative program" to the legislature so that laws the ex-servicemen "so justly deserve" could be passed. Quoted from the *Arkansas Gazette*, January 17, 1949, by Key in *Politics, Parties, and Pressure Groups, op. cit.*, p. 162n.

in conflict are sent off to reach a settlement among themselves which, if not unreasonable (and sometimes then too), the legislature will then accept.

Party leaders as legislative actors bargain with other actors, employ strategy, use or threaten sanctions, and retreat as well as attack. The one mistake not to make is to rule them out of the game altogether in states where there is a sufficient bloc of party members of both parties to constitute a nucleus of power.

The Limited Legislature

It is sometimes assumed that the state legislature is but a small version of Congress. In a formal sense the two are analogous, but in a practical sense there is a vast difference. Although Congress too has lost relative standing in the councils of government especially in the past half-century, its losses are not as striking as those of most state legislatures. There are several reasons for the marked decline in status and power of the state legislature—some aspects of which we have already discussed —and it is our purpose to reflect on some of the constitutional-political reasons behind this decline.

1. *Constitutional Limitations.* The state legislature operates within a constitutional straitjacket. It is constitutionally restrained both in what it can do and how it can be done, limited in time for consideration of what is often a very long and involved agenda.[37] These limitations, which as noted earlier were largely the product of the late-nineteenth and early twentieth-century distrust of the legislature, rested on a simple premise: to restrict the potential power and the methods and the time alloted to the legislature will mean little loss of anything useful and may prevent harmful action. To frustrate the powerful machines that often got control of the legislatures in that era, a network of devices was established to force publicity (via the mandatory roll call, for example) upon legislative activities, and to set up hurdles in the way of unusual majorities for the enactment of certain kinds of law, or even to prohibit some acts except by a constitutional amendment.

Some unanticipated consequences of these restraints have followed. Mandatory roll calls have produced no great floodlight of publicity on

---

[37] For a discussion of some of the problems of constitutional stipulation of details of procedure, see Jefferson B. Fordham, *The State Legislative Institution* (Philadelphia: University of Pennsylvania Press, 1959); especially Chap. 2, "The Legislative Process—of Men and Method."

legislative activities. The diminution of potential legislative authority has had the unintended result of lowering the prestige and status of the legislature as compared with the burgeoning power of the governor. Many procedural prescriptions are noble in design and intent but ineffectual in practice. Thus the New York Constitution requires that a bill be on "the desks of the members, in its final form, at least three calendar days prior to final passage" (Article III, Sec. 14). Formally acquiescing in but actually showing contempt for the rule, the legislature at times adjourns in effect, leaving a skeleton crew of legislators from the environs of Albany to convene and adjourn daily while the bills "mature" for later passage. A command to weigh and consider carefully does not necessarily lead to careful deliberation of a law even if all the particulars of procedure are observed, and in the last analysis these procedural demands probably have more importance as potential means of invalidation than they have as elevators of legislative morality or responsibility.[38]

The paltry salary permitted for legislators by most state constitutions makes the legislator's job a parttime task for most members. Legislative pay is hardly the only reason for the short tenure of the average legislator (in some states where the pay is low many do stay in the legislature for decades); pay is nevertheless one of the causes of amateurism of the state legislature. In only one-fifth of the states is the salary of legislators more than $2,500 a year. Some states do provide expense allowances for travel and maintenance while at the capital, but this by no means brings the remuneration to high levels. The highest salary is in Michigan ($12,500 per year), and it is $12,000 in New York and Pennsylvania. By contrast, North Dakota pays its legislators a lordly $5 a day, Arkansas pays $6 a day, and New Hampshire grants its legislators $200 per biennium with no expense allowance. It is perhaps a reflection of public attitudes toward the legislative institution that referenda to increase salaries often fail, as has happened repeatedly in California.[39] It would not be valid to infer that salary is at the root of the amateurism

---

[38] Thus in New York in 1961 a judge invalidated a statute partly on the grounds that it had not been on the desks of members in its final form before passage. See *The New York Times*, March 15, 1961.

[39] See Alexander Cloner and Richard W. Gable, "The California Legislator and the Problem of Compensation," 12 *Western Political Quarterly* 712 (1959). They note that there are other officials paid much higher salaries—Public Utilities Commissioners and Industrial Accident Board members receive $9,000 and $15,000 per year, respectively, but by a good margin the voters refused to increase legislative pay in 1960. In recent years voters have refused to increase legislative salaries in Oklahoma, New Mexico, New Hampshire, and Massachusetts. See Heard, *op. cit.*, pp. 116–17 for recent salary data or the current *Book of the States*.

of the legislature. There are other sources of frustration for legislators, not the least of which is the low prestige and limited prerogatives and power of the institution. But neither is it reasonable to count it out as one cause of amateurism.

Partly as a consequence of the amateurism of the legislature no doubt, legislative operations are often inept and bumbling. Most states provide no staff assistance to the legislator. Legislative councils have been established in many states to assist the legislature but there is considerable variation in the degree to which these bodies provide useful research and advice. Some are quite helpful; others are useless. Formal arrangements for handling bills are often chaotic; bills get lost and mislaid intentionally and unintentionally. The following news story from Indiana is extreme but not entirely atypical:

Indianapolis, March 14, 1961 (UPI)—"Well gentlemen, it appears somebody goofed." . . .

A bill passed by the Indiana Legislature and setting up a $24,000,000 highway program for the Indianapolis area vanished somewhere between the Assembly chambers and the desk of Governor Matthew Welsh.

With no bill before him, Mr. Welsh couldn't sign it and make it law. With the legislative session adjourned, no new bill could be passed for the next two years.

Perhaps this was an accident, but often constitutional limitations on a legislature invite such chicanery as "losing" bills till a deadline passes.

2. *Legislative Apportionment.* The most common restraint on the legislature until recently was malapportionment, a characteristic of all but a small handful of the states. The degree of distortion varied but at the extreme it was close to the classic problem of the rotten borough of nineteenth-century Britain—a legislative district without constituents. The beginning of the end of the problem came in 1962 when the U.S. Supreme Court decided *Baker* v. *Carr.*[40] The Court had previously been petitioned frequently to declare disproportionate allocations of seats an unconstitutional procedure, but it had persistently refused to do so, rejecting what Mr. Justice Frankfurter called a "political thicket" that the Court would be tossed into if it got involved in such cases.[41] In the *Baker* case the court held that to deny urban residents in Ten-

---

[40] 369 U.S. 186.

[41] See particularly *Colegrove* v. *Green* 328 U.S. 549 (1946). Note however, the division of the Court at that time: four to three, with one of the concurring Justices (Rutledge) concurring with the majority while rejecting their argument on the nonjusticiability of the issue. Hence the turnabout in *Baker* v. *Carr* was not without advance signals.

nessee equal representation with rural residents raised a question of "equal treatment under the law" as provided by the Fourteenth Amendment. Thus began the hundreds of law suits, constitutional amendments, and state constitutional conventions that have rewritten the legislative articles of nearly every state constitution in some degree. For the Court was not satisfied to insist that one house of a legislature must be fairly apportioned; it went on in *Reynolds* v. *Sims*[42] to insist that both houses must be apportioned according to population. Here the Supreme Court rejected the so-called "federal analogy," that is, the argument that since the U.S. Senate is not apportioned according to population neither must the state be required to apportion both houses that way. The Court found the analogy irrelevant and an "after-the-fact rationalization"; the writers of the U.S. Constitution had no intention of setting a model for state legislatures when they established the Senate. In any event the states are not federal systems of government internally, and thus the rationale for equal state representation in the U.S. Senate—namely, to protect the integrity of the states as individual units of government—is absent at the state level.[43]

Needless to say, the Court's decisions caused a great deal of turmoil and political skirmishing. It led immediately to attempts in Congress to reverse the Court's action, and for several years it appeared that the campaign might succeed, but the difficulties of passing any constitutional amendment finally made it appear unlikely that such an amendment would be passed in Congress—or accepted by the state legislatures once they had all been reapportioned. Although there was grumbling about the difficulties of reapportioning in constitutional conventions, the legitimacy of the Court brought compliance with its decision. Indeed in New Jersey, where as it happened I was a delegate to a convention to reapportion, the Supreme Court was hardly mentioned in general discussion of our problems, except for occasional criticism of it for not having stated more specific criteria for us to follow.

The end of malapportionment has brought on a discussion among political scientists as to what difference fair apportionment will make.[44] Professor Herbert Jacob, for example, cautions about expecting enormous changes in government as a consequence of reapportionment, and

---

[42] 377 U.S. 533 (1964).

[43] On the battle to end malapportionment, see Royce Hanson, *The Political Thicket.* (Englewood Cliffs, N.J.: Prentice-Hall, 1966); and Robert B. McKay, *Reapportionment* (New York: The Twentieth Century Fund, 1965).

[44] And generally speaking malapportionment has ended. See W. D. J. Boyd, "All States Have Redrawn Districts," 56 *National Civic Review* 587 (November, 1967).

the note of caution is well take, although it can be overstressed too.[45] There were ways of overcoming some aspects of malapportionment, at least in some states. If a state had a competitive party system and significant discipline and leadership in the parties, it was possible for the leaders of the party with the advantage of the malapportionment to pressure their legislative followers to go along with policies they disliked in order to safeguard against defeat in general elections. Thus, in comparing Massachusetts and Connecticut, the former with very equitable representation and the latter with very poor apportionment (until its recent reapportionment under judicial orders), one cannot find much difference in the liberality of the two state legislatures toward their cities, notwithstanding the fact that Connecticut's major cities were grossly underrepresented in one house. The reason is that the Connecticut Republican party had to compete in statewide elections and utter neglect of cities would have been fatal. On the other hand, maximum impact of malapportionment came in states without party competition and with both houses badly apportioned. In Florida, for example, where 17 per cent of the people could elect majorities of both houses, the legislature generally ignored urban problems. Yet it was wrong to assume, as some did, that the tendency for cities increasingly to turn to Washington for help was the simple result of malapportionment. City needs are more complicated than that, although apportionment was a contributing factor. For example, the system of distributing grants for highways and education were often rigged to favor the areas that benefited from the malapportionment.

Malapportionment also contributed to another problem: divided party control between governors and legislatures. V. O. Key pointed to the prevalence of divided controls and especially to the tendency for this to affect Democratic governors more than Republican ones.[46] This was because, outside the South, most rural areas tended to be Republican and therefore rural overrepresentation meant Republican legislative majorities, even when the statewide number of votes cast for Democratic candidates for the chamber vastly exceeded the total number for Republicans. With disparities in the size of districts in the order of as much as one to one hundred this was easy to achieve. Thus in some

[45] Herbert Jacob, "The Consequences of Malapportionment: A Note of Caution," 43 *Social Forces* 256 (1964); Richard I. Hofferbert, "The Relationship Between Public Policy and Some Structural and Environmental Variables in the American States," 60 *American Political Science Review* 73 (1966), and Thomas Dye, "Malapportionment and Public Policy in the States," 27 *Journal of Politics* 586 (1965).

[46] See his *American State Politics: An Introduction* (New York: Alfred A. Knopf, 1956), pp. 52–84.

states it took a landslide election to win Democratic control of the
house of the legislature that malapportionment affected—*e.g.,* Connecticut, New Jersey, Rhode Island, Michigan, and to a lesser degree
Pennsylvania and Wisconsin. Richard I. Hofferbert, however, argues
that during the last decade when malapportionment was a problem
there was no particular correlation between the degree of malapportionment and the tendency to have divided control. He showed that by
dividing the states into three groups according to the degree of malapportionment one found each group had approximately one-third of the
cases with divided control. This does not necessarily prove that apportionment does not contribute to divided control, however. In the
first place, the measure of malapportionment he used combined the
two houses of the states' legislatures in order to get a single ranking,
thereby inevitably reducing the evidence of malapportionment in a
single house.[47] Because this kind of apportionment—equitable for one
house but skewed in the other—invites divided control, it seems inappropriate to use a measure of apportionment that obscures the very
factor being studied. If one removes the southern states from consideration in view of the fact that during the years in question it was
impossible for a Republican governor to win in any of those states,
making divided control impossible, then one gets somewhat different
results. Then the bottom third of the states in terms of the extent of
divided control are with one exception (Oregon) states with one or
more houses considerably malapportioned. If a state combines a badly
apportioned house and high party competition, then the likelihood of
divided control is still greater. Indeed if one controls for party competition (and again removes the southern states), then the following distribution occurs. (The elections are those between 1954 to 1964.)

	Average Per Cent of Divided Control
Top third of the states in competition	64.0
Middle third of the states in competition	51.5
Bottom third of the states in competition	39.1

Whatever the contribution of the malapportionment was toward
divided legislative control, the virtual elimination of gross malappor-

---

[47] The measure he uses is that of Glendon Schubert and Charles Press, "Measuring Malapportionment," 58 *American Political Science Review* 302 (1964); and
for corrections, see the same volume, pp. 966–70.

tionment has not ended it. It has, however, wiped out the tendency for the hard luck governors facing opposition-controlled legislatures to be mostly Democrats. As of January, 1968, a point in time reflecting the fairly close election of 1966, there were a few more Republican than Democratic governors facing opposition control (actually 14 Republicans and 12 Democrats as the figures below indicate).

	Both Houses Democratic	One House Republican	Two Houses Republican
Democratic Governors	13	3	9
Republican Governors	10	4	9

A final point might be made about the consequences of reapportionment. We shall never be able to assert with any certainty what the precise consequences of the change have been for the obvious reason that any changes in policy or governmental practice that occur after reapportionment may be just that: events *after* and not *because of* reapportionment. Yet it is at least suggestive that in a great number of states the legislative sessions following the reapportioning there were amazing breakthroughs in policy areas where before nothing at all could be done. New Jersey is perhaps an extreme example of this, but there is no question that the atmosphere and operations of the New Jersey legislature were enormously different in the two years following reapportionment. Even in the landslides of the New Deal the Democratic party could not win control of the state Senate (apportioned on a one-Senator per county basis, regardless of population), but reapportionment helped give the Democrats overwhelming control of the Senate. The result was an avalanche of long-held-back legislation. While apportionment alone was not the "cause" of this it was a necessary contributing factor.

The Legislative
Process in
11. Local Government

THE DIFFERENCES among state legislatures practically disappear by comparison with the range of variations in local legislative institutions. In operating methods, scope of influence, range of formal authority from maximum to minimum, local legislatures fit no uniform pattern. One cannot even find a universally applicable name for them, for the common term *council* is by no means a uniform designation. The problem of assessing these varied institutions is not simplified by the fact that there are approximately 35,000 municipalities, towns, and townships —each with some kind of legislative body. To this variegated collection one should add the governing boards (again they go by many titles) of the more than 3000 counties, most of which have certain legislative powers as well as administrative responsibilities. In short, one can hardly conceive of an "average" local legislative body: the differences overshadow the similarities, although some similarities, to be sure, do exist.

All local legislative bodies that merit the name have the power to enact ordinances, as local laws are usually called, and these are as much the law of the land as any other statute. The formal procedures that must be adhered to in passing ordinances are numerous and are usually very precisely stated in the basic law of the municipality. (For example, a proposal must be considered during a stated number of open meetings of the council before it can be validly enacted.) If an ordinance is passed which fails to meet these prescriptions in every detail or to conform explicitly with the charter or state laws that set the boundaries for local enactments, it may be successfully challenged in the courts. Indeed, local legislation is more likely than state or national legislation to be overturned by the courts. Local ordinances are also often characterized by their specificity, their involvement in minute detail. They may concern a specific traffic light or the repaving of a single block, although this should not lead to the conclusion that all ordinances are concerned with petty matters. On the contrary, they can be sweeping and inclusive and may concern vitally important matters of policy. They may dictate matters of civil rights, public health, housing conditions, and business regulations, and may therefore stir controversies no less intense than those enacted by other levels of government. Local powers (see Chap. 6) are sharply restricted by the fact that local government is at the bottom of the governmental hierarchy and that superior governments have the authority to limit local powers. Naturally there are considerable differences between the range of possible enactments permitted to the council of a hamlet and that of a metropolis, but both must look outside the local community for authorization to undertake an action.

Two further attributes of councils should be cited. Local legislatures possess—at least in a legal sense however much or little in a practical sense—certain powers over financial matters. The council may be limited in what it can do to raise or lower the budget and may occasionally share power over the budget with another board specifically authorized to oversee finances for the city, but it invariably has some authority in matters of budgets, bonding, and taxation. Finally, it is not an unimportant fact that the members of these bodies are subject to popular election in almost every instance, even though the methods by which they are chosen, their terms of office, and the political circumstances surrounding the election vary infinitely.

Yet most generalizations about local legislatures encounter so many necessary exceptions that they are not very useful. It may be that when councils have been studied more systematically and extensively some more viable generalizations will emerge, but one of the most remarkable things about these institutions is how few comparative studies have been made of them. What follows then is less an effort to make universal generalizations about the local legislature than to assess the ways in which variations in formal authority, relative power, policy orientation, and other facets of the council can most effectively be analyzed. The focus is on the operational effectiveness of these bodies—on their capacity to compete effectively with other political actors and their ability to win policy contests. Hence the structure or form of local legislative institutions is treated not as a significant factor in itself but as a factor that influences the power of the council.

Obviously there are many factors that condition the effectiveness of a legislature: some are formal and legal, others are less tangible (traditions and political relationships, for example). One general observation about the relative power position of the local council should be made: local councils are today relatively less significant political forces than were their predecessors of fifty years ago. The often clumsy bicameral council of the past was a more significant center of power, if only for the reason that it had less competition. Although the old council was frequently dominated by a party machine, it nevertheless was the key source of formal power. In the intervening years, the legislative function throughout all levels of government has lost relative importance in the face of growing bureaucratic and executive authority, but the losses have been most drastic at the local level. The bad reputation of the legislature in the age of the Muckrakers had a more debilitating effect on the city council than it did on the state legislature. Distrust of the state legislature (see Chap. 10) resulted in numerous restraints on procedure and on substantive powers. The city council, while suffering similar or more extensive restraints of this kind, also had a great deal of its power removed and parceled out to commissions and special district governments of various kinds. Taxation, over which the state legislature in nearly all cases retains a general power, was often partially removed from the city council and its counterparts in counties or rural area governments and given to special district governments concerned with education and dozens of other functions.

The relative power of the council has declined so drastically that the following hypothesis will probably be proved true in the course of future studies of municipal political institutions: the council's power rests primarily in its prerogative of saying "no" when its concurrence is indispensable. Nor does it have exclusive possession of this source of power. The planning board may have to agree to zoning changes; the board of education may be in a position to veto policies the rest of the city government wants to initiate. But the point is that the council is singularly dependent upon its nay saying power, and rarely is politically significant enough to initiate policy and push it through. An elected mayor has potential initiative power—that is, he is known and can attract attention to his proposals by dramatizing his program more effectively than the more isolated members of the council. The popularity of some interests (the education leaders or the firemen, for example) provides a measure of political support for their demands. All this is denied the council, and it also lacks the institutional continuity and esprit for its cause that often animates the bureaucracy.

Councils are often remarkably timid about pushing policies. Some members of the council may take leadership positions from time to time, but they do so usually with a sense of daring adventure, for their position often appears to be quite insecure. They must, unlike many of their competitors, stand for election, and although the record of incumbents winning reelection is very good, most members apparently feel the risks of conspicuous policy leadership outweigh any potential gain in public support. Some observers apparently feel that the timidity is unwarranted—that the regularity with which incumbents are returned to office is evidence that their position is not so insecure as they often believe. But I am aware of no evidence that would convince a doubting council member that the high rate of re-election is not a result of the policy of timidity. In any event, the evidence now available does not show the council to be a very strong agency, and its major power does appear to reside in the fact that its acquiescence is needed.[1]

Factors Conditioning the Power of the Local Council

The Form of Government. Since the form of government dictates the formal authority of the council and distributes authority among elements of a government, it is patently a major factor in determining the council's relative power position.[2] It may be repeated that the term

---

[1] See, for example, the comments on local councils in the city politics studies of the Harvard University-M.I.T. Joint Center for Urban Studies edited by Edward Banfield, *op. cit.* See also the case studies reported by Warner E. Mills and Harry R. Davis in *Small City Government: Seven Cases in Decision-Making* (New York: Random House, 1962). The cases are particularly revealing of the tendency for nearly all issues to end up in the council in some form. See also Sayre and Kaufman (*op. cit.*, p. 609), where they say that the New York City Council "is more shadow than substance." See also the pamphlets on city manager governments published by the Public Administration Service in 1939–40, and Harold Stone, Don K. Price, and Kathryn H. Stone, *City Manager Government in the United States, A Review after Twenty-Five Years* (Chicago: Public Administration Service, 1940), which brings together the results of several years of study of city manager government. Both have interesting observations to make on local councils.

[2] On forms of local government generally, see Chap. 7, pp. 111–24. It should be noted too that Chap. 14 presents further analysis of the manager system in some detail, and this naturally supplements the present discussion with particular respect to the role of the council *vis à vis* the manager. It need hardly be repeated

power here has an ambiguity: power refers both to formal authorization to undertake an action—*e.g.*, the ordinance-making power—and the more dynamic sense of power which involves the probability that an actor in politics will be able to induce another to do his bidding. The council's power in the dynamic sense of the term is thus measured by the probability that it will be able to get others to submit to its will in a contest over policy. Obviously formal control over appointments, the presence or absence of a veto, the authority to initiate or to modify budgets freely are potentially important forces for determining the relative power of any governmental body. These potential powers are like ammunition, however: their possession is significant, but the effectiveness with which it is used is also important. Form and structure distribute advantages and disadvantages among the participants, authorizing and denying, giving formal opportunities to control areas of policy to some and denying them to others. But the formal grants can be hollow and meaningless: the ostensible authorization of a council or other agency to perform a specific act does not mean that it will, nor even that other agents will not assume the authority. City managers may dominate councils, or may defer to council members in making appointments, rather than use their own prerogatives, "weak" mayor systems may turn out to have strong mayors who dominate their city councils, and "strong" mayor systems can have weak mayors who defer to their councils. In short, the forms must be taken into account in assessing the power relationships in a local government, but they must be considered as conditioning factors rather than definitely determining what kind of government will result. Like a weather map, form indicates probabilities, but closer observation is needed to see where it's raining and where it's dry.

It is true, however, that some structural factors have greater potential effect than others. When governmental structure affects the essential role of the legislature and makes it, for example, both the legislature and the executive (as the commission plan of government does), then form has unusual significance. This is not to say that all commission governments are alike: it can involve a virtual dictatorship, as was the case in Boss Hague's Jersey City from the 1920's to the 1940's, or it can be a slow-moving and ineffectual government with the commis-

---

that structure does not operate in isolation from the party and interest group and belief patterns of a community; obviously this is true, however often the point is ignored in popular and occasionally also in scholarly discussion. Robert H. Salisbury presents an excellent analysis of the way in which these elements interact in his article, "St. Louis Politics: Relationships among Interests, Parties, and Governmental Structure," 13 *Western Political Quarterly* 498 (1960).

sioners acting at crosspurposes or going each his own way in his own department with little regard for the interrelationships of the policies undertaken. The increasing unpopularity and resultant abandonments of commission government suggest that the structure led to weakened and less effective government.

At the opposite extreme of concentration of power is another variation in legislative arrangements which widely disperses legislative authority: the town meeting as legislative body where every eligible voter may participate in the making of decisions. Although this is mainly a New England phenomenon, some other areas do use township meetings of generally similar character. Town-meeting systems vary widely, as one might expect. In some communities the town meeting is a lively and argumentive affair, in others it is sparsely attended and may be managed to the hilt by political factions. The fabled democracy of the town meeting is, in the judgment of two close students of the institution in Maine, a sham:

Unfortunately, the record fails to substantiate the attainment of very real democracy. Town meetings are poorly attended, manipulated by minorities, unrepresentative of the community, and cumbersome to the point of rendering town government unresponsive. There are, of course, towns where the lie is given to this generalization, but they really are the exceptions that prove the rule. The farcical nature of the town meeting is accentuated in the larger towns: those with over 5,000 population. A sampling of their town meeting attendance for the past five revealed that only one attracted as many as 15 per cent of the potential voters. . . ."[3]

Whether or not this appraisal of the town meeting is accurate, one can safely predict that it will not be believed for it flies in the face of well-settled beliefs. Romantic notions about town meetings will not let most people believe that "these governments are susceptible to all the vices of their larger urban relatives. However, even where the honesty of

---

[3] James Wilson and Robert W. Crowe, *Managers in Maine*, Government Research Series No. 24, Bureau for Research in Municipal Governments, Bowdoin College, Brunswick, Maine, 1962, p. 10. A recent analysis of Massachusetts town meetings by that state's Legislative Research Council reveals a slightly higher rate of attendance. In the 120 town meeting communities of the state the "normal" attendance was less than a quarter of the registered voters; in a majority of them less than 20 per cent of the eligible usually attend. It is interesting, however, to note that the larger communities (with more than 2000 voters) tend to have the least attendance and that the smallest ones (fewer than 500 voters) have the most. See "Report Relative to Town Meetings in Regional Schools" (mimeographed) submitted by the Legislative Research Council to the Massachusetts General Court, December, 1961, p. 39.

officials is above reproach, there is a tendency for family dynasties, as well as informal political machines, to develop."[4]

The apparent dispersal of power to the voters of towns does not necessarily mean that actual dispersal follows. There is an inevitable tendency for the permanent officials who run the government between town meetings (in New England called the *selectmen* and usually three in number: in some other areas called *supervisors* or *freeholders*) to have administrative discretion which counteracts the seeming dispersal of authority to the mass of voters. Still, the makings of revolt are at hand under these conditions; a dramatic issue or highly contentious one can bring forth large attendance at a town meeting with sometimes unexpected reversals of the usual form. Many school budgets, for example, are rejected by such means. In effect, therefore, the structure of the government potentially facilitates the dispersal of power well beyond the control of the influential official few, and this must be taken into consideration by officials.[5]

The difficulties of encouraging attendance at meetings and the further problem of handling large numbers when they do turn out have resulted in an innovation called the "representative town meeting" (commonly called the "RTM" in towns where it is used). The membership of the RTM is usually large (50–150 members in Connecticut and Massachusetts where the system is most widely used) and often attendance is poor. But the system does potentially disperse opportunities to affect policy broadly. In practice, power tends apparently to be concentrated in relatively few, although the potential for revolt is greater than might be the case with a regular city or town council.

Another structural change may soon affect municipal councils: the judicial demand that population equality be given to districts of a local legislative body, just as the courts did for state legislatures. On April 1, 1968 (in Avery v. Midland County, Texas) the U.S. Supreme Court so ruled—by a five to three vote. The full implications of the ruling are not immediately clear for the court appeared to suggest it would be lenient in applying the rule it laid down.

The Political System. The character of a community's political system is an obviously important factor for determining the political position of the council. The dynamics of political relationships in a community, the bargaining among actors and interests characteristic of

---

[4] Wilson and Crowe, *op. cit.,* p. 14.

[5] For good discussions of town meeting government, see Robert Babcock, *State and Local Government and Politics* (New York: Random House, 1956), Chap. 6; Lane Lancaster, *Government in Rural America* (New York: Van Nostrand Press, 1937), pp. 44–51, 70–79; John F. Sly, *Town Government in Massachusetts, 1620–1930* (Cambridge, Mass.: Harvard University Press, 1930).

so many American communities, patently are major determinants of the place of the council in decision-making. This comment on Chicago politics emphasizes the impact of the political system on the relative positions of the mayor and the council:

> In Chicago, political power was highly decentralized *formally* but highly centralized *informally*. The city had what the textbooks in municipal government called a "weak mayor" form of government to be sure, but it also had a powerful mayor, or, if not a powerful mayor, a powerful leader of the Council. This paradox of a "weak" government that was strong was to be explained by the presence of the Democratic machine, an organization parallel to the city government but outside of it, in which power sufficient to run the city was centralized. The weakness of the city government was offset by the strength of the party.[6]

Such factors as the party system, interest-group activity, social behavior barriers for racial groups, and other political phenomena not only condition the place of the council in the scheme of things, they also affect the kinds of policy that may be initiated. A political system that tends to be dominated by downtown business interests will probably result in a council that reflects these views and reacts favorably toward policies proposed by these interests. On the other hand, a political system heavily dependent upon ward or precinct organizations that respond to the urgings of ethnic and racial minorities whose voting power can be translated into significant influence may produce a different kind of council entirely—one that may look askance at downtown business proposals and quite favorably toward a proposal to investigate alleged police brutality to minority groups. In short, the political system affects what the government does as well as the processes by which it acts. Power, process, and policy are intermixed.

To be more specific, how exactly does the character of a community's political system affect the political position of the council? This can best be answered perhaps by classifying some of the effects that different kinds of political systems have on the council's role: (1) the council is affected by the political system's variable effects on its competitors for power; (2) the political system may result in essential domination of the council by other actors on the political scene whatever the legal distribution of power; (3) the political system may be decentralized in character and the council left in what appears to them a vulnerable position fully justifying their timidity and retreat; and

---

[6] Martin Meyerson and Edward Banfield, *Politics, Planning and the Public Interest* (New York: The Free Press of Glencoe, 1955), p. 287.

finally (4) the political system may turn on familial and social relationships (*e.g.*, the closely-knit small town) and this may make the
council the formal decision-maker for virtually all political decisions and
yet an agency reflective of strictly drawn and socially enforced limitations so stringent as to deny it the effective control over policy that it
appears formally to possess. Perhaps the variable character of the
council in municipal affairs will be best illustrated by examining these
four variants in terms of examples drawn from contemporary cities and
towns.

1. The System's Effect on Competitors. It is obvious that the
council will move up and down the scale of relative power depending
in part upon the position of its competitors for authority—mayors,
managers, interest groups, and the bureaucracy—or some element of
it. And in many ways the political system does bestow favors and handicaps on all these actors in the governmental system. Thus a political
system that reflected a strong party leadership, headed by a mayor of
considerable popularity and persuasiveness, would tend to diminish the
relative position of the council. A scholar describing the politics of
Nashville, Tennessee, comments on the dominance of the council by
the mayor, noting that the factional politics and personal popularity of
the mayor has resulted in two-thirds of the council being unwilling "to
speak or vote in a manner that might embarrass Mayor West."[7] Similarly one of the best verified propositions about the operation of the
city manager system is that the manager's relative position (and hence
also that of the council) will depend upon the community's acceptance
of the basic tenets of the system. If the politics of a community offers
organized popular support to the city manager system, the manager's
hand is stronger, for in any dispute with the council he has a trump
card to play: the council's political fear of being made to appear as
opposed to the city manager system. Hence the variable of political
attitude conditions the relative powers of the manager and the council.[8]

The effect on competitors is a broad category, of course, and one can
imagine an infinite number of ways in which competitors would be
significantly affected; indeed, the following categories are in one sense
corollaries of this more encompassing factor.

2. Domination of the Council by Others. Mayors, managers, bosses,

---

[7] Bertil Hanson, *A Report on the Politics of Nashville, Tennessee*, edited by
Edward C. Banfield (Cambridge, Mass.: Joint Center for Urban Studies of M.I.T.
and Harvard University, 1960), p. II-4 (mimeographed).

[8] See the observations on the politics of the manager system in Charles R.
Adrian, "Leadership and Decision-Making in Manager Cities," 18 *Public Administration Review* 208 (1958).

bureaucrats, interest group leaders, and other actors frequently assert a dominating power over the council in a number of significant policy areas. The dominance may be so extensive that the council is reduced to a bargainer of relatively little influence in most matters, or it may be more moderate and involve few matters. The avenues to this dominance are varied, of course. Thus the old-fashioned political boss dominated not only by controlling the selection of the members of the council but also by determining their votes on issues that were crucial to him. The essence of his control method was his position at the top of a political machine: the machine had either the authority to force its will on others or the money and influence to buy its way. Thus the Jersey City of Boss Hague was a personally dominated political system with commission members (the city was run on a commission plan rather than a mayor or manager plan) serving as subordinates of Mayor Hague.

Mayors may use other avenues than Hague's to assert political control. Mayor Richard Dilworth of Philadelphia was dependent upon a factional following of the Democratic party and an uneasy alliance with the Democratic machine headed by the late Congressman William J. Green. In New Haven Mayor Richard C. Lee controls the Board of Aldermen by combining his own personal popularity (he has won the office repeatedly by unprecedented margins) with reliance upon a political machine headed by Democratic National Committeeman John M. Golden. The members of the Board of Aldermen tend to be anonymous and nearly powerless. Dependent on the mayor for their political positions on the one hand, a majority of them are dependent on him for their income on the other. Robert Dahl remarks that 18 of the 33 aldermen as of 1958 "received income from the city; fourteen of these were employed by the city and four sold to it. Four more members had been appointed by the mayor either to Board itself or to some other board or commission."[9] Should one of the members get obstreperous he can be denied renomination without much difficulty. Admittedly the extent to which the mayor dominates the council varies with the character of the regime at any given time, for when the incumbent mayor is not a strong figure the Board of Aldermen plays a somewhat stronger role. Further evidence on this point—of variable influence and domination is also provided by events in New York City politics during Mayor Robert Wagner's term in office. In earlier years of his administration, the City Council—not a very influential body at best—was at its nadir and the Mayor's influence was strong, but when Wagner was engaged

[9] Robert A. Dahl, *Who Governs?*, *op. cit.*, p. 252. See also William Lee Miller, *The Fifteenth Ward And the Great Society* (Boston: Houghton Mifflin, 1966).

in a defensive battle to maintain his position under adverse conditions and against numerous adversaries, the council became more and more restive and resistant to his leadership. In the spring of 1961 it openly defied him on a matter of charter revision, and—although unsuccessful in direct attack—its position at the end of the controversy was probably stronger than when it began.

Other variations could be cited, of course. City managers may effectively control their councils, notwithstanding the inverse relationship that supposedly is the rule of the council-manager system, or particular interest groups (a gambling syndicate perhaps, city employees, or a group of industries) may acquire unusual power with respect to a broad range of policy. No doubt there are many ways by which dominance over a council is achieved, but for the analysis of council politics the point is that one should be alert to its possibility.

3. *Dispersed Political Leadership.* As a result of an every-man-for-himself politics that sometimes prevails, council members may feel themselves to be in unusually vulnerable spots: visible enough to be held responsible for what goes wrong, but not powerful enough to push policies that would perhaps be politically rewarding. Whatever may be said for the accuracy of this appraisal, the obvious fact is that in many communities council members do adhere to it, and the results in terms of policy evasion are significant. Exactly how widespread this is, it would be difficult to say, although it probably occurs fairly frequently. James Q. Wilson characterizes the position of the Los Angeles City Council in this fashion, bearing out the general point:

> Because of nonpartisanship and the fact that most Councilmen have personal organizations, an incumbent tends to be re-elected by overwhelming majorities time after time unless an awkward issue arises or he personally is involved in a scandal. The tactic for re-election is to avoid scandal and commitment on any dangerous issue: the Council tends to move cautiously.[10]

4. *The Politics of Family and Face-to-Face Social Patterns.* The community in which kinship and tight in-groups determine the power relationships in matters of public policy (both governmental and nongovernmental for, particularly in the small community, the two intermingle freely) has a politics that produces a paradoxical effect on the local council. Whereas it appears to be the key agency of all public

---

[10] James Q. Wilson, A *Report on Politics in Los Angeles*, edited by Edward Banfield (Cambridge, Mass.: Joint Center for Urban Studies of M.I.T. and Harvard University, 1959), p. II-6. The reports of the same series on Detroit, Minneapolis, and St. Paul show signs of similar council behavior in varying degrees.

policy-making its actual position is much more limited. Viditch and Bensman in their study of a small upstate New York town illustrate the anomolous position of the council. Powerful although the council appears to be on the surface (since virtually all public decisions for the township are made there), its actual position is much less imposing since it tends to reflect the subtly arrived at desires of a certain group of families and community businessmen. The "village board" operated on "the principle of unanimity," and such disagreement as existed in the community was not brought out at the meetings. Say Vidich and Bensman:

> Through a process of consultation prior to an official meeting and by extended discussion involving the entire group during the meeting itself, a point is reached when it seems reasonable to assume that everyone will go along with the proposed action. Only then, as a final parry, will someone suggest that a motion be made to propose the action. After a short period of silence which provides a last opportunity for further discussion prior to the motion, the motion is made. Whereupon it is assumed that the motion is passed, or, if brought to a vote, as occasionally happens, it passes unanimously.[11]

There is reason to believe that as a consequence of the particular social patterns of the smaller community, the operations of the local legislature would not necessarily conform with what one would expect for larger city councils. The personal relationships of more intimate groups, the absence of a true bureaucracy in the sense in which it exists in larger communities, and the informality of political conduct and communication might be expected to produce a quite different kind of legislative politics. It is clear too that close social contacts override tendencies to form special-interest groups and political parties are often very vague associations with scant impact on local political life.[12] Con-

---

[11] Vidich and Bensman, *Small Town in Mass Society, op. cit.*, p. 110. This volume, as noted previously, is an excellent introduction to the political and social patterns of a small community; it serves well as a counterfoil to the standard assumption that we tend to fall into—the assumption that small communities are mere replicas of larger ones. See also the more rhapsodic and favorably biased accounts of the social and political life of the small town such as Arthur E. Morgan, *The Small Community* (New York: Harper & Row, 1942); Baker Brownell, *The Human Community* (New York: Harper & Row, 1950); Richard W. Poston, *Small Town Renaissance* (New York: Harper & Row, 1950).

[12] There is an interesting parallel between these features of the American small town and the non-Western nations to which students of comparative government have been turning their attention in recent years. The newer nations often have social and institutional patterns radically different from those of Anglo-Saxon and Western European governments which had been the customary basis for comparative government analysis. Tribal or village structures do not fit interest groups concepts,

flict and—equally if not more importantly—the suppression of conflict about policy are handled by face-to-face discussion on the basis of traditional and well-understood, if unstated, social relationships among families and individuals.[13] If the evidence presented by Vidich and Bensman for their New York village is widely applicable for small communities—and it may well be—their report of "Springdale's" successful efforts to avoid local expenditures has great significance. That is, the small community often gets the state or county to assume some functions in order to avoid costs, thereby promoting centralization. Thus although small town leaders deplore the concentration of power at higher levels of government and complain of being pushed around by upper echelons, they may aid their nemesis by eagerly avoiding local expenditures. Local legislative bodies are therefore increasingly put in the position of dealing with other governments as a standard practice. Local legislative politics becomes in part a politics of intergovernmental negotiation.

Legal Authority. Little elaboration is necessary to show the relationship between the formal powers of the council and its opportunities to exert significant influence: possessing the formal authorization may not mean that the powers will be employed effectively or indeed at all, but nonpossession probably means the council will be powerless in the area concerned. The latter does not follow invariably: the council of Jersey City in the days of Hague exercised a good many powers it did not legally have, including some that the Supreme Court of the United States had to terminate, but this surely is an exceptional situation.[14]

---

for example, and very probably many aspects of the American small town should also be viewed as not fitting some of the generalizations we are accustomed to using. See Gabriel Almond and James S. Coleman, *The Politics of Developing Areas* (Princeton, N.J.: Princeton University Press, 1960).

[13] It is interesting to speculate whether the subcultures of larger communities also have a somewhat similar politics at times, at least in respect to the social and familial ties. Daniel P. Moynihan raises a fascinating point in his article "When the Irish Ran New York," 24 *The Reporter* 32 (June 8, 1961), arguing that the Irish-dominated Tammany Hall organization was really a social organization reflecting the social patterns of Ireland:

Instead of letting politics transform them, they transformed politics, establishing a political system in New York City that from a distance seems like nothing so much as the social system of an Irish village writ large. Village life was characterized by the pre-eminence of formal family relations under the dominance of the stern father. Substitute "party" for "family" and "leader" for "father," the Irish created the political machine (p. 33).

How far this can be taken is open to doubt (Boston's Irish produced a very different pattern of city politics from that of New York), but the broad similarity of the boss system and the village politics of the Anglo-Saxon-Protestant small town of today is interesting.

[14] See *Hague* v. *CIO*, 307 U.S. 498 (1939).

Typically, nonpossession of formal authority implies powerlessness to make policy.

Once shorn of authority through restrictive legislation, by transfer to special agencies or commissions, or by centralization of functions in higher governments, the city council's power is manifestly reduced. Subject to the supervision of higher governmental agencies—both judicial and administrative—the council's opportunities to use the powers it has are circumscribed.[15] Procedure of adoption as well as the content of local legislation can produce successful challenge in the courts or occasionally before state or even national administrative agencies. (The national government's supervision comes particularly in programs financed in part with federal funds such as urban redevelopment and housing projects.) Although few ordinances of a community may be overruled in a year, the lawyers who advise local councils on policy proposals and who usually are the draftsmen of the legislation are well aware of the practices of the courts and constantly advise caution and restraint. Moreover, opponents of a given policy are advised by their attorneys of the possibilities of reversing policies by resort to litigation. Thus the council has a sense of being restrained in its potential authority even beyond the language of state statutes or the local charter, for on every hand there is evidence of and warnings about probable delay and even reversal that may follow an incautious act. Such an atmosphere may do much to condition the role and policy enactments of the council, for—apart from all other reasons why the individual members of the council do not wish to be censured—it does not wish to be accused of having acted *illegally*.[16]

The Councilman's Perspective

There is no single perspective on the councilman's position and role, for this varies with the individual and his community. Yet it probably is advantageous to look at some perspectives that we can glean from the literature on the subject[17] and try to postulate some of the ways of looking at the office.

---

15 See the discussion of judicial supervision of the council in Jefferson B. Fordham, *Local Government Law* (Brooklyn, N.Y.: The Foundation Press, 1949), pp. 367–426.

16 See "Taxpayers' Suits: A Survey and a Summary," a "note" in 69 *Yale Law Journal* 895 (1960), which offers detail as to the uses of such suits.

17 The political scientist who has written most about the experience of serving on a council is Arthur W. Bromage, who served on the Ann Arbor, Michigan,

In the first place the perspective is local: the problems are immediate and the relationships between the councilman and his constituency are often close and personal. The councillor answers the telephone at any hour of the day or night to listen sympathetically to complaints about garbage collection, rowdies on the corner, potholes in the street, dangerous intersections, tax levies, zoning variances, and thousands of similar problems that are of vast importance to constituents and therefore of at least some concern to the councillor. Arthur Bromage notes that the services of the old-time ward councilman—baskets of food, rent money, and comparable favors—are no longer important, or at least did not seem to be so in his experience as councillor in Ann Arbor. But the councillor must still be a "broker": delay in paving a street may require "a little push on the wheel of scientific administration."[18] What he calls "brokerage" might equally well be labeled "politics," but the point is that the questions were ones that aroused strong feelings. They stimulated citizens to pursue their council members in order to get information, urge his intercession, or persuade him to vote in the "right" way.

The perspective of the councillor elected from the city at large and that of the one chosen from a ward are likely to be different. The ward representative is likely to have closer contacts with his constituency, and the at-large representative is probably freer to ignore neighborhood blandishments.[19] The theory is that the ward election system tends to overemphasize the "selfish" desires of sections of a city rather than consider the overall welfare of the city as the at-large representation system is supposed to do. Ward election is said to lead to logrolling, spoils-seeking, and an ardent desire on the part of councilman to get something for "his" people. Professors Anderson and Weidner say that if the councillor "must indulge in logrolling to get results, his action will be condoned by his constituents, whereas to come home with 'clean

Council. His commentary is realistic if limited in the range of analysis undertaken. See his book, *On the City Council* (Ann Arbor, Mich.: George Wahr Publishing Co., 1950), an excerpt from which is presented by Robert L. Morlan, *Capitol, Court House and City Hall* (Boston: Houghton Mifflin Co., 1954), pp. 264–67. Professor Bromage also has described his campaign for the council in "Practical Politics: Running for the Council: A Case Study," 43 *American Political Science Review* 1235 (1949).

18 From "The Councilman as a Political Broker," reprinted from *On the City Council* in Morlan, *op. cit.*, p. 197.

19 In Boston the at-large system "has turned attention away from the wards and neighborhoods. . . . In 1958 the Council passed 20 orders requesting the city to improve particular streets and intersections; before 1951 it used to pass hundreds of such orders every year." Banfield and Derthick, eds., *A Report on the Politics of Boston*, p. II-28.

but empty' hands is considered a proof of weakness in aldermen as well as ambassadors."[20] According to Professor Alderfer, the purpose of at-large systems of election, as of several other council reforms, has been to stabilize the "council so its members could be responsible and responsive to the will of the community."[21] If indeed such has been the purpose of the reformers who sought to replace the ward system, then the reasoning involved is somewhat strange. Is a ward representative not being "responsive" when he responds to the requests of his constituents, whether he acts in ways that Bromage approves or that Anderson and Weidner disapprove? If *responsive* is given its ordinary dictionary meaning ("ready or inclined to respond"), then perhaps at-large elections produce less responsive councillors. Suppose, for an example, a member of a city council representing a ward with a concentration of Negro residents responds to their demands and urges the hiring of more Negroes in the city's civil service. If the Negroes lack "their own" representative under an at-large system, they may (and in point of fact often do) find it harder to get their viewpoint strongly expressed in the council or elsewhere. Which system then is the more responsive?

The question is, of course: Responsive to what? Clearly the intent of the reformers is to diminish one kind of responsiveness. Minority groups and politicians whose success depends upon close constituency contacts reject the at-large system for the same reason that its supporters like it: it does tend to free the councillor from localized pressures.

Thus the question is one of perspective of the councillor: What should he see as his appropriate function? Should the election system be organized so as to encourage response to neighborhood gripes and desires or should it encourage representatives to overlook these pressures and take a more aloof position? The question of which of these alternative methods of election is the "right" one, or the one most likely to produce "good" government is often debated in the literature of local government. But this is not a technical question; it is a question to be answered in terms of values and goals, of policies and character of government; it is a question of whether the government will respond more to the felt needs of the lower class or those of the more organized and articulate middle and upper classes. It should not be assumed, however, that ward election systems assure minority group representa-

---

20 William Anderson and Edward W. Weidner, *American City Government* (New York: Holt, Rinehart, and Winston, Inc., 1950), p. 405.

21 Harold F. Alderfer, *American Local Government and Administration* (New York: The Macmillan Company, 1956), p. 328.

tion. Ward representatives can be neglectful as well as respectful of minority demands.[22] And the gerrymander can be used to deny representation to such groups. At-large elections appear to high-status groups as a means to goals they ardently desire: the maximization of efficiency, the elimination of "politics" from government, government by the "better" people. Probably many of these same people would deny any desire to minimize the opportunity of the depressed people of the community to have meaningful opportunities to participate in the politics of the community, but knowingly or not they do just that with this particular election reform. Some Negro politicians bitterly complain that at-large representation, use of civil service instead of patronage recruitment, and other such reforms are being adopted now that the Negro's turn has come to share in the benefits previous ethnic groups used to help themselves up the ladder of acceptability in American society. There is also ground for believing that tendencies toward apathy and alienation from the political system are promoted by the lack of contact between lower ranks of society and their representatives.[23] Migration of Negroes from the South to Northern urban centers poses some very difficult problems of social adjustment, and local government can do much to facilitate or frustrate this adjustment. A voice in city government for these citizens may be more important to the "good" government of the city than the efficiency and no-politics goals of the advocates of the at-large system.

Practically speaking, the alternatives are not limited to the ward and at-large systems, for many communities have combined the two in compromises worked out in local constitutional bargaining. In Philadephia, Buffalo, Houston, and Kansas City, for example, part of the council is chosen at large and part of it from wards. This dual system is employed in about a quarter of the mayor-council governments (the remaining percentage is about equally divided between ward and at-large elections), although in the council-manager systems only 12 per cent of the councils are drawn from both kinds of constituency and the at-large system predominates (74 per cent of all such cities elect councillors at large.)[24] Conceivably such a straddle may be a way of serving both ends,

---

[22] See, for verification of this point, the commentary on Chicago Negro politics of James Q. Wilson in his *Negro Politics, op. cit.*

[23] See the pungent comment on this general point by Robert Lane in *Political Life, op. cit.*, pp. 270–71. Murray B. Levin in *The Alienated Voter* (New York: Holt, Rinehart, and Winston, Inc., 1960), and in *The Compleat Politician* (Indianapolis: Bobbs-Merrill, 1962) makes a somewhat exaggerated case for the alienation of voters in Boston and Massachusetts respectively.

[24] *Municipal Year Book*, 1967, p. 108. It would perhaps be instructive to do some research on communities which use both kinds of representation. Are there

or it may of course fail to serve either with effectiveness. In any event assessment or comparative analysis of the three alternatives cannot be made in isolation from other governmental and political variables: the attitudes of the community, the political party system, the formal and informal place of the council in the governmental system as a whole.

The perspective of the council member is also likely to be that of a part-time, often amateur, operation. There are professionals who stay on councils for decades, of course, yet the turnover in membership is often high. The range of conflicts the council must resolve or conciliate, the technical complexity of the problems it handles, and the personal animosities and intense feelings often stirred by items on the council's agenda are more than the timid and retiring types can stand. Particularly in the larger city, the councilman has a formidable work load, an inevitable portion of abuse, and usually not very much in the way of salary. Salaries run from $17,500 in Detroit and $17,000 in Los Angeles and a few other large cities to absolutely nothing in about a fifth of all cities (mostly smaller cities, although Austin, Texas, and Hartford, Connecticut, councillors serve without pay), and in a great proportion of the cities with over 5000 population the salary is but a token payment of a few hundred dollars.[25] This is in return for regular meetings of the council (weekly in most places), committee meetings, hearings, investigations, and ceremonial obligations, not to mention the political responsibilities of communicating with the public and acting as an intermediary between the public and the bureaucracy. And there is the problem of election too. About half of all councillors serve four-year terms, so that their problems of campaigning (and equally important, particularly where politics tends to be every-man-for-himself, the difficult task of digging up perhaps several thousand dollars to finance campaigns) are not constantly at hand, but the remainder who must stand for reelection every two years must feel that campaigns are always imminent.[26]

Members of local councils, like state legislators, face disputes over the regulation of business that pit one interest against another, putting the councillor in the line of fire between embattled interests out to use the law as a crutch to support their own business or a club to beat down

---

differences discernible between the two kinds of legislators? Do other factors in the politics of a community make both kinds of councillors conform to similar patterns? Or are there differences in the outlook, council actions, and political fortunes of the two types?

[25] *Municipal Year Book*, 1967, pp. 107–09.

[26] *Municipal Year Book* carries an annual tabulation of these facts. For 1967 it was reported that 50.5 per cent of all cities over 5000 population had four-year council terms, and manager-council cities showed 57.1 per cent with four-year-terms (p. 109).

competition. The battle of New York City's automatic coin-operated laundries to avoid regulations aimed at limiting their hours of operation and requiring attendants on duty on the premises during evening hours is a good illustration. The Fire and Police and Licensing Departments supported a law to force the closing of these establishments after midnight and to keep them closed on Sunday because, it was claimed, they became hangouts for delinquents. Not surprisingly the regular laundry industry was much interested in limiting the operation of their competitors, and, although it took considerable patience and pushing to get the bill passed, it did get through the City Council first and then (after seven months' delay) it was passed by the Board of Estimate. Pressures on members of the council and the Board of Estimate (a kind of second chamber with powers greater than the council's) were intense, judging from newspaper accounts.[27] Zoning regulations, traffic control and parking facilities, building and health regulations, and many other public policies can become subjects of lusty battles between economic groups, and the local legislator, sitting in the middle, may not only have a difficult time weighing the merits of alternative proposals but is likely to get brickbats and little glory no matter what he decides.

Abuse by the disgruntled, by the losing contestant in a zoning fight or hassle over an appointment, is more or less standard fare for anyone who ventures into the public arena as a decision-maker for the community. He is fair game. As a "public servant," he is also a public target. One particular form of abuse, however, seems to be increasing in severity in recent years: the denunciation of councillors for meeting secretly. Since it raises some significant questions about democratic government generally, it needs consideration here. Newspapers in particular have complained bitterly of the denial of "the right to know," and it is not always clear whether this is the public's right to know what is going on or the newspaper's right to have access to all meetings and information. (The two, although related, are not identical, for newspapermen feel no obligation to tell all they find out, and in selecting what they choose to play down or eliminate they obviously often decide according to the political opinions of publishers and editors—thus opening themselves to the charge of violating the public's right to know.) If newspapers are feathering their own nests in some part in making this attack, they are also consistent with the stream of American political thought, particularly in its emphasis on popular sovereignty, and thus many editors who

---

[27] See the stories in *The New York Times*, February 10, February 25, and March 16, 1961, on this controversy. And see also the item of April 6, 1961, reporting an order from the courts restraining the enforcement of the act until its constitutionality can be tested.

write the scorching editorials conceal from themselves the self-seeking aspect of the attack.[28]

The common conception of popular sovereignty sustains the right of the public to know all since the legislator is but a proxy acting for the populace. Never far beneath the suface is a simple syllogism that would run, if articulated, this way: secrecy is for a purpose, an honorable purpose need not be hidden, therefore the purpose must not be honorable. In deference to this reasoning, if such it be, some city governments have legally banned secret meetings, and if councillors meet to discuss public policy in secret meetings at all they do so clandestinely and off public premises. Not wishing to appear crooked, they bar what is in many respects a perfectly natural and quite defensible parctice.

Secret sessions to consider political questions (*i.e.*, contentious matters involving the use of influence of one person or group on others) are defensible and indeed necessary for many kinds of policy-making if it is to be done fairly, equitably, and efficiently. Suppose a council has to weigh the relative merits of candidates for an appointment, say, as chief of the police force. When making such an appointment, any responsible councillor wants to know as much as he can about the character and reputation of the candidate, and therefore rumor and innuendo, perhaps quite unfounded in fact, will have to be reviewed. If it is rumored that a police captain has cooperated with gamblers, then this inevitably becomes a relevant item of speculation for the person who must approve the appointment. If the rumor is unsound and baseless, how much better to consider it privately than out in public for the press to report and others to distort! The councillor must entertain rumors and allegations, just as a prosecutor or a criminal investigator must if he is to act rationally.

Or consider a council discussing the acquisition of property by the city. Public discussion may be an invitation to speculators which will result in inflated prices for the city. Prohibiting prior caucuses may make it more difficult to achieve compromise also, since a councillor who has publicly stated an opinion will be more reluctant to reverse himself than one who told a half-dozen colleagues where he stood. This may reflect the mere weakness of man in his desire to save "face," but it is a truth about human behavior, and since compromise can often be indispensable to making policy, the closed meeting may be particularly useful.

It is of course quite true that the closed caucus can lead to a mock ceremony in open meeting, with nothing to indicate the reasoning

---

[28] Much self-rightous comment from both newsmen and officials may be found in *City Hall and the Press*, Raymond L. Bancroft, ed. (Washington: National League of Cities, 1967).

behind or the divisions among members on a proposal, and it is further-more evident that such meetings can be used for secret skullduggery that even a fool would not attempt to perpetrate in open meeting. One need not condone such practices to see the ultility of legislators foregathering to consider problems *in camera*. In preventing, or attempting to prevent such meetings, hypocrisy is invited by urging councillors to be open and frank in their public discussion on the one hand, while running the political system in such a way that to be open and frank on all matters is a sure ticket to political oblivion. The councillor who must do all his discussing and deciding under public scrutiny cannot avoid hypocrisy, for there are things he cannot and will not say since they will be politi-cally suicidal. There is hypocrisy enough in political life without en-couraging it in this fashion.

If the perspective of the member of the council contains so many negative facets, why then do candidates appear on the ballot—not just once, but in election after election? Low pay, abuse, confusion, difficulty in deciding imponderable problems, and a tremendous expenditure of time and energy are involved. Why do candidates always turn up to seek such an assignment? Some don't of course; the call of family, busi-ness, or relaxation terminates some careers in a brief time—or even before they begin. Yet there are rewards: a sense of power to affect the making of public policy; prestige which can be cashed in in different ways (a young lawyer makes his name well-known, a member of the Elks Club gets great satisfaction out of being deferred to by the boys at the lodge). There are ways in which service on the council may indi-rectly lead to other rewards—some of them dishonest (a bribe), some quite honest (higher office). Professor Stephen Bailey has described another kind of reward that serving on a city council may give, and while it sounds odd in the world of cynicism that often surrounds the city council, it is not an inappropriate point on which to conclude:

The enobling effect of a public office is one of its greatest psychic dividends. Those who believe that men seek to hold public office only because it gives them power and status do not appreciate the importance to many men of simply feeling that the job they hold makes them better members of the human race. The heightened capacity for doing good in the world is one of the key attractions of political power and, from my limited observations, is a far more fundamental factor in determining the direction of men's ambitions than the baubles and tinsel of temporary status and deference.[29]

---

[29] Stephen Bailey, *Ethics and the Politician* (Santa Barbara, Calif.: The Center for the Study of the Democratic Process, 1960), p. 10.

Politics, Executives, 12. and Administrators

OURS IS THE AGE of the executive, just as the late eighteenth and early ninteenth centuries were the age of the legislature. The existence of a large, industrial, urban, and therefore complex society has been conducive to the expansion of the executive and to the enhancement of its reputation. This did not come by default, as was to some extent the case with the power and popularity of the legislature in the early decades of our national history: the American legislature was the beneficiary of a tradition of antimonarchial and prolegislature politics in Britain. Thus, remembered antagonism to King George, combined with substantial traditions and practical political considerations, led early American institution-makers to emphasize legislative power and minimize executive authority. Fear of the executive waned slowly, and only reluctantly were the powers of the executive increased. Indeed, fear of the executive even now remains as a significant force in our politics. Thus not by default, but actually in opposition to traditional beliefs, the executive acquired new powers and won a new reputation.

American suspicion of the executive is illustrated in the early state constitutions which relegated the governorship to a position of complete insignificance.[1] In ten of the original states the legislature chose the governor and in only one was the governor given a veto power. Often executive authority was entrusted both to the governor and a council of advisers also appointed by the legislature. In short, the early governor's position was not particularly auspicious. So too with municipal executives, whose powers were negligible. The spoils system and the venality of the post-Civil War era hardly enhanced public confidence in the executive. Notwithstanding these handicaps, the executive branch has in this century grown enormously in numbers, scope of activities, power, and prestige. If the mainspring—the dominating force in the political machinery—of early American government was the legislature, the mainspring today is the executive. As the most visible element of the government, the focal point of public attention, the prime source of policy initiative and wielder of broad regulatory powers, and the responsible agent for performing a broad range of services to the public, the executive of today may or may not be a threat to liberty, but it is undeniably the successor to the legislature as the energizing element of government.

Whether the bureaucracy and the popular, perhaps demagogic, leader at the head of the executive branch are seen as threats to liberty is obviously a matter of values for the same reason that desires for expansion of governmental services or regulation are. The expansion of the executive and of governmental activity go hand in hand. Still, these are by no means the only value aspects of the executive. Some of these value questions are passed off as "mere" matters of fact, having nothing to do with value judgments. Thus it is often said that efficiency is the ultimate test of administration. Efficiency for what? Efficiency in transporting Jews to Nazi extermination camps was something in which Adolph Eichmann took pride as he sat before Israeli judges in 1961. Efficiency in the sense of speed and dispatch in the handling of public affairs—maximum results for minimum manpower and cost to the public—may mean gross arbitrariness to the citizen whose petition for reconsideration of his rights is rejected without review. To reconsider is to delay and to impose a kind of inefficiency on the system. Appeal to higher administrators or to the judiciary may be a price in efficiency that a society chooses to pay for less arbitrary government and more control over bureaucratic power. Questions of efficiency may involve rationality but that does not eliminate their value connotations. The

---

[1] For a review of the early governorship, see Leslie Lipson, *The American Governor from Figurehead to Leader* (Chicago: University of Chicago Press, 1939), Chap. 2.

study of the administrative-executive process should not obscure or evade matters of value.[2]

In order to point up some of the value premises that condition thinking about the executive in state and local government, it will be worthwhile to review the evolution of some basic concepts of the executive, highlighting major themes that continue to affect thinking and practice.[3]

Some Values and Premises Concerning the Executive

Herbert Kaufman, singling out the major values that have influenced thinking about administration as well as its organization and operation, identifies three sets of values: representativeness, neutral competence, and executive leadership:

> Each of these values has been dominant (but not to the point of total suppression of the others) in different periods of our history; the shift from one to another generally appears to have occurred as a consequence of the difficulties encountered in the period preceding.[4]

The first stage—the quest for representativeness—produced a dominant legislature and an important executive. In both state and local government the chief executive tended to be more symbolic than significant. The development of the Jacksonian spoils system and the practice of electing administrative officials (the "long ballot") were efforts to achieve representativeness. This was succeeded by a quest for neutral competence:

> The core value of this search was ability to do the work of government expertly, and to do it according to explicit, objective standards rather than to

---

[2] There is a tendency occasionally to pose a detached objectivity in assessment of values, while in reality pleading a case through subtle choices of adjectives and coloring the argument in suitable shades of meaning. Although such a tendency is well-nigh unavoidable, since those who write know and care about the subject and thus probably have some value judgments, it ought to be minimized for obvious reasons—at least when the intent is not to wage a campaign but to study.

[3] For a brief but perceptive introduction to the character of public administration and for an excellent analysis of the trends of thinking on administration, see Dwight Waldo, *The Study of Public Administration* (Garden City, N.Y.: Doubleday & Company, 1955), an excellent introduction for a student unfamiliar with the subject.

[4] Herbert Kaufman, "Emerging Conflicts in the Doctrines of Public Administration," 50 *American Political Science Review* 1057 (1956).

personal or party or other obligations and loyalties. The slogan of the neutral competence school became, "Take administration out of politics."[5]

Finally there came the quest for executive leadership, sometimes in concurrence with and sometimes in conflict with the neutral competence goals. The essence of the new quest was concentration of power in the hands of the chief executive in order to reduce the fragmentation of administrative power that the earlier concepts produced. As each stage was succeeded by another, it left behind ideals and believers that continue to shape the administrative process. It is conceivable that a fourth stage is in the process of development—it might be called a quest for political adjustment. I refer to the emphasis on political pluralism in contemporary theory and the resultant concern for the difficulties of resolving conflicts among interests and of concentrating sufficient political authority in the executive to deal with a pluralistic congeries of interests—all of which possess enough power to stall and delay and none sufficient power to dominate the others. Thus the thrust of the new approach, if such it be, is to concentrate upon the party and other political devices as means to effective leadership both within the bureaucracy and outside it. The approach has major importance for the administrative system but the tools and concepts are not traditionally those associated with administrative management, such as the executive budget or the elaboration of staff.[6]

The high point of the representativeness doctrine was in the pre-Civil War era, yet it continues to have articulate spokesmen today.[7] The quest for neutral competence became significant after the Civil War and continues to have adherents today. But the executive leadership school of thought is a twentieth-century movement.[8]

1. *The Value of Representativeness.* The desire for a representative bureaucracy stems not only from a desire to assure that the actions of the bureaucrat are in conformity with the wishes of the represented, but also reflects a negative aspect: a desire to prevent excessive power in the executive branch. Both the literature of representativeness and the political devices spawned by the movement suggest a desire to restrict the bureaucracy. Early legislative supremacy and latter-day

---

[5] *Ibid.*, p. 1060.

[6] See, for example, Richard E. Neustadt's analysis of the political realities of the presidency in his *Presidential Power: The Politics of Leadership* (New York: John Wiley & Sons, Inc., 1960).

[7] See, for example, Charles S. Hyneman, *Bureaucracy in a Democracy* (New York: Harper & Row, 1950), Chaps. 1–4.

[8] Kaufman, *op. cit.*, pp. 1069ff., discusses some interesting conflicts between adherents of the latter two sets of values.

means for legislative control over the executive are obviously restraint-oriented. Although there are great variations in the degree to which advocates of representativeness are apprehensive about the bureaucracy as a threat to liberty, they all appear to share some sense of unease about bureaucracy and desire control. Control indeed becomes the key factor. Thus Professor Hyneman says:

> Some of the recent literature of serious character relating to administration in this country supports a degree of immunity from political direction and control for administrative organizations which seems to me to be incompatible with a sound theory of democratic theory of government.[9]

Accordingly they emphasize the importance of the investigatory power (to put administrators on the carpet) and the power of the purse (in order to get at bureaucracy where it *lives*).

Although the scoffer of today finds it hard to credit, there is no doubt that the original insistence on patronage and frequent turnover of personnel in the civil service was motivated in large part by a desire to get new and different people into the bureaucracy, thereby preventing the creation of a permanent civil service. Permanence was feared because it seemed aristocratic and because it seemed likely to induce a sense of detachment from the public and its concerns—in short, it was feared that it would produce a ruling clique rather than self-rule by public participation. Of course, the concurrent desires to control jobs to fuel the party machinery and other (often less noble) objectives were present and ultimately became the dominant motivation for most patronage. Still it would not be accurate to assume that only reasons of party or personal gain motivate those who want representativeness in the bureaucracy. Ethnic minorities, for example, continue to think more or less in the same terms as the early nineteenth-century democratic zealots: the bureaucracy takes its place with the legislature or the judiciary as another place where the attitudes, hopes, and aspirations of a group of people can be represented. A place in the governmental system is an avenue to power, and, with a realism that surpasses the polite fictions of the sophisticated advocates of separation of policy and administration (the theory that the bureaucrat supposedly does not make but only enforces policy), Negroes, for example, see bureaucratic positions as a form of representation.[10]

---

[9] Hyneman, *op. cit.*, p. 48.

[10] A contributing factor in the surprise upset election of Samuel Yorty as Mayor of Los Angeles in 1961 was his promise to appoint representatives of minority

The abiding faith of Americans in the direct election of administrators is derived from concepts of representativeness. Well over half a million offices in the United States are subject to direct election, and most of them are administrative rather than legislative in character.[11] Long campaigning against the long ballot—decades and decades of denunciation in editorials, lectures, and journals devoted to civic affairs —has probably reduced the rate of increase of elective officers, but the popular faith in direct election has surely not been reversed.[12] The idea behind the direct election process is, of course, the belief that only thus can officials be held responsible to the electorate. The official subject to re-election will, it is assumed, be more responsive to the will of the people, than one who is appointed. In a simpler community where face-to-face politics makes it possible to know the personalities of office-holders and something of their activities, it is conceivable that the citizenry may be able to effect controls through direct election methods.

The evidence is overwhelming, however, that present-day governmental and political conditions do not afford the public an opportunity to know their officials and their roles. There are too many elective offices and too little public concern. In Los Angeles in 1960 there were 70 candidates and issues to be voted on, and the 1956 election in Little Rock, Arkansas, produced a ballot with 169 names—132 of them seeking uncontested election as justice of the peace.[13] From such a miscellany of names citizens cannot be expected to make choices rationally, especially where the rough guidepost of party labels is removed. Few voters take the trouble to investigate the qualifications of a horde of candidates. The 1950 contest for California State Superintendent of Public Instruction featured two candidates, one of whom was listed as the "incumbent" and the other as "educator and organizer." The incumbent won handily with 1.7 million votes, and the challenger got but 600,000 votes, but that many votes for an organizer of the Communist party in San Diego is indeed a great showing. This indicates absolutely

---

groups to positions of importance in the city government—which in fact he did do when he took office. That Negroes in Los Angeles turned away from Yorty subsequently to a significant degree illustrates another relevant point: such representation is in practical terms largely symbolic, and the contemporary Negro movement has had enough of "tokenism."

11 U.S. Department of Commerce, Bureau of the Census, 1967 *Census of Governments, Popularly Elected Officials of State and Local Government* (Washington, D.C., Government Printing Office, 1968), p. 7.

12 Childs recounts the story of the campaign in *Civic Victories* (New York: Harper & Row, 1952), Chaps. 1–5 and 9. See also his article, "Woodrow Wilson Legacy," 46 *National Municipal Review* 14 (1957), in which he stresses the role played by Wilson in the National Short Ballot Organization.

13 From an editorial in 46 *National Municipal Review* 173 (1957).

nothing about the feelings of Californians toward Communists, for an identified Communist ticket in California—as elsewhere in the United States—would garner about as many votes as a barmaid running for chairman of the Women's Christian Temperance Union. What it indicates is that the voters blindly voted for an unknown candidate.[14]

The invalidity of the direct election system may not be demonstrated by adducing evidence that voters do not know the names of the candidates they elect nor the functions they are supposed to perform, but it does suggest the case for election may be based on dubious premises. A survey in Michigan indicated that at most only a quarter of the voters could identify the incumbent holding the best-known of statewide elective positions, and a lesser proportion knew incumbents of other offices; only 4 per cent of the respondents in a poll could identify the state treasurer, although he had been in office longer than any other elective official.[15] Should the average citizen of Michigan care who is Secretary of State? The office does not intrude itself in any obvious way on his daily life and it is hardly occasion for surprise therefore that citizens are unaware of the operations if not indeed the existence of the office. Naturally they would be outraged if it turned out that the Secretary of State had connived with the state treasurer to embezzle state funds, and in the memory of such unhappy activities, a good many citizens insist on the retention of the power to elect directly these administrative officials since they feel this gives them a means to remove the unwanted and irresponsible. Indeed, in the poll referred to above, most respondents said they wanted to retain direct election, and a fifth of them wanted an extension of the principle of direct election to more offices.[16]

Support for direct election is not solely attributable to traditional

---

14 This episode I gleaned from Clinton Rossiter's *Parties and Politics in America* (Ithaca, N.Y.: Cornell University Press, 1960), p. 185. The Communist candidate had not gained these votes by stealth, however; she had announced her occupation when she filed for the office and repeated it in radio broadcasts and in newspapers during the campaign.

15 D. S. Hecock, "Too Many Elective Officials?" 41 *National Municipal Review* 449–54 (1952); see also the commentary on this poll and the problem generally in Coleman B. Ransone, Jr., *The Office of Governor in the United States* (University, Ala.: University of Alabama Press, 1956), pp. 374ff.

16 When asked about preferences on direct election, 12 per cent of the sample said too many were chosen by direct election, but 22 per cent thought too few were, 41 per cent thought the number about right, and 25 per cent did not express an opinion (Hecock, *op. cit.*, p. 453). This curbstone opinion does not have to be read as gospel truth even about the people of whom the questions were asked let alone others in the nation, but the fact that nearly two-thirds of those questioned expressed approval of direct elections to the extent then practiced in Michigan (26 elective statewide officials) is significant.

beliefs, however, for there are beneficiaries of direct election who promote the system. Candidates for elective positions—particularly where a loose factional system prevails—are ready to plead the cause of "pure democracy" in urging direct election. Positions on the ballot for lesser administrative posts (comptroller, treasurer, auditor, highway commissioner) can often be turned into lucrative income-producing sinecures. Or these positions can be the basis for sufficient popularity to try for the governorship and all the possible glories and rewards of higher office. Popular election is singularly suitable as a way into office for flamboyant types who might have no chance of being appointed. Hence support for the system both by incumbents and hopefuls is understandable.

2. *The Value of "Neutral Competence."* As the tasks of government grew in scope and complexity with the emergence of industrial society in America, it was inevitable that demand for administrative effectiveness would grow too. The bulwarks of the existing system were well-defended, however; the parties defended the patronage system staunchly; the hordes of office seekers laughed down pleas for merit systems and demands for expertise and training as qualifications for service. The misanthropic Henry Adams is perhaps too bleak for total accuracy in his description of the conditions of post-Civil War Washington, but his observation that the able never expected to be asked to serve the government was apparently the key to the mood of the times:

> As for Henry Adams [he said of himself], in fifty years that he knew Washington, no one would have been more surprised than himself had any President ever asked him to perform so much of a service as to cross the square. . . . There never was a day when he would have refused to perform any duty that the Government imposed on him, but the American Government never to his knowledge imposed duties. . . . The Government required candidates to offer.[17]

And if they hoped to get a job, they knew prior service to the party was a prerequisite. Still the conditions of the times led many to conclude that the existing bureaucracy needed complete reform. The reformers, particularly the academic ones, looked longingly to England where the reforms of the middle of the nineteenth century had converted an overstaffed, venal, and incompetent civil service to a nucleus of a trained and efficient service. And they looked too to the competent and disciplined civil service of Germany where many young Americans

---

[17] Henry Adams, *The Education of Henry Adams* (New York: Random House, Modern Library edition, 1931), pp. 322–23.

then went for advanced education. Slowly reformers made headway in the United States with such victories as the Pendleton Act of 1883 (the basis of the Civil Service system, passed largely as a consequence of President Garfield's assassination), but the pace was slow indeed. In state and local government, despite frequent defeat of the spoilsmen and the introduction of merit systems and other features of neutral competence, the battle was even more delayed; and in fact many states have not yet succumbed, retaining long lists of unclassified jobs to be distributed without regard for civil service standards.[18]

The protagonists of neutral competence were obsessed with developing scientific methods for maximizing the efficiency of the service. Leaving aside questions of values, since these were relegated to the sphere of politics and not that of administration, they concentrated on methods of scientific management. Imitating the natural sciences, they sought laws of administrative operations analogous to the laws of physics. They deduced "principles" of scientific administration, and attempted to promulgate objective, pure concepts of management. They spoke, for example, of "span of control," being the limit in number of subordinates that any administrator could effectively cope with.[19] Sober second thought challenged the validity of some of these supposedly scientific propositions, and indeed some of their original proponents backed away and hedged. They were challenged to show how an optimum span of control could be postulated, given the obvious variations in human capacities (as there are variations in the height to which human beings can jump, why not in ability to administrate?) and the manifest differences in kinds of tasks being supervised which may make control easier or more difficult. They produced no satisfactory answers, and the term, at least as a scientific principle, ceased to be employed.[20]

At the heart of the neutral competence position was the doctrine of separation of politics and administration. This separation was not

---

[18] See *The Book of the States* for current data. About one-third of the states have civil service coverage for only those employees in jobs covered by federal grant-in-aid funds. Civil service is used in slightly more than half of all smaller cities and is invariably used in the largest cities. See *Municipal Year Book* for current data. Charles Gilbert has a good discussion of party patronage in counties and towns of suburban Philadelphia; see his *Governing the Suburbs* (Bloomington: Indiana University Press, 1967), pp. 110–13, 252–59.

[19] See the arguments in *Papers on the Science of Administration*, edited by L. Gulick and L. Urwick (Chicago: Institute of Public Administration, 1937). On span of control, see V. A. Graicunas' article in that volume entitled "Relationship in Organization," pp. 181–88; and L. Urwick, "Organization as a Technical Problem," pp. 49–88.

[20] The best brief challenge to the scientific basis of administration is found in Robert Dahl's article, "The Science of Public Administration: Three Problems," 7 *Public Administration Review* 1 (1947).

stated as a demonstrable fact of governmental operations but as a normative proposition; that is, its adherents did not claim that the nature of existing government proved that government and politics were distinct. On the contrary, they saw and disliked the evident involvement of politics with administration and urged its exclusion therefrom. They conceived of the two realms as ideally distinct: let the policy-makers in the legislature state general laws and then let the administrators carry out the laws free form improper restraint or interference from the political elements. Thus Woodrow Wilson, as a young instructor in political science, wrote: "Administration lies outside the proper sphere of *politics*. Administrative questions are not political questions. Although politics sets the tasks for administration, it should not be suffered to manipulate its offices."[21] This became the major dogma of administrative reform, and, although on this too some of the leading spokesmen later hedged, they were loath to abandon it. Indeed, it is still widely accepted. Thus the late Leonard D. White observed that a "more sophisticated understanding of both politics and administration has led to much more qualification of the . . . thesis without, however, destroying its underlying validity."[22] The more "modern" position was that although it was self-evident that politics and administration would intermingle—that the ostensibly administrative act would often involve values and might in a sense be a political decision—nevertheless, the two extremes of pure policy at the one side and pure administration on the other were recognizable and ought to be kept in mind as separate factors in the governmental process. And, given that degree of distinction, it was important to keep administration nonpolitical to the extent that it was possible to do so.[23] If the politicians meddled in administration or the administrators got into the forefront of political controversies, the opportunities for making the most of efficiency without regard for issues would be diminished. The old doctrines, however muted and now

---

[21] Woodrow Wilson, "The Study of Administration," 2 *Political Science Quarterly* 197 (1887). This article was one of the earliest attempts to discuss problems of studying administration for, as Wilson pointed out, there had been relatively little systematic study of administrative procedures although other aspects of government had been studied for centuries.

[22] Leonard O. White, *Introduction to the Study of Public Administration*, 4th ed. (New York: The Macmillan Company, 1948), p. 6.

[23] See the position taken by Herbert A. Simon who argues that there is a distinction between facts and values—that the former are or can be nonvalue components with which the administrator works. See his *Administrative Behavior* (New York: The Macmillan Company, 1947), pp. 45ff., and—in collaboration with D. W. Smithburg and V. A. Thompson—*Public Administration* (New York: Alfred A. Knopf, Inc., 1950), pp. 20ff. Note also the criticism of this position by Philip Selznick, *Leadership in Administration, A Sociological Interpretation* (Evanston, Ill.: Row, Peterson and Co., 1957), pp. 74ff., and espeically pp. 79–80.

almost absent from the administration literature, still have adherents. The separation idea has supporters, particularly among practitioners: many city managers will stoutly claim they have nothing to do with policy but deal only with administration of policies set forth by the council.[24]

Dubious as the underlying tenets of the separation theory may be, its dogmas have left a curiously mixed legacy, for undoubtedly they have led to vast improvement of the conduct of public business while also tending to obscure many operational realities of the governmental process. The merit system has in fact been indispensable to the development of expertise in the modern civil service. The emphasis on training, permanence, and promotion on the basis of competence rather than favoritism and the protection from the hazards of political displacement have made for greater efficiency. Civil service tenure undoubtedly has protected some incompetents, and the lack of opportunities for career men to enter the topmost administrative posts has perhaps discouraged the ambitious and adventurous and resulted in timidity and specialization in red tape. Notwithstanding these and other difficulties, the merit system has contributed much to making a more effective bureaucracy.

The desire to get politics out of administration led to the proliferation of independent agencies in both state and local government. Some of these agencies were regulatory bodies which—partly because they performed functions of a quasijudicial character—were placed beyond the direct control of the chief executive and the legislature.[25] But many of the more or less independent commissions—and they were created by the thousands—were not concerned with regulatory activities at all. They dealt with subjects that somebody wanted to protect by insulating them from the day-to-day vicissitudes of politics. Thus education is usually given some independence in both state and local government, and other agencies of varying character—licensing boards, banking commissions, and boards concerned with such matters as parks, planning, hospitals, libraries, and so on—are given similar status. In short, to remove politics from given fields of public affairs, the agencies themselves were made independent of the policy-makers at the center of the government. By making the agencies independent and their members elective (often on nonpartisan ballots), it was hoped to reduce

---

[24] For a firm rejection of the separation idea, read Paul H. Appleby, *Policy and Administration* (University, Ala.: University of Alabama Press, 1949).

[25] For a thorough and politically realistic evaluation of state regulatory activities, see James W. Fesler, *The Independence of State Regulatory Agencies* (Chicago: Public Administration Service, 1942). Although it reports conditions of the late 1930's, its essential facts are still accurate and its insights are still pertinent.

the political factor to a minimum. Whatever the effect on the political actions of the independent agencies (and it is worth remembering that independent decision-makers still make decisions that are political), there is no doubt that one effect was clearly felt in most cities and states —a fragmentation and dispersal of policy-making responsibility. This effect, and the strong impression that it rendered government less efficient through lack of coordination, inspired the last of the great quests in the field of administration: the quest for executive leadership.

3. *The Values of the Executive Leadership School.* *Integration* is the key word: the object is to integrate administrative activities and concentrate control over them in the hands of a responsible chief executive. What was wanted was a forceful hand somewhere to pull governmental activities together since neither the courts, the legislatures, nor the chief executives of the day seemed able to do so. Both the representativeness and neutral competence had led to fragmentation which, as Kaufman puts it:

. . . bred chaos; agencies pursued contradictory policies in related fields. It fomented conflict; agencies engaged in bitter bureaucratic warfare to establish their spheres of jurisdiction. . . . It was costly. . . . And, most important of all, it led to irresponsibility. . . . No one seemed to be steering the governmental machinery, though everyone had a hand in it.[26]

From about 1910 to the present countless studies have been made of administrative organizations, and most have preached the integration-concentration line. Under Presidents Taft, Franklin Roosevelt, Truman, and Eisenhower, major studies of the federal bureaucracy were made and each of these spawned comparable studies in state and local government. The reports emphasize the importance of having an executive budget as a necessary tool for executive control over agencies rather than allowing the individual agencies to negotiate with the legislature for appropriations more or less independently of the chief executive. They also urge expanding staff assistance for the governor or the mayor so that these officials can keep track of what is going on in the executive branch and acquire information and advice from personnel loyal solely to the executive himself rather than having him depend upon what may be biased information and advice from departments whose own destinies are involved in the questions about which they must advise. The reports also urge the elimination of independent status for departments and agencies and request that they be brought under the supervision of the governor or mayor.

---

26 Kaufman, *op. cit.*, p. 1063.

The quest for executive leadership has been persuasive to many people and, as a consequence, the overall position of the executive has been strengthened. The basic logic of the quest is after all simple and at least superficially reasonable: fragmentation leads to irresponsibility, since evidently we do not know what is going on in the dozens of scattered agencies; the chief executive, on the other hand, is visible, and if he is given power to control the administrative hierarchy, he can then be held accountable through the elective process. The idea, in short, is to achieve responsibility through concentration of control. Although the doctrines have been far more popular with public administration scholars and with practitioners in the field than with legislators and suspicious people who feared undue concentration of power in the hands of any single individual, there has nevertheless been a general movement toward administrative integration. No doubt this is partly a consequence of the increasing popularity of chief executives in this century as a result of the drama that some of them have brought to the presidency, the governorship, and—sometimes—mayoralty. Modern problems of government and modern methods of campaigning have caught the public attention, and as a result no other official is as visible as the chief executive. This popularity has been helpful in the contests over rights to control the operations of the government with the legislature losing ground to the executive.

It would be wrong, however, to suppose that this movement has entirely or even largely achieved its goals. Fears of concentrating too much power (cries of "Dictatorship!" follow invariably upon the publication of reports of study commissions) are deep. These fears combine with the practical politics of agency separatism to limit the reforming movement. The clientele of agencies threatened with loss of independent status form alliances and by thus pyramiding their power often defeat reform bills in a legislature. The degree of executive power may now be greater than it was a generation ago, but it is still far short of the amount of power that the reformers in quest of executive leadership have proposed.[27]

The Task of the Executive and the Administrator

If there is little merit in making a categoric distinction between policy and administration, since the two are so intermixed, it is still significant

---

[27] Of this drive for concentration of executive control much more will be said in Chap. 13 in discussion of the development of the modern governorship.

that some activities are more concerned with policy than others are. The conduct of administrative business can become a matter of policy when it involves values of significance to the society or decisions which are of wide enough concern to make for dispute or competition. Thus what may seem minor matters of personnel within an agency may become a matter of policy—preference for veterans, for example, or the harshness or lenience with which loyalty-security safeguards are applied. And the highest executives may at times have to concern themselves with questions of a management character—that is, problems of organizational detail in critical cases that get shunted up the hierarchical ladder. But the upper executive is normally concerned with policy and value questions and lower administrators with organizational relationships. Problems of how-to-do-it predominate at lower levels and problems of values at the upper. As Philip Selznick has aptly said:

> The logic of efficiency loses force . . . as we approach the top of the pyramid. Problems at this level are more resistant to the ordinary approach of management experts. . . . *The executive becomes a statesman as he makes the transition from administrative management to institutional leadership.*[28]

The executive, Selznick says elsewhere, is concerned with the "promotion and protection of values" of the institution he heads, whereas the lesser administrator's task is "to smooth the path of human interaction, ease communications, evoke personal devotion, and allay anxiety."[29] It is perhaps unfortunate that we have not developed terminology to show these distinctions, although terminological clarity might have resulted in overstressing the distinctions and making too rigid a separation. Selznick's distinction, however, has flexibility and is a singularly apt way of characterizing the various aspects of executive process.

Equally important to remember is the fact that administrators and executives are people. Too often officials are rendered into abstractions by lumping all occupants of offices together and ignoring the tremendous variations that exist among human beings. We sometimes forget that some individuals inspire confidence and can win loyalty and support where others cannot; that some can comprehend complex situations and see the interrelationships of problems and people and plan coordinated approaches accordingly while others can neither comprehend nor plan nor explain. An individual lacking the qualities of leader-

---

[28] Selznick, *op. cit.*, pp. 3–4. (Italics in original.) This little volume contains some very penetrating thinking on problems of administration, and is highly recommended.

[29] *Ibid.*, pp. 27–28.

ship occupying an office well-endowed with formal authority may achieve remarkably little. An official who has formal power and leadership qualities but who is disinclined to use the authority he possesses will simply not be comparable to one of equal talents (or perhaps of lesser talents) who is determined to get action. The abilities, attitudes, personal traits, values—even the personal appearance—of individuals condition their effectiveness as leaders. It follows therefore that generalizations about leadership and about the effects on executive power of governmental structure or political alignments must be considered in terms of these personal variables. This may seem a painfully obvious point to make. It is perhaps so elementary that it is lost sight of by those who discuss the operations of governments, for it is certainly true that such terms as *weak mayor* or *strong mayor* are often used as though mayors came in cans like peaches, uniform in size, quality, and character.

These facts of human variability assume even greater importance when one takes into account the role of the modern executive, for the kinds of tasks to be performed require prodigious effort, energy, and patience in addition to ineffable personal qualities and abilities. The modern chief executive is the key link in government; not only does he assume a crucial role as the most visible figure in government, but he performs a broad range of functions—and failure in any one of which may be catastrophic. The larger the government, the broader the tasks, naturally. In a small community the mayor's role may be very simple and involve little in the way of chief executive activity. But as the communities become larger—when we are talking about the mayors of cities with tens of thousands of inhabitants or the governors even of small states like Vermont—the full range of tasks appears. A review of some of those tasks—or of ways at looking at the functions of the modern executive, if you prefer—is a useful preparation for consideration of the problem of executives at the state and local level.

A chief executive is, among other things, chief administrator, chief legislator, political chief, symbolic and ceremonial head of the community, chief of public safety, and chief negotiator with other governments. And to be successful in these roles he must be an effective persuader, constantly using his various wiles to get his points across and action taken. He may have to bargain, accept compromises, plead for what he can get when he can't get what he wants, defer action until the time is ripe, and choose well which role to play when. Lesser executives may have to perform some of these roles: a highway commissioner may be subordinate to the governor, but he will also have an administrative overseer role, a role in the legislative process, major political responsibilities, a certain symbolic and ceremonial role (*e.g.*, the ribbon-cutting events), a responsibility for public safety (*e.g.*, in emergencies), and a negotiator with officials of other governments or other departments. And he certainly is going to have to be a persuader—in his own administrative house, in the bureaucracy in general, in the legislature, with the public, and even with his enemies. In short, major administrators may not be chief executives, but their tasks are similar. As we descend the administrative hierarchy, the degree of responsibility declines, of course, until at the more technical and less managerial positions leadership tasks are at a minimum.

Governors, mayors, and managers are not faced with the bewildering range of duties that fall to the President, but their tasks broadly resemble his.[30] Consider briefly the nature of these several tasks: the chief administrator role for governors and mayors of huge cities is mostly a matter of negotiating with the bureaucracy and the heads of departments in trying to achieve coordination, and trouble-shooting where evidence of difficulty arises. Day-to-day administrative work—in the sense of management details—does not occupy much of the time of an effective administrator. If it does, he is risking the overall role of leadership by dealing in minutiae. The chief executive, particularly in larger governments, is likely to consider only problems of broad coordination and general supervision of major administrative operations.

The legislative role patently varies in many respects: the formal-legal position of the executive, the political position, and the personal inclinations, to mention a few. But the importance of legislative policy dictates an inevitable involvement for an executive who wants to assert leadership. Some executives, of course, will take little or no initiative in legislative matters, waiting instead to see which way the ball is going to bounce before taking a position. Yet even such an executive will probably be involved to some extent if only because the public is inclined to hold him responsible for "wrong" policy enactments however much or little he may have had to do with making the policy decision. At the opposite extreme, executives may nearly supplant the legislature in dominating policy-choices.

Patently, too, the political role of the chief executive varies widely —from a situation in which the mayor is the boss of the city's politics to one in which a reserved and reticent city manager in a city with nonpartisan elections where the formal chief executive has virtually nothing to do with the political machinery. Yet even in the latter situation the manager does play a certain political role, for his recommenda-

---

[30] See the compartmentizing of the presidential office by Clinton Rossiter in his *The American Presidency* (New York: Harcourt, Brace, and World, Inc., 1956).

tions—even if modest and minimal—are of some relevance, and in the management of the bureaucracy he assumes a responsibility for keeping the system honest and disciplined and in pursuit of specified goals. The political implications of this may be most evident when things go sour, as the political storm that ensues from revelations of wrong-doing quickly illustrates. As the most visible political figure in a city or state, the mayor or the governor tends to become a representative —that is, he is looked upon by the public and he thinks of himself as a representative of the will of his constituency. He speaks in the manner of a representative, often contending in his demands for legislative policy, that he is the representative of all the people in a way that the legislature is not.

The symbolic and ceremonial chieftainship of a state or local government obviously does not evoke deep emotions comparable to those associated with the president's symbolic role, but in many other respects the lesser executives perform similar tasks. The mayor at the banquet symbolizes the community's approval of the lodge or the charity, and the governor's presence in the town's centennial parade signifies the power and prestige of the state itself. Although it may be almost impossible to separate the symbolic aspects from the public relations and political campaigning elements of such appearances, the symbolism is still there.

The chief of public safety role is in some respects comparable to the defense responsibilities of the president. Emergencies may suddenly catapult a mayor to unprecedented leadership as he takes action to cope with a disaster or civil unrest. The range of power of the governor or the mayor may be pale in comparison with the president's role as commander-in-chief of the armed forces, yet the discretionary powers born of emergencies can be broad. Faced with violence in labor disputes or in riots from whatever source, an executive's decision is not only important intrinsically but may to an unusual extent be in his hands alone.

Finally the chief executive is a chief negotiator with other governments—a variation on the diplomatic role of the president in a sense. Since ours is a federal system, there are constant negotiations among governments. For two or more states to coordinate highway development, pollution control, or resource conservation, or to arrange reciprocity in various policies (tax laws, for example), negotiation is necessary. Municipalities and states negotiate matters of finance such as conditional grants. The mayor, with the welfare commissioner at his side, may dispute the ruling of the state welfare officials that the city will not be eligible for further grants unless it complies with some specific regulations promulgated by the state. So, too, neighboring municipalities must coordinate their activities, and their chiefs are called upon to resolve by negotiation questions such as the respective shares of towns in financing a water resources program. This is not of course to imply that the chief is the sole negotiator; on the contrary, many negotiations never involve high officials, although if the program involves difficult policy decisions it is almost inevitable that the chiefs will sooner or later be involved.

This complex of tasks requires the use of the art of persuasion. In a recent discussion of the power of a governor faced with an administrative system in which some of the administrators were not appointed by him but were themselves subject to the same election process by which he came to power, it was said that under these circumstances the governor is "reduced to persuasion." This is wholly misleading, for even a governor with great formal power to control subordinates has to rely on persuasion. Power, as we have observed repeatedly, runs not only from the top down but from the bottom up. A governor, a mayor, or a manager has to persuade his subordinates of his point of view if he hopes to achieve his ends. Although the independently elected administrator may be better able to resist, all kinds of subordinates have to be pushed. The distinction, in short, is not the persuasion but the opportunity to resist it.

As Professor Richard Neustadt has pointed out, even the president, whose authority over his subordinates is legally greater than that of most governors or mayors over theirs, must depend on persuasion to get results. Merely to order something done is no assurance it will be:

The President of the United States has an extraordinary range of formal powers, of authority in statute law and in the Constitution. . . . [D]espite his powers he does not obtain results by giving orders—or not, at any rate, merely by giving orders. . . . Presidential *power* is the power to persuade.[31]

It is true that the presidency involves particularly difficult problems of control due to the size of the federal bureaucracy and the enormous range of activities that take place in the federal government. There are many ways to evade, to hide noncompliance in so large a system. In

---

[31] Richard E. Neustadt, *Presidential Power* (New York: John Wiley & Sons, Inc., 1960), p. 10. In some respects Robert C. Wood argues a similar line with respect to the governor in his "The Metropolitan Governor" (unpublished dissertation presented at Harvard University, 1949). Wood says at one point: ". . . no metropolitan governor, and probably no governor at all, enjoys an 'area of uncritical acceptance' to his orders. . . ." Rather, he says, governors face "political repercussions and professional administrative resistance" (p. 326).

smaller governments the evasion may be somewhat more difficult, but evasion and resistance are present on all levels of government.

Whether or not subordinates comply is conditioned on many factors. How good a persuader is the governor? Does he mean what he is asking for? Is he perfunctorily responding to pressures that he does not take seriously or does he intend to fight for what he has ordered? What kinds of sanctions would he bring to bear if no action is taken? What kinds of reverse pressure can be applied to the governor if he persists? (Would a threat to resign that might embarrass the governor with adverse publicity force him to let up?) Is the order really "right" from the point of view of the subordinates? If it seems the "right" thing, there may be no resistance at all, even though the subordinates may not personally like the order. Obviously the character of the political system in which the governor, mayor, or manager is operating will condition the chances of his effectuating policies without serious resistance. Where the party system is strong enough to reward the ambitious with re-election or advancement, subordinates may comply readily simply because this is a sanction not lightly ignored. These and other factors of practical political maneuvering—the playing of the game of politics with its stakes and opportunities for bargaining—are constant elements of the process of persuading and leading that increasingly we expect or demand of chief executives.

13. The Governor and State Administrators

THE "IDEAL" GOVERNOR has the looks of Adonis, the stamina of a marathon runner, a reputation for honesty, integrity and independence, political acumen of the highest order, ability to entertain and to educate, and the capacity to appear concerned with the problems of everyone while remaining calm and collected in the midst of a political whirlwind. Judging from the images candidates and incumbents seek to project, these are the approved attributes of a governor. Specifications vary from state to state, depending upon political and social traditions. Being a hillbilly songster can be a liability or an asset, depending on the locale, but a certain resemblance to the prototype of American male good looks seems appropriate everywhere. The office having become more and more personalized as it becomes increasingly the most visible office in state government, gubernatorial campaigns—particularly since the advent of television—emphasize personal appearance.[1]

The ideal governor's reputation for being independent, fearless, and honest is not made any simpler by the demand that he be at the same time an effective political operator. There is a considerable

---

[1] Let the scoffer look at any issue of the *Book of the States* where the photographs of governors are presented. More than half of the pictures show reasonably handsome men; others not thus naturally endowed are often grandfatherly figures. The light-and-shadow artists who take official pictures are acutely aware of the governor's need for an effective official photograph; these are not casual snapshots.

[337]

leniency on the part of the public toward a respected political figure—acts commonly considered "dirty" politics may be excused as necessary compromising when attributed to a hero. Still, the need to maintain a front of independence and aloofness from routine political maneuvering is hardly facilitated by the governor's need to compromise, push, persuade, and use bait and punishment to achieve his purposes.

The governor thinks of himself as a representative of the people—as apparently the politically articulate expect or demand him to be. Hence the ideal governor is responsive to the public demands and seeks to give the impression that he is concerned with every man's problem and that not only his office but his own broad shoulders are appropriate repositories for the worries and fears of the people.[2] Note the following from an editorial on former Governor of New Jersey, Robert B. Meyner:

> In office his was the tested formula for popularity: tireless attendance at gatherings large and small, sedulous attention to correspondence, meticulous observance of amenities.
>
> He came to terms with party bosses, while preserving a reputation for independence. He has so thinned out his image that he won over the progressive concerned with human welfare and the conservative concerned with property.
>
> His youthful energy delighted the young, his marriage [while in office] enchanted the romantic, his concern about the aged, the disabled, the underpaid and under-privileged touched the public conscience.[3]

Accordingly, the governor's office receives bulging bags of mail—much of it dealing with subjects the governor has neither authority nor capacity to do anything about. The governor's list of callers suggests he is willing to see anybody in the state who has a problem: sixth-graders visiting the capitol, ward-heelers eager to report back to the boys "what the governor said when I was talking to him yesterday," dignitaries from the Congo, lobbyists, legislators, administrators, reporters, academic interviewers, aggrieved citizens whose problems the bureaucracy has perhaps dealt with for weeks or months.[4]

---

2 Robert C. Wood's "The Metropolitan Governor" (unpublished dissertation presented at Harvard University, 1949), makes a telling argument, backed with substantial supporting evidence, for the proposition that in the three states he analyzed (New Jersey, Connecticut, and Massachusetts) the "representative" role of the governor tends to predominate over his other roles.

3 From the *Newark Evening News*, January 20, 1958.

4 Coleman B. Ransone presents evidence from several states as to the time allotted by governors to visitors to his office. A New Hampshire governor spent an average of 20 hours a week thus engaged, and he found in the states he investigated

But whose "ideal" governor is this? Is this the governor who appears in the standard description of an executive in charge of administrative operations of the state? or the governor imagined by the constitution-makers who assigned him (and denied him) specific constitutional authority? It is neither. Rather the foregoing describes another kind of "ideal," one that reflects the apparent inclinations of the interested part of the public. The best test of whether or not this is what apparently is desired is the extent to which governors obviously try to fit themselves to this model. Even casual observation suggests that they do.

This does not mean that there are no onerous administrative problems to cope with, no hard-fought battles with interest groups, no contests of will and guile with the legislature or within the party organization. And it certainly does not mean that governors are Cheshire cat smiles without substance, ideas, or policy convictions. Policy is the business of the governor: he makes it and he is constantly aware that it can make or break him. Running for office is not just a matter of looking handsome in a toothy way on a television screen, but a year-round activity inevitably involving policy decisions. A battle over state highway appropriations in Iowa, a contest over the University of Massachusetts' budget, a donnybrook in Georgia over segregation legislation —all may demand the utmost in leadership, skill, and patience on the part of the governor, for a "reasonable" settlement of the question may be indispensable to a governor who wants always to be thought "successful." Success is not composed of front and pretense (although admittedly it may partly be that); it is also struggles over public policy. The governorship is preëminently a political office.

The Politics of the Governorship

People increasingly speak of a law being "passed by the governor." In sarcasm the storekeeper tosses coins into a can labeled "Sales Tax" and says, "A penny for the Governor." A cabbie in New York said after Rockefeller's proposal of a tax increase: "So this rich character gets elected and right away he's got his hand in my pocket."[5] Sophisticates may not use such terms, and those who do presumably know the legislature exists too, yet the tendency to equate policy-making with the

the "average American governor sees from 10 to 25 persons a day." *The Office of Governor in the United States, op. cit.,* pp. 125, 137.

[5] Stuart Alsop, *Nixon and Rockefeller* (Garden City, N.Y.: Doubleday & Company, 1960), p. 167.

most visible element of the government is understandable, if mistaken. This "common man's" assessment may in a given case be inaccurate —the governor may lack the political means or the personal inclination to cut the sweeping figure suggested by the common conception—but the popular image nevertheless has a significant potential in the game of politics. For the governor can convert the popularity of his office into direct support for his policies, or he may be able to convince his adversaries that a basis of support for his position exists to be exploited, perhaps to the detriment of those who impede him.

Moreover, when a governor is not inclined to use the potential of his office for leadership, when he settles back into a caretaker role, this almost inevitably will have serious consequences for the operations of state government simply because the expected leadership role is not being filled. The demands of the role are onerous after all, and, as Karl Bosworth has pointed out, some governors are incompetent to fill the bill and others retreat into merely tending the store if they are rebuffed in early efforts to achieve leadership.[6] A stalemate of contesting interests or of competing administrative agencies may go unresolved for the lack of effective leadership. Or less than responsible elements may find in the vacuum of leadership an opportunity to shift policies subtly (or not so subtly) toward certain contractors, liquor interests, gamblers, or others from whom a killing can be made. This is not to say that governors never have been known to partake of such operations themselves —for they have, but far more rarely than underlings. The problem of getting re-elected or of getting elected to another post higher up the political ladder tends to keep governors out of such involvements. An alert and forceful leadership discourages not only the dishonest but also the militantly selfish interests that may grab an opportunity to insure their future position while leadership is not likely to be used against them. What better evidence of the ultimate significance of gubernatorial leadership than the fact that its absence has great effect on the conduct of government?

What resources are necessary for a governor who wants to make the most of his leadership position? What tools, methods, powers, and qualities can be called upon to build support for the governor's position? To lead, of course, is not merely to push bills through the legislature, although that is the stereotype measurement of gubernatorial leadership. Leadership may involve stopping the rackets from getting the gambling legislation they want, defending an administrator who has

---

[6] See his essay on "Law-Making in State Governments," in *The Forty Eight States, op. cit.*, pp. 108–09.

stepped on toes but who has done what the governor thinks is right, negotiating with warring elements to get a peaceful resolution of a controversy (between interest groups or between governmental agencies, for example) without doing damage to political machinery that will have to be used tomorrow. He may have to initiate or promote what others have initiated. The variable character of the leadership role therefore demands many resources, many kinds of bait and many ways of using it. In a rough way these resources may be classified according to whether they are (1) personal, (2) party-oriented, (3) publicity devices, (4) or legal-constitutional.

1. Personal Resources. It is obvious, of course, that a governor must be inclined to assert himself—to feel sure that he ought to lead —if he is to be effective. This is a matter of values, of approach to political realities, and different governors have manifested different views. Some aspire to no more than a modest overseer's role. Others may feel that the only route to political success, given the political conditions of the state, is to stir no fuss, to anger no one, to bide one's time and wait for promotion to the United States Senate with its power, prestige and six-year term of office. Other governors, whether as conservatives like J. Bracken Lee of Utah or liberals like Richard Hughes of New Jersey, feel it is their duty to step out front and insist upon leading.

To be such a leader demands more than will and conviction; it also demands certain ineffable traits of personality that some men have and others lack. These qualities are exceedingly hard to describe for they are elusive, subjective matters of emotion and personality. How is it that some men inspire loyalty and tireless support while others cannot? In manner, bearing, and behavior some individuals are attractive and stir the imagination and create a willingness to follow. In personal relations, in public appearances—the dynamic transmission of feelings in a speech illustrates the kind of quality involved, through examples of confidence and command, and by infusing a sense of mission in others, some individuals radiate a magnetism that is an essential ingredient of leadership.

Leadership may also require a willingness to take risks, to choose a path and stick to it rather than to permit the forces of the moment to set the course. Capacity to decide and persist once a decision is made, even in the face of formidable opposition, is important, and yet this needs to be combined with a capacity for seeing when persistence no longer makes sense and a feeling for the politically possible that moderates firmness so as to prevent it from deteriorating into mere stubbornness.

The following remarks made by former Governor Gaylord Nelson of Wisconsin to the assembled state Chamber of Commerce reflect a kind of candor and willingness to attack that is uncommon in a governor or any other politician, but it may also reflect the kind of brass necessary to get political action in a stagnant environment. Nelson said:

> I am going to speak frankly and bluntly to you tonight. I am going to be critical, and I think that's only fair, because you have been pretty blunt and pretty critical of me for a long time. . . .
> I found out from reading your bulletins that the "business interest" in government . . . as expressed by your organization, is a shockingly short-sighted, selfish and narrow interest.
> I found in your bulletins an astonishing lack of attention to and concern for the urgent problems facing the state—the problems of educating our children, caring for the mentally ill and the elderly, building highways, conserving our natural resources, and other challenges that confront us. . . .
> Businessmen can contribute much to politics and government. You can exercise a great deal of influence. You can even influence Democrats, believe it or not. But you aren't doing it now and you won't do it in the future unless you broaden your horizons and deepen your concerns. . . .

The effective leader must also possess the ability not only to comprehend a broad range of issues but also to speak reasonably clearly about them. A political leader is also an educator, and the higher the leadership position the more crucial the educational role, for he must himself acquire an understanding of many propositions and then convey not only their essence but also their importance to others. An executive in a press conference who indicates he does not quite know what a policy matter is all about thereby announces to his antagonists (and, importantly, to his own subordinates) that he is not much concerned with it and may not be willing to invest much of his leadership capital in support of it.

From these and other resources a governor can build up what Professor Neustadt has called—with reference to the president—a "professional reputation"—the attitudes of other players of the political game toward the skills and capacities of the president. His reputation is a composite of expectations of others in government as to whether the chief has the tenacity and the ability to make trouble for those who do not respond to his bidding.[7] By the same token, a governor who

---

[7] This is akin to Carl J. Friedrich's "law of anticipated reactions," as Neustadt points out. See Friedrich's "Public Policy and the Nature of Administrative Responsibility," 1 *Public Policy* 3–24 (1940).

has developed a professional reputation for using skillfully and fully the resources he has to punish his adversaries and reward the cooperative may achieve his ends with a minimum outlay simply because it is anticipated that effective follow-through action will be forthcoming. A reputation for backing down, for avoiding situations involving him in publicized dispute, may mean that the governor's adversaries will ignore or refuse to go along with him since they doubt his willingness to persist in his own policy requests. Reputations may be intangible and based upon gossip and rumor, but they may nevertheless be the foundation of gubernatorial power or weakness.

2. *Party Resources.* Party organizations exist in every state and, notwithstanding the variations among them, they set the patterns of competition for office if nothing else. For this reason if for no other, parties are important determinants of the potential power of a governor. Whether the party is a loose congeries of factions in mutual competition and with little sense of organizational unity or a relatively strong and well-organized grouping of politicians, the governor must take cognizance of it and its elements. Both in gaining office and in carrying out his program, parties and factional elements thereof are basic to a governor's operations. In some states the party machinery is a major source of power for a governor; in others the formal state organization may mean next to nothing whereas the faction with which the governor is associated may be a tool of gubernatorial leadership. A governor alienated from major elements of his own party may turn about and use the parties as whipping boys, vaunting his independence and seeking public support through condemnation of parties. The fact remains, however, that any governor is elected as either a Democrat or a Republican, and thereby acquires obligations, associations, varying degrees of commitment to the party's organized existence, as well as opposition both within his own party and from the opposition party (if one exists). These are the byproducts of a campaign for the office, byproducts that go to the governor's mansion with him on inauguration day to grow or diminish as his term proceeds.

It is sometimes said that one of the roles of the governor is that of "leader of the state party." This is backed up with the evidence so familiar to television viewers who have seen governors rallying the forces of state delegations at national party conventions. But the fact is that few if any governors are really the undisputed single leaders of their state parties. At most they are chief among various party leaders within the state parties, for there are many leaders in the large, factionally- and regionally-divided parties in the states today. Any governor has to deal with rather than command the other major leaders in his party.

The power of former Governor Thomas E. Dewey of New York was legendary, and in fact he probably was one of the most powerful and effective of modern governors, but his power was necessarily shared with other Republican leaders. He had and used disciplinary power in his party, and yet to employ that power he had to cooperate with lesser leaders in the party. The realities of state party operations are such that no governor enjoys undisputed control over his party.[8]

A strong party organization that has prospects of getting or holding power in a state with at least somewhat competitive parties can be the basis of considerable power for a governor. A party with any control over the access to positions of power in government has the means to reward the faithful and punish the recalcitrant. And if the governor is on good terms with the bulk of the party's leadership, this disciplinary power can be a weapon in his hands. It need not be used daily to be effective. Like all punishments it fits the rule of anticipated reactions: if it *has* been used recently it *may* be brought to bear again, so perhaps what the governor is urging is right after all. Administrators, legislators, and interest group leaders—as well as political underlings—learn to respect such power.

It should not be assumed that this kind of power is never vested in a governor of a one-party state. Professor Robert Highsaw, an observer of Southern politics, has said that:

It is fairly standard practice now for executive leaders to make a careful tabulation of legislative votes on gubernatorial programs and to tell dissenting legislators that, if attitudes and votes are not changed, they will get no more jobs for constituents, no more state-aid for rural roads in their districts, no more of the favors that are the lifeblood of state legislators. This relationship is not subtle; it is direct, brutal; and it is effective. Executive politicians now can—and do—back recalcitrant legislators against the wall and read the "riot act" to them.[9]

Naturally a governor, South or North, can have the riot act read effectively in his behalf only when he has strong organizational backing. He

---

[8] See Ransone's discussion of governors and their relationships with parties and factions (*op. cit.*, pp. 185ff). See particularly his quotation from former Governor Walter J. Kohler of Wisconsin regarding the latter's methods of influencing the legislature through such devices as personal attendance at Republican legislative caucuses and meetings with party leaders (pp. 206–07).

[9] Robert B. Highsaw, "The Southern Governor—Challenge to the Strong Executive Theme," 19 *Public Administration Review* 7 (1959). Reprinted in *American State Politics*, Frank Munger, ed. (New York: Thomas Y. Crowell and Co., 1966), pp. 74–80.

cannot deny the favors to some and grant them to the faithful without organizational support for his decisions.

There is another side to the coin, however: the party may minimize the governor's power. When the governor lacks rapport with major party leaders, he may be the victim of stalling and blocking operations and may lose his effectiveness as a leader. There is almost always a certain reserve in relationships between formal party leaders and governors, for the latter tend to think of themselves as somewhat apart from the party both in a personal sense and officially as well. Similarly, professional politicians are wary of governors—especially of those who did not come up the ladder through the organization but who came to the office from "outside" (from the business world, for example). Mutual distrust can flower into antagonism, and under these circumstances arguments against placing "too much power" in the hands of the governor can be most persuasive to the suspicious politician.[10]

Nor should it be forgotten that in the competitive states there is an opposition party with every hope of making the incumbent governor look like something less than a great success. And governors are frequently faced with legislatures, one or both of the houses of which are controlled by the opposition party. Not infrequently an opposition party will turn down a proposal precisely because it is sponsored by the governor. Often the same proposition subsequently proposed by their "own" governor will be passed without dissent. It is sometimes possible to split the opposition party in the legislature and by bargaining or use of patronage to lure opposition legislators, but it must be admitted that the kinds of bargaining this sometimes involves are not particularly savory aspects of politics.[11]

3. *Publicity as a Policy Resource.* The whole state is the governor's constituency and therefore no governor dares to look only to his own party ranks or to other officials in his efforts to shape policy. The facts of modern pluralistic government necessitate looking to a broad public, winning support from enough influential persons to have an effect on

---

[10] This was markedly true of former Governor Chester Bowles's relationships with some elements of the Democratic party in Connecticut. Bowles had come to the office after a successful career in advertising and wartime administrative duties in Washington. More recently Govenor Nelson Rockefeller, who came to the New York governorship from philanthropy and sporadic service in Washington, had similar problems with the regulars in the state Republican party.

[11] Massachusetts and Connecticut governors are frequently faced with this problem, and the bargaining indulged in to get action despite the opposition party frequently results in the most dubious swapping policies with attendant disregard of the consequences for public policy. See Lockard, *New England States Politics, op. cit.* Chaps. 6, 10. It happens elsewhere too, of course.

others who share policy-making prerogatives. The media of modern communications, ubiquitous though they seem, never reach the whole public, although enough interested people are aware of state politics to have an effect on many kinds of policy. Or at least there is evidently a sufficiently strong conviction among politicians that there is always danger of public awareness to make callous disregard of public attitudes risky. So there is a constant effort to get to the people with the "real" truth about this or that problem, hoping that this will build a basis of support for proposals. The simple fear of election defeat assures a hearing for any point of view that is shared very widely, regardless of what is demanded—from antiobscenity laws to the construction of a zoo.

In the game of publicity, the governor has certain advantages over his opponents. His visibility—the fact that he is the most widely known state official—makes his remarks more newsworthy than those of lesser actors in the political game. Even though newspapers can intentionally obscure—even as they can "make,"—news by featuring or burying stories, the governor's press conference is still a major newsbeat and the press attends faithfully. The press, even those newspapers whose owners and editorial writers vigorously oppose an incumbent governor, has to give some kind of space to the governor's pronouncements if they are at all significant. Through television, radio, and public appearances; by press releases and other literature; and through the use of his staff as a mail-answering and complaint-hearing crew, the governor has ample opportunity to be heard.

Publicity can be the basis of power, but it is not without limits. Much of the public is after all immune to the daily outpouring of information and pleading. And the aroused interests that demand action on labor laws, agricultural policy, or aid to education are likely to be vociferous and drown out those who may have some interest but whose intensity of feeling about the issue cannot compare with that of the directly involved groups. And only on relatively few matters can a governor use direct publicity with success, for in marginal matters effort to arouse interest is unlikely to be worth the effort. Some governors seem to rely on their public relations staff to produce great volumes of material for distribution to the press, apparently persuaded that the volume of publicity will in itself have effect. They may possibly be right. But more important to the governor's publicity efforts is a sense of when to speak out and when to shut up—and this is a natural gift that public relations advisers cannot supply.

4. *Legal-Constitutional Resources.* According to the dictionary, *authority* means "legal or rightful power, a right to command or act."

In this sense the "authority" of governors varies considerably: some have fairly broad authority to do certain official acts at their own discretion and to have formal command over subordinates; some have to share many aspects of formal authority with other executives and boards. That the constitution assigns a power does not nessarily mean that the assignee will be able to use it, nor does the constitution's neglect to assign a power necessarily mean that he will not have it. Thus the legislature of Connecticut is nominally given the power to appoint the state auditors (one Democrat and one Republican) but not within the memory of any living politician has the Connecticut legislature ever really made this choice: the party leaders and the governor, in collaboration with the more powerful of legislators (who are also party leaders), actually choose auditors. Similarly, a governor may be denied the formal rights to command an independent agency, but the realities of state politics may make independent agencies no less subordinate to the governor than those legally under the governor's command.

My argument is then that the granting of powers is the beginning and not the end of power allocation. And I emphasize the "convertibility," so to speak, of these powers, because there is a particularly strong tendency in the study of state and local government to assume that the formal granting of powers is in fact the essence of the ultimate power relationship. Nothing could be further from the truth. Let us examine some of the powers granted and denied to governors by constitutions and statutes and assess some of the significant variations in the utilization, atrophy, and alienation of those powers.

Without attempting to classify all of the constitutional and legal authority of the governor in the typical state, one can single out three categories of authority that have particular importance to the governor in maximizing his leadership potential:[12] (a) The power to appoint and remove personnel; (b) the concentration of specific authority to set policies in certain areas or, conversely, the parceling out of relatively independent policy-making authority to boards, commissions, or individual officials; and (c) the executive veto of legislative acts.

(a) *The power to appoint and remove.* Compared with the power of the president to appoint and remove his cabinet and other political executives in the national government, the authority of most governors to choose and remove their own subordinates is relatively limited—in

---

[12] It may be argued that these categories exclude some kinds of power that have significance—e.g., the governor's authorization to command National Guard units in an emergency or his right formally to address the legislature. The categories are not intended to be totally inclusive but illustrative of the kinds of powers most commonly identified as tools of effective gubernatorial leadership.

some cases sharply limited. Some subordinates are elected, some appointed by the legislature, some may be picked by boards or commissions rather than by the governor. And where they are appointed by the governor their terms of office may not coincide with gubernatorial terms, leaving a new governor with department heads chosen by his predecessor (who may have been of the opposite party). Just over half of the 1180 major administrative posts in state government for which data are available are filled by gubernatorial appointment—sometimes without further approval, more frequently with some kind of second check by the legislature or a governor's council.[13] The heads of more recently created agencies tend to be appointed by the governor, whereas the older offices (e.g., secretary of state, attorney general, and treasurer) are likely to have been designated as elective by older constitutional provisions and thus remain elective for no better reason than that the constitution says so. (Is there any better reason why the secretary of state should be subject to election when he performs largely routine and clerical-record keeping duties whereas other administrators who perform more significant duties are otherwise chosen?) As a matter of fact, the list of administrators subject to gubernatorial appointment contains most of the heads of agencies concerned with such matters as labor, banking, highways, health, taxation, budgeting, welfare, and public utilities.[14]

For reasons that are fairly obvious, certain administrative posts are frequently subject either to popular election or are appointive by the boards or agencies that have quasiautonomous control over the subject matter. Education is a politically favored subject and therefore just under one-half of the commissioners of education are popularly elected and the other half (except for seven who are appointed by governors) are chosen by boards of education.[15] So too with agriculture (12 of them are elected) and public health (18 health department heads are chosen by their special boards). The situation may be summarized this way: just over half of all major administrators are appointed by governors, usually subject to approval by the legislature; just under a fifth are elected (19 per cent as of 1966); and the remainder are either picked by boards or

---

[13] This is a calculation from data presented in the *Book of the States*, 1966–67, pp. 138–39. The list includes 29 different offices and in 100 instances the *Book of the States* indicates it has no information on method of selection.

[14] The number of states selecting administrators with gubernatorial involvement in the appointment process are as follows: taxation, 35; administration and finance, 28; budget directors, 26; labor, 40; health, 30; welfare, 28; highways, 23; banking, 38; and public utilities, 31.

[15] There is apparently a trend away from popular election of state superintendents of education, since 21 are now elected, whereas 32 were in 1946. See the Bureau of the Census publication, *Elective Offices of State and County Government* (Washington, D.C.: Government Printing Office, 1946).

by the legislature.[16] The significant point in terms of gubernatorial power is that the list of elective officers contains some offices of relatively little concern to the governor (secretary of state and treasurer, for example), and the list of appointive ones contains the departments and officials of most concern to the governor insofar as he is involved in administrative management. This is a point to keep in mind in view of the arguments commonly made regarding the reorganization of the state administrative machinery.

What of the governor's power to remove officials? In many states the governor's right to remove is even more restricted than his right to appoint. Removal may require the concurrence of the senate, or the showing of cause—that is, incompetence, neglect of duty, or malfeasance. Whereas the President of the United States is assumed to have full power to remove political executives whom he appoints, there is no comparable assumption for most governors. The necessity to show legal cause for removals certainly reduces the direct control potential of the governor. But one cannot speak in absolutes about this. The sweeping language of Chief Justice Taft in stating the doctrine of absolute removal power for the President is politically unrealistic. He said in the case of *Myers* v. *United States* that it was vitally important that if the President loses "confidence in the intelligence, ability, judgment, or loyalty of any . . . subordinate . . . he must have the power to remove him without delay."[17] No doubt the firmness of the Chief Justice's opinion was the product of frustrations and problems he had had as President (he had removal power but it did not solve his staff problems), but the very character of those frustrations points to a lesson he apparently did not learn: the power to remove is only part of the means of control.[18] Its existence does not necessarily grant and its absence does not necessarily deny the opportunity for control. The president does not often directly remove a subordinate; probably he does so no more frequently than does the average governor, for removals are signs of difficulty, an implicit admission that something is wrong within the government, and ammunition to the opposition for the next campaign.

---

[16] The percentage of elected officials has declined since 1960 but this is due to the fact that many new agencies are now covered by the tabulations in the *Book of the States. See loc. cit.*

[17] 272 U.S. 52 (1926).

[18] In the famous Glavis-Ballinger controversy of 1909–10, President Taft's power of removal was perhaps the least important of all the means at hand for asserting effective control over the subordinate administrators who were disputing public policy on natural resources. See the case study in Harold Stein, *Public Administration and Policy Development* (New York: Harcourt, Brace, and World, Inc., 1952), pp. 77–87.

Therefore the polite resignation, with letters of thanks and warm best wishes exchanged (however bitter may have been the recriminations and arguments that preceded the hearts and flowers stage), is preferred.[19] Having said all this, however, it remains true that formal tenure can be a great asset to an administrator who comes into direct conflict with a governor; it can be a tool with which to fight back.

The governor's control over general patronage—not just the appointment of major administrators—also has significance for his leadership potential. Patronage is one of the prizes that politicians seek; their prestige and power rests, or, significantly, seems to them to rest, on the opportunity to pass out jobs to the "deserving." It is particularly true in parts of the country that are economically depressed (large parts of the South, for example, or the hard-pressed coal mining regions) that marginal patronage jobs are important to the underemployed, if not unemployed. And it follows that if voters need the jobs at all, politicians see high value in the passing them around. The jobs are not usually directly handled by the governor, but he can make appointments available to cooperative politicians and deny them to the resisters.

As Professor Frank Sorauf has observed, patronage is in general decline in importance. Most Americans, he points out, look at patronage as a "short-term desperation job alternative" if they are interested in it at all, for the mores of our day frown on patronage and the insecurity of such posts is unattractive.[20] Parties are now more ideologically oriented instead of being issueless and largely concerned with favors and rewards, and even the staffing of party organizations now depends not so much on the patronage seeker as on "volunteer and ad hoc political groups and personal followings." For party workers of the kind most needed, the lower-paid and menial patronage positions are useless, although for the more specialized jobs there are more seekers than qualified seekers.[21] No doubt this general description of the decline of patronage as falling as much by its own lack of utility as by the attacks of the reformers is accurate. Yet to pronounce the end of patronage as a politically significant tool would be premature. There are some states with almost no patronage available to the governor and the party or

---

19 To illustrate, consider the unconventional behavior of Governor Lester Maddox of Georgia who, when dissatisfied with the performance of the Department of Industry and Trade, simply fired its director and the chairman of its board. Maddox, being a nonpolitician, did not take the normal course of arranging for calm resignations.

20 Frank Sarauf, "The Silent Revolution in Patronage," 20 *Public Administration Review* 28 (1960), 30.

21 *Ibid.*, pp. 31–32. See also the suggestive argument of James Q. Wilson in his article, "The Economy of Patronage," 69 *Journal of Political Economy* 369 (1961).

faction to which he belongs, but in most states there are hundreds of jobs subject to political appointment rather than being under the civil service-appointment-by-examination rule. In half the states less than half of the state employees are covered by civil service rules, and in 12 states less than a quarter are so covered.[22] Since civil service coverage is required for personnel in agencies financed even in part by federal grants in aid, there are some states that protect only such employees and no others, with minor exceptions (such as the state police, perhaps). (Some 18 states provide only this minimal coverage.) In all the states combined it appears that 1,016,000 of the 1,873,000 state employees (that is, some 54 per cent) are under civil service.[23]

The extent to which patronage is significant politically varies of course from state to state. Research by Daryl Fair suggests there is no correlation between the effectiveness of state parties and the amount of patronage available to state parties.[24] Another factor is the turnover of personnel with a change of administration and in some states this is high (as in Pennsylvania and several southern and western states[25]), and in others the authority of the civil service commission is sewed up so tight that neither the governor nor anyone else can interfere with appointments in lesser positions. The Michigan civil service commission, for example, has a constitutionally guaranteed independence. It does not even have to haggle with the legislature for operating funds, since it is assured by the constitutional amendment that established it of 1 per cent of the administrative payroll of the state. Of the sweeping powers of the Michigan commission, Professor Charles Adrian observes that it "can increase salaries of civil servants without consulting the governor or the legislature and controls 92 per cent of all state jobs. Only two nonclassified positions are allowed in each department."[26] This is an extreme example perhaps, but it does suggest that the political tools of a Michigan governor are obviously different from those of his

---

[22] This is calculated from data on public employment in the *Book of the States,* 1966–67, pp. 153–61. The calculations were made from tables presenting the numbers of public employees covered by various merit systems as percentages of the total number of state employees (not the number of "full-time equivalents" which would include part-time nontenure workers). The figures are obviously estimates in some instances and the calculations should therefore not be taken as absolutely accurate, although as used here the data are reliable.

[23] This is calculated from the data cited above from the *Book of the States,* 1966–67, pp. 158–66. The information is reported as of August, 1965.

[24] Daryl Fair, "Party Strength and Political Patronage," 45 *Southwestern Social Science Quarterly* 264–71 (1964).

[25] See Frank J. Sorauf, "State Patronage in a Rural County," 50 *American Political Science Review* 1046 (1956).

[26] Adrian, *State and Local Governments, op. cit.,* p. 341.

Pennsylvania counterpart. The problems are also different, of course, for patronage can be disruptive when competition for scarce jobs flares up in disputes. Whether the ultimate loss through squabbles is more or less than the gain to the governor in bait to offer the faithful is not an easily answered question, although the answer no doubt depends in part upon other political traditions and practices of the state. Thus, in Connecticut, the lower ranks of the state's employment system are almost entirely covered by civil service, and "political pull" is worth little in getting a state job, yet the governor's position is strong without the lesser patronage. He has upper-level patronage in fair quantity. In states lacking the kind of party system that enhances the Connecticut governor's position, patronage may still be a significant tool.

(b) *The concentration or dispersal of powers.* Literature on the governorship comes largely from two sources: practitioners in administration and political scientists in research or academic positions. Both kinds of writers show a remarkable consistency on the question of whether formal constitutional-statutory power should be concentrated in the governor's hands or dispersed to individual agencies. They are overwhelmingly in favor of concentration of powers in the governor, and only a handful dissent.[27] Thus in state after state administrative reorganization drives, from the first notable one inaugurated in 1917 by Governor Frank O. Lowden of Illinois down to the flurry of reorganization commissions that set to work in the post-World War II era, have stressed the need to put more formal authority in the hands of the governor.[28]

Although these drives have done much to enhance the formal authority of the governor in the last fifty years, there has been steady

[27] Nearly any textbook on state government illustrates this observation, as do those on public administration which advocate similar concentration in the federal government. A few political scientists dissent, such as Francis Coker who as far back as 1922 objected in an article called "Dogmas of Administrative Reform," 16 *American Political Science Review* 399 (1922). Harvey Walker has raised doubts on several occasions, as for example in his "Theory and Practice in State Reorganization," 19 *National Municipal Review* 253 (1930); Charles Hyneman was irreverent in his article "Administrative Reorganization: An Adventure into Science and Theology," 1 *Journal of Politics* 62 (1939). The unorthodox view may be growing in popularity now (as evidence the works of Highsaw and Wood, cited above), but the predominant thesis of the literature is very much proconcentration. A brief restatement of the concentration thesis is in Terry Sanford's *Storm over the States* (New York: McGraw-Hill Book Co., 1967), pp. 184–205.

[28] On the history of the Lowden reorganization and of many successor drives in other states, see Leslie Lipson's *The American Governor from Figurehead to Leader;* Ransone's *The Office of Governor in the United States* (especially Chap. 9); John A. Perkins, "Reflections on State Reorganizations," 45 *American Political Science Review* 507 (1951); and Karl Bosworth, "The Politics of Management Improvement in the States," 47 *American Political Science Review* 84 (1953).

resistance to the proposals of the concentrators. The opponents of enlarging the governor's powers may have lacked academic and other scholarly supporters to state their position in learned journals or in those of reform organizations such as the Council of State Governments and the National Municipal Association, but their opposition has been formidable. Why this opposition to programs intended to increase the efficiency and responsibility of state government, as the reformers claimed their reforms would do? What, that is to say, are the political motivations of the reformers and their opponents which have produced these battles in state after state year after year?

To answer that question it is necessary to ask and answer several others. First what is the extent of dispersal of administrative authority in the states? What are the reasons behind the dispersal—that is, why did it happen in the first place? What are its consequences? And what are the implications of the concentration of power?

The variations in formal authority among the fifty governors are so vast as to make it difficult to describe the degree of dispersal or concentration of powers. The formal appointive and control power of governors is cleverly assayed by Professor Schleslinger, who assigns an index number to each state according to the extent of gubernatorial control. New York, Illinois, and New Jersey rank at the top, while Mississippi, South Carolina, Texas, and North Dakota are at the bottom.[29] Still it is clear that no governor has the broad range of formal authority possessed by the President of the United States. There are independent regulatory commissions and government corporations in the national government that are nominally beyond his direct control, but the constitution vests in him "the executive power" which has been interpreted to mean full authority to conduct the business of the executive branch. Governors, on the other hand, often share their authority over such matters as state fiscal policy with officials who are elected along with the governor and whose formal rights to act are no less clearly constitutional mandates than those of the governor. Or if there are few or no other elected administrative officials, the governor may lack the power to control the making of a budget, or there may be a series of constitutionally guaranteed funds ("earmarked" is the common term) set aside for specific agencies without regard to competing needs or economic conditions or any other consideration the governor or legislature might think compelling enough to warrant reallocation of

---

[29] Joseph Schleslinger, "The Politics of the Executive" in *Politics In the American States*, Herbert Jacob and Kenneth Vines, eds., (Boston: Little, Brown & Co., 1965), pp. 207–37.

resources. As noted previously, only seven governors appoint their own superintendents of education, and only half of all governors choose their own men to run the departments of agriculture. Also, the terms of office of some administrators do not coincide with those of governors, so that a new governor may have to work with an appointee of a previous administration. A governor's power to choose administrators may also be hedged about with statutory restrictions that almost remove the power to select by specifying in great detail the qualifications and background of those eligible. At the ultimate extreme of dispersal of authority, the Alabama State Health Officer is chosen by the Medical Association of Alabama: choice by a private organization!

As an example of a state where the formal powers of the governor are fairly limited, consider these observations by a legislative investigatory group in Florida: "The Governor, charged by the Constitution as Florida's chief executive, has no direct authority over the Cabinet or the activities in the several departments headed by these cabinet members."[30] A cabinet meeting there, according to Professor Ransone:

. . . is not like that in other states in that it is not looked upon as a meeting of the governor and his chief advisers but rather as a meeting of the major executive officials of the state with the governor presiding as chairman. The so-called "chief" executive has a vote and undoubtedly has a great deal of influence but can be, and sometimes is, outvoted by his colleagues.[31]

Why this tendency toward separatism for agencies and the dispersal of power? Why do agencies and their supporters seek to reduce to a minimum any control or influence from other elements of the government? To pose the question is to suggest the answer: both the bureaucrats and their clientele naturally believe theirs to be a special aspect of government which they know others are not equally sympathetic toward. They therefore seek to insure the maintenance of existing advantages free from the interference. As a Mississippi agency head reported to a group investigating the possibilities of integrating functions in that state's government:

I think this is one of the very best things that has ever been done in the State of Mississippi and I have long been of the opinion that this work should have been accomplished in the past. However, my department is of a type, character and kind that cannot be consolidated with any other agency, as its

30 Quoted in Ransone, *op. cit.*, p. 261.
31 *Ibid.*, p. 262.

duties and functions are unique, and a reduction of personnel or a transfer of any duties of this department would work a hardship and prevent certain citizens from receiving benefits to which they are entitled.[32]

Ludicrous, perhaps, but a nearly universal attitude.

The politics of administrative operations makes independence a desirable goal. The clientele served by the agency want independence, fiscal and otherwise, so that their favored agency will not have to take the chance of being abandoned, short-changed, diverted to other activities, or reduced in effectiveness by some future governor or majority of legislators who may be misguided enough not to see the merits of the unit in question. Therefore, anticipating tomorrow's possible problems, they put their agency as far beyond the daily vicissitudes of competitive politics as possible. The common argument is that the agency in question is unique, performs very special functions, and therefore needs to be protected from "politics" so as to conduct its business effectively. And if the special agency's forces are particularly strong (as agricultural and educational interests are in most states) then there is a likelihood of some degree of insulation.[33] The common fear of politicians and spoilsmen can be exploited in combination with emphasis upon the special characteristics of an agency that render it "nonpolitical" and for that reason justly deserving of an independent status.

What are the practical consequences of separatism? What power can a governor have who must operate a government staffed in part by top administrators whom he has not appointed and cannot remove, divided into separate and semiautonomous units with powers granted independently of him, and even financed in part by prearranged allotment of funds which he cannot affect? When the case is painted in its darkest hues, one would assume that no governor thus encumbered could ever achieve any significant leadership either within the executive branch or elsewhere. But, again, it does not follow that the lack of a specific authority to control an agency implies actual inability to do so.

---

[32] Quoted by Karl Bosworth, "The Politics of Management Improvement in the States," 47 *American Political Science Review* 84, 90 (1953). An almost equally amusing reason for not increasing the New York governor's control over welfare administration came from that state's Chairman of the State Board of Social Welfare. *The New York Times* (September 12, 1962) reported him as saying "The vastness of the state welfare program makes it imperative that the responsibility for naming the commissioner and administrative board not fall on one man."

[33] See the excellent brief statement of the tendency to separatism in state administration by York Willbern in *The Fifty States and their Local Governments*, James Fesler, ed., (New York: Alfred A. Knopf, Inc., 1967), pp. 345–63.

Thus the legislative inquiry group quoted above on the plight of the Florida governor also observes that:

Only through his prestige, personally, and party leadership can the Governor assume the responsibility vested in him by the Constitution but also denied him by that same instrument in providing for the election of cabinet officials.[34]

And they add that his position has been such that he does achieve coordination among these independently-elected officials.

Another example illustrates this point. Professor W. W. Kaempfer describes an institution in West Virginia government called the Board of Public Works (which literally it is not), consisting of the governor and six other administrative officials, including the separately elected superintendent of schools and the commissioner of agriculture. The Board has control over the budget-making process, certain personnel decisions and certain other less crucial matters. The governor sits as just another member of the board, and although he does preside, he can be and occasionally is outvoted by his fellow members. Standard theories of public administration would write this off as a hopeless means of administration—boards cannot administer, governors ought not to have to put their powers in commission since it invites conflict of interests within the executive, and so on. Not satisfied with the standard theory, however, Kaempfer took a careful look at the actual operations of the Board and reports several interesting observations. First the board does not administer and does not sit as a cabinet to "advise" the governor. "Criticisms based on the Board's administrative work largely miss their mark; its usefulness turns instead on its policy-making functions."[35] Second, the Board does not appear to limit the governor with regard to the budget. (". . . [T]he governor is seldom frustrated by Board action [with regard to the budget]."[36]) Third, he concludes that in view of the separately elected officials who share power with the governor, perhaps the Board serves to moderate the potential division that might otherwise occur by producing collegial or collective decisions for which the whole executive accepts responsibility.[37]

---

34 Ransone, op. cit., pp. 261–62.
35 W. W. Kaempfer, The Board of Public Works, West Virginia's Plural Executive (Morgantown, W. Va.: Bureau for Government Research, West Virginia University, 1957), p. 70.
36 Ibid., p. x.
37 Ibid., pp. 119–20. Having weighed the Board's role carefully and finding it not to be the bugbear that the traditionalists would have one suppose it to be, Kaempfer for reasons that are not apparent to me concludes his study by saying,

Similarly, Professor James Fesler, commenting on the status of independent regulatory commissions in the states, makes some observations that deserve to be quoted at length. These agencies have a greater degree of insulation than most of routine operating agencies, since the regulatory bodies often have a quasi-judicial status to reinforce their independence. Fesler says:

The so-called "independence" of state regulatory agencies is more myth than reality. . . . The degree to which each department or commission enjoys a quasi-independence depends not only upon statutes, but upon the mental and moral caliber of the agency heads, their financial status, their desires for further political careers, their views about public policy toward regulated interests, the attitude toward the agency of politicians and regulated interests, and the existence of specific methods by which these politicians and pressure groups can impress their wishes on the agencies. . . . In a state in which the governor controls a large bloc of legislators, there is a natural tendency for the regulatory agencies to knuckle under to the governor's wishes. But if the agency cannot call the governor's friends its friends, or if the governor is an undesirable ally, the agency must redouble its efforts to establish its own contacts with the legislature and the persons that have great influence politically. To call a regulatory department or commission "independent" does not free it from this necessity of winning friends so as to influence legislators.[38]

In short, an independent agency—like any other actor in the political game—has to concern itself with the political realities that exist: if the governor has political power, the agency may "knuckle under" to him: if he lacks power, the agency will likely turn elsewhere to seek the support it needs to sustain itself in the competitive world of budgets, patronage, and the authority to expand operations or to grow in personnel and importance. Therefore, whether or not the formal dispersal of powers of a state government is a true dispersal of powers depends upon factors beyond that of direct authorization. The character of the state's political system and traditions, the factional or party position of the governor as well as his personal attitudes and abilities, the galaxy of interest groups that compete and how they do so—these

---

"If West Virginia state government is not to stagnate, perpetuating its faults as well as its virtues, the Board of Public Works will eventually be modified or even abolished" (p. 124). See his other recommendations regarding the utility and operations of the Board in his concluding chapter.

[38] James W. Fesler, *op. cit.*, p. 61.

are the kinds of criteria that determine whether or not apparent dispersal is actual dispersal.

This does not mean that the actual dispersal of power is of no consequence; on the contrary, when there is a lack of effective control over some areas of policy the implications can be most serious. The creation of a licensing board or an agency to regulate insurance operations or public utilities involves the creation of a set of rules for the protection of the society. The licensing boards concerned with hairdressers or real estate salesman are intended—or at least are promoted as means—to protect the public by demanding high standards. If, however, the boards are taken over by the professions or businesses that supposedly are being regulated, the regulations may become meaningless, or standards for getting a license may be so impossible to meet that there is little chance of entering the business. Thus the sanctions of the state serve to sustain a monopolistic policy of exclusion. Or an independent public utilities commission may forget the broader welfare of the community in its favoritism toward the utilities it in effect represents. As Fesler aptly says: ". . . the freeing of a policy determining agency from immediate contact with the politicians in the governor's mansion and in the legislative halls often throws the agency into the hands of the special interests it is supposed to regulate."[39] If, on the one hand, there is wide public support for autonomy for departments of education, which are deemed vital because they deal with our children and ought therefore to be kept free of "politics," on the other hand there is a possibility of so much autonomy that the public has little to say about educational policy. In education particularly—although not exclusively—the professionalism of teachers often supplants public judgment. The teachers in Texas, for example, had the political strength to get passed a statute requiring that the state superintendent of schools be a professionally trained educator. A minimum of a Master's Degree and an eligibility "for the highest school administrator's certificate" were made prerequisites for the job.[40] The argument is that education is so technical and professional in character that only a professional can supervise it. (Would it not follow, by such reasoning, that only a general should be Secretary of Defense? Yet as Talleyrand said, "War is much too serious a thing to be left to military men.") Expertise

---

[39] *Ibid.*, p. 65. Fesler also advances the interesting thesis that it might be wiser to give independence to the routine service agencies of government where the "experts and technicians" would have a fair chance to control operations rather than giving independence to the regulatory bodies where special interests loom so importantly in daily operations.

[40] Willbern, *op. cit.*, p. 362.

can be a set of blinders as well as a useful tool; self-interest clothed with public authority is powerful medicine.

An instance of educational independence in Connecticut further illustrates this point. In 1955 the Board of Education at the urging of its professional staff decided to establish a requirement of five years of college for school teachers, which the Board could do by administrative ruling rather than through a statutory enactment. The promulgation of administrative rules in Connecticut is followed by submission of the rules to the General Assembly (legislature) for its consideration. Accordingly this rule was presented to the Education Committee late in the 1955 session, and after considerable discussion in the committee, much of it decidedly negative in tone, the suggestion was made that this rule be vetoed. But the committee was told it could not do that now, for the rule was not yet formally promulgated. When would it be, it was asked? Well, some weeks hence, after the legislature had adjourned. Thus the rule would have been in operation for some 18 months before the biennial legislature would have an opportunity to review the policy again, and if it wanted to reverse the policy then it would have to attack an existing rule that would have gained support by its having been in operation for a year and a half.

Hence the steady demand in nearly all states for increasing the power of the governor to assert control over the scattered elements of state government and the consequent enlargement of his powers. Illustrative of the desire to strengthen the office is the increasing tendency to lengthen the term of office; as recently as 1938 a majority of the governors were elected for two-year terms, now they serve four-year terms in more than two-thirds of the states. The longer term manifestly strengthens the governor's hand: he can take the longer view and will be around long enough to punish his enemies and reward his friends.[41] What then are the implications of the strengthening of the governor's powers? In some respects the changes have clearly improved management of state administration and have reduced friction in government. Improvements have been apparent in New Jersey since the 1947 Constitution integrated 100 scattered agencies into no more than 20 departments under the governor's control. In Connecticut, for example, the governor now appoints his major administrative subordinates and their terms are essentially concurrent with his, rather than the system of

---

[41] Presently 36 states use four-year terms, although in 13 states the governor is forbidden to succeed himself and in 10 others may serve only two consecutive terms. All the states forbidding two consecutive terms are southern or border states with the exception of Indiana and Pennsylvania. See *Book of the States* for current information.

overlapping terms that previously led to so much friction when governors of one party had to get along with administrators from another. (Political realism was the order of the day when this change was instituted, for approval of the governor's nominations may be given by either house of the legislature. He may thus send the names to the house controlled by his own party.)

But some of the fondest hopes of the reorganizers for sharp clarity of responsibility have not been realized. The kind of "solution" to the problem that they often envisaged is impractical, a mirage that always vanishes in the heat of political realities. Part of the difficulty rests in their conception of the governor as a full-time administrative supervisor which he is not and cannot be. His duties as "representative of the people," as the political leader of the state, and the hard facts of a huge and sprawling bureaucracy simply make it unlikely that any governor can act as a day-to-day administrative overseer.[42] It is the constant complaint of the reorganizers, for example, that the governor is nominally the supervisor of perhaps a hundred or more agencies, and that he cannot possibly see that many people and keep track of their work. True, he can't. But does it necessarily follow that he will have any more accurate track of their doings if he has only twenty men reporting to him on the activities of them all? The practical realities of the operation of the governor's office are not those of the reorganizer's theory: the governor does not know what is going on until there is some reason to have to pay attention to a trouble spot in the administrative system. Wood goes so far as to say that:

It is not even important that he perform adequately the managerial tasks which the law deems necessary. *It is the governor's status among the informal groups which elect him that is the crucial factor in his success.*[43]

He is a political leader and not an organizational manager, and by the yardstick of public approval or disapproval as applied in elections, he would probably be rated a miserable failure if he concerned himself with all the details of management that the reorganizers sometimes seem to think he should.

There is also a fairly standard tendency among reorganizers to overemphasize the formal at the expense of the operating realities.[44]

---

[42] Robert Wood presents telling evidence to sustain this point in *The Metropolitan Governor, op. cit.*, where he studied the administrations of half a dozen governors and found that none fitted the corporate manager image.

[43] *Ibid.*, p. 328. Italics in original.

[44] See, for example, A. E. Buck's *The Reorganization of State Governments in*

That a governor seems to have weak formal controls over a given segment of policy may mean little if he has in his files an undated letter of resignation from the head of an agency—a letter which he demanded as the price of the appointment in the first place.[45] Reorganizers often draw handsome organization charts, showing the existing or planned relationships among administrative agents. Boxes and lines run neatly from the top where the voters select the governor and the governor appoints various officials; other boxes are placed to one side indicating an independent position by virtue of the direct election of a board or a commission, and so on down to the bottom of the chart. But the pretty images of the organization chart may be wholly misleading. Human beings with human needs, interests, drives, ambitions, emotions occupy the boxes, and they sometimes act as though unaware that lines had been drawn to keep them in their places. Perhaps the best analogy is the diagram of a planned football play. The coach sketches it to illustrate what each man is to do, but the diagram of the actual play as it transpires on Saturday afternoon differs for it takes into account the quarterback who fumbled the ball, or the linebacker who saw the strategy and spoiled everything. Political quarterbacks also fumble, subordinates sometimes grab the ball from the captain, and linebackers spoil well-laid plans. Professor Leslie Lipson makes essentially this point in the closing paragraph of his book on historical development and modern reorganization of the governorship:

The major premise of the whole [reorganization] movement was: strengthen the governor, put your trust in the governor. It is not unfair to say that some have betrayed the trust. Where reorganization and legislative leadership have failed, it has been largely due to the governor's incompetence. Was it not a naive faith which led Wilson to assert that reorganization was the key to the whole problem of restoring democratic government? Results have shown that tinkering with the machinery is not enough. One can at will reorganize a departmental structure; one cannot reorganize a tradition of politics. . . .[46]

There is also, of course, a frank fear that the governor will acquire a dangerous amount of power—power that would make him into a

---

the United States (New York: Columbia University Press, 1938). Or read some of the state "Little Hoover Commission" reports and observe how politically unrealistic many are.

[45] Fesler asserts this to be a common practice (*op. cit.*, p. 62). President Coolidge is reputed to have used this tactic.

[46] Lipson, *op. cit.*, p. 268.

virtual dictator. While this charge is sometimes phony and is frequently used irresponsibly and demagogically by special interests wishing to protect their advantages, it is not necessarily always a ruse by any means. Robert B. Highsaw has grave reservations about the concentration of powers in the hands of Southern governors. The basic axiom of reorganization is that responsibility can be fixed by concentrating on the governor who is directly elected and therefore subject to public control. But, says Highsaw, among the Southern states only in Texas and Arkansas is the governor allowed to succeed himself in office, and the factional one-party politics of the South tend to push problems of administrative responsibility into the background and emphasize segregation, state's rights, and personalities. He says:

It is my contention that the result of executive integration in several southern states has been a chief executive often unrestrained by either the legislature or public opinion. Although this result means that the governor has the power to and often does promote integration of executive authority in line with general concepts of modern administration, it may also make for less rather than more administrative responsibility in the Southern states. . . .

On the whole, the idea that a strong executive with clear lines of integrated authority will best guarantee public interest oriented administration is importantly challenged by the experience of southern state governments today. The political power of the governors in the region, checked principally by a growing professionalization among program administrators and intergovernmental relationships along program lines, casts at least the shadow of a doubt on the universality of this concept.[47]

It can hardly be said that political campaigns in the Northern states regularly turn on questions of administrative responsibility, although Highsaw is undoubtedly right that two-party competition would be more likely to highlight malfeasance or nonfeasance in office than one-party politics does. In any event the careers of the Long family in Louisiana, the Fergusons in Texas ("Ma" Ferguson served as Governor of Texas as a stand-in for "Pa" Ferguson after the latter had been impeached for misuse of state funds—her slogan was "Two Fergusons for the Price of One"), and some others of slightly less flamboyant character but with no higher scruples lend cogency to Professor Highsaw's contention. Alabama's Governor George Wallace, his opponents claim, exercised excessive power in both his own and his successor wife's administrations. But Huey Long was perhaps the only modern governor who established a quasidictatorship in a state. Other governors

---

[47] Highsaw, op. cit., pp. 7, 11.

might not achieve that extreme, but a tradition of politics that has known—and, if it does not condone, at least fully expects—widespread corruption does not make concentration of gubernatorial power an unmixed blessing.

Opposition to concentration of power in the governor's hands also comes from conservatives who often see the governor as their natural enemy because he is particularly susceptible to the blandishments of urban and metropolitan interests. The legislature, given its diversity of representation, is less likely to respond to the demands of labor unions, welfare system promoters, and other government service-action advocates who want to spend more money and institute or tighten regulatory powers. The governor who runs in the state at large and who must therefore be respectful of urban-metropolitan problems is inclined to take policy positions that may alienate conservatives. Perhaps the best evidence of this is the extreme displeasure voiced by some California conservatives to Governor Ronald Reagan whose policies, while hardly radical, still disappointed ideological conservatives. Special interests with a vested concern for an agency whose independance is threatened by an enlargement of gubernatorial control form a coalition with conservative-rural and conservative-urban interests to defend their common cause.

As a resource of gubernatorial power then, the granting of formal authority to control subordinates has importance; the long controversy over the scope of those powers is evidence of that. That controversy also suggests that there is no single "solution" to the question of how much power should be concentrated and where or how much it should be dispersed. The search for "the" solution is misleading since the conditions of political competition and the traditions of politics vary greatly among states. In truth, of course, the word *solution* is itself misleading; this is the kind of problem to which there will never be a "solution" for its character changes constantly with new concepts, new uses of power, different relationships evolving to change the components of the equation. How can one "solve" a problem when the values of its elements change constantly? One presumably seeks an optimum arrangement for the time and place and people involved, respecting their values, fears, needs, and aspirations, as much as possible.

(c) *The veto as a resource.* If Lord Bryce was correct at the time he said of the veto that it was "in ordinary times, a governor's most serious duty, and chiefly by discharge of it is he judged," this is surely no longer the case.[48] The rise in power and prestige of the office

---

[48] James Bryce, *The American Commonwealth*, 2nd ed. (New York: The Macmillan Company, 1910), p. 500.

has obscured the veto; other sources of power are much more important. This is not to say that the veto is either unused or unimportant. It can be an important resource for the simple reason that in most states the veto comes close to being absolute. In a majority of the states a veto can be overridden only when two-thirds or more of the legislators elected (not just those present and voting as is the case in Congress) vote to override.[49] Not only in those states where great unanimity is necessary to prevail over a veto, but even in states where the veto is easier to override (numerically at least), there is surprisingly little tendency to do so. Thus in Connecticut a simple majority of the members present may override a veto, and yet it cannot be said that the veto is insignificant there. It is used occasionally to weed out legislation that the governor (or his staff who review bills for him) thinks undesirable. When the governor is of the same party as the majority of one of the two houses, vetoes are sustained in that house; when the governor is of the same party as the majorities in both houses, the veto is virtually unused: the governor's staff are in constant communication with legislative leaders so that dubious legislation is rarely sent to the governor. When, however, the governor faces a legislature both houses of which are controlled by the opposition, he does use the veto more frequently and as might be expected, it is often overridden. Such a party division between governor and legislature is rare, having occurred only once in this century. Finally, and very importantly, the governor can use the veto freely after the legislative session is over and overriding is impossible.

Professor Frank W. Prescott has provided basic data on the use of the veto which illustrates the relatively small use the veto receives. In a survey of the Southern states over a ten-year period he found only 1501 of 100,019 bills had been vetoed. Of these only 101 vetoes were overridden, and even that figure is misleading since 59 of them came from Florida, most of them coming in a single session feud between the legislature and the governor over local bills and claims bills.[50] In a subsequent study of all states, roughly the same findings resulted: in 1947 there were 1253 vetoes of which only 22 were overridden.[51] It is true that where the veto is difficult to override it may assume more importance than these figures suggest. Actually it may not be

---

[49] In Alaska a vote of three-quarters of those elected is required to override; in five states a vote of three-fifths is necessary; and in seven others only majorities are required. See the *Book of the States* for current data on the veto.

[50] Frank W. Prescott, "The Executive Veto in Southern States," 10 *Journal of Politics* 667 (1948).

[51] Frank W. Prescott, "The Executive Veto in American States," 3 *The Western Political Quarterly* 99 (1950).

used so much to stop bills that got passed as to persuade legislatures to alter bills under consideration in order to suit the governor. To assess its use in such behind-the-scenes situations is difficult, but it clearly is frequently so used.

Furthermore, it should be recognized that in many states the veto is used to save face for harried legislators. They pass legislation and fully expect the governor to veto it and would indeed be surprised if he did not. Such bills apparently account for part of the large number of vetoes in New York and California. "Dodge" bills are often presented to the governor in the last days of a legislative session so that their promoters will not have the embarrassment of trying to get the bill passed over the veto. In a few states this can be handled through the "pocket" veto, similar to that possessed by the president; if not signed within a specified number of days, a bill dies automatically.

A variant on the straight veto is the power (possessed by four out of five governors) to veto items in appropriations bills. By this means limitation on expenditures by selectively culling out the unwanted items is feasible, and in some instances—in California and Pennsylvania, for example—it is so used, but in most states it has not been widely employed. This is undoubtedly often a reflection of the political realities by which budget making takes place; the governor and the legislators cooperatively produce a budget and the governor does not welch on agreements by vetoing items. Still the potential of selective nullification is a bargaining asset for the governor in his budget battles.[52]

Sweeping generalizations about the major importance of the veto in establishing a governor's power frequently fail to take account of North Carolina where there is no veto. The governor of North Carolina is not evidently much less effective in his legislative leadership than other governors. Indeed, his effectiveness apparently surpasses that of some governors who do have a strong veto. This of course does not show that the veto is of no consequence; rather it suggests that it is —like all other resources—not an absolute. If other sources of power are sufficient to permit gubernatorial influence in the legislature—as appears to be the case in North Carolina and in Connecticut, where a simple majority can override—the veto is obviously not indispensable. Lacking the veto, certain other governors—particularly those whose

---

[52] There is still another variant in the veto power—the so-called executive amendment whereby the governor returns a bill with a provisional amendment, the acceptance of which by the legislature will avoid an outright veto. This is used in Alabama, Virginia, Massachusetts, and New Jersey. Virtually the same thing is regularly done elsewhere, although informally.

other resources are notably less impressive—might find legislative leadership very difficult to achieve.

The Governor's Perspective:
The View from the Executive Suite

Professor Thomas Eliot, an erstwhile Congressman, tells of a colleague describing the governorship as a fate worse than death—never a peaceful minute, no time to be with the family, constant party hassles, and so on. Never would he take such a job. "As he paused for breath," says Eliot, one of his fellow-representatives said slyly. "Joe, Joe, don't close the door too tight." The speaker "stared solemnly into the future, and then said in his deepest voice: 'Well, if *duty* calls - - -.' "[53] "Duty's" call need not be a loud shout for the ambitious politician to hear; the lure of the office is strong whatever its difficulties. For the prestige of being governor and of being called "Governor" for the rest of one's life are like magnets, and the office is a notable stepping stone to the United States Senate, the judiciary, and even the biggest prize in American politics—the presidency. Moreover, the pay and perquisites of the office are in most states quite attractive.[54]

The governorship, particularly in larger states, is undergoing the same kind of transformation that has overtaken the presidency in this century: it is only partly an office held by an individual, it is also an institution that embodies the gubernatorial authority but is not restricted to the nominal occupant of the office. The governor operates through his staff whose duty it is to protect, advise, and operate for him. In smaller states the staff amounts to a few clerical personnel and perhaps one or two professionally trained assistants; in the larger ones as many as forty or more aides of various kinds serve the governor.[55] Experts on the law, public relations, budgets, administrative problems, and politics, along with typists, messengers, and switchboard operators keep the institution going. It is obvious that a governor cannot personally cope with the flood of bills sent to him in the last weeks of a

---

[53] Thomas Eliot, *State and Local Supplement to Governing America: The Politics of a Free People* (New York, Dodd, Mead and Co., 1961), p. 63.

[54] Executive mansions are provided in most states and the salary runs from $10,000 (in Arkansas only) to as much as $50,000 (New York). Four other states provide $40,000 or more, and the median salary is $25,000.

[55] See Ransone, *op. cit.*, Chap. 10, which presents a long discussion of staff.

session. He may have as many as four or five hundred separate pieces of legislation to sign or veto—in some states, within ten days of their presentation to him. He would require aid even if he were not rushed, for the technical character of many bills is such that he has to depend upon the advice of his legal or other aides to tell him whether to sign or veto.

Staff assistance may also supplement or, in some cases, supplant the line agencies in advising the governor or negotiating for him. This is particularly true when the governor has no confidence in an administrator who may be of the opposite party or faction and thus more an opponent than an associate. Under these conditions the governor may send one of his staff to Washington to negotiate about federal projects for the state rather than dispatch an official more directly involved. Or his staff may be set to the task of finding information about a problem, perhaps duplicating the work of an agency. The staff answers his mail, arranges his schedule, soothes the irate, mediates disputes in his behalf, and does a certain amount of sleuthing to uncover dubious practices that may cause him embarrassment. This is the classic service that staff is constantly supposed to perform: to act as eyes and ears for the chief (the term *staff* comes from military usage, of course). Staff as full-time "coordinators," more or less as conceived in reorganization literature, are rare. The staff provides information and intelligence services on an ad hoc basis: a problem arises and it is investigated. In reality the scope of state operations and the size of most staffs prevent the allocation of personnel to the coordination task as a regular assignment. Rather the tendency is to put out the fires that are burning brightest and attracting most attention. Staff members may attempt to quiet intraadministrative conflicts, head off malpractices by indirect use of the governor's authority, or bring matters to his personal attention.

But above all the staff protects the governor. "Do you have to see him personally? Can't I take care of this for you?" is a constant refrain. A staff is chosen for its loyalty as well as its ability and they try, like faithful guardians, to keep harm and danger away from their charge. What this means is a life of exhilarating exhaustion for the staff, an inevitable degree of uncertainty for the governor, and frustration for subordinates, pleaders, and newsmen who want access to the inner office.

Since everyone wants to have the governor attend his special affair, the governor receives infinitely more invitations than he can possibly accept. Al Smith, before he gained fame as a presidential candidate in 1928 was a notably successful governor of New York, and, like all governors, was harried by admirers. He said in his autobiography:

At a public dinner I once said, jokingly, that the constitution of our state should be amended to provide for the election of two governors—one to attend the business of the state and the other to attend public and social functions not directly connected with the business of the state. I was prompted to make that remark by the enormous volume of invitations, supplemented by personal requests, that come to public men to attend all kinds of functions. Even a slight acquaintance at times leads people to believe that the governor should attend a wedding in the family or a christening. Invitations to attend the laying of cornerstones for private buildings, private charitable enterprises, meetings of trade bodies, anniversary celebrations of all kinds, testimonial dinners, requests for the use of the governor's name for drives for charitable and religious purposes or for donations, all pour into the governor's office. . . .[56]

So the office of governor is a magnet, an institution, a misery, and a delight. It attracts the devoted and the hard-working as well as the demagogic, the ambitious, and the incompetent.[57] It has gained in popularity and in power consistently over recent decades, and the prospect would appear to be good for a continuation of that process. So long as the state itself is a significant instrument of government, the probability is that the focus of attention will stay on the handsomest suite of offices in the state capitol building where, smiling and available, sits the governor with the state flag decorously draped a few feet behind his shoulder.

The Politics of State Administrative Operations

Some years ago a scholar-participant in state administration made an observation which he thought reorganizers might well keep in mind:

---

[56] Alfred E. Smith, *Up to Now: An Autobiography* (New York: The Viking Press, Inc., 1929), pp. 297–98.

[57] There are a number of good biographies of governors that will give insights into the operations of the office. See, among others: W. T. Hutchinson, *Lowden of Illinois* (Chicago: University of Chicago Press, 1957); Bernard Bellush, *Franklin D. Roosevelt as Governor of New York* (New York: Columbia University Press, 1955), Frank Freidel, *Franklin D. Roosevelt: The Triumph* (Boston: Little, Brown and Co., 1956); James Kearney, *The Political Education of Woodrow Wilson* (New York: Appleton-Century-Crofts, 1926); Wilbur Cross, *Connecticut Yankee* (New Haven: Yale University Press, 1943); and Walter Edge, *A Jerseyman's Journal* (Princeton, N.J.: Princeton University Press, 1948). On the general background of governors, see Joseph Schlesinger's *How They Became Governor* (East Lansing, Mich.: Michigan State University, 1957), which also contains an extensive bibliography on governors.

. . . taken function by function, the services of state government are more often than not carried on satisfactorily, in spite of their not being properly grouped and related to one another and to the chief executive.[58]

This unorthodox assertion is worth pondering, for—despite the "improper" organization of much state administration and regardless of the maligning it receives—the administrative operations of state governments are often marvels of social control with relatively little abuse of authority. When one thinks of the operations of state government, involving some one and a half million public employees and carrying on tasks of myriad diversity and incredible scope, the wonder is not that it has some difficulties but that it works at all.

This is not to say there are no difficulties. Irresponsibility, arrogance, malingering, timidity, corruption, and red tape exist in every state. The bill of particulars in condemnation of bureaucracy is, however, contradictory. On the one hand it is accused of being a Frankensteinian monster endangering the society with its all-inclusive power over every activity and, on the other hand, as being timid, wastefully idle, and unwilling to exercise the powers that it has against the malpractices a critic wishes curbed. Bureaucracy can hardly be simultaneously a ruthless and tyrannical usurper and also a collection of timid, evasive, lazy people. These are the categories of politicking, of course, and are more appropriate to pleading a case than to serious analysis. Closer to the needs of students of bureaucracy are basic facts about its operations, seeing it neither as an aggressive monster nor as a refuge for timidity. What does it do? How does it use its own resources in seeking answers to questions of public policy? What are the characteristics of the administrative political process?

Observe, to begin with, the enormous scope of the modern state bureaucracy.[59] The very range of its activities suggests the innumerable ways in which the pressures of interest groups fall on the bureaucracy, and the ways in which the bureaucrats themselves—both through attempts to change policy as regards their agency and through the application of the existing policies—are constantly involved in the use of influence to affect the behavior of others. Thus the huge educational system of the United States is under the general supervision of state agencies. Large staffs are used to oversee local educational programs

---

[58] John A. Perkins, "Reflections on State Reorganizations," 45 *American Political Science Review* 507 (1951).

[59] The easiest way to get a general view of the administrative complex of any given state is to check a copy of a recent issue of the state manual, red book, or similar collection of basic facts on the government.

and practices, and the state is responsible for most of the college education in the country. The state provides public safety through the police
forces, correctional institutions, public health programs, the National
Guard, and other operations. Welfare programs are numerous, contentious, and important: aid to handicapped, aged, blind, unemployed,
and destitute persons; to veterans; and to dependent children. The
range of regulatory functions is similarly broad and troublesome: business controls (banking, public utilities, insurance), labor-management
regulations, licensing boards for professions and occupations particularly
affected with the public interest (medicine, law, and education, on the
one hand; real estate, liquor stores, and barbering, on the other). The
development and conservation of resources and the promotion of economic growth consume vast sums of money with programs involving
fish and game protection, highway construction and maintenance, agricultural experiment stations, conservation, parks, and water resources,
together with the more recent "development commissions" created to
conduct the state's competitive bid for a larger share of industry and
business. And the bigger the system gets, the more important become
the housekeeping and management services of the government—the
tax, treasury, fiscal control (auditor's staffs), purchasing, personnel,
and clerical operations. To repeat: the wonder is not that there is some
lack of coordination and occasional bumbling or malfeasance; the wonder is that the whole system works at all.

And the further wonder is that anyone ever conceived of such a
complex set of operations as not being involved in politics. As one looks
at administrative operations, one is impressed with the lines of political
relationship radiating in all directions. Consider an administrator in a
welfare or highway department, for example. He has a loyalty to his own
department, and naturally feels that its share of the budget is worth
fighting for since what it is doing for the public is vitally important. The
sense of mission naturally varies with individuals but some sense of
attachment to the cause is virtually inevitable even if for no other
reason than self-promotion, since the bigger the operation the more
important a role an ambitious administrator is likely to play. So he is
eager to protect the interests of his agency, and to do so he is aware
of the legislature, the governor, and the major administrative officials
who may influence budgets or administrative power (budget officer,
commissioner of finance and administration, key members of the
governor's staff). By the same token, his relationships with the clientele
groups that support welfare or highway operations are vitally important.
For if on the surface the administrator is barred from open politicking
and must operate subtly and out of the spotlight, there is no such

inhibition where the clientele are concerned. The contractors who build roads, for instance, are ready to spend money freely and to use every promotional device known to man to get a bigger highway appropriation. The welfare department has its allies among the professional organizations of social workers and among labor unions and other welfare-service-oriented groups that will press the department's interests. As a means of both gaining support and carrying out agency policies, the departments have relationships with the personnel of other governments—with the staff of the federal agency through which flows the grants in aid that are indispensable to the program, and with the local administrators who may need to be encouraged to do a job more effectively or cajoled into cooperation on some policy innovation.

In addition to the external political operations, administrators must concern themselves with internal political relationships. By this I do not mean what is commonly called "office politics" in the sense of the maneuvering of personnel or the petty jealousies and aspirations that have to be taken into account in running any small unit (or large one either for that matter). Rather I am referring to the kinds of relationships and maneuvering necessary to get an administrative organization to do what someone determines it should do. Efficiency in the sense of getting the job done well and economically is but one objective of such relationships; the administrator also needs to control the operations of the agencies in order to get coordinated actions consistent with the intent of the organization as a whole. Persuading subordinates to conform to policies is a task of major proportions in some cases simply because in a large department there may not exist any unanimity of attitudes on policy matters. Intradepartmental conflict can be a serious impediment to operational effectiveness and the typical bureaucrat may find that his loyalties are divided and that he himself is drawn both to the goals of a broader organizational position and to the support for the desires of his particular unit. (Thus a decision to curtail state support for country roads and to take over the previously supported roads and make them part of the state system could set up a tangle of mixed motivations in administrators who had been dealing with county officials and who have reasons, both personal and professional perhaps, for bucking the desires of the larger departmental organization.) If the creation of a huge bureaucracy brings benefits, it also produces problems of control, coordination, and costs. And the costs are not in money alone for the society also pays a price in that restraints are sometimes imposed arbitrarily. To create a state police system may be important to the peace and good order of a society, but the essence of such a law enforcement agency is a range of discretionary authority to apply the law to individual cases, and it is in the nature of human beings to misuse power sometimes. Discretionary authority can be partial authority that sees some infractions and overlooks others; power over prisoners can be turned into brutality.

To minimize the inefficiency of administration, to assert control over improper or inconsistent actions, demands a wide array of means of persuasion and restraint. So impressed were earlier students of administration with the need for controls to achieve efficiency that they constructed a set of basic "principles of administration" and began to talk of a "science" of administration. The goal was unattainable, as we have already observed, but some of their work remains useful to the student of administration operations if it is considered not as gospel but as analyses of and insights into the relationships involved in administration.[60] It is unnecessary for present purposes to review all these basic "principles," but a look at some of them will illustrate some of the political problems involved.

To achieve control over operations in administration it is important to *organize* jobs in such a way as to cut duplication to a minimum, make possible specialization of functions, and provide general supervision over operations so as to know when things are going wrong. To erect this into a principle of organization—that is, to decree "functional" organization or to insist on "unity" of command—may be nonsense, but to ignore organizational needs may be ruinous. To say that administration must be organized functionally (setting up the units of administration according to functions performed and collecting similar functions within a single agency) is to raise problems of how the functional alignment is to be made. The function of legal advice, for example, can be organized so as to put a lawyer with each subunit or to have one large organization of lawyers who serve all elements. Either form of organization allows for specialization, and there is no way—in terms of "function"—to say which is the better. The realities of competition for control over personnel are more likely to be decisive here than any abstract "principle."

Or consider the principle of unity of command. It is often claimed that it makes for bad administration to have any subordinate serve more than one master, that to do so is to invite conflict of orders. But it is obvious that most individuals in any kind of complex organization will take orders from more than one person. The administrator in an

---

[60] A brief account of some of these concepts is found in Waldo, *The Study of Public Administration, op. cit.*, Chap. 4. A fuller analysis is presented by the same author in an earlier work, *The Administrative State* (New York: The Ronald Press Company, 1948).

agricultural agency gets orders from the attorney general, the auditor, the governor's staff, and his immediate superior—and these orders are presumably all obeyed or ignored depending upon the urgency of the demand, not on the source from whence they came. By the same token, it is sometimes argued that a board or commission is unfit to conduct administrative operations. Such a collegial body, it is contended, may be internally divided and therefore may be ineffective in managing an agency whereas a single person has no such limitation. But as Professor Charles S. Hyneman said long ago, there is nothing about the case for such unity that need convince a skeptical mind. The case for the incapacity of boards to do administrative work is at least shaken by the fact that thousands of multimember boards do operate reasonably effectively in this country and no one has yet shown with any convincing evidence that they will not work.[61] In the pursuit of "representativeness" of the bureaucracy, it is frequently contended that it is wiser to vest powers in a board so that different points of view (or different interests, if you prefer) may be represented. In any event a board at the state level rarely administers: full-time staffs, headed by an administrator called an "executive director" or by some such title, do the administrative work which is supervised by the board.

Delegation of power and advance planning of work are obviously essentials of administration of any kind. To do either effectively it is necessary also to develop effective communications within the administrative organization. It does little good to plan if there are no effective means for communicating the plans, and it is impossible to delegate effectively unless there is some means of communication between the person who delegates and the person to whom power to act is delegated. And the larger an organization grows, the more difficult and costly (in terms of money, time, and added personnel) is the communication problem. In no small measure the necessity to communicate is the source of the red tape of which each of us complains when we fill out forms with five carbon copies. The carbons are often necessary so that knowledge of what is transpiring can be circulated to those who need to know in order that they not act at crosspurposes. (Red tape may also result from attempts to spread responsibility and pass the buck up the line and as such is evidence of bureaucratic timidity and track covering.)

There are other ways of controlling and directing administration. Ultimately sanctions against the violator of orders or the uncooperative, or positive sanctions through rewards to the effective and obedient

---

[61] Charles S. Hyneman, "Administrative Reorganization: An Adventure into Science and Theology," 1 *Journal of Politics* 62 (1939).

can be employed. Promotion of commitment to the program, the development of an *ésprit de corps* within an organization, and the intangible but important consequences of personal leadership which inspires loyalty and effort are all contributory to control. An equally important (if not in the final analysis a more important) factor making for control is a cultural milieu reinforcing the inclination of the subordinate to go along if the directions are reasonably clear. In a social system harboring deep animosities—such as those existing in most present-day colonial bureaucracies—one cannot count upon obedience as routine behavior. Under these circumstances the opposite—covert disobedience, even sabotage—is almost routine. By the same token, a tradition that puts honesty on a pedestal and ruthlessly crushes the corrupt official facilitates control by an honest one, but a traditional pattern of acceptance of peculation and action against only the more flagrant forms of corruption may make it nearly impossible for an official to control his subordinates, no matter what devices he employs. Since attitudes vary from state to state, problems of control obviously vary too.

Thus, with regard to administrative politics—as with other elements of the governmental process—the character of the operation is dependent not only upon the structural pattern but also upon the qualities of the individuals involved and the traditions and political habits of the society. These set the contour map around which individual parts of the governmental process inevitably fit themselves. A thorough study of the administrative operations of a state will illustrate this far more convincingly than any textbook chapter can possibly do.

14. Municipal Executives and Administrators

ENORMOUS AMOUNTS of energy and emotional fervor have been poured into debates on which is the "best" form of local government. The strong mayor and the weak, the commission plan and the city manager system, all have been promoted with evangelistic zeal and opposed with equally resolute conviction. Through it all runs an apparent belief that the form of a government is *the* crucial variable determining the ultimate character of a community's government. Overemphasis on form and structure has been attacked often enough in these pages to obviate the need to repeat the point here, but the literature and the "common knowledge" about the municipal executive are so form-and-structure oriented as to make appropriate a caveat against accepting some of the standard generalizations instead of demanding more rigorous proofs.[1]

For all the debate about the various types of local executive, amazingly little effort has been devoted to intensive comparative studies of these officials. Rather, the tendency has been to postulate an executive with specific formal authority, then to debate the relative merits of types

[1] Evidence of the emotionalism and shallow and unproved generalizations is readily available to any who will take the trouble to read a few issues of the standard journals of local government—the *National Civic Review* (previously the *National Municipal Review*) and *Public Management*.

of government in terms of that hypothetical executive. Of course, a certain amount of empiricism was involved in the formulation of the new systems that replaced the prevailing pattern of nineteenth-century local government: a strong council, and a chief executive competing with many other elected administrators but usually not acting as a political leader. The reformers knew what they wanted to get rid of—in that sense the new creations resulted from empirical observation. But after that early stage of observation and experimentation with new forms, the literature of local government reflects not continuing empirical evaluation of operating systems so much as extrapolation of the *logical* consequences of the structure of governments. Interest turns to deduction from postulated relationships rather than analysis from observed relationships. Executives become symbols, counters about as real as the pieces of cardboard with which we played "Monopoly" as children. Mayors are classified as weak or strong without regard to the manner in which their powers are employed, without regard for the political system of which the mayor is inevitably a part. City managers, too, are condemned as backstage operators dominating the council, or presented as "mere" experts using their specialized knowledge to achieve "objective" administration. Collegial leadership, such as the commission plan involves, is said to be unworkable for lack of focused leadership, disregarding the leadership (whatever its consequences) that the late Boss Hague exercised while a member of the Jersey City Commission.

This is not to say that the facts of structure are unimportant. They are relevant facts, to be sure, but they are the *beginning* of analysis of the manner in which a local government operates. Formal authorization is a basis of power—not the only basis, but one of the resources to be employed to get others to do the bidding of a political actor. The game of politics has to be played in terms of—even if by devising detours around—the contours set by the structural pattern of government. Thus, with regard both to particular communities and to a broad overview of the local executive, it is useful to know the pattern of distribution of authority. So long as one keeps in mind that the facts of organization are the beginning not the end of analysis, the fact that mayor-council, manager council, and commission plans are distributed in certain proportions among the 18,000 municipalities of the country becomes useful information. So, too, the proportions of mayors with and without vetoes over council actions. On the basis of the facts about the existence of the veto power can be built a more significant analysis of what mayors manage to do with the veto; the formal powers lead to analysis of the operational facts of the system, the pattern of relationships among the actors in local government. The scarcity of detailed operational analysis admittedly makes it difficult to arrive at valid generalizations about operations, but that does not render this a less valuable aspect of the study of local executives. It does, however, mean that one is forced, upon examination of both the available facts and the generalizations that have been made, to ask more questions than one answers, to pose problems for investigation rather than to show reasonable certainties that have been verified by comparative analysis.

Thus the present discussion begins by giving an overview of the local executive, showing the proportions of various types of executives and pointing up some of the peculiarities of the local executive position. Some features of the mayoral position are then presented, with illustrations from a few cities having different kinds of mayors. The same treatment is given to the manager's role with emphasis on the ongoing debate about the ultimate political implications of the position. After a short discussion of collegial executives, the chapter concludes with an analysis of the municipal bureaucracy and the head bureaucrats who operate it.

The Municipal Executive: An Overview

In one sense it is nearly impossible to present an accurate picture of the municipal executive. We do not know enough about the operational details of the thousands of governments in this country to make such description feasible. Even if we knew far more than we do about the manner of operation of these numerous governments, easy generalization would still elude us, given the wide variations among these governments. Yet from the facts of formal structure—the grants and denials of executive authority—and from what can be said tentatively about the operations of municipal executives, one can piece together a jigsaw puzzle image of the position. There are pieces missing, to be sure, some of them most puzzling and intriguing, but a rough representation does emerge.

In some respects the local executive is just another chief executive. His duties are the familiar ones with which we have dealt in the preceding two chapters—persuading, calming, stirring up, compromising, representing—in a word, leading. Now the extent to which executives lead, both because of their personal attributes and because of the political system within which they work, obviously varies greatly. Some men who have the resources for strong leadership lack the will to use them; others who desire to push lack the resources; and so on, with many variations between these two poles. As executives, they are all involved in administrative supervision to some extent, but it is probably true that the degree of actual involvement with day-to-day administration varies inversely with the size of a community: that is, the likelihood of a chief executive's being deeply involved in day-to-day administrative problems is small in the larger city, greater in the small town.

The reasons for this are obvious. The big-city mayor is like the governor, as we pointed out in the last chapter—so much involved in broader policy disputes that he usually has neither the time nor inclination to involve himself in the minutiae of administrative operations. He has staff assistance for the routine aspects of administration that he must deal with, and except for the crisis situation—when serious difficulties with mismanagement or corruption forcefully bring his attention to administrative details in a given agency—he is little involved. It is apparent that the city manager in the larger city is likely to be more involved with administrative supervision than his mayoral counterpart, but even the manager cannot involve himself in detailed operations to any great degree lest he risk loss of ultimate authority that comes from allowing subordinates sufficient delegated authority to manage the details. Managers in large communities, as will be more fully elaborated below, are policy leaders, too; they cannot remain tied down by detail. The small-town executive is, however, very likely to be engaged in administration. The scope of administrative operations in a small town is such that they can be encompassed by a single person, in a general way at least, and lack of staff may force the executive into administrative supervision. Naturally the extent to which this proposition holds true will vary with the individual and the conditions: some executives cannot avoid getting involved in details (indeed, some may take refuge in them); others, unconcerned, neglect them almost entirely. Quite without regard for personal inclinations, however, the proposition does seem to be true that the degree of involvement in administrative management varies inversely with the size of community.[2]

There are similarities between the rules of local executive and executives at other levels of government, but there are some differences. It appears, for example, that the political position of the local executive is more vulnerable than those of the government or the President. If one judges by the willingness of mayors to risk their political resources in proposing programs or initiating ventures that may draw fire, one can deduce at least that the executives themselves believe their positions

---

[2] Limited observation and logical inference support this proposition, but it certainly could bear verification by comparative research.

to be vulnerable. Unwillingness to be caught in a crossfire of criticism is obviously not unique to municipal executives; others play it safe for the same reasons. But the record of re-election of placid, stay-out-of-trouble types has apparently suggested that it is the road to success for many, perhaps most mayors. No doubt the clamor of protest seems loud to a local executive whether he has proposed an innovation or not, for the very fact that the clamor is localized must make it seem all the more intense. The governor has the insulation of his staff and the buffer of distance to modulate the volume. But the mayor's office is close at hand, and his appearance at several functions each week of the year makes him available for private gripes about the tax rate, garbage collection, street lights, slum clearance, welfare case load, and so on endlessly. Many a mayor and city manager resort to unlisted telephones to fend off the middle-of-the-night callers who want to complain about noise in the streets, a clogged sewer line, or some other annoyance. Robert Moses has said of the mayors in New York City: "By comparison the Governor up in Albany is a hermit."[3]

It is noteworthy, too, that the local executive does not have the same kind of official prestige that a governor or the President has. As symbolic embodiments, as heads of state, the latter officials have standing prestige, and an opportunity to be heard, accorded as much to the office itself as to the individual incumbent, and this can be put to good use in political combat. The mayor has perhaps a small token quantity of this representative-of-our-fair-city quality about his office, but the supply is not enough to get him far in a fight. The pompous nonentities that often fill the mayor's chair have induced enough joking references to "Hizzoner The Mayor" and comparable ridicule that no mayor can hope for quite the same power of symbolic imagery that goes to higher executives.

Moreover, the mayor and the city manager do not usually have the range of power over the operations of city government that governors and the President have. If state government is beset by separate and independent commissions, most city governments are even more beset.[4] As a rule, at least some of the operational agencies of the govern-

---

[3] Robert Moses, *La Guardia, A Salute and a Memoir* (New York: Simon & Schuster, 1957), p. 18. Reprinted from an article in the *New York Times Magazine*, September 8, 1957. See also Charles Garrett, *The La Guardia Years, Machine and Reform Politics in New York City* (New Brunswick, N.J.: Rutgers University Press, 1961).

[4] That independently elected and separately financed commissions and boards are endemic in local communities (in both manager and mayor cities) is clear, but over-all statistics on the prevalence of such bodies in the cities of the country have not, to my knowledge, been assembled.

ment (the education department, for example) have fiscal and policy independence, and in some cities an amazing range of independent agencies exist. This does not mean that a politically effective executive will have nothing to do with the making in these agencies, but if the political position of the executive is not secure, then the lack of formal power certainly will likely diminish the probability of his exerting influence on independent agencies.

In a majority of cities (more than 5000 population) there is no long list of administrative officials subject to direct election. At the opposite extreme, about 90 communities elect four or more officials in addition to the mayor and the council.[5] The election of administrators has declined gradually over the years, particularly where the manager system has been introduced. Insofar as the manager system concentrates administrative power in the manager's hands, elective offices tend to be eliminated. The strong-mayor plan also involves reduction of the elective list. But a marked difference still exists between the mayor and the manager system in this respect as is apparent from the data below, which show the percentages of cities in various population groups that elect two or more officials other than the mayor and the council:[6]

Population Category	Per Cent of Manager Cities	Per Cent of Mayor Cities
50,000 and over	16.9	41.5
25,000 to 50,000	19.3	36.5
10,000 to 25,000	16.0	35.4
5,000 to 10,000	19.5	33.8

A city that elects two, four, or even six of their administrators directly, as sometimes happens, does not necessarily have a government that flies off in all directions. Some of the elective offices are of relatively little consequence. Whether a city clerk, whose role usually is that of chief record keeper, is elected or appointed matters little in the long run, except to the politicians who either seek the office or want to control access to it; certainly it is not usually a vital factor in the operation of the city's government. Similarly, the office of treasurer, the one most

---

5 Data from the *Municipal Year Book*, 1966, pp. 98ff.

6 *Ibid*. The 243 cities using the commission plan of government fall about half-way between the other two types, so far as this factor is concerned: 24.3 per cent of those cities elect two or more officials. These data do not include elective boards and commissions, only administrators as such.

frequently subject to popular choice, is usually not one in which major policy decisions are made; it is on the contrary a ministerial post, unless the responsibility for budget-making is vested there, which occasionally but rarely happens. The matter can become more serious, however, when officials controlling major policy-making agencies are elected.

More important to the government of a city than the long ballot are the questions of how the chief executive is to be chosen and whether or not the executive is to be collegial—that is, whether a mayor, manager, or commission shall be in charge of administration. As we observed while discussing the constitutional patterns of municipal government, the city manager system has spread rapidly since it was inaugurated in 1908. Table 14-1 gives a general view of the distribution of the various types in various population groups of cities.

TABLE 14-1
Types of Local Government by Population Groups*

Population Group	Percentage of Mayor-Council Gov'ts.	Percentage of Commission Gov'ts.	Percentage of Manager-Council Gov'ts.
Over 500,000	76.9	3.8	20.0
250,000 to 500,000	40.7	11.1	48.1
100,000 to 250,000	35.4	12.5	32.0
50,000 to 100,000	37.0	9.7	53.3
25,000 to 50,000	36.1	10.8	52.8
10,000 to 25,000	48.7	9.0	42.4
5,000 to 10,000	65.1	4.8	30.0
All cities over 5,000	51.8	7.9	40.3

* *Municipal Year Book*, 1967, p. 103. For several reasons these data do not include 100 of the 3189 cities having more than 5000 population. See source for explanation.

From the table one can see that the mayor-council system is used in a bare majority of cities, and that it is most prevalent in cities of 25,000 or less and those of more than a half-million people. The commission form of government is employed in less than one city in ten— losing ground rapidly, it declined by 22 per cent between 1956 and 1961. Finally, 40.3 per cent of all cities over 5000 use the manager system, the growing popularity of which is suggested by the following:[7]

---

[7] *Municipal Year Book* for 1945, 1954, 1961, and 1967. There are reported to be 618 municipalities with less than 5000 population that also have manager systems. See *Year Book* 1967, p. 90. In addition there are 39 county managers—18 of them in North Carolina. *Ibid.*, p. 89.

	1914	1924	1934	1944	1954	1961	1966
Number of Manager Cities:	31	273	444	613	731	1114	1245

Both the formal and informal powers of the various executives under the three systems of government naturally vary widely. Some city managers have as many competitors for administrative authority as do weak mayors, and some mayors are provided managerial assistants (usually called the Chief Administrative Officer, of which more will be said later). There are variations in the voting powers of mayors in council meetings and in the use of the veto. In about half of all manager cities mayors can vote on all issues, but only to break ties in the other half; few commission plan mayors have the power to break ties, whereas two-thirds of the mayor-council mayors do. About two-thirds of all mayors in mayor-council cities have a veto; about one in ten of the commission-plan mayors and less than a third of the manager-plan mayors have this power.[8] What use is made of this power naturally varies widely from community to community; merely to know that these proportions of cities with or without these powers exist tells one very little. The application of the power in practice is the significant point.

The Mayor as Chief Executive

It is sometimes said that the difference distinguishing the mayor-council from the manager-council government is that the former retains the traditional American principle of separation of powers and that the latter system has legislative supremacy. The reasoning is that the mayor stands in somewhat the same theoretical position as does a governor or the President, both of whom deal with a separate legislative body in a government where both branches have independent authority and neither is in subordination to the other. In manager-council government, however, the manager is seen as an expert administrator, who is analogous to a prime minister in a parliamentary system, at least in the sense that he is subordinate to the legislative body.

But the distinction is more apparent than real. On the one hand,

---

[8] *Municipal Year Book*, 1967, pp. 104–05.

specialization of governmental tasks has produced in the British government a distinct differentiation of roles as between the executive and the legislative elements of government, the classic interpretation of the British constitution notwithstanding. By the same token, it is nonsense to talk of American government at the national or state level as if the executive and legislative branches were islands apart. As Richard Neustadt has said of the federal government: "The constitutional convention of 1787 is supposed to have created a government of 'separated powers.' It did nothing of the sort. Rather it created a government of separated institutions *sharing* powers."[9] Exactly the same thing can be said of mayor-council relationships. True, they are apart in a sense, indeed often in violent conflict (although some of this is sound and fury only), but they are harnessed to the same load and must share power not only between themselves but with other governmental elements and with nongovernmental elements as they all bargain, deploy, and maneuver in the making of public policy. So, too, with managers and their councils. Managers have their separate bailiwicks to defend against council interference, and the council has its provinces and prerogatives. Cooperation, conflict, maneuver, and pressuring are as characteristic of manager-council relationships as they are of other executive-legislative relationships. The theory of absolute subordination of the manager to the council is not even good theory, for it presupposes an executive who is supine and without any notions of his own which, if it were in fact to prevail, would surely spell the defeat of the system in the long run—perhaps not a very long run, either.

Far more promising as an analytical approach to the two forms of government is an evaluation of the fact that the mayor is subject to popular election, the manager is not. Direct election involves a major source of power; yet, paradoxically, it also harbors potential weakness. Popularity is itself a reservoir of power, and a popular mayor can make much of his public endorsement. Opponents perforce respect popularity, for it can be translated into votes and into pressure for compliance with the mayor's desire. Moreover, the ethos of American democracy makes it morally right and inwardly satisfying to go along with a popular leader; complementally, a mayor who has won by a good margin and who feels he has substantial support may feel morally as well as politically justified in pressing his demands because he has sanctification by way of the ballot. Under certain circumstances this can produce strong and resourceful leadership—true whether the objectives of the leadership are ignoble or grand.

---

[9] Neustadt, *Presidential Power, op. cit.*, p. 33. Italics in original.

It does not, however, follow that leadership necessarily inheres in the system of direct election. The system opens the way to resourceful leadership—no doubt more so than any other kind of local governmental structure yet tried in this country. But it does just open the way—it does not assure that it will be forthcoming. For in many communities the rule becomes "Risk Not, Lose Not." If the vox populi can inspire leadership, it can also encourage evasion. If those who stick their political necks out for policies that are unpopular seem invariably to get them chopped off, and those who avoid contentious issues are rewarded with re-election, the lesson for the ambitious is quickly apparent: endorse popular issues to keep in the public eye, but never promote a controversial one. Communities appear to go through cycles of evading and avoiding until some crisis arises or until difficulties are so pressing that the need for action finally steels the nerve of some political entrepreneur who then risks bold proposals and actions. Then the cycle repeats itself. This phenomenon is by no means limited to the city with the mayor-council system of government, of course, but the difficulties of hideaway leaders do seem to stand as a countervailing possibility to the leadership potential of popular election.

Direct elections cannot help being at least in part popularity contests. If a candidate is affable, has joined the right lodges, has been a regular communicant at his church, these are assets on election day. That such seemingly irrelevant qualifications are criteria for judging mayoral candidates distresses many observers of local government, for it seems a most inept way of choosing a man to administer a multimillion-dollar operation. And it is undeniably true that sometimes popular election brings to office men lacking in administrative ability or honesty, or both. Granted an infallible method of selecting executives in business, government or elsewhere has yet to be devised, yet if one assumes that the essence of the mayor's task is to be an administrative overseer it seems that more propitious methods of choice could be found. In fact, the method of choosing city managers is unquestionably more orderly and more likely to produce trained administrators than is the elective process.

But does it follow that the appropriate criterion is the question of administrative expertise? It is obvious that other criteria are used. For the mayor no less than the governor is commonly conceived to be a representative. He is chosen in part because voters believe he shares their values, their aspirations, and their attitudes. They wish him to be responsive to their preferences; accordingly, candidates complete in pledging to do just that. The components of voter motivation in making choices among potential candidates are enormously complicated, and one is well advised to be chary when generalizing about them, but it does seem justified to say that voters usually do not much concern themselves with the relative managerial talents of candidates. Indeed, most voters would probably be ill-equipped to do more than judge between the grossest extremes of excellence and ineptitude in managerial capacities. What therefore may seem irrelevant criteria to one who assumes administrative ability to be the crux of mayoral qualifications may be quite relevant to the person seeking a mayor to represent him and act more or less consistently, with his (the voter's) preferences. Thus the question of criteria is a question of values.

In this connection it is significant to recall a point made earlier: the larger the city, the less likely it is that a mayor will in fact involve himself in the minutiae of administrative detail. This does not mean that he has no concern with management problems—inevitably he will often be involved in administration matters, but he will be more concerned with the broader problems of the government than with operating details. He will be attempting to convince others of the rightness of programs, promoting school-bond campaigns or urban renewal programs, seeking to get the governor's support for a state highway bypass to relieve downtown traffic, mediating between real estate developers and the city planning board about a new project, etc. These are the kinds of political problems the mayor works on, and as a result he has neither much time nor much need to involve himself in the workings of the police department or the treasurer's office. As Sayre and Kaufmann sum up the problems of the New York Mayor: "It is political help (in the broadest sense of the word 'political') rather than managerial assistance that the Mayor most needs."[10] In short, mayors at least in the larger cities are, like governors, far more concerned with being policy formulators than being administrative managers.

This does not mean that ability and a reputation for intelligence and decisiveness are unimportant attributes for a candidate. It is apparent that the urban community of today is no longer the city of a half-century ago, when ethnic minorities were herded to the polls by political bosses to vote in blind obedience. A new era has come to urban politics. The day of the ethnic politician who could identify with minority groups and do little more is gone. James Michael Curley's formula of a touch of brogue, some recognition, a little gravy, and a patronage job no longer works—indeed, it had ceased to work for Curley himself and forced him to retire long before he wanted to. It

---

[10] Sayre and Kaufman, *Governing New York City, op. cit.*, p. 668.

is likely that a candidate for mayor of Boston who seemed invincible in view of his fitting the standard patterns of the Boston politician and in the formidable backing he had, lost the election of 1959 because he

. . . fitted too well the image of the Irish politician that the Irish electorate found embarrassing and wanted to repudiate. . . . It appears . . . that the nationality-minded voter prefers a candidate who has the attributes of his group but has them in association with those of the admired Anglo-Saxon model. The perfect candidate is of Irish, Polish, or Jewish extraction, but has the speech, dress, and manner and also the public virtues (honesty, impartiality, devotion to the public good) that belong in the public mind to the upper class Anglo-Saxon.[11]

It is appropriate to emphasize differences among mayors in operation, not only because there are enormous differences among them but because this offers a convenient way of analyzing the office. Although mayors might be classified in many ways the following categories will serve to illustrate the major variations—the reformer, the program-politician, the evaders, and (inelegantly) the stooges.

1. *The Reformer Type.* Invariably dramatic and often demagogic, always courageous but inclined to moralistic tilting with windmills, the reform mayor is surely one of the more colorful breeds of American politician. The flaming political success of some reformers has led lesser imitations to talk the language of the reformer, confusing spectators about the genuine and the bogus reformer types. But the prototype of the reform mayor is unmistakable and genuine—he rides to power against sin, promising to clean the Augean stables promptly and dramatically. Flamboyance aside, the successful reformer is a competent politician; his success depends upon his ability to weld together a following—both a wide following in the community and a narrower set of devotees who carry out the operations of the reform administration.

The conditions of urban politics at the turn of the century offered more than ample grounds for the reformer's art. All across the nation reform movements—both lasting and fleeting—sprang up and challenged entrenched political machines. The number one requisite for these movements was a colorful and resourceful leader as the focus

---

11 Edward C. Banfield, "The Political Implications of Metropolitan Growth," 90 *Daedalus* 61, 72 (1960). See Murray B. Levin, *The Alienated Voter* (New York: Holt, Rinehart and Winston, Inc., 1960) for a view of the 1959 election that in part confirms and in part denies Banfield's interpretation.

for attention, someone to provide leadership and to take office as mayor once the dragon was slain. Thus "Golden Rule" Jones of Toledo, Ohio, and his friend Tom Johnson of Cleveland were dramatic and successful leaders who inspired devoted followings and passionate opposition as well, but their popularity made them unbeatable at the polls. Jones acquired his nickname from his simple belief in the New Testament principle; his sympathy and love for the downtrodden immigrants and his relentless efforts to improve their lot made him unchallengeable politically. Johnson, a wealthy owner of transit franchises, gave up his monopolistic operations to go into politics after being converted to Henry George's single-tax ideas. Lincoln Steffens, while making his muckraking tour of American cities, called Johnson the best mayor in the United States. Brand Whitlock, a disciple of Jones and close friend of Johnson, succeeded Jones as the mayor of Toledo and continued to win public support with reformist ideas. Significantly, none of these reformers was a doctrinaire supporter of nostrums for "solution" of municipal problems.[12]

No other reformer—past, present, or even, one is tempted to say, in the probable future can quite match Fiorello La Guardia of New York. Flamboyant egoist, demagogue, driving political master, and chief flagellant of the party leaders of New York City, La Guardia stands alone.

It must be admitted that in exploiting racial and religious prejudices La Guardia could run circles around the bosses he despised and derided. When it came to raking ashes of Old World hates, warming ancient grudges, waving the bloody shirt, tuning the ear to ancestral voices, he could easily outdemagogue the demagogues. And for what purpose? To redress old wrongs abroad? To combat foreign levy or malice domestic? . . . Not on your tintype. Fiorello La Guardia knew better. He knew that the aim of the rabble rousers is simply to shoo into office for entirely extraneous, illogical and even silly reasons the

---

[12] Whitlock's fascinating autobiography stands beside Steffens' as required reading for those who want a view of the conditions of municipal government and politics fifty years ago: *Forty Years of It* (New York: Appleton-Century-Crofts, Inc., 1914). Whitlock's discussion of Jones (pp. 112–50) and of Johnson (pp. 151–75) are particularly recommended; on his own mayoralty, see pp. 180ff.

He says at one point: "I shall not attempt in these pages a treatise on municipal government. . . . Nonpartisanship in municipal elections, municipal ownership, home rule for cities—who is interested in these? . . . One cannot discover a panacea, some sort of sociological patent medicine to be administered to the community, like Socialism, or Prohibition, or absolute law enforcement, or the commission form of government" (p. 215).

municipal officials who clean city streets, teach in schools, protect, house and keep healthy, strong and happy millions of people crowded together here.[13]

La Guardia attracted not only a popular following among voters (he was Mayor from 1934 to 1945) but devoted and unusually able lieutenants. As Rexford Tugwell points out, La Guardia had to depend upon these people who in many respects knew more about the government of the city than he did—but none of them could be elected mayor. It took the personal qualities that this man possessed to make a personal organization and a personal movement to hold power and to do things for the city. As Tugwell also says:

It is hard to estimate even roughly now how many words La Guardia devoted to telling New Yorkers about their city and its operations. There must have been millions about the budget alone, and anyone who thinks it easy to talk about finances and hold the attention of voters is innocent indeed. And especially if budgets are not your own best subject.[14]

There are other reform mayors, of course, some of them currently operating or only recently departed for other activities. Richardson Dilworth in Philadelphia carried on the reform mayor role that Joseph Clark relinquished when he went to the United States Senate. Neither Clark nor Dilworth has the flamboyant qualities of La Guardia, but both came to and held power because of their crusade against a corrupt Republican organization that had long dominated Philadelphia politics. Both demonstrated that an upper-class Yankee Protestant is not disqualified from political leadership in the large cities of the East.[15] The late DeLesseps Morrison, once a reform mayor of New Orleans, demonstrated that ability and upper-class status are no disqualification even in the rough and demagogic politics of Louisiana's largest city. And John V. Lindsay, upper-class, Republican, and Protestant, (definitely a minority type in New York City) won and exploited the reform potential of the mayoral office in the nation's largest city.

The decline of the old-fashioned machine has reduced the reformer's opportunities to ride the white charger against bona fide bosses, for an essential precondition to effective reform mayor operations is a suffi-

---

13 Moses, op. cit., pp. 37–38.

14 Rexford Tugwell, The Art of Politics, As Practiced by Three Great Americans: Franklin Delano Roosevelt, Luis Muñoz Marin, and Fiorello H. La Guardia (Garden City, N.Y.: Doubleday & Company, 1958), p. 131. See Chaps. 12–15 particularly for an analysis of what made La Guardia such a phenomenal and intriguing figure.

15 On Clark and Dilworth, see James Reichley, The Art of Government: Reform and Organization Politics in Philadelphia (New York: Fund for the Republic, 1959).

ciently deteriorated political climate to make the public receptive to the reformer's charms. Yet when political stagnation sets in, as it had in New York when Lindsay ran, the cry of bossism is still effective.

2. *The Program-Politician Type.* It is not quite accurate, perhaps, to say there is a stereotype of incompetence associated with the mayoralty, but something close to that seems to prevail in many minds. The maledictions pronounced on urban government in its truly unholy past still cling and are applied today as if no change had occurred in the intervening years. Thus, Robert S. Allen in the introduction to his book *Our Fair City*, asserts that there had been no essential change in American local government in the forty-three years since Lincoln Steffens had pronounced the American city "corrupt and content." "There is not a major city in the country," said Allen, "that does not possess . . . a dismal record. Nauseous misrule, fleeting, and often inept, reform, and then back to the old garbage cans. Still 'corrupt and content' is distinctly the underlying motif of municipal rule in our country."[16]

Writing off contemporary urban government as misrule and mayors as incompetents is not justified, however. Admittedly there are many American cities run by less than Periclean standards, but the picture of universal misrule is inaccurate. Seymour Freedgood, writing in *Fortune* in 1957, expressed a view remarkably unlike Allen's. Observing that the large cities (those over half a million population) are hard pressed by suburbanization, financial problems, state limitations and so on, Freedgood says they need "top notch leadership," and adds:

They have it. Since the 1930's, and at an accelerating rate after the second world war, the electorate in city after city has put into office as competent, hard-driving, and skillful a chief executive as ever sat in the high-backed chair behind the broad mahogany desk. At the same time they have strengthened the power of the office.

This has not been a victory for "good government." To most people, good government is primarily honest and efficient administration, and they believe that the sure way for the city to get it is to tighten civil service, eliminate patronage, and accept all the other artifacts of "scientific" government, including the council-city-manager plan. But today's big city mayor is not a good government man, at least in these terms, and if he ever was, he got over it a long time ago. He is a tough-minded, soft-spoken politician who often out-

---

[16] Robert S. Allen, *Our Fair City* (New York: Vanguard Press, 1947), p. 15. If Allen would not still in the 1960's defend such a position, there are others who would.

rages good-government people, or, as the politicians have called them, the Goo-Goos.[17]

The tough-minded, soft-spoken, hard-driving politician has turned up, not only in the big city, but in more than a few smaller communities in the last decade. The office of mayor seems to have intrinsic challenge and is as well an inviting stepping stone to higher political rewards. Candidates accordingly have included some able aspirants. Program-oriented in order to attract support, ready to work with a political organization and to use patronage and other traditional tools to get and hold office but unready to depend upon these alone, the program-politician type of mayor is a leader and a promoter. Freedgood describes tellingly the characteristic traits of the breed:

The profile of today's big-city mayor—with one difference—is quite similar to that of the chief executive of a large corporation. Typically, the mayor is a college graduate, usually with a legal or business background and is now in his late fifties. He puts in hard, grinding hours at his desk, sometimes six or seven days a week, and his wife suffers as much as his golf game. The difference is in salary: he usually makes $20,000 to $25,000. . . .

"Public relations" take a big chunk of his time. He is aggressively press-conscious, holds frequent news conferences, often appears on TV-radio with his "Report to the People"; and from his office flows a flood of releases on civic improvements. About five night a week there are civic receptions, banquets, policy meetings, and visits with neighborhood civic groups. In between he may serve as a labor negotiator, or a member of the Civil Defense Board. . . .

Despite the fact that His Honor is likely to be a Democrat, he gets along well with the businessmen, though he is apt to feel that they have a lot to learn about political decision-making. . . .

Above all the mayor is a politician. True, he may have risen to the office on the back of a reform movement. But he is not, as happened too often in the past, a "non-political" civic leader who rallies the do-gooders, drives the rascals out of City Hall, serves for an undistinguished term or two, and then withdraws—or gets driven out—leaving the city to another cycle of corruption. Instead, he fits the qualifications of the mayors whom Lincoln Steffens called on the public to elect: "politicians working for the reform of the city with the methods of politics." His main interest is in government,

---

[17] Seymour Freedgood, "New Strength in City Hall," 56 *Fortune* 156 (November, 1957), reprinted in *The Exploding Metropolis* (Garden City, N.Y.: Doubleday & Company, 1958), p. 63. Quoted by courtesy of *Fortune* Magazine, © 1957, Time, Inc. All rights reserved.

not abstract virtue, and he knows that the art of government is politics.[18]

It would be easy to cite a long list of competent program-politician type mayors. William B. Hartsfield, twenty-four years the mayor of Atlanta, is a good example; he led Atlanta into the ranks of the metropolitan cities, giving it improved management and budgeting procedures, providing leadership for urban renewal, recreational, cultural, highway and other projects. "An unabashed ham," wrote a *New York Times* reporter on the occasion of Hartsfield's announcement of his retirement, "He often put [that quality] to use when it seemed in the city's interest."[19]

A comparable mixture of ham, determination, hard work, and resourceful leadership make Richard C. Lee of New Haven, Connecticut, one of the more remarkable mayors of recent years. Urban renewal has been the cornerstone of Lee's political career, and so successful has he been in promoting renewal in New Haven that he has acquired for the city more federal aid per capita than any other city in the land and he has also parlayed the remaking of the downtown core of the city into a political bonanza. Hard-headed bankers and businessmen, not usually accustomed to giving campaign backing to liberal Democrats, have backed him financially and otherwise in his successive re-election campaigns between 1955 and 1967. (He first won the office in 1953, having lost twice in earlier bids—once by a heartbreaking two votes.) Predecessors had been satisfied to muddle along, allowing a slow deterioration of city assets, offering little leadership. Lee reversed this process, asserting strong leadership and beginning to reconstruct the city—doing so, moreover, without raising tax rates.[20]

One could cite others: Mayor Raymond Tucker of St. Louis, an erstwhile professor of engineering; Murray Seasongood and Charles Taft, the only outstanding mayors that come to mind who served in manager cities; or Frank P. Zeidler or Daniel Webster Hoan of Milwaukee. Even though it was apparently not expected by many observers, the current mayor of Chicago has turned out to be an extraordinarily effective executive. As Freedgood has said, "When he was elected many people believed he would sell City Hall to Cicero [meaning the gangsters] without a qualm. Instead, Daley went along to a remarkable extent in putting into effect reform legislation that

---

[18] *Ibid.*, pp. 67–68. Quoted by courtesy of *Fortune Magazine.* © 1957, Time, Inc. All rights reserved.

[19] *The New York Times,* June 11, 1961.

[20] See the profiles by Joe Alex Morris, "He is Saving a 'Dead' City," 230 *Saturday Evening Post* 31 (April 19, 1958); and Jeane R. Lowe, "Lee of New Haven and His Political Jackpot," 215 *Harper's Magazine* 36 (October, 1957). See also Robert Dahl, *Who Governs, op. cit.,* pp. 118–21, 200–14.

tightened and improved the structure of Chicago's city government."[21] He may not be elegant in speech (he is reported to have said at a "town-and-gown" dinner at the University of Chicago, that "We will go on to a new high platitude of success"), but his control over the political organization of the city and his determination to achieve improvements in the city appear to be getting results.

There are others, leaders distinguished by the common drive to move the city ahead, or at least in some direction that it was not going in before. In this sense they might be labeled liberal or progressive in outlook and program. But the driving, tough leadership mantle does not belong solely to the progressive. Mayor J. Bracken Lee of Salt Lake City, for instance, is a professed and active conservative. As strong and resourceful a mayor as any of the progressive types, he won the office over a liberal Democrat in 1959, having campaigned against heavy spending in government, a goal he has vigorously pursued ever since. In his first budget he cut a quarter of a million from the requests, and got into a row with a popular chief of police and fired him over the prospective budget cuts in the police department. This and some other maneuvers have stirred up hornets' nests of opposition, but has won him support at the same time.[22]

3. *The Evader Type.* It is difficult to compose a list of well-known evader types; their careers do not commend them to national audiences. Indeed, it is the capacity *not* to attract notoriety or excessive publicity as pushers of anything notable that is their major stock in trade. To assure their tenure they avoid commitments, seek zealously to placate disputes, and follow the lead set by councilmen or other actors. Of course, all mayors use the evader routine on some issues; the conditions of political competition demand it occasionally. But there is a difference between being evasive occasionally and being evasive permanently.

The evasive stance is most common in smaller communities that are not growing or that have not developed serious problems of slums, racial conflict, finances, traffic bottlenecks, transit failures, and the like. But the larger cities have nurtured the type also, however serious their problems. New York City has had such mayors. Vincent R. Impellitteri, who ran in 1950 as an Independent against candidates from the divided and discredited Democratic organization and a Republican, won the election. He seemed not to know what to do with his prize. He "retreated into his self-described role as presiding officer of the Board of

---

[21] Freedgood, *op. cit.,* p. 74.

[22] See the typically *Time*titled article, "Nettled Nickle-Nipper," 75 *Time,* 14–15 (April 4, 1960), on Lee's successes and problems.

Estimate, sharing initiative and responsibility generously with any who would ease his burdens of accountability."[23]

The weak mayor system seems at times to discourage mayors from even attempting leadership, since their resources for backing up their initiatives are limited, but weak-mayor system or strong there is also involved a matter of basic attitude and a calculation of the probable consequences of risking leadership resources. It is claimed that P. Kenneth Petersen, until recently mayor of Minneapolis, one of the few large cities with what approximates a classic form of weak-mayor government, zealously avoided commitment on issues. Alan Altshuler in a study of Minneapolis politics attributes the following strategy to Petersen:

He does not actively sponsor anything. He waits for private groups to agree on a project. If he likes it, he endorses it. Since he has no formal power with which to pressure the Council himself, he feels that the private groups must take the responsibility for getting their plan accepted. He never attempts to coerce aldermen. Instead, he calls them into his office to reason with them. . . . The Mayor has let citizens' groups use the facilities of his office to work out solutions to certain pressing and highly controversial problems. Such solutions are often then seized upon by him and by the Council and adopted without amendment.[24]

Others claim that Petersen did not even employ the resources at hand such as press conferences to embarrass the council when it was vulnerable.

Some mayors ride into office as reformers but end up as evasive, long-term tenants at city hall. Such was the long career of Jasper McLevy of Bridgeport, Connecticut. Running as a Socialist candidate in 1933, he won the office because he was neither a Democrat nor a Republican in a city where a corrupt dual machine had discredited both major parties. He held the office for the next twenty-four years. Notwithstanding his Socialist label, his tenure was marked by penuriousness that would have done credit to the arch-conservative J. Bracken Lee, by the creation of a well-oiled local organization to support his biennial candidacy, and by a gradual decline of conditions in the city until another reformer displaced the reformer-turned-evader.

One final example may serve to illustrate another variation in the

---

[23] Sayre and Kaufman, *op. cit.*, p. 697.
[24] Alan Altshuler, A *Report on Politics in Minneapolis* (Cambridge, Mass.: Joint Center for Urban Studies of M.I.T. and Harvard University, 1959), pp. II, 14–15 (mimeographed).

pattern. Mayors of Chicago, according to Meyerson and Banfield in their study of a Chicago public housing controversy, were traditionally eager to make the most of public housing projects: "Back in 1915 Mayor William Hale [Big Bill, the Builder] Thompson had demonstrated a formula for winning elections which had proved itself time and again; it called for (among other things) assiduous cultivation of the Negro vote and an energetic appeal to the booster spirit which gloried in vast public works. Politicians of both parties had not forgotten this time-tested formula, and public housing seemingly fitted the formula perfectly since it was presumed to appeal both to Negroes and to boosters.[25] But Mayor Martin H. Kennelly fooled those who predicted he would behave as his predecessors had. In time the promoters of public housing realized he was not going to be mayor in the same sense that his predecessors had been, "or, indeed, in any sense at all. Until 1948 it was reasonable for them to suppose that the Mayor was the person with whom a general understanding would have to be reached. But when it became evident that the city government was to be run by the 'Big Boys' of the Council, it would not have been easy for the heads of the [Housing] Authority, even if they had tried, to reach an understanding with them."[26] Bereft of the focused leadership of the mayor's office, the program drifted, and in good measure so did the city itself.

4. *The Stooge Type*. Happily, today there are probably few examples of this species. It took the old-fashioned machine to pull off the election of a pliant, controlled candidate to the office of mayor. Once chosen, the proxy mayor would be careful to do the bidding of the boss who called the signals from the background. The old Philadelphia organization and that of Edward Crump in Memphis, Tennessee, handpicked minions for the front office to respond puppet-like to the bidding of the real political power source. Not only party organizations and factional groups managed to get pliant mayors to do their bidding—it has often been claimed with considerable truth that business groups achieved the same sort of dominance over "their" mayors, and apparently the underworld on occasion achieved similar control.

No doubt the practical relationships of the "subordinated" mayor with his masters were not entirely one-sided; the possession of the formal authority of office counted for something, at least, and there

25 Martin Meyerson and Edward C. Banfield, *Politics, Planning and the Public Interest* (New York: The Free Press of Glencoe, Inc., 1955), p. 61.

26 *Ibid.*, p. 258.

was always the possibility of a break with the masters and an attempt to strike out independently. Many mayors tried to get out from under such domination—some were successful for brief periods, but the odds were against it. The reason is simple: if the political conditions of a community are such that an organization has strong enough control over access to office to choose a compliant stooge, then it is likely that the power can be used to squash a rebel.

How widespread this phenomenon is today, it is difficult to say. Probably there are communities where in essence this does prevail, although it is difficult to believe that any political organization today can muster the quasitotalitarian sweep of powers that sustained the old-fashioned proxy mayor and backstage boss relationship. Doubtless the relationship where it exists today is a modified one, best described perhaps as a cooperative relationship with dominance of the mayor on most but not all questions.

Mayors: A Problem of Power

For the reformer, program-politician, and evader alike (we may ignore the stooge for present purposes), the nub of the mayor's problem is power: how to acquire it, use it, retain it. The major problem of the mayor is not actually to think up matters to initiate, if he is inclined to strike out with new projects, for others will supply him with a long list of alleged crucial matters to be promoted. It is not in the sense of originating that an innovator-mayor plays his role, rather he applies his power resources to the promotion, publicizing, organizing and financing of the projects that others suggest. In short, the crucial factor is not origination but power to promote. The same is true of the task of maintaining adequate municipal services, keeping the city's real estate and social conditions from deteriorating, and financing the operations of city government—all require a basis for power and the resourcefulness to apply it.

Not only are the mayor's problems imposing, his competitors are formidable. The bureaucrats, entrenched behind their well-carved niches in the law and desirous of protecting their advantages, have their own resources. Professionalism both raises the standards of performance of functions and rigidifies the hierarchy of administration, resulting in islands of power relatively beyond the control of outside forces. Wallace Sayre says that "The next big concern for the big city electorates is how to curb the bureaucrats, how to keep the experts under control, how to keep them from making all the decisions."[27] There are other competitors, of course. The council, other elective officers, labor or business groups, the assembled PTA's, the state legislature or the governor—all can and do mix into local politics, and may set themselves against the mayor. The range of competitors is in fact equivalent to the number of potential political actors, and it is a constant task of the mayor to get as much cooperation as he can muster and as little dissent.

The formal authority to take actions independently of other actors or to command others to conform to his decisions is, as we have noted, one of the significant sources of mayoral power. The possession of a veto, power to draft the proposed budget, to appoint and remove administrative officials are naturally means to power. In all probability the very possession of these powers tends to enhance the mayor's effectiveness even without his having brought them into use—the fact that he has them constitutes a threat. Lacking them, the mayor is weakened, not only because he lacks ultimate tools with which to reinforce his demands in certain instances, but also because a tradition grows up which sanctions a second-balcony seat for the mayor when the political play is being staged. In Minneapolis, a mayor lacks many of the prerogatives that other mayors in cities of comparable size regularly have. Only two administrators are directly elected (the treasurer and comptroller) and they have little policy significance, but the school board, library board, park board, and part of the Board of Estimate are directly elected. The mayor's removal power extends only to the head of the police force, the Civil Defense director, and his own secretary. With council consent he appoints members of five commissions, but the council selects the remaining top officials, most of them under civil service rules. The mayor therefore has no patronage and relatively little formal control over administration, particularly in view of the fact that the council has primary control over the budget (agencies submit their budget requests directly to the council, there being no budget agency).[28]

Understandably this limits the potential power of the mayor, and few holders of the office have managed to make it a position of effective leadership. Hubert Humphrey is among the few reputed to have achieved leadership as mayor of the city. The political traditions of the city sustain the long ballot and the decentralization of power; when-

---

[27] Quoted by Freedgood, op. cit., p. 79. Freedgood cities an instance in 1954 in which the mayor of Jersey City had to battle the State Civil Service Commission for the right to fire his own deputy mayor.

[28] Altshuler, op. cit., pp. II, 1–4.

ever it is proposed to increase the mayor's power, an outcry against dictatorship always rises and defeat follows. A 1959 proposal to increase mayoral powers was soundly defeated in a referendum. The campaign against it was led by city councilmen and some labor leaders combined with conservative elements. The city's research engineer was for many years a major adviser to the council on budget and a wide range of other matters, a role performed from a protected position under civil service rules. Given the vacuum of leadership, this experienced civil servant acquired modest influence. It is true, however, that Humphrey managed to exert strong leadership notwithstanding these limitations. Still the political traditions and the nonpartisan-splintered-factional political organization of the city weaken the mayor, as a rule.

At the opposite extreme, the strong mayor's position is enhanced by the grant of formal powers to control administrative subordinates, to use the veto, patronage, and wide appointive and administrative powers. A mayor who has the personal inclination to lead and who has political backing to sustain his position, is able to dominate the council and the bureaucracy with some consistency. Mayor Lee of New Haven has most of these powers. When he sought wider powers in a charter reform movement, he was turned down by the voters, partly, perhaps largely, because many of the organizational Democrats feared Lee and opposed the change. With his ample power he dominates both the council and the bureaucracy. For example, he appoints the Board of Education and by appointing sympathetic members to it he trimmed the power of a superintendent of schools who under earlier mayors had gradually become the master of the board.[29]

In order to assist the mayor of the large city with its multiplicity of pressing problems, many cities have provided what is called a Chief Administrative Officer (CAO) who, as a subordinate of the mayor, assumes general responsibility for overseeing administrative operations. The CAO acts as the mayor's deputy in administrative matters, making appointments with the approval of the mayor, and generally serving in a staff role for him. In New York City the office has been filled with distinguished and able administrators—such as Luther Gulick, widely known as a student and practitioner of administration—and they have performed valuable services for the mayor. Sayre and Kaufman observe

---

[29] Later Lee took a different attitude about charter reform, and has been quoted as saying "It fills me with a frenzy of indifference." On Lee and his use of leadership skills, see William Lee Miller, *The Fifteenth Ward and the Great Society* (Boston: Houghton Mifflin Co., 1966), Chap. 12. This is particularly revealing of how Lee refrained from using his power—in the school busing controversy—as well as how he does use it, for example, in urban renewal.

that the CAO and his office have become, notwithstanding the opposition of the entrenched bureaucrats who welcome no competitors,

... the most fully realized assets of the Mayor's office. They have become the Mayor's most active problem-solvers, especially in matters requiring interdepartmental agreements or departmental reorganizations. They have yet to weather a change of administration, but Mayor Wagner's successor will have strong incentives to retain an important instrument of leadership if he wishes to be Mayor rather than merely the presiding officer of the Board of Estimate.[30]

With some exceptions, the CAO system has been adopted only in the larger cities, but it is there, of course, that the need for greater expertise in the handling of a complex and huge administrative apparatus is most evident. As a halfway compromise between the strict manager system and the mayor system it is possible that it will spread to other communities. In some California cities, the CAO's position is apparently somewhat like that of a city manager with limited powers. There is, however, an invitation to conflict in the position of the CAO. If he acquires enough influence to be effective and thus a certain standing with other officials, it may be difficult for the CAO to remain loyal to the mayor when they disagree. Nevertheless, the prospects for the spread of this device would seem good for it offers the mayor the benefit of greater freedom to concentrate on policy and an opportunity to improve management practices.[31]

Whatever the apparatus for administrative supervision in City Hall, it is obvious that the character of the party-political system of the city will be a decisive influence in the mayor's power position. In some communities, as we have observed, party organizations are not involved in the politics of the city at all; in others the party organization is clearly an important basis of strength. In Los Angeles, for example, parties count for almost nothing in municipal affairs, but in Chicago and New Haven, the party is at the core of the mayor's power. In New Haven the mayor has power apart from the strong Democratic machine

---

[30] Sayre and Kaufman, op. cit., pp. 665–66.

[31] On the system and its adoption and operation in such cities as New York, Boston, Los Angeles, Louisville, Newark, New Orleans, Philadelphia, San Francisco (where it originated), see Wallace Sayre, "The General Manager Idea for Large Cities," 14 Public Administration Review 253 (1954); a response to the implied criticisms of the manager system in the above was written by John E. Bebout, "Management for Large Cities," 15 Public Administration Review 188 (1955); see also John C. Bollens, Appointed Executive Local Government: The California Experience (Berkeley, Calif.: University of California Press, 1952).

in the city, but his alliance and close cooperation with the boss of the Democratic party in the city is an important source of authority, notwithstanding the undercurrent of distrust of him on the part of many of the seasoned politicos.

Finally, mayors derive power from their own personal attributes and actions. Through charismatic qualities of leadership not only may a mayor persuade his close associates but he may build a base of support—as La Guardia did—in the public with his appeals. In addition to this psychological attraction, mayors also—and especially so in nonpartisan election cities—develop personal organizations that sustain their campaign drives and rally support for their programs. Thus Mayor Daley of Chicago greatly enhances his formal position through his tight control over the Chicago Democratic machine.[32]

City Managers and Politics

As we observed some pages back, the city manager system has had a phenomenal growth in popularity in the last half-century, booming from a handful of manager cities in 1913 to about 2000 today.[33] The distribution of manager cities across the country has been far from uniform, however. The plan has been exceedingly popular in some states, but has yet to gain a single city convert in others. Indeed, over half the manager systems are located in seven states, a degree of concentration that has not changed significantly in the last twenty years: six states in 1940 had exactly 50 per cent of the nation's managers; in 1967 the proportion was 48 per cent.[34] Conversely the system has made little impression in about half the states: the twenty states with the fewest managers had less than 7 per cent of the nation's managers, and in the bottom half of the states only 10 per cent of the manager systems were located.[35] In one sense it is not surprising that manager

[32] On Daley's use of the machine, see Edward C. Banfield, *Political Influence* (New York: The Free Press, 1961), Chap. 8.

[33] This figure varies from the data in the brief table on p. 382 because now included are communities under 5000—to be exact 2,066 places have managers. See *Municipal Year Book*, 1967, p. 87. Incidentally the record says that 90 places have abandoned the plan by popular vote over the years.

[34] Not quite the same list of states, but nearly so: in 1940 the champion manager states were Michigan, Virginia, Florida, Texas, California, and Oklahoma; by 1967 Pennsylvania and Maine had displaced Oklahoma and Virginia. California now has 273 manager cities; Texas, 169; Maine, 150.

[35] The states with the lowest number of manager systems, as of 1961, were: Hawaii and Indiana, none at all; Alabama, Arkansas, Delaware, Idaho, Mississippi,

systems tend to be bunched in some states, for in most states the adoption of the system is possible only when enabling state acts have been passed. If the politicians at the state level take a dim view of the manager system, which is, after all, a fairly common view and, no strong movement has forced them to retreat from their opposition, then adoption may be difficult or even impossible. (Indiana's law-makers still do not permit the system, and in Rhode Island it has been possible to adopt manager charters only within recent years.) Also there are fashions in form of government, as people involved in local govern-ment swap ideas and neighboring communities imitate each other. In the decade 1940–50 the number of city managers in Maine increased from 21 to 104. In any event there are some 50 million people living in city manager communities, enough to make the movement and its implications of serious concern to any student of government.

1. *The Managerial Job.* Managers, or most of them at any rate, are trained in administration, hired for their expertise in good measure, if not entirely so. Although most city managers in the early days were trained as engineers (about two-thirds of the managers prior to 1939 were engineers), the more recently hired manager is more likely to have been a graduate of a university program specifically designed for city manager training or at least will have concentrated on public adminis-tration in college rather than on engineering subjects.[36] On the whole the salary level for managers is reasonably high, although there are complaints that it is not high enough.[37] Managers expect to start their careers either as assistants in large cities or as managers in small com-munities, with the hope that they will then graduate to larger cities. Promotional turnover and other transfers therefore result in a certain transiency among managers, although the average tenure of managers is not so brief, and more than a quarter of those active today have served in their present assignment for more than five years.[38]

Montana, North Dakota, Rhode Island, South Dakota, and Wyoming, none with more than five managers. It would not seem warranted to jump to the conclusion that these are states with few managers because they are rural and have few towns and cities; some of the states with equally sparse cities and no more population have many managers.

[36] For a survey of the backgrounds and conditions of employment of managers, see the article "An Analysis of City Managers," 36 *Public Management* 5 (1954).

[37] *Municipal Year Book*, 1967, p. 118. For a manager's conception of his job (and some complaints), see C. A. Miller, "The City Manager's View of His Job," 41 *Public Management* 10 (1959). The median salary in the largest cities is about $27,500 a year; in medium-sized cities (25,000 to 50,000) the salary is about $16,800—which, interestingly, is considerably more than that of mayors in mayor-council cities of the same size.

[38] The tabulation of tenure presented in the *Municipal Year Book* exaggerates the length of tenure since it covers the tenure of only those who died, retired, or were

At the heart of the manager's job is the task of overseeing administrative operations, and in most manager cities the manager does have a fairly wide range of formal authority to command his administrative hierarchy. Usually there are relatively few elective officials, and although there are independent authorities, commissions, and boards in most manager systems, this practice seems less prevalent than in mayor-council cities.[39] Moreover, the manager has in most communities wide discretion to appoint his subordinates, although this is occasionally shared in some degree with the council. Preparation of the budget and of detailed studies on pending questions, both at the request of the council and on the manager's initiative, is standard practice. Inevitably the manager is deeply involved in the financial operations of the city, usually playing a major role in financial decisions both immediate (in the sense of setting a tax rate, or deciding to authorize bonds for school improvements or park development) and for the future (planning the retirement of bonds or spacing capital projects by priority of need). These are decisions made formally and finally by the council, but managers usually supply information and advice at the least and mastermind decisions at the most.[40]

Formally, the manager's position is tenuous and dependent upon his satisfying the council with his conduct of office. Most managers are not appointed for any specific term (some 13 per cent were said to have definite terms in a 1954 study[41]) but can be removed usually by a straight majority vote, less frequently by an unusual majority, and occasionally only after a hearing to show cause for the removal. Informally the manager has considerable insurance against "irresponsible" removal, and in fact he has considerable ammunition to use against any attempt—responsible or not—to remove him. Against an "irresponsible" removal attempt, growing out of spite, or out of resistance by the manager to pressures from the council which he feels he must

---

removed during the preceding year, thereby concentrating on older managers. In 1967 these managers had had an average tenure of somewhat over six years per city served. The *Public Management* survey cited above reported a median term of four years per city for the 801 managers it analyzed. On tenure and termination as related to several city characteristics, see Kammerer, *et al., op. cit.*

[39] In 1940 Stone, Price, and Stone reported on the numbers of agencies independent of the manager in a sample of fifteen cities. In cities under 50,000 population nearly half of all agencies and departments were independent of the managers, and in cities above that size the independent agencies were one-third of the total. The authors also observed that "Managers seemed to get more headaches from the independent offices than from all the other departments put together; in trying to deal with these offices, as they had to, they frequently got into public controversies." *City Manager Government in the United States, op. cit.*, p. 152.

[40] *Ibid.*, Chap. 6, deals with the financial policy role of managers.

[41] "Analysis of City Managers," *op. cit.*, p. 6.

resist (for the appointment of an incompetent as head of the public works department, perhaps), the manager has considerable leverage to use. His partisans will support him and those who seek to wield the bludgeon may themselves get a knock on the head. Managers also can and often do, when they are pressed hard by their opponents on the council, subtly make the attack on the manager an attack on the system of government.

The City Manager, Administrative Theory, and Political Power[42]

Although the formal structure of the city manager government has not changed much since the system originated half a century ago, its theory and practice have changed considerably. That the operational patterns and theoretical conceptions of manager government should change is no occasion for surprise—no institution with a dynamic role to play could fail to change in such times. The rise of the metropolis, the development of suburbs, the growth of planning, the initiation of urban renewal—all have had their impact on the manager system as on other institutions of local government. Also, significant developments in administrative theory have contributed to the revision of manager theory. The theory of absolute separation of policy and administration —once a key idea of protagonists of the manager system—has been abandoned by nearly all administrative theorists. Even the leading spokesmen of the manager profession have joined in the abandonment. In essence, changes in administrative theory have eroded much of the theoretical foundation on which the manager system was originally erected.

This changed conception of the place of the manager in the political life of a community cannot be dismissed as unimportant on the ground that theoretical constructions are matters apart from the day-to-day operations of officials in a city manager government struggling with "here-and-now" problems and not given to cogitation on administrative or other abstractions. On the contrary, the behavior of all agents in the local political process is conditioned by their conception of appropriate roles for themselves and others and by their respect or con-

---

42 With some alterations the ensuing discussion of manager theory is drawn from a previously published article, "The City Manager, Administrative Theory, and Political Power," in 77 Political Science Quarterly 224–37 (1962) and is reprinted here with the kind permission of its editors.

tempt for the principles underlying any governmental system. Behavior follows belief and belief reflects theory, however vague or profound the comprehension of the theory may be. Doctrinal shifts filter down slowly from learned journals and the exchanges of theoreticians, but ultimately they do have an effect. The principles of the city manager system may have sunk to the cliché level by the time they reach some of the practitioners who are influenced by them, but the effect is no less important. Changes in conception of the managerial role inevitably affect what an actual manager will feel it is his duty to do (or not do), for he—like every human faced with a dilemma—seeks a rationalization to explain and justify its resolution to himself and to others. (There is a "feedback" process too: that is, observations and reports from the field condition theory which then guides future action.)

Herbert Kaufman traced three lines of development of administrative theory and speculated on some of the "emerging conflicts" that these diverging lines of thought and action were producing.[43] His categories were broad, but they fit perfectly the shifts of doctrine concerning the manager system in the past half-century. Kaufman (see Chap. 11) identified three separate "quests" that had motivated theorists and practitioners alike in the history of American government: the quest for representatives, the quest for neutral competence, and the quest for executive leadership. Each theme, he noted, has been dominant at various times although never to the absolute exclusion of the others. Early emphasis on representativeness (as seen in the long ballot, for example) gave way to a drive for neutral competence (*e.g.*, the demand for civil service careers and training for administrators). Governmental fragmentation and irresponsibility later produced a new theme: the demand for concentration of power in the hands of the chief executive (*e.g.*, the plea for integration of administration under a strong executive).

The Manager and "Neutral Competence" Theory

The manager plan, dedicated to competence and "objectivity" in management, is the apotheosis of the quest for neutral competence. Believers in the separation of politics and administration (and this included most of the great names of political science in the years when

---

[43] Herbert Kaufman, "Emerging Conflicts in the Doctrines of Public Administration," 50 *American Political Science Review* 1057 (1956).

the manager system was emerging) took readily to the manager plan; it seemed an ideal way of proving that it was possible to remove "politics" from administration. This was after all an age of emerging emphasis on specialization and expertise, and it must therefore have seemed that trained technician-managers, independent of the "political" council in matters of administration, would produce "nonpolitical" government. Leonard White, writing when the manager movement was young, said:

It ought to be possible in this country to separate politics from administration. Sound administration can develop and continue only if this separation can be achieved. For a century they have been confused, with evil results beyond measure. . . . [City] managers have an unparalleled opportunity and a deep obligation to teach the American people by their precept and conduct that their job is to administer the affairs of the city with integrity and efficiency and loyalty to the council, without participating in or allowing their work to be affected by contending programs or partisans.[44]

Faith in the doctrine of separation died hard among reformers and the more traditionally oriented managers, and indeed some cling to the doctrine even yet. In 1940, when Stone, Price, and Stone turned out their detailed comparative study of the manager system, they adhered to the idea of separation, although the book otherwise reflected a political realism unusual in the literature on the subject. They admitted that not all cities had achieved a proper separation but gave nosegays of adjectives to those that came closest. It is revealing to note that they slip into description of the character of the electoral process rather than of the decision-making process when they seek to demonstrate the separation of politics and administration. They speak of a "complete distinction between politics and administration" that developed in cities which "conducted their political campaigns entirely without reference to the city manager or the administration. . . ." Under these conditions "the city manager and his relations with the council never became a political issue."[45] This, it scarcely needs be said, is no evidence that the conduct of the government in these cities left administration and politics in separate categories. It merely says that the manager did not become involved in open controversy, which is not the same thing as saying that the manager had nothing to do with the

---

[44] Leonard White, *The City Manager* (Chicago: University of Chicago Press, 1927), p. 301.
[45] Stone, Price, and Stone, *City Manager Government in the United States, op. cit.*, pp. 248–49.

formulation of policy or that the administrative decisions of the city did not involve the significant use of influence among competitors for the prizes at stake in a city—to use the language of Sayre and Kaufman's *Governing New York City.*

In order to go on believing that administration and policy were separate entities, it was helpful, perhaps necessary, to think in rigidly structural terms. Early students of the manager plan—and even more so the reformers promoting it—tended to see the system in static terms, emphasizing the formal relations between manager and council rather than considering its more dynamic aspects. Thus Stone, Price, and Stone say that it "seems obvious that in the last analysis the city manager has absolutely no independence and exercises his authority only at the pleasure of the council, for the council may discharge him at its discretion, and he has no legal recourse."[46]

It does not seem obvious at all. A city manager with long tenure and support among influential community leaders has a considerable base of power from which to act. He may not be independent in the sense that he can ignore the council (few executives in democratic systems can for that matter), but to cite the fact that the manager has no "legal recourse" is to miss the political essence of the relationship. The many case studies in city manager government of recent years (*e.g.,* Frank Abbott's telling study of the Cambridge City Manager[47]) demonstrate beyond doubt that a manager is an actor in the politics of a city. It is hard to imagine a council that would move against a manager without taking account of the resources for counterattack at his disposal. Whether or not this is independence in the legal sense of the term is the least of the matter; the calculation of the power resources is more significant by far. It is always possible, subtly or otherwise, to convert an attack on a manager into an attack on the manager system —or at least to convince a good many manager-system supporters that it is indeed the system that is under attack. And this, as candid councillors will admit, can be a political force of considerable moment. The

---

[46] *Ibid.,* p. 250.

[47] See Harold Stein, ed., *Public Administration and Policy Development* (New York: Harcourt, Brace, and World, Inc., 1952), pp. 573–620. Evidence of the popularity that the manager sometimes has is found in an episode in Milford, Connecticut, which upon abandoning the manager plan and adopting a mayor-council government, elected its outgoing city manager to the office of mayor. And it did so in spite of the fact that the manager had to run as a write-in candidate, having been pushed off the ballot through a court action by the political parties on the grounds that he had filed his nomination petition in an invalid manner! The manager-mayor was Charles R. Iovino, who won the election with a good margin. See *The New York Times,* November 8, 1959.

legally prescribed remedy—removal by majority vote—gives no hint of the political difficulties that dissuade councillors from taking that step.

As the hortatory and formalistic approach to local government has slowly been replaced by concentration on operational realities and decision-making processes, the theory of separation has inevitably suffered. The changes in methods of inquiry as well as the jettisoning of the normative element (promoting separation as well as looking for evidence of it) doomed the theory.

Although the doctrine was accepted by early managers, the system had not long been in operation before managers began to debate the principles of separation. Having tested the precepts in practice, they debated among themselves as to the appropriate role of the manager, and particularly they questioned the extent to which a manager should allow himself to become involved in open contests over public policy. At first a conventional line, consistent with the separation doctrine, prevailed—although over the complaints of a minority who disliked so neutral a role. The prevailing doctrine, enunciated in the first Code of Ethics was that the manager should remain apart from political controversy: "No manager should take an active part in politics."

Each annual convention of the International City Managers Association produced a new round of discussion on the point, however. It was agreed that the manager should stay out of partisan politics and council election campaigns. But there was far less agreement on whether the manager should influence the choice of community policy goals and actively promote them. Public speech-making and open support of policies agreed upon by the council became common practice and was supported in the professional manager journals. Some managers had always been active promoters, but many (no doubt most of them, in fact, since the majority of managers were trained as engineers) had done little to promote policies, serving instead as expert-caretaker-administrators.[48] The advocates of a freer role for the manager won out in the redrawing of the Code of Ethics in 1938 and added considerably stronger language to describe the managerial responsibility for leadership:

---

[48] It is particularly interesting that the first man ever to serve as a city manager (Charles E. Ashburner in Staunton, Virginia, in 1908) cared little about administrative detail and had a passion for constructive work. "With the greatest of emphasis and decisiveness" Ashburner told Leonard White, "By God, I go into a town to build! When I can't build, I get out.'" White later adds that Ashburner "gives little thought to the detail of management." *Op. cit.*, p. 94.

The City Manager is in no sense a political leader. In order that policy may be intelligent and effective, he provides the council with information and advice, but he encourages positive decisions on policy by the council instead of passive acceptance of his recommendations. . . . The City Manager keeps the community informed on municipal affairs but keeps himself in the background by emphasizing the importance of the facts.

The negative tone of the denial that the manager is a political leader is deleted in the 1952 version of the code; instead there is an affirmation that the manager is a "community leader" who "submits policy proposals to the council and provides the council with facts and advice on matters of policy to give the council a basis for making decisions on community goals. . . ." At another point in the code the following is added:

The city manager keeps the community informed on municipal affairs. He emphasizes friendly and courteous service to the public. He recognizes that the chief function of local government . . . is to serve the best interests of all the people on a nonpartisan basis.[49]

City Managers on Contemporary Manager Theory

The very fact that the code has been revised twice suggests that the managers themselves have derived from their practice some new notions on theory and are thus contributing to its evolution. Indeed some managers have now denied the validity of some of the first precepts of the system. Thus in 1959 two city managers said:

When the modern political scientists state that administration is part of the political process and that administrative agencies are engaged in politics, they mean that administrative officials and their staffs are inescapably a part of the total process of government which includes the determination of policy. The new definition seems to the city manager perfectly evident and arguments to the contrary uninformed.[50]

This should not be taken to mean that the managerial profession now embraces open political participation, nor even that the idea of

---

[49] Hugo Wall presents a more detailed survey of these changes in his article, "Changing Concepts of Managerial Leadership," 36 *Public Management* 50 (1954).

[50] C. A. Harrell and D. G. Weiford, "The City Manager and the Policy Process," 19 *Public Administration Review* 109 (1959).

the political content of administration is widely accepted. Thus another manager comments:

> We have passed from the clear and definitive separation of policy and administration . . . [to the idea] that the two are but aspects of a whole approach, commingling in the heady wine of practice. Be that as it may, the council-manager plan's unique contribution is the establishment of a formal polarity by which general policy matters flow to the consideration of the elected representatives and administrative details gather themselves together at the desks of the appointed officials.[51]

In short, as the distinctions between the more political and the more administrative elements of the governmental process are emphasized— as is the evident tendency in manager government—the concept of separation subtly re-enters. The case is made for "polarity" of aspects of government rather than for absolute distinctions. Yet in terms of the dilemmas of power—the contests over desired prizes that bring political influence into the situation—the polarity has little meaning. Budget-making is a matter of both policy and administration. The desk that the duty of budget-drafting lands on does not classify the subject according to its essential quality, as a vigorous fight over teachers' salaries well illustrates. The problem is that the manager's desk is both administrative and political, and where it matters most the polarity argument has little bearing.

Still another manager illustrates the problems of managerial leadership with a finesse that would have charmed Machiavelli himself. Dismissing two types of manager-leaders as ineffectual (one, "who leads with his neck" and has the facts but is sometimes "statistically right and politically wrong"; the other, who really doesn't lead at all but passively waits the bidding of the council), he then describes his ideal manager. The ideal type should be a good "salesman" and should have the "ability to set goals; that is, to determine the final objectives which underlie any successful program." He should keep in harmony with the council for:

> With the manager playing a large role in developing policy, decisions must be sound because the council in the end will be judged by the public on its over-all policy decisions. *Indeed, in a sense, the success or failure of a city council is a definite responsibility of the manager.* It is difficult for a city council to stand up and defend a city policy when it is not "saleable." . . .

---

[51] William A. Sommers, "Council-Manager Government: A Review," 11 *Western Political Quarterly* 137 (1958).

A manager should stay in the background—should push and lead through the council and the staff. *The council is elected for leadership.* This should be accomplished through others, avoiding differences whenever possible. It is practically axiomatic that in most council-manager differences, the manager generally comes out second and goes out first. When the manager is right, few people remember; when wrong, no one forgets. . . .[52]

Recognizing that brickbats come to the adventurous and unsuccessful policy promoter, Leonard White urged a diametrically opposite course of action for managers. To supplant the council as leader when the council fails may be a sore temptation, White said, but to take this course:

. . . will sound the death knell of the manager plan as now conceived, for a manager who undertakes civic leadership stakes his position on the acceptance of his program by the voters. If his program is rejected, and no man can supply effective leadership without openly courting the possibility of rejection, he sacrifices his position as manager.[53]

City manager Matthews (quoted above on the manager's responsibility to develop policy) and some others suggest a way around the dilemma posed by White, suggesting that the manager push policies by strongly endorsing points raised by his staff or by council members. Charles Adrian, in his intensive five-year study of three operating manager systems, found a consistent pattern of managerial promotion of policy through others. He observes that there:

. . . appeared to be a psychological advantage to the manager if he could place himself in the position of defending a policy developed by [administrators, advisory groups, or private groups]. He would take a strong stand, but could use the protective coloration of saying, "professional planners tell me . . ." He would, in other words, take a public position of *leadership* in policy matters, but preferred to attribute policy innovation to technical experts or citizens groups.[54]

Although many contemporary managers speak of their duty of "seizing the initiative," of "taking the government to the people and . . . presenting it in symbols they know and understand," and of being "hu-

---

[52] Steve Matthews, "How Managers Lead," 50 *National Civic Review* 294 (1961), at 295–97. Italics added.

[53] White, *op. cit.*, p. 301.

[54] Charles R. Adrian, "A Study of Three Communities," 18 *Public Administration Review* 216 (1958).

man" so as to win public popularity and support, the case histories of managers who have gone too far out on the limb of policy innovation without substantial backing apparently has convinced managers of the need for due caution before venturing forth.[55]

"Neutral Competence" v. "Executive Leadership"

Are there implicit difficulties in the effort to achieve neutral competence simultaneously with executive leadership? Are the two quests incompatible? Does the maintenance of neutrality forbid the development of vigorous leadership? Executive leadership certainly appears to be a "need" in modern society where bureaucracy rises in importance, the legislative branch declines, and pluralism seems to distribute power widely, rendering more significant the centralization and focusing of power that a strong executive can achieve. To curb and occasionally to stimulate the bureaucracy, to persuade warring factions that concessions are necessary, to rise enough above the fray to acquire visibility convertible into political influence, may well be the functions the chief executive can fulfill more capably than any other political agent can. A "neutral" avoider of initiative cannot be a chief executive in this sense, a point well-illustrated by colorless mayors who do not exploit their potential.

There is an obvious temptation for a manager to assume a leadership role when other elements of the political system fail to provide it. Thus, a manager said in an off-the-record session that "when the carpetbagging housing developers come in and begin to spoil your town, you don't fuss about what's policy and what's administration, you do something to stop them." The same city manager described his personal campaign to achieve racial integration of fire houses in his city. With tough policy directives and threats of disciplinary action, integration was readily achieved. When it was all over, he told the city council what he had done. He claimed this was a personnel matter and therefore not "policy", although the same issue had caused an acrimonious two year long political battle in Los Angeles.[56]

---

[55] D. G. Weiford, "The Changing Role of the City Manager," 36 *Public Management* 170 (1954); Carleton Sharpe, "What It Takes to Be a Good Administrator," 35 *Public Management* 246 (1953).

[56] On the Los Angeles affair, see Frank P. Sherwood and Beatrice Markey, *The Mayor and the Fire Chief* (University, Ala.: University of Alabama Press, 1959), I.C.P. Case No. 43.

To what extent in fact do managers get themselves involved in politics? Usually they eschew involvement in partisan politics entirely, of course, but they patently do become involved in the politics of major decision-making for their communities. No official vested with authority to draft a tentative budget can be considered beyond the purview of politics, for he must make tentative decisions that have a way of becoming permanent ones. Decisions to include an increase in teachers' salaries, recommendations to borrow to develop water facilities, refusal to recommend a new park—all are political decisions as we have used the term in this book. As Professor Karl Bosworth has rightly said, managers are not "simply master mechanics of bureaucratic routine. . . . City managers . . . must seek to be among the best politicians in town, for their work deals with the satisfaction of the wants of people who have the privilege of discussing and voting about his work."[57] And as many case studies of the operations of managers have illustrated, the manager is in jeopardy—or at least his program is—unless he shows an awareness of the need to cultivate support and use his bargaining and maneuvering capacities to the fullest.

In Cambridge, Massachusetts, for example, the manager system was inaugurated in 1940, and as the first manager a local businessman and former Army Colonel, John Atkinson, was chosen. The community had bitterly divided over the question of the manager plan and its accompanying Proportional Representation system of election; the old line Democratic politicians and their faithful lined up in opposition, while the proponents depended upon the leadership of members of the Harvard and M.I.T. faculties. The manager was, inauspiciously, elected by a 6 to 3 vote in the council. Atkinson was a man of ability, courage, and determination, and he had considerable political support as he set about the task of improving conditions in the city's government, for the conditions had been anything but laudable. A shake-up in the Police Department and the City Hospital brought improvements; other changes, including tighter budgeting and management, resulted in a lower tax rate. Atkinson soon got wide support, but his worst problems were ahead. A warning of the storm came early over a dispute concerning raises for the police and fire department personnel. It was Atkinson's

---

[57] Karl Bosworth, "The Manager Is a Politician," 18 *Public Administration Review* 216 (1958). This brief article is a penetrating survey of the development of the managerial idea. See also the companion pieces in the symposium of which it was a part: Charles R. Adrian, "A Study of Three Communities" (*op. cit.*, pp. 208–13) and Dorothee Strauss Pealy, "The Need for Elected Leadership" (*op. cit.*, pp. 214–16). Kammerer, *et al.*, deal with this general point in their *City Managers in Politics, op. cit.*

position that as the official charged with supervision over personnel and responsibility for the budget, the initiative for pay increases would have to come from him. The council, as the legislative body with power to enact ordinances, saw the matter differently, perhaps partly because of the numerous policemen and firemen and their families in the electorate. This dispute was compromised during the war years, but a new battle erupted after the war when the manager was challenged with new demands for wage increases—not only for policemen and firemen, but for teachers as well. The matter of who had the right to act was brought to the courts and the manager won the suit. In the end salaries were negotiated among the contending parties, including the organized teachers, firemen and policemen. Whether Atkinson was right or wrong in his actions, it can hardly be said that his was a "nonpolitical" role, not at least if the word *political* is to have any meaning.[58]

Another striking case of a city manager in the position of political leader is the role of City Manager Joseph M. Mitchell of Newburgh, New York; a Hudson Valley town of about 31,000. During 1961 Newburgh came to the attention of the nation through its campaign to reduce expenditures for public welfare by cutting off the relief rolls those who were deemed not to need or deserve aid. The proposed new welfare rules aroused a storm of protest (state welfare officials acted to stop the new program), but at the same time it led to the lionization of Mitchell by conservative opponents of welfare spending. Both sides of the dispute exaggerated their respective positions in typical fashion. The proponents were trying merely to get rid of chiselers (at one point the city manager ordered relief recipients to pick up their checks at the police station, where they were questioned by the police— a procedure the mayor tried, unsuccessfully, to stop) and to promote simple morality by threatening unmarried mothers with refusal to aid dependent children born after due notice of the new policy. The opponents were apprehensive over the denial of aid to blameless children and warned of retrogression to Elizabethan Poor Laws. With most newspapers in the country reporting and editorializing on the story, the focus of attention was on the city manager and not on the directly

---

[58] The source of this episode is an excellent case study which treats the case much more fully: Frank C. Abbott, "The Cambridge City Manager," in *Public Administration and Policy Development, op. cit.*, pp. 573–620. See the briefer but also useful case study of the "Manager Under Fire" by James Wilson in *Cases in State and Local Government*, edited by Richard T. Frost (Englewood Cliffs, N.J.: Prentice-Hall, Inc., 1961), pp. 17–27. Interestingly, Kammerer, *et. al.*, found that a manager's tenure was likely to be shorter in cities where mayors are directly elected than in those where the council picked the mayor, *op. cit.*, pp. 79–83.

elected mayor, William Ryan, who opposed the project, nor on the four council members, who all agreed to it.

Mitchell became city manager in 1960, and at the time the city councillors were concerned over the problem of high costs of welfare aid, and Mitchell's outlook seemed appealing to the council. In a speech before a local group soon after assuming office, Mitchell gave his philosophy with regard to welfare, explaining that ever since the 1920's: "Criminal lawyers and all the mushy rabble of do-gooders and bleeding hearts in society and politics have marched under the Freudian flag toward the omnipotent state of Karl Marx." He announced his intention to do something about the city's welfare program which, he said, was bringing "the dregs of humanity into this city. . . ."[59] Whatever the extent of his responsibility for the initiation or ultimate execution of the program, the impression the public got was that the manager was the chief cog in the operation, an impression not diminished by his decision at the height of the controversy to go to Washington to be hailed by conservative Senators and to deliver a speech before a conservative group's convention.[60] Significantly, the Executive Committee of the International City Managers Association censured Mitchell for "unethical conduct" for taking part in "partisan politics" and specifically for "offering just prior to the November Council election, 'to resign his position as manager if certain members were not elected, calling for the re-election of specific candidates, and challenging the Mayor of Newburgh to resign if his candidates were not elected.' "[61]

Mitchell's behavior is atypical, of course, and serves only to illustrate what managers typically do not do. What they appear increasingly to be doing, however, is assuming a larger responsibility for leadership although in a less controversial manner. But if managers do more openly become "politicians," can they retain the aura of neutrality that affords them the opportunity to make the most of managerial expertise? Perhaps the more appropriate way of putting the question is this: Under what circumstances can the manager contribute enough leadership to

---

[59] Quoted by Meg Greenfield in "The 'Welfare Chiselers' of Newburgh, New York," 25 *Reporter* 37 (August 17, 1961).

[60] The story can be followed as it unraveled in the almost daily stories in *The New York Times* during June, July, and August, 1961. Most of Newburgh's new welfare rules were invalidated by court order.

[61] *The New York Times*, November 28, 1961. Mitchell's reply was that this was just one of the many efforts being made nationally to discredit the Newburgh welfare plan by one means or another. He also pointed out that the whole convention did not censure him but just a "small committee." The policy was later reversed and Mitchell left his post.

cope with the existing problems and yet not get into difficulty by alienating elements in the community so as to spoil his effectiveness as an expert in management? The answer, at least in part, appears to be that carrying off both these roles will be hardest where (1) the social divisions in the community are deepest and (2) the gravity (and therefore the divisiveness) of the issues are most serious. The difficulty of the manager system in getting a foothold in larger cities is in part a reflection of this fact, as well as a result of blocking actions of city political machines. Moreover, the higher rate of abandonment of the manager system in large cities suggests the same conclusion: the deeper the social schisms the tougher the leadership role.[62]

Meyerson and Banfield claim that the efficiency-low-cost-businesslike government themes of manager government are popular in "communities where middle- and upper-class people have an overwhelming preponderance of political power" and not so acceptable to the citizens of more urbanized and polyglot cities.[63] Possibly the distinction between the types of cities reflects the social divisions that make leadership so difficult in the larger cities rather than the appeal of the middle-class slogans and goals, but the point is moot since obviously both factors are involved.

The interesting question for the future of the manager plan is whether or not the trend of population migration outward along the lines of transportation radiating from the metropolitan centers will produce more homogeneous communities. If the homogeneity factor increases, then perhaps manager government may grow even more rapidly than in the past and the strain posed by the neutrality-leadership conflict may not be the deterrent that it appears to be in theory. Surely the main tendency of suburbanization has so far been to produce greater homogeneity if for no other reason than that the poorest elements cannot afford to commute and the few Negroes who can afford it are systematically excluded from the suburbs. On the other hand, the arrival of Southern Negroes and hill country whites and Puerto Ricans in Northern cities (in the Newburgh welfare controversy one of the sources of irritation was the animus toward incoming Negroes and Puerto Ricans), will surely work in the other direction.

---

[62] From data in Arthur Bromage's study of manager plan abandonments one can calculate a rate of abandonment in cities under 100,000 population at about 3 or 4 per cent of those adopting. But in the case of the 40 cities with population in excess of that figure, the rate of abandonment is about 15 percent. See his *Manager Plan Abandonments* (New York: National Municipal League, 1954), pp. 6–9.

[63] Martin Meyerson and Edward Banfield, *Politics, Planning and the Public Interest* (New York: The Free Press of Glencoe, Inc., 1955), p. 290.

The homogeneity factor can hardly be predicted with certainty, but one may be reasonably sure that there will be many communities which will not often present the manager with the necessity for a controversial decision. But when other communities, both urban and suburban, face up to the problems of adjusting to life within a metropolitan area, to rapid population growth, to failing water supply, racial conflict, and to the need to rebuild the slums that generations of unplanned expansion have produced, will they respond to the siren call of strong "executive leadership" or not? Will manager cities, when faced with major and divisive problems, respond as other kinds of American government have increasingly done in this century, by turning toward the chief executive as a representative, policy-initiating, policy-promoting center of power? Diffusion of leadership is an endemic problem in manager cities for the council commonly lacks a basis of power from which to lead and rarely do manager-city mayors succeed in establishing the leadership base that, for example, Cincinnati mayors have set for themselves. Will managers feel justified in becoming stronger leaders since they feel the "need" for policy innovation and "justification" in modern manager theory and current executive leadership trends eleswhere in American government? Quite apart from the customary question which comes from friend and foe alike of the manager system—whether the system is "democratic" when the manager's power grows—is it possible that currents in community development and changes in the internal political characteristics of the system now endanger its effectiveness?

The answer to such questions can only be speculative. One can be reasonably sure that the logic of the situation will not be the decisive influence, or else the system would have floundered long ago on the rocks of erroneous assumptions about the separation of politics and administration. But traditions and beliefs do affect the way a governmental system works. In formulating tentative answers to the operational problems of the system in the future, it would be well to keep in mind these beliefs and common tendencies: (1) the favorable reputation that the manager system undeniably has for efficiency and honesty, and which will sustain managers when they are hardpressed; (2) the increasing deference to expertise and experts in matters of economics, industry, personal life, and in government as well; (3) the patently strong trend toward emphasizing executive leadership over legislative power, reserving to the former the initiative and to the latter a veto role; (4) the significant traditional attachment of the American people to the elective process as a means to popular control over leaders.[64] In any given community the dynamics of its political system (interests, personalities, particular problems, local traditions) will define the limits of leadership effectiveness, and yet these local factors will operate within the context of changing conceptions of the manager system and the currents of popular belief about government and politics.

Collegial Executives:
Policy and Administration Unified

Although it is customary to think of executives as single individuals —the mayor, manager, governor, and president spring to mind— there are thousands of collegial executive agencies operating in this country. Towns and townships usually have some form of collegial executive such as the Board of Selectmen in New England and town trustees (or comparable titles) in the northeastern and midwestern states where organized township governments exist. Most of the 3000 counties are governed by elective boards (a few are operated by appointive boards), and tens of thousands of special districts are largely operated by elective boards.[65] And in urban areas just under 250 cities are governed by commissions. If one took seriously the frequent assertions that collective administrative operations are somewhere between difficult and impossible, one might assume the government of commission cities and of rural and small town America to be one great chaos, but of course it is not. Disputes do arise between board members, and often there

---

[64] It has been contended that the manager system suffers no particular handicap from the lack of direct elective relationship with the voters—or at least none attributable to the fact that a traditional American desire for the direct election of executives exists. There is, it is clamed, also an American tradition of appointed executives that is in its way equally deep, as for example the apponted superintendent of schools serving an elected school board. (See, for example, Sommers, *op. cit.*, on this point.) The superintendent is, however, probably conceived as more strictly a subordinate official than is a city manager, and this is likely to be more and more true if the managerial leadership role continues to grow. An appointive and apparently subordinate executive is consistent with American practices and beliefs, but an appointive executive who is not evidently a subordinate may be less acceptable. Is there not a significant difference between European deference toward professional municipal executives and the American attitude toward executives? A German burgomeister subject to recall election is hard to imagine. An American appointive political leader is not inconceivable—witness the manager himself—but the best evidence of the inconsistency of such an office with tradition is the ardent effort devoted to keeping the manager from being identified as a politician.

[65] See Paul W. Wager, ed., *County Government Across the Nation* (Chapel Hill, N.C.: University of North Carolina Press, 1950), for a description of both county and township government.

is patently a lack of coordination in activities, but such conditions affect other kinds of government as well.

In most of the municipalities or special districts governed by boards, the scope of problems to be dealt with is relatively restricted, and the amateur boards that govern are small in size and able to communicate readily with each other on most matters that arise. Thus the possible difficulties often do not develop for the simple reason that decisions are made collegially.[66] Yet difficulties arising from the lack of focused executive direction and from a lack of coordination do seem to be common when the government grows large and complex. Thus York, Pennsylvania, a city of 55,000, found difficulties in operating under the commission system and abandoned it in 1959. Commissioners administering individual departments were inclined to be concerned with their own bailiwicks and unconcerned with other parts of the government. It was charged that "the mayor had no veto power and had public responsibilities incommensurate with his power; that budget-making was log-rolling by councilmen; and that coordination and leadership were almost impossible to achieve."[67]

In view of the declining number of commission governments, it appears that something like this set of "faults" is increasingly being found with the system in the larger cities, and often in the smaller ones as well. This may lead to the gradual disappearance of this form of local government, but the collegial executive in county, town, and special district government may be expected to remain intact for some time to come, notwithstanding the innovation of the town manager and the county manager plans that in recent decades have won adherents. As pointed out previously over 600 municipalities with less than 5,000 population have managers as did 39 counties in January 1967.

The Politics of Municipal Administration

More than half of all public employees are on the payrolls of municipalities. Neither the huge federal bureaucracy nor that of the state governments comes close to matching the size of the local bureaucracy nor indeed the scope of the activities of local administration. The 6.4 million employees of local government (as of 1966) were engaged in an incredibly wide range of activities, although the tabulation in Table

---

[66] See the discussion of small town government in Vidich and Bensman, *op. cit.*

[67] Sidney Wise, "York Gets a New Charter," in *Cases in State and Local Government, op. cit.*, p. 7.

14-2 shows that over half of all employees are in education. The tired old joke may bemoan the inability to get them to do anything although

TABLE 14-2
Distribution of Leading Types of Employment in Local Government*

Type of Employment	Percentage of Employees Engaged
Education	55.1
Hospitals and Health	6.7
Police Protection	5.7
Highways	4.6

* Calculated from data in *Statistical Abstract*, 1967, p. 439.

"I told them down at City Hall," but the fact of the matter is that much does indeed get done at City Hall. Recreation, libraries, public utilities (86 per cent of the cities over 5000 operate some kind of public utility), public health and hospitals, and all the governmental staff (such as accountants, planners, lawyers, tax collectors, personnel staff, and so on) required to keep the other elements in operation pose a formidable organizational problem.

Many people do not recognize how complex the organizational problem of a large bureaucracy can be. Local government operations are possible to finance and manage only because cities do not operate the way New London, Connecticut, was described as operating before a new charter terminated its town meeting government. The rich detail of the mess that prevailed illustrates the organizational problems of municipal government:

Financial administration under the old town meeting form of government in New London was a confused and unintelligible hodgepodge. Many persons, elected and appointed, had something to do with finance, and not one of them had enough of the records to know the financial position of the city at any one time. Revenues were not forecast, and expenditures were not estimated before the year started. In other words, there was no budget; instead, departmental appropriations were made at irregular intervals, and deficiencies were made up at the end of the year by further appropriations....

Under the town meeting government almost any employe was able to buy supplies for the city, because the only check was the signature of any three elective officials; this requirement proved no barrier, for there were eighty such officers. Almost no records were kept of what was bought, and often there was no way to tell whether a bill had been paid. Accounting practice was an individual matter, and only a few officers bothered to keep records of expenditures. The local and state audits were not much more than tabulations to find the difference between receipts and disbursements.[68]

It now seems incredible that any city of 30,000, as New London was at the time of the description (1920), could have been run in such a disorganized fashion. And indeed much of the boodling and corruption of earlier days were attributable to the lax controls and sloppy administrative practices. The improvements in personnel management, recruitment, training, control, and coordination that characterize contemporary government are indispensable to the conduct of the wide range of activities of today's governments. Let no one assume, however, that a price is not paid for the erection of this system of controls and professionalization. Not necessarily a price in money—on the contrary, the new system has usually saved money and indeed it can be said to have made possible the financing of such a wide range of services because it does eliminate waste and make the most of specialization and expertise. The price rather has been in rigidifying administration. Red tape, delay, buck-passing, and civil service protection of incompetents are but part of the story. More significant is the drive for autonomy that seems to be the passion of all bureaucrats and their clientele supporters. As has been pointed out, the drive for independence has resulted in agencies having separate financial resources, internal control over personnel and policy, and a minimum of supervision and direction from traditional executives and legislators. This has gone to the last extreme in the various "authorities" which acquire independent power to issue bonds and to build bridges, highways, housing projects, and such— all without the appropriation of money by councils and without co-ordination of policy with other agencies. In short, for the efficiency and "businesslike" qualities of the independent authority, the society pays a price in loss of control over where, how, when, and for what its money is to be spent.[69] But it should not be assumed that only authorities gain independence. The mayor of New York has to fight a running battle to maintain some control over the police department. The political power of the department is such that all mayors have to keep reassuring the public they are not interfering improperly when they attempt to decide police policy.[70]

---

[68] Stone, Price, and Stone, *op. cit.*, pp. 121–22.
[69] More is said of the authority's operation in Chap. 16.
[70] See *The New York Times*, December 2, 1967, article "Firmer Hand for Leary" which presents interesting evidence on this point.

Bureaucrats are, as we have said, important actors in the political game. The leaders of agencies are actors seeking funds, personnel, and power to perform their tasks. The director of city hospitals may be an eminently qualified doctor with great expertise and ability as a medical administrator, but if he has no political acumen, no feeling for how to gain public support or how to maneuver with the budget director, the mayor, or manager, then the hospital services will suffer while the parks department or some other agency with a cannier leader will get the appropriations. This may sound crass and irrational, but it is nevertheless realistic.[71]

Contests over salaries, retirement benefits, hours of work, vacation, sick pay, and other details of employment are important matters to the civil servant, and in keeping with the trends of modern economic development, public employees—like those in private employment—have formed unions to promote their interests. Hence such organizations as the American Federation of State, County and Municipal Employees, the International Association of Fire Fighters, the Fraternal Order of Police, and large numbers of local unions represent all kinds of public employees. The larger the city the more common are unions, as might be expected, and the greater the likelihood that the national unions will be present; in smaller communities local unions are more common. Formal recognition for bargaining purposes is common, and dues check-off for union members and permission to do organizational work in city time are reported for high percentages of cities covered in one study of union developments.[72] The usual distinctions between bargaining by public employees on the one hand and bargaining in industry are gradually disappearing. Strikes, once almost unheard of in public employment, are becoming commonplace. Teachers, social workers, transit employees, firemen, policemen, and others have in recent years gone on widely publicized strikes. They strike notwithstanding laws that forbid it; their leaders go to jail for contempt of court, but the strikes go on. One source reported 25 teacher strikes

---

[71] Fuller discussion of the manner in which local bureaucrats play the game seems unnecessary here since the pattern is essentially similar to other, previously described, bureaucratic-political operations. For a good analysis of the manner in which bureaucracies operate in an actual city, there is no better source than Sayre and Kaufman's *Governing New York City*, *op. cit.*, Chaps. 8–11. For details of the formal organization of various elements of the administrative hierarchy of local governments generally, see the latter quarter of almost any standard textbook in local government which presents in considerable detail formal descriptions of police, fire, utility, and other functions.

[72] See Winston W. Crouch, "Employee Organizations in Council-Manager Cities," *Municipal Year Book*, 1967, pp. 137–45.

between September 1967 and March 1968, lasting from one day to three weeks and involving over 140,000 teachers.[73]

Inevitably unions are concerned with local politics not only as competing forces in policy contests but also in campaigns for office. Public workers are carefully cultivated by candidates in many communities, for their direct concern with salaries and conditions of work makes the public employee a likely target for appeals in municipal elections. Naturally also the leaders of organized public workers play up that concern to get as many concessions as possible from candidates, both before and after elections.[74]

One of the goals of the leaders of bureaucrats is the furthering of civil service status and the elimination of patronage jobs, And in many cities there is remarkably little patronage left for the politicians to dispense. The job that used to go to Cousin Lefty's boy just out of the Navy is now open to him only if he passes a civil service examination—but once on the payroll, he need have no concern about losing the job. Still, the inference that there is no patronage left in local politics would indeed be wide of the mark, for a cursory survey of data on civil service systems suggests that a great many cities do not have civil service coverage for unskilled workers, utility employees, and others. Many cities provide coverage only for firemen or policemen. As a rule, the larger cities have the broadest coverage and the smaller ones the least. Indeed, less than half of the cities from 10,000 to 25,000 population had any civil service coverage at all as of the end of 1966.[75]

---

[73] Education Commission of the States, *ECS Bulletin*, vol. 1, No. 5, undated, not paged.

[74] On the politics of the "Organized City Bureaucracy," see Sayre and Kaufman, *Governing New York City, op. cit.*, Chap. 11.

[75] *Municipal Year Book*, 1967, p. 161.

Politics
and the
15. Judiciary

ON A TUESDAY in October of 1938 an elderly woman was murdered in Kalamazoo, Michigan; within hours a seventeen-year-old boy with a seventh-grade education was arrested and taken to a Kalamazoo jail. He "was questioned on the night of his arrest until approximately 2 or 3 o'clock in the morning of the following day. On [Wednesday] he was questioned from approximately 8 A.M. until 10 P.M. [Thursday] he was questioned from approximately 8 AM until noon and again in the afternoon when he orally confessed."[1] On Saturday in a brief proceeding, during which the defendant waived his right to have counsel represent him, he was found guilty and sentenced to life imprisonment. It subsequently appeared, however, that the confession of guilt had been induced by fears, instilled by the sheriff, that unless he did plead guilty there might be a riot where his safety could not be assured by the sheriff's forces. Said the defendant, "After the man tell me he couldn't protect me then there wasn't nothing I could do. I was mostly scared than anything else [sic]." Holding that the boy had been denied the assistance of counsel, the Supreme Court reversed the conviction *after he had spent nineteen years in prison*.

"*LONG ISLAND MAN HELD 50 DAYS, HEARS ARREST*

---

[1] *Moore v. Michigan*, 355 U.S. 258 (1957).

[423]

WAS ERROR," said a 1961 headline of a mistaken identity story; *"NO TRIAL IN YEAR, YOUTH, 18, FREED"* said another. A man was freed after four years in a hospital for the criminal insane because he had persisted in a fantastic tale which he insisted was true but only convinced psychiatrists he was mad. Finally a woman lawyer believed his story proved its truth and won his release. As a Puerto Rican who spoke little English he had not been able to persuade anyone of the truth of the reason for his assault on a boarder in his home. His story was that the boarder had stolen his wife by taking blood from his own arm and drinking it in his beer to demonstrate his virility. The victim said, "the doctor told me that if I forgot that story, they might let me go, but the truth is the truth no matter what anyone says." In a campaign for court reform, an advertisement asserted that a nineteen-year-old girl "was left paralyzed from an accident compounded by gross negligence in a New York hospital" and was advised 12 years later to accept an inadequate settlement "rather than face the delay of another protracted trial."[2]

Justice is fallible. Elaborate protections for the innocent, founded on ancient traditions and firmly stated constitutional principle, must meet society's insatiable appetite for punishing the guilty; fair play for the wronged but impecunious party to a dispute comes hard when poverty combats corporate millions. Trials are contests—adversary proceedings, the lawyers say—where the quest for truth competes with the quest for victory.[3] Moreover, a trial is a human process, necessarily involving distortions by prejudice, ambition, avarice, and ignorance. The perfect system for divining the just answer to all disputes has yet to be found, but in some manner every society must resolve disputes, determine guilt and innocence, and paradoxically protect both the society at large from the wrongdoing of the individual and the

---

[2] These items are from *The New York Times,* for the respective dates of October 30, December 1, 1961; September 28, 1962; and November 6, 1961.

[3] The late Judge Jerome Frank made much of this point in his book, *Courts on Trial* (Princeton, N.J.: Princeton University Press, 1949). See particularly Chap. 6. He quoted a judge, who began his speech at a Bar Association meeting by declaring that our trials are an "orderly inquiry for the discovery of truth," but who a little later cautioned lawyes never on crossexamination "thoughtlessly [to] ask the one question which will supply an omission in our opponent's case." "So here you have a judge," said Judge Frank, "who, after seriously depicting a trial as an "inquiry for the discovery of truth," goes on to encourage lawyers to avoid bringing out the truth." The human aspects of the law have often been well-stated in fiction, if also often grossly distorted there. The best "legal" novel I know is James Gould Cozzens' *The Just and the Unjust* (New York: Harcourt, Brace, and World, Inc., 1942). Its verisimilitude is astounding, and its insights into the strains and moral dilemmas of a murder trial and its understanding of the court as a social system are penetrating and revealing.

individual from the collective mischief of the society or groups thereof. A community may rightly be judged by the fairness and effectiveness with which it handles these tasks for *all* its citizens. As Sybille Bedford has said:

The law, the working of the law, the daily application of the law to people and situations, is an essential element in a country's life. It runs through everything; it is a part of the pattern, like the architecture and the art and the look of the cultivated countryside. It shapes, and expresses, a country's modes of thought, its political concepts and realities, its conduct. . . .[4]

Politics and the Judicial Process

If courts are properly seen as the agents of essential services to the society, how then can the title of this chapter be appropriate? Why speak of "politics" of the judiciary? To many readers the very notion that politics has anything to do with the judiciary will seem shocking, akin perhaps to the idea of using profanity in church. Yet as the word is used in this book, *politics* is inevitably associated with the judiciary since it involves the exercise of power over the behavior of others. As Sayre and Kaufman put it:

Like all other governmental officials and employees engaged in the quest for the stakes of political contest, judges and their staffs are both claimants and distributors. The special character of the judicial process sets them apart from those whose primary functions are the formulation and management of government programs. . . . Nevertheless, they are participants in the political contest, involved as fully as all the others who take part in it. Many individuals and groups expend a great deal of energy trying to influence court personnel (from judges down); judges and other court personnel, in turn, exert all the influence they can bring to bear upon some other contestants when certain questions are to be decided. Judges and their staffs are not without their modes of exercising influence, nor are they invulnerable to the pressures of others.[5]

---

[4] Sybille Bedford, *The Faces of Justice* (New York: Simon & Schuster, Inc., 1961), p. 101. This little volume of commentary on British, German, Austrian, Swiss, and French courts is impressionistic but its straightforward descriptions are particularly instructive to an American who may, by looking at other courts, better appreciate both the values and the deficiencies of our own courts.

[5] Sayre and Kaufman, *Governing New York City, op. cit.,* p. 522.

Judges bringing pressure to bear and being vulnerable to pressure —surely these are not the marks of a "good' judicial system? Questions of good or bad aside for the moment, one fact cannot be escaped: placing power in the hands of judges invites the use of pressure. A judge in a Southern community, possessing the power to rule for or against segregation, feels the pressure of his community even if the local citizenry can in no way affect his tenure. "The judge can never forget," says Jack Peltason, writing about the lonely and vulnerable spot of the Southern judge ruling in a desegregation case, "that any action of his against segregation will threaten his easy and prestigious acceptance by the community."[6]

A judge presiding at the trial of an infamous defendant, charged, let us say, with the sadistic murder of a child, likewise feels the pressure of the community. Newspapers often ride a judge mercilessly when they feel he has used his discretion wrongly—by not being tough enough, for example. The applying of overt pressures in newspaper editorials and the playing up of a point of view in news stories are not uncommon. Judges, especially those subject to election (but by no means only those), can hardly ignore these pressures.

Interest groups have long used the "Brandeis brief" (originated by Justice Brandeis when he was an appellate lawyer and consisting of detailed economic and social evidence and argument to support the reasonableness of legislative judgment) to supplement their legal arguments.[7] Judges commonly participate in campaigns for court reform: they have been known to be interested in court patronage, and they sometimes display concern about judicial salaries in a discreet fashion. In short, there are ways in which judges use and are subject to the methods of pressure and persuasion. Most of these methods the public accepts, but there are others that are not acceptable, even though— strictly speaking—some of them may be legal (consulting with a state

---

[6] Jack W. Peltason, 58 Lonely Men, Southern Federal Judges and Desegregation (New York: Harcourt, Brace, and World, Inc., 1961), p. 9. A little later, speaking of "less gentle pressures," he says, "Judges who have issued antisegregation orders, however mild, have been forced to discontinue the public listing of their telephones to avoid anonymous and obscene telephone calls made round-the-clock" (p. 10).

[7] See the extended analysis of these methods in matters of desegregation by Clement Vose in his book, Caucasions Only (Berkeley, Calif.: University of California Press, 1959). See also his article, "Litigation as a Form of Pressure Group Activity," 319 Annals of the American Academy of Political and Social Science 20 (1958), and reprinted in Walter F. Murphy and C. Herman Pritchett, Courts, Judges and Politics (New York: Random House, 1961), pp. 283–94. See also Vose's article "Interest Groups, Judicial Review, and Local Government," 19 Western Political Quarterly 85 (1966).

party leader about a legislative apportionment case before the court, for example).

Apart from "pressure," however, the values and general political orientation of a judge has significance for the way he will react to issues before him. Stuart S. Nagel has demonstrated distinct partisan differences in voting tendencies of supreme court judges on fifteen kinds of cases. Particularly in matters of "administrative regulation of business, unemployment compensation cases and employees injury cases" he found a strong tendency for judges who were known to be Democrats to decide for the administrative agency and the workers, while Republicans showed an opposite tendency.[8] He adds that this does not indicate that "some judges consciously vote for or against a party line," rather it indicates general differences in the values of Democrats and Republicans that have significance in the courtroom as they have elsewhere.[9]

It should not be forgotten, when the politics of the judicial branch are considered, that the prosecution is part of the judicial process. And in most states the office of the prosecutor has been highly politicized. Indeed it is a stereotype of an office which will pay an ambitious politician the reward of publicity. The catalogue of famous political leaders whose careers were advanced by service as prosecutors is long and includes such figures as Senator Robert La Follette, Governor Thomas E. Dewey, and Chief Justice Earl Warren. A study some years ago of the prior careers of governors indicated that law enforcement careers were common in the backgrounds of governors who served between 1870 and 1950, and furthermore that the incidence of this increased in recent decades. Some fifty prosecutors of one kind or another had gone directly to the governor's chair.[10]

The prosecutor's office is not only a position from which to advance politically, however. It is a source of great political power—unhappily, a power sometimes misused. Since the prosecutor can decide

---

[8] Stuart S. Nagel, "Political Party Affiliation and Judges' Decisions," 55 *American Political Science Review* 843, 845 (1961). His sample includes 298 judges of supreme courts, both federal and state, but of course only nine of the judges were from the U.S. Supreme Court.

[9] *Ibid.*, p. 847.

[10] See Joseph Schlesinger's *How They Became Governor* (East Lansing, Mich.: Governmental Research Bureau of Michigan State University, 1957), p. 76. His data on law enforcement officers include judges and other officials (such as police commissioners) and gives no indication whether the prosecutor's office itself has had a comparable increase in incidence in gubernatorial backgrounds. See particularly Chap. 4. Schlesinger develops these points more fully in his *Ambition and Politics: Political Careers in the United States* (Chicago: Rand McNally, 1966), but he still does not distinguish prosecutors from other law enforcement officers. Note that high percentages of men later to be governors and U.S. senators served as law enforcement officials. Pp. 91–92.

whether to press a charge or not, he makes a quasijudicial decision before formal judicial proceedings open. His range of discretionary authority is enormous. Although he is subject to criticism if he uses this discretion in a flagrantly unfair way, the fact is that discovery of his misuse of power is exceedingly difficult. He can reject complaints, refuse to initiate a prosecution, give a one-sided case to a grand jury, or decide not to prosecute a case even if it is formally on the records (*nolle pros* is the legal term for such a decision). He also can bargain about presenting a lesser charge which may insure the likelihood of a conviction or may equally be used as favoritism. It is obvious too that during the conduct of the trial and in the sentencing of the convicted he has considerable opportunity to use his judgment—fairly or unfairly.

Thus political leaders may use pressure and persuasion to get the prosecutor not to prosecute at all or to reduce charges. The incidence of such intervention naturally varies with the political climate of a community. Prosecutors rationalize their exceptions by persuading themselves that the special "exceptions" are few among the numerous cases they handle. Moreover, if they receive a few requests from political friends, they are no less frequently asked to do exactly the same thing by ministers and other "proper" people in the community. The following comment from a politician-academic is worth a second thought in this connection:

I once asked a municipal judge in Middletown [writes Stephen K. Bailey who was once mayor of that Connecticut college town of 30,000], to tell me what pressures were most constant in trying to influence his impartial administration of justice. He thought a minute and then said, laughingly, "the university deans and the town clergy." But why should he have laughed? Certainly few would question the motives of deans and clergy in attempting to save the reputations of individuals known to them, and under their keep, who have been accused of wrong-doing. But what of the wrong-doer who has no "friend in court"? Anyone who has ever watched a municipal court in action over a period of time knows that "political influence" is frequently a corrective for the partial justice that results from the rich litigant's capacity to purchase superior legal talent. Middle-class justice is not always equitable to the poor. This is not to condone political influence in courts of law, it is to suggest that without political influence certain inequities might be greater than they are and that those inequities need as much attention as overt or covert political influence.[11]

---

[11] Stephen K. Bailey, "Ethics and the Politician" (Santa Barbara, Calif.: Center for the Study of Democratic Institutions, 1960), p. 5.

If the office lends itself to favoritism and unfair discrimination among those charged with crime, it is no less significant that defendants may be victimized by prosecutors eager to make a "record" of toughness and numerous convictions for the sake of political advancement. Thus a Texas prosecutor took the witness stand to testify that he had intentionally withheld from a trial information acquired in an interview with a witness to a murder which would have indicated mitigating circumstances that, under Texas law, would probably have spared the defendant a death penalty. He also admitted coaching the witness not to volunteer the information. The United States Supreme Court reversed the conviction, but one may assume this practice is not confined to this Texas prosecutor.[12] A southern prosecutor who showed too much sympathy for a Negro accused of crime would be endangering his political career—or, if he would not in fact be doing so, in many regions he might well assume that he was going to suffer political retribution.[13] Although the following is less true today than when Raymond Moley said it thirty years ago, there remains much truth in his judgment that ". . . the American prosecutor emerges as a completely political official."[14]

As the evidence of numerous crime surveys and legislative investigations proves, the political element does not end with the prosecutor's office: the police are involved too.[15] Crime, it is well to remember, is one of our largest national enterprises, involving hundreds of millions of dollars every year. (Frank Costello is said to have had an annual gross income in excess of $30 million from his personal gambling empire during the 1950's.) The Mafia in its multifarious activities, both legitimate and criminal, has many ways of winning official cooperation— and not just from policemen but from many highly placed officials. On more petty levels, however, there is a constant problem of keeping the police force "straight." The efficient, fair, and honest conduct of a police department is inevitably and constantly challenged by forces that tend to make it just the opposite: ineffective, unjust, and corrupt. For the policeman and the detective also have discretion-

---

[12] See *Alcorta* v. *Texas*, 355 U.S. 28 (1957).

[13] See Claude Sitton, "When a Southern Negro Goes to Court," *The New York Times Magazine*, January 7, 1962.

[14] Raymond Moley, *Politics and Criminal Prosecution* (New York: Minton, Balch and Co., 1929), p. 94. See also his *Our Criminal Courts* (New York: Minton, Balch and Co., 1930). John B. White, *Criminal Law in Action* (New York: Harcourt, Brace, and World, Inc., 1934), also presents a dated but, in many respects, still accurate picture of the criminal courts.

[15] See *Justice*, Report of the U.S. Commission on Civil Rights, 1961, Chaps. 2, 6, 8.

ary powers that they exercise beyond the public view. Moreover, the restraints of professional ethics which condition the behavior of a judge are likely to be less important where a policeman is concerned. This is not to say that a policeman's loyalty to his job and departmental *esprit* are unimportant—on the contrary, they are more likely to be decisive. But the policeman is often underpaid and deals with sordidness and corruption as a daily routine, thus he faces the strongest temptations to sell his discretion to those who can buy it. Given the strains to which their integrity is regularly put, the surprising thing is not that some succumb but that more do not.[16] There are, it is true, signs of hope in the improved training (including college programs) of policemen, but the improvements are counterbalanced by deteriorating and crime-inducing conditions in central urban areas that complicate the task of even the most superbly equipped (mentally and otherwise) police officers.

Police forces are increasingly a political problem in cities with a substantial Negro population for the obvious reason that the police stand as representatives of a society with which a significant part of the black community is at war. Police have not treated Negroes the same as whites, just as no other part of the white community has treated Negroes the same as whites. As a result, the police are feared and hated by Negroes—even while they desperately need the police to protect them from the rampant crime of the ghetto. Brutality by policemen may not be as universal as some Negroes maintain, but neither is it as nonexistent as some police officials claim; it has been enough of a fact of life to help trigger many, perhaps most, of the riots of recent years. So antagonistic toward the police are many black persons that a minor traffic incident can trigger a riot as happened in Watts in 1965 (and the year before in Philadelphia). It is inconceivable that these attitudes toward policemen are figments of the imagination.

One attempt to limit the brutality of police has been the police review board, an agency outside the police force through which charges of brutality can be processed. But the police stanchly oppose such agencies and have largely succeeded in defeating them. In New York City in 1966 an intensive campaign of propaganda against a review board succeeded in defeating it in a referendum. The keynote of the campaign was "safety in the streets," and because the review board was fixed in the public mind as an impediment to the effectiveness of the

---

[16] See the comment of the late William H. Parker, once Los Angeles' Chief of Police, in *The Police* (Santa Barbara, Calif.: Center for the Study of Democratic Institutions, 1962).

police in providing that safety it is not surprising that the board lost out, despite its illustrious supporters. It is interesting to note that there was considerable support for the police and antagonism for the board in some Negro neighborhoods, presumably reflecting the greater fear of criminals than the police.[17]

Another possible channel for appeal from the police and other forms of official abuse is the ombudsman. In Scandinavia the office of ombudsman has existed for about a century. His function is to hear any and all complaints about the behavior of public servants, to investigate the charges, and if they prove accurate, to recommend corrections. Britain has installed an ombudsman with limited powers as have some other Commonwealth nations, and it is being urged in American states and cities. It has been tried in Nassau County on Long Island, New York, where a former judge served from May 1966 until the experiment was ended by referendum in 1967. Although the police were specifically not within the jurisdiction of the Nassau County ombudsman, the police nevertheless campaigned against it and may thus have contributed to its defeat.[18]

State and local police agencies have been forced by the U.S. Supreme Court to alter their procedures in criminal investigation and prosecution. Each of these cases has raised an outcry that criminals are being coddled, that the hands of the protectors of society are being tied at the very time when crime is booming, that the courts are permitting "legal jailbreak" and the like. Coddling or not, however, the Supreme Court has set some new standards for criminal law at the local and state levels.

---

[17] See also Joseph Lyford, *The Airtight Cage* (New York: Harper & Row, 1966), p. 280, where he comments on an attitude survey in a New York neighborhood which indicated little feeling of antagonism about brutality and much concern about the lack of protection. This does not appear to me to be in contradiction to the observation that there is resentment about brutality. Given the conditions of the ghetto it is quite conceivable that the average person would be more concerned about his personal safety than the likelihood that he would be abused by the police. Evidence of considerable antagonism toward the police is found in overt behavior at scenes of ghetto arrests. As one Irish cop told Lyford, "A white policeman is crazy to get involved in a tough situation if he is in a Negro or Puerto Rican slum area. The experienced cop will tell the young cop to move on. . . . It's not that a white man doesn't want to help a black man, but the people the cops are trying to help turn them against them" (p. 293). See also the evidence from the Watts riot in Robert Conot, *Rivers of Blood, Years of Darkness* (New York: Bantam Books, 1967). For an account of police station confession extortion, see C. P. Crow, "Justice of Sorts," *The Reporter*, December 14, 1967, pp. 37–41.

[18] *The New York Times*, November 20, 1966, and November 8, 1967. See for general discussion of the office, Walter Gellhorn, ed., *Ombudsmen and Others: Citizen Protectors in Nine Countries* (Cambridge; Harvard University Press, 1966), and Stanley V. Anderson, ed., *Ombudsmen* (Englewood Cliffs, N.J.: Prentice-Hall, Inc., 1968).

For example, it has ruled that a person charged with a crime must be provided counsel at public expense if he lacks the funds to hire one for himself. The Court also held that the state may not use in a trial evidence illegally seized (holding the state to the same rules under the Fourth Amendment that apply for U.S. trials). Then it held in 1964 that a person who was being questioned in a murder investigation must be given the opportunity to talk with an attorney when he requests it, particularly when he is not informed that he has the right to remain silent if he so desires. Then two years later in a somewhat similar case the Court went still further, holding that a suspect must be informed of his right to remain silent and must be given the opportunity to have an attorney present during an investigation.[19] Reversals of convictions on these and other grounds have led to angry complaints from state judges, prosecutors, and police officials, not to mention state's rights politicians in general. For the most part, however, these rulings merely hold lower courts and police to the same rules of conduct as are provided for federal courts and investigators. And the evidence is not at all conclusive that the new standards where confessions are concerned will greatly reduce the ability to convict the guilty. Some judges and scholars have contended that the interference will be negligible, although the police may have to labor harder to find evidence when the accused does not confess. Judgment on this will have to await more experience, but clearly there is some risk of not gaining convictions of guilty persons just as conversely there is less risk of convicting the innocent.

In recognition of the interrelated problems of bench, bar, and police practice, the American Bar Foundation is currently undertaking a major study of the administration of criminal law. Their preliminary research suggests several tentative observations: that there is a wide range of variation in practice among cities, that major shortcomings exist in some aspects of criminal justice, and that some notable progress has been made toward solving the problems that were chronic a few decades ago. Although there are certainly grave problems in the areas of the investigation, apprehension, prosecution, trial and post-trial management of the criminally accused and/or convicted person, the facts presented in the lengthy seven-volume preliminary survey give ground for believing that the deplorable conditions of a few decades ago are now less prevalent.[20]

---

[19] The four cases cited were *Gideon* v. *Wainwright,* 372 U.S. 335 (1963); *Mapp* v. *Ohio,* 367 U.S. 643 (1961); *Escobedo* v. *Illinois,* 378 U.S. 478 (1964); and *Miranda* v. *Arizona,* 384 U.S. 436 (1966).

[20] I refer to the mimeographed and privately circulated "Pilot Project Report" of the American Bar Foundation, entitled "The Administration of Criminal Justice

Judges, "Independent" or "Representative": A Judicial Paradox

There is something ironic about American attitudes toward the judiciary. We speak of an independent judiciary as one of the notable achievements of American government, yet in practice much has been done that undermines its independence. Hence the paradox: we have great respect for the judiciary and have sought to insulate judges from routine political pressures, but at the same time we have thrust them into the political arena. Although the American judge has a broader range of discretionary power than the judges of other nations, the very obverse of independent discretion—popular election of judges—is common here but unknown elsewhere. If, on the one hand, our constitutionalism involves a heavy judicial element and therefore unusual judicial authority, the exercise of that sweeping power invariably calls forth demands for curbing the judicial branch. Popular sovereignty slogans, fired at the bastions of judicial independence, have frequently hit their targets with telling effect.

Perhaps it is the very fact that judges have such broad political power that has made easier the application of popular sovereignty ideas —through popular election, short terms of appointment, and the drawing of judges from the ranks of political lawyers rather than through the development of a more bureaucratic cadre of judicial expertise as is common in Europe. No doubt a major role in "politicizing" the selection of judges belongs to party politicians who aimed at control over offices and patronage rather than restraints on judicial discretion. Nevertheless, politicians often achieved their objectives, one may reasonably infer, because the proposals were in harmony with popular sentiments.

The late Chief Justice of the New Jersey Supreme Court, Arthur T. Vanderbilt, once argued that it has been the "American way" to vest the protection of basic constittuional rights in a judiciary "not subject to any pressures, even those of the people." "While at times," he wrote, "some have questioned whether the judiciary should be independent of popular control in a democracy, the need of such independence seems self-evident for the protection of individual and minority

in the United States," which includes studies made in Wisconsin, Michigan, and Kansas. Two parts of the project have now been published under the editorship of Frank J. Remington. See Wayne R. La Fave, *Arrest* (Boston: Little, Brown, 1965) and Donald Newman, *Conviction* (Boston: Little, Brown, 1966).

rights."[21] This was more self-evident to Vanderbilt than it has been to many distrustful and aggrieved pleaders for restraints on the judiciary. In one sense to say that the courts are "not subject to pressures" runs contrary to demonstrable fact. It is, after all, a fact that the predominant means of selection of judges in four out of five states is election; indeed, only in seven states in the Northeast, two in the South, and in Hawaii are more judges appointed rather than elected.

Chief Justice Vanderbilt recognized the pressure implications of direct election of judges, of course, and was indeed arguing (in the context of the remarks quoted above) for appointment rather than election. Nor was he any stranger to political life in view of his deep involvement in New Jersey politics. Yet the argument he advanced for total independence lacks realism unless it be taken as a plea against direct and extensive involvement by judges in routine political affairs— in effect, political party leadership from the bench. This is probably what he did mean, and yet taken at face value his words are far more sweeping and unqualified.

Pressure will be present in some form or degree, regardless of how judges are chosen. The point is that pressure, where the judiciary is concerned, is different from pressure in other parts of government. The awesome regalia of the judge, the deferential language of the court, the respect for judicial privacy, the code of secrecy that prevails where judicial decision-making is concerned, and the many centuries of tradition of judicial behavior sustained by the "canons" of the bar associations—these and many other facets of the American judiciary set it apart from other institutions. Even where judges are elected, their campaigns are usually in a lower key, more restrained and aloof than ordinary campaigning.[22]

So strong are these traditions that the pressurer hesitates to approach a judge or does so as discreetly as possible. And the judge in turn tends to become unapproachable. As Chief Justice Vanderbilt himself said, "The Common law tradition of independence has resulted by and

---

[21] *Judges and Jurors: Their Functions, Qualifications and Selection* (Boston: Boston University Press, 1956), p. 50.

[22] Evidence confirming this is presented by Claude J. Davis from a questionnaire sent to West Virginia judges. About half of his respondents appear to have done little campaigning; only 14 of the 52 replying made speeches and only 12 used newspaper advertising. See his *Judicial Selection in West Virginia* (Morgantown, W. Va.: Bureau for Government Research of West Virginia University, 1959), p. 38. Further evidence is presented by E. W. Bashful in his *The Florida Supreme Court: A Study in Judicial Selection* (Tallahassee, Fla.: Bureau of Governmental Research, 1958), Chap. 3. "Incumbents," he writes, "have regarded it as below the dignity of the court to wage a campaign for office in which bitter attacks were made on the personal and professional integrity of their opponents" (p. 38).

large in good judges [notwithstanding the prevalence of direct election]
being the usual matter and exceptions being rare, especially at the
higher levels."[23] In fact, it has turned out that there have been recorded
unexpectedly good performances by judges whose appointments were
tainted by dubious influences. "One judge," according to Adolph Berle,
"whose appointment was at least partially forwarded by the famous
underworld character, Frank Costello (at all events, the judge thought
so), has turned in an unexceptional record of judicial probity."[24] Traditional respect for the judicial office has its effect on the judge—the
donning of the judicial robe casts its spell. He will be very circumspect
about the company he keeps, fearing always that the finger of suspicion
will be pointed at him, thereby robbing him of his air of neutrality
that he feels he must maintain. The comments of Judge Bernard Botein
make the point well:

Where and with whom to lunch . . . poses a problem for judges. . . . A
judge is sometimes embarrassed when he enters a public restaurant without
a luncheon companion. Someone is bound to sing out, "Are you alone,
Judge? Why don't you join us?"

"Us" may include some persons unknown to the judge. He may be
asked to sit with a person of dubious repute. . . . A judge is especially sensitive
to certain externals. He is animated only partly by a desire to shield his own
reputation; he also strives constantly to sustain public confidence in the
court system. . . .[25]

Though a judge may avoid "pressure" in any direct way, he may
nevertheless be covertly subjected to it. Inasmuch as the judiciary has
broad power to make public policy, organizations of various kinds make
every effort to combine their forces when they come to the judicial
phase of a struggle over policy making. Because stalling and modification of policy through appeals are so easy in American law, and because high-priced legal talent may affect a decision, it pays to use the
courts to try to win a payoff. And all kinds of groups do so, as Clement
Vose, among others, has pointed out. He points out that many important issues of municipal law are hammered out by the National Institute of Municipal Law Officers (commonly called NIMLO) and
carried by it through the levels of the judicial hierarchy. In zoning law

---

[23] *Ibid.*

[24] Adolph Berle, "Elected Judges or Appointed?" *The New York Times Magazine*,
December 11, 1955.

[25] Bernard Botein, *Trial Judge* (New York: Simon & Schuster, Inc., 1952), pp.
320–21. See particularly Chap. 18 on "Influence and the Courts."

and many other municipal matters NIMLO comes to the aid of municipalities, and so do other interested parties. In one case cited by Vose involving acreage zoning *amici curiae* briefs were filed with the Pennsylvania Supreme Court by two suburban towns, the Pennsylvania Local Government Conference, the Pennsylvania Planning Association and a wealthy lawyer from the town in question.[26] While the presentation of supplemental briefs does not assure victory—especially when the other side has the money and support to do likewise—it is clear that organized, coordinated, and expensive efforts are devoted to influencing judicial decisions in legal and aboveboard fashion.

Disorder in the Court?

Every year several million pieces of litigation originate in state and local courts—how many, no one knows exactly.[27] The range of subjects involved almost defies categorization: heinous crimes, brawls over grandfather's estate, the validity of a sewer tax levy, a divorce suit, commitment of the insane, and so on *ad infinitum*. The network of courts that adjudicate these myriad cases is a nightmare of diversity and dissimilarity—especially to the tidy of mind for whom the confusion of names and organizational structure are an affront. State court systems have been unusually resistant to change, consequently the structure of courts are often ill-adapted to the needs of the litigant—the question, that is to say, is more than one of logical orderliness. A student of the marvelously diverse state judicial systems said: "In 1950 state courts had about the same structure and powers as they had one hundred years before. They presented a notable example of the toughness of our legal institutions as contrasted with the movement that went on in substantive policy."[28] Partly as a consequence of this the United States has proportionately far more judges than other nations; judicial offices are rarely abandoned but are supplemented from time to time.

In order to discuss the operational and political significance of the

---

[26] Vose, "Interest Groups, Judicial Review . . . ," *op. cit.*, p. 90.

[27] James W. Hurst cites an estimate made in 1933 of about a million cases in courts of general jurisdiction and "many millions in minor courts" in *The Growth of American Law* (Boston: Little, Brown & Co., 1950), pp. 170–71. In New Jersey alone, during the 1958–59 court term some 600,000 cases—exclusive of parking violations—were handled. More than 160,000 civil cases alone were instituted. See the detailed *Annual Report of the Director of the Courts* (Trenton, N.J., 1959), p. 3.

[28] James W. Hurst, *The Growth of American Law*, *op. cit.*, p. 88.

structural arrangements of American state and local courts, it is necessary first to say something rather specific about the kinds and interrelationships of existing court systems so as to clarify terminology and present a general sketch of the court system for those unfamiliar with its contours. The following rough outline may serve that purpose.[29]

Strictly speaking there are no local courts. All courts, except federal ones, are subject to state legislative control, and apply state and local law subject to higher state court review. Yet, paradoxically, the structure of our court system is oriented toward the locality. Judges for courts with very limited jurisdiction are local judges in the sense that they are often locally chosen, and that they serve small areas. This is the usual arrangement for courts of very limited jurisdiction: Justice of Peace court, Mayor's court, police court, recorder's court, municipal court— the terminology is richly varied.[30]

These courts represent the bottom of the judicial hierarchy; above them are other courts of original jurisdiction (as opposed to appellate jurisdiction) which cover wider geographical areas and wider subjects of jurisdiction. Next, in many states are intermediate or regional appellate courts that hear appeals from lower courts, although in most states there is a single intermediate appellate court that hears nothing but appeals. In the more populous states the single appeals court is separated into "divisions," accomplishing essentially the same end as the regionally or otherwise divided appellate courts.[31] Above all these courts, of course, is the court of last resort of the state, usually called the supreme court. Appeal from the state supreme court can only be to the United States Supreme Court and then only if the loser presents a federal question (under either the United States Constitution or federal statutes) of sufficient significance, in the opinion of at least four of its nine members, to warrant the attention of the Court.[32]

Among state courts there are many kinds of distinction beyond those

---

[29] *Ibid.*, Chap. 5, and Lewis Mayers, *The American Legal System* (New York: Harper & Row, 1955), Chap. 2 and pp. 55–79 fill in the background of our state judicial institutions very well. Henry J. Abraham's *Courts and Judges* (New York: Oxford University Press, 1959), provides a useful guide to terminology.

[30] See the publication of the Council of State Governments on "State Court Systems," 1960 edition, Table 1, for a listing of state courts. The number of kinds of courts ranges from three or four in a few exceptional states to eight or more in 17 states. See *Martindale-Hubbell Law Directory*, Vol. III (Summit, N.J.: Martindale-Hubbell, Inc., issued annually), for annual review of court structure of individual states, brief description of jurisdiction of all courts.

[31] See Mayers, *op. cit.*, pp. 76–79, for a brief but useful survey of appellate courts.

[32] Sometimes review of an appeal is not left to the discretion of the Supreme Court but is mandatory. These, however, are now rare cases.

of hierarchy and jurisdiction. Some courts consider only criminal matters, while others consider only civil disputes (which may be between governments, between governments and individuals, or between individuals, and involves either a court order aimed at redressing some wrong or an order—called an injunction—to prevent the carrying out of an act that will cause irreparable harm to some party). Some courts sit both as civil and criminal courts—but never simultaneously, of course.

Other courts have highly specialized jurisdiction. Some consider only matters pertaining to juveniles, usually doing so in less formal ways than those used by ordinary courts so as to emphasize correction of the problems of the delinquent rather than punishment as is (rightly or wrongly) the emphasis in courts for adults. Some states have instituted family courts, which take the problems of the family and treat them on a unified basis rather than parcel out to various courts the actually interrelated problems of, for example, juvenile delinquency, divorce, guardianship of children who are orphans or neglected, and alimony payments. Probate courts consider matters of estates and the settlement of wills. Other specialized courts and some administrative agencies that verge on being courts (agencies for determining workman's compensation cases, for example) exist in various states. Thus each state has its unique system of court structure, jurisdiction, procedure, and terminology.

The scope and volume of judicial business has grown enormously in the last half-century, and the difficulties of a judicial system resistant to change and often subject to jerry-built additions here and there without regard to rational structure have become more evident. It is therefore not surprising that there have been demands by legal and other groups for revision of the court system. Reformers have emphasized—and perhaps overemphasized—the difficulties of jurisdictional complexity and the general untidiness of judicial organization. Overlapping jurisdiction, a multiplicity of courts the supposed judges of which are sometimes woefully incapable of dealing competently with the questions that come before them, undue expense of court proceedings, and opportunities for extended delay as cases get caught in the intricacies of an elaborate network of courts—such are some of the indictments brought against the courts. Roscoe Pound, later to become Dean of the Harvard Law School and one of the century's great legal scholars, fired an opening shot (with no apparent direct effect) in a speech to the 1906 meeting of the American Bar Association on the 'causes of popular dissatisfaction with the administration of justice."[33]

---

[33] That speech is excerpted in Murphy and Pritchett, *Courts, Judges and Politics, op. cit.*, pp. 41–46.

Before looking at organized efforts that have been made to reorganize the court systems of the states—efforts which reveal much of the political essence of the courts—it would be well to assay first some of the shortcomings that are said to characterize courts today. First, it is said that the delay in getting decisions in cases is unduly long. Second, it is argued that the jury system and some other aspects of the typical American court inhibit rather than facilitate fair trials. Third, it is charged that justice is often prohibitively expensive for the wronged party in a civil suit or the defendant in a criminal trial. Fourth, it is claimed that the courts are assigned impossible tasks to perform. Fifth, it is alleged that the methods of choosing judges are such that incompetence or worse is to be expected all too often on the bench.

1. *Delay in the Courts.* "Justice delayed is justice denied." The ancient adage is no mere homily but a statement of bitter fact. A litigant who must wait months or even years before his case can be heard is often placed in a difficult position. Consider the plight of a person, injured through the negligence of another, disabled and therefore unemployed and facing heavy medical bills, but utterly unable to get court action. He is pushed to make a settlement—a less than equitable one perhaps—rather than wait for a just verdict.

There are many jurisdictions in which just this kind of situation faces litigants—often the delay in bringing a civil case to trial (particularly if the plaintiff seeks a jury trial which may be his right but may put him still farther down the waiting list) is to be counted not in months but years. Some New York court calendars in recent years have been so crowded that a delay of more than five years was possible. A 1958 survey of the calendars of some 100 courts indicated an average delay of 6 to 19 months before cases could be brought to trial. The delay was greatest in populous metropolitan counties (in some counties with over 750,000 population the wait might be in excess of four years, with an average of 18.8 months), while in smaller counties it was less (in those under 500,000 population the average delay was just under six months).[34] Imagine the difficulty in getting reliable testimony about events that transpired two to five years previously. Memories are fickle, witnesses die or disappear. Injustice results and the prestige of the courts inevitably suffers.

Why these delays? In one sense the answer is simple: we are given

---

[34] "State Trial Courts of General Jurisdiction, Calendar Status Study—1958" (New York: Institute of Judicial Administration, New York University, 1958), p. ii. The survey covers a six-year period and indicates a gradual decline in length of delay. Ten years later, however, the problem continues to be severe in many jurisdictions.

to suing each other about everything imaginable. Suits are brought for an infinite number of reasons—for political reasons (over voting rights, election frauds, or to stop a governmental action), for reasons of recovery for negligence, over property disputes, contractual obligations, and a thousand other reasons. But the main cause of the log jam in the courts is the automobile negligence case. About half of all civil cases are automobile negligence suits, where somehow responsibility for an accident must be ascertained and compensation set for the losses to the injured party. With over a hundred million licensed drivers on the highways and over a million accidents per month it is no surprise that the courts of the nation are overburdened.

But why not simply increase the number of judges and eliminate the backlog of cases? This has been proposed and tried in some states, but the backlog has not disappeared.[35] In New Jersey between 1949 and 1967 the number of judges handling civil cases was doubled but the number of civil cases increased by four and one-half times. See Figure 15-1. In addition to the simple increase in number of cases, the backlog problem is also caused by the unavailability of lawyers to try cases. This is not a problem of shortage of trial lawyers but a result of the capacity of a few lawyers to corner the market in negligence cases. Once a lawyer or law firm has gained a wide reputation for success in such cases, the prospective clients line up outside their doors; and as a consequence, assignment judges trying to set trial schedules have to battle with a pair of overworked lawyers who plead the necessity to be at other trials whenever the judge tries to set a date. The lawyers make loud noises about the injustice to their clients if the judge puts on pressure, and the inevitable consequence is postponement.

How can the problem be resolved? There is a solution, although it will cause so much dislocation of firmly fixed interests that it may never be tried. More and more critics of the automobile negligence problem are calling for the substitution of a simpler settlement procedure similar to the workman's compensation system. Instead of a person insuring himself against a charge of negligence he would insure himself against his own losses much as he does with his fire insurance. Then it would be unnecessary to determine the cause of the loss or

---

[35] Some years ago it was contended that the addition of just a few new judges in Manhattan—where delay is notoriously bad—would eliminate the backlog within a few years. But the rising rate of negligence suit generation doomed this proposition. Even doubling the number of judges in some other jurisdictions did not cut out the backlog. See Hans Zeisel, Harry Kalven, and Bernard Buchholz, *Delay in the Courts* (Boston: Little, Brown and Co., 1959).

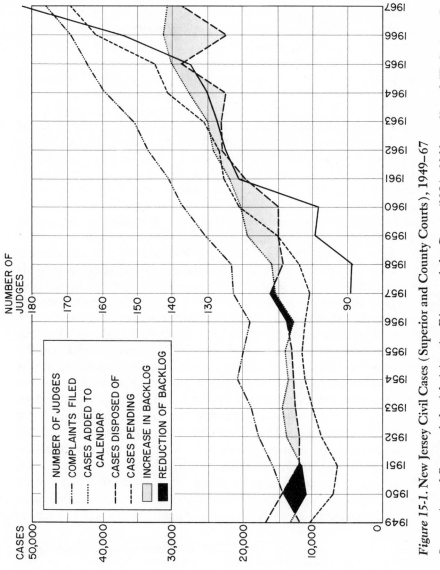

Figure 15-1. New Jersey Civil Cases (Superior and County Courts), 1949–67

Source: *Annual Report of the Administrative Director of the Courts* (N.J.), 1966, p. 69; and "Preliminary Report," 1967.

[441]

responsibility for it but only the amount of damage suffered.[36] Liability coverage might be retained for damages exceeding a certain amount— $10,000 has been suggested—but for amounts below that level a much quicker and ultimately fairer settlement would become possible. The proponents of the reform believe it will greatly reduce the cost of insurance and make it comparable to medical insurance plans where the ratio of premiums to amounts recovered in losses would be nearer to one-to-one rather than the two-to-one found in one study of automobile insurance. One thing is certain, however; by removing almost half of the civil cases from the docket a dramatic decrease in the backlog of cases would follow.

But this will be difficult to achieve for a number of reasons. For one thing some participants benefit from delay. As a result of long delay an insurance company may be able to reach a less costly settlement out of court where the pressure is heavily on the injured party to settle because he cannot afford to continue to sustain losses without compensation. Furthermore, the insurance fraternity is apprehensive about the uncertainties of the new proposal—fearful that high awards might result in ever higher premiums and equally or more frightened of the possibility that government itself might institute the new arrangement and leave only the liability element to the private insurance industry. It is true, however, that some of the more progressive companies have expressed interest in the new scheme and are investigating it. Another major source of resistance are lawyers who concentrate on negligence cases. Often these suits are taken on a contingency basis—that is, the lawyer gets a certain percentage of the award if he is successful, and the percentage can run from a quarter to a half of the amount. (Some of the most successful practitioners levy a further fee in addition to the contingency percentage to reduce their risk.) In any major metropolitan area this is a multimillion dollar annual income and the recipients are articulate, powerful, and very well placed to prevent this disaster. Finally, although a considerable number of persons inescapably are involved in the difficulties of negligence litigation each year, it remains difficult to mount a campaign for change. It is not a cause that arouses much emotional involvement—unlike the regulation of drugs, pure food, or even automotive safety—and as a result the advocates of reform

---

[36] For a brief account of the problem and more detail on the proposed remedy, see Daniel P. Moynihan, "Next: A New Auto Insurance Policy," *The New York Times Magazine*, August 27, 1967. See also Robert E. Keeton and Jeffrey O'Connell, *Basic Protection for the Traffic Victim: A Blueprint for Reforming Automobile Insurance* (Boston: Little, Brown, 1965).

face difficulty in mounting an attack on the formidable defenders of the status quo.

2. *Fair Trials.* It is sometimes true that the accused person is, for a number of reasons, put under unfair duress. Forced confessions, illegally gained evidence, perjured witnesses, and confused or prejudiced juries sometimes result in less than justice for the defendant. Public sentiment seems to sustain official use of illegal or unethical means of getting convictions where deep animosity toward the defendant seems to make any means acceptable to the end of vengeance.

In civil cases juries sometimes have to cope with highly technical questions of medicine or engineering for which they have no background, and accordingly it is claimed that civil juries are less an aid than an impediment to a fair trial. Thus Judge Frank made a strong case against the jury, arguing that it is neither competent to find facts nor able to comprehend the legal proceedings in which it participates. Juries, he contended, are likely to find facts to sustain the conclusion they wish to reach. "They determine that they want Jones to collect $5000 from the railroad company, or that they don't want pretty Nellie Brown to go to jail for killing her husband; and they bring in their general verdict accordingly."[37] The legal terminology of the lawyer and of the judge's instructions to the jury are beyond their comprehension, he claimed:

To comprehend the meaning of many a legal rule requires special training. It is inconceivable that a body of twelve ordinary men, casually gathered together for a few days, could, merely from listening to the instructions of the judge, gain the knowledge necessary to grasp the true import of the judge's words. For these words have acquired their meaning as the result of hundreds of years of professional disputation in the courts. The jurors are usually as unlikely to get the meaning of those words as if they were spoken in Chinese, Sanskrit, or Choctaw.[38]

In England and in Europe generally the jury has lost popularity and is rarely used. In this country the use of juries in civil cases has declined markedly. Use of the jury is no longer universal practice in criminal law. It is still the common means of trying a murder case, but in other matters waiver of the jury right is a common tendency. Jury trials tend to be longer, more expensive (although part of the expense is indirectly met by the hapless juror who sacrifices his normal income and serves at a nominal rate of pay), and in some kinds of cases not desirable from the

---

[37] Frank, *op. cit.*, p. 111.
[38] *Ibid.*, p. 116.

point of view of the defendant. There are also problems of the discriminatory selection of juries which are at times so serious as to cause
the reversal of a conviction.

Nevertheless, the trial jury still has its staunch defenders and not
alone from the ranks of the traditionalists who revere it more as an ancient
heritage than upon utilitarian grounds. Many defend it as an effective
way of getting mercy and the human element into the cold logic and
rigor of the judicial process; to them "trial by one's peers" is intrinsically
an important factor in a just trial. Murphy and Pritchett reflect this
point of view, saying that juries:

. . . inject a popular, nonprofessional element into the administration of
justice. Judges have their foibles, their prejudices, their professional biases.
Long-continued exposure to the criminal population may harden their sen-
sibilities. The system of punishment may itself be overrigorous and need
in application the ameliorating influence of laymen who reflect the opinions
of the time.[39]

No doubt a judge can develop a better capacity for ferreting out a
lie than can a juror, but it is an open question whether he will likely
be more insensitive than jurors to the plight of one who perhaps
deserves a "break." In any event it may safely be said that popular
sovereignty ideas (which the trial-by-peers argument reflects) are rein-
forcements here for both traditionalists and practical lawyers for plain-
tiffs who know very well that a jury is "good for" more money than a
judge when the plaintiff is a sweet humble widow and the defendant an
impersonal corporation.

3. *The Costliness of Justice.* The costs of litigating a claim are often
greater than the claim is worth, even when the claim runs to hundreds or

---

[39] Murphy and Pritchett, *op. cit.,* p. 316. See also Judge Botein, *op. cit.,* Chap.
13, "Jurors Are Nobody's Fools." In all candor, however, the Judge's evidence,
presented to sustain his favorable opinion of juries, leaves the impression that quite
frequently jurors are indeed somebody's "fools." That lawyers believe in and bank
on the gullibility of jurors is hardly to be denied, although one may dispute how
often emotionalism and trickery do in fact deceive. He presents a better case in
some respects in an article, "A Judge Votes for the Jury," in *The New York Times
Magazine,* September 11, 1960.

Some of the charges brought against the trial (petit) jury are also leveled at the
grand jury whose function it is to bring in a formal indictment, or accusation of
probable guilt, against a suspect. The grand jury, like the petit jury, is losing ground,
however, and in many states the "information" substitutes for the grand jury's
"indictment," and this merely involves the filing of a formal charge by the prosecutor. These details of procedure, interesting although they are, fall outside the
purview of the present subject and are not discussed here.

even thousands of dollars; the costs of defense in a criminal proceeding (and especially of appeal, should that be necessary) may be far beyond the means of a defendant. The major sources of expense are two: (1) the costs of the court as such (filing fees, witness costs) and (2) the costs of counsel and evidence (through the services of accountants, investigators, expert witnesses).[40] The first category of expenses is usually manageable, but the second may be prohibitive. Hiring well-qualified lawyers in a serious case may be the *sine qua non* of success, but expert counsel services are expensive (often $300 a day or more) precisely because they are expert and are in great demand.[41] Moreover, the costs of posting bail in criminal cases may be so high as to force the accused person into jail when he is even relatively poor. In recent years, as a result of experiments through the Vera Foundation of New York City, the New York police are finding that the release of many of the accused without bail is possible. By the mere process of a brief investigation of the person being held it becomes possible to ascertain who can reasonably be released and relied upon to show up for trial. Indeed it was discovered that the rate of failure to show up without bail was as good as the rate of failure and bond forfeiture in the pre-existing system.[42]

Several solutions to the problems of the costliness of justice are in operation but none is wholly satisfactory. Some states provide a public defender for the indigent and give him the necessary staff to conduct investigations and properly defend the accused, but such liberality is rare. Too often the public defender's office is starved for funds and all too often the only counsel the accused gets is the hurried assistance of an overworked and underpaid attorney who assists him in making a passable plea of guilty. But even where this system works well, or where lawyers through their bar associations undertake to provide assistance by rotating the burden of defending the indigent among themselves, the problem of conducting civil suits still remains. There are philanthropic legal aid societies, but these usually restrict their services to matters of small claims, or to questions most likely to arise for, say, a tenement dweller without funds—small loans, installment payments, unpaid wages, and the like. Not all cities have legal aid facilities, and many appear to operate on a provisional basis without full-time paid

---

[40] See Mayers, *op. cit.*, pp. 296–301 on the costs of court proceedings.

[41] See William M. Beaney, *The Right to Counsel in American Courts* (Ann Arbor, Mich.: University of Michigan Press, 1955), for a good review of the problems of providing counsel.

[42] See the testimony of Herbert Sturz, executive director of the Vera Foundation, before the U.S. Senate Subcommittee on Executive Reorganization, December 13, 1966, published in the Subcommittee's Hearings entitled, "Federal Role in Urban Affairs," part 13 pp. 27–40.

staff to take charge; some operate as law school clinics.[43] Under the anti-poverty program there have also been established a number of legal clinics for the poor, some of them so successful that they are deeply resented by the politicians they have attacked.

None of these solutions is adequate to the problem, or certainly none has been sufficiently developed to even the balance for the less well-off litigant. One need not be indigent in the strict sense for this to be a problem; the middle-income person with a legitimate case that may take years to settle and great sums of money to pursue properly is in a better position than the indigent person who seeks to recover unpaid wages, but the net result is not very different. One answer to the former problem—that of the person with a major suit to try but no funds to pursue it—is the contingency fee practice whereby the client agrees to split the money of the court's judgment with the attorney, who will forfeit his fee if the suit is lost. This practice can lead to obvious abuse when the ambulance-chasing lawyer exploits it, but it remains one way of coping with the problem of expense. Legal scholars insist that the costs of litigation—counsel fees, costs of presenting appellate briefs and records of lower courts and so on—are essentially irreducible. One lacking expertise in the law is hard-pressed to refute the argument, and yet it is common for critics to question the necessity of some of the practices of the bar and to doubt the utility of some judge-required or legally stipulated complexities that seem to serve no evident purpose. Yet it ought to be pointed out that part of the relatively higher costs of litigation in this country is the consequence of allowing a much wider opportunity for new trials and appeals with resultant emphasis at each step along the way on the possibility of establishing reversible error that may win an otherwise hopeless case. That is to say, trials are tests of the procedures of the court as much as of the substance of the case.

4. Judicial Assignment: The Impossible. As a result of tradition, default, or ill-fated expansion of jurisdiction, American courts entertain a great many kinds of cases for which they are notably unsuited. Of course, what a court is "suited" to do is hardly a clearly defined set of categories, but the practical problems of handling some kinds of cases are such that not a few judges and lawyers are beginning to raise questions about the capacity of courts to handle them.

Consider, for example, the criminal court dealing with gambling, narcotics, and alcoholism. The daily lineup before a city magistrate of the night-before haul of drunks from the streets is a sad spectacle. Judges

---

[43] Albert P. Blaustein and Charles O. Porter present a helpful, brief analysis of legal aid operations in their book, *The American Lawyer* (Chicago: University of Chicago Press, 1954), Chap. 3.

react differently to the human flotsam who stumble before them for judgment. Some judges joke with the familiar repeaters who are regularly dragged off the streets often more for their own safety than anything else. "Well, hello, Charlie; back again, hey?" police magistrates have been known to say. Fully recognizing the futility of thirty-day jail sentences, they nevertheless hand out such punishment—which of course does nothing toward solving the problems of the chronic alcoholic. Alcoholism in its chronic stages is not a judicial problem but a medical one, and yet in the police courts of the nation literally thousands of alcoholics parade past judges every day in a process that makes about as much sense as the passing across the stage of intentionally meaningless characters in an existentialist drama. The Vera Institute is also trying to do something constructive in this area. In late 1967 it instituted a program in which Bowery drunks (in Manhattan) are picked up by non-uniformed police, taken to a medical center where doctors, social workers, psychiatrists and others offer voluntary assistance. This may offer some hope for a solution.

The narcotics law violation may represent a more insidious form of crime, but the incapacity of courts to deal with the narcotics addict is no less evident. Jailing a person who has succumbed to narcotics will certainly not solve his problem. Although some progress has been made toward the treatment of addicts as medical rather than criminal cases, it remains true in most states and indeed to a considerable degree in every state that courts are called upon to handle narcotics problems that they are unable to cope with.

In matters of gambling, courts are often put on the spot, as are police officials, because the law requires them to suppress what the community does not wholeheartedly wish to suppress. A good proportion of the population gambles and will insist on doing so whatever the law may say. And to complicate the matter further, the state authorizes, and regulates, certain kinds of gambling. It draws millions in revenue from horse racing, but at the same time holds betting away from the tracks to be illegal. The public does not always see the distinction—nor does it want to see it, particularly in the case of such games of chance as bingo in which thousands of people participate and certainly see nothing wrong. States like New Hampshire and New York, which have lotteries, are trying to encourage gambling with one agency while trying to suppress it with another!

This is not an argument for legalizing all gambling, for it presents social evils of considerable moment that entirely transcend the argument that gambling is intrinsically sinful. But when the court is handed the task of coping with a problem, such as gambling, which the community

is not at all certain it wishes to curtail, the courts are placed in an unfortunate position. Like the efforts to enforce prohibition during the
1920's, the judiciary is unquestionably weakened when asked to perform
such a task, for its prestige is lowered, its discretion has to be stretched
to the maximum, and the invitation to corruption is all too tempting.

Finally, certain kinds of semiadministrative tasks are dumped into
the laps of the judges that might better be placed elsewhere. In zoning
matters, for example, and in other municipal questions the courts act
as arbiters. Often the judge is ill-equipped to handle such matters. Thus
at the federal level there is no doubt that the Supreme Court's assumption of responsibility for terminating segregation in the schools of the
South will greatly affect the role of the courts not only in the South but
elsewhere. The working methods of the judiciary are not well-suited to
the management of so difficult and complex a social engineering job as
the desegregation of schools. A convincing argument can be made for
having the courts undertake the task, particularly in view of the de-
faulting of other branches of the government, but the difficulty remains
for state and federal courts face handling such matters.

Although most social-legislation jurisdiction placed in state courts is
usually not so contentious as the segregation question, judges face many
cases for which they have little competence and in which they are in
effect invited to substitute their judgment for that of local officials or
administrators. The general distrust of bureaucrats and of local government in general has resulted in a heavy responsibility for judges who must
sit in review of administrative or local governmental decisions. Often
it is not just a question of statutory interpretation—although that
ostensibly is the occasion for the review—but of substitution of judgment. Tax and zoning appeals or suits to challenge the use of funds
are good examples of this practice. To have a court sit as a super-city
council is not necessarily a better way of handling local problems than
to leave them for local decision, and it certainly does not assist the courts
in measuring up more effectively to the tasks that are more traditionally
and obviously judicial in character.

5. *Selection of Judges.* Some years ago a committee of the American
Bar Association circulated among lawyers a questionnaire on "Judicial
Selection and Judicial Conduct," seeking to "determine, as far as possible,
the extent to which judges become parts of a political administration or
parts of a political hierarchy, because of the methods by which they are
appointed or elected."[44] The reporter of the results of the inquiry, a

---

[44] Philbrick McCoy, "Judicial Selection and Judicial Conduct, A Preliminary
Report of the Survey of the Legal Profession," 24 *Southern California Law Review*
1, 2 (1950).

judge in California observed that it seemed "evident from the replies to the questionnaire that the quality of justice and of judges . . . can be measured with some degree of certainty by the method by which a judge is selected."[45] The strange thing about the evidence cited in the judge's report, however, is that it completely refuted his argument. The article contained no evidence whatever to prove that the method of selection as such resulted in more or less competence, more or less "quality of justice and judges." There was ample evidence that in some respects the courts of the various states fell short on one or another of the "Canons of Judicial Ethics," but the pattern of shortcomings indiscriminately

To prove that the method of choosing judges has either a deleterious included states with all kinds of selection systems—election, appointment by governors, by legislators, and various combinations of these. or salutary effect on the quality of justice is by no means a simple undertaking. Too often promoters of one method of choosing judges use as an illustration of a good method the excellent judges in a given state and as evidence of bad methods the poor judges of another state. This, on the surface, would seem to be a quite sensible way of making inferences about the matter, but on further examination the "proof" seems less convincing. For the choice of examples of good and bad judges (leaving aside for the moment the difficulties of evaluating judicial qualities) are often quite unsystematic or biased samples that prove nothing. Moreover, even if greater care is exercised in drawing a sample of illustrative judges, there remains a problem of demonstrating that the method of judicial selection is the crucial variable. How is one to sort out the relative influence of the general political milieu of the state as differentiated from the method of choice? In hard fact, it is exceedingly difficult to be certain that any one method will produce better judges, yet the great American fascination with gimmicks of governmental procedure has led to heavy emphasis on means of choice. Consequently there has been much reasoning of the *post hoc, ergo propter hoc* sort in writing on the subject.

Does it follow then that the method of choice is irrelevant? Not at all; it is rather a factor to be weighed within the context of other factors conditioning judicial conduct. Any system of choice should be evaluated by the manner in which it works in practice, for often apparently different systems work similarly and vice versa. Thus an election system that involved the nomination of judges during party conventions and relatively uncontested general elections may resemble an appointment system more than it does an election system with open, personal-appeal

---

[45] *Ibid.*, p. 5.

campaigns by judges in nonpartisan elections. In short, the key is not the way the selection system is organized but the way it operates.

In roughly four out of five states judges are chosen in some kind of election rather than by appointment, although the methods of election vary greatly from state to state. Some elections are partisan, some non-partisan; some judicial offices are presented on separate ballots or even at separate elections, while others are listed with the rest of the ticket in general elections.[46] Often in practice there is no contest for judicial offices since the parties agree to double endorsements of judicial candidates. Whatever the system's details, there is always a potential for political pressure on the judge since in all systems he runs the gantlet of popular approval at the polls. The following comment from a judge who felt pressures upon him to decide judicial questions favorably toward potential supporters in his campaign for re-election may overstate the case, but in the rough and ready politics of West Virginia it may not be so out of the ordinary:

All in all, it's a harrowing experience to have to go through a political campaign for a judgeship to succeed yourself when you have arrived at an age that any thought of trying to practice law again is frightening and after you have given so many years to being neutral that your skill as an advocate has all but left you, and when you have held an office that does not, because of the smallness of the salary, permit you to build up an estate to tide you on, and when you have developed the fault of being so proud that it would be repulsive to you to beg or sell pencils on the street. You reach the place where you could well feel that you just had to win. And this is not a whole-some attitude to be in for one has to maintain his dignity and equilibrium in all areas of being fair and unprejudiced.[47]

In practice, it appears that the chances of a judge's being cut down at the polls are not very great. The incumbent often is not challenged within his own party for the nomination and when the general election comes the incumbent's standing as a judge seems to sustain him against challengers, if indeed there is one. The data in Table 15-1 on judicial elections in Kansas demonstrate this point. Incumbents running for re-election in the period from 1930 to 1956 apparently faced little chance of defeat:

---

[46] See Evan Haynes, *Selection and Tenure of Judges* (Boston: Little, Brown, & Co., 1944); Arthur Vanderbilt, *op. cit.*, pp. 32–51; and for a thumbnail sketch of current methods, see the latest volume of the *Book of the States*.

[47] Davis, *op. cit.*, p. 37.

TABLE 15-1
Incumbent Judges Facing Contests in Two Kansas Courts, 1930–56*

| | Total Number of Incumbents | Number Opposed in | | Number Defeated in | |
		Primaries	General Elections	Primaries	General Elections
Supreme Court:	29	4	26	0	2
District Court:	309	34	86	9	13

* Research Department, Kansas Legislative Council, Publication 211, "Selection of Judges," 1956, pp. 17–20. The data indicate that the extent of competition for judicial office has declined over the years. In the elections between 1908 and 1928 the percentage of incumbents defeated in both primary and general elections was 14.3 per cent; in the period from 1930 through 1956, the rate was 7.1 per cent. See Davis, *op. cit.*, pp. 29–30, on the degree to which candidates for judicial office were opposed in West Virginia in the 1952 election (slightly more than half had no general election opposition).

Even small risk of defeat, however, can unsettle the calm demeanor of a judge who desperately wants to hold his job. There appears to be a general inclination for judges to avoid highly contentious cases shortly before their re-election, but even with due caution the possibility does exist of becoming the object of a newspaper crusade for tougher decisions, or the object of political pressures of other sorts. It is the possibility of such events that are regularly cited as the prime reason for abandoning the election system and the substituting of appointment or some combination of appointment and election to minimize the chances of undue pressure. Appointment, may not, however, remove pressure, although it may in some cases make it less obvious.

The most widely heralded method of escaping political pressures in the selection process is the so-called Missouri system which involves appointment of judges by the governor from a list of names submitted to him by a commission composed of judges, members of the bar, and laymen appointed by the governor. After a judge has been appointed and has served for a time, his name is placed on the ballot and the voters decide whether or not he should be retained in office for a regular term. He has no opponent—the voter merely checks "yes" or "no." Continuance in office for successive terms is acquired by placing the judge's name on subsequent ballots. First approved in 1940, the system appears to be generally approved, although it is significant that it has been restricted to the upper-level courts and those courts of the metropolitan regions of the state; all efforts to extend the system to other

Missouri courts have failed. There are complaints that a judge in effect gets a life term since it next to impossible to defeat a man with no opponent running against him. Only one judge has ever been defeated under this procedure. In California where a roughly similar system is in effect for upper-level courts, no judge has been defeated since the institution of the plan in 1934. Of course, whether this is grounds for complaint depends upon the point of view; seekers after long and un-disturbed tenure would hardly count this a disadvantage, but the person who wishes some public participation in judicial selection and inevitably therefore some public pressure on the judge may not be satisfied with this aspect of the system.

It is also said that the governor of Missouri tends to appoint from the list only candidates from his own party, which is hardly occasion for surprise, although to the ardent advocate of absolutely nonpartisan choice it is grounds for concern. In fact, however, there does appear to be a tendency for governors to go outside their own parties, especially in recent years, just as presidents usually choose their federal judges from their own parties but often sprinkle in members of the opposition.[48]

The last point made—that even the Missouri system tends to result in judges who are from the "right party"—is significant and revealing. For the almost inescapable conclusion is that a political system and a political tradition such as ours tends to turn judicial offices in some degree into partisan offices. The prospect would be brighter for reforming the Ameri-can judiciary into a panel of neutral experts, like the judge-technicians of Europe, if our courts resembled those of Europe more than they do. So long as our courts are involved in quasilegislative activities in the final determination of public policy, we will tend to reinforce—not to undermine—the tradition of politically accountable judges as opposed to independent-expert judges.

Adolph Berle is essentially correct when he argues that "both the

---

[48] See Jack W. Peltason's excellent study of the campaign to initiate this new system in his monograph, "The Missouri Plan for the Selection of Judges," 20 *University of Missouri Studies* (1945). The bitterest opposition came from the members of the bar who may have felt that their chances of getting on the bench would not be enhanced by the change. See also William J. Keefe's article, "Judges and Politics: The Pennsylvania Plan of Judge Selection," 20 *University of Pitts-burgh Law Review* 621 (1959). This is the Missouri system, appropriately restyled by the state Bar Association when it was approved by them for Pennsylvania in 1947; Keefe used a questionnaire to find out the attitudes of legislators and judges about the proposed system. In essence they do not like it—both judges and legis-lators registered heavy majorities in favor of continuing direct election. The Alaska constitution adopted the Missouri system essentially, but progress elsewhere has been meager.

appointive and the elective methods really mean that judges are chosen by the chieftains of the political parties. . . ."[49] We may move away from this slightly with such schemes as nonpartisan elections and the Missouri plan, but even these devices must operate within the political milieu of a state and in all fifty states that means party systems of some kind. To illustrate the point, consider the refusal of California's judges to adopt all of Canon 30 of the Canons of Judicial Ethics. They refused specifically to endorse the rule that a judge should not seek any other office while sitting as a judge. Perhaps, says a commentator, this was due to a provision of the California constitution making it legal for certain judges to seek other offices, or perhaps it was "because the present lieutenant governor and the present mayors of Los Angeles and San Francisco were judges of the Superior Court when they were elected to their present offices. . . ."[50] Perhaps.

There is too much patronage at stake, even if nothing else were involved, for party politicians in most states to be unconcerned with judicial selection. Not only do judges control a great number of clerkships and other court positions, but some of the most lucrative of all patronage jobs are within the gift of the judge—temporary appointments as receivers, trustees, appraisers of estates, and so on.

Consider the job of an appraiser of deceased persons' estates. It is difficult to ascertain just what the practice is in the various states— statutes in 35 of the 50 states are silent on the point—but in many states appraisers of estates are paid a percentage of the total value of the estate, which—in the case of a million dollar estate—is a most interesting prospect to a lawyer or a real estate man. It is no accident that more states elect judges of probate courts than any other kind of judge, since in four of the states in which most judges are appointed the probate judge is on the ballot.[51] The elective status of the office is zealously defended by political organizations for the obvious reason that direct elections help protect a useful source of reward for the faithful. Speaking

---

[49] Berle, *op. cit.*, p. 26. Stuart Nagel (*op. cit.*, pp. 848–50) however, offers some evidence to suggest that appointed judges are somewhat less likely than elected ones to vote consistently with the "party patterns," although the reasons offered for the differences are largely speculative.

[50] McCoy, *op. cit.*, p. 20. It should be noted that California judges are elected on nonpartisan ballots, although it is not inconceivable that the serpent of ambition should enter California's nonpartisan paradise.

[51] That is, in Connecticut, Maine, South Carolina, and Vermont. After lengthy and utterly futile efforts to uncover more detail concerning judicial assignment of appraisers, I gave up; the data are apparently not readily available—perhaps for good reason.

of appointing receivers and comparable patronage posts, Judge Botein says:

In making many of these appointments most judges I know, including myself, accept and recognize recommendations from the party of their affiliation. They require that the person to be designated be honest and competent. Judges will also appoint friends on the same basis, and encourage deserving young lawyers by thus recognizing them.[52]

Suggestive of their involvement in party affairs are the state judges' frequent contributions to the party in campaign season; in some states judges are assessed (informally) a certain percentage of their salary as an annual contribution.[53] In New York City, according to Sayre and Kaufman:

A man who wants to be a judge must normally be a party insider, and, in addition, must be prepared in many cases to donate substantial sums of money to the organization of the appropriate party leader whose influence will be the chief factor in his nomination for appointment or election. . . . Clearly, one of the primary reasons the court system is of such profound concern to the parties is that this is where a part of their money comes from.[54]

Ambition for promotion, gratitude for having been helped to the bench by the party, and not infrequently a sense of general involvement with the party—all motivate the judge to reach for his checkbook when the organization calls for money.

In summary then, the judiciary has its political element in two senses: first, in that it constitutes and involves prizes and stakes that men compete for inevitably, and, second, that the judiciary has the authority to make decisions about important political questions. Political influence therefore will have something to do with the judiciary regardless of the method of choosing judges. In the last analysis the extent and methods of involvement of political influence in the courts depends largely on the kind of political system the community has. The traditions of the community, the public respect for the judge's office, the common code of behavior toward judges and of judges toward others—these are the forces that condition the political aspects of the judiciary.

---

[52] Botein, *op. cit.*, p. 311.

[53] McCoy (*op. cit.*, p. 27) quotes one of the respondents to the Bar Association poll of lawyers as saying, "All judicial candidates in Cook County [Chicago] make contributions to party funds; in fact they are assessed a per cent of their salaries."

[54] Sayre and Kaufman, *op. cit.*, pp. 542–43.

The Politics of Judicial Reform

Efforts to reform state court procedures and organization have been going on for at least half a century. Campaigns have been conducted by the American Bar Association, several specialized legal foundations and associations, many individual lawyers and jurists (like the late Chief Justice Vanderbilt of New Jersey who devoted much of his time during the last twenty years of his career to the study, practice, and promotion of court reform) and groups like the League of Women Voters. When the reform spirit has grown sufficiently in a state, ad hoc organizations are created to push reform in the legislature or through the various stages of constitutional reform.

What have these groups sought? Their objectives are essentially to achieve (1) simplification and unification of the court system, (2) improved administrative management of courts, (3) insulation of the courts from political influences, and (4) the concentration of the judicial system in fewer and more competently staffed courts (in effect an attack on the justice of peace and comparable courts of limited jurisdiction).

1. Simplification and Unification. The problem of complexity of American courts is not aided by the fact that ours is a dual court system following from the eighteenth-century decision to create a separate system of lower federal courts rather than depending upon state courts for federal proceedings as the constitution permitted and as some other federal nations have done. But apart from this complicating factor— and it can lead to serious difficulties for the unhappy individual whose case gets shunted back and forth between federal and state courts because judges cannot agree which has jurisdiction over the dispute[55]— there are ample sources of confusion in the haphazard organization of the courts of many states. The problem is that courts have been added on demand but rarely are abolished, partly because the possessors of the offices and their associates manage to protect their vested interest.

Overlapping jurisdictions make it uncertain to which court a litigant should go, and sometimes not even an experienced attorney can

---

[55] William W. Crosskey in his book, *Politics and the Constitution in the History of the United States* (Chicago: University of Chicago Press, 1953), pp. 25–27, cites the case of a railroad worker who lost a leg in an accident at the age of 22 and who appeared to have valid claim to compensation for the injury but whose case dragged from federal to state to federal courts until finally nine years later he was told that the statute under which it was ultimately determined he could get a remedy was no longer applicable as a result of expiration of the time during which application under it could be made. The case in *Chicago and Midwestern Railway v. Bolles*, 284 U.S. 74 (1931).

be sure where to bring a case. The lack of integration of functions of courts may mean that a single set of problems—of a family in process of dissolution, for example—have to be dealt with in several separate courts. If these courts cooperate with each other, equitable and appropriate disposition of the problem is possible, if difficult; but if the courts refuse to cooperate, no solution is feasible. (And judges tend to be not only jealous of their jurisdictional provinces but convinced of their ability to solve problems in *their* way.) Maxine B. Virtue, after studying the judicial system of Detroit, commented on several consequences of confused jurisdiction (cases brought in the wrong courts; lack of jurisdiction to handle adequately cases of juveniles, alcoholics, or the mentally afflicted who are properly before certain courts) and added that "the most serious area of duplication and conflict, however, involves domestic cases with family or sex problems, as to many of which any of several courts may exercise jurisdiction."[56] Cooperation among these courts, according to her research findings, is lacking.

The existence of such conditions in many states has led to drives for unification and simplification through the elimination of some courts entirely, the rationalization of jurisdiction, and the placement of all judges under the general supervision of the Chief Justice of the State so as to achieve uniform practices and high standards of conduct. Although there have been varying degrees of success with reform in such states as New Jersey, Wisconsin, Missouri, New York, and Connecticut, there have been more failures than victories.

The effort to reform the courts of Illinois illustrates the problems facing reformers.[57] First, reform could only be achieved by constitutional amendment, which in Illinois is very difficult to accomplish, and that of course gave a great strategic advantage to the opponents of change. Second, the protagonists of reorganization were dedicated to the removal of politics and politicians from the court system, but the very extent of political involvement of that state's court personnel inevitably meant that eradication would be exceedingly difficult if for no other reason than that the latter had the best of political connections. The reform elements, to cite a third debilitating factor, never managed to enlist

---

[56] Maxine B. Virtue, *Survey of Metropolitan Courts, Detroit Area* (Ann Arbor, Mich.: University of Michigan Law School, 1950), p. 269.

[57] The following brief recapitulation of a long story is based upon an excellent case study in Gilbert Y. Steiner and Samuel K. Gove's *Legislative Politics in Illinois* (Urbana, Ill.: University of Illinois Press, 1960), Chap. 7: "The Legislature Proposes a Judicial Reorganization," although the verb *proposes* in the chapter title should not be interpreted to mean that the legislature initiated the idea. It "proposed" reform only in the sense that it ultimately and reluctantly approved for submission to the voters a constitutional amendment on the subject.

wide support among the interest groups of the state. The reform drive was in fact primarily the work of leaders of the state Bar Association, and particularly of leaders of the Chicago bar. While these leading lawyers did have the support of the League of Women Voters and a few other small groups, more significant is the fact that many lawyers actively opposed the change and that labor and major ethnic groups could not be recruited as backers.

The campaign opened in 1950 when Governor Adlai Stevenson proposed judicial reform and requested work on it by the staff of the University of Illinois Law School. In the next four biennial legislative sessions the reform question was before the legislature in some form, although in serious guise only in 1953, 1955, and 1957. The legislative hurdle was a high one for the legislators themselves were among the foremost political leaders of the state, or—where they were not that —they had close contact with politician-judges who were threatened by the bill. It was an:

". . . impressive complex of vested interests that the bar leaders sought to destroy," say Gilbert Steiner and Samuel Gove, analysts of the long struggle. "Almost three hundred elective offices in the full- and part-time judiciary would ultimately have been wiped out in favor of a lesser number of appointed judges. . . . In addition, active justices of the peace and police magistrates numbering at least 450 were put in jeopardy."[58]

After the proposal had been defeated in 1953 and 1955, it became apparent that the one thing the political leaders would not accept was total abandonment of direct election of judges. The party leaders would candidly admit, when pushed, that the parties actually chose judges, and they saw no reason to believe this ought to become the prerogative of the bar association—which, they claimed, would be the consequence of the proposed new system. It is true that there were pious defenses of the "right" of the people to vote for judges (matching in fatuousness the claim that this was the "most perfect Judicial Article that any state has ever had offered to it") but this was window-dressing, not to be taken very seriously.[59] Thus Richard Daley, before he became mayor of Chicago (thus changing his role in the contest), said:

All candidates for judgeships should be initially elected in primary and general elections. . . . I have the utmost confidence in the ultimate decision

---

[58] *Ibid.*, pp. 167–68.
[59] *Ibid.*, p. 184.

of the American people going to the polls with this God-given right on election day.[60]

Compromise on the selection question was a prerequisite to success on other aspects of reform.

With the question of the method of selection deferred (and to be decided later by a two-thirds vote of the legislature and concurrence in a referendum by majority vote), the other aspects of reorganization finally won legislative approval in 1957. The once "most perfect" amendment had now been modified so as to make it palatable enough to get it by the legislature, although in the process it lost its original sponsor and designer (who joined the opponents, feeling that the amendment was no longer worth supporting). The decisive factor for passage of the bill in 1957 was that both the Republican Governor of Illinois and the Democratic Mayor of Chicago backed the modified proposal and used their powers to get legislative approval. Not particularly pleased about losing patronage and power, the leaders nevertheless were cognizant of the serious problem of the existing system, particularly the long delay in Cook County courts. Rather than face reprisals for refusal to meet these problems, the leaders now pushed rather than opposed the reorganization. Hence the amendment passed. But to no avail. In the subsequent referendum the proposal won a majority of those voting on the amendment but nevertheless failed since that majority was not equal to a majority of all those voting in the election.[61] In November 1962 the people finally accepted a sweeping reform of Illinois courts, but the fact that this was a twelve-year campaign suggests the difficulty involved.

2. *Improved Court Administration.* The management of court business was not in the past considered an important phase of judicial activity. The number of courts and the volume of business in most states was such that "bureaucratization" (so to speak) of judicial management was not considered. But as the number of courts has increased, and as the complexity of the law has grown in response to the demands of a large and interrelated society, the need for greater control within the judicial branch has been emphasized.[62] Several techniques have been employed to achieve more centralized control over judicial activity. The Chief

---

[60] *Ibid.*, pp. 182–83.

[61] Amendment in Illinois can come only by a two-thirds vote in the referendum or by a majority on the question equal in number to a majority of those voting in the election for General Assembly.

[62] See, for a discussion of the problem, Justice Arthur T. Vanderbilt, ed., *Minimum Standards of Judicial Administration* (New York: New York University Law Center, 1949), Chap. 2.

Justice in many states has been given general authority to oversee the judicial branch in collaboration with a council of judges who recommend uniform procedures. Occasionally the Chief Justice or the presiding judge of a division of courts acquires the power to assign extra judges to courts with overloaded dockets so as to reduce delay. Administrative officers have been appointed in 29 states to gather data and publish court records and supervise general budgeting and other details of the state court operations.[63] Through records thus assembled, knowledge of what is going on permits a more effective utilization of judicial manpower, and progress toward more nearly uniform standards. In some states, such as New Jersey, very detailed reports are published showing the volume and disposition of cases, income and expenditures and other facts for every court in the state.[64]

Significantly, the result of this judicial supervision—because it is a public record—can minimize the opportunities for a local judge to dispense justice as he sees fit. Some years ago, the Chief Justice of Connecticut acquired wider powers to oversee judges of minor courts and he promptly irritated them by calling public attention to the practice of reducing serious traffic violations to minor ones, adding that such reductions would be subject to inspection and that explanation to him might be called for. Defense attorneys and minor court judges growled about "dictatorship" but the practice of making special exceptions for favored defendants decidedly declined. Similar grumbling has been heard elsewhere. When reform advocates talk about "uniform standards" as a goal of administrative court reform, it is not just bookkeeping and formal procedure they have in mind; they also intend an attack on unfair and discriminatory application of the law. This may not be apparent in the language of the reformers, but it is intended. Thus Judge Botein, speaking as an advocate of judicial reform for New York State at a press conference just prior to a referendum on a constitutional amendment (and flanked by former Governors Herbert H. Lehman and Thomas E. Dewey), promised that passage of the amendment would produce more centralized administration of the courts in order to "establish uniform standards and policies for the 1500 courts contained in twenty-one separate and autonomous court systems of the state."[65]

---

[63] This is a relatively recent development; of the 29 states, 25 have adopted this law since 1950. See the current tabulation of Administrative Offices in the *Book of the States*.

[64] See the extremely detailed reports of the Administrative Director of the Courts of New Jersey with their coverage of the hundreds of thousands of cases in all courts.

[65] *The New York Times*, November 3, 1961. On hand at the session were representatives of the League of Women Voters and the Committee for Modern Courts,

"Uniform standards" can mean "heat" on a nonconforming judge.

3. *Insulation from Political Influence.* Campaigns to achieve insulation have been discussed above, particularly in connection with the controversies over the appropriate means of selecting judges. No further elaboration of the point is necessary here, except to emphasize that it is among the objectives of most reformers and that it is therefore both a positive and a negative force so far as the prospects for passage of reforms are concerned. Obviously this appeals to many people since it pushes the court away from the political world, but it is equally true and perhaps more significant that the tendency toward insulation does not sit well with political leaders who see not a blessing but a threat in this element of the reform program.

4. *Concentration of Courts and Improvement of Judicial Competence.* In essence, this aspect of the reform drive seeks to eliminate amateur judges and replace them with full-time, professionally trained judges. The justice of the peace court, an institution of honored and ancient lineage going far back in Anglo-Saxon legal history, is today a joke—and a grim one at that—in many small towns of this country. The chicken farmer or the grocer, popular with their fellow citizens, gets elected justice and acquires thereby only a limited jurisdiction over matters of law. But they do sit on many cases and their training in the law is often so scant that the brand of justice dispensed is often less than creditable. Often ignorance or response to local sympathies (which can be both negative—in the sense of unfairly discriminatory—and positive—in the sense of being merciful out of a knowledge of local social conditions and relationships) can lead to highly irregular judicial proceedings.[66] Justice courts are not courts of record—that is, no record of the courts' detailed proceedings is taken. If there is an appeal from a justice court decision, it must be an appeal for trial *de novo* (*i.e.*, a complete retrial of the issue). This is, of course, expensive and time-consuming.

Although almost any court is subject to corrupting influences, the minor and amateur court seems more than usually subject to perversion. In Suffolk County, New York (on Long Island), a state investigation some years ago turned up systematic ticket-fixing practices on

---

both of which organizations the Judge singled out for their major contributions for court reform. The reform amendment passed the following Tuesday by a wide margin.

[66] Several episodes in Cozzens' *The Just and the Unjust* illustrate this well. A brief, factual survey of *The Justice of Peace Court in Kansas,* by Ruth Wetmore (Lawrence, Kan.: University of Kansas Governmental Research Center, 1960), presents a useful guide to the office in one state.

the part of justice of peace who had unwisely left in their records clear evidence of their corruption. The investigator's report contains photostated memorandums of justices of peace, policemen, and local politicians asking for special treatment for the favored few which the justices admitted granting. Thus one justice sent a note to another saying:

Dear ———:

As per your request, I am forwarding herewith troopers summons #K193536 issued to. . . . Thanking you for the courtesy extended me and assuring you of my willingness to cooperate should you wish to make a like request at a later date, I am

Very truly yours,

———

Justice of the Peace

The defendant referred to was charged with speeding seventy-five miles an hour. He received a suspended sentence and was not even required to appear before the justice. The justice also admitted he had not marked the violation on the back of the defendant's license as required by state law.[67]

Such practices as these have done much to promote the end of the justice court. In Connecticut, for example, the justice courts along with the traditional city police courts were abolished at the beginning of 1961, and in the place of all the former minor courts there was installed a system of district courts, each with legally trained, full-time judges and prosecutors.[68] Yet the survival capacity of local courts resembles the nine lives of a cat. Coups such as the reformers pulled off in Connecticut happen rarely.

Who could oppose the replacement of amateur with professional courts? And who would have the gall to object to centralization of judicial administration in order to raise the standards of justice and to achieve uniform practices? Who would object to clarification of the lines of jurisdiction of courts by weeding out the less necessary courts and rationalizing the jurisdiction of the remaining ones? The answer, on reflection, is obvious: someone whose influence, rewards, and prizes, may be threatened by the changes. Also, values other than efficiency may be involved in assessing the operations of the courts. A strong sense

---

[67] J. Irwin Shapiro, Commissioner of Investigation, "Report of Investigation of the Enforcement of the Vehicle and Traffic Laws of the State in the County of Suffolk" (mimeographed), February 17, 1956, pp. 48–49.

[68] The new law abolished 168 justice and municipal courts, replacing them with 44 District Courts.

of localism, an ardent hope of patronage or promotion, the fear of centralization in any form, an attachment to traditional and familiar ways —all these and other motives for resistance are common.

Proponents of reform often face considerable difficulty because there is no single interest associated with the reform movement. The need for reform is not obvious to the average individual, partly because he rarely has anything to do with courts and does not wish to. He may not know the late Judge Learned Hand's reasons for wanting to avoid litigation but he undoubtedly agrees with his observation: "I must say that, as a litigant, I should dread a law suit beyond almost anything else short of sickness and death." And those who are willing to organize for court reform often find it difficult to agree on the reforms they commonly approve—they all want reform but their desires are not only different but often contradictory. Moreover, the opponents of reform are usually strategically located in the legislature and within the party systems, making the reformers' task the more difficult. Periodic success in achieving reforms always seems to renew the vigor of reformers in other states, however, and the tactics and strategic moves of the successful are studied for renewed assaults. And so with each renewed wave of political skirmishing, the paradox grows stranger: courts, supposedly nonpolitical, are the objects of political controversy in a drive to take the politics out of the judiciary.

16.

The Politics
of Metropolitan
Government

WHEN THIS CENTURY dawned six in ten Americans lived in the country, mostly on farms. Not until 1920 did census-takers find a majority of the population living in urban communities, and a generous proportion of these lived in towns of 2500–5000 population, or in something short of cosmopolitan surroundings. The galloping pace of urban and metropolitan area growth in the decades since 1920 make the figures for that census seem almost quaint. By 1950 two-thirds of the people were urban, and for the first time a majority lived in metropolitan areas. By 1960 two-thirds of the nation lived in metropolitan areas (roughly defined as a region containing a central city of 50,000 or more plus the fringe areas surrounding the center.)[1] Indeed at present it is estimated that over 60 per cent of the nation's population occupies only 10 per cent of its land. (See Figure 16-1)

---

[1] The formal definition of the metropolitan area is considerably more complex, involving, among other criteria too numerous to go into here, the relative density of population in the fringe areas and the volume of nonagricultural work force within the area; it is also possible for a metropolitan area to consist of two cities with a combined population in excess of 50,000, plus the surroundng area. The proper title of the area is now "Standard Metropolitan Statistical Area," which replaces the previous term, "Standard Metropolitan Area." For the definition of and data on the current status of metropolitan areas, see the publication of the Bureau of the Census called *1960 Census of Population, Supplemental Report*, PC (S1)-1, "Population of Standard Metropolitan Statistical Areas, 1960 and 1950" (Washington, D.C.: Government Printing Office).

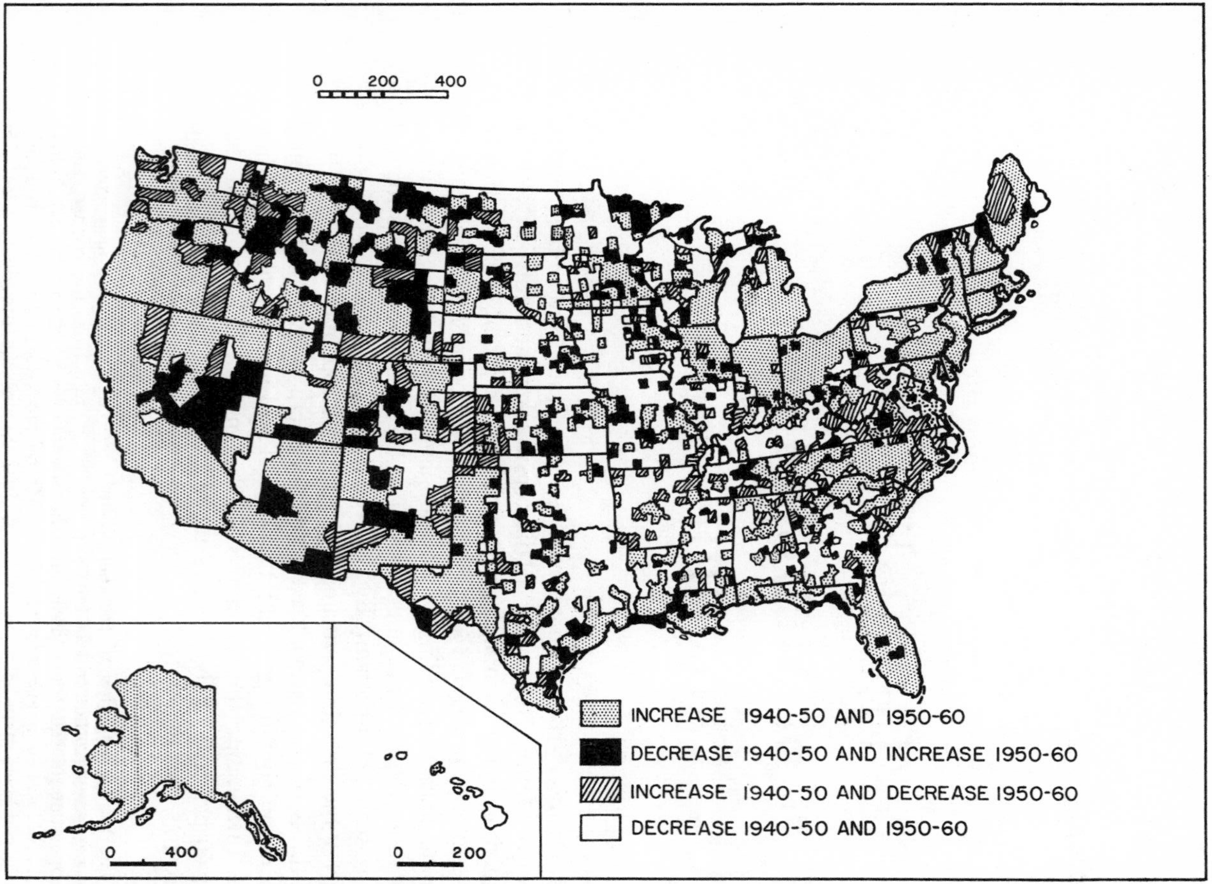

Figure 16-1. Population Trends, by Counties, 1940–60

Source: *U.S. Bureau of the Census.*

INCREASE 1940-50 AND 1950-60

DECREASE 1940-50 AND INCREASE 1950-60

INCREASE 1940-50 AND DECREASE 1950-60

DECREASE 1940-50 AND 1950-60

0   200   400

0   200   400

0   200

This apparently is but the beginning of the process of metropolitan concentration of population. Students of demographic trends foresee more developments like the East Coast "Megalopolis," so-called by Jean Gottman.[2] Already the home of 38 million residents, this sweeping complex of city, town, suburb, and countryside extends from lower New Hampshire to upper Virginia and from the Atlantic Ocean to the Appalachian foothills. Comparable concentrations are developing around the Great Lakes and on the California coast, and in the future seems evident that not only will present megalopolises grow but others will come to qualify for that awkward-sounding title.[3] It is self-evident that the metropolitan community will be about the only kind conceivable when the present population (at 200 million in 1967) doubles within a relatively short period of time. The Director of the Bureau of the Census has made the awesome prediction that the population of the United States "would grow to 400,000,000 during the lifetime of a child now [1961] five years old."[4] The New York metropolitan area is expected to reach a population of 23 million by 1985 (an increase of 5.3 million over 1965), and New Jersey planners project a population growth to 12 million by 1985 (from 7 million in 1967).[5]

Looking forward to tomorrow's troubles is, however, a guessing game. Population forecasting is no amateur's game (*cf.* the wide-of-the-mark romance of Edward Bellamy's *Looking Backward*, of 1888), and even experts sometimes outdo the weatherman in their flights of fancy. Short-range prediction can be made with reasonable accuracy, however, and those who deal with the problems posed by the present conditions and immediate growth face an awesome challenge. For present purposes, therefore, the inquiry turns to the nature of the existing metropolitan area and the directions in which it appears to be moving.

If population growth is an index of community vitality, the modern metropolis is the vital element of the country, for the rate of growth there vastly exceeds that of the rest of the nation. In fact some 85 per cent of the total increase in national population between 1950 and 1960 occurred in metropolitan areas. Moreover, in most of these areas it was primarily the rings around the major centers that attracted the new settlers. Superficially it appears that the rate of growth between 1950 and 1960 in the outer rings was 4.5 times that of the centers or, putting

---

[2] Jean Gottman, *Megalopolis: The Urbanized Eastern Seaboard of the United States* (New York: The Twentieth Century Fund, 1961).

[3] The term derives from the Greek word *megas* meaning "large" or "a million"; *metropolis* also derives from the Greek—the root word being *meter* ("mother").

[4] *The New York Times*, September 25, 1961.

[5] See Port of New York Authority report "The Next Twenty Years," 1966.

it another way, that the peripheral areas acquired three-quarters of the net gain. But once these figures are adjusted for annexations by central cities of once independent outer-fringe areas, the net gain outside the center city is clearly much greater than it first appeared. After this adjustment is made, according to Leo F. Schnore, "the outer growth is forty times as fast as that of the center." The rings "captured 97 per cent of the total metropolitan increase."[6]

The older and larger central cities, as noted previously in other contexts, are not growing. Indeed, during the 1950's only eight metropolitan areas of the then 212 showed a tendency toward "centralization" of population. Note, however, that central cities in the West and South have expanded more rapidly than cities in other regions.[7] The cities of the northeastern and north central regions (e.g., New York, Chicago, Boston, Philadelphia, and Pittsburgh) have reached at least a temporary

| | Shares of Growth in Population 1950–60 | | Per Cent of Metropolitan Area Population within the Rings | |
	Cities	Rings	1960	1950
U.S.	3.3%	96.7%	53.0%	41.4%
Northeast	−14.2	114.2	51.0	42.7
North Central	− 4.3	104.3	49.7	36.9
South	8.7	91.3	53.8	40.2
West	15.3	84.7	60.6	48.9

saturation point and are relatively static compared with their fringe areas, which continue to grow apace. (Note that the figures in the table show the respective proportions of growth, not rates of growth.) In the South and West, the central cities continue to grow (and in a few cases at faster rates than their own fringe regions), but even in these regions the centers normally grow at a more moderate rate than their rings. Observe too that the actual proportions of population in the center city and the rings do not vary greatly from region to region, the only significant variation being the western areas where the wide, open

---

[6] Leo F. Schnore, "Municipal Annexations and the Growth of Metropolitan Suburbs, 1950–1960," 57 *American Journal of Sociology* 406, 409 (1962).

[7] The table is adapted from one presented on p. 410, *ibid*. See also his data (p. 407) which demonstrates the regional variations in the proportion of population that is metropolitan: New England 79 per cent; North Central, 60.1 per cent; the South, 48.1 per cent; and the West, 71.8 per cent. All these regions refer to the standard Census Bureau classifications of states.

spaces have invited sprawling not only of the outer rings (attested to by the elaborate multilane highway systems radiating from each city) but of the center city itself. In general, western cities are much less densely populated at the center than eastern ones.

It does not by any means follow that the 231 metropolitan areas of 1967 are essentially alike. They share some characteristics, to be sure, but —like all communities or complexes of communities—they are unique in their structures, social patterns, and economic and political activities. A group of sociologists has recently underscored the wide range of variations among them.[8] Some are primarily manufacturing centers with relatively little in the way of central service activity for the regions around them. Others are both manufacturing centers and regional centers. Still others are regional capitals of social, economic, and political importance to their regional matrixes but are not important production centers themselves. That there are such wide variations is important to bear in mind in discussing and analyzing metropolitan areas, for the problems or the potentialities of one may not be those of another.

Nor should it be assumed that there is homegeneity within a given metropolitan area. Although the point seems painfully obvious, some observers seem to assume a general identity of qualities for the suburban rings around a metropolitan center. Nothing could be further from the truth, of course. There are highly industrial, densely populated cities within the "fringe" regions of many metropolitan areas alongside the more conventional "suburb." Thus Newark and Jersey City are part of the New York metropolitan region, along with the wealthy dormitory communities on Long Island, up the Hudson, or in Westchester County; in the Chicago metropolitan region are both Gary with its smoking steel mills and Evanston with its wealth. Robert C. Wood, in his study of the New York metropolitan area, devoted his attention to these variations and demonstrated enormous differences according to the degree of industrialization, the age of communities, the income levels, housing density, and community size.[9]

---

[8] As a good antidote against overemphasis on the similarities among metropolitan regions, see Otis D. Duncan, William R. Scott, Stanley Lieberson, Beverly D. Duncan, and Hal H. Winsborough, *Metropolis and Region* (Baltimore: Johns Hopkins University Press, 1960). Their detailed data on 51 different metropolitan regions are useful for the comparative analysis of areas. *See also Metropolitan Social and Economic Disparities: Implications for Intergovernmental Relations in Central Cities and Suburbs,* Advisory Commission on Intergovernmental Relations, Report A-25, 1965.

[9] Robert C. Wood, *1400 Governments: The Political Economy of the New York Metropolitan Region* (Cambridge, Mass.: Harvard University Press, 1961), Chap. 2 especially. On the general character and the governance of metropolis, see Scott Greer, *Governing the Metropolis* (New York: John Wiley & Sons, Inc., 1962);

Given the fact that the American governmental system as a whole is highly decentralized, it is inevitable that the growth of the metropolitan region has resulted in the creation of a vast number of governmental units. Perhaps the best indication of the lack of any kind of rationalized overall control of the development of metropolitan areas is that the United States Census Bureau regularly conducts a *census* of local governments in the metropolitan areas. A centralized system would never conduct a "census" of governments but it would merely check its organization chart for the answer to "How many?"

The number is quite imposing. The last count was taken in 1962 when 18,442 different units of local government were found within the then 212 metropolitan areas.[10] In the New York metropolitan area Robert C. Wood studied "1467 distinct political entities . . . each having its own power to raise and spend the public treasure, and each operating in a jurisdiction determined more by chance than design."[11]

These numerous governments present a less than tidy picture. Jurisdictional overlap, duplication of services, lack of coordination, and absence of centralized supervision are common complaints. The proximity of these municipalities, it is charged, produces problems but their independence prohibits appropriate response. The degree to which this is a serious problem we may defer for the moment, although in doing so let it not be assumed that the problems are self-evidently what the objectors believe them to be.

Quite apart from the question of the multiplicity of governmental units in metropolis, there are other serious policy contests raised by the very concentration of so many persons, buildings, and activities in so small an area. We have already dealt with some of these problems for such a complex of problems could hardly have been bypassed in any analysis of the governing of states and municipalities. Indeed, the aches and frictions of social life are nowhere more acute than in these burgeoning areas.[12] The problems of the metropolitan region are critical for several reasons: great density of population, rapid growth, and equally rapid and sweeping social change. Jane Jacobs, discussing social instability in some New York City neighborhoods, cites the stark fact that:

Michael Danielson, *Metropolitan Politics* (Boston: Little, Brown and Co., 1966); and John C. Bollens and Henry J. Schmandt, *The Metropolis: Its People, Politics and Economic Life* (New York: Harper & Row, 1965).

[10] See Bureau of the Census, *1957 Census of Governments*, Vol. 1, "Governmental Organization" (Washington, D.C.: Government Printing Office), p. 1.

[11] Wood, *op. cit.*, p. 1.

[12] See Jeanne Lowe, *Cities in a Race with Time* (New York: Random House, 1967).

In the upper West Side of Manhattan, a badly failed area where social disintegration has been compounded by ruthless bulldozing, project building and shoving people around, annual pupil turnover in schools was more than 50 per cent in 1959–60. In 16 schools, it reached an average of 92 per cent. It is ludicrous to think that with any amount of effort, official or unofficial, even a tolerable school is possible in a neighborhood of such extreme instability...."[13]

The eruption of one rotten city center after another in riots may have begun to get these truths across to white America.

In earlier chapters we have dealt with many of the problems that arise in metropolitan areas, but we have not considered them as "metropolitan" problems. Rather they were discussed as general problems of public policy-making, not matters complicated by the complex of governments in metropolitan areas. In order to analyze some of these problems and the methods of dealing with them, it is appropriate to sketch in first the shifting perspectives of leading analysts and observers of metropolis during the past six decades and then to survey some of their approaches to explanation of what the metropolitan region is and what cures are appropriate for the ills it is thought to suffer.

The Metropolitan Center and Its Region: Shifting Perspectives

The large city is no new development; ancient Rome and other classic cities were large and had incredible population density. The modern metropolis is a late-nineteenth and twentieth-century phenomenon, however. As Lewis Mumford points out, the nineteenth century began with no city in the Western world having as many as a million inhabitants.[14] Industrial capitalism in Britain, America, and Europe was an incentive to population concentration. Nineteenth-century transportation was sufficiently crude that concentration of industry near fuel and raw materials was economically advantageous. By the end of the century,

---

[13] Jane Jacobs, *The Death and Life of Great American Cities* (New York: Random House, 1961), p. 113. See also Jonathan Kozol, *Death at an Early Age* (Boston: Houghton Mifflin, 1967); Herbert Kohl, *36 Children* (New York: New American Library, 1967); and Elliot Liebow, *Tally's Corner* (Boston: Little, Brown, 1967)—among many other sources.

[14] Lewis Mumford, *The City in History, Its Origins, Transformations and Its Prospects* (New York: Harcourt, Brace and World, Inc., 1961), p. 529. Rome in the first century may have had as many as a million inhabitants but this appears to have been the limit until well into the nineteenth century.

nine Western cities had more than a million people, and by this time the growth of suburbs in the modern sense had begun.

Suburbs, after a fashion, had existed for centuries; rural retreats from the plague in the thirteenth century were incipient suburbs. Escape from the noise, smells, filth, and disease of the plague-ridden medieval city could hardly have seemed more pressingly desirable than sanctuary from the highly profitable but miserable center of the nineteenth-century industrial city.[15] The aristocratic escapee from the earlier city was no daily commuter; the nineteenth-century businessman, however, was one—for him the daily rounds at the office were mandatory. The dormitory suburb of the nineteenth century came with the development of transportation technology. The railroad, whose noise already disturbed the solitary peace of Thoreau's sojourn at Walden Pond, was to provide means for stretching the dormitory range of daytime inhabitants of the city to unprecedented lengths.[16] Still, the suburb of the railroad and the rapid transit system were one thing, and the suburb of the automobile is quite another. After about 1920 the automobile opened new suburbans worlds. In numbers of people affected, in territory covered, in sheer cost, and in both suburban and central city confusion, nothing ever matched the influence of the automobile.

The family car was the pogo stick for the leap to sprawling suburbia. Public officials cater to the suburban dweller (and the prospective suburbanite) with highways to the hinterlands and at least minimal downtown accommodations. Some cities, particularly those that grew mainly in the age of the automobile, are completely oriented toward rubber-wheeled travel. Thus no less than two-thirds of the central area of Los Angeles is devoted to roads, garages, and other amenities for cars. Some other cities, those that were large before Henry Ford's marvel of the production line changed life patterns in the United States, are half-strangled five days a week (literally from the gasoline fumes, figuratively from the traffic jams) when the eight-lane highways disgorge an incredible number of cars into the narrow confines of the city. Because the automobile offers, for all the traffic jams and danger that may often be involved, great convenience and apparent low cost of travel, the number of passengers on commuter transportation systems declines,

---

15 *Ibid.*, pp. 487ff.

16 It is appropriate to note that the once remote Concord of Thoreau's Walden Pond is now a green oasis in the middle of a thriving suburbia, and that modern defenders of the pond have recently battled county authorities who cleared part of the woods in order to provide access to the lake for emergency vehicles for the inevitable mission of resuscitating the victims of drowning—there now being a developed swimming area where once nothing but the dipping of Henry's oar disturbed the loons.

and the road jam increases accordingly. Consequently there are louder demands for still more highways, and, once built, these invite more people to join the commuter traffic lanes. Thus onward and upward goes the spiral. Nor is this phenomenon limited to the United States—it seems to be universal, even in defiance of public policy at times.[17]

To catalogue the political, social, and economic causes of metropolitan centrifugal tendencies is easy, but to perceive the meaning and the consequences of the movement is another matter. A proposal to develop a new highway system in the environs of any major city automatically gets formidable backing: from truckers, real estate interests, harassed drivers, automobile and oil industries, road and bridge contractors, and associated labor unions, to mention just a few. Evidence of the potential power of this lineup of interests is the fact that they won the needed support of the Eisenhower Administration (which repeatedly called for de-emphasis on federal activities) for the largest peacetime undertaking (at least in financial terms) in the history of the national government. This is the Federal Aid Highway Act of 1956 which established a $45 billion program of federal assistance to states for highway construction.[18] How such legislation gets passed and how the suburban sprawl continues we can see, but the consequences of these developments are not so clear. The real estate developers' promotional literature presents a rosy picture of suburban bliss, while rhetoric like that of Harrison Salisbury of *The New York Times* presents another view. He warns of a universal Los Angeles:

. . . nestled under its blanket of smog, girdled by bands of freeways, its core eviscerated by concrete strips and asphalt fields, its circulatory arteries pumping away without focus . . . the prototype of Gasopolis, the rubber-wheeled living region of the future.[19]

---

17 And it is a spiral that one may confidently expect to go on for some time. As Paul Ylvisaker has recently added: "I would guess . . . that the same will eventually happen in Madras and Moscow, when per capita income reaches the point where their residents can make a first down payment." See "The Miraculous City," *50 National Civic Review* 587 (1961), 593.

Even before cars become numerous in Moscow the urban sprawl problem became serious despite official efforts to stop urban growth. Moscow's growth rate, despite official policy against it, has been the same as the New York region in the years since World War II. See 10 *Metropolitan Area Digest* (July–August, 1967), p. 6, and *The New York Times*, November 13, 1966.

18 See Daniel P. Moynihan's critical assessment of the Act and its operation in his article, "New Roads and Urban Chaos," 22 *The Reporter* 13–20 (April 14, 1960).

19 Quoted in *ibid.*, p. 20.

Yet the romantic and the rhetorical are worth little in assessing the trends of metropolis. It is in fact all too easy to take a detached, apparently rational view of the developments, and to charge planners, mayors, or some other scapegoat with failure to provide supervision and logical direction to a set of processes that are beyond their power to command. There are no czars of urban affairs—and, if there were, their capacity to control metropolitan growth would have to be both dictatorial and omniscient to satisfy some critics of metropolitan developments. Therefore in the ensuing discussion of various conceptions of metropolitan development it is appropriate to have a skeptic's eye out for the unstated assumption, the too-detached "logical" analysis that ignores political realities and human fallibility.

It would not be accurate to say that there was no recognition of the growing metropolitan area half a century ago, but there was little recognition of the implications of this growth. City fathers, land speculators, commercial investors, and others certainly recognized and took pride, profit, and pleasure in the expansion, but few saw the ultimate cost or the consequences of what they were caught up in. Those who did begin to see made little impression on the rest.

Perhaps the man who saw and understood most clearly was Patrick Geddes, whose essentially organic conception of the city was a natural product of his earlier career as a botanist.[20] Geddes saw, as others had not and some still do not, the interdependent qualities of a natural-cultural region. Drawing an analogy between the life sciences and the study of urban civilization, he sought the fullest range of conditioning forces as the basis of his analysis. He omitted nothing: geography, meteorology, topography, esthetics, botany, economics, politics, culture, history, traditions—every factor that appears to contribute to making a region what it is. Only by analyzing detailed information on all these various aspects of life can the regional community be understood in its reality—the essential interrelationship of hinterland and center, of economic, social, and physical elements.

It is largely from the work of Geddes that the school of regionalists sprang. Men like Lewis Mumford were enormously impressed by Geddes and they in turn impressed others with the concept of regionalism. It might even be contended that they went "too far" in that they not

---

[20] A reading of Phillip Boardman's biography of Geddes is worthwhile for anyone interested in the development of modern metropolitan-urban life: *Patrick Geddes: Maker of the Future* (Chapel Hill, N.C.: University of North Carolina Press, 1944). Geddes was an unusual and fascinating man, and not the least interesting part of his life is that in this age of excessive specialization he was the master of many fields of knowledge and integrated them in a most salutary way.

only accepted the essential truth of the proposition that there are close connections between all elements of a region but went on to the less convincing contention that only by full and conscious recognition of all elements of regional interrelationship would it be possible to organize a sense-making community.

Thus one need not quarrel with Mumford's definition of the region:

Rationally defined, the locus of human communities is the region. The region is the unit-area formed by common aboriginal conditions of geologic structure, soil, surface relief, drainage, climate, vegetation and animal life: reformed and partly re-defined through the settlement of man, the domestication and acclimatization of new species, the nucleation of communities in villages and cities, the re-working of the landscape, and the control over land, power, climate, and movement provided by the state of the technics.[21]

The difficulty, however, is that regions are not sharply defined, particularly when the technology of the modern age makes intercommunication expand beyond all hitherto conceivable ranges. The pattern of regional interrelationship soon produces schizophrenic border areas which are in one area for one purpose and in another for others. Water supply areas do not necessarily match those for milk supply, food wholesaling, or recreation. In the East Coast megalopolis, attempts at neat regional demarcation must fail, for the whole area is not a single region, and the ties among communities do not fall into a neat series of unities but a congeries of overlapping associations.

One may therefore raise a point of doubt when the strict regionalist advocates the complete abandonment of the "artificial" existing political boundaries and their replacement by regionally logical units. Mumford calls for an:

. . . effective re-definition of regional areas—a scientific re-mapping of these areas and a political and cultural *re-willing* of them—[as] one of the essential preliminary tasks toward building up a co-operative and serviceable civilization. For as a man can have no fruitful traffic with the world around him, until he has a firm core of personality, so the region cannot engage in the necessary interchanges and intercourse with other regions until it possesses an integrated life, on its own solid foundations.[22]

---

21 Lewis Mumford, *The Culture of Cities* (New York: Harcourt, Brace and World, Inc., 1938), p. 367.
22 *Ibid*, p. 369. Italics in the original. See Chap. VI on "The Politics of Regional Development."

The case for re-creation of the political world suffers from over-rationalization; regional units are not clearly definable, and even if they were, the drastic recarving of the political universe necessary to achieve the most logical pattern would be exceedingly difficult to produce. Near-dictatorial power and revolutionary reconstruction of the political system would be needed. The remedy may be worse than the disease. Indeed Mumford himself recognized this in a modified way when he looked back upon the design he had drawn for the powers of an over-seer of regional redevelopment for Honolulu. Mumford set forth a plan for making over Honolulu after his survey there in 1938 and he proposed the appointment of a driving and powerful Plan Director with a ten-year term of office and very wide authority; on publication of his report in 1945 he said he "would now be inclined to throw safe-guards around such a personality" as his Plan Director would have to be.[23]

This is not to deny the great importance of regional concepts. To grasp the relationships between areas and between various aspects of nature and culture is indispensable to understanding the metropolitan area. But it does not necessarily follow that the existing metropolitan areas are inchoate monstrosities since they obviously and probably nec-essarily do not conform neatly to the conceptualized "region" of the planner's own construction.

Concepts of regionalism guided the thinking and organized ef-forts of many civic-minded groups outside the ranks of government be-fore they had much impact inside city and town hall. For decades local groups such as the New York Regional Plan Association, supported re-search projects and made recommendations concerning metropolitan trends. In due time many harassed city fathers and officials of the burgeoning suburbs got interested in the deeper meanings of metropoli-tan growth—deeper meanings, that is, than the traditional booster spirit and commercial opportunism. In the post-World War II years, first sociologists and then popular writers more concerned with best-seller lists than insight, produced dozens of books filled with gloomy pronouncements on "suburban culture" and its implications.

Then the civic-minded in many central cities came to the shocked realization that the city was no longer growing. This was hard to believe for men to whom galloping growth was not only familiar but for gen-erations a basic tenet of business and government planning and action. City officials came to full cognizance of the trend when population de-

---

[23] See Lewis Mumford, *City Development* (New York: Harcourt, Brace, and World, Inc., 1945), pp. 139–40, 147.

cline led to the prospect of reduced state subsidies. New York City officials were unwilling to believe that their population had not gone on
growing after the 1950 census and in 1957 contracted for a special
census by the U.S. Bureau of the Census to prove that they had not
lost population. The result was double disappointment: they had to pay
for an enumeration that confirmed the exodus and suffer a loss of
subsidies.[24]

By midcentury, businessmen, public officials, taxpayer associations,
and the civic-minded generally became more serious than ever about
the consequences of metropolitan change and development. Different
vantage points produced different priorities of problems, of course, but
the insistent demand for services in the developing towns and for minimal conditions of public safety and order in the decaying centers placed
such demands upon the public treasury that the problems could not
be ignored by anyone with even the slightest awareness of public affairs. A look at some of these problems may serve to illustrate the
broader metropolitan political problem.

Metropolis: A Pattern of Problems

For present purposes, a "metropolitan problem" may be defined as
any issue of sufficiently wide impact within a metropolitan area to
make it significant to individuals in the whole area or at least to those
living beyond the confines of the community or communities within
which the issue arises. This is not a restrictive definition, to be sure.
It would include the location of a shopping center in Town A which
could have a significant impact on Towns B and C where business
conditions, housing demand, traffic flow, and many other related problems might thus be created. But it is intended to exclude, for example, an issue such as the level of teacher salaries in Town A which
may be high enough to encourage demands for raises elsewhere. The
"significance" and the "directness" of the impact are not such as to
make teacher salaries a "metropolitan" problem in the strict sense.

The remaining metropolitan problems are so numerous that even
to list them is difficult. It would be more appropriate for present purposes to cite and briefly assess some of the more significant ones in
order to show the nature of the tasks of the metropolitan area govern-

---

[24] See Sayre and Kaufman, *op. cit.*, p. 18.

ments. Three examples, transportation and water problems and racial conflict will illustrate the point.

(1.) *Transportation.* It is hardly necessary to prove that the transportation problem is metropolitan in character inasmuch as it was chiefly the transportation system that made the metropolis possible. Transportation is a front rank issue in all metropolitan areas, as the decline of rapid transit and commuter railroads and the constant expansion of automobile travel present standard sources of vexation. As indicated previously, there are inexorable pressures upon public officials to develop highways which have the inevitable effect of undercutting other transportation facilities. When the trains and subways face economic difficulty there is demand for public subsidies to sustain them in order not to make the highway traffic problem still worse, so the net effect is to encourage subsidies to both kinds of travel, for the enormous public expenditures for highways are also subsidies to motorist and truckers. Total costs are rarely met by the user taxes, except on toll roads and bridges.

An indication of the trend away from rapid transit facilities in four cities can be seen in Table 16-1, which uses the traffic volume of 1940 as an index of 100. Notice that the population in the outer rings of the cities has gone up and that of the centers has declined while the volume of traffic on the rapid transit system has not increased (as one might expect if one did not calculate the impact of the automobile), but has declined sharply.

TABLE 16-1
The Decline of Rapid Transit Facilities in Certain Cities (1940-Index of 100)*

	Population Trend 1950–60		Index of Traffic		
	Inner City	Outer City	1924	1936	1960
Boston	−15%	+17%	130	100	68
Chicago	−3.5	+71	120	130	58
New York	−3	+73	96	88	76
Philadelphia	−5	+46	175	106	77

* The data in the table are derived from information presented by Thomas Conway, Jr., "Rapid Transit Must Be Improved to Alleviate Traffic Congestion," 26 *Traffic Quarterly* 103 (1962).

New York City has a higher proportion of daily users of public transportation than any other large city (one survey indicated that

83 per cent of New York's commuters used public facilities[25]) but even there the proportions are changing. Robert Wood reports the following trend:

Between 1948 and 1958 the number of commuters moving daily by private automobile through the Holland and Lincoln Tunnels and over the George Washington Bridge [between New Jersey and New York City] increased from 15,500 to 33,000. . . . At the same time rail commuters between New Jersey and New York City declined in number from 101,600 to 69,00.[26]

The increasing use of the automobile alarms many observers of the metropolitan scene who plead for some way of discouraging auto travel and getting commuters back on the train. But the odds are not with the reformers, at least not at present. Many rapid transit systems are not very rapid; a *Fortune* survey of some years ago indicated that the average speed of movement for public transportation vehicles at rush hour was less than that of the private car. In only three of the 25 cities checked (in New York, Newark, and San Francisco) did the public transportation move more rapidly than private cars; in some cities (*e.g.*, Cleveland, Houston, and Denver) cars moved at more than twice the speed of the public transportation rider.[27]

Metropolitan centers also have transportation problems that transcend their areas; that is, the metropolitan area as a center of economic life for the nation becomes a transportation crossroads and as a result the strictly local problems of the metropolitan area become enmeshed with wider transportation problems. Metropolitan commuter problems and questions of long distance travel and the movement of goods by rail, water, and air become inseparably intermixed. Long-distance freight hauling is profitable; short-distance commuter hauling is apparently not. Thus the problem is whether or to what extent the railroad should be forced to jeopardize its financial or competitive position by providing commuter services it would rather abandon. In Congress friends of railroads get involved in metropolitan transportation prob-

---

25 The Editors of *Fortune*, *The Exploding Metropolis* (Garden City, N.Y.: Doubleday Anchor Books, 1958), p. 38. Chap. II, "City and the Car," is particularly pertinent to this discussion.

26 Wood, *1400 Governments, op. cit.*, p. 124. See pp. 123–44 for an excellent discussion of New York's transportation problems. The trend has slowed since 1958. The Tri-State Transportation Commission (N.Y., N.J. and Conn.) estimates that the average weekday number of trips in the region will rise to 50 million by 1985 (from 33,500,000 in 1963), and that 76 per cent of all trips will be by automobile in 1985 (compared to 70 per cent in 1963.) See Tri-State's *Regional Forecast, 1985*, p. 4.

27 The Editors of *Fortune, op. cit.*, pp. 38–41.

lems, and suddenly the Interstate Commerce Commission is an important actor on the metropolitan transportation stage. Consider the intensity of passion that can be aroused by a proposal to locate a jet airport in a suburban area; a problem of national and international economic importance becomes a metropolitan problem with great storms of protest and much maneuvering on all sides. The point is clear: all phases of metropolitan transportation present public officials and interest groups with vast problems of cost, unforeseeable consequences, and deep conflict that are not readily resolved.

The problem of cost is vexatious in the extreme. In the first place the direct costs of transportation facilities are enormous. Digging tunnels under rivers, constructing multilane highways which may necessitate the destruction of millions of dollars worth of property, subsidizing directly and indirectly various forms of transportation—all these run up astronomical bills. How to divide these costs? Is the central city to pay a proportionate share of facilities that produce more central city problems? Can high-tax suburbs, without industrial property to tax, make contribution equal to their benefits? And how are the non-monetary costs to be calculated? What are the social and psychological costs of pushing people out of their homes for multilane highways? How can one calculate the cost to a grocer or barber whose building, clientele, and livelihood are all swept away by the eminent-domain-backed bulldozer?

Little wonder therefore that there is bitter debate about transportation policy. Obviously there are many agencies with some authority to affect (if not always to effect) policy. But there is no metropolitan region with a single body entrusted with full authority to decide transportation policy. (If there were such a body no one would trust it, which is a chief reason why one does not exist.) Even when an agency like the Port of New York Authority (a joint New York–New Jersey agency established through a compact between those states) is authorized to coordinate and manage many different aspects of transportation policy, the agency avoids overall control. The challenge is too great, the difficulties of making clear overall policy are beyond the actual grant of authority of the agencies since it cannot control the tangential policy aspects that condition transportation decisions, and its jurisdiction does not extend to the whole region. Thus the Authority has become the partisan of one particular kind of transportation—the automobile. The Authority has done much to promote highway travel and little to coordinate transportation policy.

Ultimately it is difficult to set transportation policy for the overriding reason that there is no single agreed-upon set of priorities concerning the question. There are many interests to be served, many conflicting groups seeking different goals, many governmental and inter-governmental bodies and political interests involved.[28] The probable consequences of a given policy are not always entirely clear, and even where they are relatively clear there may not be agreement among all the participants as to the desirability of the consequences. In short, the problem is a very complex one and its complexity is not the sole result of the absence of a single overreaching agency of control. Transportation policy is not transportation policy alone: it is planning policy, housing policy, tax policy, recreation policy, and so on. And on each of these there are conflicts on values, vested interests, and deep commitments. Conflict about transportation policy is naturally intense. Parceling out authority is therefore not the whole problem by any means. On the contrary, the inability to concentrate power in any agency is as much a reflection of the basic problem as it is a source of aggravation of the difficulty.

2. *Water Management.* The voracious appetite for water of the modern metropolis poses a serious problem, one to which passable resolution must be found for a metropolis to exist. As Roscoe Martin says:

. . . it is the fate of *homo metropolensis* to wander the asphalt desert, cup in hand, in search of water to slake his thirst. This is true particularly of the denizens of New York City, which has spent a good share of its time and treasure since Manhattan was New Amsterdam in quest of a suitable water supply.[29]

It is an even more critical problem for cities located in the semiarid southwestern quadrant of the nation where drought means dry river beds and recurrent crisis. Metropolitan demands in those areas must compete with irrigation needs. Even where there is adequate rainfall for a moderate-size city, the concentration of population in metropolitan regions drives the water table lower and lower, particularly in view of the demand for water for industrial purposes and for the operation

---

[28] The extreme complexity of metropolitan transportation politics is attested to by two recent works. See Jameson W. Doig, *Metropolitan Transportation, Politics and the New York Region* (New York: Columbia University Press, 1966); and Michael N. Danielson, *Federal-Metropolitan Politics and the Commuter Crisis* (New York: Columbia University Press, 1965). The first deals primarily with rail and rapid transit facilities of the New York Region, the second with the commuter railroads and the role of the national government in metropolitan transportation policy.

[29] Roscoe Martin, *Water for New York: A Study in State Administration of Water Resources* (Syracuse, N.Y.: Syracuse University Press, 1960), p. 123. See Chap. V for a general discussion of New York City's water supply problem.

of the gadgetry of modern life (the air conditioner, for example). Consequently, the metropolitan area looks to broader and broader regions to supply its needs. As Robert Wood points out, water politics are complicated by the necessity to reach well beyond the metropolitan area for water sources:

Whereas the planning and construction of rail and road facilities takes place primarily within the geographical boundaries of the [New York Metropolitan] Region, the physical development of the largest sources of water supply must take place outside the Region's twenty-two counties.[30]

Competition among metropolitan areas ensues as each seeks to guarantee its foreseeable needs. Also, reservoirs eat up farm land and may convert a fishing and recreation site into a fenced-in and forbidden oasis, secure against human contamination. This calls for sacrifices that the nonmetropolitan dweller is often loath to make and which he often has the necessary political resources to forestall. To quote Wood again, "A householder in Hunterdon County, New Jersey, does not actually want anyone in Hoboken to die of thirst but neither does he want the Hoboken reservoir in his basement."[31] The drought in the northeast from 1962 through 1966 caused a crisis of inter-metropolitan area competition for the water in the Delaware River. Finally with federal government participation a compact was signed providing rational allocation of the precious resource.[32]

Increasing demands and dwindling supply are not, however, the only problems of water management. Water also can produce hydroelectric power, thereby introducing not only other agencies of government but strong interest groups whose contests over electrical power naturally toss them into contests over the management of water flow. The reverse of water shortage—the devastating floods of spring— further complicates water politics. A continuing difficulty in metropolitan areas is the contamination of water through practices that not only diminish potential water supply but otherwise endanger public health. Every hour, millions of tons of raw and untreated sewage and industrial wastes pour into rivers and lakes with resultant contamination that makes many a stream little more than a slow-moving open sewer. Fish die and the recreational value of water sites is either re-

---

[30] Wood, *1400 Governments, op. cit.,* p. 145. See pp. 144–55 for a general analysis of the New York Region's water problems.

[31] *Ibid.,* p. 119.

[32] See the forthcoming Inter-University Case Study, "The Delaware Drought Emergency: Water Politics, Strategy and Innovation" by Richard A. Hogarty.

duced or eliminated. The Secretary of the Interior Udall estimated in 1968 that a five-year program to clean up the nations water ways would cost between $26 and $29 billions.[33]

Governmental action to prevent pollution is difficult for several reasons. In the first place local governments, not wishing to spend the necessary money to treat their sewage, rank among the foremost of the polluters. (The sewage will, after all, plague the towns down the river more than it will the polluting town.) Second, industrial polluters resist spending the money to clean up their wastes and threaten to move to a more congenial community if state or local agencies insist on being "unreasonable" about demanding clean water. Finally, there are sources of pollution from indissoluble detergents. In many areas undissolved detergents enter suburban wells and come bubbling out of the kitchen faucet.

It is obvious that developing adequate water facilities for a metropolitan area is very expensive. The facilities necessary to transport billions of gallons of water to metropolitan areas and to assure pure and potable supplies are costly to establish, maintain, and operate. It is not inconceivable that some of the general supply problem may yet be alleviated by the invention of an economically feasible method of desalting ocean water, but thus far the methods devised are far too expensive to compete with natural supplies, expensive as these are in some areas. It is the opinion of one group of investigators of water problems that there is more reason to hope for "solution" of water problems through devices to save wastage of water (as through seepage from reservoirs and water mains) than through sea water conversion, the high capital and power costs of which render the process noncompetitive with natural supply.[34]

There are also severe intrametropolitan conflicts implicit in the water management field. Parts of metropolitan regions may compete for available resources, and indeed the central city may possess preëmptive water rights on lands within the suburban region, the rights having been acquired long before the suburbs existed. Or the central city may have built water facilities and be unwilling to share them with suburban

---

[33] *The New York Times*, January 25, 1968.

[34] Jack Hirshleifer, James C. De Haven, and Jerome W. Milliman, *Water Supply, Economics, Technology, and Policy* (Chicago: The University of Chicago Press, 1960), p. 366. Indeed the authors of this volume present the novel argument that the gravity of the water supply problem has been overemphasized, and they sustain their position with considerable evidence and sound reasoning. They are not, of course, saying there is no problem, but are instead contending for an approach which weighs the economics of water supply against other needs of the community. They illustrate their argument with lengthy case studies for different areas of the nation.

communities or be unwilling to do so at costs the suburbs will accept. It is true that when the problem gets critical enough united action often follows. Faced with compelling needs cooperative effort to develop common facilities for the metropolitan region have frequently resulted. County governments may also assume the basic responsibility where counties cover enough territory.[35] Suffice it to say that the nature of the problem—limited supplies and interrelated consequences of water policy on a whole region—is such that it provides a classic form of metropolitan problem. Many levels and agencies of government necessarily are involved; decisions must await the negotiation of conflicting interests; and this in turn must await recognition that the problem is a genuine one that cannot be "solved" by individual communities acting separately.[36]

3. *Racial Conflict.* The American metropolis is segregated and is becoming more so as Negroes depart the South for northern center cities and whites flee to the suburbs. "In 1910," say Karl and Alma Taeuber in *Negroes in Cities*, "no city in the United States had as many as 100,000 Negro residents, and 73 per cent of Negroes were rural. In 1960, 73 per cent of Negroes were urban—five large cities contained more than one of every six Negroes, and more than one-third of the nation's Negroes lived in 25 large cities. When Myrdal's *An American Dilemma* was published in the early 1940's, the focus of national concern with problems of the Negro's position in American society was largely on Negroes in the rural South. But by the mid-1950's, national attention was centered on Negro problems in Birmingham, Little Rock, Detroit, Chicago, New York, Los Angeles and other cities throughout the country."[37] If in the mid-1950's we were beginning to think of the serious problems of the Negro in cities, it was surely only a beginning. By the late 1960's the problems had become so grave that concern— although not always comprehension—about them became nearly universal.

---

[35] See Roscoe Martin and Frank Munger, eds., *Decisions in Syracuse* (Bloomington, Ind.: University of Indiana Press, 1961), Chaps. IV, V, for analyses of how the Syracuse metropolitan region met the sanitation and water supply problems.

[36] The bibliography on water supply and management problems is too extensive even to attempt a presentation here; one source, however, would be of value to the student of the subject: a symposium on "Water Resources" in 22 *Law and Contemporary Problems*. See particularly E. A. Engelbert, "Federalism and Water Resources Development" (p. 325); L. E. Craine, "The Muskinggum Watershed Conservancy District: A Study of Local Control" (p. 378), and H. C. Hart, "Crisis, Community and Consent in Water Politics" (p. 510). See also Hirshleifer, *et. al.*, *Water Supply, op. cit.*

[37] Karl and Alma Taeuber, *Negroes in Cities* (Chicago: Aldine Publishing Co., 1965) p. 14. The Taeubers present a sophisticated analysis of the prevalence of racial housing segregation in cities.

The riots that have troubled every summer in recent years are the product of many complex forces, but at the root of them all is a basic fact of life in the United States: Negroes are discriminated against in gross and subtle ways from the moment of birth. Although attitudes toward Negroes have improved to an extraordinary degree in the years since the end of World War II, the change has meant little to a large segment of the nonwhite population. State and local governments have, for example, enacted and enforced dozens of statutes against racial discrimination in housing, employment, and public accommodations. The laws have meant decent homes for some, and access to better jobs and to restaurants or hotels for others, but the numbers helped, in contrast to the masses denied assistance, are pitifully small.[38] Fifteen years after the school desegregation decision the numbers of Negroes in segregated schools is larger than in 1954, and especially so in metropolitan centers. Because unemployment rates are normally twice as high for Negroes as for whites, because educational levels are low for Negroes, because accumulated bitterness has crushed "ambition" in the middle class sense out of many male Negroes—because of these and other developments, the United States for the first time in its history faces a proletariat somewhat in the sense in which Marx meant the term: a dispossessed, jobless, alienated mass of people who are becoming increasingly rebellious.

The alienation has in part been induced by what may be called a revolution of rising expectations, as that term is used in reference to the developing countries. The Negro's expectations have been aroused by what he sees when he leaves the ghetto and what he sees portrayed on television: luxury seems to abound for the white but not for the ghetto-bound black. (In truth there are far more whites than Negroes with poverty level incomes, but that is not of interest to the Negro who has the impression—correctly—that most blacks are poor and most whites are not.) It appears that two patterns of development are taking place in the Negro community. On the one hand many Negroes are pulling out of the poverty class and achieving a certain economic success, but on the other, within the core of the ghetto the situation appears to be growing worse than before. This is borne out by a special census in Cleveland in 1965. In the heart of the ghetto median incomes actually declined between 1960 and 1965, whereas in the more marginal areas of Negro population the median incomes went up slightly. There was a greater decline in the incidence of poverty among

---

[38] Duane Lockard, *Toward Equal Opportunity* (New York: The Macmillan Company, 1968).

Negroes outside the core of the slum than even for whites in the city. The average weekly income of the female-headed household was a mere $37.50, and despite a decrease of core area population there was an *increase* in the number of poverty-stricken children.[39]

Thus a rebellious mass is concentrated in metropolitan center cities where it cannot escape. As the center turns black, the suburban rings stay white. As of 1960 a majority of all white metropolitan residents lived in the suburbs (52.2 per cent), whereas 80 per cent of nonwhite metropolitan residents lived in the center cities. Indeed, because white migration to the suburbs has been so rapid, the actual proportion of Negroes in the suburbs has been declining from census to census rather than increasing.[40]

The racial crisis is the most excruciating problem that faces the metropolitan area in the years ahead. Although the problem is only partly of the metropolitan area's own making, metropolitan officials will have to be major agents of its resolution. That is, the plight of the nonwhite is fundamentally the product of centuries of history and im-bedded beliefs and defeats, and the metropolitan contribution to the problem is largely a matter of continuing to do what has always been done about the Negro—ignoring him when not actively discriminating against him. Thus business packs up and moves to the suburbs where the beckoning open land and multilane highways make for profits and a contented work force. The decision to abandon the city is made in terms of profit and not its possible consequences for the population that is left behind to fend for itself now that the factory jobs are gone. Yet necessarily it will be the metropolitan area that must provide answers to these problems if they are to be found. State and federal funds may help finance solutions but it will be primarily local agencies that do the work in education, housing, skill training, welfare, recrea-tion, to mention just a few programs.

But the political difficulties in moving toward an accommodation between the black and white elements of the metropolitan area are monstrous. White antagonism toward Negroes, already a staple feature of the American mentality, is only exacerbated by the riotous behavior of nonwhites. Consequently persuading whites to pay taxes to solve this problem is going to become even more difficult than in the past. More

---

[39] See Walter Williams, "Cleveland's Crisis Ghetto," 4 *Transaction* 33–42 (September 1967).

[40] Taeuber, *op. cit.*, p. 57. The percentage of nonwhites in metropolitan areas but outside the central cities was 8.9 in 1900 but only 4.5 in 1960. See also John H. Strange, "Racial Segregation in the Metropolis," in Michael Danielson, ed., *Metropolitan Politics* (Boston: Little, Brown, 1966), pp. 41–52.

likely there will be demands for more forceful suppression rather than a demand for resolution of the impasse.[41] The prospect of school integration—both North and South—seems to frighten white parents into frenzied activity. In New Jersey in the 1967 legislative campaign the state commissioner of education said in a speech to school administrators that the boundary lines of school districts could not be considered sacrosanct if the problem of school segregation was to be met and resolved. An outcry continued for weeks with demands for the commissioner's resignation, and for reassurance that city children would not be taken by bus to the suburbs (or even in some cases into the rural hinterland). Admittedly this was campaign season, when exaggeration spreads like mosquitoes in the tropics, but the attack struck fear in the hearts of politicians (especially in view of the numerous defeats of candidates of the Governor's party). Those fears will live on to complicate any possibility of dealing with the school problem.

There is indeed no solution in sight for the racial unrest of the metropolis, and none is likely to be found soon. Surely the election of Negro mayors (as happened in Gary, Indiana, and Cleveland, Ohio, in 1967) will be no answer, for it is a reasonable guess that within a year or two these will be the most frustrated politicians in the land: they will be expected to produce for their people far more than there are resources or means to achieve. Once again the Negro is likely to feel that sense of letdown, of defeat again after hope seemed to be justified.

These examples show some of the difficulties metropolitan areas face. One could add others. There is, for example, the sometimes critical problem of unequal financial resources, which naturally is intertwined with other problems. This inequality is the product of what one might call "unnatural" or unbalanced communities in the sense that some municipalities may have no tax-paying industrial property located within their boundaries but do have great demands for services (education, sanitary facilities, fire and police forces) as a consequence of a rapidly expanding population. Residential property taxes under such conditions rocket upward and the house-holder's burden becomes onerous. If a huge factory locates in Town A, its tax rate may drop, since the services provided for most industrial property do not cost a government as much as the revenues received in property taxes. But in adjacent Towns B and C, the influx of new residents who work in Town A's new factory may aggravate the tax problem since the services

---

41 See Tom Hayden, *Rebellion in Newark* (New York: Random House, 1967); and Robert Carnot, *Rivers of Blood, Years of Darkness* (New York: Bantam Books, 1967).

rendered to residential housing usually cost more than the revenue produced—or at least will cost enough to raise taxes. One town's relief is another's grief. The similar and familiar problem of the metropolitan center providing services to suburban dwellers who are beyond its power to tax is another example. The city provides an art gallery, a zoo, and police, sanitary, and other expensive services to the suburban visitor but cannot recoup a proportionate share of the cost from him.

One could also cite instances of unnecessary duplication of services in metropolitan areas, of waste through inadequate coordination of planning (*e.g.*, public utilities dug up and relocated or expanded as a consequence of blindly made decisions that foresight through coordinated planning might have obviated). Or one could point to waste and distress caused by inadequate coordination of land-use planning. A factory planted across the town line from a residential neighborhood would have most destructive results, since noise, traffic congestion, smoke, and smells are no respecters of political boundaries.

To cite further examples would be superfluous. The problems are of such gravity and pervasiveness that an enormous amount of energy and brain power—not to say promotional emotion—has gone into the devising of the optimum "solutions." To these "solutions" and their assessment we now turn.

The "Solution Syndrome": Attitudes and Approaches

As we have said before, there is a particularly American faith in and fervor for devising new governmental structures and new systems to deal with difficult political questions. The devising goes on within a stable framework of relatively unchanging institutions, and perhaps it is this stability that encourages imaginative attempts to find a new way to "solve" problems. Moreover, the filling of a continental sweep of territory which governments invited experiment and ingenuity, particularly since states were independent in such matters and were not subject to central control as to form and structure of government. Whatever the origins of faith in the rational mind as a solution-deviser, it certainly can be said that the metropolitan area has been no exception to the standard rule: when a problem arises, find a "reform" that will "solve" it.

Although one may look askance at some of the more simple-minded attempts to arrive at "the" answer to metropolitan problems, since the oversimplifications usually convert reality into make-believe, one cannot deny the significance of either the specific proposals made or the general attempt to devise corrections. The contribution of the solution-maker is likely, however, to be important only to the extent that he comprehends both the issues at hand and the nature of the community with which he deals. Skepticism is warranted when the advocate of a solution sees it as universal cure-all. This suggests, after all, that the solution-deviser has misconceived the situation, for about the best one has reason to hope for in this process is a "resolution" of present conflicts of values in terms of an existing situation. The situation will change and today's "solution" may have to be reconsidered, for solutions are a response to a dynamic configuration of the forces of the time. And the political realities of a metropolis are, of course, anything but static; they are inevitably dynamic precisely because of the socioeconomic forces of a metropolis which itself changes constantly—in population, economic activity, and social patterns and tensions.

Consequently it is well to examine any proposal for solving metropolitan problems in three ways: in terms of the realism with which the problem itself is conceived; in terms of the probable effectiveness, political consequences, and other costs of the solution; and finally in terms of the feasibility of applying the solution in the real world.

Accordingly there follows a review of some leading "solutions": (1) annexation, (2) metropolitan districts and public authorities, and (3) integrated government.

1. *Annexation.* This is a deceptively simple answer to metropolitan problems for it involves the absorption and incorporation of new territory into the existing city. Seeming to wipe the slate clean of the intermunicipal conflict and the need for intergovernmental negotiation, annexation was common, particularly in the nineteenth century. Usually there was some opposition from the fringe areas which preferred to maintain their independence rather than be swallowed up in the larger city, as in the case of Brooklyn's resistance to being consolidated with New York City in the late 1890's.[42] Fringe area resistance became increasingly effective in this century, no doubt in large part because of the change in the nature of the metropolitan area. The newer far-flung suburban network is not the gradual expansion on the edge of the city that the nineteenth century had known. The new suburb is not only farther away but is likely also to be built in the area of an existing local government unit rather than in open unincorporated countryside. Hence there is not only citizen demand to guard the autonomy

---

[42] See Sayre and Kaufman, *op. cit.*, pp. 11–17. Formal consolidation came in 1897.

and fiscal independence of the new suburb from the encroaching center city, but also an existing set of public officials and local customs and investments (psychic as well as economic and social) to be protected.

So the annexation process slowed down. In many parts of the nation annexation is now almost unknown; in some it occurs infrequently; in a few states is it a very significant practice. In Virginia, where annexation is accomplished through a judicial proceeding, and in Texas, where it is effected by ordinance without the necessity of a referendum for approval, the process is widely used. Between the 1950 and 1960 censuses there were 22 large cities (over 250,000 population)—most of them in the South and Southwest—which gained more than 10 per cent in population through annexation.[43] Many commentators are inclined to lament the increasing opposition to and decreasing incidence of annexation, since they see it as a way of minimizing intermunicipal conflict. To be sure, the absorption of outlying areas does decrease intergovernmental conflict, but it is not self-evident that it will produce the increased efficiency or administrative improvement often expected of it. If the newly encompassed area is markedly different from the center, it does not necessarily follow that the center-dominated government will be better able to manage its own or the added area's government more effectively. Annexation may bring in its train some disadvantages of considerable moment for the people involved, and at times these may outweigh the benefits.

Consider, for example, the management of the schools of a metropolitan community. It would seem that there would be gains from making the system larger, allowing for specialization of talents and the provision of elaborate programs (e.g., through educational television programming) through a reduction in the unit costs. The demise of the one-room school and its replacement by the consolidated school system

---

[43] Ann R. Miller and Bension Varon, "Population in 1960 of Areas Annexed to Large Cities of the United States between 1950 and 1960 by Age, Sex, and Color," Technical Paper No. 1, Population Studies Center, University of Pennsylvania, 1961, Table A (mimeographed). Some of the increases were spectacular—Phoenix gained 75.7 per cent in this fashion and Tampa 51 per cent. Still, 27 of the 52 cities studied showed no annexation at all or accretions of less than 5 per cent thereby.

On methods of annexation and for an excellent review of annexation in general, see Victor Jones's long essay, "Local Government Organization in Metropolitan Areas: Its Relation to Urban Redevelopment," in The Future of Cities and Urban Redevelopment, edited by Coleman Woodbury (Chicago: University of Chicago Press, 1953), pp. 550–72. See also Professor Jones's earlier volume on Metropolitan Government (Chicago: University of Chicago Press, 1942), which is still an important work on the general subject of metropolitan affairs even though it is now more than twenty-five years old. For legal detail on annexation, see Frank S. Sengstock, Annexation: A Solution to the Metropolitan Area Problem (Ann Arbor, Mich.: Michigan University Law School, 1960).

illustrate the point. But the catch is that greater and greater concentration does not always result in greater efficiency. Without a doubt some of the worst-run of the nation's school systems are in the large cities and some of the best are in suburbs. Naturally there are many factors influencing these differences, but it would be foolish to overlook the costs of bureaucratization that accompany hugeness. The larger the school system is, the more likely the disease of rules-paralysis and the myopic incapacity to see and respond to problems. The larger the system, the less likely that one element of it will know what another is doing. Neighborhood groups, unhappy about falling plaster in classrooms or rats in the cafeteria, will have a hard time getting their complaints registered at city hall; in the smaller community, access to school leaders and public officials through PTA and similar groups is possible and responsive action more likely. Following at least in part such ideas as these a special committee proposed a decentralization of the huge New York City school system, in 1967. It was also intended to permit ghetto parents to have some say in the operation of neighborhood schools.[44]

The point is, of course, that in some respects annexation is likely to be an advantage since it reduces the conflict points and may aid in achieving coordination of policy-making, but it does not follow in every case—or in any given case before it is carefully examined—that there are net gains to be had by annexing just as it does not follow that there are inevitable and invariably convincing benefits from retaining suburban independence.

2. *Metropolitan Districts and Public Authorities.* In the years since World War I, the metropolitan district and the public authority have been increasingly employed to deal with certain kinds of problems. Usually having a semiautonomous position, both the district and the authority commonly have independent revenue sources and often borrowing power as well. Organized in many different ways, these agencies inevitably vary greatly in their operations, depending upon the extent to which they are given independent fiscal powers, whether their members are directly elected or appointive, and the kinds of authority they are granted (not to mention the degree to which they are accepted locally). Most of them are service rather than regulatory agencies, more likely to be concerned with water, sewage, recreation, and transportation rather than with city planning or pollution control (although special districts with such functions do exist). Since authorities and districts

---

[44] Mayor's Advisory Panel on Decentralization of New York City's Schools, *Reconnection for Learning*, Nov. 1967.

commonly exist within municipalities (*e.g.*, school districts, park authorities, and so on), it is surprising that the metropolitan district is no commoner than it is. John C. Bollens, the foremost scholar on the subject, finds special districts in about one-fourth of all metropolitan areas, and in about three-quarters of the largest metropolitan areas.[45] On reflection, however, there is no reason to be surprised that metropolitan districts are rarer than intramunicipal districts, since the metropolitan districts require the collaboration of two or more municipalities and this is achievable only under special conditions. Thus, for presumably the same reason, metropolitan districts and authorities are usually limited to a single function rather than vested with interrelated functions. Some authorities are creatures of the states, although this does not eliminate the municipalities of a metropolitan area from the negotiations and politicking that go into the legislation for the creation of, appointment to, or operation of the metropolitan authority or district. Understandably, it is difficult to get agreement between two or more states in order to establish a bistate or multistate authority. Usually Congress gives its approval to such compacts in *pro forma* fashion so that congressional involvement does not greatly complicate the proceedings, but this is not invariably true; at times Congress has balked.

As single-purpose agencies, districts and authorities lack the power to undertake integrated planning. They sometimes lack financial resources and legal authority to perform even their directly assigned tasks. Still they do provide a kind of intermunicipal and supramunicipal institution to tackle regional problems, and since broader agencies are hard to establish, the district and the authority often serve a useful role. As John Bollens has said, "in spite of their limited functional scope and their frequent deficiencies in formation, structure, or finances, metropolitan districts represent the nearest existing approximation to areawide government in many metropolitan areas."[46]

The typical metropolitan district is independent of the remainder of the governmental system in the metropolis. This is particularly true of the interstate metropolitan district where the members of the agency are unlikely to have been chosen locally, but are usually appointed by the governors of the states involved. Remoteness from the people most directly concerned is thus a common charge. This independence of local controls need not undercut the popularity of the authority (as the Port of New York Authority has demonstrated) but does raise

---

[45] John C. Bollens, *Special District Governments in the United States* (Berkeley, Calif.: University of California Press, 1957), p. 67.

[46] Bollens, *op. cit.*, p. 92.

questions about the responsiveness of the agency to democratic control. Of course, such agencies are not given independence in order to make them democratically responsive agents, rather they are made independent—in part at least—in order to bypass existing democratic governing processes. It is the intent—explicit or implicit—of the originators of these institutions to place them beyond the influence of "politics," and therefore in some respects beyond democratic controls. The typical rationale emphasizes technical considerations and minimizes value conflict and therefore political control as well.[47]

Evidence indicates that a considerable degree of practical autonomy and independence is often achieved. In no small part this independence results from a good reputation built on a record of achievement in the building and operating of needed facilities. Of course, some of the reputation derives from skillful public relations operations. And there is no questioning the fact that the common practice of freeing authorities from dependence on the budget allows them a freedom of operation that is denied to other bodies. Independent authority to borrow, to collect tolls for services, and otherwise control their own finances offers a considerable advantage over the agency that has to compete for funds in routine budget negotiations. The story of the Port of New York Authority is not typical for it has greater autonomy than most such interstate agencies, yet its history illustrates the degree of independence a well-financed and well-run authority can achieve.

By any standard, the Port of New York Authority is big business. The value of its holdings is almost $2 billions and its outstanding bonds are worth $1 billion. Annual income in 1967 was $207 million and the scope of its activities is equally impressive: control and management of 24 major projects: airports, bridges, piers, tunnels, bus and freight terminals, heliports and a world trade center scheduled for completion in 1972. Included are such landmarks as the George Washington Bridge, John F. Kennedy International Airport, and the two Hudson River tunnels. If the Authority is a bigtime operation, it has bigtime salaries to match, for among its 7600 employees there were over two dozen earning in excess of $27,000 a year. Austin J. Tobin, Executive Director, receives $70,000 a year, the second-highest salary of any American public official (only the President of the United States earned more).

Established by interstate compact in 1921, the Authority is formally controlled by a twelve-man board, appointed for overlapping terms and

---

[47] For analysis of interstate agencies of this sort, see Richard H. Leach and Redding S. Sugg, Jr., *The Administration of Interstate Compacts* (Baton Rouge, La.: Louisiana State University Press, 1959), especially Chap. 5. See also Victor Jones, "Local Government Organization . . . ," *op. cit.*, pp. 573–86.

in equal proportions by the Governors of New Jersey and New York. The Governors have a veto on the minutes of actions taken by the Authority and the legislatures of the two states have to authorize new undertakings. The Authority nevertheless has considerable discretionary power. Governors rarely veto an act of the Authority even when they disagree, and the legislatures have small say about the policies of "their" agency. Thus in 1958 the New Jersey Legislature was trying to work out a policy to save commuter railroad operations in the state. The Port Authority's Executive Director, Mr. Tobin, was pressed by the legislators to admit that he could legally divert some of the surplus of the Authority to this problem. Tobin strongly denied he could do so, contending that deficits in this field excluded the Authority, which could only undertake self-sustaining projects. Although he insisted that Port Authority policy was made in Trenton and Albany, he still resisted the legislators' plea for help, saying the Authority had gone as far as it could.[48] The Authority did, however, enter a deficit-producing venture in the field of commuter transportation within two years. Tobin had claimed that no nonprofit-producing venture was feasible, but after the legislature agreed to limit expected transit deficits to no more than 10 per cent of the Authority's reserve fund, the Authority did what it claimed it could not.

The Authority's subjugation to the governors and the legislatures of the two states is often more formal than real. Fiscal independence, a good reputation, and skillful management have made it a giant among the actors in New York metropolitan politics, and every municipal leader or interest group that has tangled with the Authority is well aware of its potential. It has public status combined with freedom from some of the standard restraints (such as the necessity to levy taxes, get budget approval from a legislature, or have its leaders face the public in an election) plus great economic resources with which to undertake impressive, public-satisfying programs. The business community has in general felt kindly toward the Authority as a well-run organization, and it has had warm support from the metropolitan newspapers as well. With these assets, its competitive position is formidable.[49]

Over the years the Authority has been friendly to automobile travel and distinctly cold toward rail transportation, although its leaders defend "balanced transportation," claiming that a metropolis not only needs many forms of transportation but that "each mode is particularly

---

48 See Doig, op. cit., pp. 184–87.
49 Tobin claims the press is an avenue of exchange between PNYA and the public and he revels in the fact that in one period "1400 favorable editorials" about PNYA appeared in regional papers. See Doig, op. cit., p. 263.

suited to serve certain transportation needs and is relatively unsuited to serve other needs."[50] The "recognition" of interrelationship, according to many critics, has been more formal than real, since the Authority has until very recently avoided involvement in commuter transportation except automobile and bus transportation. This has made the fiscal position of the Authority secure, for rail facilities are deficit-ridden whereas bus and auto tolls on bridges and tunnels make the bonds of the Authority gilt-edged investments. The more bitter of its critics have charged that the Authority is more concerned with its fiscal commitments than with its role as a transportation agency.[51]

Along with its popularity, the Authority has acquired considerable enmity during its four decades of operation. The ranks of the enemy have included the many who have been displaced by the Authority's use of eminent domain power and many public officials who tried to persuade the Authority to do something the Authority did not want to do. It is worthwhile to underscore the point that the Authority is not omnipotent—for it surely is not; it is a major force in metropolitan politics but it has restraints on its powers and competitors whom it must take into account. Some of the popular criticisms of the Authority have seen it as an utterly unrestrained source of power, a contention no doubt encouraged by the outraged remarks of governors, mayors, major interest groups, and legislators who have sought to bargain with the Authority. The long controversy over whether the Authority should take over the Hudson and Manhattan Railroad and expand its facilities constitutes a good case in point. Many influential figures and major interest groups pressed for Authority action, but its leaders resisted. It was their contention that the Authority's charter forbade it to enter into any arrangement that might make its overall deficit exceed its surpluses from its profit-making operations. This might have happened if the Authority had assumed responsibility for all commuter-operations, but a far more limited proposal was at stake.

In the end the Authority did consent to take over the deficit-ridden line, but not until pressures had mounted high and other difficulties had weakened the bargaining position of the Authority. In addition to the pressure exerted by Governor Meyner of New Jersey and—to a lesser

---

[50] Austin J. Tobin, "Balanced Transportation—Metropolis 1980," An Address to the Convention of the American Society of Civil Engineers, October 18, 1961, p. 4 (mimeographed).

[51] For a journalistic attack on the Authority, see Edward T. Chase, "How to Rescue New York from Its Port Authority," 220 *Harper's Magazine* (June, 1960), pp. 67–74. A defense of the agency is Frederick Bird's *A Study of the Port of New York Authority* (New York: Dun and Bradstreet, 1949). See Jones, *op. cit.*, pp. 583–86. For an excellent commentary on the authority, see Doig, *op. cit., inter alia.*

extent—by Governor Rockefeller of New York, the Port Authority faced other forces that inclined its leaders to change their position. They wanted, for example, support for their proposal to build a jet airport in the metropolitan region, and to do this they needed support from the very politicians who wanted the Authority to help with the commuter problem. Also, members of the congressional delegation from the metropolitan area—led by Representative Emmanuel Celler, the powerful Chairman of the House Judiciary Committee—began a congressional investigation of the Authority. Tobin, requested by the investigating committee to release the records of the Authority, refused, and in August of 1960 he was charged with contempt of Congress. (A conviction followed, but it was subsequently reversed.) The next month the Authority told New Jersey officials that it now thought it possible for the Authority to take over the long-since bankrupt Hudson and Manhattan Railroad and to expand its facilities and create a "loop" transit system between the Jersey shore and Manhattan.[52] Singularly committed to maximizing a set of carefully selected goals and mindful of the political advantage of a good reputation, the Authority again demonstrated its capacity to steer a course that made "political sense," a course that preserved its organizational integrity even at the cost of some of its transportation goals. The Port of New York Authority is a classic study in administrative-political effectiveness—whatever else may be said of it.

3. *Integrated Metropolitan Government.* Since annexation is out of the question for most metropolitan areas and since special districts and authorities tend to be single-function agencies without the ability to coordinate policy with regional comprehensiveness, other answers and solutions have been sought. An important and eminently reasonable-sounding proposal has been that of integration or federation in some form. Suggesting some kind of agency representative of the whole metropolitan area which would be vested with authority to make policy for the whole area in selected fields, the proponents of integration have argued that it would lead to greater efficiency, economy, and rationality in metropolitan policy. Typical of this approach is the case made by Luther Gulick, who wants to combat the "breakdown of local government in metropolitan regions." He finds a "governmental vacuum" (some gov-

---

[52] After more than another year's negotiation, terms were agreed upon for Authority acquisition of this railroad. See Doig, *op. cit.*, for a discussion of the long negotiations between the Metropolitan Rapid Transit Commission and the Port Authority. This underscores the great strength from which the Authority could bargain. More was involved in the short-run failure and dissolution of the Commission than the potential power of the Authority, but this surely was a prominent factor.

ernmental services and functions are simply not performed at all in the metropolitan region); a "fractionalization of assigned duties" (the problems of metropolis have "coalesced" but jurisdiction has remained unchanged); a "political imbalance" (governmental units with "unbalanced population and a truncated economy, neither of which is equal to the governmental activities now required"); and a "lack of clear-headed and courageous political leadership and a recognition that we face a metropolitan problem."[53]

Accordingly, Dr. Gulick proposes a "Metropolitan Council" with broad legislative powers whose policies would take precedence over those of local communities. The Council would be

. . . made up entirely of elected officers. Some might well be directly elected by districts or at large, some might serve *ex officio* on the basis of their election to some other local governmental office, such as existing city mayors and county commissioners and presidents. Several of these Metropolitan Councils will have members from two or more states, creating a new set of governmental and legal problems for America.[54]

In one form or another, this suggestion has been offered for most major metropolitan regions in the nation. Yet when it is put to a referendum, it usually meets with hostile majorities. In some areas it is proposed that the county be given general jurisdiction over the affairs of the region; in others the inauguration of new "federal" governing arrangements is proposed. But whatever the form, the reaction has, with a few exceptions, been negative. The usual course of events is that at first little attention is paid to the plea for unification, but in time news media, public officials, or other business or community leaders take over promotion. Then an official proposal is made and a campaign ensues with a certain degree of rational argument and at least an equal amount of exaggeration of the probable benefits and the liabilities of the proposal. Ultimately the matter comes to a vote and that is the end of it.[55]

---

[53] Luther Gulick, *Changing Problems and Lines of Attack* (Washington, D.C.: Governmental Affairs Institute, 1957), p. 9.

[54] *Ibid.*, p. 27. The same proposal is discussed at slightly greater length in Gulick's contribution to the symposium, "Metropolis in Ferment: Metropolitan Organization," 314 *Annals of the American Academy of Political and Social Science* 57 (1957), pp. 63–65. See also his more recent reflections in his *The Metropolitan Problem and American Ideas* (New York: Alfred A. Knopf, Inc., 1962).

[55] Victor Jones presented a clear portrayal of this negative response over twenty years ago, and the situation has not changed significantly since. See his perceptive review of the sources of antagonism to this reform in *Metropolitan Government, op. cit.*, Chap. 9, 10, 11. See also the data on integration efforts in the period 1950–61 presented in the report of the Advisory Commission on Intergovernmental Rela-

Why is there such bitter opposition to so salutary and rational a set of reforms? The answer is that they are not seen as salutary and rational by those most affected, whose own goals, they fear, the proposal will more nearly defeat than serve. Nor is it just a matter of suburban resistance to big-city encroachment; in many instances the central cities are equally reluctant to merge. Events in St. Louis, where integration has been firmly rejected, led observers there to turn a fancy phrase in generalizing that:

The chaste suburbs have generally been regarded as balky brides-to-be in metropolitan marriages but now the rakish central cities have also assumed the role of reluctant grooms. This series of setbacks may indicate that metropolitan governmental relations are becoming more inflexible, and that instead of progressing closer to agreement, the present pattern of local political pluralism had become institutionalized to the point where only catastrophe or the imminent threat of it will bring radical readjustment.[56]

Observers of Cleveland's fruitless efforts to achieve integration also found little distinction between suburban and central-city voter response to integration proposals. In Cleveland, the major division of voters on this question was in terms of class, education, and occupation rather than region—the lower-class elements voted "no" and the upper-class elements "yes."[57] Negroes, as they gain more political power in central cities, are disinclined to support integration which might threaten their relative increase in political weight. And for the same reason, suburban elements are often apprehensive of integration moves that may force them to compete politically with urban Negroes and lower-class whites.

---

tions, "Factors Influencing Voting on Governmental Reorganization in Metropolitan Areas," May, 1962. This reports on 18 reorganization movements, ten of which failed. See also the bibliography on these campaigns.

[56] Henry L. Schmandt, Paul G. Steinbicker, and George D. Wendel, *Metropolitan Reform in St. Louis: A Case Study* (New York: Holt, Rinehart, and Winston, Inc., 1961), p. 70. The authors look not only at the publicity and the referendum election results but also at the details of political maneuvering involved in working out a formal proposal in this highly illustrative case study. See also Daniel J. Elazar, *A Case Study of Failure in Attempted Metropolitan Integration: Nashville and Davidson County, Tennessee* (Chicago: University of Chicago Press, 1961). In July of 1962 the "failure" was erased when the voters approved consolidation in another referendum.

[57] See Richard A. Watson and John H. Romani, "Metropolitan Government for Metropolitan Cleveland: An Analysis of the Voting Record," 5 *Midwest Journal of Politics* 365 (1961). The one geographic correlation they did find to be significant was a higher percentage of "no" votes in all villages than in central city or suburban city. In nine of ten referenda between 1933 and 1959, they found village residents more opposed than city-dwellers (p. 378).

Toronto, Canada, led the way among major cities in making a bold experiment with a "Metro" government having the inclusiveness and unification that integration promoters advocate. Integrated government for Toronto's 1.5 million inhabitants was not the product of a persuasive referendum campaign, however; on the contrary it was the result of a command by the provincial legislature. In 1950, after long and futile negotiations between municipalities for a formula for integration, the Premier of Ontario warned the city and its suburbs that unless they acted the Provincial government would. They did not move but the Province did; in 1953 the Municipality of Metropolitan Toronto was created, and on July 1 of that year Toronto and its twelve suburbs became a new governmental unit.

The separate municipalities did not cease to exist, however, and some of their functions were not transferred. They retained authority to operate fire departments, to distribute water, to provide local street maintenance and garbage collection, and, importantly, to manage their own schools. To the new "metro" government went authority to borrow all money on behalf of the lesser units; to provide water supply, sewerage services, major roads, police, and a licensing agency; to operate all public transportation facilities except taxis and railroads, and to decide whether or not to build new schools. Also, significantly, there is a Metropolitan Planning Board, although the localities still have planning authority. Tax collecting remains the function of the individual municipality, and the bill for Metro is paid through proportional assessments on the tax rates of the local governments.

The governing body, the Metropolitan Council, has 32 members: twelve from the city and the remainder from the suburbs. This was a change from the original plan which provided equal city and suburban representation. Equal representation continues, however, on the powerful Executive Committee of the Council.[58] The chairman of the council for its first eight years was Frederick C. Gardiner, and by all accounts he dominated the council and was in no small measure responsible for the success and the popularity of the system.[59]

What conclusions can one draw from this experiment? First, it is

[58] On these 1966 changes and other aspects of Metro, see Harold Kaplan, *Urban Political Systems, A Functional Analysis of Metro Toronto* (New York: Columbia University Press, 1967). See also Frank Smallwood, *Metro Toronto: A Decade Later* (Toronto: Bureau of Municipal Research, 1963).

[59] Some notion of the man and his Robert Moses-like qualities come through in his speech to the National Conference on Metropolitan Problems at Michigan State University in 1956; see *Proceedings* (New York: Government Affairs, Inc., 1957), pp. 56–60. See also Kaplan, who says Gardiner practically never lost a legislative contest. *Op. cit.*, Chap. 3.

obvious that if the political traditions of the state permit an imposed solution from outside, it is possible to achieve changes which in a more pluralistic and decentralized system would simply be impossible. (Except for the interstate areas, there is, however, no *legal* reason why a similar act could not be passed in most American state legislatures.) Second, it would seem to suggest—as does the case of the Port of New York Authority and Robert Moses' operations in the New York area— that freedom from the restraints of democratic accountability can make the uninhibited agency look like a marvel by comparison. (It is significant that Gardiner of Toronto resisted changing the charter to provide for the popular election of the "super-mayor," as the chairman of the council is sometimes called. Popular election might enhance the responsiveness of the official in political terms at the sacrifice of some of the free-wheeling opportunities that indirect choice affords.) Third, Harold Kaplan, a careful student of the experiment, concludes that it has been reasonably effective in the realms it has functioned in, but that in some key and difficult areas it has abstained: *e.g.*, land use control and regional planning. Like some American special authorities, it has excelled in public construction. It does not appear to be wildly popular, although suburbanites support it rather than face amalgamation with the city.[60]

At first glance the county seems a likely instrument with which to transcend the parochialisms of metropolitan local governments. It is after all an existing governmental unit within whose borders are contained the lesser municipalities. Why not merely add to county responsibilities and thus integrate functions? In practice this has been very difficult to do. In the first place, where integration has been most vociferously called for (the largest metropolitan areas), regions usually consist of not one, but many counties. (The New York region covers 22 counties. There are no other counties comparable to Los Angeles County with its more than 4000 square miles of area and more than 6 million population). County government's poor reputation has not recommended it as a likely agency to receive new and complicated responsibilities. County commissioners in most parts of the nation are marginal politicians, commonly associated with patronage politics and the management of smalltime administrative duties. The officials of county government normally lack the initiative and leadership necessary to promote a wider county role and the advocates of integration are disinclined to promote the county as the vehicle of integration since

---

[60] Kaplan, *op. cit.*, pp. 246–63.

integration itself is hard enough to sell without having to fend off attacks on the county.

Nevertheless, it is true that counties are effective governments in some areas, and that in rare cases metropolitan responsibilities have been vested in counties. In 1949 a complete county-city consolidation was approved in Baton Rouge, Louisiana, and consolidations were approved for Nashville and Davidson County, Tennessee in 1962. This was a total consolidation into a single government.

Two other developments in county government should be noted: the "Lakewood Plan" and the Dade County, Florida, Miami "Metro" experiment. The Lakewood Plan refers to a scheme whereby municipalities hire the county to perform certain functions on a contract basis. The city of Lakewood, California, was incorporated in 1954 and promptly turned over many of its functions to Los Angeles County to perform on a contract basis. Since then a number of other cities in that area have followed Lakewood's example. Municipal contracting for services did not originate with Lakewood, but was in use as early as 1907 when early contracts were made for county assessment and collection of taxes for municipalities.[61] By the time Lakewood incorporated, there were "over 400 service agreements . . . in effect with the forty-five cities that existed [in Los Angeles County] at that time. The number of contracts has nearly doubled since 1954. . . ."[62] The Lakewood innovation differed from earlier county-city contracts in that it included a broad range of services, including police and fire protection, "based upon a single multifunctional contract that sets forth in considerable detail the administrative relationships, and costs are set forth in terms of units of service—permitting the city to determine the level of service it will purchase."[63]

Apparently the Lakewood plan has been an invitation to formerly unincorporated areas in Los Angeles County to incorporate in order to avoid annexation by other cities, to improve certain services, and to assure local control over local affairs. The rate of incorporation has in any event increased rapidly—from 45 in 1954 to 70 in 1960. Although the benefits of large-scale organization and lower unit costs of some

---

[61] See Samual K. Gove, "The Lakewood Plan" (Urbana, Ill.: Institute of Government and Public Affairs of the University of Illinois, 1961), p. 8. See also the more recent article by Richard M. Cion, "Accommodation Par Excellence: The Lakewood Plan," in Michael Danielson, ed., *Metropolitan Politics, op. cit.*, pp. 272–80. Cion shows how ridiculous the process can become as incorporation is used to protect suburban enclaves.

[62] Gove, *op. cit.*, p. 11.

[63] Winston W. Crouch, "The California Way," 51 *National Civil Review* 139, 143 (1962).

services (jail facilities, police protection, traffic signal maintenance, and tax and health services, for example) may go to the communities, some critics wonder whether there may be a compensating disadvantage in the invitation to multiplication of local semiautonomous governing units. This multiplication, they contend, may complicate integration more than contracting facilitates it. In an area where there is little un-incorporated area remaining, and where the county is not too discredited to be built upon, the development of a contractual system may offer an ameliorative opportunity.

The Dade County "Metro" experiment is a looser federal system than the one in Toronto. After a constitutional amendment in 1956 per-mitted Dade County to draft and adopt its own system of government, the new system was approved in a referendum (by a close margin) in 1957. The county government took over a number of functions from the 26 local governments in the metropolitan region (now containing about 1.5 million residents), including maintenance of water supply and sewerage systems, traffic control, administration of traffic courts, and county-wide planning. The charter permitted the expansion of the county's general functions, leaving vague exactly how broadly the county might interpret its authority. With the expansion of its powers into several matters previously subject to local jurisdiction, the in-evitable challenging litigation began. Florida courts read the law gen-erously and the county (or "Metro" as it is commonly called) was permitted considerable latitude for expansion. Antagonists of Metro were rebuffed by the court as it validated county adoption of building codes, a zoning appeals system, public works projects, and the en-forcement of a traffic code.[64]

The coming of metropolitan county government to Miami did not mean the consolidation of all local functions (as it had in effect in the 1897 annexation-consolidation actions in New York City). Rather, it meant the transfer of some functions to the county and the retention of others in the 26 municipalities. Because the local governments con-tinue to exist and to exercise general powers, they have been able to resist Metro encroachment. Resistance to Metro has come largely from threatened municipal officials who want to retain their positions. The

---

[64] Basic sources on the Miami experiment include the excellent analysis of the system's leadership by Edward Sofen, "Problems of Metropolitan Leadership: The Miami Experience," 5 *Midwest Journal of Political Science* 18 (1961); the same author's more extensive description of the system in his *The Miami Metropolitan Experiment* (Bloomington: Indiana University Press, 1963). See also for a com-parison of the Miami, Nashville, and Toronto Metro experiments, Daniel Arant, "Metro's Three Faces," 55 *National Civic Review* 317–24 (1966).

ease with which a court challenge of Metro authority or an amendment to the basic law can be initiated (the latter, by getting some 14,000 signatures from the more than 400,000 voters), have put weapons in the hands of antagonists. Resistance has also taken the form of continued operation of functions that supposedly have been terminated by the courts. In the short run, the lack of direct representation of municipalities on the county commission may weaken the powers of resistance, for the apportionment system grants a municipality representation only when its population exceeds 60,000. Only three communities have reached that size (Miami, Miami Beach, and Hialeah), which has resulted in a commission of 13 members, ten from districts and three from the larger cities. In time, however, other communities will undoubtedly acquire direct representation since the area as a whole has been growing since 1940 at an average rate of 7 per cent annually.

Evaluation of the work of Metro is difficult at this early stage, but there does at least appear to be majority approval on the part of those aware of the system—a point the antagonists have insisted on having proved repeatedly in their forced referenda, each campaign seeking essentially to restore the *status quo ante* 1957. In 1958, an amendment was proposed to restore local "autonomy," but this was beaten by a comfortable margin of 24,000 votes. By 1961, however, a number of factors appeared to have weakened the hand of the backers of the system: a reappraisal of property had increased the valuation to $5000 or more on many of the more than 35,000 homes that had been entirely excluded from property tax payments because they fell below the state exemption limit of $5000; the Metro traffic court had aroused displeasure not only because it had removed some local revenues in fines but also because it had acquired a reputation for vigorous enforcement of the law; the system was viewed with dissatisfaction by those who felt that it had not moved fast enough in accomplishing promised improvements in mass transportation, and water and sewage problems; and, finally, the long controversy between the county manager and the county commission was producing widespread dismay.[65] The election of 1961 did not defeat the system, however badly it scared Metro's protagonists due to their scant margin of victory (48 per cent of the vote favored amendments intended in effect to abolish the system).

Why was it possible to institute a metropolitan government in Miami when the same proposal has been rejected in so many other cases?

---

[65] See T. J. Wood, "Dade Charter Survives Test," 50 *National Civic Review* 609 (December, 1961). Wood cites data from survey research revealing the expected lack of passionate concern about Metro on the part of average citizens.

The answer provided by one close observer of the experiment, Professor Edward Sofen, is that the peculiarities of Miami politics made it possible.[66] It is not only an explosively expanding community, it is also a community without firmly organized interest groups and without clearly identified leadership. There is no manufacturing of any importance, political party organizations are unusually weak, there are no powerful labor unions, ethnic minorities are not important politically, and the business community is divided and lacks the ability to assert leadership. The newspapers, in Sofen's opinion, tend to fill the leadership-promotional role to a considerable degree. Elsewhere the existence of strongly entrenched parties, firmly established local traditions, and strong local interests, will probably continue to be barriers to "Metro" adoption.

Metropolitan Government Reconsidered

The twentieth-century view of the metropolis has undergone several significant changes: from recognition of potential to recognition of problems to concentration on structural revision to alleviate the problems. It now appears that another viewpoint is emerging, one that questions the accuracy of the customary problem diagnosis and challenges the standard remedies. Three representatives of revisionist persuasion recently wrote an article criticizing the traditional view which, they said,

. . . assumes that the multiplicity of political units in a metropolitan area is essentially a pathological phenomenon. The diagnosis asserts that there are too many governments and not enough government. The symptoms are described as "duplication of functions" and "overlapping jurisdiction." Autonomous units of government, acting in their own behalf, are considered incapable of resolving the diverse problems of the wider metropolitan community. The political topography of the metropolis is called a "crazy-quilt pattern" and its organization is said to be "organized chaos." The prescription is reorganization into larger units—to provide 'a general metropolitan framework' for gathering up the various functions of government. A political system with a single dominant center for making decisions is viewed as the ideal model for the organization of metropolitan government.[67]

---

[66] Sofen, "Problems of Metropolitan Leadership . . . ," *op. cit.*, pp. 20ff.

[67] Vincent Ostrom, Charles Tiebout, and Robert Warren, "The Organization of Metropolitan Areas: A Theoretical Inquiry," 55 *American Political Science Review* 831 (1961).

The doubters are probably a minority among those who speculate on metropolitan problems, but the unexpected man-bites-dog quality of their case deserves attention. Thus Jane Jacobs, after reviewing the work of various students of metropolitan integration, comes to the conclusion that the voters are right in consistently rejecting metropolitan consolidation moves. They are right, she says, "because in real life we lack strategies and tactics for making large-scale metropolitan government and planning work."[68] She questions whether an impenetrable administrative maze of a huge metropolitan government would be any better than the "crazy-quilt of township and suburban government."

Others argue that the metropolitan community is not in fact a "community" and that efforts to get it to act as a single entity fail because the metropolitan citizen lacks the sense of community necessary for an effective government. Edward Banfield further contends that the class and race distinctions that divide the metropolitan center and its fringes are so deep as to make an integrated government inevitably difficult if not impossible to achieve.[69] Democrats tend to control the center cities and Republicans the suburbs and neither will risk steps that might jeopardize their respective power enclaves.

Beyond race, class, and partisanship, there are other sources of center city-suburb conflict that not only have prevented merger but would continue to plague an integrated government. As Banfield points out:

If overnight all of the people of the central cities were transformed into middle-class white Protestants, there still would be a basis for conflict between them and the suburbanites. It would still have to be decided, for example, whether thousands of central city residents should be relocated to build expressways to give suburbanites quicker access to the city as well as how taxes to pay for such improvements should be levied. In St. Louis a metropolitan transit scheme failed of adoption recently apparently because of fears that improved service for suburbanites would be paid for by the fares of central city residents.[70]

If there is an advantage to being able to take an overview of the whole metropolitan region, there is a concurrent disadvantage in having to encompass a broad range of policy questions that pit antagonistic elements in all-out conflict. If the logic of integration has appeal, there is also some persuasiveness about the counterproposition that the

---

[68] Jacobs, op. cit., p. 425.

[69] Edward Banfield, "The Politics of Metropolitan Area Organization," 1 Midwest Journal of Political Science 77 (1957). See also Morton Grodzins, The Metropolitan Area as a Racial Problem (Pittsburgh: University of Pittsburgh Press, 1958).

[70] Banfield, "The Politics of Metropolitan Area Organizations," op. cit., p. 88.

smaller unit of government poses fewer divisive questions because it is likely to contain a more homogeneous collection of people. Right or wrong, the case against consolidation says in effect that, like India and Pakistan, it is better to remain separate if the price of unification is disunity.

Moreover, the pleaders for reconsideration of the metropolitan "problem" ask for re-examination of the diagnosis: Is the metropolis in as chronic a situation as is sometimes claimed? There are many kinds of intergovernmental cooperation among the governments of the typical metropolitan area, and the number and intricacy of these is increasing, and at least part of the reason for the increase is the apprehension of local leaders that unless they do cooperate they may sacrifice local control to higher echelons of government. How far these interconnecting links go toward rationalizing metropolitan government is a matter for debate, but the existence of the links should not be overlooked:

Contrary to the frequent assertion about the lack of a "metropolitan framework" for dealing with metropolitan problems, most metropolitan areas have a very rich and intricate 'framework' for negotiating, adjudicating and deciding questions that affect their diverse public interests. . . .[71]

Evidence to sustain this has been provided by a group of scholars studying the relationships among governments in the Philadelphia area. Thus George S. Blair found 693 interjurisdictional agreements in the five-county Philadelphia metropolitan area in 1959—a 59 per cent increase over the number of existing agreements in 1952. He found evidence:

. . . to suggest that the most successful areas of interlocal cooperation relate to those services which supply the necessities of community life— police and fire protection, public education, sewage disposal. Certainly the number of agreements in such areas far outnumber those in other areas where mutual administrative advantages could accrue—as in joint purchasing, personnel administration, etc.[72]

---

[71] Ostrom, Tiebout, and Warren, *op. cit.*, p. 842.

[72] George S. Blair, "Interjurisdictional Agreements in Southeastern Pennsylvania" (Philadelphia: Fels Institute and University of Pennsylvania, 1961), p. 129. See also Oliver P. Williams, "Intergovernmental Cooperation for Disposal of Sewage: Southeastern Pennsylvania" (Philadelphia: Fels Institute and University of Pennsylvania, 1961); Jeptha J. Carrell, "Interjurisdictional Agreements as an Integrating Device in Metropolitan Philadelphia" (unpublished Ph.D. dissertation presented at the University of Pennsylvania, 1952). See also O. P. Williams, T. R. Dye, H. Herman, and C. S. Liebman, *Suburban Differences and Metropolitan Policies* (Philadelphia: University of Pennsylvania Press, 1965); and Charles Gilbert, *Governing the Suburbs* (Bloomington, Ind.: Indiana University Press, 1967).

Other studies have found networks of interrelationships of comparable extent—in New York State, in Cleveland, in Syracuse, for example.[73] The case study analysis of a series of problems faced in the Syracuse area reveals not only the number of links between local governments but the pattern of conflict and cooperation between officials of those units. Interestingly, one of the more fruitful avenues of achieving co-operation was the Republican party organization, which was strong both in the center city and in the suburbs.[74]

Finally, it is necessary to distinguish between problems, as Edward Banfield and Morton Grodzins say, which "exist in metropolitan areas" and "problems which exist by virtue of the inadequacies of govern-mental structures in the metropolitan areas." Thus, they contend, "lack of playgrounds within easy reach of mothers and children may indeed be a problem in metropolitan areas; it is not, however, a problem which requires for its solution any reorganization of governments."[75] Gener-alization on which problems fall inside this circle and which fall out-side is not easy, but it is clear that a skeptical mind could turn aside as unproven a great many of the assumptions and inferences made about what are "significant" problems that need a metropolitan solution.

It should be repeated here that there is by no means a uniform ac-ceptance of this "new view" of the metropolis. There are many who persist in their opinion that structural reforms are mandatory. Thomas H. Reed, for example, recognizes the obstacles to reform and ruefully accepts the fact that it "may well be another twenty years before genuine reform measures are widely adopted." But he is unshaken in his con-viction that the "adoption of a rational form of metropolitan govern-ment, geared to the movement of population and to other socio-economic conditions of today, is a great and worthy enterprise."[76] Robert Wood identifies several lines of attack on the integrationist

---

[73] Guthrie S. Birkhead, "Interlocal Cooperation in New York State, Extent of Cooperation and Statutory Authorization for Cooperative Activity," New York Department of Audit and Control, 1958; Joint Legislative Committee on Metro-politan Area Study, "Metropolitan Action" (mimeographed), 1960; Matthew Holden, "Intergovernmental Agreements in the Cleveland Metropolitan Area," Study Group on Metropolitan Organization, 1958; Roscoe C. Martin and Frank J. Munger, eds., Decisions in Syracuse (Bloomington, Ind.: Indiana University Press, 1961).

[74] See particularly Harold Herman's chapter, "Cooperation, Contract or Consolida-tion," and the two chapters by Lewis P. Welch on county government reorganiza-tion, in Martin and Munger, op. cit.

[75] Edward Banfield and Morton Grodzins, Government and Housing in Metro-politan Areas (New York: McGraw-Hill Book Co., 1958), p. 32. This volume is a useful sorting out of relevant and irrelevant governmental factors in public policy on metropolitan housing.

[76] Thomas H. Reed, "A Call for Plain Talk," 51 National Civic Review 119 (1962), 128.

movement and responds to them, defending a more rationalized kind of metropolitan government and emphasizing that there are not one but many ways of achieving:

. . . metropolitan government defined as the new and broader use of government as an instrument for shaping the urban environment. But underlying each of these approaches is one common denominator: the conviction that in the end we do not have to drift; that we can rationally and reasonably direct the course of action; that we can use our affluence and technology to build better urban communities than our forefathers did; that we can make local government responsible and effective once again.[77]

Which is the stronger case? Anyone who has read the preceding part of this chapter with any care will know that I am inclined to accept the proposition that rationalization of metropolitan government will not only be difficult to achieve but might in some cases do more harm than good. I am accordingly disinclined to accept the "need" for a consolidated or rationalized metro-political structure. But to render a categoric answer to the question of which of the two cases is the stronger requires that the positions be stated in an oversimplified way. And if the positions are simplified the answer can only be misleading for the problem is not a simple one. Therefore, the point to be emphasized is that the best way of examining this matter is not in terms of sharply drawn alternatives but in a pragmatic fashion. That is, the prescription must be written in terms of the specific situation, not in categoric terms. In some communities certain problems will demand more centralized metropolitan control and it will be feasible, perhaps because of the gravity and self-evident seriousness of the problem, to get action. In others the problems will be less demanding and no action will be possible.

It is well to remember that there are worse things than inefficiency and asymmetrical or seemingly illogical government designs. Among the hard realities of metropolitan politicking, it must be accepted that a great proportion of the population will not care in the least whether there is consolidation or not. Still, those who take positions one way or another are influenced by a wide range of values, fears, selfish motives, and possession or lack of information. It seems perfectly clear that many persons would readily sacrifice lower cost and greater efficiency in government in order to have either the illusion or the reality of local

---

[77] Robert Wood, "There Are Many Roads," 51 *National Civic Review* 129 (1962), 174.

control over local matters. Before they sacrifice the opportunity to decide locally, the citizen and the public official representing him will have to be convinced that the risks of not consolidating will be too great to bear.

And the cost of refusal to centralize will not be too great to bear for some time to come. First, there are ameliorating forces, as noted above, which permit more rational decision-making even though there is no centralization. Not only are intergovernmental contracts and agreements offering formal ways of interlocking public policies within areas, but there are also informal ways of cooperation that may in the long run prove more effective. One of the more hopeful signs is the development of ad hoc committees of chief executives of municipalities in metropolitan regions where the executives meet, share information, and attempt to work out common approaches to common problems. Thus the Metropolitan Regional Council in New York has been operating since 1956 as a voluntary consultative group representing 16 cities and 21 counties in the region.[78] In San Francisco the Association of Bay Area Governments has been in operation since January 1961, and its purpose is:

. . . to facilitate study of metropolitan matters and to determine functions that the cities and counties may perform jointly. . . . In no sense is it a new unit of government. It is dedicated to attempting to achieve a concert of action among the member governments, each acting within its own area and by means of its own employees and facilities.[79]

Through this organization operations got underway to provide the area with a rapid transit system, a much-needed development. In many other areas similar agencies are being created, and although their potential depends upon many imponderables, it is not inconceivable that they may contribute something toward minimizing the effects of sheer ignorance of metropolitan conditions on the part of metropolitan officials.

Second, the costs of decentralization will continue to be bearable, both because the costs are hidden and because we are affluent. If the costs of metropolitanization continue to be subsidized, obscured, and unrecognized, and if the financial ability to pay the costs continues to

---

[78] It must be admitted, however, that the MRC is a weak reed; fear that it might gain power undercut it in Suburbia.

[79] Winston W. Crouch, "The California Way," 51 *National Civic Review* 139 (1962), 144. See also Victor Jones, *Associations of Local Governments: Patterns for Metropolitan Cooperation* (University of California, Public Affairs Report, April, 1962).

exist, then it would not appear likely that the cost factor will precipitate a change. If costs can be met, then tangible pleasures, vested interests, and apprehension of the unknown are formidable adversaries when pitted against proposals to "rationalize" and make more logical a governmental system whose untidiness and unwieldiness may be far more apparent to the conceptualizer than to the individual citizen or the official immersed in immediate problems.

Third, there may well be alternatives yet to be devised that may play a role in coping with the disparities of the metropolitan region. For example, in state after state it is becoming fashionable to create a department of urban affairs (or some similar title). These agencies may be able to play an important role in encouraging the communities in various regions to cooperate more fully. And if the federal government should turn to a tax-sharing system and grant to the states considerable amounts of cash that is not tied to specific programs, it might be possible for the states to use the carrot of assistance to encourage joint planning and development. I grant, however, that this will take some doing. The communities both at the center and the periphery of the metropolis have vested interests in land use control, which they give up hesitantly indeed.

Thus the suburb is reluctant to give up its power over the zoning of land. If laws on zoning are too lax, a jungle of hot dog stands and gas stations can create an aesthetic horror around, for example, a newly developed park. Or to the contrary zoning laws can be rigged to keep the indigents (black or white) out of a town that establishes three- or four-acre zoning for houses worth a small fortune. It is possible that in time the state may have to blow the whistle on such practices. If the problem of the central city ghetto becomes too intense, it may be necessary to permit some residential diversification in suburbia. And when a state invests hundreds of millions of dollars in a recreational site it may be reluctant to see its handiwork despoiled by zoning that invites aesthetic disaster. It might become not only politically possible but necessary to act to review zoning laws. (When I said this to a large meeting of planning board members in convention a few years ago, I felt the kind of hostility and shock that might be expected in church if the minister began telling an obscene story.)

What goes for suburbia where such possible future state controls are concerned may conceivably also hit the center city, although again the vested interests in allowing madcap development are strong. A few years ago esthetes howled over the construction of the huge Pan Am building over train tracks adjacent to the Grand Central Station in what is one of the most congested urban spots in the world. Despite the heavy concentration of population in that spot, the building was to be over 700 feet high and the largest business office building in the world. (All this on a 3.5 acre site!) And a few years after this building (with its added noise-making heliport on its roof) went up, someone then came up with another proposal to build still another office building, this one literally on top of Grand Central, thus adding new congestion and confusion. (This proposal was made just after the Port of New York Authority got clearance to build twin towers 110 stories high—the World Trade Center—in lower West Side Manhattan, to be the world's largest building. One is reminded of Frank Lloyd Wright's grim satire: a building a mile high in which a whole city would live and work.) But the city collects taxes on these architectural monuments to concentration and it doesn't want limitations that will cut its desperately needed revenues. But the cost to the city as a whole in traffic, population density, and aesthetic values may yet cause outside interests to intervene.

The Politics of Metropolitan
Intergovernmental Relations

There is a remarkable similarity between the politics of international relationships and the politics of metropolitan intergovernmental relations. There are, admittedly, differences too, but the unexpected resemblances are both interesting and instructive. Thus international politics is made awkward by and yet must find ways of coming to grips with the tremendously important fact that while all nations have that form of independence of action called sovereignty, there is in fact no complete freedom of action for any nation. Neither the alliances it makes nor the adversaries it faces—to say nothing of the forces of its own international politics—permit the free-choice role that the canons of nineteenth-century jurisprudential theory postulated for nations. Nor, when one stops to think about it, does the American state possess the kind of total authority to manipulate the municipal government implied by Dillon's rule which is a kind of local analogue of Austinian theory. By the same token, it is one of the problems of international politics that in formal terms all nations have equal standing (and therefore equal power potential), and yet this formal equality flies in the face of enormously different physical and economic power potentials among nations. So too New York City and a suburban dormitory town of a few thousand are both municipal entities in the New York region, and each has not only status but a legal and political potential that the other must respect. As small nations in the United Nations Assembly employ their national identity as a source of power in competition with the superpowers, so the small municipalities have legal rights under the laws and state constitution that the city, although vastly larger, wealthier, and politically more powerful, must perforce take into account.[80]

There are also interesting analogies between general approaches to international and metropolitan politics. Inis L. Claude in his book, *Swords into Plowshares,* identifies three general orientations toward international politics—that of the power-realists, that of the world government advocates, and that of the pragmatists. There are interesting parallels between these and certain outlooks on metropolitan affairs. Without going into detail, one can see a parallel between the power-realists (who, Claude says, see in the system of nation-states an inevitable conflict which commands a prudent policy of concentration on survival), and those who would let metropolitan affairs be settled by each governmental unit protecting its own interests, forgetting supergovernment ideas. By the same token, there is a parallel between the world government enthusiasts (who believe chaos will result unless there is world government to cope with what they deem equally inevitable internation clash) and the proponents of integrated metropolitan government. Finally Claude identifies a third approach to international politics—one which refuses to accept the inevitability of conflict and holds out for the feasibility of modifying the relationships of nations "even while the present system remains unchanged in its fundamentals."[81] This group is comparable to the metropolitan pragmatists who hold the view that there are ameliorating moves open for dealing with genuine metropolitan problems short of allout integration.

One can also see interesting comparisons between the general political processes at the two levels. In both cases bargaining and negotiation are necessary. Bargaining is complex at both levels because it involves bargainers who cannot be sure that the bargains they make will be safe from the point of view of their own political futures. Bargaining goes on in an atmosphere of varying degrees of tension and always with a

---

[80] See, for example, Inis L. Claude's *Swords into Plowshares* (New York: Random House, 1956), and note how many analogies with metropolitan politics one can find in his theoretical analysis and description of international organizational politics. Matthew Holden also compares metropolitan and international politics in "The Governance of the Metropolis as a Problem in Diplomacy," 26 *Journal of Politics* 627–47 (1964).

[81] Claude, *op. cit.,* p. 14. See pp. 13–14 for his summary presentation of these broad types.

considerable degree of ignorance of the facts of the matter at hand. Captives of preconceived ideas find it hard to negotiate beyond certain self-imposed barriers. Firm convictions about local integrity or the necessity to relinquish no authority neatly parallel concepts of national honor and sovereignty.

Bargaining is obviously affected by different power potentials of the governments involved. In relations between municipalities, or between state or national government and municipalities, there are often gross differences between the "potential" power of the bargainers. A state government dealing with a municipality has infinitely greater potential power resources to draw upon than has the municipality. And yet the state has to temper the use of its authority and may often seek some compromise rather than face a showdown on a given issue. If, for example, a state official is dealing with several municipalities on water pollution problems in a metropolitan area, the official may have the authority to command the municipalities to cease polluting streams, but he may be hesitant to use his authority. A blunt command may stir a hornet's nest of protest and result in a general weakening of the agency or program since legislators may react negatively to the controversy that ensues. It hardly need be pointed out that there are interesting parallels with international politics where underdeveloped nations successfully bargain with richer and more powerful nations.

Thus formal controls and formal authority may be more illusory than real. Formal authority to abolish local governments is meaningless because in practice it cannot be employed. Like the power of impeachment in the federal government, it exists but is unused. In practical terms, however, formal power to abolish local governments is irrelevant: the point is that the state has the formal as well as the practical power to grant or deny powers and functions to localities, to prescribe methods of operation, and otherwise to condition the operations of local government. The state, in other words, has a strong base of power in its constitutional authority to assert certain kinds of control over local government. The locality likewise possesses a reciprocal base of power in that state officials are apprehensive about the possibility of popular dissatisfaction over too stringent use of state authority. Widespread belief in "home rule," however dimly understood, is a base of local power which the superior government must inevitably take into account.

If formal powers are but an element of the bargaining process to be evaluated alongside a host of other factors such as tradition, adherence to localism, the inducements of grants-in-aid, the blandishments and recurrent campaigns of reformers, then it does not appear likely that "solutions" in the often hoped-for sense will ever be found. As has been pointed out often in this volume, problems are more likely to be "resolved" (*i.e.*, compromised, ameliorated, or otherwise tentatively taken off the prime agenda) in respect to existing circumstances and conflicting values and desires than any orderly syllogistic thinking. More rational approaches than those in common use in the metropolis can easily be imagined, and in time many of the imagined approaches will turn into practical methods, but as surely as they are tried some will fail, some will persist awhile and then become anachronisms. For the metropolis does not stand still; its essence is change and development. This process of rethinking, bargaining, persuading, influencing, is what we have been talking about throughout this assessment of state and local *politics*.

BIBLIOGRAPHY

The following references are intended to guide research efforts on the fifty states and some selected cities on which useful materials are available. The selections are therefore arranged by states and cities rather than topically. Full bibliographic information on a given title or series is presented only at the first reference to it. See the Index for references to bibliographic footnotes.

State Politics References

ALABAMA

Earle, Valerie A., and Chester B. Earle. *Taxing the Southern Railroad in Alabama,* rev. ed. (I.C.P. Case Series, No. 18.). University, Ala.: University of Alabama Press, 1959.

Hamilton, Charles V. *Minority Politics in Black Belt Alabama.* (Eagleton Cases in Practical Politics, No. 19.). New York: McGraw-Hill Book Co., 1960.

Key, V. O., with Alexander Heard. *Southern Politics.* New York: Alfred A. Knopf, Inc., 1949, Ch. 3.

ALASKA

Slotnick, Herman. "Alaska: Empire of the North." In *Western Politics,* edited by F. H. Jonas. Salt Lake City, Utah: University of Utah Press, 1961, Ch. 2.

ARIZONA

Morey, Roy D., *Politics and Legislation: The Office of Governor in Arizona.* Tucson: University of Arizona Press, 1965.

Rice, Ross R. "Amazing Arizona: Politics in Transition." In *Western Politics,* Ch. 3.

————. "Bibliography of Arizona Politics." 11 *Western Political Quarterly,* Supplement 13 (1958).

ARKANSAS

Key, V. O. *Southern Politics,* Ch. 9.

CALIFORNIA

Anderson, T. J. "Bibliography of California Politics." 11 *Western Political Quarterly,* Supplement 23 (1958).

Anderson, Totton James. "California: Enigma of National Politics." In *Western Politics.* Ch. 4.

Bollens, John C. and W. W. Crouch, *The Governments of California.* San Francisco: H. Wagner Publishing Co., 1966.

Buchanan, William. *Legislative Bipartisanship: The Deviant Case of California.* Berkeley, University of California Press, 1963.

Carney, Francis. *The Rise of the Democratic Clubs in California.* (Eagleton Case No. 13), 1958.

Harris, Joseph P. *California Politics,* 3rd ed. Stanford, Calif.: Stanford University Press, 1963.

Jacobs, Clyde E., and John Gallagher, *California Government: One Among Fifty.* New York: Macmillan, 1966.

Lee, Eugene C. *The Politics of Nonpartisanship.* Los Angeles: University of California Press, 1960.

Leuthold, David A. *et al. California Politics and Problems, 1960–63: A Selective Bibliography.* Berkeley: University of California Press, 1965.

Pritchell, Robert J. "The Electoral System and Voting Behavior: The Case of California's Cross-Filing." 12 *Western Political Quarterly* 459 (1959).

————. "The Influence of Professional Campaign Management Firms in Partisan Elections in California." 11 *Western Political Quarterly* 278 (1958).

Radabaugh, John S. "Tendencies of California Direct Legislation." 42 *Southwestern Social Science Quarterly* 66 (1961).

Swisher, Carl B. *Motivation and Political Technique in the California Constitutional Convention, 1878–79.* Claremont, Calif.: Pomona College, 1930.

Velie, Lester. "The Secret Boss of California." *Collier's* (August 13, 1949), pp. 12–13, 71–73; (August 20, 1949), pp. 12–13, 60–64.

COLORADO

Gomez, Rudolph. "Legislative Voting Behavior in Colorado," 17 *Western Political Quarterly* 70–72 (Supplement), 1964.

Martin, Curtis. "Bibliography of Colorado Politics." 11 *Western Political Quarterly* Supplement 51 (1958).

———. "Colorado: The Highest State." In *Western Politics*, Ch. 5.

Schur, Morris J. *Selected Bibliography of Colorado State and Local Government.* Boulder, Colorado: Bureau of Governmental Research and Service, Colorado University, 1964.

CONNECTICUT

Barber, James D. *The Lawmakers.* New Haven: Yale University Press, 1965.

Lieberman, Joseph I. *The Power Broker: John Bailey, Modern Political Boss.* Boston: Houghton Mifflin, 1966.

Lockard, Duane. *Connecticut's Challenge Primary.* (Eagleton Case No. 7), 1959.

———. "Legislative Politics in Connecticut." 48 *American Political Science Review* 166 (1954).

———. *New England State Politics.* Princeton, N.J.: Princeton University Press, 1959, Chs. 9, 10.

Lyford, Joseph P. *Candidate.* (Eagleton Case No. 9), 1959.

Sikorsky, Igor I. *Convention at Large* (Eagleton Case No. 32), 1964.

DELAWARE

Dolan, Paul. *The Government and Administration of Delaware.* New York: Thomas Y. Crowell Company, Inc., 1956.

FLORIDA

Doyle, Wilson K., *et al. The Government and Administration of Florida.* New York: Thomas Y. Crowell Company, 1954.

Key, V. O. *Southern Politics.* Ch. 5.

Price, H. Douglas. *The Negro and Southern Politics: A Chapter in Florida History.* New York: New York University Press, 1957.

GEORGIA

Gosnell, Cullen B., and David C. Anderson. *The Government and Administration of Georgia.* New York: Thomas Y. Crowell Company, Inc., 1956.

Key, V. O. *Southern Politics.* Ch. 5.

HAWAII

Meller, Norman and Daniel W. Tuttle, Jr. "Hawaii: The Aloha State." In *Western Politics.* Ch. 6.

IDAHO

Huckshorn, Robert J. "Decision-Making Stimuli in the State Legislative Process," 18 *Western Political Quarterly* 164–85 (1965).

Martin, Boyd A. "Idaho: The Sectional State." In *Western Politics*.

——. and R. D. Humphrey. "Bibliography of Idaho Politics." 11 *Western Political Quarterly* Supplement 54 (1958).

ILLINOIS

Fahrnkopf, Nancy, and M. C. Lynch, eds. *State and Local Government in Illinois, A Bibliography.* Urbana, Ill.: Institute of Government and Public Affairs, University of Illinois, 1965.

Garvey, Neil F. *The Government and Administration of Illinois.* New York: Thomas Y. Crowell Company, Inc., 1958.

Fenton, John. *Midwest Politics.* New York: Holt, Rinehart & Winston, 1966, Ch. 7.

Gove, S. K., ed. *State and Local Government in Illinois: A Bibliography.* Urbana, Ill.: Institute of Public Affairs, University of Illinois, 1953, with 1958 Supplement.

Keefe, William. "Party Government and Lawmaking in Illinois General Assembly." 47 *Northwestern University Law Review* 55 (1952).

Littlewood, Thomas B. *Bipartisan Coalition in Illinois.* (Eagleton Case No. 22), 1960.

MacRae, Duncan, Jr., and James A. Meldrum. "Critical Elections in Illinois: 1888–1958." 54 *American Political Science Review* 669 (1960).

Ranney, Austin. *Illinois Politics.* New York: New York University Press, 1960.

Steiner, Gilbert Y., and Samuel K. Gove. *Legislative Politics in Illinois.* Urbana, Ill.: University of Illinois Press, 1960.

INDIANA

Fenton. *Midwest Politics.* Ch. 6.

McNeil, Robert, *Democratic Campaign Financing In Indiana.* Princeton, N.J.: Citizens Research Foundation, 1966.

Munger, Frank. *The Struggle for Republican Leadership in Indiana, 1954.* (Eagleton Case No. 23), 1960.

Standing, William H., and James A. Robinson. "Inter-Party Competition and Primary Contesting: The Case of Indiana." 52 *American Political Science Review* 1066 (1958).

IOWA

Gold, David, and John R. Schmidhauser. "Urbanization and Party Competition: The Case of Iowa." 4 *Midwest Journal of Political Science* 62 (1960).

Ross, Russell M. *The Government and Administration of Iowa.* New York: Thomas Y. Crowell Company, Inc., 1957.

Schmidhauser, John. *Iowa's Campaign for a Constitutional Convention in 1960.* (Eagleton Case No. 30), 1963.

KANSAS

Bart, Peter, and Milton Cummings, Jr. *The Transfer of the Kansas State Civil Service Department.* (I.C.P. Case Series, No. 31), 1955.
Cape, William H. *Constitutional Revision in Kansas.* (Governmental Research Series, No. 17), Lawrence, Kan.: University of Kansas, 1958.
Smith, Rhoten A., and Clarence J. Hein. *Republican Primary Fight: A Study in Factionalism.* (Eagleton Case No. 11), 1958.
Titus, James. "Kansas Governors: A Résumé of Political Leadership." 17 *Western Political Quarterly* 356–70 (1964).

KENTUCKY

Fenton, John H. *Politics in the Border States.* New Orleans: The Hauser Press, 1957, Chs. 2, 3.
Jewell, Malcom E. "Party and Primary Competition in Kentucky State Legislative Races." 248 *Kentucky Law Journal* 517 (1960).
Reeves, John E. *Kentucky Government.* Lexington, Ky.: Bureau of Government Research, University of Kentucky, 1955.

LOUISIANA

Fenton, John H., and Kenneth N. Vines. "Negro Registration in Louisiana." 51 *American Political Science Review* 704 (1957).
Havard, William C. "From Bossism to Cosmopolitanism: Changes in the Relation of Urban Leadership to State Politics." 353 *Annals* 84–94 (1964).
Howard, P. H. *Political Tendencies in Louisiana, 1812–1952.* Baton Rouge, La.: Louisiana State University Press, 1956.
Key, V. O. *Southern Politics.*
Sindler, Allan P. "Bifactional Rivalry as an Alternative to Two-Party Competition in Louisiana." 49 *American Political Science Review* 641 (1955).
———. *Huey Long's Louisiana.* Baltimore: John Hopkins Press, 1956.

MAINE

Lockard, Duane. *New England State Politics.* Ch. 4.
Walker, David B. *Politics and Ethnocentrism: The Case of the Franco-Americans.* (Government Research Series, No. 23). Brunswick, Me.: Bowdoin College, 1961.
———. *A Maine Profile: Some Conditions of the Political System.* Brunswick, Me.: Bureau for Research on Municipal Government, Bowdoin College, 1964.
Wilson, James, and Robert W. Crowe. *Managers in Maine.* (Government Research Series, No. 24). Brunswick, Me.: Bowdoin College, 1962.

MARYLAND

Fenton, John. *Politics in the Border States.* Chs. 8, 9.

Friedman, R. S. *A Selected Bibliography of Maryland State and Local Government.* College Park, Md.: Bureau of Government Research, University of Maryland, 1956.

Hanson, Royce. *Fair Representation Comes to Maryland.* (Eagleton Case No. 35), 1960.

MASSACHUSETTS

Eliot, Thomas H. *Reorganizing the Massachusetts Department of Conservation,* rev. ed. (I.C.P. Case Series, No. 14), 1960.

———. *The Van Waters Case,* rev. ed. (I.C.P. Case Series, No. 22), 1960.

Huthmacher, J. Joseph. *Massachusetts People and Politics, 1919–1933.* Cambridge, Mass.: Belknap Press, 1959.

Latham, Earl and George Goodwin. *Massachusetts Politics.* 2nd ed. Medford, Mass.: Tufts Civic Education Center, Tufts University, 1960.

Levin, Murray. *The Compleat Politician.* Indianapolis, Ind.: Bobbs-Merrill, 1962.

Litt, Edgar. *The Political Cultures of Massachusetts.* Cambridge, Mass.: Massachusetts Institute of Technology Press, 1965.

Lockard, Duane. *New England State Politics.* Chs. 5, 6.

Mallen, John P., and George Blackwood. "The Tax That Beat a Governor: The Ordeal of Massachusetts." In *The Uses of Power,* edited by Alan F. Westin. New York: Harcourt, Brace, and World, Inc., 1962, Ch. 6.

Pesonen, Pertti. "Close and Safe State Elections in Massachusetts." 7 *Midwest Journal of Political Science* 54–76 (1963).

MICHIGAN

Fenton, John. *Midwest Politics,* Ch. 2.

Fischer, Floyd C. *The Government of Michigan.* Boston: Allyn and Bacon, 1965.

Friedman, Robert S. *The Michigan Constitutional Convention and Administrative Organization.* Ann Arbor, Mich.: Institute of Public Administration, University of Michigan, 1963.

Halperin, Samuel. *A University in the Web of Politics.* (Eagleton Cases in Practical Politics, No. 14), 1960.

LaPalombara, Joseph G. *Guide to Michigan Politics,* rev. ed. East Lansing, Mich.: Bureau of Social and Political Research, Michigan State University, 1960.

Sarasohn, Stephen B., and Vera H. Sarasohn. *Political Party Patterns in Michigan.* Detroit: Wayne State University Press, 1957.

Schubert, Glendon A., Jr. *The Michigan State Director of Elections.* (I.C.P. Case Series, No. 23), 1954.

Thomas, Norman C. *Rule 9: Politics, Administration and Civil Rights.* New York: Random House, 1966.

Turano, P. J. *Michigan State and Local Government and Politics: A Bibliography.* Ann Arbor, Mich.: Institute of Public Administration, University of Michigan, 1955.

Ulmer, Sidney. "The Political Party Variable in the Michigan Supreme Court." 11 *Journal of Public Law* 352–62 (1963).

White, John P., and John R. Owens. *Parties, Group Interests and Campaign Finance: Michigan '56.* Princeton, N.J.: Citizens Research Foundation, 1960.

MINNESOTA

Fenton, John. *Midwest Politics*, Ch. 4.

Flinn, Thomas. *Governor Freeman and the Minnesota Budget.* (I.C.P. Case Series, No. 60), 1961.

Mitau, G. Theodore. "The Governor and the Strike." In *Cases in State and Local Government*, edited by Richard T. Frost. Englewood Cliffs, N.J.: Prentice-Hall, Inc., 1961, Ch. 17.

———. *Politics in Minnesota.* Minneapolis: University of Minnesota Press, 1960.

MISSISSIPPI

Highsaw, Robert B., and Charles N. Fortenberry. *The Government and Administration of Mississippi.* New York: Thomas Y. Crowell Company, Inc., 1954.

Key, V. O. *Southern Politics*, Ch. 11.

Silver, James W. *Mississippi: The Closed Society.* 2nd ed. New York: Harcourt, Brace and World, 1966.

MISSOURI

Fenton, John H. *Politics in the Border States*, Chs. 6, 7.

Karsh, R. F. *The Government of Missouri.* Columbia, Mo.: Lucas Bros., 1966.

Salisbury, Robert H. "Missouri Politics and State Political Systems," *Research Papers, 1958.* Columbia, Mo.: Bureau of Government Research, University of Missouri, 1959.

MONTANA

Payne, Thomas. "Bibliography of Montana Politics." 11 *Western Political Quarterly* Supplement 65 (1958).

———. "Under the Copper Dome: Politics in Montana." In *Western Politics*, Ch. 8.

Renne, Roland R. *The Government and Administration of Montana.* New York: Thomas Y. Crowell Company, Inc., 1958.

NEBRASKA

Breckenridge, A. C. *One House for Two*. Washington, D.C.: Public Affairs Press, 1957.

NEVADA

Driggs, D. W. "Bibliography of Nevada Politics." 11 *Western Political Quarterly*, Supplement 73 (1958).
————. "Nevada: The Silver Dollar State." In *Western Politics*, Ch. 9.
Mack, E. M. *et al*. *Nevada Government*. Caldwell, Idaho: Caxton Printers, 1953.
Ostrander, Gilman M. *Nevada, the Great Rotten Borough*. New York: Alfred A. Knopf, 1966.

NEW HAMPSHIRE

Lockard. *New England State Politics*. Ch. 3.

NEW JERSEY

Frost, Richard T. "The New Jersey Institutions Case." In *Cases in State and Local Government*, Ch. 18.
————. "Stability and Change in Local Party Politics." 25 *Public Opinion Quarterly* 221 (1961).
Hogarty, Richard A. *New Jersey Farmers and the Migrant Housing Rules*. (I.C.P. Case Series No. 94), 1965.
Lockard, Duane. *The New Jersey Governor*. Princeton, N.J.: Van Nostrand, 1964.
McKean, Dayton David. *The Boss*. Boston: Houghton Mifflin Co., 1940.
————. *Pressures on the New Jersey Legislature*. New York: Columbia University Press, 1938.
Pomper, Gerald. "New Jersey County Chairmen," 18 *Western Political Quarterly* 186–97 (1965).
Rich, Bennett M. *The Government and Administration of New Jersey*. New York: Thomas Y. Crowell Company, Inc., 1957.

NEW MEXICO

Holmes, Jack E. *Politics in New Mexico*. Albuquerque: University of New Mexico Press, 1967.
Irion, Frederick C. "Bibliography of New Mexico Politics." 11 *Western Political Quarterly*, Supplement 77 (1958).
————. "New Mexico: The Political State." In *Western Politics*, Ch. 10.

NEW YORK

Ahlberg, Clark D., and Daniel P. Moynihan. "Changing Governors—and Policies" 20 *Public Administration Review* 195–204 (1960).

Caldwell, Lynton K. *The Government and Administration of New York.* New York: Thomas Y. Crowell Company, Inc., 1954.

Herzberg, Donald G., and Paul Tillett. *A budget for New York State, 1956–1957.* (I.C.P. Case Series, No. 69), 1962.

Martin, Roscoe C. *Water for New York: A Study in State Administration of Water Resources.* Syracuse, N.Y.: Syracuse University Press, 1960.

Miller, Howard F. *The Shredded Wheat Property.* (I.C.P. Case Series, No. 54), 1960.

Moynihan, Daniel P., and James Q. Wilson. "Patronage in New York State, 1955–59." 58 *American Political Science Review* 286–301 (1964).

Moscow, Warren. *Politics in the Empire State.* New York: Alfred A. Knopf, Inc., 1948.

Straetz, Ralph A., and Frank J. Munger. *New York Politics.* New York: New York University Press, 1960.

Zeller, Belle. *Pressure Politics in New York.* Englewood Cliffs, N.J.: Prentice-Hall, Inc., 1937.

NORTH CAROLINA

Bowman, Lewis, and G. R. Boynton. "Coalition as Party in a One-Party Southern Area . . ." 8 *Midwest Journal of Political Science* 277–97 (1964).

Hodges, Luther H. *Businessman in the Statehouse: Six Years as Governor of North Carolina.* Chapel Hill, N.C.: University of North Carolina Press, 1962.

Key, V. O. *Southern Politics,* Ch. 10.

Rankin, Robert S. *The Government and Administration of North Carolina.* New York: Thomas Y. Crowell Company, Inc., 1955.

NORTH DAKOTA

Huntington, Samuel P. "The Election Tactics of the Non-Partisan League." 36 *The Mississippi Valley Historical Review* 613–32 (1950).

Morlan, R. L. *Political Prairie Fire: The Nonpartisan League.* Minneapolis: University of Minnesota Press, 1955.

OHIO

Aumann, Francis R., and Harvey Walker. *The Government and Administration of Ohio.* New York: Thomas Y. Crowell Company, Inc., 1956.

Fenton, John. *Midwest Politics.* Ch. 5.

Flinn, Thomas A. "The Outline of Ohio Politics." 13 *Western Political Quarterly* 702 (1960).

———. "Continuity and Change in Ohio Politics." 27 *Journal of Politics* 185–91 (1965).

Key, V. O., Jr. "Partisanship and County Office: The Case of Ohio." 47 *American Political Science Review* 525 (1953).

Rose, Albert H. *Ohio Government, State and Local*. 3rd ed. Dayton, Ohio: University of Dayton Press, 1966.

OKLAHOMA

Patterson, Samuel C. "The Role of the Lobbyist: The Case of Oklahoma." 25 *Journal of Politics* 72–92 (1963).

Thornton, H. V. *An Outline of Oklahoma Government*. Norman, Okla.: Rickner's Book Store, 1956.

Walker, Robert S., and Samuel C. Patterson. *Oklahoma Goes Wet: The Repeal of Prohibition*. (Eagleton Case No. 24,) 1960.

OREGON

Baker, Gordon E. "Reapportionment by Initiative in Oregon." 13 *Western Political Quarterly* 508 (1960).

Balmer, Donald. *Financing State Senate Campaigns: Multnomah County, Oregon*. Princeton, N.J.: Citizens Research Foundation, 1966.

Seligman, Lester G. "Political Recruitment and Party Structure: A Case Study." 55 *American Political Science Review* 77 (1961).

———, and Martha Swanson. "Bibliography of Oregon Politics." 11 *Western Political Quarterly*, Supplement 110 (1958).

Swarthout, John M. "Oregon: Political Experiment Station." In *Western Politics*, Ch. 11.

PENNSYLVANIA

Cooke, E. F., and G. E. Janosik. *Pennsylvania Politics*. rev. ed. New York: Holt, Rinehart and Winston, Inc., 1965.

Hacker, Andrew. "Pressure Politics in Pennsylvania: The Truckers vs. the Railroads. In *The Uses of Power*, Ch. 7.

Keefe, William. "Parties, Partisanship, and Public Policy in the Pennsylvania Legislature." 48 *American Political Science Review* 450 (1954).

Smith, Reed M. *State Government in Transition: Reforms of the Leader Administration, 1955–59*. Philadelphia: University of Pennsylvania Press, 1963.

Sorauf, Frank J. "State Patronage in a Rural County." 50 *American Political Science Review* 1046 (1956).

Tanger, Jacob, *et al. Pennsylvania Government: State and Local*, 3rd ed. University Park, Pa.: Penns Valley, 1950.

RHODE ISLAND

Lockard, Duane. *New England State Politics*, Chs. 7, 8.

SOUTH CAROLINA

Eisenberg, Ralph. "The Logroll, South Carolina Style." In *Cases in State and Local Government*, Ch. 13.

Hendricks, Peter W. *The South Carolinian and His Government*. Chapin, S.C.: Privately published, 1966.
Key, V. O. *Southern Politics*, Ch. 7.

SOUTH DAKOTA

Clem, Alan L. *Legislative Power and Reapportionment in South Dakota*. In *Public Affairs*. Vermillion, S.D.: Government Research Bureau, University of South Dakota, 1961.
Farber, William O., Thomas C. Geary, and William H. Cape. *Government of South Dakota*. Sioux Falls, S.D.: Midwest-Beach Co., 1962.

TENNESSEE

Goodman, William. *Inherited Domain: Political Parties in Tennessee*. Knoxville, Tenn.: Bureau of Public Administration, University of Tennessee, 1954.
Greene, Lee S., and Robert S. Avery. *Government in Tennessee*. 2nd ed. Knoxville, Tenn.: University of Tennessee Press, 1966.
Miller, William D. *Mr. Crump of Memphis*. Baton Rouge, La.: Louisiana State University Press, 1964.
Key, V. O. *Southern Politics*, Ch. 4
Parks, Norman L. "Tennessee Politics Since Keefauver and Reece." 28 *Journal of Politics* 144–68 (1966).

TEXAS

Benton, Wilbourne E. Texas: *Its Government and Politics*. rev. ed. Englewood Cliffs, N.J.: Prentice-Hall, 1966.
Key, V. O. *Southern Politics*, Ch. 12.
MacCorkle, S. A., and Dick Smith. *Texas Government*, 5th ed. New York: McGraw-Hill Book Co., 1964.
McClesky, Clifton. *The Government and Politics of Texas*, 2nd ed. Boston: Little, Brown & Co., 1966.
Mills, Warner E., Jr. *Martial Law in East Texas*. (I.C.P. Case Series, No. 53), 1960.
Patterson, C. P., S. B. McAlister, and G. C. Hester. *State and Local Government in Texas*, 3rd ed. New York: The Macmillan Company, 1961.

UTAH

Jonas, Frank H. "Bibliography of Utah Politics." 11 *Western Political Quarterly*, Supplement 132 (1958).
———. "Utah: Crossroads of the West." In *Western Politics*, Ch. 12.
———, and Garth Jones. "J. Bracken Lee and the Public Service in Utah." 9 *Western Political Quarterly*, 755–65 (1956).

VERMONT

Garceau, Oliver, and Corinne Silverman. "A Pressure Group and the Pressured: A Case Report." 48 *American Political Science Review* 672 (1954).

Lockard. *New England State Politics*, Ch. 2.

VIRGINIA

Gates, Robbins L. *The Making of Massive Resistance: Virginia's Politics of Public School Desegregation 1954–56*. Chapel Hill, N.C.: University of North Carolina Press, 1964.

Key, V. O. *Southern Politics*, Ch. 2.

WASHINGTON

Avery, Mary W. *Government of Washington State*. Seattle, Washington: University of Washington Press, 1967.

Baker, Gordon E. *The Politics of Reapportionment in Washington State*. (Eagleton Case No. 3), 1960.

Bone, Hugh A. "Washington State: Free Style Politics." In *Western Politics*, Ch. 13.

——, and W. H. Leavel. "Bibliography of Washington Politics." 11 *Western Political Quarterly*, Supplement 151 (1958).

Ogden, Daniel M., Jr., and Hugh A. Bone. *Washington Politics*. New York: New York University Press, 1960.

WEST VIRGINIA

Davis, Claude, *et al. West Virginia State and Local Government*. Morgantown, W. Va.: Bureau for Government Research, 1963.

Fenton. *Politics in the Border States*, Chs. 4–5.

Kaempfer, W. W. *The Board of Public Works, West Virginia's Plural Executive*. Morgantown, W.Va.: Bureau for Government Research, West Virginia University, 1957.

Ross, William R. *An Introduction to the Electoral Process in West Virginia*. Morgantown, W.Va.: Bureau for Government Research, West Virginia University, 1962.

WISCONSIN

Epstein, Leon. *Politics in Wisconsin*. Madison, Wis.: University of Wisconsin Press, 1958.

——. *Votes and Taxes*. Madison, Wis.: Institute of Governmental Affairs, University of Wisconsin, 1964.

Fenton. *Midwest Politics*. Ch. 3.

Patterson, Samuel C. "Patterns of Interpersonal Relations in a State Legislative Group: The Wisconsin Assembly." 23 *Public Opinion Quarterly* 101 (1959).

Sykes, Jay C. *Wisconsin Gets a Sales Tax* (Eagleton Case No. 38), 1965.

WYOMING

Beall, Charles P. "Wyoming: The Equality State." In *Western Politics*, Ch. 14.

John B. Richard. *Government and Politics of Wyoming.* Dubuque, Iowa: W. C. Brown Book Co., 1966.

Trachel, H. H. "Bibliography of Wyoming Politics." 11 *Western Political Quarterly*, Supplement 164 (1958).

Trachel, Herman H., and Ralph M. Wade. *The Government and Administration of Wyoming.* New York: Thomas Y. Crowell Company, Inc., 1956.

City Politics References

On city politics the Joint Center for Urban Studies of the Massachusetts Institute of Technology and Harvard University has published an excellent series of descriptive works on twenty-two communities—large and small. Available only in mimeograph form, the reports follow a similar format so that comparison is facilitated. Professor Edward Banfield, the general editor of the project, used some of these works in the preparation of his *Big City Politics*, which is cited below under the appropriate cities. The mimeographed originals covered the following cities and are not cited otherwise in this bibliography.

Boston, Mass., 1959
Cincinnati, Ohio, 1959
Denver, Colo., 1959
Detroit, Mich., 1959
El Paso, Tex., 1963
Houston, Tex., 1960
Kansas City, Mo., 1959
Los Angeles, Calif., 1959
Manchester, N.H., 1961
Miami, Fla., 1961
Milwaukee, Wis., 1961

Minneapolis, Minn., 1959
Nashville, Tenn., 1960
New Castle, N.Y., 1961
Philadelphia, Pa., 1963
Salt Lake City, Utah, 1961
San Diego, Calif., 1962
Seattle, Wash., 1961
St. Louis, Mo., 1959
St. Paul, Minn., 1959
Washington, D.C., 1962
Worcester, Mass., 1960

ATLANTA

Banfield, Edward C. *Big City Politics.* New York: Random House, 1965, Ch. 1.

Hunter, Floyd. *Community Power Structure.* Chapel Hill, N.C.: University of North Carolina Press, 1953.

Jennings, M. Kent. *Community Influentials: The Elites of Atlanta.* New York: Free Press, 1964.

Walker, Jack L. *Sit-ins In Atlanta* (Eagleton Case No. 34), 1964.

BALTIMORE

Flemming, G. James. *An All-Negro Ticket in Baltimore.* (Eagleton Case No. 10), 1960.

BELOIT, WISCONSIN

Mills, Warner E., Jr., and Harry R. Davis. *Seven Cases in Decision Making.* New York: Random House, 1962.

BIRMINGHAM

Earle, Chester B., and Valerie A. Earle. *The Promotion of Lem Merrill,* rev. ed. (I.C.P. Case Series, No. 20), 1960.

BOSTON

Banfield, Edward C., *Big City Politics*, Ch. 2.

Levin, Murray B. *The Alienated Voter: Politics in Boston.* New York: Holt, Rinehart, and Winston, Inc., 1960.

Meyerson, Martin, and Edward Banfield. *Boston: The Job Ahead.* Cambridge, Mass.: Harvard University Press, 1966.

CHICAGO

Banfield, Edward C. *Political Influence.* New York: The Free Press of Glencoe, Inc., 1961.

DeGrazia, Alfred. "The Limits of External Leadership over a Minority Electorate." 20 *Public Opinion Quarterly* 113 (1956).

Gosnell, Harold F. *Machine Politics: Chicago Model.* Chicago: University of Chicago Press, 1937.

Gottfried, Alex. *Boss Cermak of Chicago: A Study of Political Leadership.* Seattle: University of Washington Press, 1962.

Meyerson, Martin, and Edward C. Banfield. *Politics, Planning and the Public Interest.* New York: Fress Press of Glencoe, Inc., 1955.

Rossi, Peter H., and Robert A. Dentler. *The Politics of Urban Renewal.* New York: The Free Press of Glencoe, Inc., 1961.

Wilson, James Q. *The Amateur Democrat: Club Politics in Three Cities.* Chicago: University of Chicago Press, 1962, Ch. 3.

————. *Negro Politics. The Search for Leadership.* New York: The Free Press of Glencoe, Inc., 1960, Chs. 3, 4, 6.

CINCINNATI

Straetz, Ralph A. *PR Politics in Cincinnati.* New York: New York University Press, 1958.

CLEVELAND

Norton, James A. "Referenda Voting in a Metropolitan Area." 16 *Western Political Quarterly* 195-212 (1963).

Sacks, Seymour, and William F. Helmuth, Jr. *Financing Government in a Metropolitan Area: The Cleveland Experience.* New York: The Free Press of Glencoe, Inc., 1961.

Watson, Richard A., and John H. Romani. "Metropolitan Government for Metropolitan Cleveland: An Analysis of the Voting Record." 5 *Midwest Journal of Politics* 365 (1961).

DALLAS

Thometz, Carol E. *The Decision Makers. The Power Structure of Dallas.* Dallas, Tex.: Southern Methodist University Press, 1963.

DENVER

Bridge, Franklin M. *Metro-Denver: Mile High Government.* Boulder, Colo.: Bureau of Governmental Research and Service, 1963.

DETROIT

Banfield, Edward C., *Big City Politics*, Ch. 3.

Mowitz, Robert J, and Deil Wright. *Profile of a Metropolis.* Detroit, Mich.: Wayne State University Press, 1962.

Wilson, James Q. *Negro Politics: The Search for Leadership*, Ch. 2.

KANSAS CITY

Gabis, Stanley T. "Leadership in a Large Manager City: The Case of Kansas City." 353 *Annals* 84-94 (1964).

LITTLE ROCK

Alexander, Henry R. *The Little Rock Recall Election.* (Eagleton Case No. 17), 1960.

Silverman, Corinne. *The Little Rock Story*, rev. ed. (I.C.P. Case Series, No. 41), 1959.

LOS ANGELES

Banfield, Edward C. *Big City Politics*, Ch. 5.

Governor's Committee on the Los Angeles Riots: *Violence in the City: an End or a Beginning.* Los Angeles, 1965.

Sherwood, Frank P., and Beatrice Markey. *The Mayor and the Fire Chief.* (I.C.P. Case Series, No. 43), 1959.

Wilson, James. Q. *The Amateur Democrat*, Ch. 4.

———. *Negro Politics, The Search for Leadership*, Ch. 2.

MIAMI

Banfield, Edward C. *Big City Politics*, Ch. 6. Sofen, Edward. *The Miami Metropolitan Experiment.* rev. ed. New York: Doubleday Anchor, 1966.

Wood, Thomas, J. "Dade County: Unbossed, Erratically Led." 353 *Annals* 64-71 (1964).

MILWAUKEE

Maier, Henry W. *Challenge to the Cities*. New York: Random House, 1966.

MINNEAPOLIS

Altshuler, Alan. *The City Planning Process*. Ithaca, N. Y.: Cornell University Press, 1965.

MUNCIE, INDIANA

Lynd, Robert, and Helen Lynd. *Middletown*. New York: Harcourt, Brace, and World Inc., 1929.
————. *Middletown in Transition*. New York: Harcourt, Brace and World, Inc., 1937.

NASHVILLE, TENNESSEE

Grant, Daniel R. "Metropolitics and Professional Political Leadership: The Case of Nashville." 353 *Annals* 72-83 (1964).
Hawkins, Brett W. "Public Opinion and Metropolitan Reorganization in Nashville." 28 *Journal of Politics* 408-18 (1966).

NEWARK, NEW JERSEY

Governor's Select Commission on Civil Disorder, *Report For Action*, Trenton, N.J.: Office of the Governor, 1968.
Kaplan, Harold. *Urban Renewal Politics: Slum Clearance in Newark*. New York: Columbia University Press, 1963.

NEW HAVEN

Farrell, Gregory R. *A Climate of Change: The New Haven Story*. New Brunswick, N. J.: Urban Studies Center, Rutgers University, 1965.
Dahl, Robert A. *Who Governs?* New Haven: Yale University Press, 1961.
Hazen,, Robert N. "Oak Street, New Haven, Connecticut." In *Cases in State and Local Government*, Ch. 27.
Miller, William L. *The Fifteenth Ward and the Great Society*. Boston: Houghton-Mifflin, 1966.
Muir, William K., Jr. *Defending "The Hill" against Metal Houses*, rev. ed. (I.C.P. Case Series, No. 26), 1959.
Wolfinger, Raymond E. "The Development and Persistence of Ethnic Voting." 59 *American Political Science Review* 896-908 (1965).

NEW YORK CITY

Blaisdell, Donald C. *The Riverside Democrats*. (Eagleton Case No. 18), 1960.

Garrett, Charles. *The La Guardia Years: Machine and Reform Politics in New York City*. New Brunswick, N.J.: Rutgers University Press, 1961.

Hapgood, David. *The Purge that Failed: Tammany V. Powell*. (Eagleton Case No. 15), 1959.

Lowi, Theodore J. *At the Pleasure of the Mayor: Patronage and Power in New York City, 1898-1958*. New York: Free Press, 1964.

Peel, Roy V. *The Political Clubs of New York City*. New York: G. P. Putnam's, 1935.

Sayre, Wallace S., and Herbert Kaufman. *Governing New York City: Politics in the Metropolis*. New York: Russell Sage Foundation, 1960.

Shaw, Frederick. *The History of the New York City Legislature*. New York: Columbia University Press, 1954.

Thomas, Samuel F. *Nassau County: Its Governments and Their Expenditure Patterns*. New York: New York City College Press, 1960.

Wilson, James Q. *The Amateur Democrat*, Ch. 2.

————. *Negro Politics: The Search for Leadership*, Ch. 2.

Wood, Robert. *1400 Governments*. Cambridge, Mass.: Harvard University Press, 1961.

PHILADELPHIA

Banfield, Edward C. *Big City Politics*, Ch. 7.

Gilbert, Charles E. *Governing The Suburbs*. Bloomington, Ind.: Indiana University Press, 1967.

Reichley, James. *The Art of Government*. New York: The Fund for the Republic, 1959.

Robinson, Marianna, and Corinne Silverman. *The Reorganization of Philadelphia General Hospital*. (I.C.P. Case Series, No. 47), 1959.

Williams, Oliver P. *et. al. Suburban Differences and Metropolitan Policies: A Philadelphia Story*. Philadelphia: University of Pennsylvania Press, 1965.

PITTSBURGH

Keefe, William J., and William C. Seyler. "Precinct Politicians in Pittsburgh." *35 Social Science 26* (1960).

ST. LOUIS

Banfield, Edward C. *Big City Politics*, Ch. 8.

Salisbury, Robert H. "The Dynamics of Reform: Charter Politics in St. Louis." *5 Midwest Journal of Political Science 260* (1961).

————. "St. Louis Politics: Relationships among Interests, Parties, and Governmental Structures." *13 Western Political Quarterly 498* (1960).

Schmandt, Henry J., Paul G. Steinbicker, and George D. Wendel. *Metropolitan Reform in St. Louis: A Case Study*. New York: Holt, Rinehart, and Winston, Inc., 1961.

SALT LAKE CITY

Huefner, Dixie, S. A *Report on Politics in Salt Lake City*. Cambridge, Mass.: Joint Center for Urban Studies of Massachusetts Institute of Technology and Harvard University, 1961.

Williams, J. D. *The Defeat of Home Rule in Salt Lake City*. (Eagleton Case No. 2), 1960.

SEATTLE

Banfield, Edward C. *Big City Politics*, Ch. 9.

Bender, Charles W. *Report on the Politics of Seattle*. Cambridge, Mass.: Joint Center for Urban Studies of Massachusetts Institute of Technology and Harvard University, 1961.

Peabody, Robert L. *Seattle Seeks a Tax*. (I.C.P. Case Series, No. 49), 1959.

SHREVEPORT, LOUISIANA

Vines, Kenneth N. *Two Parties for Shreveport*. (Eagleton Case No. 12), 1959.

SYRACUSE, NEW YORK

Fiser, Webb S. "Urban Renewal in Syracuse." In *Cases in State and Local Government*, Ch. 26.

Munger, Frank J., *et al. Decisions in Syracuse*. Bloomington, Ind.: Indiana University Press, 1961.

WICHITA, KANSAS

Harder, Marvin A. *Nonpartisan Election: A Political Illusion?* (Eagleton Case No. 5), 1958.

INDEX

A

Abbott, Frank C., 119n, 405, 412n
Abraham, Henry J., 437n
Adams, Henry, 324
Addams, Jane, 211n
Adrian, Charles, 138n, 212n, 215, 216n, 217n, 222n, 254n, 270n, 313n, 351, 409
Advisory Commission on Intergovernmental Relations, 105n, 495n
Agger, Robert, 134n, 138n
Aiken, Charles, 87n
Alcorta v. *Texas*, 429n
Alderfer, Harold F., 105n, 310n
Alexander, Herbert, 193n
Allen, Robert S., 207, 389
Almond, Gabriel, 307n
Altshuler, Alan, 393, 396n
American Municipal Association, 123

Anderson, William, 32n, 44, 46, 119, 309
Annexation, 487–89
  bibliography on, 488n
Appleby, Paul, 327n
Apportionment, 289–93
Arant, Daniel, 500n
Articles of Confederation, 73
Ashburner, Charles E., 406n
Ashwander v. *T.V.A.*, 87n
Association of Bay Area Governments (San Francisco), 507
Atkinson, John, 411
Avery v. *Midland County*, 301

B

Babcock, Robert S., 101n, 301
Bachrach, Peter, 139n
Bailey, Stephen, 146, 315, 428
Bailey v. *Drexel Furniture Co.*, 78n
Bain, H. M., Jr., 222n

[533]